Invisible Hands

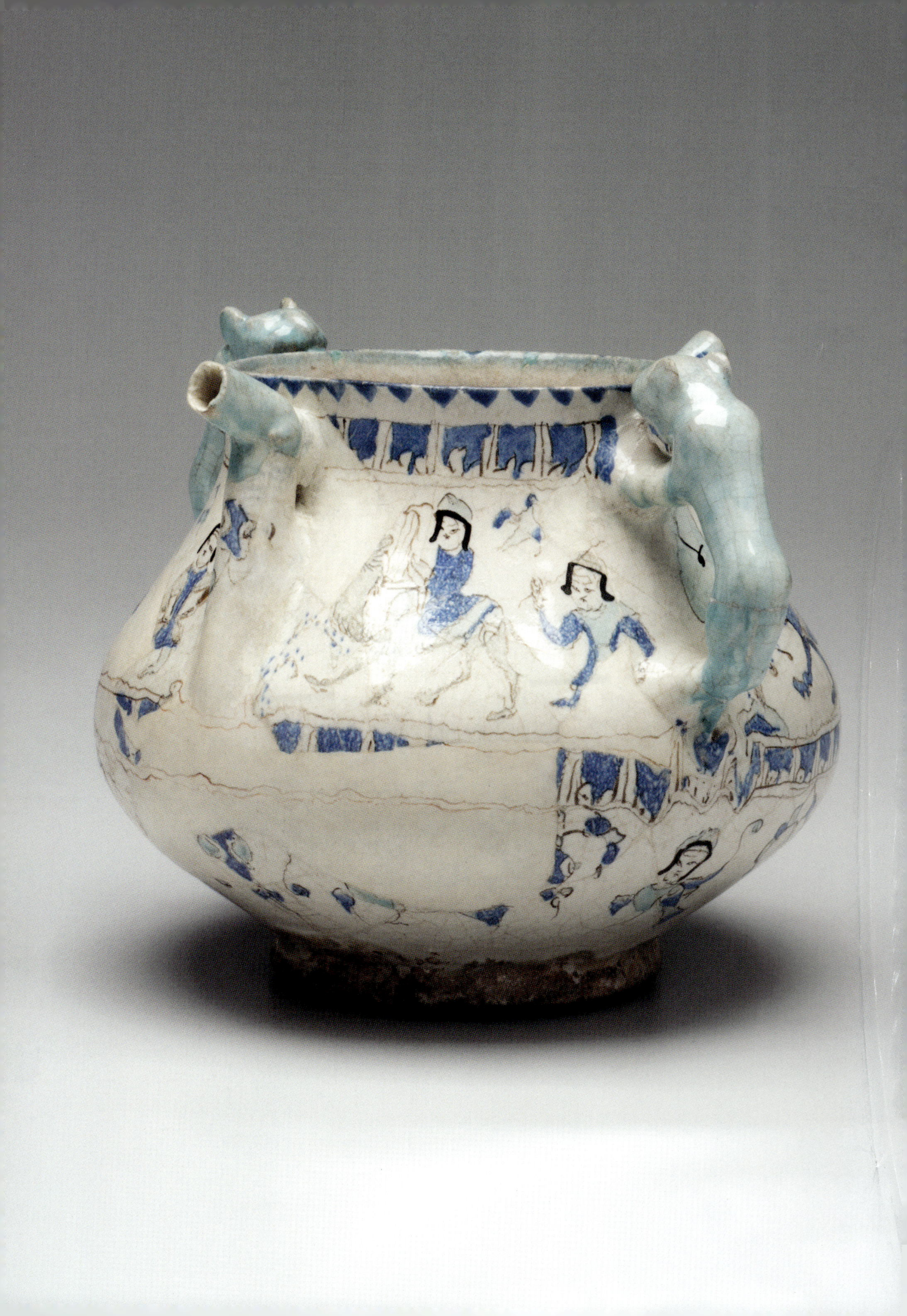

Invisible Hands

FABRICATION, FORGERY, AND THE ART OF ISLAMIC CERAMICS

Margaret S. Graves

PRINCETON UNIVERSITY PRESS
PRINCETON AND OXFORD

Published by Princeton University Press, 41 William Street, Princeton, New Jersey 08540

In the United Kingdom: Princeton University Press, 99 Banbury Road, Oxford OX2 6JX

GPSR Authorized Representative: Easy Access System Europe - Mustamäe tee 50, 10621 Tallinn, Estonia, gpsr.requests @easproject.com

press.princeton.edu

Brethren of Purity epigraph from *On Composition and the Arts*, trans. Nader El-Bizri (Oxford University Press, 2018), 150–51

Illustrations in front matter: p. ii, detail of fig. 3.28; p. vi, detail of fig. 1.6B

Illustrations in chapter openers: p. 28, detail of fig. 1.11; p. 62, detail of fig. 2.38; p. 122, detail of fig. 3.39; p. 184, detail of fig. 4.16; p. 220, detail of fig. 5.26; p. 264, detail of fig. 6.3

Jacket images: (*front*) Detail of fragments from a disassembled so-called mina'i ware bowl, Iran, 1180. © The Fitzwilliam Museum, University of Cambridge. (*back*) Bottle, glazed stone-paste(?) with modern materials and gilding. Height approx. 28 cm. Cincinnati Art Museum, Museum Purchase, 1952.257. Photograph by Rob Deslongchamps, courtesy of Cincinnati Art Museum

ISBN 9780691279749
ISBN (e-book) 9780691279756

Library of Congress Control Number: 2025933393

British Library Cataloging-in-Publication Data is available

Editorial: Michelle Komie and Annie Miller
Production Editorial: Sara Lerner
Text and Cover Design: Monograph / Matt Avery
Production: Steven Sears
Publicity: Jodi Price

This book has been composed in Source Serif

Printed in Italy

10 9 8 7 6 5 4 3 2 1

MIX
Paper | Supporting responsible forestry
FSC® C016466

Know, my brother, that all the people are makers and merchant-traders, rich and poor. For the makers are those who labour through their bodies and the use of their tools to set the forms, engravings, dyes, and shapes in their products. Their purpose is to be remunerated for their manufactures in [serving] the goodness of worldly living. The merchants are the ones who trade through demand and supply transactions, and their aim is to seek increases in what they receive over what they give. The wealthy are the ones who possess these natural and manufactured objects, and the objective of collecting and preserving them comes out of a concern they might fall into poverty.

—THE BRETHREN OF PURITY, *Epistle 8*, tenth century

Don't try to fake it, try to invent it.

—KUBACHI PROVERB

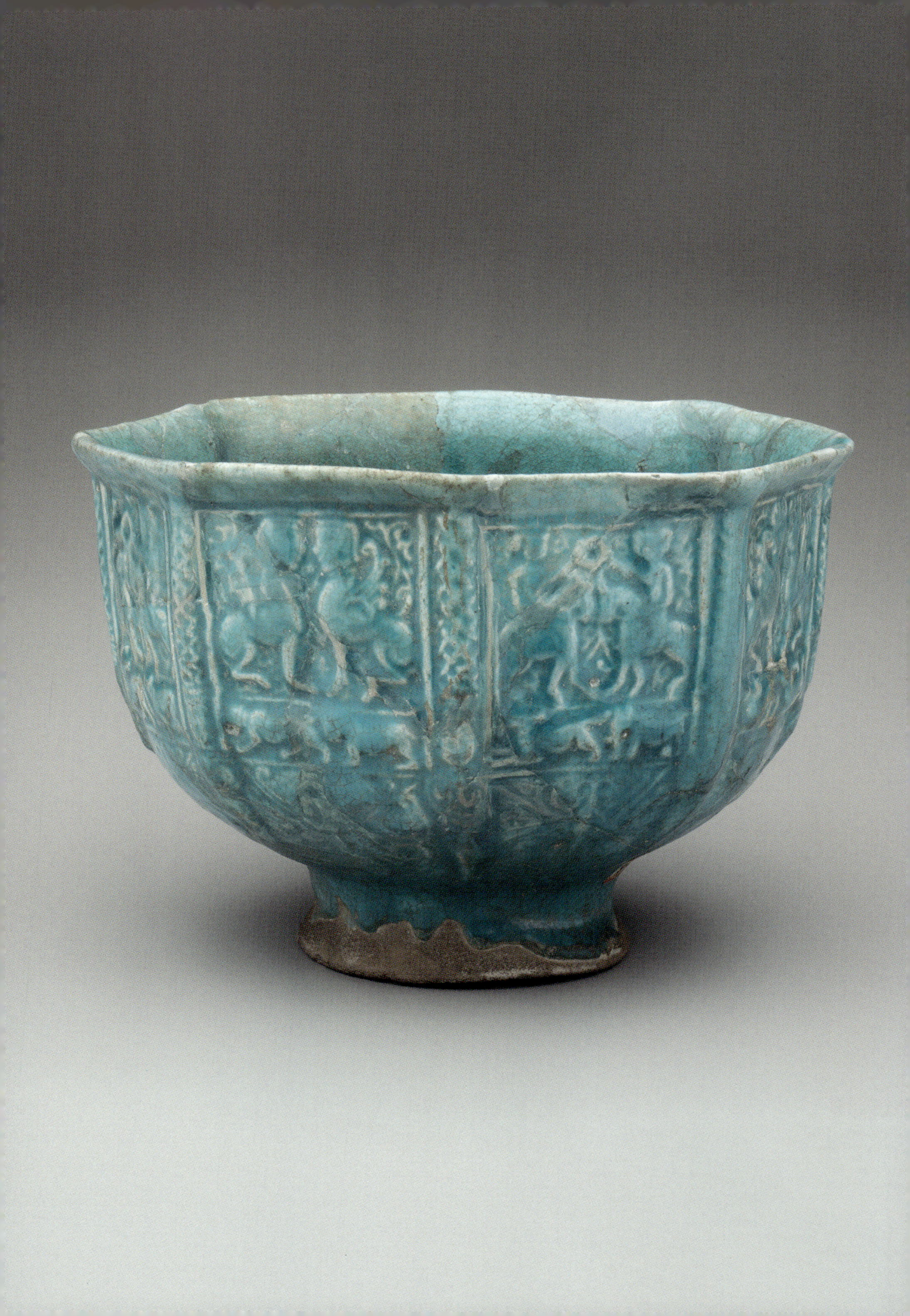

Contents

Note on Transliteration

For the transliteration of words, names, and titles from Arabic, Persian, and Ottoman Turkish, this text follows a modified version of the transliteration system used by the *International Journal of Middle East Studies*, without macrons and diacritics apart from those indicating *ʿayn* (ʿ) and *hamza* (ʾ). The exception is quotations from secondary sources that use macrons and diacritics in their own transliteration, which have been retained. Words from foreign languages have been italicized unless they appear in standard English-language dictionaries, in which case they are given in Anglicized form without italicization. The ceramic term *minaʾi* appears frequently throughout and has not been italicized after first use. Translations are by the author unless otherwise indicated.

Invisible Hands

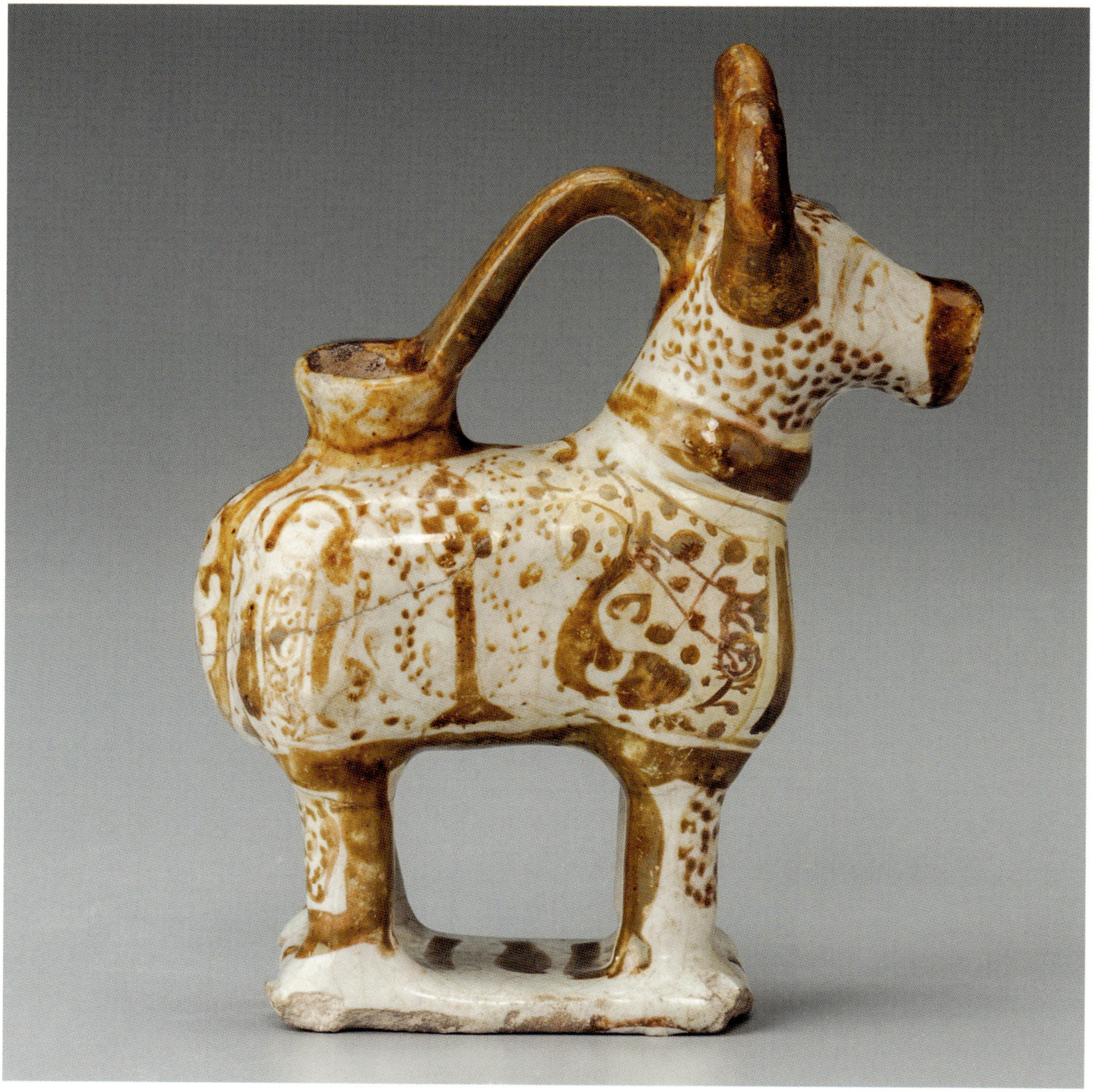

1.1. Aquamanile, glazed stonepaste with overglaze luster and modern material. Original material attributed Iran, late 12th/13th century. Height 14.6 cm. Eskenazi Museum of Art, Indiana University, 60.58.

Introduction

FICTIONS OF CAPITAL

Time is the most precious capital, and with it every happiness is acquired, but little by little it dissipates.

—AL-QAZWINI, *The Wonders of Creation and Marvels of Existence,* thirteenth century

Capitalism's fictitious objects have left strange traces in the archives of modern history. In the courts of eighteenth- and nineteenth-century Syria, moneylenders circumvented Islamic law's formal proscription on earning interest by inserting imaginary commodities into loan agreements. In contracts for *bayʿ wafaʾ* (a type of loan secured against immovable property), fictitious goods enabled creditors to charge and receive interest. In the eighteenth century, these financial fictions were measured in quantities of soap; in the nineteenth, clocks.[1] James Reilly has shown that the "price" of the imaginary clock or watch (*saʿa*) in those nineteenth-century contracts amounted to interest or profit for the creditor, paid to them in monthly installments, with the arrangement openly acknowledged in some documents as an artifice.[2] Timepieces were presumably chosen for this role because they represented small, eminently exchangeable high-value assets—a neater fiction to conjure into existence than piles of nonexistent soap. It is hard to imagine a better symbol of capitalism's chimeric powers of generation than all those imaginary clocks lying forgotten in court archives, quietly ticking out the accelerating time of money.

This is a book about faking, forging, and fictionalizing medieval ceramics from the Islamic world. It is also a book about extracting, buying, selling, and investing in antiquities, and the curious physical transformations that money can effect upon objects. In the collected corpus of Islamic ceramics, two kinds of history—the long art histories of material objects, and the economic history of the colonial-era Middle East—fuse into each other. Together they tell the story of an entire body of craft skills that has been disavowed, concealed, and forgotten; crafts that have the power to create glamour and enchant onlookers, make the broken become whole, cast the shadows of time where they have not yet fallen, and launch a thousand imagined pasts. Some of the smallest exemplars of these skills, like the little aquamanile explored in depth in chapter 3, have the most to reveal when we attend to them closely (fig. I.1). But I have opened this book among the imaginary clocks of finance because they represent the strange structures that beat the heart of the antiquities market. The dizzying instabilities of the modern financial industry and its capacity to create money out of nothing—money that can then disappear again when markets collapse—are important to this story. Even more important than imaginary money, though, is the nature of assets, and what happens when the physical matter of history—here mostly potsherds, but elsewhere manuscripts, architectural decoration, and all the other residues of the physical past—gets translated into numbers and entered onto a balance sheet.

This introduction sets the stage by asking when and how and why people have fabricated and then circulated physical history, especially that which purports to represent the past of the region known conventionally as the Middle East, as well as what we should call it and why it matters. First, it briefly explores the words we use to describe inauthentic artworks, before turning to the political and cultural economies in which they have been created and circulated, and the material challenges faced by those craftspeople who turned their skills to the creation of fictive antiquities. It then explores the reprographic technologies and visual remediation that helped bring both the modern antiquities market and its attendant spectrum of forged, doctored, and fabricated material culture into being. Finally, the introduction returns to the financial industry's extraordinary powers of transubstantiation that turn artifacts into assets, showing how these have underpinned the workings of the antiquities market from the past to the present, underwriting all the subjects of this book in the process.

Fake, Forgery, Fabrication

Every collection of historic ceramics from the Islamic world will contain composite objects, pastiches, and perhaps some whole-cloth forgeries, but not every custodian of those pieces is in a position to tell the stories that hide behind the glamorous surfaces.[3] Research in collections and archives requires time and money for travel to far-flung institutions, while technical analysis can be prohibitively expensive and difficult to arrange if you don't have laboratory facilities on your doorstep. More insidious are the barriers to transparency about condition that come from private interests and impact even public museums via donors, dealers, trustees, and the collectors who might one day be persuaded to donate or sell their artworks to the institution. Put bluntly, the collectors' market for Islamic ceramics has a tremendous interest in maintaining the fiction of the intact object, and it is very difficult for scholarship to operate completely outside of that ecology.

A vast range of deceptive modifications have been practiced on the ceramics of the premodern Middle East as they made their way to market, and huge amounts of skilled labor have been expended on making these objects of desire. That labor has rarely been recognized for what it is: a major form of embodied craft skill. The commercial narratives of the antiquities market usually prefer to gloss over modifications, while scholarship has, with a few specialized exceptions, expended most of its energy on parsing out original material from modern interventions and trying to clean the present off the past. Both have tended to ignore the unknown artisans who did this work, frequently treating their art as a distasteful or distracting interruption in the life of the object. Only a few art historians, Oliver Watson chief among them, have sought transparency about physical condition within the corpus of Islamic ceramics as a means of telling a larger art history of collected objects.[4] This book, then, is not only about ceramics but also about acknowledging skills that have not yet received their due. It is also about the unstable natures of history and authenticity, and what it means to try to extract those intangible things from physical artifacts that have journeyed through a modern global marketplace. Therefore, the first point of order is to clarify terminology. I attempt to set the terms as simply as possible before turning to the vexed question of how we write about inauthentic artworks.

Almost every study of inauthenticity in art acknowledges the slippery nature of the available terminology, and many authors have laid out their working parameters for words like "fake" and "forgery" at some length. Dictionary definitions are not as helpful as one might hope, but in standard English-language contexts there is an overall difference in tenor between the words "fake" and "forgery." A fake is something that is not what it purports or is purported to be, and the word can be used for a bewildering variety of things from handbags to body parts to social self-presentation. A forgery is something made in fraudulent imitation of something else with the specific and deliberate intention to deceive. Thus, "fake" is a status that an object could acquire through lots of different routes, including postproduction sleight of hand on the market. The status of forgery, on the other hand, is definitively dependent on the initial intent of the maker(s) at the point of production. For something to be a forgery, it must have been intended from the moment of its inception and creation to be perceived by a human audience as something it is not.[5]

Throughout this book I have reserved the relatively narrow term "forgery" for clear-cut cases where objects have demonstrably been made from scratch with an express intention to deceive. Several such cases are discussed in this introduction. I have veered away from the word "fake," with its confusingly broad applications, except when referring to general phenomena. "Fake" tends to subsume all nuance and particularity into negative judgment, eliding the very activities that this book seeks to excavate: that is, the physical alteration and invention of historical ceramics for sale on the antiquities market. An extraordinary number of degrees and types of remaking are possible with old ceramics, as this book shows, and determining intention to deceive is often contingent on both material and transactional evidence. To this end, I have favored "fabrication" as a word that brings the material skill and improvisational ingenuity of all such interventions back into view.

There is, of course, a substantial literature on the forgery of art and antiquities, with varied aims and intentions. Much of the writing from the early twentieth century is premised on educating the buying public so they can learn to spot the inauthentic.[6] Such primers frequently incorporate an element of the "gotcha" narrative, taking pleasure in exposing the tricks that might catch out the unwary. Often, this type of writing lingers over the ingenuity of the forger and the credulity of those who were taken in—especially when the latter were supposed to be experts. The gotcha element in these texts is ostensibly part of a didactic and educational mission to aid potential buyers, but much of the time it seems geared toward entertaining a readership fostered on detective

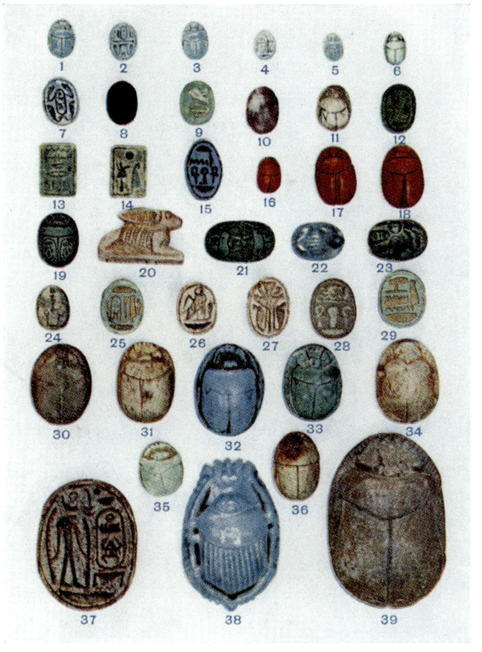

I.2. T. G. Wakeling, *Forged Egyptian Antiquities* (London: Adam and Charles Black, 1912), plate VIII.

fiction and the "indiciary paradigm" of physical clues.[7] One such example of early forgery literature, T. G. Wakeling's color-illustrated *Forged Egyptian Antiquities* of 1912, states its mission to be educational—in large part so that experts such as him will be spared the social discomfort of being asked to give opinions on forgeries unwittingly purchased by travelers in Egypt, like the endless new-made "Ancient Egyptian" scarabs being produced by local and European craftsmen (fig. I.2).[8] But in reality, most of the audience for this book must have been the library-going public of Great Britain, unlikely to travel to Cairo to buy antiquities but able to enjoy Wakeling's anecdotes of detective work and exotic roguery from the comfort of their own homes. The twin threads of buyer's guide and gotcha narrative are intertwined throughout the history of forgery literature as a genre, and have also found expression in a number of exhibitions calling attention to fakes and forgeries in art.[9]

Within the literature of collecting and connoisseurship that surrounds the so-called decorative arts—ceramics, woodwork, metalwork, glass, stone-carving—much of the writing on fakes and forgeries has concerned itself with policing the evidence base and cleansing it of inauthenticities. Less often stated is the rude economic truth underpinning some of those anxieties: exposure of faking and forgery can decimate the financial value of investments. Across the entire globe, the nineteenth- and twentieth-century antiquities markets turned historical artifacts into financial assets. The "decorative arts"

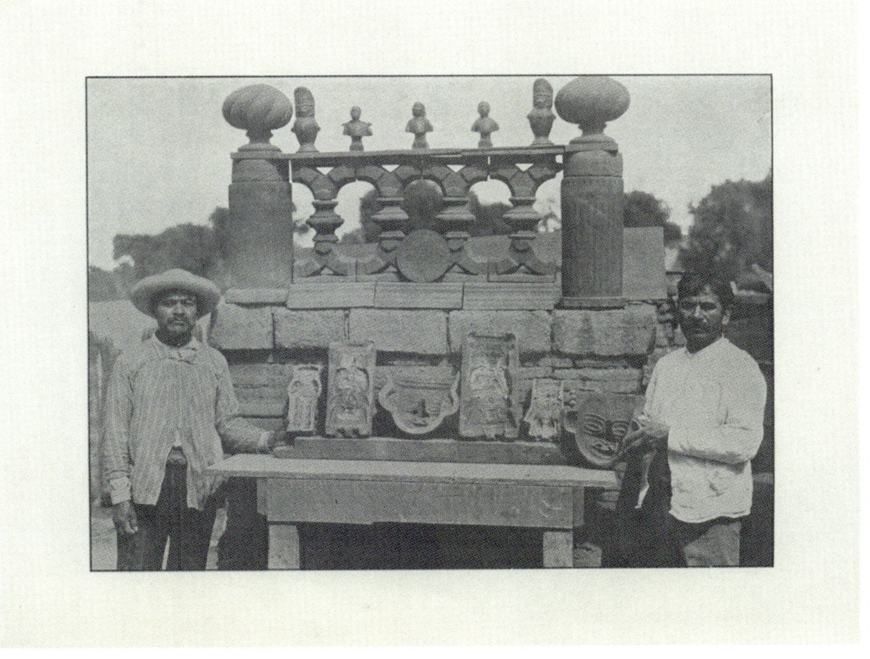

I.3. Leopoldo Batres, *Antigüedades mejicanas falsificadas: Falsificación y falsificadores* (Mexico City: Fidencio S. Soria, 1910), plate 5.

were extracted from every corner of the earth, creating new industries of faking and forgery, and with them, new genres of writing about inauthenticity.[10] The 1910 publication of Leopoldo Batres's book *Antigüedades mejicanas falsificadas*, with over two hundred objects from the Museo Nacional de México illustrated in photographic plates, exemplifies one of the didactic strains in forgery study. Through its text and illustrations the book makes itself a specimen cabinet of paradigmatic falsifications, as the author parses the inventory of the museum's archaeological collections, sifting new antiquities from old and establishing his own authority as the adjudicator of authenticity.[11] It even includes photographs of the Barrios brothers of San Juan Teotihuacan with the molds they used for manufacturing new-made "antiquities" from earthenware, giving a rare glimpse of individual craftsmen and their modes of working within a frenetic antiquities market (fig. I.3).

Finally, there is another distinct strand in art forgery studies that has tended to focus on the philosophical implications of forgery, riffing on the borderlines between truth and falsehood.[12] A small group of celebrity painting forgers come up over and over again within this subgenre, especially Hans Van Meegeren and Elmyr de Hory, the latter being the focus of Orson Welles's film *F for Fake*. More recent figures, including Wolfgang Beltracchi and Pei-Shen Qian, are surely already being incorporated into this canon as well.[13] This branch of forgery literature delights in staging the forger as a master trickster, a twisted genius making collectors and institutions dance to his tune and leading us all into an existential hinterland of unstable realities. Within this celebratory discourse the forger is always a man, and most often a white European. This particular branch of writing about art forgery may offer a certain kind of entertainment, but it does not generate a lot of insights among the so-called decorative arts. These usually come to us unauthored and therefore, forged or not, cannot be turned so easily into fodder for narratives of individual genius.

The question of creators looms large in this book, although they remain elusive. The invisible hands of colonial-era ceramics fabrication are usually not filled out with names, identities, families, or written records of what those craftspeople thought about the world they lived in and the work they did. We can catch stray glimpses of them, however, in the background of certain episodes from the history of antiquities forgery, and it is to such concrete episodes that this introduction now turns. The motivations for creating and circulating new "antiquities" that supposedly originated in the ancient and medieval Middle East have been many and various. For the Europeans and North Americans who constituted the primary market for most such ventures from the second half of the nineteenth century onward, the Middle East was a region of the mind that mixed together the Holy Land of Biblical origins, Europe's exotic "Other," and a vast quarry for the extraction of history. When those projective desires met local craft knowledge, the result was a market in fabricated history.

Writing New Histories in Stone and Clay

The modern science of archaeology developed in part out of quests by European Christians to confirm the veracity of the Bible. This created a special platform for forgeries that purported to confirm or invoke Biblical history, especially those that bore "ancient" writing. By the era of the European Enlightenment, when texts and material objects were becoming formalized as evidentiary categories and collecting cultures were starting to solidify into structured markets, quests for Biblical proof were already giving rise to forgeries. Sometimes these were made far from the Holy Land itself. One of the great hoaxes of the eighteenth century was the Lügensteine ("lying stones") created in 1725 to dupe Johann Bartholomew Beringer (1667–1740). These falsified fossils were manufactured by Beringer's colleagues at Würzburg University and distributed around Mount Eibelstadt for his specimen seekers to find, with the express intention of discrediting and humiliating Beringer. (Academics can be *so* cruel.) The prank became a career-damaging scandal when Beringer decided to publish his remarkable collection as a book, complete with printed plates. In addition to highly fanciful carvings of insects, plants, animals, and even heavenly bodies petrified in stone, one group of the Lügensteine comprised, in Beringer's words, "magnificent tablets engraved in Latin, Arabic, and Hebrew characters with the ineffable name of Jehova" (fig. I.4).[14] The nature of fossil formation being as yet undetermined, Beringer speculated that these characters could have been formed through the action of light carrying impressions of words and imprinting them onto matter—an idea that must have seemed no more or less incredible than other theories of immanent geological trace emerging in the fevered academic environment of eighteenth-century Europe.[15] The state of flux around fundamental questions of matter, belief, and the legibility of stones made the Lügensteine hoax possible in the same instant that it also made Beringer's acceptance of it risible among his peers.

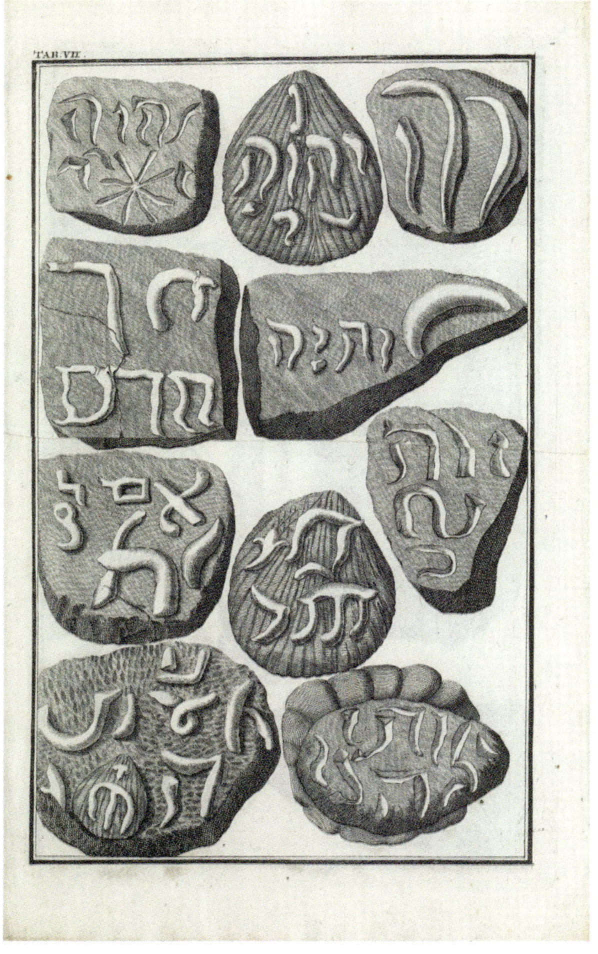

I.4. Johan Bartholomäus Adam Beringer, *Lithographiae Wirceburgensis, Ducentis Lapidum Figuratorum* (Würzburg: Mark Anton Engmann for Philipp Wilhelm Fuggart, 1726), plate 7.

One hundred and thirty-five years after the Lügensteine were carved, two stones inscribed with Hebrew script (both modern and archaic) were supposedly found in earthworks in Ohio in 1860. The most famous of these is the so-called Decalogue Stone (fig. I.5), an arch-shaped piece of black limestone carved with an inscription in archaicizing Hebrew characters and a vaguely Near Eastern-ish image of a standing man (the latter quite possibly cribbed from *Discoveries Among the Ruins of Nineveh and Babylon*, published in 1853 by Sir Austen Henry Layard, English excavator and founding chairman of the board of the first Ottoman Bank).[16] Although the Ohio stones were quickly recognized as forgeries in some quarters, in others they were heralded as proof of a theory that the earthworks and mound structures of pre-Columbian North America were built not by indigenous peoples but by the Lost Tribes of Israel.[17] The Ohio stones were created at a time when archaeology was in its infancy in the United States and arguments about the origins of humanity—and especially the nature of "the races"—were violently animated by the immediate political issue of slavery.[18] Risible as the Lost Tribes theory may sound to some, it is a foundational tenet of that remarkable document of nineteenth-century American religious fervor, The Book of Mormon. The

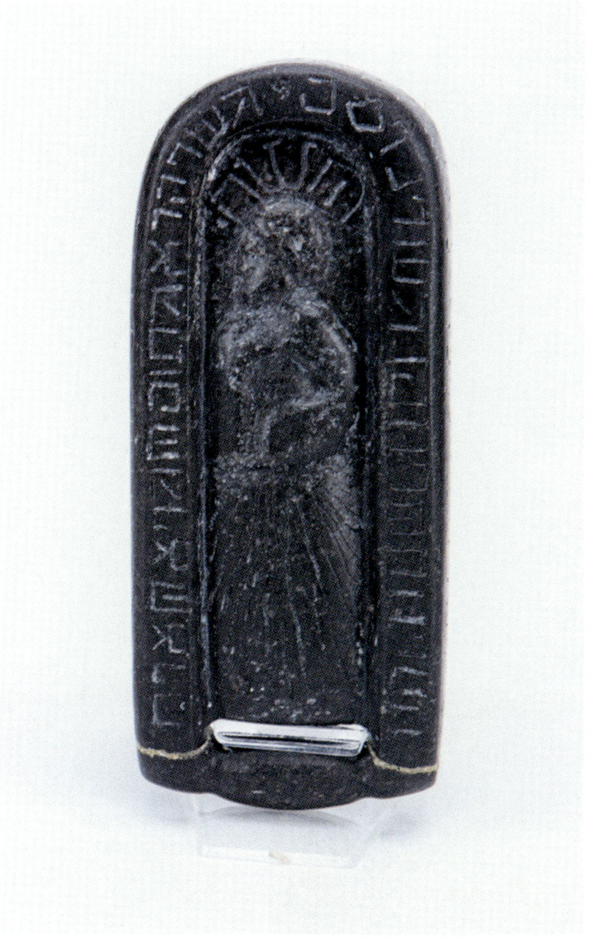

I.5. Decalogue Stone, carved limestone. United States, ca. 1860. Johnson-Humrickhouse Museum, Coshocton, Ohio.

Decalogue Stone might originally have been a prank, like Beringer's Lügensteine, but it has come to be an object of belief that represents a deeply held version of history.

As the creators of the Lügensteine and the Ohio Decalogue Stone well knew, carved stone inscriptions carry their own authority within Judeo-Christian environments, where the archetype of the stone tablets of Moses is reliably present in the collective consciousness. Stonecarving is, however, very difficult to do skillfully—see the clumsy letters on the Decalogue Stone—and it is easy to see why antiquities forgers might favor more plastic media.[19] After encountering these two early forgeries crafted in stone to serve as "evidence" in intellectual and theological debates, it is striking that large-scale market-driven forgeries of the later nineteenth century were often conducted through clay. In theory, unglazed earthenware presents the least technically demanding medium of pottery forgery, but its deceptive simplicity has lured some craftspeople and dealers into overestimating their own ability to turn a convincing modern forgery out onto the market—especially in the perennially appealing realm of the figurine.[20]

In the 1870s and '80s, hundreds of so-called Asiatic Terracotta forgeries of Greek earthenware sculptural figurines were offered for sale to European and Ottoman collectors (fig. I.6).[21] The scale of production and success of the deception was such that some 20 percent of the figurines of this type in the Berlin Antikensammlung have been shown by thermoluminescence testing (see chapter 5) to be modern creations.[22] Certain private collectors fared even worse: all fifteen of the figure groups of this type bought by the Havemeyer family of New York are now thought to be modern.[23] The identities of the craftspeople responsible for the forged Asiatic Terracottas were never settled, but Athens has been suggested as the likely point of origin. Hypotheses of the time included an Italian with high-level training in sculpture who established a forgery workshop in the city that then undid itself through its own overproduction. One wonders, however, if this projection of Italian artistic supremacy over Greek is based on evidence, prejudice, or a mixture of the two.[24]

The late nineteenth-century Asiatic Terracottas illustrate an important material truism of ceramics forgery, one that appears again in this book. They sometimes incorporate deliberate fractures and repairs, which can be an integral part of the forger's process.[25] In the twentieth century, forged antiquities were sometimes even given to professional restorers in a damaged state so their reconstruction from fragments would be documented, making the restorer into a witting or unwitting "launderer" of authenticity.[26] In the case of the Asiatic Terracotta forgeries, one identifiable characteristic is a tendency—against all logic—for the breaks in the earthenware body to lie on the backs and bases of the figurines and not on projecting parts, or for heads and arms to be delicately broken off and reattached without any disfiguring

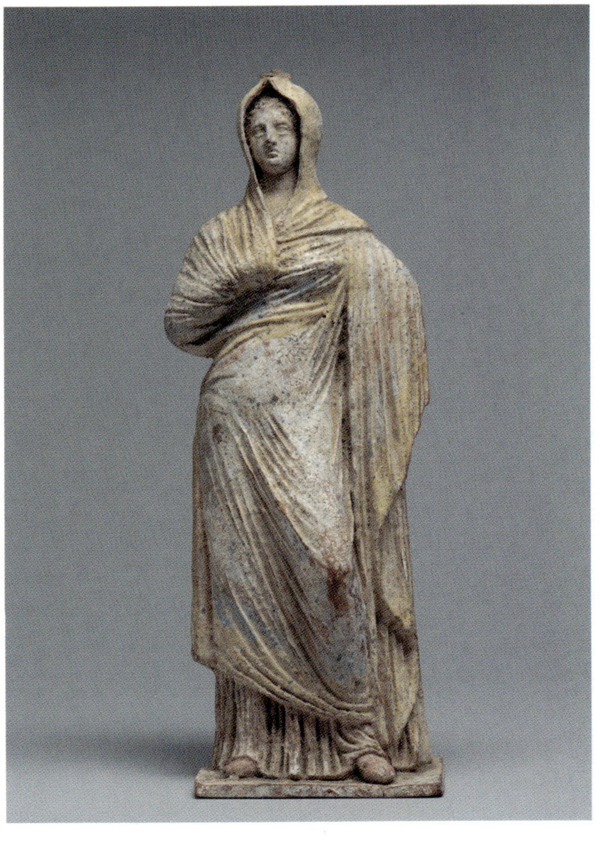

I.6. So-called Asiatic Terracotta forgery, fired earthenware with pigment. Probably Greece, late 19th century. Height 25.5 cm. Harvard Art Museums/Arthur M. Sackler Museum, 1920.44.98, Gift of the Misses Norton.

loss of material. As a contemporary commentator noted, "[the modern craftsmen] had not the heart to damage the more dignified portions of their works, the freely-modelled parts that had cost them so much trouble. We see, therefore, in spurious figures and groups fractures which confine themselves, in a manner contrary to all reason, to the base or the back of the figures or groups, while they dexterously avoid the heads, hands, wings, fans and other projecting portions."[27]

Salim al-Kari, Islam Akhun, and the Value of the Past

Around the same time that the unknown creators of the Asiatic Terracottas were laboring over their figurines, the lure of unglazed earthenware led a Jerusalem artist named Salim al-Kari and his collaborator, the antiquities dealer and sometime missionary Moses Wilhelm Shapira (1830–1884), to invent an entire material history in clay. Like the creators of the Asiatic Terracottas, they might possibly have escaped detection for longer if they had not produced such large quantities of material. Al-Kari, whose name identifies him as a craftsman (from the Arabic *kar*, meaning work or workmanship), was an Arab Christian with a business making icon paintings to sell to the Orthodox Christian pilgrims who streamed to the city of Jerusalem.[28] His partner-in-production Shapira is now remembered mainly for his role in a Biblical papyrus forgery of 1883. Shapira was born to a Jewish family in what is now Ukraine before migrating to Jerusalem and converting to Protestant Christianity in the mid nineteenth century.[29] As is shown in chapter 1, these points of religious and ethnic identity have potential significance in the turn-of-the-century antiquities market.

Al-Kari and Shapira's intervention into the rising antiquities market of the 1870s was sparked by the excitement surrounding a genuine ancient artifact, the Moabite stele. This black stone slab, found in Dhiban (in modern-day Jordan), first came to antiquarian attention in 1868. It was inscribed in an ancient Semitic language in the ninth century BCE; its content, which parallels the Biblical account of the Moabite king Mesha, was immediately seized upon as confirmation of the veracity of the Bible. Recognizing the frenzied desire among European collectors for more of the same, al-Kari and Shapira began in 1872 to manufacture thousands of modern Moabite artifacts, a large tranche of them being bought by the Royal Museum in Berlin in 1873. Charles-Simon Clermont-Ganneau, a French dragoman (translator for merchants and government agents) living in Jerusalem, unmasked the affair and exposed al-Kari and Shapira's fraud in a series of publications. He tracked al-Kari's activities through conversations with the potters of Jerusalem, who told him that al-Kari and his father used local clay to create figurines and tablets to which al-Kari added pseudo-Canaanite characters. Many of these characters were copied from the genuine inscription on the Moabite stele but applied to the pottery in mostly nonsensical order. By Clermont-Ganneau's report, al-Kari also worked with local potters who made wheel-thrown vessels for him, which he then adorned with "inscriptions" before firing the pieces in their kilns. The pottery was artificially aged after firing by soaking it in a nitrate solution to mimic deposits found in the soil at the area of its purported discovery.[30] Shapira and al-Kari even went as far as staging excavations in the 1870s,

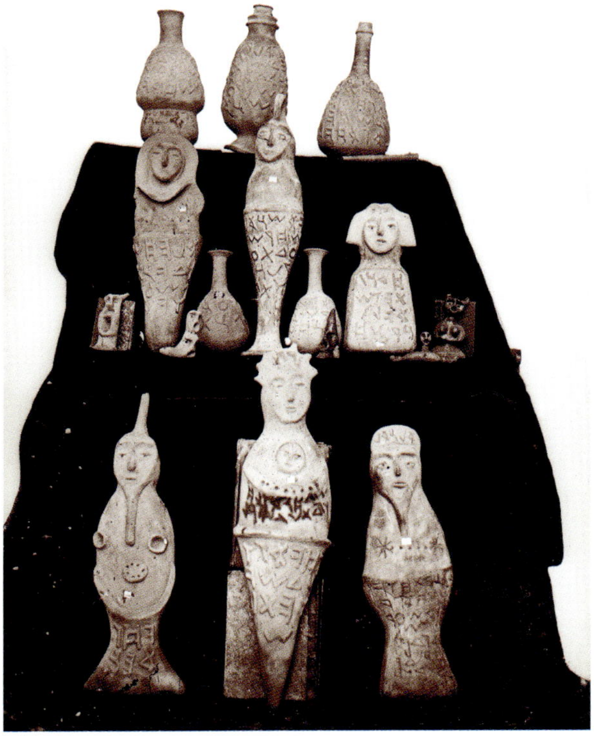

I.7. *Moabite Pottery in Mr. Shapira's Shop*. Photograph by H. H. Kitchener, 1874. Palestine Exploration Fund, PEF-P-5111.

with their new-made antiquities carefully buried beforehand, to demonstrate the authenticity of their goods to excited buyers.[31]

Records of the "Moabite" pottery made by al-Kari and sold by Shapira survive in a remarkable group of drawings and watercolor paintings made by a British lieutenant named Claude R. Conder. To judge from the paintings by Conder, Shapira's stock included not only the public-facing figurines recorded in two surviving photographs (fig. I.7), but also a backroom supply of sexual subject matter (fig. I.8). Five extant sheets of Conder's paintings are labeled "Phallic"—some of them also annotated "not to be published"—and depict animate phalluses, figures with exaggerated genitalia, and a startlingly graphic earthenware pudendum.[32] Conder's paintings and the surviving photographs of Shapira's Moabite stock reveal inventive hands at work in clay, trying to create things that looked convincingly "primitive." And yet the pieces now immediately betray nineteenth-century sensibilities, especially when viewed *en groupe*. This is evident not only in the prurient subjects and the oddly modern-looking hooded eyes of some of the figures, but also in the exaggerated presence of outsize, undamaged letters on the front and back of the objects, applied in barbotine or incised into the clay body. Tellingly, it is as if the inscriptions had been intended from the outset for mediation through print or photographic reproduction, for the delectation of philologists and armchair travelers.[33] The creators of these modern "Moabite" materials likely drew upon the hodgepodge of available reproductions of ancient artifacts coming to light in the arms race of nineteenth-century archaeology

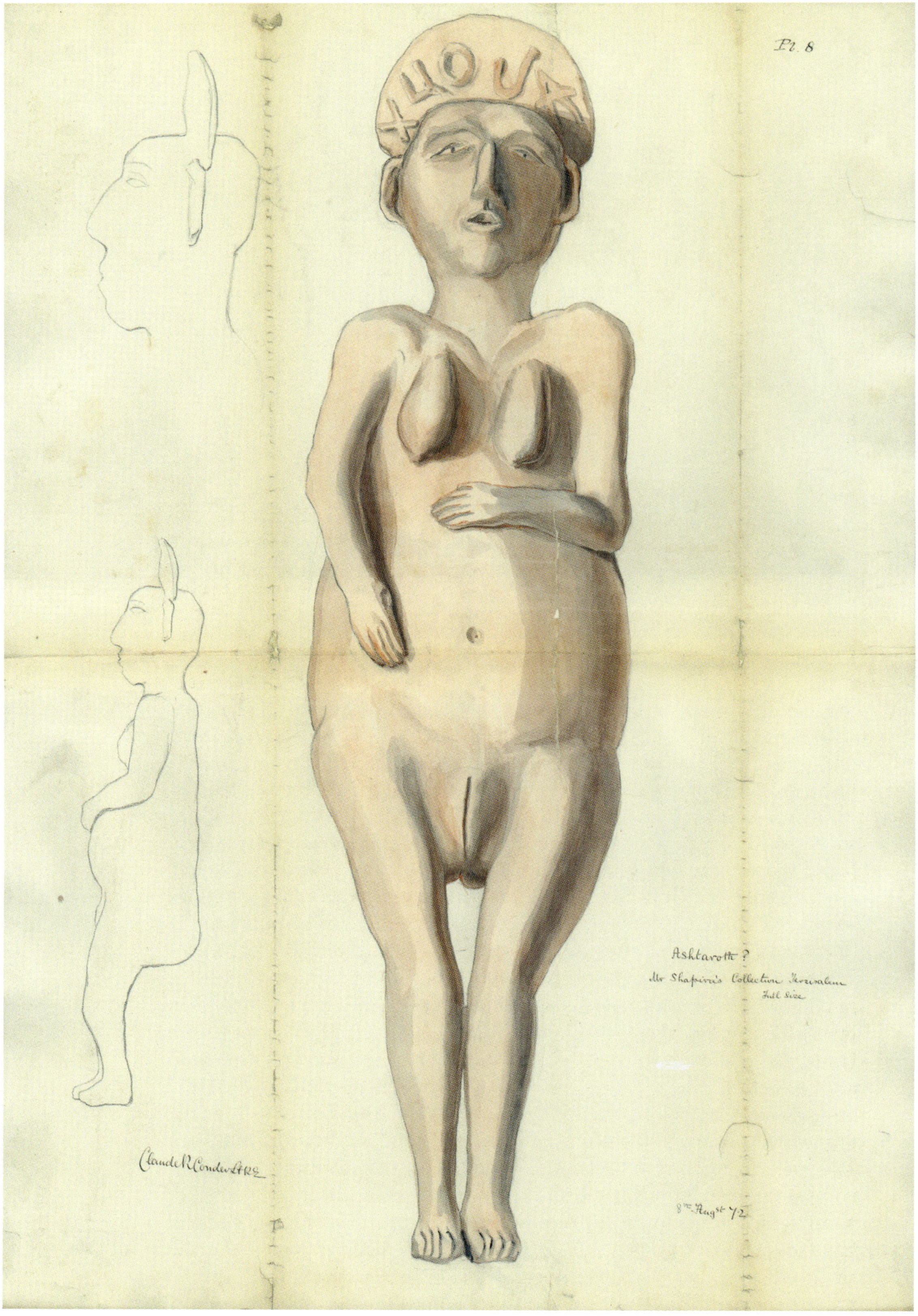
Pl. 8
Ashtaroth ?
Mr Shapira's Collection Jerusalem
Full Size
Claude R Conder Lt RE
8th August 72

in the Holy Land and Mesopotamia, in addition to firsthand viewings of the Moabite stone itself.[34]

Perhaps inevitably, Shapira's name has come to have its own luster on the market. As Michael Press has shown, objects that may have nothing to do with him are now promoted and sold as "Shapira forgeries."[35] The trope of the lone male forger-genius is so appealing, and so powerfully lodged in the modern imagination, that it tends to bend the evidence around it to fit itself. It also carries some distinctly racialized baggage. When Clermont-Ganneau wrote up his investigation of the Moabite pottery in tones of high indignation in the late nineteenth century, he was confident the main craftsman and real mastermind of the episode was al-Kari—in spite of the somewhat predictable protestations from some European commentators that "it is impossible to conceive that an Arab created these quantities of statuettes and vases covered with Moabite inscriptions."[36] But when the affair has been presented in more recent writings as an enjoyable trickster romp, the portion of genius has accrued to Shapira. In recent accounts al-Kari has become Shapira's mute factotum, the unthinking hands to Shapira's brain.[37] It is a striking truth of antiquities forgeries that the indigenous craftsman may be permitted center stage when blame is being apportioned, but once the balance has settled in favor of genius, he will usually be eclipsed by the nearest white or white-approximating man, often an extraterritorial dealer or equivalent figure.

That said, one of few subaltern figures of the colonial era who is now recognized in the annals of forgery in his own right is Islam Akhun (active ca. 1894–1901). At the eastern end of the Islamic world, the oasis town of Khotan in modern-day Xinjiang became a locus for foreign collectors at the end of the nineteenth century as the British and Russian empires played out the territorial maneuvers of the Great Game.[38] Observing the prices foreigners would pay for the historical manuscripts that had started to come to light in the Taklamakan desert—and that none of those foreign buyers could read the pages they were so keen to acquire—Islam Akhun and his collaborators manufactured a series of manuscripts written in made-up scripts. At first these were handwritten, before someone realized blockprinting on artificially aged paper was a more efficient means of production (fig. I.9). One report from the time tells that the woodblocks were prepared by a cotton-printer, giving a tantalizing glimpse of local craft knowledge, tools, and materials being repurposed to the new commodity system of the global antiquities market.[39]

For a few years Islam Akhun and company were able to sell a substantial number of these forged manuscripts and woodblock books to foreign diplomats and travelers, before suspicions became too great. In 1901 the Hungarian British traveler Aurel Stein confronted Islam Akhun with the deception and induced him to tell the whole story, which Stein then published.[40] More recent research shows that Islam Akhun's workshop did not limit itself to the now well-known manuscript and blockprint forgeries, but also produced and sold fired earthenware objects.[41] Forgeries of antique earthenware figurines and vessels were being made concurrently in Russian Turkestan, and it is hardly surprising that Islam Akhun and his workshop would have tried their hand at earthenware figurines as well.[42] The most arresting to come to light so far is the wonderful and absurd figurine of the evil king Zahhak of Persian myth, held in the Hermitage Museum since its acquisition in the early

I.8. Claude R. Conder, *Ashtaroth? Mr. Shapira's Collection, Jerusalem.* Watercolor painting. Jerusalem, 1872. Palestine Exploration Fund, PEF-PI-233.

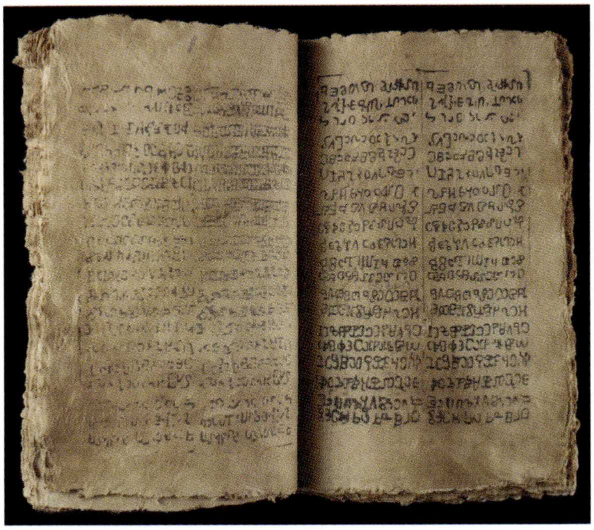

I.9. Islam Akhun and workshop, manuscript forgery, woodblock print on paper. Sold to George Macartney in Kashgar, 1896. Length 21 cm. British Library, Or.13873/2.

twentieth century from Nikolai Fyodorovich Petrovsky (1837–1908), Russian consul to Kashgar (fig. I.10). The large scale and unwieldy form of this figure must have presented serious challenges for firing, and its successful execution certainly attests to the involvement of knowledgeable potters. Painstaking research by Pavel Lurje and his colleagues has revealed the path traveled by this and related earthenware objects now in St. Petersburg and Berlin, a path that leads back directly to the Khotan workshops of Islam Akhun and his collaborators.[43] Thermoluminescence testing in 2013 confirmed what stylistic analysis and archival research already announced: the Zahhak figurine was last fired between 100 and 150 years ago, and is not an antiquity but a modern forgery. Most interesting is a point raised by the Russian scholars: the Khotan Zahhak forgery is neither a direct imitation of any genuine historical material nor one aligned along the edges of any identifiable categories of local antiquity. Rather, it is a creation of the imagination built from ideas about the pre-Muslim past of the region that were held by its late nineteenth-century Muslim inhabitants.[44] Unglazed, fired earthenware proved to be the perfect plastic medium for confecting a highly imaginative piece of physical history that could be sold to eager agents of empire.

In economic environments where the artifacts of the past had some monetary value in immediate society but enormous value to foreigners, Salim al-Kari, Islam Akhun, and others correctly estimated that successful forgeries could be made from base materials with some local exchange value but no international worth, like clay, wood, and paper. The abstract financial value of antiquity was thus successfully embodied, via the labor of colonial-era craftspeople, into new commodities. Sometimes those workshops amalgamated different historical epochs into their products. An undated glass negative shows a particularly curious example of historical blending in Islamic ceramics forgery (fig. I.11). The plate comes from the archives of Antoin Sevruguin (1851–1933), a Russian of Armenian-Georgian descent who ran a successful photography business in Tehran in the late nineteenth and early twentieth centuries. It is one of a set that show historic ceramics photographed in studio settings, including vessels and dishes that were in the possession of well-known dealers by 1910 and 1912.[45] The photographs were presumably com-

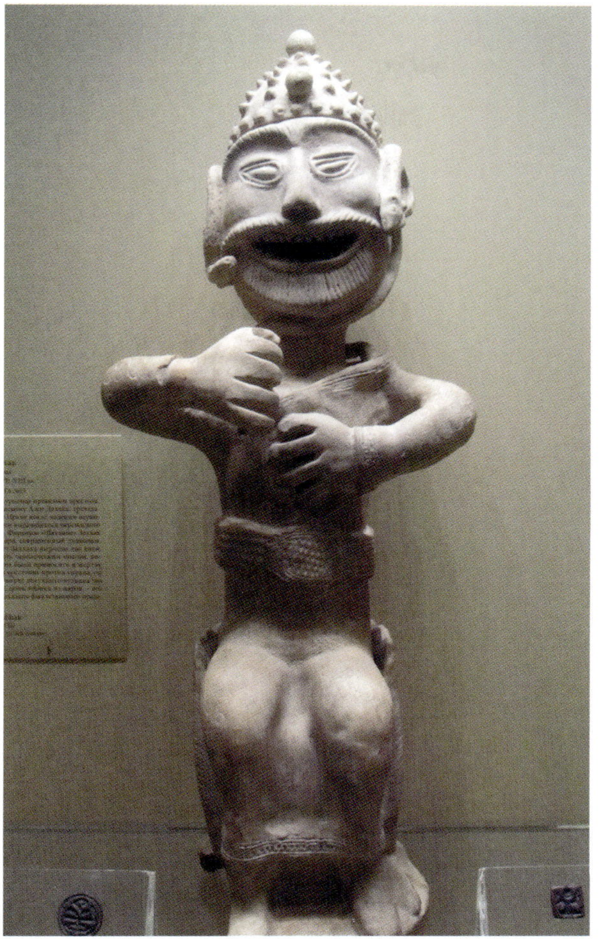

I.10. Islam Akhun and workshop, Zahhak figurine, fired earthenware. Khotan, late 19th century. Height 61 cm. State Hermitage Museum, St. Petersburg, ГА-3053.

missioned before 1910 for circulation on the market to potential buyers and they were probably taken in Sevruguin's Tehran studio.

The appearance of the large monochrome glazed jar in the center of the negative plate clearly indicates that it was created in the modern era and intended to look archaic. The processes of making (and identifying) fabrications and forgeries are treated at length in chapter 3; here it is enough to say that questions are immediately raised by the very crudely rendered turbaned figures, birds, and animals that have been pastily applied to the body of the jar. These do not fit with any known ceramics tradition from the premodern Islamic world and look more like pastrywork than a potter's art.[46] The problems do not stop with the figural imagery. Like some of the Asiatic Terracottas, the jar has been deliberately broken into large pieces before being ostentatiously stuck back together, making a show of its fragmentation without causing it to sustain any actual loss. Finally, and most startlingly, a curious addition sutures a much older historical period into an otherwise vaguely medievalizing invention. The characters around the neck of the jar are obviously intended to mimic the cuneiform script of ancient Near Eastern clay tablets, a script used from around 3000 BCE to the first century CE. They have, however, been made at an enlarged scale and in positive by applying strips of clay onto the surface of the jar, in contrast to real cuneiform which is inscribed

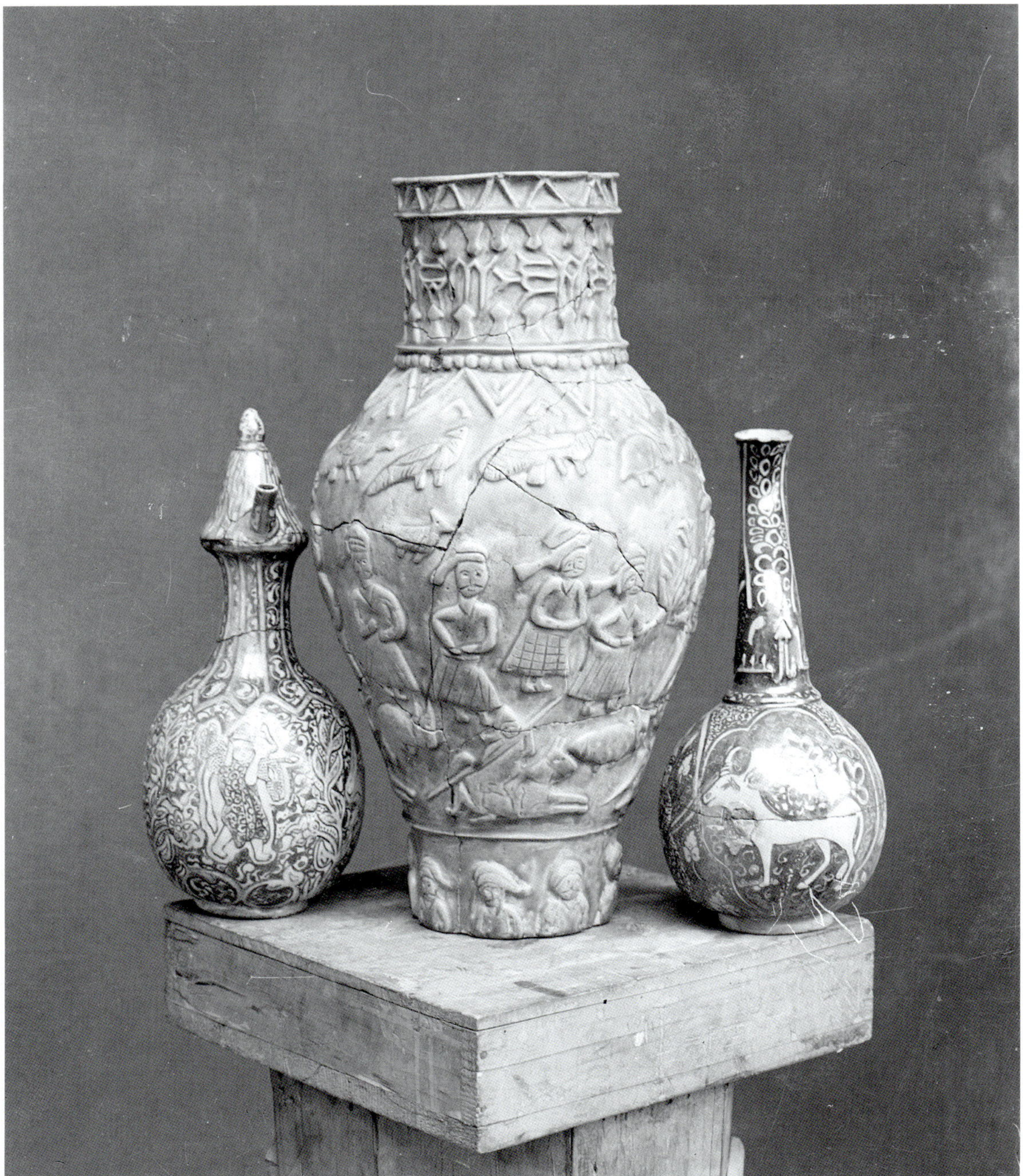

I.11. Studio photograph of ceramics. Positive image from glass plate negative, probably taken before 1910 in Tehran. Antoin Sevruguin/National Museum of Asian Art Archives, Smithsonian Institution, Myron Bement Smith Collection, Gift of Katharine Dennis Smith, 1973–85, FSA_A.04_2.12.GN.26.05.

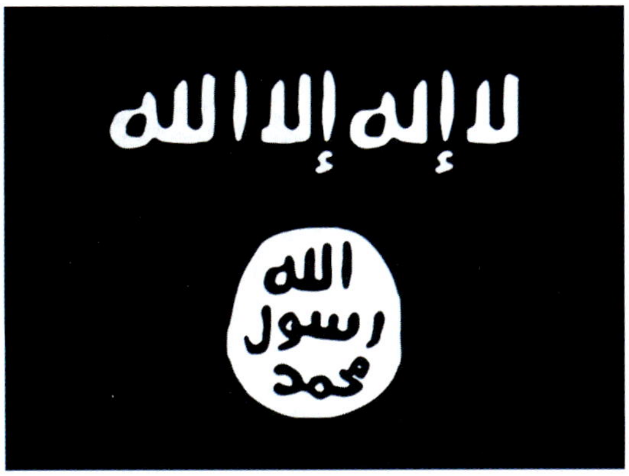

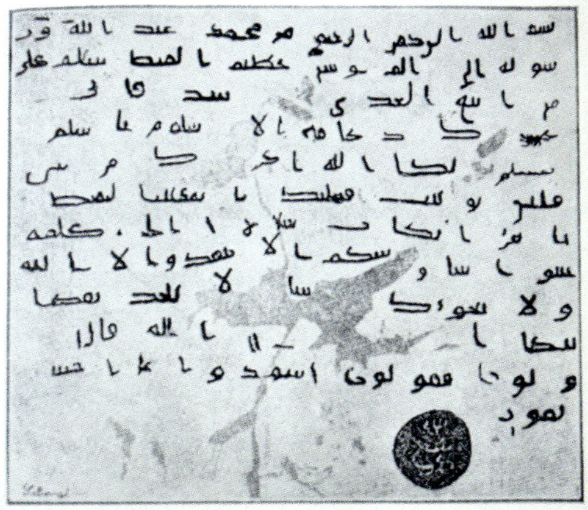
LETTER OF THE PROPHET TO THE "MUKAUKIS," DISCOVERED BY M. ÉTIENNE BARTHÉLÉMY; BELIEVED BY SEVERAL SCHOLARS TO BE THE ACTUAL DOCUMENT REFERRED TO IN THE TEXT.
From the "Hilal," Nov., 1904.

I.12. Flag of Islamic State of Iraq and Syria (ISIS) and other terrorist organizations.

I.13. So-called Letter from the Prophet to the Muqawqis of Egypt, after a drawing published in *Hilal*, 1904. D. S. Margoliouth, *Mohammed and the Rise of Islam* (New York/London: Putnam/Knickerbocker Press, 1905).

by pressing into a clay surface with a wedge-shaped stick. The out-of-scale pseudocuneiform characters around the neck surely derive from print reproductions of ancient inscriptions and, like the Moabite forgeries, they seem to anticipate the jar's own remediation and circulation through photography and print media. They may well have been drawn from the images of cuneiform inscriptions found in the publications of the Iranian scholar Fursat al-Dawla (1854–1920), such as his 1896 *Asar-i ʿajam*.[47]

The mawkish cuneiform jar seems to have sunk without trace sometime after its photographic portrait was made in Tehran, or at least, I have not been able to trace it. Latter-day fundamentalists have, however, ensured that the nineteenth-century heyday of market forgeries in Middle Eastern antiquities will continue to resound in the present. The scandalous mess of looted artifacts, new-made "antiquities," and forged documentation at the Museum of the Bible looks set to continue unfolding—and generating new forgeries—for years to come.[48] But the acquisitive greed of collectors is not the only route by which religious forgeries continue to have traction. Around the same time that the Museum of the Bible's founder, Steve Green, was asking no questions about his newly acquired antiquities, the neocaliphal terrorist group ISIS adopted a nineteenth-century forgery as the central device of their official flag (fig. I.12).

The so-called seal of Muhammad was imprinted on a letter that purported to be an original document sent from the Prophet Muhammad to the governor of Egypt in the seventh century. The subject of huge excitement when it was "discovered" in Egypt in 1854 and subsequently sold to the Ottoman sultan in 1858, the letter enjoyed only a few years of celebrity before the consensus started to turn against its authenticity. It is now recognized by most experts as a forgery, quite possibly manufactured by its "discoverer," a Frenchman called Etienne Barthélémy. The emblem on the ISIS flag is in fact a remediation at several removes from Barthélémy's fraud, being copied not from the document itself but from early twentieth-century drawings of it that subsequently gave rise to further copies in physical and digital media (fig. I.13).

As Ahmed El Shamsy observed in his study of the flag, "Countless postcolonial states were built on colonial mythologies created and developed by Orientalist scholars. Yet the fact that the Islamic State—a group obsessed with its own authenticity and freedom from outside influences—fell for a 150-year-old European fraud is not without irony."[49]

Perhaps, though, it is not so much ironic as inevitable. The modern fetishization of authenticity and evidentiary proof and the conversion of that impulse into tangible material is, after all, what brought the Lügensteine and the seal of Muhammad alike into existence.[50] And when the "evidentiary impulse" of modernity meets the commodity systems of late imperial capitalism—the same systems that shaped the colonial states of the Middle East and their economies—the outcome is inescapable. The market will produce tangible objects that meet the desires of consumers, titillating them with artifacts that support their preferred version of history and offering them the chance to hold that desired past in their hands and wield it. The "seal of Muhammad" proved attractive to nineteenth-century collectors and twenty-first-century fundamentalists alike because it looks so satisfyingly archaic—the result of its having been created for a modern world that equates the appearance of antiquity with the latter-day virtue of authenticity.

F for Photography

Already in this introduction, the technologies of print and photography have surfaced several times as vital components in the translation of artifacts to commodities. The inbuilt relationship between photography, print publication, and the collectors' market in fine ceramics is visible from the very start of the new technology. The first fascicle of the first photographically illustrated book, William Henry Fox Talbot's *The Pencil of Nature* (1844–46), gives two of its five plates over to the carefully arranged contents of collection cabinets. One of these is devoted entirely to glazed fine ceramics (fig. I.14). The objects have been arranged on dark shelves, carefully prepared to provide a strong contrast with the pale forms of the pieces. Although they mimic the appearance of an opened cabinet in a stately drawing room, the photographs were in fact taken outdoors—quite possibly in the courtyard at Lacock Abbey, Talbot's ancestral home.[51] The resulting plates are, simultaneously, luminous records of the new technology's capacity to render reflective surfaces and precise details of design, and documentary inventories of commodities.

Talbot himself recognized documentation of property as one of the great potentials of the new medium, specifically citing it as a potential application of photography in his comments accompanying the image of the china cabinet. He writes that "The more strange and fantastic the forms of [the collector's] old teapots, the more advantage in having their pictures given instead of their descriptions. And should a thief afterwards purloin the treasures—if the mute testimony of the picture were to be produced against him in court—it would certainly be evidence of a novel kind."[52] Photography was thus immediately and presciently identified by Talbot as having an evidentiary function in both a particular legal sense—the hypothetical trial of a thief—and the more generalized aspect of documenting property and validating ownership. Thus, in the first book to be published with photographic illustrations, owner-

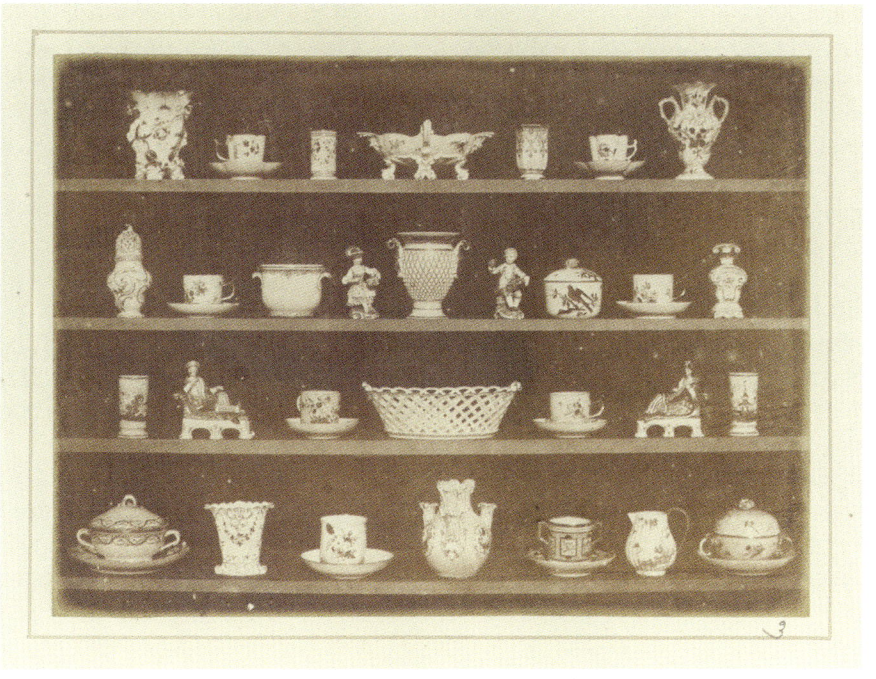

1.14. "Articles of China." Photograph by William Henry Fox Talbot, 1844. *The Pencil of Nature* (1844), plate III, fascicle 1. Getty Museum Collection, 84.XZ.572.

ship of fine ceramics acts as the premier means for demonstrating photography's potential documentary value to those who collect and own art and antiquities.[53]

Talbot's image is directly analogous to country-house practices of visible storage for collected objects of "decorative art," whereby a china cabinet becomes a kind of visual inventory for an owner who will notice if something goes missing from his "stock." In the photograph, the absence of any indication of the surrounding supports for the shelves—which may well have been rather makeshift and unattractive—advances the ceramics themselves into a realm of pure commodification, abstracted from much real sense of physical setting or potential use.[54] The image of the china cabinet received favorable comment from audiences of the time. Reviewers noted the precision with which the photographic process had been able to render individual objects entirely legible in form and pattern in spite of their tiny dimensions on the page, the author of the *Athenaeum* review even observing that they "improve under examination with a powerful lens."[55] The connoisseur's eye had found a new training ground.

Prescient though he was about the usefulness of photography for documenting art ownership, Talbot perhaps did not foresee another, closely related paradigm shift that photography would enable—that is, the massive acceleration of the forger's art. The business of faking and forging art and antiquities is, as seen in chapter 1, quite old; however, the expansion of print and above all photography accelerated such practices exponentially.[56] To trace the colossal impact of photography on practices of forgery and fabrication, we must turn to the pages of a most unusual early twentieth-century publication. The *Mitteilungen des Museen-Verbandes als Manuskript für die Mitglieder* (Communications of the Museum Association in Manuscript for Members, hereafter the *Mitteilungen*) was privately printed in Hamburg from 1899 to 1939 for the Association of Museum Officials for Defence against Fakes and Improper Business Practices.[57] The journal circulated to a membership of museum directors and curators in Germany and elsewhere in Europe who met annually; the society also maintained in Hamburg, and subsequently in Berlin, a physical archive of photographs and documentation of suspected or proven art forgeries, cross-referenced in the reports circulated in the *Mitteilungen*. The archive disappeared in World War II, probably destroyed in Allied bombing, but copies of the publications survive. Oliver Watson, as curator at the Victoria and Albert Museum, had access to the secret journal through the museum's library holdings and was the first to make use of it in the study of Islamic ceramics forgery.[58] Today the entire run of the journal has been digitized by Heidelberg University and provides an extraordinary record of the prewar antiquities market's shadow side.

Created as a private route for sharing information about forgeries being offered for sale and the means of their detection, the entries in the *Mitteilungen* range from brief warnings about specific objects to full transcriptions of lectures. In the earliest years of its publication, the expected code of confidentiality among the journal's subscribers seems to have been taken as read. From 1903 onward, however, all issues include a stern masthead notice reminding readers that "the association expects its members not to deposit [copies of the journal] in libraries and to take precautions to prevent the association's printed matter falling into unauthorized hands or even into the trade."[59] The game of cat and mouse between museums and forgers was on, and each side was trying to stay one step ahead of the other by keeping secret what it knew.

Information was prime currency in this scramble. The *Mitteilungen* made it possible for museum directors and curators to share not just the names, locations, and sales pitches of those trying to sell goods that weren't what they claimed them to be, but also the techniques being used in manufacture and the means by which those could be detected. At first the journal was not illustrated, but as reprographic capabilities expanded through the first decades of the twentieth century, photographic illustrations appeared more frequently. In word and image, the four-decade print run of the journal exposes an extraordinary range of suspect material swirling in the eddies of the market: prehistoric tools, Japanese woodcuts, Swiss furniture, Roman bronzes, Bohemian glass, Italian relief carving, and every kind of ceramic from Spain to China. Virtually everything that collectors desired would turn up faked, sooner or later. Reading through the entries, it becomes clear that print publication and especially photographic reproduction were the engines that drove it all. Time and again the expert reports note that models used by forgers can be identified with reproductions in books, from the designs on new-made Attic vases to "prehistoric" engravings on fragments of bone.[60] Print and photography were important means by which information could be shared among those seeking to detect forgeries, but they were also the fabricator's best friends.

A particularly neat illustration of the fabricator's reliance on published photographs can be seen in a rather Disneyesque bull figurine published in the journal in 1929 by the scholar of Islamic art and curator of the Islamic department in the Kaiser-Friedrich-Museum in Berlin, Friedrich Sarre (fig. I.15).

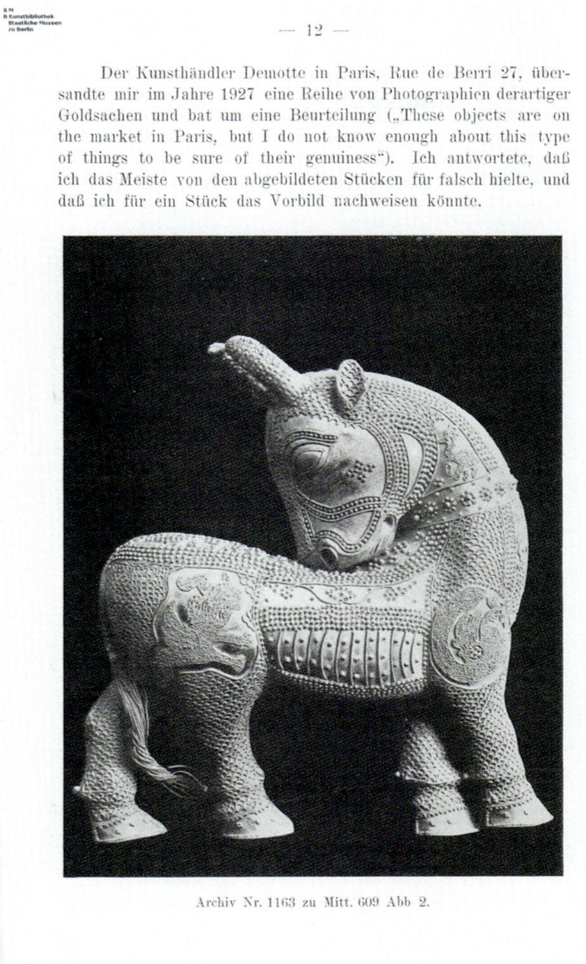

— 12 —

Der Kunsthändler Demotte in Paris, Rue de Berri 27, übersandte mir im Jahre 1927 eine Reihe von Photographien derartiger Goldsachen und bat um eine Beurteilung („These objects are on the market in Paris, but I do not know enough about this type of things to be sure of their genuiness"). Ich antwortete, daß ich das Meiste von den abgebildeten Stücken für falsch hielte, und daß ich für ein Stück das Vorbild nachweisen könnte.

Archiv Nr. 1163 zu Mitt. 609 Abb 2.

I.15. Forged figurine in gold, offered on the market in 1927. After Friedrich Sarre, "609. Persian Style Forged Precious Metal Work," *Mitteilungen des Museen-Verbandes als Manuskript für die Mitglieder* (May 1929), p. 12.

Made from gold and supposedly found at Rayy in northern Iran, it was offered for sale by the Paris dealer Demotte in 1927—right around the same time that other gold figurines and large-scale figural sculptures in stucco, all of purported medieval Iranian origin, were circulating through European and North American dealer networks.[61] Medieval Iran was having a "sculpture moment" on the market. The curious proportions of the bull figurine, with stumpy legs and a huge head turned backward, make sense only when one reads Sarre's note in the 1929 volume of the *Mitteilungen*. He points out that the modern maker of this object was probably working from a photograph of a relief-carved bull at Persepolis that had been published in Sarre's own book, *Arts of Ancient Persia*, in 1922 (fig. I.16). In the book, Sarre's published photograph of the Persepolis relief had cropped out the lion that attacks the bull from behind, leaving much of the composition obscure and forcing the forger to make up a body for the creature while adapting the head from that of the contorted bull in the frieze.[62]

Modern reprographics and the ever-increasing circulation of photographic images in the late nineteenth and early twentieth centuries generated more and more models for copyists to work from.[63] But photography was more than

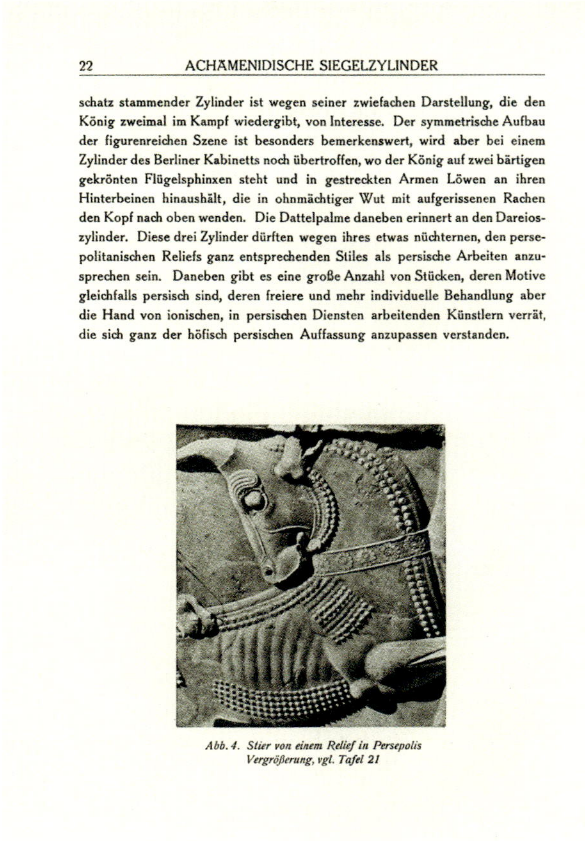

22 ACHÄMENIDISCHE SIEGELZYLINDER

schatz stammender Zylinder ist wegen seiner zwiefachen Darstellung, die den König zweimal im Kampf wiedergibt, von Interesse. Der symmetrische Aufbau der figurenreichen Szene ist besonders bemerkenswert, wird aber bei einem Zylinder des Berliner Kabinetts noch übertroffen, wo der König auf zwei bärtigen gekrönten Flügelsphinxen steht und in gestreckten Armen Löwen an ihren Hinterbeinen hinaushält, die in ohnmächtiger Wut mit aufgerissenen Rachen den Kopf nach oben wenden. Die Dattelpalme daneben erinnert an den Dareios-zylinder. Diese drei Zylinder dürften wegen ihres etwas nüchternen, den persepolitanischen Reliefs ganz entsprechenden Stiles als persische Arbeiten anzusprechen sein. Daneben gibt es eine große Anzahl von Stücken, deren Motive gleichfalls persisch sind, deren freiere und mehr individuelle Behandlung aber die Hand von ionischen, in persischen Diensten arbeitenden Künstlern verrät, die sich ganz der höfisch persischen Auffassung anzupassen verstanden.

Abb. 4. Stier von einem Relief in Persepolis
Vergrößerung, vgl. Tafel 21

I.16. Relief carving at Persepolis in Friedrich Sarre, *Die Kunst des alten Persien* (Berlin: Bruno Cassirer Verlag, 1922).

just a sump of raw material for the forger. Increasingly, it was also the instrument of passage from physical object to virtual commodity. The identification of artifacts with their photographic images—images that tended to monumentalize their subjects through certain conventions of lighting, angle, and scale[64]—meant that the photograph became the premier document of commodity ownership, just as Talbot had foreseen. Moreover, it also meant that ownership was no longer mediated solely or even primarily through the physical object; rather, it was mediated through the image of the object. Within the commodity system of the antiquities circuit, representation through print and photographic imaging increasingly substituted for—and ultimately eclipsed—the physical presence of the object.[65] As one recent scholar of Iranian art has succinctly put it, "Exhibitions come and go and what remains is a catalogue."[66] This commodification of physical artifacts—the process that turns them into assets of virtual value, mediated by their own images—brings us back full circle to the curious fictions of capitalism with which this introduction began.

Transubstantiation: Artifacts to Assets

One of the oddest truths underpinning modern life is that most money in the world exists only as numbers. It comes closest to having any reality only at the point of transaction. A famous quote—often misattributed to a director of the Bank of England—states this truth in bald terms: "The modern banking system manufactures 'money' out of nothing; and the process is perhaps the most astounding piece of sleight of hand that was ever invented. . . . Some 80 percent of what a modern community uses as money is not, strictly speaking, 'money' at all, but merely a transferable entry scribbled in a bank's ledger."[67] Mark Carney, former governor of the Bank of England, recently confirmed this when he observed that 85 percent of what we think of as "money" in the banking system is numbers created by the banks themselves through lending against illiquid assets, like company shares, real estate, and even antiquities.[68]

This is the alchemy that turns physical artifacts into antiquities and thereby virtual commodities—that is, objects of desire, accumulation, and investment. The concept of the asset is key to this. When a physical object like a thirteenth-century Iranian luster bowl enters the antiquities market, it becomes an exchangeable asset with a ledger value that exists increasingly independently of its physical self. Simultaneously, to become an asset in this way it must be shorn of its originary context, just as money acquired through criminal activity must be if it is to be successfully laundered. For example, if the bowl gets mired in debates about the legality of its extraction from Iran, it will become difficult or impossible for its current owner to exchange it, at least within the public and legal levels of the antiquities market. In short, its commodity status will falter and its value as an asset will therefore be placed in jeopardy. I say more throughout this book about provenience (the precise location of archaeological recovery) and provenance (the chain of ownership that establishes a historical artifact as a legally exchangeable commodity, rather than a recently looted object). Here, the important point is that turning historical artifacts into exchangeable assets depends overwhelmingly on severing them, physically and intellectually, from their original contexts. Architectural monuments must be fragmented and ripped apart, manuscripts taken from libraries and often dismembered, ceramic sherds disassociated from archaeological stratification and often reconfigured into an artificial whole, like our hypothetical luster bowl.[69]

The market requisite for severance from context lays bare a fundamental point of tension between the scholarly disciplines of archaeology and art history today. Modern academic archaeology varies in its practices but most, if not all, current methodologies are premised on the accurate documentation of extraction context wherever possible. Maps, findspots, stratigraphy, and assemblage data are now part of archaeology's stock-in-trade (although, as chapter 2 shows, this was certainly not always the case). In some contemporary iterations of archaeology, the archaeological context could even be considered the primary subject of study, ahead of the individual artifact. The discipline of art history, on the other hand, has historically placed the interpretation of images at the center of its models of meaning, and has not always paid close attention to the physical histories of its subjects. In recent years there has been a distinct "material turn" in art history as well as an accelerating awareness of collecting histories—especially for works harvested from colonial contexts—and the contours of the field are changing rapidly. But while the highly destructive nature of early archaeological extraction makes the damage done in the past exceedingly visible, art history's paradigmatic subjects of study—easel paintings and other forms of transportable image—

circulated above ground from the moment of their creation onward. This has perhaps conditioned art historians to think of their subjects as inherently and unproblematically mobile, meaning that the distorting and even destructive effects of the discipline have not been as immediately evident nor as widely discussed as they are in archaeology. One outcome is that while both disciplines were born out of collecting cultures, much of art history remains imbricated with the market in ways that academic archaeology does not, or at least not to the same degree, and it is within art history that the fictions of capital still circulate most freely. Our thirteenth-century luster bowl, transformed from archaeological subject matter (sherds with a context, even if unrecorded) into an art historical object (a bricolaged vessel with an attractive design and no context), is now free to enter the market.

As with other kinds of asset, once the monetary value of an antiquity has been established, it can be altered by subsequent transactions without the physical reality of the object changing at all. Those value-changing transactions are not limited solely to buying and selling. The most dramatic example of this in recent times is the much-contested *Salvator Mundi* painting, which increased enormously in financial value once it was included in the National Gallery's 2011 Leonardo da Vinci exhibition and thereby publicly validated as an autograph original by Leonardo himself.[70] This is an extreme example of what I will call a "scholarly transaction," a category that includes cataloguing, publication, and display. These can affect the value of any antiquity, including our hypothetical thirteenth-century luster bowl, by adding information, authority, and pedigree to it, augmenting its status as an asset and ultimately its financial value.[71] Scholarly transactions—especially successful exhibitions and their catalogues—can even create new asset classes by demarcating a particular type of object as interesting or important and therefore valuable.[72]

Because scholarly transactions can be used to "launder" the market profiles of unprovenanced antiquities once they have entered circulation, exhibitions, publications, and entrance into a "good" collection are classic routes for generating an asset-worthy pedigree. This pedigree can eventually serve to displace or obscure awkward questions about provenience and provenance. This is especially true for objects originating in areas like the Middle East or Southeast Asia, where modern geopolitics and historical instabilities have created low market expectations for documentation and a laissez-faire attitude among many buyers.[73]

The same routes that launder the provenance of looted objects can also be used to get inauthentic objects into circulation. When a reputable scholar publishes the first study of a collected object and implicitly or explicitly represents authenticity, condition, and/or provenance as unproblematic, the piece is then usually considered free to continue onward, passed as "safe" for scholarship and exhibition. A completely untroubled passage might be rare in reality for ultrahigh-value assets—again, witness the *Salvator Mundi* painting, which has garnered plenty of comments about its (in)authenticity—but it is possible for low-to-mid-value assets like our medieval luster bowl.[74] This means that scholarly publication can have significant implications for the financial value of antiquities. It is hardly surprising that private collectors have long paid to have their collections published in beautifully produced catalogues, written by eminent scholars. In this way, the transubstantiation of artifact to asset can be completed.[75]

There is also a deeper level to this interplay between the curious alchemies of finance and those of the antiquities market. At every turn in the modern antiquities trade, from the nineteenth century to today, the instruments of finance do not just provide parallels to the market; rather, they are its actual substrate. It is no coincidence that the heyday of fabricating Islamic ceramics—and antiquities forgery in the region more generally—coincided with the rapidest expansion of modern European-style banking into the Middle East, from about 1870 to 1914. It was this financial system that created the full-blown antiquity-as-asset, making it possible for fragments of physical history to become an internationally tradable, value-bearing asset class, and rendering historical time itself an exchangeable form of capital. Critical to the expansion of modern banking and the antiquities trade alike in this new frontier was the establishment of what are essentially fictive forms of money: bills of exchange, for example, were introduced to the Ottoman Empire by European bankers who sought to stabilize a fiduciary currency system by regulating the exchange market.[76] Stocks, bonds, mortgages, formalized credit facilities, and exchange systems of asset valuation all play their part in the histories told within this book, as the economic landscape of the Middle East underwent irrevocable changes with the introduction of new financial practices.[77] Relevant histories of banking in the region are developed more fully in chapter 1, as the ground is laid for the large-scale translation of artifacts to assets within the tilling fields of the Middle Eastern antiquities race.

Invisible Hands

This book presents a history of Islamic ceramics as modern subjects of extraction, fabrication, collection, and imagination. It seeks to illuminate the previously disdained craft enterprises of fabrication and forgery, and to reinstate those enterprises into the history of art as crucial forms of artistic skill that demand closer study. To do so, the book travels across several different registers, from materially focused art histories (albeit applied to unorthodox subjects) to political and social economies. The conventional narrative would tell us that craft skills and artisanship were swept away in the Middle East in the second half of the nineteenth century, drowned by the wave of manufactured goods that arrived via industrialization and the asymmetric trade treaties of colonialism. There is much truth in this, but it is only part of the story. As this introduction has already shown, some craft skills were in fact redirected toward a new market generated by the colonial project and its fanatical harvesting of artifacts: the faking, forging, and fictionalizing of antiquities, especially ceramics. To probe the challenges that colonial modernity presents to the discipline of art history, we must look more closely at the thousands of brittle objects that moved through it and were remade in its image. Islamic ceramics came to be canonized as an art form through processes of extraction and fabulation that made the new old and the old whole again; these processes were enacted by invisible hands that created an entire asset class for circulation in a globalizing antiquities market.

A foundational premise of this book is that the global antiquities market is rooted in colonial models of resource extraction, nourished by the instruments of the modern finance industry. Chapter 1, "Middle Eastern Antiquities: The Making of a Modern Marketplace," lays out the long prehistory of collecting that produced a marketplace so receptive to the fabricator's craft. It presents the history of Islamic art collecting as a history of commodification, viewed through three distinct temporal episodes. First, the chapter traces the convergence of colonial ventures, resource extraction, finance, and forgery in the early modern scramble for antiquities in the Middle East and considers the types of objects that were most desired by those early collectors. This is followed by a study of the confessional groups that moved from early modern mercantile success to prominence in both the antiquities trade and the modern banking industry, within the late nineteenth-century Ottoman Empire and Iran. It asks who achieved success in that environment, and why those two trades were frequently conjoined. The chapter finishes with a case study on the rise and fall of one incredible, emblematic object in the early twentieth-century art market: the so-called chalice of Antioch, a late antique Syrian silver vessel that was at one point marketed as the most sacred and storied object in Christianity. Through these three aperçus, a multilayered, longue durée view of social networks, political structures, and economic institutions comes to light, exposing the deep foundations of a quintessentially modern marketplace and the fabricated antiquities that moved through it.

Between the 1880s and 1914 the market for Islamic antiquities from the Middle East exploded, fueled by the increasing interest of European and North American collectors and the development of ever more efficient technologies of transportation and communication. Chapter 2, "Objects of Desire, In and Out of Time," focuses on this critical era of market acceleration to produce an extractivist history of Islamic ceramics. In this chapter, vessels and tiles are presented not in the tidy evolutionary sequence of the sales catalogue but as a resource that was violently harvested and processed in largely undocumented circumstances, all within the space of a few decades. The absence of scientific archaeological information dogs the field of Islamic art history, and we have not always been keen to acknowledge the sans-papiers nature of most of our materials. Chapter 2 addresses this by piecing together the scattered evidence to tell the story of above-ground ceramics harvesting from collections and shrines and below-ground commercial extraction from historical sites, defying tidy chronologies and keeping one eye on the places where inauthentic objects appear in that record. Along the way, the chapter interweaves close studies of superlative individual objects to show what drove this frenzied harvest, as collectors clamored for more.

Chapter 3, "Making Gold from Base Matter: Potsherds, Paint, and Patience," is the fulcrum of the book. To make the case that ceramics fabrication was an important site of craft skill, it is essential that the reader should appreciate how that work was done. A quite astonishing range of craft practices, representing untold hours of work and experimentation, were dedicated to the creation of seemingly whole ceramic objects for the antiquities market. To make these visible, this chapter coordinates several different kinds of detective work: close looking, laboratory analysis, scientific imaging, and archival research are used in concert to dive deeply into the self-effacing methods by which ceramics were made anew. Deliberately framing a new vocabulary for the phenomena it describes, the chapter sets out three main modalities of fabrication in historic ceramics from the Islamic world: bricolage, skin-swaps, and the coup de théâtre of true forgery, complete with the artificial shadows of time.

After economies, extraction, and fabrication, chapter 4 turns to the human networks that created and floated these objects and secured their status as assets. "The New Babylon: Dealing in an American Century" follows the shifting financial focus of the global art market from Paris and London to New York and, eventually, the mid-twentieth-century American Midwest. Built on archival research conducted in collections across the United States and Europe, the chapter begins in the Middle East by examining the changes that antiquities collecting brought to local economies, querying what we can know about the craftspeople involved and mapping the locations of Islamic ceramics fabrication. Switching next to the dealer network, correspondence archives bring to light the means and methods by which a host of individuals pitched their wares and made their fortunes in a transnational network that mobilized social as well as financial capital. The last part of the chapter homes in on the emblematic ceramics collection of one of the most celebrated Middle Eastern antiquities dealers of all time, Dikran Kelekian (1867–1951). The changing fortunes of Kelekian's collection, traced through multiple museum archives, serve as a mirror of the twentieth century's global economic transformations, as his pieces travel from the Middle East to Paris, London, and eventually New York, finally coming to rest in the civic museums of the Midwestern United States.

Finally, in chapter 5, "The Riddle of Raqqa" returns to an object class that has recurred at points throughout the book—so-called Raqqa ceramics—and a dealer who made his first appearance in chapter 1. This chapter challenges the art historical consensus about the highly coveted ceramics of Raqqa, now represented in several major US museums. The study is centered upon an unpublished collection of Raqqa ceramics on the Indiana University campus that traveled through the same routes as much better-known examples in more famous institutions. It traces the story of the Indiana pieces back to Raqqa through three anachronic episodes: the arrival of the pieces in Indiana in the 1970s; analysis conducted on campus between 2016 and 2021; and the extraction and circulation of the famous ceramics of Raqqa between the end of the nineteenth century and the interwar years. Using laboratory analysis and provenance research, it questions the stories that dealers and art historians have relied upon to explain the miraculously intact and perfect condition of some of these medieval survivals, and mounts an alternative explanation for their immaculate appearance.

Within all this there remain the material poetics of the objects themselves. When done well, the craft of ceramics fabrication creates works of compelling virtuosity that defy easy comprehension and suture multiple temporalities into a single whole. The extraordinary material durability of fired clay lures us into thinking that we can somehow reconstruct the past from it completely; that if we had but world enough and time, we could perfectly recreate both the object and its life story from the shattered and degraded pieces, the imperfect archaeological record, the lopsided archive, and the doctored display object. We couldn't, of course, but there is a great deal to be gained in trying. In truth, the histories of premodern ceramics are as fractured as the objects themselves; and like ceramics, histories can become distorted when we try to piece them back together from fragments.

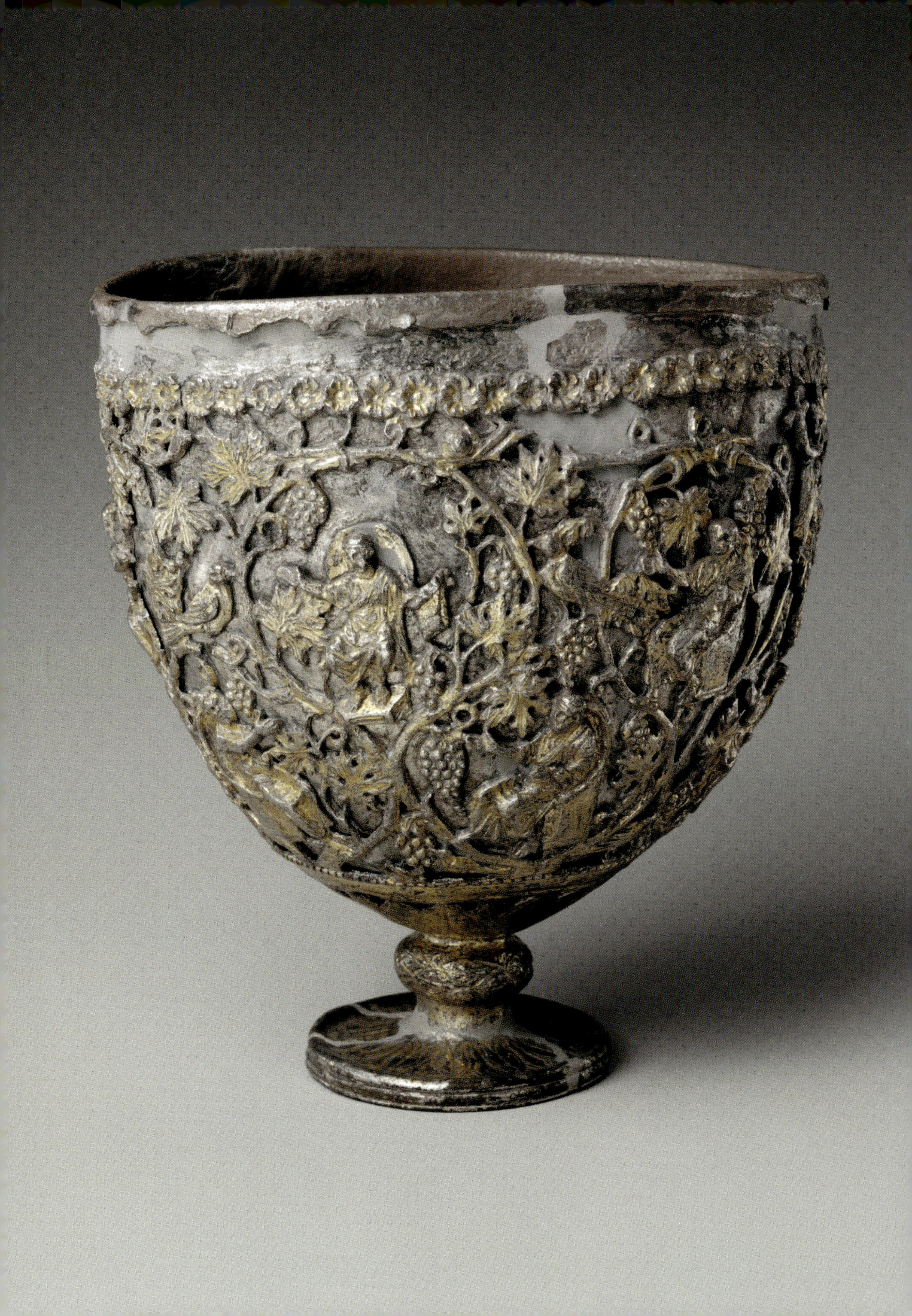

1 Middle Eastern Antiquities

THE MAKING OF A MODERN MARKETPLACE

Pay attention to the business of commerce. It is different from other occupations. It needs various types of knowledge. Among them [are] knowledge of jewelry and mines, the assay of gold and silver; but foremost is that of accounting, being the foundation of commerce.

—AMIN AL-ZARB'S TESTAMENT TO HIS SON, 1886

The story of Middle Eastern antiquities as transhistorical commodities goes back as far as tomb-robbing does. In most early contexts, however, the robbers' quest was focused not on the artistry of individual artifacts but on the reuse value of materials—especially precious metals that could be melted down and reused or, in ancient Egypt, the relatively rare commodity of wood, which was recycled in myriad ways.[1] Early tomb-robbing, such as took place in late New Kingdom Egypt (ca. 1295–1070 BCE), could sometimes also be the means of putting crafted objects of high social and material value, including vessels and jewelry, back into economic circulation and/or making them available for reuse in subsequent burials.[2] Nonetheless, those activities did not constitute an antiquities market in the same sense that we would use the term today, being primarily oriented toward reuse and recycling rather than acquiring and amassing artworks as assets that could be hoarded, circulated to increase value, or liquidated. To trace a more direct prehistory of the colonial-era market in Middle Eastern art and antiquities, we must turn to the Mediterranean region of the early modern era, and above all to the hunt for the physical remnants of antiquity, beginning in Renaissance Italy.

This chapter presents a commodity history of Middle Eastern antiquities, encountering them not as the exalted objects of connoisseurship but as the raw material of a collecting industry that emerged in tandem with, and continues to be entangled with, finance capitalism and international banking. From the early modern period to the present day, the antiquities market has been interlaced with the finance industry through the promotion of antiquities as an extractable and refinable resource and an asset class, creating an environment especially receptive to fictive objects. That entanglement inheres not only in the abstract realms of investment and valuation but also in the persons of individual collectors and dealers, many of whom had or have financial careers or connections of one sort or another.

This chapter unfolds that history through three distinct episodes. First, it explores the early modern development of a European market in Middle

Eastern antiquities, looking particularly to the activities of the English peer Sir Thomas Howard, Earl of Arundel (1585–1646) as an aperçu through which financial frameworks, colonial enterprises, and craft practices of restoring and faking can be glimpsed in early convergence. Initially, European antiquarian collecting in the Islamic world was most attentive to manuscripts, coins, and carpets, with other forms of art and "curiosities" emerging in a more ad-hoc way as objects of desire and status. Only in the later nineteenth century did historic Islamic ceramics fully enter the commoditized sphere of antiquities trading, a phase of excavation and circulation explored in full in chapter 2.

The second part of this chapter switches focus from early modern collectors to the expanding mercantile networks of the eighteenth, nineteenth, and early twentieth centuries, pausing to consider the questions of identity that these raise. From whose hands did Middle Eastern antiquities enter transregional markets? From which communities did those brokers and dealers come, and why? Over time, Europeans increasingly tapped into existing markets as well as generating new systems of extraction and routes of circulation, and by the turn of the twentieth century huge quantities of material had passed from the Middle East into European and North American collections.[3] For reasons that are examined below, certain communities—especially Eastern Christians of various denominations—rose to prominence as interlocutors between East and West in this globalizing marketplace. International trade and banking provided the physical and virtual networks of transportation and value exchange that moved antiquities through the commercial metropoles of Aleppo, Cairo, Damascus, Istanbul, and Tehran.

To illustrate in detail the workings of these early twentieth-century economic networks, and to reveal their transformative powers, the third and final part of this chapter is a close study of one remarkable object and its modern history: the so-called chalice of Antioch. At once a genuine early Christian artifact and a fabulous creation of the modern art market, the chalice's passage from northern Syria to Aleppo, Paris, and finally New York has generated a narrative that is almost farcically cinematic. On its way to becoming one of the most famous and controversial objects of the early twentieth century, the chalice took in bankers and financiers, staged discoveries, mortgaged hoards of silverwork, and a family firm of dealers that reappears later in this book. Extraordinary showmanship was used to foment religious fervor as the chalice's folkloric and (ultimately unrealized) financial value went up in leaps and bounds along the way—until it ended up a victim of its own overpromotion, its stock fizzling out in mid-century Manhattan.

Harvesting Middle Eastern Antiquities in the Renaissance

By the second half of the fifteenth century, an age of enthusiastic digging and collecting was well underway in Rome. Italian nobles competed for antiquities in the city, especially monumental marble sculpture, with personal status increasingly projected through ownership of the classical past.[4] Some early collectors of antiquities in Italy, including such notable figures as sometime merchant Cardinal Pietro Barbo (1417–1471; Pope Paul II from 1464), began to look farther afield, across the eastern Mediterranean. As well as the Roman antiquities harvested closer to home, Barbo collected coins, gems, small

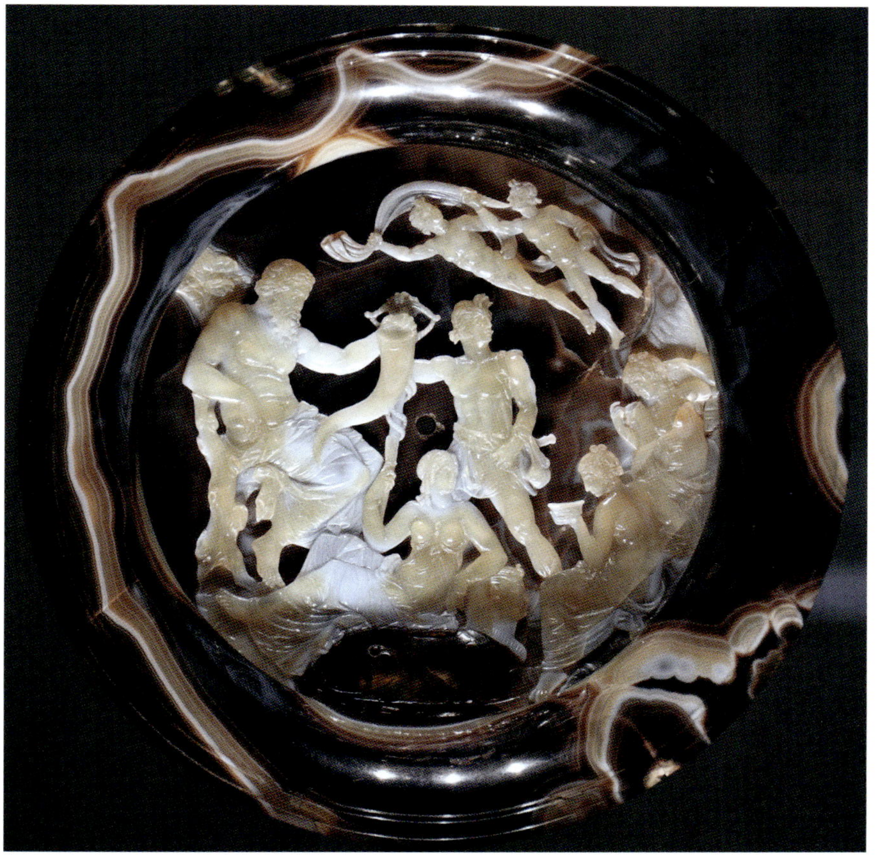

1.1. Tazza Farnese, sardonyx cameo vessel. Attributed 2nd century BCE, Alexandria. Diameter 20 cm. Naples, Museo Archeologico Nazionale, Inv. 27611.

bronze objects, carved ivories, and other items gathered from Asia Minor.[5] His interests, like those of other Renaissance-era antiquities collectors in Europe, lay primarily in the ancient Greek and Roman empires; one of his most famous possessions was the celebrated Tazza Farnese, a large carved agate cameo depicting allegorical figures, created in second-century BCE Ptolemaic Egypt (fig. 1.1).[6] The remarkable trajectory of the Tazza Farnese saw it transmitted from one illustrious owner to another, apparently spending time in the courtly collections of Timurid Central Asia in the early fifteenth century—during which period a strikingly precise ink drawing was made of it, surviving in a Timurid album now in Berlin (fig. 1.2).[7] The Timurid drawing of the Tazza makes clear that an early modern regard for classical antiquities was not limited to Europe, and opens a narrow but tantalizing window onto entangled Eurasian views of classical artifacts as subjects of wonder and elite possession. Meanwhile, the Tazza itself seemingly journeyed from Timurid Herat to Naples and onward to Rome, through fifteenth-century routes as yet largely unknown.

The Tazza Farnese arrived into a politically volatile Italian peninsula where age-old fascinations with the artifacts of the past were consolidating into categories of exchangeable goods. Classical antiquity was gaining such associative value that its material remains became trophies of personal education as well as visible signs of professional success and spending power. Gem cabinets, coin collections, and sculpture gardens developed as the loci of collections,

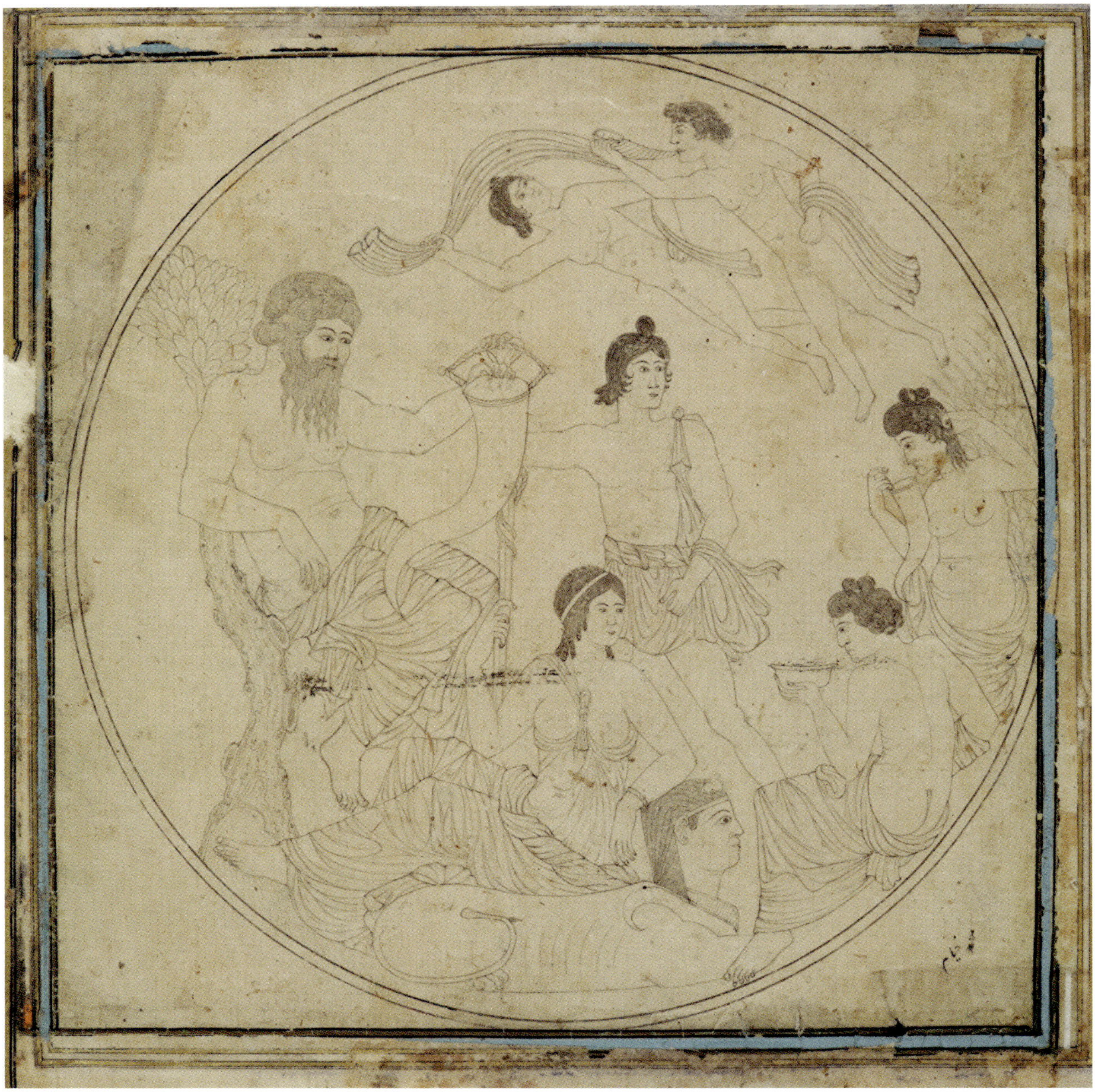

1.2. Drawing of the Tazza Farnese, ascribed to Muhammad Khayyam, ink on paper. Attributed Samarqand or Herat, ca. 1400–1450. Staatsbibliothek zu Berlin, Preussischer Kulturbesitz, Diez A fol. 72, p. 3, no. 2.

and with these there came forgeries. For example, a counterfeit coin with forged Greek letters (*falsificatum cum litteris grecis*) is recorded in the 1457 inventory of Barbo's numismatic cabinet, and coin forgeries intended to dupe collectors were seemingly in circulation even before Barbo's time.[8] The identification of supposedly antique coins as falsifications raises interesting questions about early modern conceptions of authenticity, which could apparently include quite freely reconstructed statuary (see below) but did not accommodate coin forgeries. Right from the inception of what we might call modern collecting practices, antiquities were traded through a market that was ready to respond to demand by supplying material fashioned through all sorts of means. From the Renaissance to the present day, the antiquities market not only has facilitated the exchange and transformation of objects but also has brought objects into existence.[9]

Of course, while there is much to say about the antiquities market as a system, all the movements that took place within that system were the outcome of activities by individuals. The label "antiquarian" is sometimes used to denote any humanist scholar of the Renaissance era and it has an air of lofty detachment from the present, but the so-called antiquarians of Renaissance Italy included many men who acted as dealers and brokers of antiquities and played a very active role in the burgeoning antiquities market.[10] These individuals, from a range of socioeconomic and cultural backgrounds, had to have wide professional and social networks across the trade as well as the buying classes, and in an economic environment dependent on a volatile and hazardous credit system it made sense for merchants and artisans to diversify. Accordingly, some in sixteenth-century Rome kept a stock of antiquities as a "complementary investment to their main business."[11] As Barbara Furlotti cogently observes, the dealer-antiquarians of sixteenth-century Italy "functioned as the hinges between distinct social planes that were normally separated from one another and facilitated interchanges between otherwise disconnected social and cultural environments."[12] This book will show that such a description could be applied equally to those figures who moved objects between the excavation sites of the Middle East and the vending capitals of Europe and the United States in the late nineteenth and early twentieth centuries, with added complexities of ethnic, linguistic, and religious difference at play. The label "antiquarian," with its grand scholarly aura, was often self-applied by those colonial-era dealers.

To return to the cradle of the global art market in the early modern Mediterranean: mercantile networks and scholarly historicism made antiquities from the region ever more visible and desirable throughout the seventeenth century—especially to wealthy western European audiences. The architecture of ancient Greece and Rome became established as part of the education of European elites via the so-called Grand Tour, generating acquisitive desires for the physical remains of classical antiquity. Whole buildings are not easily transportable except in images, but architectural fragments, including figural sculpture and inscriptions, are movable. Many were carried off to colder climates by such rapacious art collectors as Sir Thomas Howard, Earl of Arundel, long before the much more infamous removal of the Parthenon marbles from Athens by the Earl of Elgin.[13] In a celebrated portrait of 1618, Arundel is shown seated, with a late sixteenth-century carpet from northwestern Iran

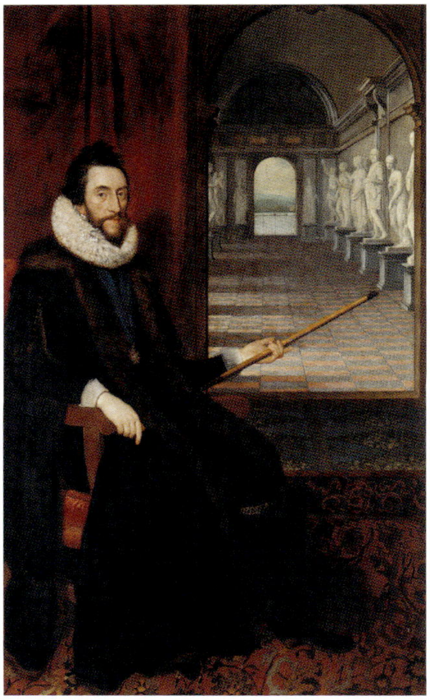

1.3. Daniel Mytens, *Thomas Howard, 14th Earl of Arundel*. Oil on canvas. England, ca. 1618. Length 207 cm. Accepted in lieu of tax by H.M. Government and allocated to the Gallery, 1980. National Portrait Gallery, 5292.

below his chair. He gestures with his earl marshal staff of office toward a gallery of classical statuary, viewed through a curtain as if it were a picture within a picture (fig. 1.3).[14] Within the gallery, receding lines of sculptures mounted on pedestals lead across the checkered floor toward an arched opening overlooking a river, indicating that the setting is likely Arundel House (no longer extant) on the Strand, looking out onto the River Thames.

The conjunction of ancient Rome and the early modern Iran of Arundel's time, via the collected commodities of statuary and carpet, is a striking one. Some of the statues in the painting (several of which are now in the Ashmolean Museum in Oxford) probably came from Arundel's 1613–14 visit to Rome, and much has been written about the Earl's sculpture collection in relation to his role as "the first great English art-collector."[15] Far less has been said about the carpet, although as Lindsay Allen and Moya Carey recently pointed out, its alignment with Arundel's Roman statuary in this painting is "a sign that [both the carpet and the statues] formed part of a shared constellation of globally-circulating objects in contemporary discourse."[16] The very fact of a contemporary Iranian carpet playing a significant role in a painting that inaugurates, via classical statuary, the new concept of the aristocratic English art collector shows how deeply embedded were the craft products of the Middle East within the mercantile commodity networks of western Europe. It also shows that they had not yet reached the center stage occupied by classical antiquity.[17]

Arundel's host during his 1613–14 visit to Rome was the art collector, banker, and financier to the Vatican, the Marchese Vincenzo Giustiniani (1564–1637). Giustiniani helped arrange a permit for Arundel to perform excavations on the Forum Romanum, a remarkable concession to be granted to a foreigner.[18] There, the earl reportedly uncovered several sculptures, which were then sent back to England. It has been repeatedly suggested, however, that the savvy financier Giustiniani "planted" antiquities in the Forum for Arundel to discover, presumably in the hope of pleasing and thereby gaining influence over the important English Catholic peer.[19] This does indeed seem a likely explanation for Arundel's improbably immediate and spectacular excavation success in the feverish collecting environment of Rome, a city that had already been picked over during the sixteenth century when it became "a vast excavation site."[20]

Many of the pieces Arundel acquired on his Rome excursion have been restored since antiquity, including documented seventeenth-century restorations performed in Arundel's time—and presumably at his request—intended to render damaged statuary complete. A shipping inventory dated to March 1635 gave a Walloon sculptor working in Rome, François Dieussart, permission to export "a group of Echo and Narcissus, two Sibyls, the head of a putto and an assortment of legs and arms intended for those statues at Arundel house in need of limbs."[21] Some of the restorations significantly changed not only the appearance but also the identity of the artifacts, like the statue of "Cicero" whose head, including Cicero's defining wart, is of modern manufacture, probably made in the seventeenth century.[22] Preferring "anachronistic but intact statues to fragmentary originals," Arundel was in step with other collectors of the period, and the resultant modus operandi of suturing new parts to old fragments foreshadows much of the work done to Islamic ceramics.[23]

Like some other collectors of the time, Arundel soon turned his attentions eastward. Frustrated by failures in the Roman market and the Papal prohibitions against exporting antiquities, Arundel commissioned Sir Thomas Roe, the English ambassador in Constantinople, and others to bring him antiquities from Ottoman territory.[24] Eventually he sent his own agent, Rev. William Petty (1585–1639), into Ottoman Greece and Turkey on the quest for "books, medalles or stone which may be founde."[25] Arundel and Petty followed a deepening set of paths from Europe into Ottoman territories in what would become, in the eighteenth and nineteenth centuries, a "scramble for the past" across the Ottoman Empire, from the Mediterranean littoral to Mesopotamia.[26] Western Europeans writing from within this scramble frequently posited the peoples of the Ottoman Empire and elsewhere in the Islamic world as indifferent or even hostile toward the remains of the past that they lived alongside, sometimes invoking the orthodox Islamic prohibition of figural images as supporting evidence and justification for removal to western European collections. Those tropes are periodically contradicted, however, by reports of local resistance to the removal of statuary and architectural material, and its incorporation into everyday life through legends and beliefs.[27] European writers in the later nineteenth century, at a time of openly nationalist competition over antiquities to stock metropolitan museums, would blame the Ottoman government for failing to protect the empire's physical heritage and for its lack of interest in museum development outside of the imperial capital.[28]

Returning to the seventeenth century, Petty's methods for extracting statuary and inscription panels from Ottoman territory in the seventeenth century were successful, if also highly questionable by today's standards.[29] An anonymous tract attributed speculatively to him, *Of Statues and Antiquities*, gives instructions on how to conceal the value of excavated antiquities from Turkish audiences and what to use to bribe Ottoman officials, as well as describing how those sculptures that couldn't be carried off whole should be cut "asunder with iron saws and sharp sand" for transportation with tackles, pulleys, and carts.[30] One paragraph neatly summarizes the value table of an emerging commodity system for the physical remains of antiquity:

> The things to be sought for are these following: Statues clothed & naked, but the naked ones are of greatest value, Heads of all sorts that can be found, marbles carved with halfe round figures, which are called Basso, Relevo, Pili of Marble histored, which are like troughs of marble carved with figures, Vazes, Altars, or pedestalls with any kinde of carved work on them, or if the vazes be plaine, they are to be esteemed. Likewise beasts of all kindes for tombs or sepulchers, The most ancient are to be desired, for as for those done in latter times, of the Easterne Emperors they are of small value. Inscriptions of all sorts, and if a statue have an inscription on the pedestall or Bases, it is the more rare. or if a pedestall be standing with anie inscription on it, & neare it by digging, a Statue chance to be found it is of the like value. Besides all these, there are to be provided manie great blocks of severall grecian marbles to mend & repaire the statues, & other things aforesaid. All things of brasse work that can be found, as Statues, heads, pieces of Basso Relevo, and likewise all little figures in brasse or lampes, vazes Instruments for sacrifice, medalls or whatsoever else can be gotten, if they be of metall, are of great value.[31]

Of Statues and Antiquities is a guide to effective management of resource extraction, the resource being antiquity itself. In this regard it is extremely revealing of the paradigm that European collectors and their agents were bringing to bear on the eastern Mediterranean past and its physical remnants: carved stones were resources that needed to be extracted from their native context in order to be rendered properly visible and valued correctly. Like any cash crop, antiquities were often shipped in a raw or semiraw state for processing, a stage of refinement that would take place closer to the imperial center. In this case, "processing" includes both the physical reconstruction/refinement of statuary and architectural fragments and cleaning of coins and metalwork, and the intellectual "processing" that takes place when an object is placed into scholarship and begins to circulate in publication and citation as a named, categorized, and owned artifact.

Arundel also trained his sights on antiquities even farther east than the Ottoman Empire. In 1637 he persuaded King Charles I of England to send a painter to Iran in company with an Iranian merchant who styled himself the Safavid ambassador. The young painter was tasked with creating drawn records of ancient buildings, as well as

> procuring such [antiquities] as are fitt for us to be brought away to ye sea side on land—the Antiquities we principally desire are Antique statuaes whose heads or peeces Baise Relioug ["basso relievo," i.e., bas-relief], subscriptions or such like in Marble or brasse, any great or small Vessels of Aggats, Brasse or Marble any Antique Coins or gravings in any kind of Aggat or any Metall any instruments for . . . or such like As also any excellent auntient Bookes in ye Persian Arabian or Greeke Language.[32]

The scheme came to nothing and the young painter died at Bandar ʿAbbas on the Persian Gulf in December 1637 without reaching his destination. Nonetheless, the episode shows the interest taken at the highest levels of English society in sourcing antiquities from an increasingly wide geographic range. Arundel's interest in the ruins of Persepolis in particular was undoubtedly fueled by the first images of the Achaemenid site—famed as the location of Alexander the Great's conquest of the Persians—to appear in print in Europe in 1634.[33]

Importantly, the proposed English mission to Iran was not only intended to gather visual records and physical works of art from the Safavid heartland. The last item on Charles I's directive for the Persian mission was a curious instruction to explore the possibilities of setting up an English colony on Madagascar. Like the command for Persian antiquities, this too seems to have come direct from Arundel, an investor in English ventures in the Atlantic and Indian Ocean trade routes. He campaigned energetically for the establishment of a colony on Madagascar.[34] Like the Persian antiquities collecting initiative, the Madagascar scheme ultimately came to nothing. But if it had been realized, it would have attempted to replicate the colonization of North America in a new, idealized island paradise—and would have incurred the wrath of the British East India Company, who strenuously objected to this threat to their monopoly.

Viewed in toto, Arundel's seventeenth-century hunt for antiquities, from Rome and ever eastward, has all the ingredients of more recent markets in antiquities: reported "excavations" that may or may not have been what they seemed; restoration that in some cases radically modified artifacts; a resource-extraction model for the physical remains of the past; and the direct alignment of antiquities acquisition with colonial ventures.

Before turning to the collecting of Islamic artifacts, it is worth pausing to consider the transportation risks attendant on treating antiquities as an extractable resource. Large-scale sculpture and materials en masse had to be transported by water, via routes that were not always easily navigable and using vessels and rafts that were not necessarily well suited to the task. In 1625 Petty lost "many things" he had gathered on Samos when they were washed overboard on the sea voyage to Ephesus, near modern-day Selçuk on the west coast of Turkey. He seems to have been able to retrieve some of them from the coastal seabed, but the episode suggests such mishaps may have been fairly frequent.[35] There must have been plenty of unrecorded episodes, too, of materials that were lost in transit. The most famous transportation failure in Middle Eastern antiquities collecting took place in 1855, when a massive quantity of Mesopotamian antiquities was lost into the Tigris at Qurna, a town near the confluence with the Euphrates. The pieces had been excavated from the Assyrian sites at Khorsabad and Hillah (Babylon). Rafts carrying four enormous, monumental stone sculptures and 150 crates of stone carvings and metalwork sank when villagers near Qurna boarded and scuttled the boat of a Monsieur Clément, who had been employed by the French government to sail the excavated material through hostile territory to Basra for its eventual passage to France.[36] Two of the sculptures and about thirty crates were saved, but the rest went to the bottom of the river.

Collecting Islam in Early Modern Europe

The European pursuit of remnants of the Greek and Roman empires within now Muslim lands was slowly augmented by a growing interest in the textual and material records of the Islamic world itself. This was evidenced in Charles I's 1637 request for "auntient Bookes in ye Persian Arabian or Greeke Language" to be acquired in Iran, as well as Roe and Petty's efforts to acquire "an olde and greate manuscript in Arabicque," along with multiple manuscripts in Greek, from the Patriarch of Greece.[37] In seventeenth-century Europe, at the same time that the modern ideal of the art collector and the structures of the antiquities market were taking shape, the Islamic world was beginning to emerge as a subject deemed worthy of serious philological, historical, and doctrinal study, as well as the focus of ongoing political concerns. European scholars grappled with the Arabic, Persian, and Turkish languages, and the end of the seventeenth century saw the publication of the first full translation of the Qur'an into a European language (1698, by Lodovico Marracci), and the 8,158 articles on Islamic topics in the monumental *Bibliothèque orientale* (1697, by Barthélemy d'Herbelot and Antoine Galland).

The 1650–1750 heyday of the "Republic of Arabic Letters" in Europe, as Alexander Bevilacqua has recently termed it, was formed through a network of European scholars who sought to investigate "Oriental" letters, practices, and customs, and especially the Islamic faith.[38] Although many of them identified Islam as a form of imposture, their individual and collective efforts to access, translate, and reckon with source texts in a range of languages were genuine attempts to create knowledge and understanding of a religious and cultural tradition that they saw as being both different from, and analogous with, their own. This florescence of scholarship fed, and was fed by, a search for manuscripts that could be acquired and taken to European libraries. Diplomacy, too, was an important route by which objects from the Islamic world—including but certainly not limited to manuscripts—arrived in European collections.[39]

Importantly, this expansion of European interest in the physical history of the Islamic world coincided with the growth of antiquarianism within the Islamic world. Earlier records of encounter with the monuments of past cultures had generated what has sometimes been framed as antiquarianism. This model could be applied to the carefully choreographed reuse of spolia, for example, the reused Roman pediment in the entrance to the Bimaristan (hospital) of Nur al-Din in Damascus, founded 549 H/1154 CE.[40] By the early modern period there was a distinct and multifaceted tradition of Islamic antiquarianism, much of it bound up with the concept of *athar* or *asar* ("traces"; "vestiges") and the remainders of the past encountered in physical monuments and materials.[41] This emic engagement with Islamic and pre-Islamic pasts may also have included the production of historicizing artifacts. Recent analysis suggests that a paper manuscript in the University of Tehran library collections, executed in imitation of a very early script and dated in inscription to the ninth century but clearly not an authentic work of that period, was likely produced in the late sixteenth or seventeenth century.[42] This example highlights the culturally specific nature of historicizing practices before the full arrival of the modern antiquities market, especially within an Islamic tradition where practices of scribal copying were understood as a means of demonstrating one's own mastery, connecting with past masters, and appropriately materializing the text.[43]

Unlike statuary and monumental architectural inscriptions, manuscripts are easy to transport. Merchants could carry them without difficulty, and they were also offered for open sale in spectacular numbers on the Istanbul book market.[44] Antoine Galland (1646–1715), author of the first European translation of the *One Thousand and One Nights* tales, made several stays in Istanbul and other cities of what is now Turkey during his buying missions for the French royal house. Writing about the Ottoman capital in 1685, he described how the city attracted scholars from all over the empire while at the same time serving as the hub for book collections brought from cities captured by the Ottoman armies, bringing together works "as much from Egypt, from Syria, from Arabia and Mesopotamia as from Persia itself, where the Turkish armies once advanced considerably."[45] Many prestigious books plundered from libraries during the Ottoman conquests ended up in the Ottoman imperial collections, but countless others made their way onto Istanbul's thriving book market, and from thence, eventually arrived in European collections.[46]

The scale of European collecting would only increase in the nineteenth century, with European scholars and institutions increasingly interested in the "classical" era of Arabic and Persian intellectual history (a contested period label, but usually understood to be pre-1450), and ready to take advantage of any neglect at libraries held by pious and even royal institutions in the Islamic world.[47] In such a marketplace, corrupt custodians could do great damage in uncatalogued libraries. In Tehran, one Qajar official placed in charge of the royal library from 1896 stole hundreds of manuscripts and sold them to Jewish and Armenian dealers in the city, who then sold them to Europeans in the various foreign embassies in the Qajar capital or smuggled them out of the country to Paris.[48] Similar occurrences took place in other important libraries of the Islamic world when custodians sought to supplement their incomes by selling stolen manuscripts in a hot market.[49] By the end of the nineteenth century, tens of thousands of manuscripts had left the Islamic world for Europe, in what Ahmed El Shamsy has vividly described as a "book drain" by nineteenth-century collectors who "sought Oriental books as the raw material for the construction of a taxidermic replica, a stuffed corpse of the Islamic cultural edifice to be placed in the mental museum of European thought."[50]

As well as books, European scholars and collectors also sought antique coins and inscribed plaques and gems from the Middle East. These eminently portable objects combined precious materials with aesthetic interest and documentary data, enabling the reconstruction of dynastic histories of the region. As such, coins were prime subjects of early modern connoisseurship. (Not coincidentally, forged antique coins were the first class of artifact to receive systematic analysis in Renaissance Italy as a form of forgery.)[51] Early European interest in Arabic texts inscribed on coins and plaques even prompted a famous sixteenth-century forgery, the so-called lead books of Granada, which purported to contain a Christian gospel written in archaic Arabic on twenty-one circular lead plaques. The episode played a significant role in stimulating early modern Spanish Oriental scholarship and prompted heated debates about the status of Arabic as a language of Christian groups as well as Muslims, revealing the close relationships between the early modern pursuit of knowledge, the formation of group identities, and the practices of forgery.[52]

The use of coins as subjects of historical inquiry was certainly not limited to early modern European antiquarianism. Writers in the Islamic tradition, notably the fourteenth- and fifteenth-century North African polymaths Ibn Khaldun (d. 1406) and al-Maqrizi (d. 1442), had already used coins as documents for the writing of history.[53] Their interests lay in exploring the legal status of different types of coinage and its role in economic and social stability. In the later European context, by contrast, where numismatics was established partly as a means of learning the conventions of classical Greek and Roman art, coin collectors focused primarily on imagery, documentary inscriptions, and the creation of taxonomies.[54] To many collectors, coins were romantically connected with historical events and personages, acting as points of contact between the present and a past that could potentially surface in any field or vineyard. Coins, the most concrete representatives of economic systems, constituted one of the most defined and desirable categories of early modern collecting. All along the edges of the Mediterranean, mercantile interactions with the Islamic world brought old coins into European hands.[55]

The growth of European numismatic scholarship on Islamic coins was, like the Republic of Arabic letters in Europe, a networked endeavor made possible through print publications.[56] A copperplate print published in 1752 in the Leipzig scholarly periodical *Das Neueste aus der anmuthigen Gelehrsamkeit* may be the earliest European reprographic illustration of Islamic coins (fig. 1.4). It depicts both sides of six copper coins with Arabic inscriptions in the Viennese imperial collections, accompanied by a plea from Vienna for "the masters of Oriental languages" in the Leipzig circle of numismatists to send any thoughts on the inscriptions to the editors for publication in the journal.[57] The 1752 print marked the decisive arrival of Islamic coins in the graphic media and scholarly discourse of the European Enlightenment, after more than a century of piecemeal but increasingly focused collecting. The onward trajectory of coin collecting, in the Middle East as well as Europe, would see numismatics blossom as a subspecialization of the historical sciences. Deniz Türker has recently shown how the activities of government official Abdüllatif Subhi Paşa (d. 1886) enshrined coin collecting at the core of mid-nineteenth-century Ottoman historicism.[58] Subhi's own collection of coins and manuscripts constituted a "protomuseum" and important site of scholarly discourse, before its liquidation and dispersal through sales held in his lifetime and after his death. The balance of his collection of Islamic coins, consigned by the Ottoman Bank, was auctioned in 1899 at Sotheby's to a clientele that included the young Calouste Gulbenkian (1869–1955), who would go on to assemble a celebrated coin collection as well as other famed art collections.[59]

The entanglement of money and antiquities collecting is rendered very literal in the case of numismatics, for its objects of study are units of finance in a triple sense. They are literally currency, with each coin representing a unit from a historical exchange system in which it held buying power. At the same time, they also carry a material value that can be unmetaphorically liquidated if necessary. Finally, they are value-bearing commodities in the antiquities trade. Other sorts of antiquities from the Islamic world, especially

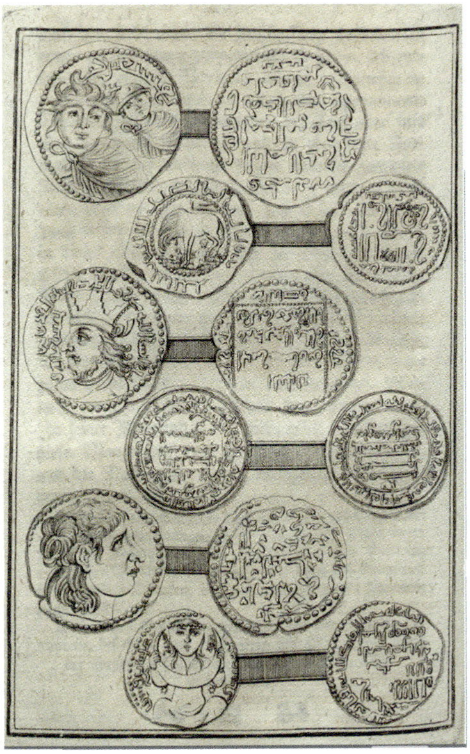

1.4. Copperplate print showing Islamic coins, including three from the Artuqid dynasty, *Das Neueste aus der anmuthigen Gelehrsamkeit* 6 (Leipzig: Ben Bernhard Christoph Breithopf, 1752).

manuscripts, were also reckoned in financial terms from the inception of European collecting in the region. As a truly internationalized antiquities market emerged in the last decades of the nineteenth century the connections between financial markets and the antiquities trade became ever more pronounced, crossing emergent national boundaries and often running between particular identity groups.

Identities in a Colonial Marketplace

Reading through accession records in museum archives, it does not take long to notice that certain ethnoreligious groups predominated in the late nineteenth- and early twentieth-century international market in Middle Eastern antiquities. Most obviously, many notable dealers have Armenian names. Other Eastern Christian communities are also represented, including Maronite and Melkite Arabs and Orthodox Greeks, as well as Iranian and Levantine Jews to a lesser degree. The success of those communities within the modern antiquities market can be attributed to two conjoined factors that I discuss in more detail below. In brief, the first factor is access to established transregional exchange networks and credit systems based on trust. These were critical to the physical movement of antiquities. The second factor is polyglotism, which was utterly essential to successful navigation of the supply chain. At the same time, there is also a much more disquieting commonality across several of these groups: many of them have experienced disenfranchisement, displacement, persecution, and even genocide, generating diasporas across the globe.[60]

To consider the first factor, dealer success in the burgeoning antiquities market was dependent on access to, and successful navigation of, trade networks and credit agreements that were often maintained through familial and kinship ties.[61] These networks had deep roots in early modern mercantilism. Most famously, the Armenian communities of Iran were so well known for their trade networks that in 1603 the Safavid ruler Shah Abbas forcibly moved thousands of Armenians from Julfa in northwestern Iran to the newly created Isfahan suburb of New Julfa, as part of his grand vision for Iran's commercial development and control of the silk trade. Armenian families were deeded the land at New Julfa; in return, "they were locked into a mutually advantageous partnership by becoming a 'service gentry' to the crown, which used them as commercial and diplomatic agents in relations with Europe."[62] Through established family networks and a risk-sharing system of commercial investment agreements known as *commenda*, New Julfan families maintained and extended overland trade networks across Eurasia, expanding with the Iranian silk economy.[63] Those networks ran around the Indian Ocean, into Russia, China, and Southeast Asia, and through Mesopotamia to Europe, with nodes in the Mediterranean port cities of Izmir, Venice, and Marseilles, as well as Aleppo—the major hub for Iranian silk export to Europe through the seventeenth century.[64]

Similarly, the Melkite, Maronite, Armenian, and Jewish communities of Greater Syria operated within trans-Mediterranean trading networks that had begun developing long before the modern antiquities market came into existence.[65] These minority trading groups—especially Melkite Catholics—were the beneficiaries of Ottoman legal advantages given to dragomans (translators for European merchants). This status gave rise to a commercial elite of multilingual minority traders.[66] Aleppo was a particular hub for Melkite trade families, along with smaller communities of Maronites and Armenians.[67] One multilingual Maronite man from a merchant family in Aleppo, Hanna Diyab, describes how, staying in Marseilles in 1708, he "began to receive invitations from all the merchants of Aleppo [currently in Marseilles] who knew me. All of them treated me honorably: *khawājah* Bazan, *khawājah* Simon, *khawājah* Bonifay, *khawājah* Roux, and *khawājah* Samatan, who was my dearest friend in Aleppo."[68] (*Khawajah* is an honorific title for a merchant, derived originally from Persian via the New Julfan traders.) The impression one receives from his travelogue is of a Mediterranean crisscrossed by intersecting strands of linguistic, cultural, regional, and professional kinship, moving goods across and around the liquid space of the Inner Sea.

The end of the eighteenth century and the decades that followed witnessed momentous political events that partially dismantled both the Ottoman state and its network of maritime and trade relations: Napoleon's invasion of Egypt, the Greek War of Independence, the rise of Egyptian nationalism under Muhammad Ali, and the French conquest of Algeria.[69] With the Gülhane edict of 1839, the Ottoman administration in Istanbul began a process of reform and modernization that sought to secure the empire's political sovereignty. However, as Bruce Masters has pointed out, some of those Ottoman reform policies accelerated the incorporation of parts of the empire into the late nineteenth-century capitalist system, thus carrying them into dependent relationships with the economies of Europe that were outside of the sultan's control.[70] As European economic power waxed, commercial life in the Ottoman cities of the Arab provinces and especially Aleppo was transformed. The export of raw materials from Aleppo dried up as trade expanded in Damascus and other cities, and the rising import of manufactured goods was increasingly controlled by foreigners, leading some of the local Christian and Jewish trade families to leave the city for Egypt, France, England, and elsewhere.[71] At the same time, however, new opportunities for wealth sprang up where they had not previously existed, like the growing banking sector and the antiquities market, and some families moved successfully into these new roles.

Individual facility with multiple languages and/or having translators in the family were also necessary to subaltern success in the lopsided economic order of colonialism, giving a potent advantage to communities with traditions of multilingualism.[72] Religious identity played an explicit part in many of these linguistic-economic equations, especially after the Anglo-Ottoman treaty of 1838 made the Ottoman Empire "the most extreme example of a free-trade regime in the world" at the time.[73] In this new trading ground, European merchants seem to have preferred commercial contact with non-Muslims and especially Christians, thus positioning Armenian, Greek, and Levantine Christians to act as polyglot middlemen.[74] Some successful antiquities dealers started out as dragomans, their multilingualism enabling them to serve as interpreters, guides, and brokers for European or American antiquities hunters. The Turkish-born Armenian Daniel Zado Noorian (1865–1929), for example, would go on to run an antiquities business in New York after working in his youth as interpreter for American archaeological missions to Ottoman Mesopotamia in the 1880s and early 1890s. Instrumental to his success was fluency in at least four languages: Armenian, Turkish, Arabic, and English.[75]

Noorian appears, indistinctly, in a photograph taken by John Henry Haynes at the ancient site of Sippar in Iraq, only identifiable through an accompanying entry in Haynes's journal: "Dr. Ward, Daniel & Arabs taken unconsciously hence the short exposure" (fig. 1.5.). The hierarchy of address makes the status of each person in the photograph clear: "Daniel," called by his Christian name, is lodged socially between the properly titled Dr. [William Hayes] Ward and the undifferentiated ethnic block of "Arabs," hired local men who made up much of the team's workforce. Judging from the Americans' penchants for pith helmets, as seen in other photographs taken on this mission, Noorian is probably the shorter of the two men at center, his brimmed hat obscuring the face of the pith-helmet-wearing Dr. Ward next to him.[76] From the 1890s to his death in 1929, Noorian sold Middle Eastern antiquities to various institutions across the United States, including a spectacular group of Islamic ceramics sold to the Detroit Institute of Arts in 1925 (fig. 1.6).[77] Noorian took the contacts and experience he accumulated as a young man in Iraq—including knowledge of excavation management and export practicalities, and the relative desirability of different types of antiquity for European and American collectors—and turned it to good account in the booming antiquities market of the late nineteenth-century United States.

As well as the ability to communicate across the ethnic and social strata of the antiquities supply chain, polyglotism enabled individuals to maintain several different registers of correspondence. For example, the dealer-collectors Hagop Kevorkian (ca. 1872–1962) and Calouste Gulbenkian exchanged a series

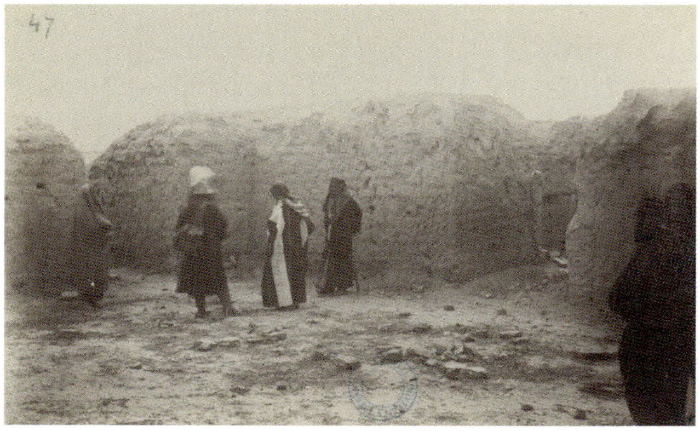

1.5. Untitled photograph taken by John Henry Haynes at Sippar, Iraq, 1884. Photographs of Asia Minor, #4776. Division of Rare and Manuscript Collections, Cornell University Library.

of business letters in Armeno-Turkish (Ottoman Turkish written in Armenian script), a form of communication that may have helped keep their trade correspondence relatively private.[78] On the demand side, the rise of the United States as the premier market for antiquities meant that English eventually came to replace French as the lingua franca of wealth—although French, Italian, and German all continued to be major languages of the international antiquities trade well into the twentieth century.[79] The prevalence of French manuals within the nineteenth-century "how-to" literature on ceramic restoration (see chapter 3) suggests that French was also an important language of craft expertise in the burgeoning trade in historical Islamic ceramics, real and fabulous, just as it was within the rising craft of photography.[80]

Finally, one must also consider the reports of links between specific ethnic or religious communities and antiquities forgery. The Jewish community of Hamadan in Iran is repeatedly linked in nineteenth-century travel literature with the forgery of antique coins for the international antiquities market. In the late 1880s Charles James Wills wrote that these forgeries were "sent in large quantities to Baghdad, Teheran, Ispahan, and Constantinople, and sold there to the unsuspicious or ignorant European. [Captain Pierson] told me, too, that Hamadan has a great reputation for the finding of real antiquities, and that many of the Jews actually paid a small sum for the privilege of searching the ground in certain spots, taking the chance of a find or a blank day."[81] Separately, Joachim Ménant attributed forgeries in Babylonian and Assyrian cylinder seals, plaques, and stelae in the 1880s to "a family of Persians established at Kerbella [Karbala]," whose work was traded through the Baghdad antiquities dealers.[82] With the negative judgment of forgery always present, explicitly or implicitly, in these reports, it is usually hard to know where any reality ends and the religious and racial prejudices of the writers begin.[83] One should not, however, overlook the likelihood that, just as with many other forms of skilled craft, antiquities forgery probably often was a family or kinship business. Training in manual crafts is often passed down through families or within small kinship groups, and practitioners of an illicit or semilicit craft like antiquities forgery would have extra imperatives for working with trusted close kin. Like banking and the antiquities trade, forgery is also a livelihood that depends on maintaining outsider trust in a system of valuation—with the ever-present threat that value will collapse if trust is lost.

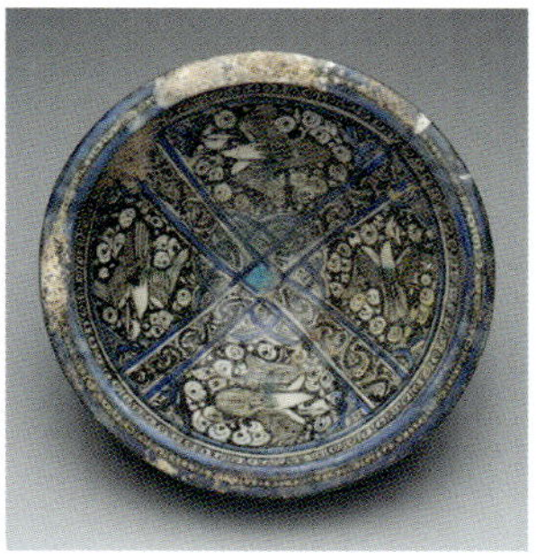

1.6A. Bowl, glazed stonepaste. Attributed Iran, late 13th or 14th century. Diameter 29.2 cm. Detroit Institute of Arts, 25.53.

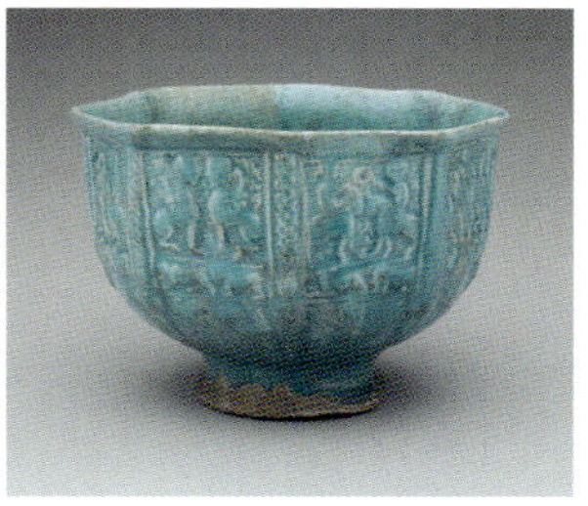

1.6B. Bowl, molded and glazed stonepaste. Attributed Iran, 12th or 13th century. Height 12.9 cm. Detroit Institute of Arts, 25.54.

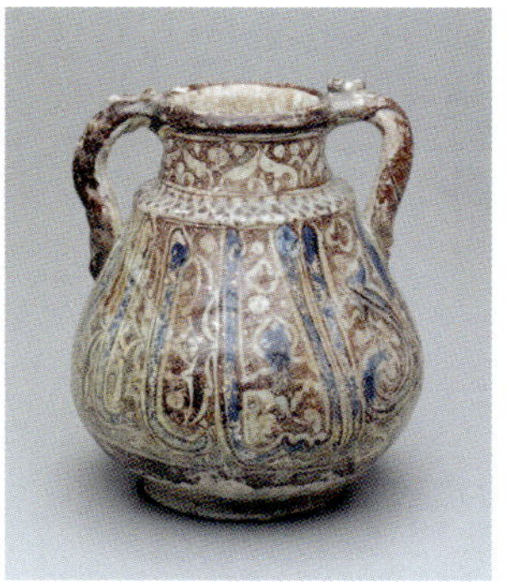

1.6C. Handled jar, glazed stonepaste with overglaze luster (so-called Raqqa ware). Attributed Syria, late 12th or early 13th century. Height 25.4 cm. Detroit Institute of Arts, 25.55.

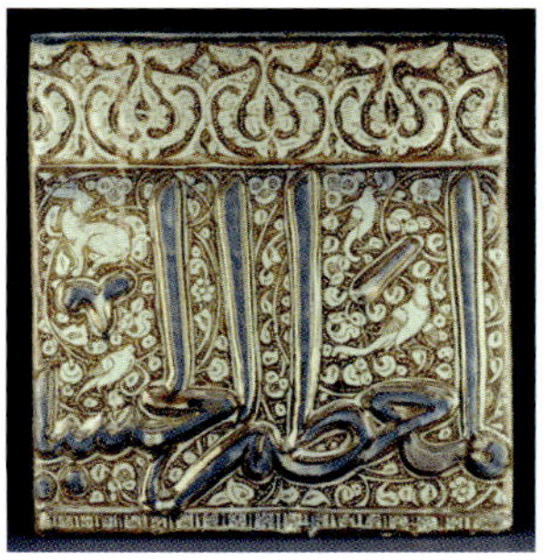

1.6D. Tile, glazed stonepaste with overglaze luster. Attributed Iran, late 13th or early 14th century. Length 34.3 cm. Detroit Institute of Arts, 25.56.

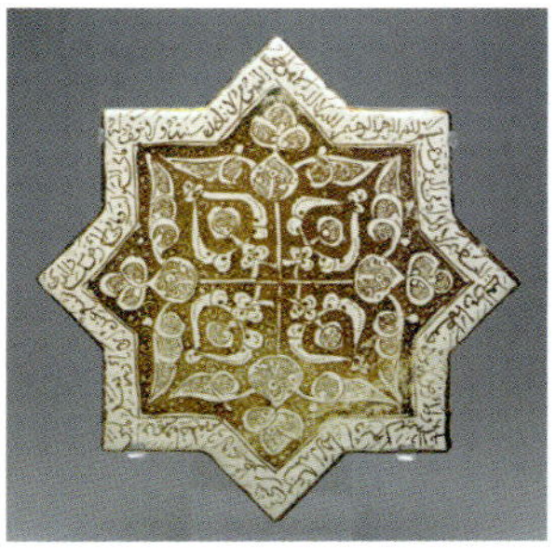

1.6E. Tile, glazed stonepaste with overglaze luster. Attributed Iran, ca. 1262, from the shrine of the Imamzadeh Yahya at Varamin. 30.5 x 31.1 cm. Detroit Institute of Arts, 25.57.

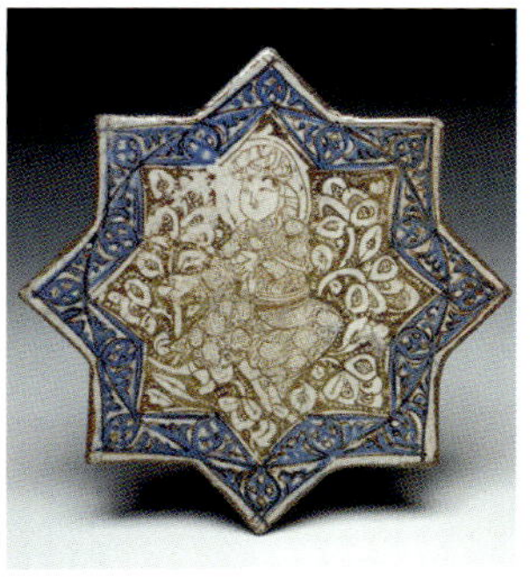

1.6F. Tile, glazed stonepaste with overglaze luster. Attributed Iran, early 14th century. 21.3 x 21.6 cm. Detroit Institute of Arts, 25.58.

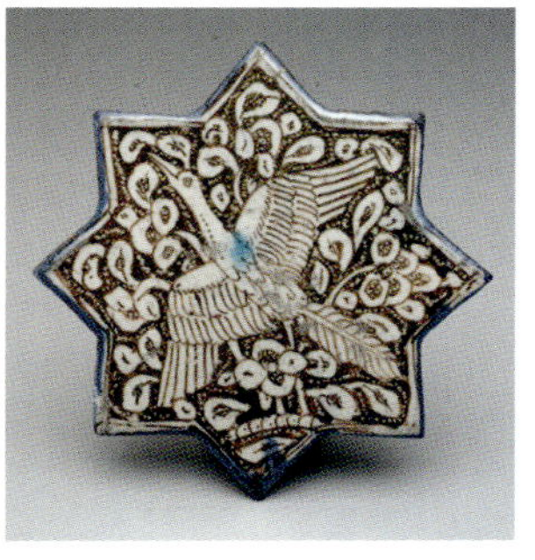

1.6G. Tile, glazed stonepaste with overglaze luster. Attributed Iran, late 13th century. 15.2 x 15.2 cm. Detroit Institute of Arts, 25.59.

Banking and Antiquities

Banking and the antiquities trade have long gone hand in hand, frequently being practiced within the same families or even by the same individuals. Strikingly, some of the same non-Muslim ethnic groups who were most successful in the antiquities trade also became particularly visible for their success within the modern banking institutions of the Middle East. There is a long history of non-Muslim moneylenders and currency traders in the Islamic world, often connected with the Islamic religious prohibition on *riba* (excessive gain, traditionally deemed to include charging interest on loans) although that is only part of the story. The success of Eastern Christian and Jewish individuals and families within the emerging financial industry also reflects the earlier success of those same groups in building kinship-based transregional credit systems and risk-sharing trade mechanisms, as described above.[84] Banking was a fully internationalized venture by the late nineteenth century, and the finance machine turned anything and everything—including preexisting mercantile networks and social structures—into profit.

The rise in the Middle East of new professions associated with international trade—broker, overseas commission agent, merchant banker—took place in tandem with the establishment of European-style banks and fully fledged imperial banks in the region. The Crédit Lyonnais, Wiener Bankverein, and other European financial houses all rushed to establish themselves within the Ottoman Empire in the last years of the nineteenth century and the beginning of the twentieth, along with newly created interests like the Deutsche Palästina Bank, Deutsche Orientbank, and the Bank of Salonica.[85] The biggest bank in the region, however—indeed, one of the biggest in the world by 1900—was the Imperial Ottoman Bank, founded in Istanbul in 1863. It was created as a hybrid venture between London, Paris, and Istanbul, and regarded with envy from Germany. The bank was born not only of the competing interests of European financiers but also of the explicit desire of the Ottoman sultan Abdülmecid I (r. 1839–1861), voiced in the Reform Edict of 1856, that "institutions such as banks will be established in order to correct the coinage of my Sublime State and to give credit to its financial affairs."[86] Often perceived as a foreign entity of questionable patriotism, the Ottoman Bank was nonetheless sufficiently important for a view of its headquarters in Istanbul to be included among the nearly two thousand photographs that make up the extraordinary, panoptical record of Ottoman territory in the photographic albums produced for Sultan Abdülhamid II (r. 1876–1909) (fig. 1.7).

In Iran, the first European-style bank was the New Oriental Bank Corporation founded in 1888; this was followed very soon by the Imperial Bank of Persia, founded in 1889 as a state bank of issue. The Imperial Bank was founded on a concession to Britain, and its head office and board of directors were located in London.[87] As in the Ottoman Empire, the monetary system in mid-nineteenth-century Iran had been somewhat chaotic. All sorts of currency, local and foreign, were in circulation within the country, especially Russian roubles in the north and Indian rupees in the south. This kept the trade of *sarraf* (moneylender/moneychanger) an active and profitable one, but by the last decades of the century it was no longer tenable. The centralized administration of money got underway in the 1870s, to be followed by the founding of the imperial bank.[88] By 1928 the Imperial Bank of Persia had twenty-four branches in Iran and a broad range of activities. Its credit facilities played an important role in financing the expanding carpet industry, for example, in the years before World War I, as well as in the export of opium to East Asia and cotton to Russia.[89]

The necessity for these seismic transformations in financial life was, of course, the rise of a capitalist world economy. The advent of telegraphic and postal services and the changes this connectivity had wrought in business made unitary and stable monetary economies an absolute necessity for Middle Eastern powers if they wanted to stay afloat within a capitalist world order. The Imperial Ottoman Bank and the Imperial Bank of Persia both sought to convert local populations to European-style banking and its orthodoxies, introducing credit and saving systems that were markedly different from those traditionally practiced locally. This was a huge undertaking; both banks ini-

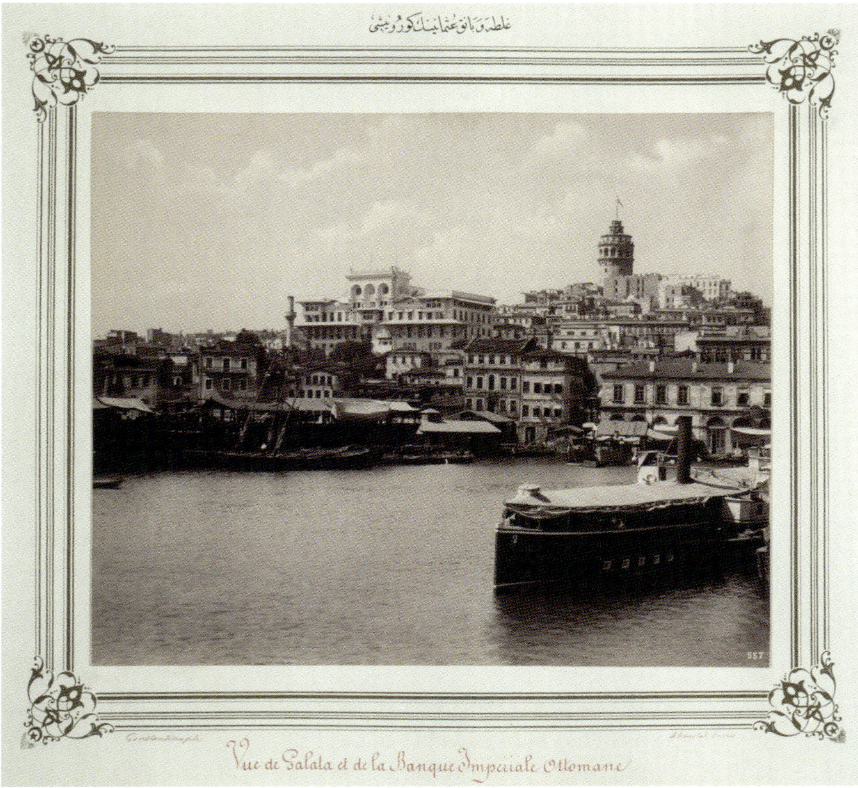

1.7. *View of Galata and the Imperial Ottoman Bank*, photograph by Abdullah Frères, taken between 1890 and 1893. From the Abdülhamid II albums. Library of Congress, www.loc.gov/item/2003667957/.

tially pursued buy-in from local elites as a means of promoting the new financial order.

Both the Ottoman and Persian imperial banks provide windows through which the social hierarchies of their empires can be glimpsed. In both cases, stratification on ethnic, linguistic, and confessional terms was strongly in evidence in both the employee base and the clientele. At the Ottoman Bank, although the most senior positions were often held by Europeans, the bank also employed local staff in managerial positions from an early date, almost all of them non-Muslims: typically, they were Armenians, Greeks, Jews, and Christian Arabs.[90] The British overlords of the Imperial Bank of Persia, on the other hand, reserved its managerial posts exclusively for Europeans. At the branches, the mirzas (acting as interpreters and intermediaries) were Persian, while the bulk of the lower-level local staff was made up primarily of Armenians in the north, and Armenians, South Asians, and Jews in the south.[91] The priority given to white Europeans can be seen by looking at the faces and positions of individual staff members in an undated photograph of the Tehran staff of the bank in the Antoin Sevruguin archives (fig. 1.8). As for clientele, demographics for the account holders of the Persian bank are hard to come by, but within the Ottoman bank it is striking that there was a major overrepresentation of foreign clients relative to their actual demographic weight in the population at large. Local non-Muslims were also somewhat overrepresented in the bank's clientele, while the Muslim majority of the population was underrepresented.[92]

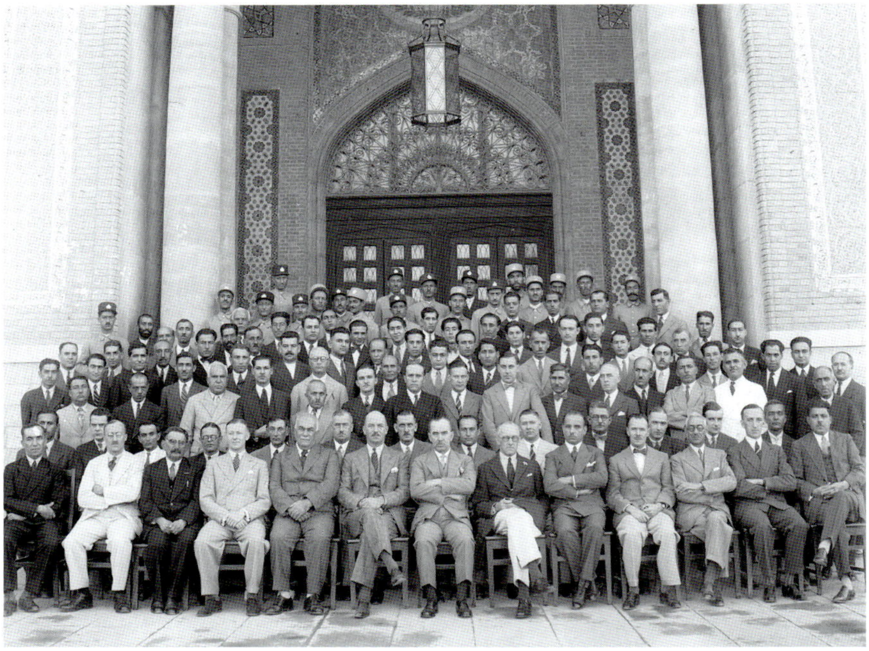

1.8. The staff of the Imperial Bank of Persia, early 20th century. Positive image from glass plate negative. Antoin Sevruguin/National Museum of Asian Art Archives, Smithsonian Institution, Myron Bement Smith Collection, Gift of Katharine Dennis Smith, 1973–85, FSA A.4 2.12.GN.30.09.

The notable presence of the Armenian community within banking and the antiquities trade alike is symptomatic of the larger successes of that community within colonial-era economies of the Middle East. The very visibility of that success, however, was a lightning rod for ethnicist tensions within the Ottoman Empire that would culminate in the horrors of the Armenian Genocide. One of the best-known dealers in Middle Eastern antiquities of the twentieth century and a pivotal figure in this book, Dikran Garabad Kelekian (1868–1951), was an Armenian from Kayseri in central Turkey whose father is usually described as a banker. Kayseri had a large Armenian population in the nineteenth century and was the birthplace of several other notable antiquities dealers, including Hagop Kevorkian (whose brother Carnig was also an antiquities dealer), the Indjoudjian brothers, Agop (1871–1951) and Meguerditch (1884–1927), and possibly also Kirkor Minassian (ca. 1874–1944).[93] The family of Calouste Gulbenkian was originally from nearby Talas. In a dark sign of things to come, however, Kayseri was the site of a massacre of Armenian citizens by Turkish militias in 1895. Waves of violence toward Armenians swept across the Ottoman Empire in the late nineteenth century and presaged the genocide that would begin fully in 1915.[94] Many Armenian families in the region who were able to do so left the empire for Europe, Russia, the United States, and elsewhere, taking their trade expertise with them to new cities.[95] Some who had already established themselves in Paris, including the Indjoudjian brothers, may have returned to the region after the massacres of the 1890s to acquire antiquities.[96] The routes traveled by just one potent artifact—eight pages of canon tables from the Zeytun Gospels—through the terror and chaos of the genocide has recently been documented by Heghnar Zeitlian Watenpaugh, revealing an extraordinary story of passage that must have been repeated many times over by an untold number of objects.[97] The resonances of the persecution and genocide of Armenians by the Ottoman state reappear throughout this book, a painful thread that cannot be extricated from the modern histories of antiquities trading in the Middle East.

Levantine and Greek Christians also established themselves in finance and trade, and, like some of the Armenian Christian families within the Ottoman Empire, went on to leverage their trade and banking connections in the antiquities business as the market expanded. A case in point is an Aleppine family who appears again in chapter 5: the Marcopolis, originally from Chios, Greece.[98] They had settled in Aleppo by the eighteenth century and for several generations acted as hereditary consuls of Venice.[99] In some sources they are noted as Italian nationals; in others, subjects of the Austrian emperor;[100] and branches of the family also settled in Mosul and Beirut.[101] The Aleppo listings in *Abdou's International Directory* for 1910 include members of the Marcopoli families under "exporters," "banks and bankers," "commission agents," and "merchants," indicating their wide reach.[102] T. E. Lawrence wrote that the Marcopolis were "the big dealers in Aleppo," and Gertrude Bell and Charles Lang Freer both make note in their early twentieth-century travel diaries of visiting the Marcopoli premises to view antiquities for sale.[103] An image of the antiquities showroom of André Marcopoli—probably in the grand Khan al-ʿUlabiyya, occupied by the family since the mid nineteenth century—survives on a commercial postcard showing the attractions of Aleppo, of a type designed for business owners to insert an image of their own concern alongside the city's great monuments (fig. 1.9).[104]

The connections between modern banking and the antiquities market can be traced most clearly in Egypt. Egypt's economic integration with European financial systems was quite pronounced by the late nineteenth century, with Alexandria and especially Cairo established as major banking cities.[105] In Alexandria the banking sector was dominated by the Greek community that settled there from the mid nineteenth century, beneficiaries of a late Ottoman system of tax concessions to foreigners to stimulate trade and investment.[106] Financial family networks in Cairo, most visible among Jewish banking families, provide the most easily traceable points of intersection between banking

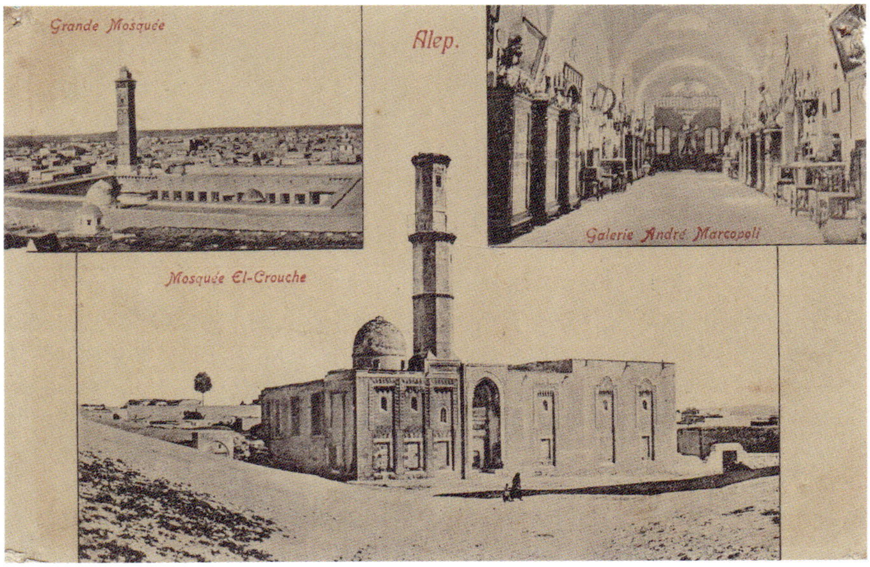

1.9. Postcard showing the Marcopoli showrooms in Aleppo. Early 20th century.

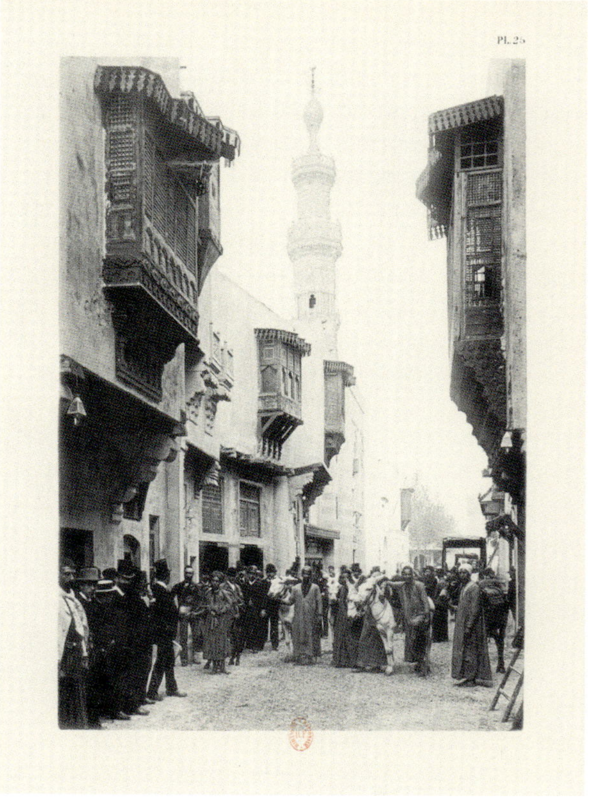

1.10. *Rue du Caire.* Photographic plate in Alphonse Léopold Marie Delort de Gléon, *L'architecture arabe des khalifes d'Égypte à l'Exposition universelle de Paris en 1889: La rue du Caire* (Paris: E. Plon, Nourrit et Cie, 1889), plate 25.

and antiquities collection; a few examples suffice to give a sense of the overlap between these modern industries of asset accumulation and exchange.

The Islamic art collector and director of the London merchant banking house S. Japhet & Co., Ralph Harari (1892–1969), is most famous in Islamic art history for his ownership of the so-called Harari hoard, a group of twenty exceptional silver vessels attributed to eleventh- or twelfth-century Iran (reportedly found "in Northern Persia" inside an earthenware vessel).[107] He was the son of Victor Harari Pasha (1858–1945), a child of Levantine Jewish immigrants to Cairo, who served in the Egyptian Ministry of Finance before leaving to preside over various of Ernst Cassel's financial interests, including the National Bank of Egypt.[108] Jacques (Jack) Mosseri (1884–1934) came from another Jewish banking family of Cairo, and between 1909 or 1910 and 1912, when the market for Middle Eastern antiquities was positively frenzied, acquired thousands of pieces of Geniza material in Cairo with the French archaeologist Raymond Weill.[109] A third and particularly illustrative Cairene banking connection is found in the person of Baron Alphonse Delort de Gléon (1843–1899), the funder and promoter of the famous "rue du Caire" at the 1889 Paris Exposition Universelle. This popular fabrication of a Cairene street in the Paris Expo incorporated architectural salvage from real Cairene buildings (fig. 1.10).[110] As well as being a civil engineer and early collector of Islamic art, the wealthy Gléon was also cofounder of the Crédit Foncier Égyptien (est. 1880), Egypt's first European-style mortgage bank[111]—which was, in turn, the employer of the banker and famous antiquities dealer Maurice Nahman (1868–1948), a major trader in ancient Egyptian antiquities. A Cairo resident, reportedly of Macedonian, Greek, and/or Syrian Jewish ancestry and part of the extended Mosseri banking family, Nahman worked as head cashier at the Crédit Foncier Égyptien for forty-one years.[112] He launched his own antiquities dealership in 1890, trading from a neo-Mamluk mansion he built in central Cairo.

Many more examples could be found of direct connections between the worlds of banking and antiquities trading that emerged in the Middle East prior to World War I, but those given here are sufficient to show the complex and varied nature of the entanglements between the two trades—which should be properly considered as a continuum, rather than two separate industries. It is clear that ethnicity and confessional identities played important roles within that continuum in ways that are not always easy to reconstruct. To show how these things played out, the last part of this chapter zooms in to a case study of one famous antiquity to show not only how questions of identity and social connection worked on the ground, but also how the developing financial instruments of credit and asset valuation constituted the very substrate of the modern antiquities market.

Fahim Kouchakji and the Antioch Chalice

Fahim Kouchakji (1886–1976), a central figure in chapter 5, was a member of the firm Kouchakji Frères, a family of antiquities dealers from Aleppo. The family name itself is remarkable: it must come direct from the Ottoman Turkish word *kaçakci*, meaning "smuggler." One wonders what the motivations were for keeping, or even choosing, this name. As the moniker for an internationally successful family of antiquities dealers, it certainly suggests a more plain-speaking era than our present one.[113]

Marilyn Jenkins-Madina was the first to point out that Fahim Kouchakji played a significant part in the dispersal of so-called Raqqa wares on the international antiquities market.[114] His role in that episode—and its surprising coda in Indiana—is explored in full in chapter 5. Outside the circles of Islamic ceramics collecting, however, he is most famous for his role in the discovery, promotion, and sale of one (in)famous object: the so-called chalice of Antioch, acquired from Kouchakji by the Metropolitan Museum of Art in New York in 1950 (fig. 1.11). A silver assemblage standing about twenty centimeters high, it is composed of a plain and rather crudely worked vessel inside an elaborate openwork outer shell, mounted on a foot. The gilded, chased openwork of the outer shell bears a vine scroll design inhabited by animals, birds, and twelve clothed human figures seated in chairs. These days the piece shares a case with other examples of Byzantine silverwork in the Metropolitan Museum, and one could easily walk right past it in the dim light of gallery 300. In the early years of the twentieth century, however, the Antioch chalice was a celebrity object of the first order, commanding a central vitrine to itself and attracting crowds wherever it was displayed. "Tout le monde connaît le calice d'Antioche," wrote Charles Diehl in 1926, and he was not wrong.[115] Its most high-profile appearances were at the Exposition internationale d'art byzantin in Paris in 1931 and the Chicago World's Fair in 1933.[116] In Paris, the chalice was presented to the public by itself on an elevated pedestal and under a specially constructed miniature baldachin, a mode of presentation

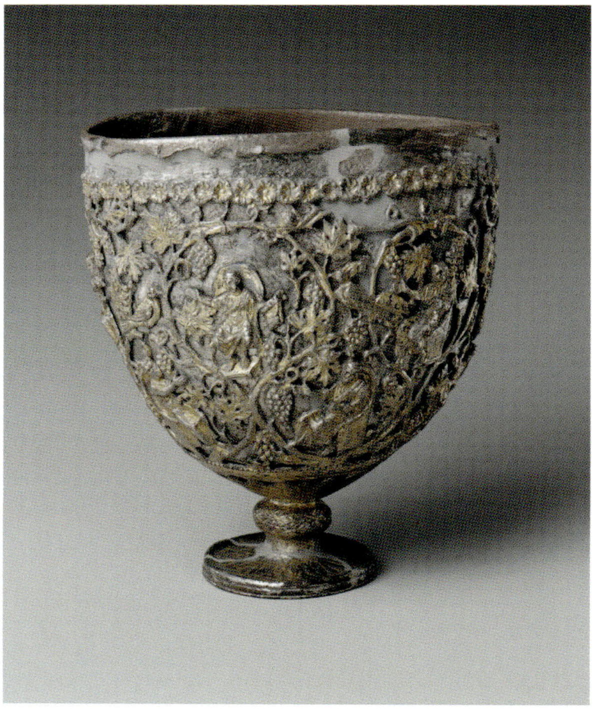

1.11. The so-called chalice of Antioch, silver with gilding. Attributed Kaper Karoan (modern Kurin, Syria), first half of the 6th century. Metropolitan Museum of Art, The Cloisters Collection, 50.4.

1.12. Installation view, *Exposition internationale d'art byzantin,* 28 May–9 July 1931, Pavillon de Marsan. Paris, Musée des arts décoratifs, Album Maciet 309bis/5.

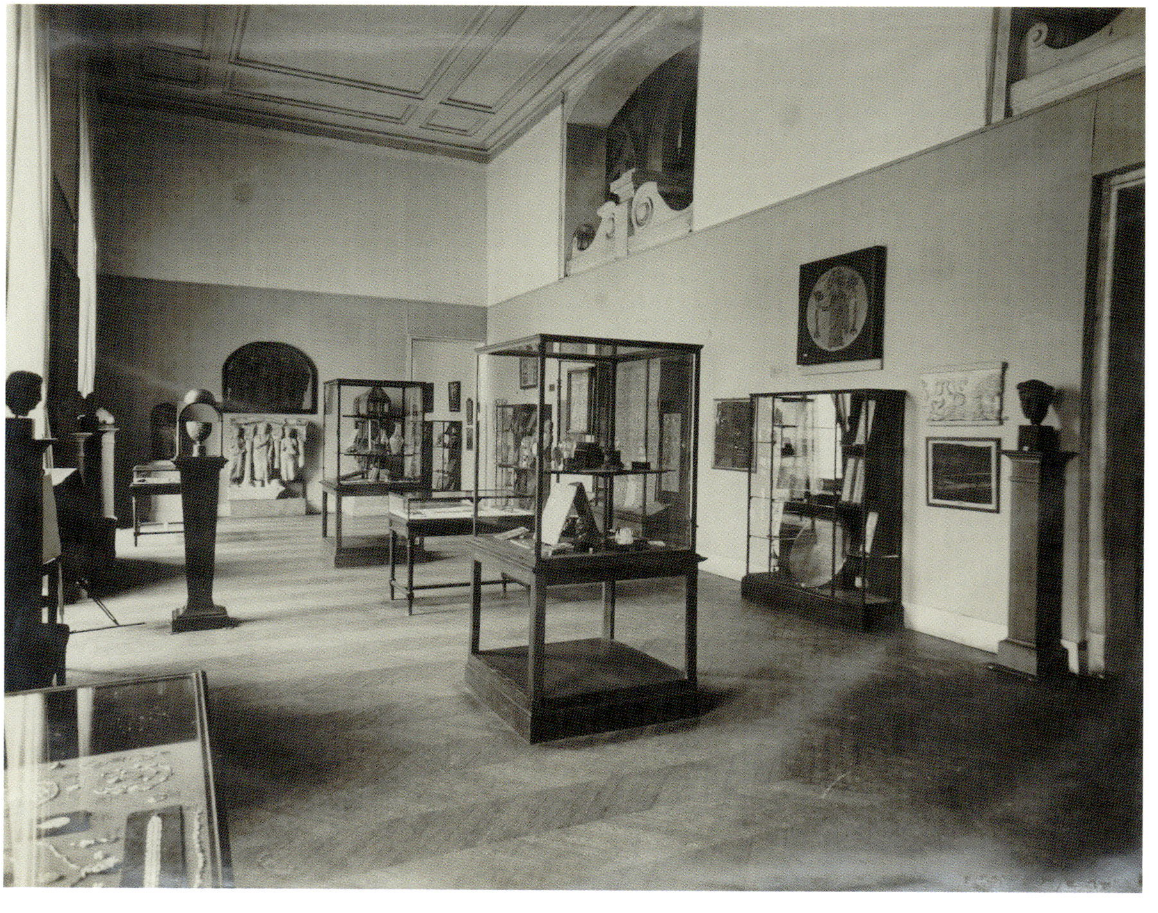

that deliberately underscored its sacred aura in contrast to the more "scientific," unadorned vitrines of the other objects grouped together for display (fig. 1.12). At the height of its fame, the Antioch chalice was both decried as a modern forgery and acclaimed as a religious relic, capable of moving the pious to tears.[117]

The strange twentieth-century history of this object sheds light not only on the background and sales practices of the Kouchakji family firm, including Fahim's role in establishing a successful business trading Middle Eastern antiquities in the United States, but also on the greater landscape of the antiquities trade in late Ottoman Syria at its most frenetic, in the decade and a half leading up to World War I. Several factors coincided to produce a maelstrom of excavation, dealing, smuggling, and collecting in the prewar eastern Mediterranean littoral. Islamic art was growing as an area of commercial interest alongside more established interest in other "Oriental" cultures, especially the pre-Islamic Middle East, long appealing to western Christian collectors who sought tangible access to Biblical antiquity. Megawealthy American collectors, including J. Pierpont Morgan and Charles Lang Freer, were buying hand over fist in this new frontier of antiquities. Dealers used all their resources to outwit the Ottoman authorities and extract historical material for sale to wealthy individuals and institutions—most of whom were less concerned about the legality of their acquisitions than they were about successfully getting them out of the Ottoman Empire and into their own possession.[118]

For the sake of clarity, I begin with the ending of the convoluted story of the chalice. Although presented as a first-century relic supposedly found at the early Christian site of Antioch (now Antakya in eastern Turkey), this ambitious claim was contested from its first appearance in print in 1916. The site and circumstances of discovery are discussed in some detail below; as for dating, by the middle of the twentieth century, scholarly consensus had settled on a fourth-, fifth- or early sixth-century date for the chalice, the latter being widely accepted today.[119] Moreover, the piece is probably not a chalice at all. Marlia Mango has suggested, quite convincingly, that it was created as an openwork lamp, originally intended to hold a glass bowl for a floating wick but fitted at some point in its history with a plain inner cup of hammered silver.[120]

To resume calling it by its stage name, the Antioch chalice as an object of fame and notoriety was the product of what might be called a creative partnership between Fahim Kouchakji and Gustavus A. Eisen (1847–1940). Much about this partnership, however, remains somewhat opaque, including who knew what about the real circumstances of the object's discovery. Eisen was born in Sweden and is probably better remembered as a biologist than as an antiquarian. His research on earthworms and raisin production earned him membership in the California Academy of Sciences but gave way in later life to publications on art and antiquities, from ancient glass beads to portraits of George Washington.[121] Eisen formed a close relationship with Fahim Kouchakji and his wife, Evelyn—so much so that he lived in the Kouchakjis' apartment on Park Avenue and was being looked after by them up to his death in 1940 at the age of ninety-three.[122] Eisen tells that he first encountered the chalice in 1915, "while inspecting some other objects in the same [i.e., Kouchakji's] collection."[123] He went on to work with Kouchakji on other materials besides the publication and promotion of the chalice, for example, providing forewords for the catalogues of Kouchakji's 1916 and 1918 sales.[124] Kouchakji, for his part, is credited with "assisting" Eisen in his 1927 two-volume publication of premodern glass, a work aimed at collectors and including many pieces in Kouchakji's collection. Among these are some modern forgeries of Roman "gold-glass" that raised doubts early on among museum curators; one of these was later gifted by Fahim Kouchakji to the Corning Museum—an institution to which he also sold a considerable number of pieces of ancient glass.[125]

Discovery Stories: The Syndicate of Sixteen

Eisen published numerous writings on the chalice between 1916 and 1933.[126] Within these, the all-important story of the object's discovery changed in subtle but important ways over time. In his first publication of the piece in 1916, Eisen reported that the chalice and other pieces were "procured by the present owners, Kouchakji Frères in Paris, directly from the excavators in 1910 ... [they] were all found together by Arabs digging a well at Antioch, on the Orontes in Syria, in 1910."[127] But in Eisen's extremely luxurious and expensive two-volume book on the chalice, published in 1923 by Kouchakji Frères (with a foreword by the polemical art historian Josef Strzygowski, who had his own agenda about the agency of eastern lands in early Christian art very much in view), the story had changed slightly but significantly. The chalice was no longer bought by the Kouchakji family directly from those who found it, but instead it and the other pieces in the group were now supposed to have been bought from intermediaries:

> This silver treasure was discovered in 1910 by Arabs digging a cellar or well in the city of Antioch on the river Orontes in Syria. The exact site they refused to reveal. While occupied with their work they came upon some underground chambers, more or less encumbered with debris, in which the pieces were embedded.... The whole objects were divided among the finders but changed hands several times until finally they belonged to as many as sixteen different owners, some of them being held conjointly. It was at this stage that the treasure was procured by Kouchakji Frères of Paris and New York.[128]

> The Chalice and six other objects were procured from the Arabs by the two brothers, Salim and Constantin Kouchakji, who assembled the units and in time forwarded them to their brother George in Paris.... [T]he Chalice and the other objects were kept in Paris, but at the outbreak of the Great War and on the eve of the battle of the Marne were, for greater safety, forwarded to his brother, Habib Kouchakji, and to his son, Fahim Kouchakji, in New York, where they have remained until now.[129]

By 1926 the sixteen intermediaries had become a syndicate in the retelling of the tale. "The chalice was found in 1910 by Arabs, who did some excavating in Antioch on the Orontes in Syria. The finders sold it to a syndicate of sixteen of their compatriots, who in turn disposed of it to the present owners [i.e., Kouchakji] in Paris."[130] Another version of the story, published in 1931 and probably written by Fahim Kouchakji or provided to the anonymous author by him, says that the treasure was found in the ruins of a fourth-century church at Antioch, only to be stolen "by Arabs and recovered only with much difficulty," soon after its discovery.[131] And in 1933, when the chalice went on display at the Chicago World's Fair, Eisen repeated the 1926 story, a "syndicate of sixteen Arab compatriots" who brought the silver objects "to Aleppo, Syria, and sold them in turn to Kouchakji Frères."[132] The story of indirect purchase from a syndicate of sixteen appears once more in a *New Yorker* piece by staff writer and well-known humorist James Thurber. In his review of the chalice's display at the Brooklyn Museum in 1936, Thurber says that he asked Fahim Kouchakji "if he knew the name of the particular Arab who dug up the Chalice. 'I have no idea,' he said. 'It was found by a syndicate of sixteen Arabs.'"[133]

In this fog of unreliable reportage, the story circulated by Eisen and Kouchakji came over time to bear all the hallmarks of the "discovery story," a trope of collecting literature. As Melanie Holcomb has succinctly put it, this trope usually presents "a peasant or labourer who makes the discovery; a finder who may or may not be aware of a treasure's monetary value but who rarely understands its cultural value; a dispute over ownership, either among locals or with government officials; the acquisition by someone—frequently an educated European—aware of the treasure's importance who saves it, with implied heroism, from oblivion."[134] In the case of the chalice, the racial stratifications of the late Ottoman context are underscored by the repeated assertion that the finders, along with the intermediate layer of owners (whether they be thieves or a syndicate), are always simply "Arabs." The heroic recognizer of the object's true worth, in contrast, is Fahim Kouchakji, whose Aleppine family was Catholic (probably Melkite) and whose ethnicity is hard to categorize from his Arab first name and highly unusual Turkish surname.[135] In the telling and retelling, the trope of the discovery story positions Kouchakji and his family as members of an urbane, floating class of educated and cultured Christian internationals, equally at home in Aleppo, Paris, or New York. In Manhattan, the reportedly well dressed and handsome Fahim Kouchakji might read as exotic, cosmopolitan, and cultured, with the sense of the familiar afforded by a Christian identity, but a name, ethnicity, and accent unplaceable, and thereby open to Orientalist projection. Fahim Kouchakji's social success can be surmised from a comment by a former associate, who described him long after the fact as a man "who lived in New York and, I believe, dealt in a very superior manner in his Park Avenue apartment in antiquities."[136]

As well as exposing the racial hierarchies of the late Ottoman Empire, Eisen and Kouchakji's discovery narratives make intriguingly frequent use of the word "syndicate." It is a significant word choice. The term came into English usage in the second half of the nineteenth century to designate "a combination of capitalists or financiers entered into for the purpose of prosecuting a scheme requiring large resources of capital, esp. one having the object of obtaining control of the market in a particular commodity."[137] It is, in short, a word—and an idea—brought into being by modern finance capitalism. Its repeated invocation in the story of the chalice's discovery and early ownership shows how models derived from the finance industry were directly shaping the activities (real or invented) of regional actors within the exploding antiquities market of the early twentieth century. It is likely that the syndicate of sixteen had some basis in reality, for there is evidence that the Kouchakjis may have acquired parts of the silver find from several local dealers who traded in and around Aleppo but did not have the international reach the Kouchakjis were establishing.[138] There was money to be made in a tiered system that added financial value at each layer of remove from the original labor of the finders.

Creating the Legend and Obscuring the Kaper Koraon Find

While the story of the chalice's discovery might change in Eisen's various publications, the thrust of his argument was always the same. Using tools of analysis that were esoteric by any standards—including the identification of "occulted spirals" in the faces of the silver-gilt figures (fig. 1.13) and "the lift of inhalation" supposedly animating their tiny, draped bodies—Eisen advanced the theory that the outer cup was made within the first century CE by a Greek Christian artist who had seen Christ with his own eyes. In the 1923 luxury two-volume publication, Eisen marshals close-up photography and highly fanciful etchings to argue that the figures on the outer cup are identifiable, veridical portraits of Christ, the Evangelists, and some of the Apostles. Reviewers of the time noted with amusement and sometimes alarm that the supposed veracity of the etchings (fig. 1.14), by Margaret W. Kinney, was undermined as soon as the viewer even glanced at the enlarged photographs of the object found in the same volume (fig. 1.15). Kinney's etchings demonstrate perfectly how the desire to perceive a particular quality can shape an artist's rendering of her subject.[139]

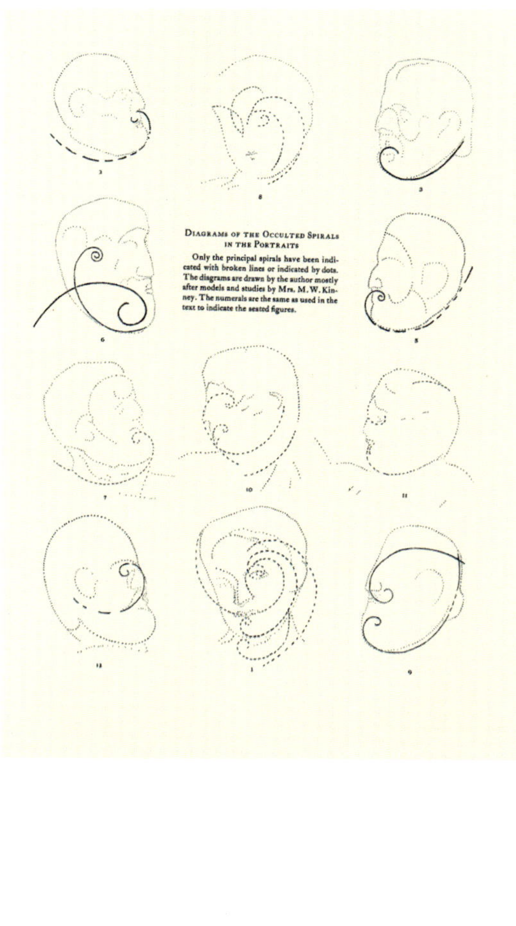

1.13. Gustavus A. Eisen, *The Great Chalice of Antioch, on Which Are Depicted in Sculpture the Earliest Known Portraits of Christ, Apostles, and Evangelists* (New York: Kouchakji Frères, 1923), vol. 1, unnumbered plate.

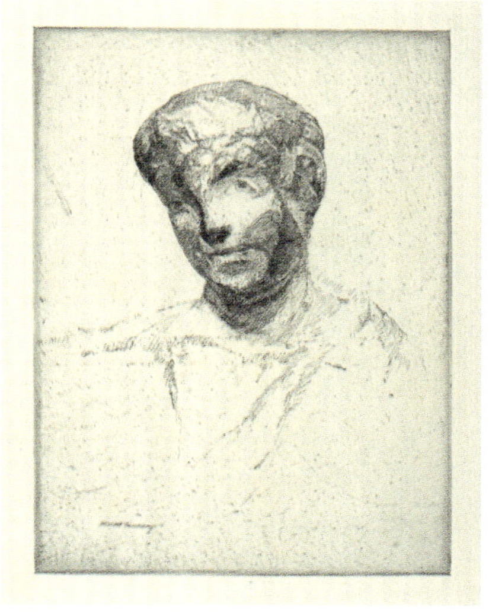

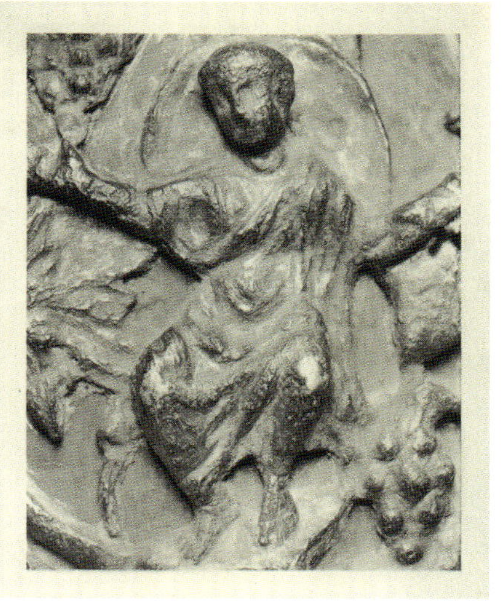

1.14. Margaret West Kinney, "Christ as a Youth," in Gustavus A. Eisen, *The Great Chalice of Antioch, on Which Are Depicted in Sculpture the Earliest Known Portraits of Christ, Apostles, and Evangelists* (New York: Kouchakji Frères, 1923), vol. 2, plate 56.

1.15. "Christ as a Youth." Photographic detail in Gustavus A. Eisen, *The Great Chalice of Antioch, on Which Are Depicted in Sculpture the Earliest Known Portraits of Christ, Apostles, and Evangelists* (New York: Kouchakji Frères, 1923), vol. 2, plate 26.

The inner cup is presented in even more fevered terms. A chapter summary from the 1923 publication—described by a contemporary as "expensive, verbose, and sometimes unscholarly"[140]—captures Eisen's breathless lines of reasoning and their startling climax in the identification of the chalice with the most storied artifact of Christianity:

> Part VII
> THE INNER CUP
> CHAPTER XX
>
> THE INNER CUP HASTILY MADE—A SACRED RELIC. Its Two Distinct Units—A Cup and Its Holder—Hastily Made—Unfinished—Never Repaired—Plainly Made—The Inner Cup but not the Holder Mutilated for Relics—The Cup is Older than the Holder—Similarity to First Century Vases and Cups—Antique Cups with Holders in Open Work—The Artistic Quality—The Cup a Sacred Relic—Must Have Been Connected with the Person of Christ—Vessels Connected with Christ Mentioned in the New Testament—The Vessels of Joseph of Arimathea—Can They Be Connected with the Antioch Chalice—Sacred Vessels as Amulets of Early Christians—Openly Worn in the Time of Constantine—An Identification of These Objects Possible—Their Relationship to the Chalice—Perhaps the Cup of the Last Supper.[141]

That's right. Eisen's grand, incredible claim was that the inner chalice was the Holy Grail itself, the cup that caught the blood of Jesus Christ at his crucifixion. The outer cup, Eisen proposed, contained the earliest depictions of Christ and the Apostles, observed from life. A tour de force of willful projection written across 185 enormous pages, the 1923 publication marshals interminable passages of description in the place of evidentiary argument, combining a rather laborious prose style with the ecstatic subjectivity of a religious vision.

Eisen's erratic and idiosyncratic methodologies in the publication, as well as the total absence of any images of comparative material, were criticized enough by some contemporary reviewers and need not be expanded here.[142] The debates around the chalice and Eisen's publication of it even induced Kouchakji to self-publish an undated, defensive booklet of carefully selected quotes from reviews of the two-volume 1923 publication.[143] Yet in spite of all the ink spilled over the chalice's purported identification with the Holy Grail, the reliability of reports on the chalice's discovery at Antioch were less widely questioned—although not completely ignored. As painstakingly reconstructed by Mango, three sources in the 1920s gave separate reports of other sites in Syria that had supposedly seen the real discovery of the chalice. Leonard Woolley in 1924, Charles Diehl in 1926, and René Mouterde also in 1926 attributed the find to, respectively: the town of Maʿarrat al-Nuʿman, south of Aleppo; a site near the village of Karah, west of Hama; Serjilla, north of Hama; or Tell Bissa, south of Hama.[144] Woolley's report is particularly notable for its illustration of the layered pricing structures of the international antiquities market: "It was discovered, together with a silver cup or bowl and a silver crucifix, by a peasant, who sold it for £3 to a man at Ma'arit il Na'aman, who sold it for £70 to a group of three antiquity dealers at Aleppo; these sold it to Messrs Kouchakji Frères for £120."[145]

If not Antioch, where? In spite of the various suggestions aired in the 1920s, the question was not systematically explored until Marlia Mango published *Silver from Early Byzantium* in 1986. In that book she presented a strong case for the chalice's likely site of discovery as the area around Stuma, a village halfway along the road between Idlib and Riha in northern Syria, rather than Antioch, which lies some distance away to the northwest. Mango's masterful detective work proposes that the chalice and the other objects grouped with it in the so-called Antioch treasure were probably part of a larger, single find of silver objects dedicated to the treasury of the village church of St. Sergius at Kaper Koraon (modern Kurin, near Stuma). The finds in this group were divided via the art market after their discovery in 1908, passing first through a network of dealers in Aleppo and then onward through Paris and New York. The group came to be known to collectors as a series of allegedly separate discoveries, the so-called Hama, Stuma, Riha, and Antioch treasures. The dealers active in the dispersal of the objects in this subdivided cache include several whose names appear elsewhere in this book: Hagop and Garbis Kalebdjian, the Marcopoli family, Joseph Demotte, Joseph Brummer, Alexander Imbert, and above all, the Kouchakjis.[146]

The obfuscation of the cache's origins must have come about partly through the desire to avoid confiscation—a very real risk as the Ottoman authorities tried to stem the flow of antiquities out of the empire, especially after the 1906 antiquities law prohibited the export of newly discovered antiquities without the express permission of the Sublime Porte. The deception went as far as staging the "Hama treasure" as a discrete group of ancient church property, supposedly buried in the nineteenth century and rediscovered in 1910. With its credentials thus established as property of the church prior to the implementation of the 1906 law, its owners—the Kouchakji family—were able to sell it.[147] It would also have made sound commercial sense for all involved to orchestrate the dispersal of the large Kaper Koraon cache through different "treasures," marketable in tranches to European and American buyers as excitement mounted, rather than flooding the market with it all at once.

Furthermore, in the case of the chalice and the associated "Antioch treasure," there was an obvious desire on the part of the Kouchakjis to create an advantageous association with the sacred relic mythos of Antioch, a renowned site of early Christianity. Identifying the chalice with the much more obscure site of its likely actual discovery would hardly aid in its promotion as a masterpiece of metalwork and early Christian relic of the utmost sanctity.

The Antioch Chalice as International Commodity

Reading contemporary reviews of the 1923 book and of the whole controversy, one becomes aware how strongly Kouchakji's project was pitched toward not only a new class of megarich financier-collectors but also a public steeped in the early twentieth-century evangelical Christianity of the United States. Indeed, in a letter of 1924 posted on a family blog, Fahim's brother Henri wrote to their younger brother Emile that the 1923 publication was so expensively produced that its price made it unsaleable in France—but sale in America should be easier.[148] The chalice's public appearances were highly choreographed. In the Paris exhibition it was presented in isolation under a miniature honorific canopy, like a church relic (see fig. 1.12), while its 1933 appearance at the Chicago World's Fair included atmospheric music to usher visitors into an appropriately reverential state. This mode of presentation sat badly with some scholars of art and archaeology for many of the same reasons it was successful with reviewers from *America* and *Ladies' Home Journal*.[149] A young woman called Elizabeth Huff, later a notable scholar of East Asian art and literature, was employed by Kouchakji as a summer lecturer to accompany the chalice during its presentation in Chicago. She recalled an atmosphere of theatrical religiosity inside the Hall of Religion, where the chalice was displayed with a range of other artifacts of North American Christian devotion. In an interview conducted in 1977, when asked whom she met during her stint in Chicago, she replied:

> Mostly it was just the people working in the pavilion—the man who was explaining the Lord's Prayer engraved on the head of a pin [laughter], that sort of thing. And there was a—it may have been the Mormon tabernacle, I don't know—something done in ivory to scale. As I recall, an organ played softly in the background. Oh dear! I don't know how I endured it all. [Laughter][150]

The other critical component of the chalice's story is the role of financial institutions in the chain of ownership and transfer of the objects themselves. Beyond the finance-capital framework invoked through the purported "syndicate of sixteen" Arab owners, the networks and actors of modern international banking underpin the whole story of the silver cache and its dispersal. In an interview Mango conducted in 1985 with George Antaki, grandson of the owner of the Homsi Bank in Aleppo, Antaki stated that in 1910, when the Kouchakji family was bidding for pieces in the "Hama treasure" section of the cache, they simultaneously mortgaged the Antioch chalice to the Homsi Bank, presumably using it as collateral to fund their acquisition of the Hama treasure. The Kouchakjis then sold much of the Hama treasure to Tawfic Abucasem, director of the Imperial Ottoman Bank branch in Hama in

1910 and later director of the same bank's Port Said branch.[151] Presumably, the Kouchakjis used some of the money they received from selling the Hama treasure to Abucasem to buy back the Antioch chalice they had mortgaged to the Homsi Bank. The Antioch chalice was then moved onward to New York, probably through Paris, then seemingly back to Paris for restoration work, and finally back to New York again as World War I threatened Europe.[152]

By his own account, Fahim Kouchakji trained in banking at the Crédit Lyonnais in Cairo from 1903 to 1909, before joining the family business of antiquities dealing.[153] The Crédit Lyonnais was one of the early twentieth century's largest and most powerful financial institutions and helped cement France's reputation as "banker for the world."[154] Its branches served, as did those of other banks, as repositories and safehouses for increasing numbers of antiquities. Dikran Kelekian not only requested international clients to make their payments to his Paris business through the Crédit Lyonnais but was also storing his collection of Islamic ceramics in the vaults of the Crédit Lyonnais when the Victoria and Albert Museum's representatives visited him in Paris in 1909, to begin negotiations over the loan of his ceramics collection to London (see chapter 4).[155]

The role of banks in the Middle Eastern antiquities trade, however, went far beyond their utility as safe storage. The Crédit Lyonnais was perhaps the most aggressive of a crop of institutions that rapidly expanded modern high-risk investment banking practices alongside traditional, low-risk deposit banking in the Middle East. Egypt, with its crushing debt to European powers and its volatile economy precariously dependent on the cotton crop, was particularly important to the bank's rapacious international ambitions. The Alexandria office of the Crédit Lyonnais opened in 1874, followed by branches in Cairo—specifically to give the bank greater proximity to the Egyptian government—and Istanbul in 1875, and at Port Said, the new-built entrepôt of the recently opened Suez Canal, in 1877.[156] The Crédit actively sought to undermine the Imperial Ottoman Bank, for example by capitalizing on the latter's instability when the political and economic crises precipitated by state-sponsored massacres of Armenian Ottomans led to a run on the Imperial bank in 1895.[157] If Fahim Kouchakji had indeed worked in the Cairo branch of the Crédit Lyonnais, he would likely have had advantageous connections to financial institutions (and their owners) around the region. Moreover, working in an international commercial-cum-investment bank such as the Crédit Lyonnais would have given Kouchakji insight into the developing financial structures of credit, advance, asset valuation, and international exchange that could be employed to further his family's success in the globally expanding antiquities market. Doubtless this helped take their operations from local to international via the establishment of the family's trading premises in Paris and New York (by 1908 and 1910 respectively).[158] No ambitious antiquities dealer in the early twentieth century could afford to be ignorant of the workings of international banking and the operations by which capital could be leveraged and assets transferred across national borders, and having an intelligent young banker in the family would have been a great advantage to the Kouchakji Frères.

The Kouchakjis hoped to sell the chalice to the most (in)famous financier of them all, J. Pierpont Morgan.[159] Given Morgan's blizzard of buying between

1900 and 1912, his interest in artifacts of early Christianity, and his role in establishing the asset value of objets d'art within a globally exploding antiquities market, it is quite likely that the Kouchakjis had him in mind as their intended purchaser for the chalice from very early on.[160] Unfortunately for them, their chances were destroyed when the billionaire art collector died in 1913. Three years after Morgan's death, however, Eisen's first article on the chalice was published. A blaze of publicity for the Kouchakjis' prize piece was now guaranteed, ramped up by the continuing stream of publications from Eisen and his increasingly explicit argument that the chalice was the Holy Grail itself.

* * *

Today, the Antioch chalice has come to rest in a quiet vitrine in the Metropolitan Museum. By the time the museum bought it in 1950, expert opinion had come down decisively against claims that this battered vessel was the Holy Grail. It seems never to have quite realized the dreams that Fahim Kouchakji and his family must have had for it in the earlier decades of the twentieth century. Marlia Mango's research has revealed, in as much detail as will likely ever be possible, the pathways by which it traveled from rural Syria to Manhattan; these routes reveal the modus operandi of the antiquities market within the economies of late colonialism. As it had been since the early modern period, antiquity continued into the twentieth century and beyond to be treated as a physical resource: extractable, refinable, and convertible into an asset class.

One of the most important differences, however, between the emergent antiquities trade of Lord Arundel's time and the fully fledged international market of Fahim Kouchakji's was the increasing sophistication and complexity of modern finance capitalism and banking as the machinery that drove it all. The exchanges that took place through the hands of diggers, brokers, dealers, and bankers saw the chalice launched on an economic trajectory of virtual valuation, its status moving from physical resource in the ground to mobile commodity above ground. As it crossed into a realm where financial value was being actively constructed and increased by an international network of collectors like J. P. Morgan, it entered the world of the virtual object, the artwork-as-commodity moving within a self-perpetuating realm of reprographic images. In this virtual world all sorts of fictions could be sustained, up to a point, but identifying the Antioch chalice as the Holy Grail turned out to be a bridge too far. The next chapter keeps this framework in view as it turns to the many and varied forms of ceramic production from the Islamic world that came to be valued in the modern antiquities market. These reached the international stage in successive waves of different "types" associated (sometimes spuriously) with particular sites, each of which was promoted as enthusiastically as its individual exemplars were ambitiously reconstructed.

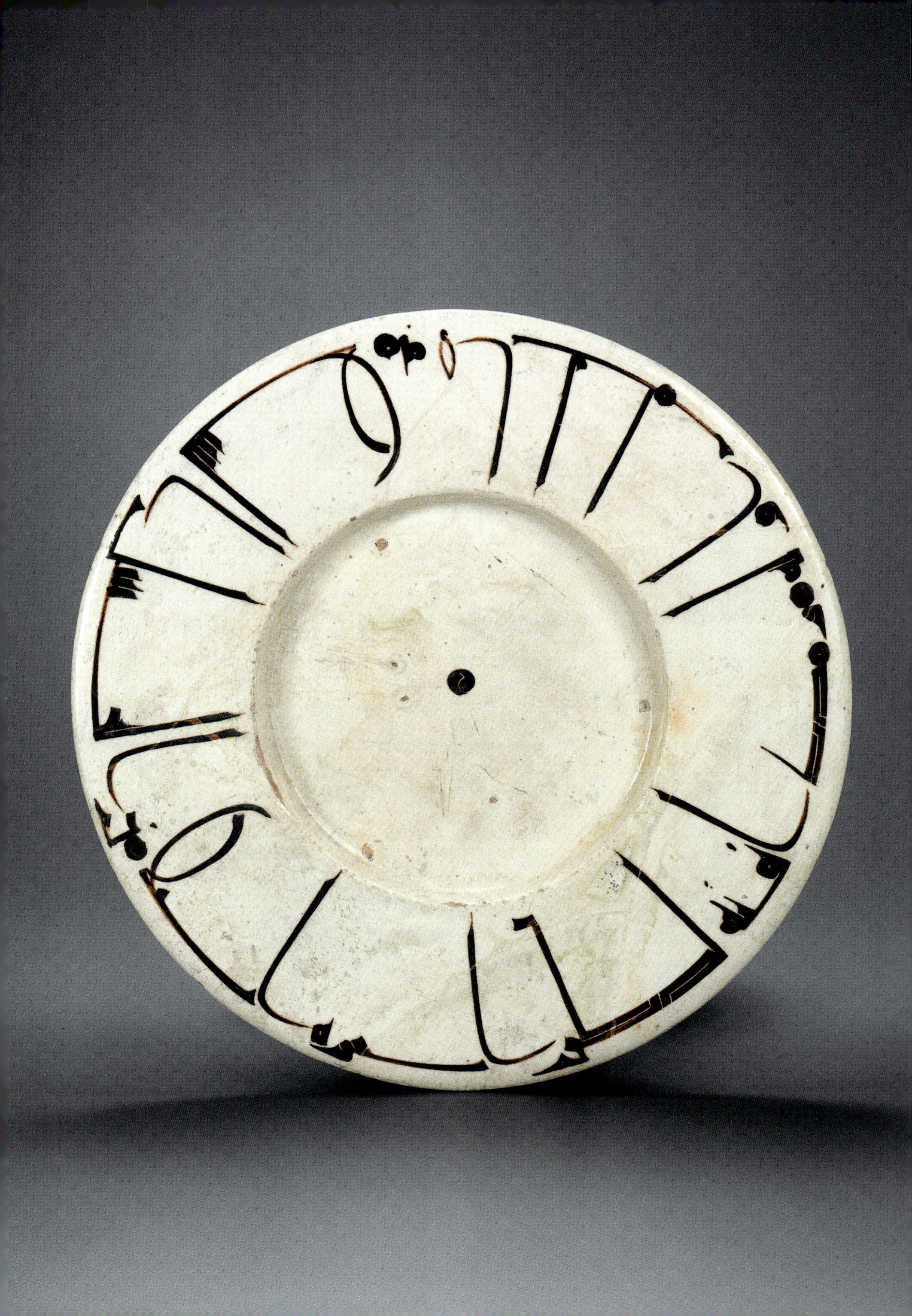

2 Objects of Desire, In and Out of Time

AN EXTRACTIVIST HISTORY OF ISLAMIC CERAMICS

But you can't overthrow the past: It's more kingly than kings. You have to make your peace with it.

—SIGIZMUND KRZHIZHANOVSKY, *In the Pupil*, 1927

Chapter 1 explored the market for Middle Eastern antiquities, how it emerged, and how it worked for celebrity objects like the Antioch chalice. Chapter 2 now delineates the modern formation of a collectors' canon of what are commonly termed "Islamic ceramics." That canon was shaped first and foremost by the labor of diggers, restorers, dealers, and brokers, as waves of commercial and clandestine extraction launched tranches of ceramics from one area after another onto the market, creating a perfect environment for the fabrication and fabulation of objects. Whatever aesthetic judgments the arbiters of collecting taste exercised when they selected one object over another in the salerooms of Europe and North America, they were only applying the last in a long line of filters to a material corpus that had been heavily mediated before it even reached their hands.

Ceramics have long been objects of desire and wonder. Their incredible material longevity means that they also have a big impact on our reconstruction of premodern history, from archaeological records of settlement to narratives of taste and economies for luxury goods.[1] Medieval sources attest to a seemingly universal regard for the East Asian ceramics that were exported across Eurasia, as well as the high status of fine wares produced in Egypt, Syria, Iran, and elsewhere within the Islamic world. "In Cairo they make all types of pottery [*sifalina*]," wrote the Persian traveler Nasir-i Khusraw in the middle of the eleventh century, "so fine and translucent you can see your hand behind it when held up to the light."[2] The fame of some rarefied ceramic traditions meant that prized types traveled widely in their own eras of production, a fact amply attested by the archaeological presence of, for example, medieval Iranian lusterware vessels and tiles at sites across Eurasia.[3]

The emergence of premodern Islamic ceramics as an asset class in the international antiquities market, in contrast, was a somewhat uneven process. Long after the establishment of collecting in ancient Greek and Roman ceramics, the international market only developed momentum around premodern Islamic ceramics in the middle decades of the nineteenth century, and then only in the field of early modern production.[4] This trend emerged in part from the burgeoning focus of nineteenth-century European ceramics fanciers on early modern majolica from Italy and "Hispano-Moresque" lusterwares from Spain. Turkish and Iranian ceramics of the fifteenth to eighteenth centuries got bundled in—rather haphazardly at first—with their European coevals. The trade in historical ceramics from the Middle East accelerated greatly from the 1870s, as the early modern focus and ad-hoc collecting of "curiosities" by travelers gave way to more systematic campaigns of commercial extraction of medieval material, from the tiled walls of standing monuments and from archaeological sites that had previously yielded occasional surface finds.

Despite the truly staggering number of Islamic ceramics that entered collections from the 1860s onward, the medium was not very comfortably synthesized at first into the growing scholarly field of "Islamic art history." A developmental narrative for Islamic ceramics first began to emerge in specialist publications in French in the 1840s and in English in the 1850s, aligning with the early dominance of French and British collectors in this area. German collectors followed only somewhat later, and more slowly.[5] Because it has been shaped by the proclivities of those early collectors, the extractivist history of Islamic ceramics presented in this chapter places an unavoidable focus on what is now the Islamic Republic of Iran. This territory was the source of many of the most coveted and collected medieval ceramic types from the Islamic world to hit the international market. Of course, other regions also yielded up fired treasure for tourists and dealers, from Egypt, Turkey, and the eastern Mediterranean to Central Asia, and those major sites and traditions also figure in this chapter. It was the products of medieval Iran, however, that really consolidated "Islamic ceramics" as a collectors' canon with a distinct profile in the world of collecting and display.

While I explore the extraction history of this disorderly corpus, I also want to show why modern buyers cared so much about this material and were ready to pay sometimes extraordinary sums for pieces of old pottery. There have already been many catalogues that celebrate the premodern ceramics traditions of the Islamic world, often organizing themselves around a well-established canon that runs in a tidy, evolutionary line from ninth-century Iraq to seventeenth-century Iran. I do not intend to replicate the work done in those publications.[6] But without understanding the underlying wonder of the original material, none of the modern craft skills expended on fabulating these objects—detailed in full in chapter 3—will make sense. Accordingly, in this chapter I have tried to bring attention along the way to details and to special material qualities, to account for the spell these objects have cast over audiences past and present and also to point to the places where imitative fabrications could grow. Throughout, I have used archaeological literature wherever possible to provide empirical "control" data for comparison with all the objects that have surfaced through the market with nothing but hearsay to attribute them to one site or the other.

As this chapter surveys the horizons of ceramics extraction in the Middle East from the 1860s to the 1930s, it moves from the above-ground liquidation of extant collections and despoliation of monuments to below-ground digging and harvesting of sites for ceramic remains, with tranche after tranche entering the market under conditions that were often almost completely opaque. In the process, it interweaves several different types of history: the lore of dealers (often the only information accompanying pieces that have surfaced on the market); the scattered eyewitness evidence of travelers, collectors, and other observers; archaeological literature past and present; and, always, the objects themselves.

Above Ground: Liquidation, Circulation, Imitation

In an article published in 1923, Friedrich Sarre (1865–1945)—then director of the Islamic department at the Kaiser-Friedrich-Museum in Berlin—reviewed the market for Islamic ceramics over the previous decades. One senses his retrospection was prompted by the growing signs of slowdown in a market that had seen an absolute frenzy of extraction over many years, peaking in the decade and a half running up to World War I. In particular, Sarre noted something already briefly mentioned above: until about 1890, by his reckoning, most collectors of ceramics from the Islamic world had been primarily interested in the products of the sixteenth to eighteenth centuries, especially Turkish (i.e., Iznik) tiles and vessels and Safavid Iranian blue-and-white wares, but not older material.[7] When the diplomat Julien de Rochechouart (1831–1879) described *faïences anciennes* in Iran in the 1860s, it was clear he was writing about the wares of the sixteenth century and later that had survived above ground, and not the medieval wares that have come to be more celebrated today.[8] Unlike medieval ceramics, the early modern wares that captivated the first wave of European collectors in the nineteenth century were circulating above ground, in considerable numbers and in good condition, because they had been preserved in collections in their regions of production, as well as farther afield.

The celebrated kilns at Iznik in Turkey, at their sixteenth- and early seventeenth-century technical peak, had produced glazed stonepaste vessels that were collected by elites throughout the Ottoman Empire and beyond. Many made their way to Italy, where they were greeted with admiration and attempts at emulation that spread through Europe.[9] Seventeenth-century blue-and-white ceramics from Iran also entered European collecting circuits shortly after their production. This was especially evident during the hiatus in production at the Jingdezhen kilns in China, when the Dutch East India Company tried from 1652 to 1683 to fill the ceramic export gap with Persian wares (although these were often circulated as Chinese products).[10]

With the nineteenth century came more systematic and avaricious collecting. By the 1850s, collectors in Europe were beginning to focus their attentions not only on the globally dispersed Iznik and Safavid wares, but also on household collections of seventeenth- and eighteenth-century wares in Iran. There were active, longstanding, and effective local systems of circulation that included the widespread institution of the *dellah/dallal* (broker) who arranged sales of personal goods, as well as the practice of monetary loans secured against movable property (pawning) known in Arabic as *al-bayʿ bi-al-dayn*, and specialized trades like the corporation of the *chini-forush* (china sellers) in Isfahan.[11] Local sites of exchange and accumulation supported household collecting among elites—especially of books and small objects—

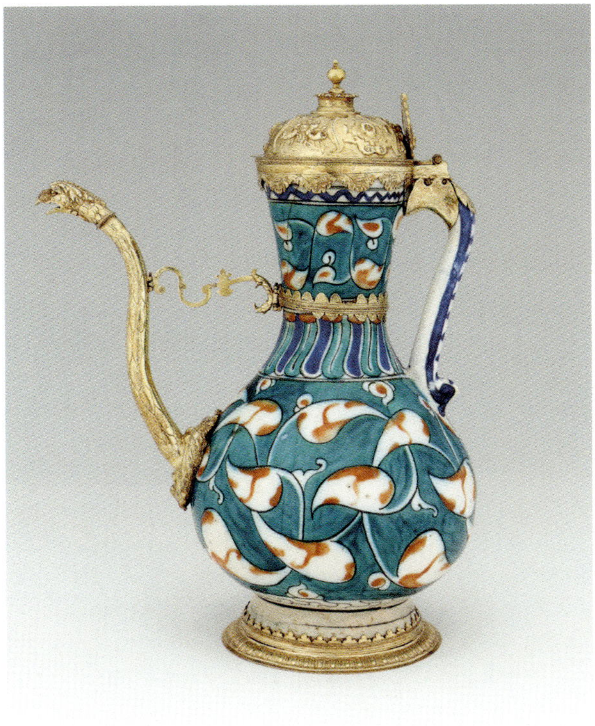

2.1. Jug, glazed stonepaste with silver-gilt mount. Jug attributed Iznik, Turkey, ca. 1585; mount made in London, dated 1597–98. Height 32.7 cm. British Museum, AF.3132.

that demonstrated personal status and educational refinement as well as business success.[12] Viewed in this light, some of the nineteenth-century collecting of Middle Eastern ceramics by Europeans represents not so much a rupture as an extension of longstanding local practices, albeit under increasingly unequal economic conditions.[13]

A wide variety of early modern forms survived more or less intact in these above-ground contexts. In the case of Iznik ware, Nurhan Atasoy has already pointed out that many more vessels of this type have survived outside Turkey than inside the region of their production. She attributes this primarily to the fires and earthquakes of Istanbul, with European collecting in the eighteenth and nineteenth centuries a secondary factor.[14] Some sixteenth-century vessels made at Iznik traveled long distances very soon after they were created. One jug, attributed on stylistic and technical grounds to production at Iznik circa 1585, acquired an elaborate silver-gilt mount in London with a hallmark dating it to 1597–98, as well as a possible connection to the lord treasurer of Queen Elizabeth I (fig. 2.1). The mounted Iznik jug—and the small known group of others with similar mounts—would have been used for drinking beer, a staple across sixteenth-century English society.[15] The longstanding European admiration for Iznik ceramics that fitted this prized jug with its very costly silver-gilt mount also gave rise, eventually, to a scholarly debate in the late nineteenth and early twentieth centuries about where such ceramics were actually produced—a debate heavily shaded with anti-Turkish/anti-Ottoman racism. Erroneous attributions of the Iznik wares to Greece and Iran circulated well into the twentieth century, despite the emerging evidence for their production in Turkey. Some commentators clearly struggled to believe that a "non-Aryan" people could have produced such beautiful ceramics.[16]

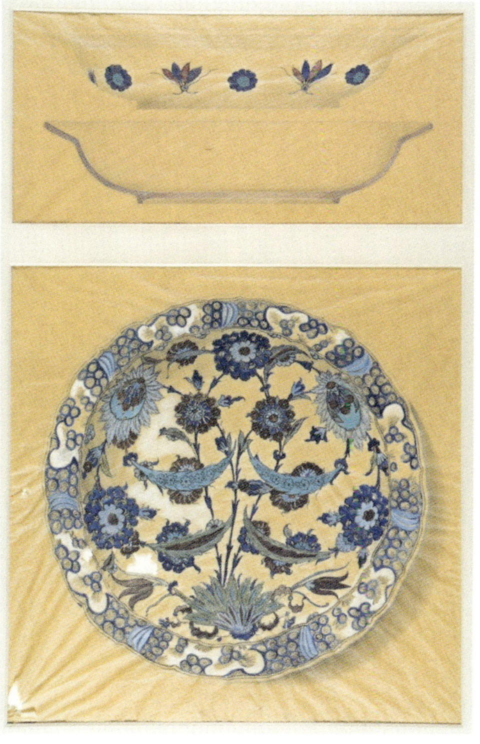

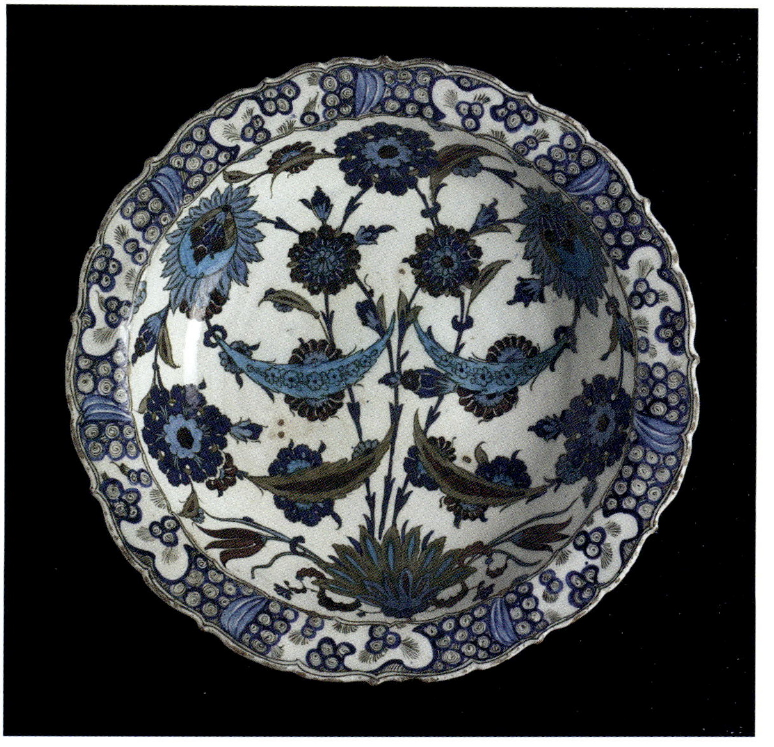

2.2. Blanche F. Hunter, illustration of Iznik plate. Watercolor on paper. London, 1897. Victoria and Albert Museum, 385A-1897.

2.3. Dish, glazed stonepaste. Attributed Iznik, Turkey, 16th century. Diameter 35 cm. British Museum, G.22.

As the nineteenth-century collectors' market turned its attention to Iznik ware, high-quality imitations of sixteenth- and seventeenth-century Iznik designs were being produced in Europe. Manufacturers included Edmé Samson (1810–1891) and his son Émile (1837–1913; discussed further in chapter 3), Théodore Deck (1823–1891), Léon Parvillée (1830–1885), and the Cantagalli brothers, Ulisse (1839–1901) and Romeo.[17] While the Samson company was notorious for deceptive practices, others, like the Cantagalli brothers, were apparently quite scrupulous about adding their maker's mark to every imitation that left their factory. They could not, however, control what dealers did with their pieces after purchase, including attempts at removing or covering the maker's mark.[18]

In a particularly interesting case of international copying documented by Oliver Watson, ceramists in Isfahan at the end of the nineteenth century produced imitations of sixteenth-century Iznik wares to order for a British import-export agency called Wright and Hansford. To make these vessels, the Isfahani potters worked from copies of drawings that had been commissioned by the V&A in 1896–97 for circulation to British design schools as exemplars for students (fig. 2.2). The drawings depicted genuine Iznik pieces in the Godman collection (fig. 2.3), and it is not totally clear how copies of the drawings made their way to Isfahan via Wright and Hansford. When production was complete and the finished pieces sent to London, several of the modern Isfahani imitations of Iznik ware were then bought by the V&A (in full awareness of what they were), only to be deaccessioned years later. Having been cut loose from the documentation that would have explained when and where they were made, at least one of them made its way onto the lower end of the antiquities market in the mid twentieth century

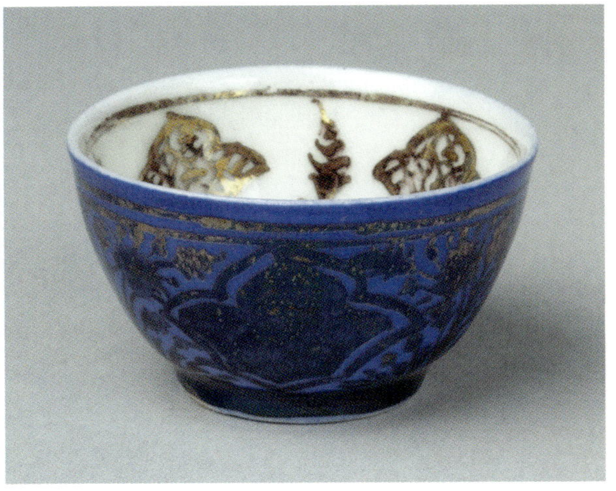

2.4. Cup, glazed stonepaste with overglaze luster. Attributed Iran, 1650–1700. Height 4.1 cm. Victoria and Albert Museum, 7495–1861.

and was presented there as a sixteenth- or seventeenth-century Iznik original.[19] Thus an object that was originally bought and sold under its true material identity—a late nineteenth-century Iranian copy of a sixteenth-century Turkish dish—had become, through a subsequent transaction, a fraud. As is discussed further in chapter 3, the precarious realm of copies and imitations shadowed the antiquities market throughout the nineteenth century and beyond, with decontextualized objects frequently crossing the authenticity threshold from "copy" to "original" through acts of human misdirection or misapprehension.

Early modern vessels like the Iznik jug fitted in England with silver mounts naturally frame questions about consumption: not just the commercial consumption of ceramics, but also the bodily consumption of their contents. Beer may have been popular in London but in seventeenth-century Isfahan, delicate little stonepaste coffee cups mimicked the form of the Chinese porcelain ones that were exported around the Indian Ocean as the coffee trade blossomed (fig. 2.4). The Iranian versions of this form often received the addition of bold decoration in luster, adding glimmer to clink.[20] The seventeenth-century Iranian cup illustrated in figure 2.4 entered the South Kensington Museum (now the V&A) in 1860, relatively early in the annals of modern Islamic ceramics collecting. It was acquired in Italy, then the primary entry point to Europe for goods from the Islamic world.[21] Other early modern Iranian types that caught the European imagination included the still-enigmatic "Gombroon" wares, named after an old English designation for the Iranian port city of Bandar ʿAbbas (fig. 2.5). These were admired for their resemblance to Chinese porcelain and at one point circulated on the market as medieval products, but are now attributed to early eighteenth-century Iran.[22] The very fine walls of these stonepaste vessels are "fenestrated" with pierced designs executed so delicately that the glaze layer pools in them to form tiny panes through which the light can shine; many of them also have minimal linear designs in chromium black that contrast sharply with the pure greenish white of the glaze. This example has slumped a little on its stem-foot in the kiln (always a risk with very fine walls), giving it a slightly drunken list that belies the glossy perfection of its alluring, "lettuce white" surface.

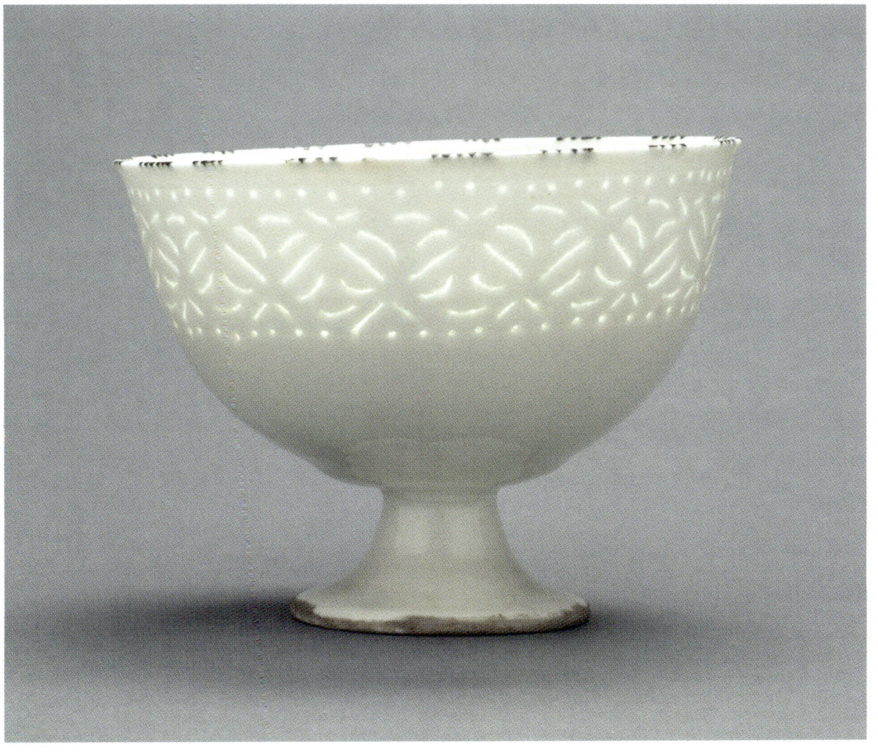

2.5. Footed bowl with pierced decoration, stone-paste with chromium black under clear glaze. Attributed Iran, late 17th–early 18th century. Height approx. 16 cm. Cincinnati Art Museum, Museum Purchase, 1952.270.

In the asymmetric economies of the late nineteenth century, faced with a rising interest among foreign buyers for historic ceramics, it is easy to see how domestic collections of early modern ceramic dishes, cups, and bottles in the Middle East came to be liquidated and to circulate on an increasingly global market. Tiles and tile panels, however, raise more pressing questions about physical extraction. While the sourcing of early modern tiles did not necessarily follow the same pattern of wholesale despoliation that fed the market for medieval tiles from Iranian shrines (discussed below), there is no doubt that looting was and continues to be a factor.[23] The famous Ottoman antiquities law of 1906, which placed a complete ban on the export of cultural property from the empire, was the last in a series of increasingly stringent legal statutes intended to curb the looting of artworks and architectural decoration from Ottoman territories (although it has often been pointed out that those same statutes were overturned by the sultan when it suited him).[24] The 1906 law was the first to provide full coverage for Islamic-era antiquities in the Ottoman territories and it created clearer parameters for the protection of applied architectural decoration on historic buildings, including tile panels on mosque walls.[25] Clearly, the despoliation of monuments was an increasing problem in the last decades of the Ottoman Empire.[26]

At the same time, architectural tilework programs have historically been stripped, renovated, or moved and reused for all sorts of reasons, especially in the seismically active and fire-prone environment of Istanbul. Winter and time also take their toll on exterior revetments.[27] Long-established practices of reuse and repurposing mean that many thousands of previously used tiles and tile fragments are stored at the Topkapı Palace, for example, and processes of

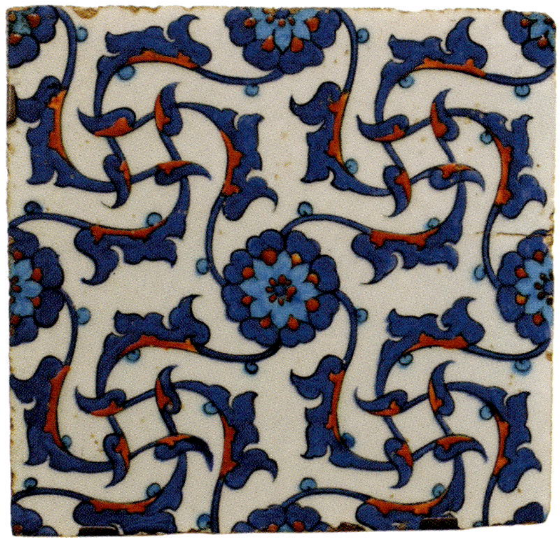

2.6. Tile, glazed stonepaste. Iznik, Turkey, 1560s, design associated with the Rüstem Pasha Mosque, Istanbul. 24 x 25 cm. Aga Khan Museum, AKM862.

periodic renovation undoubtedly released individual tiles onto the market.[28] Deliberate overproduction of certain designs at the Iznik kilns, especially in the 1560s, also seems to have created surplus tiles that eventually made their way into salerooms and collections. This appears to be the case for several of the tile designs seen at the Rüstem Pasha Mosque in Istanbul, of which there are exemplars in multiple collections that don't show any signs of having been taken from the walls of the mosque itself (fig. 2.6).[29]

But even if individual tiles haven't been wrested off walls, they inevitably suffer from loss of context when presented as singular entities within a museum display. Close looking at one Rüstem Pasha tile reveals the qualities that made these so desirable to collectors as discrete objects: the fineness of drawing, precision of design, purity of painted colors, and the luminosity of the white stonepaste body. But on the wall of the mosque, the centripetal design of the intertwining leaf sprays is almost hypnotic in repetition, with the design seeming to oscillate slightly as it joggles the eye back and forth (fig. 2.7). This critical aspect of the design—its capacity to create visual overwhelm through a complex repeating pattern—is virtually impossible to reconstruct from an orphaned tile, no matter how good the viewer's imagination may be. Aggregate effects are very often a defining feature of the conceptualization and use of ceramics—not just tiles, but vessels too. Yet the dislocating force of the collecting industry replaces aggregate aesthetics with spotlit singularity, often rendering original modalities of creation, use, and viewing almost impossible to reconstruct.

A Caucasian Mystery

Alongside these routes for the circulation of early modern ceramics within and beyond the Islamic world, we must set what is still the most mysterious collection liquidation in the history of Islamic ceramics. "Kubachi wares" are a large group of mid-fifteenth- to seventeenth-century Iranian ceramics that first began to enter the antiquities market in the late nineteenth century.[30] They are so called because they come from still-enigmatic domestic collections held entirely in Kubachi in Daghestan, a village above the tree line in the North Caucasus.

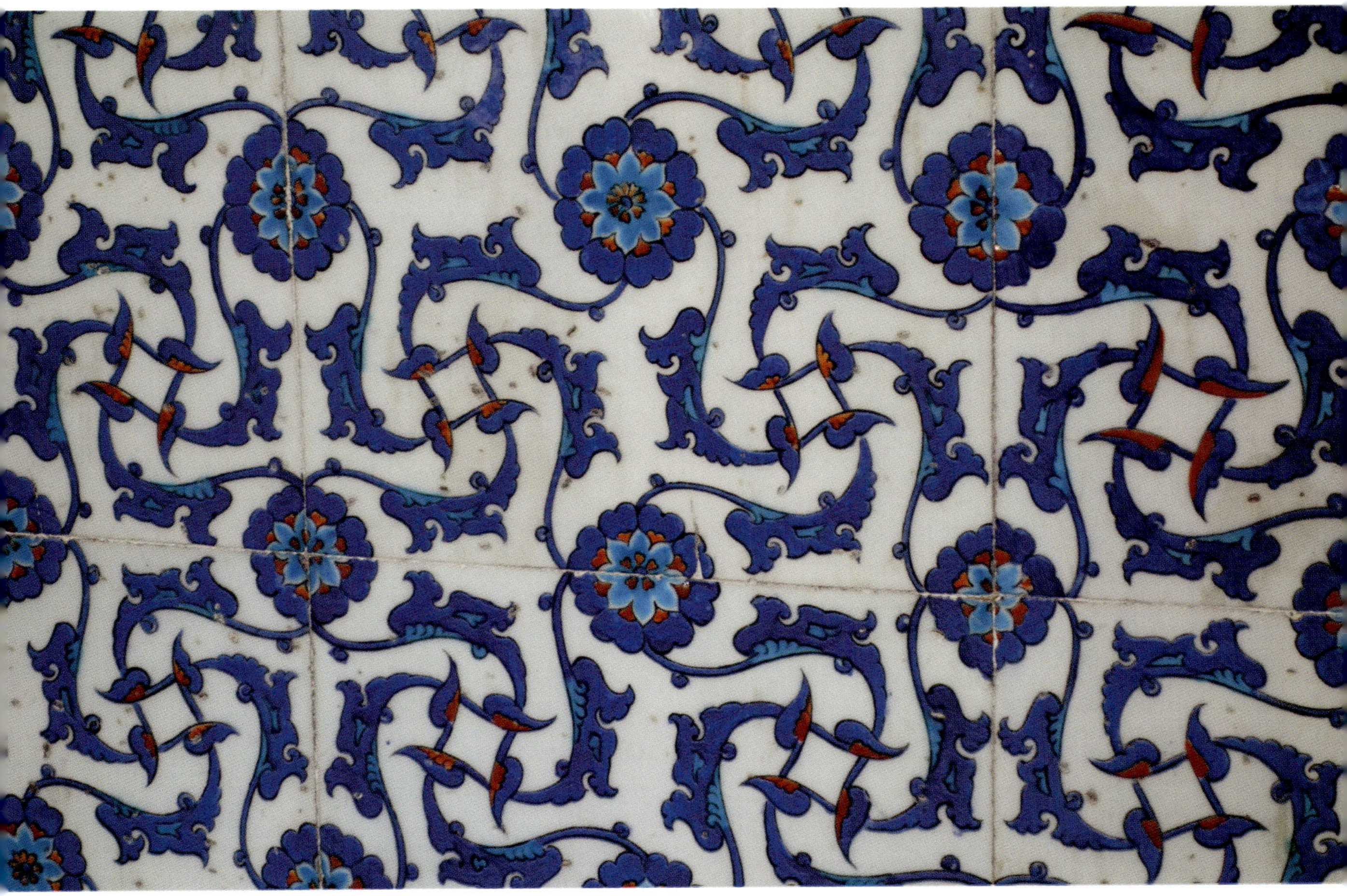

2.7. Tile frieze, glazed stonepaste. Rüstem Pasha Mosque, Istanbul; tiles Iznik, 1560s. Photographed by Melanie Gibson.

Kubachi has played a larger role in the annals of art history than one might expect of such a small and remote settlement, and much has been written about its hyperlocalized craft specializations. It was the site of a striking medieval tradition of stonecarving, preserved in tomb markers and carved masonry blocks.[31] Metalworking in the village also seems to go back to the medieval era,[32] and Kubachi was famed during the nineteenth century and into the Soviet era for its live craft tradition of silverworking in small arms and jewelry.[33] Historical artworks from the village, which included not only locally made objects but also repurposed medieval metalwares from Mosul and Iran, were bought up by the Hermitage Museum in the early twentieth century.[34] During that collecting bonanza the museum also accessioned several modern inlaid metalwork vessels from a local industry of historicizing production, probably without initially realizing that they were of modern manufacture. One of these, now in the Hermitage Museum, is inscribed in Arabic with a false date of 671 H/1272–73 CE in silver inlay.[35] Most recently, the longstanding enigma of Kubachi resurfaced in a series of carved stone arches traded through London dealers in the 2000s, some of them with vague attributions to "palace buildings" of medieval Central Asia. The source of those highly decorated arches turned out to be Kubachi (and possibly other villages in Daghestan): not medieval and not palatial, they were in fact domestic fireplace surrounds made in the eighteenth or nineteenth century.[36]

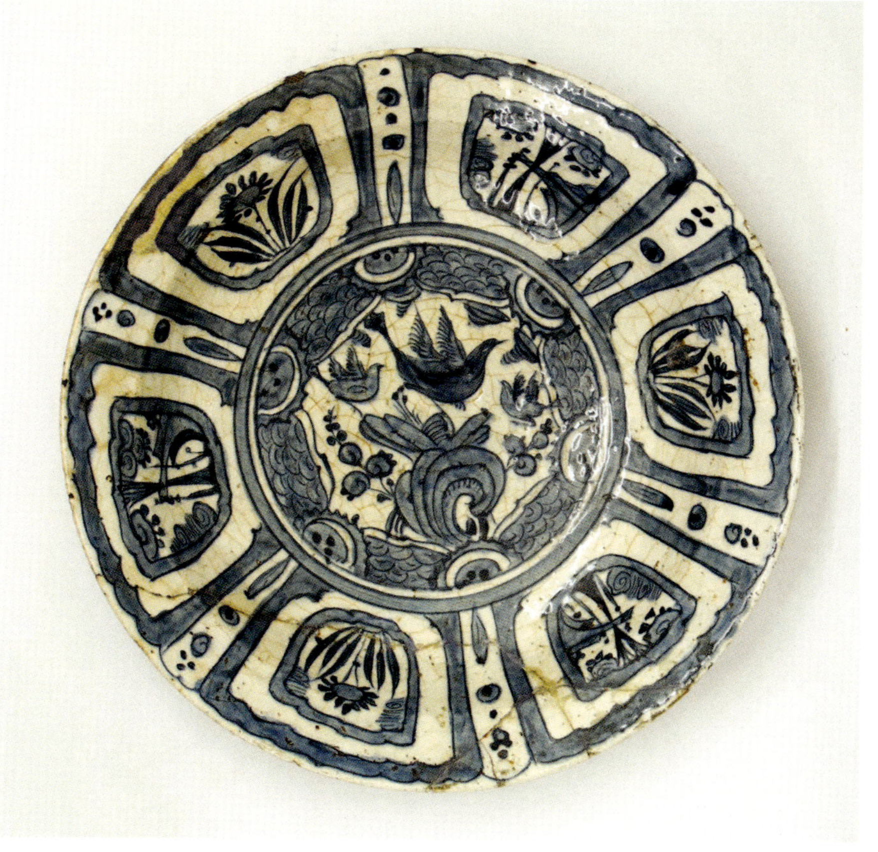

2.8. Dish, stonepaste with cobalt design under clear glaze (so-called Kubachi ware). Attributed Iran, late 17th century. Minassian Collection, Brown University, M.039.

To this small village with an outsized artistic profile, then, we can add, in the late nineteenth century, the surprising presence of hundreds of Iranian stonepaste ceramics from the Safavid era (1501–1736).[37] These included, among other types, blue-and-white dishes of a production attributed by Golombek and Mason to Isfahan, circa 1680, with petal-shaped panels and chinoiserie designs borrowed from the so-called Kraak ware made in China for the export market (fig. 2.8).[38] Most strongly associated with the Kubachi collections are large polychrome dishes, also attributed by Golombek and Mason to seventeenth-century Isfahan, that are painted under a thick clear glaze with black, blue, and turquoise pigments and red and ocher slips (fig. 2.9).[39] The painting of some of these polychrome wares relates closely, in both subject and style, to images created for the burgeoning market in *muraqqaʿ* (album) paintings in seventeenth-century Isfahan. For example, the repeated image of a curly-locked young man in a rich turban is found on Kubachi dishes and album paintings alike. Not shown are the defining characteristics seen on the reverse of the dishes that were found at Kubachi: drill holes in the feet, for suspension by cords that enabled them to be hung on walls, and a layer of grease or grime visible on the raw fabric at the foot and often penetrating the pronounced craquelure of the glaze.[40] These grimy surfaces were ascribed by an early commentator to the fact that in Kubachi the dishes were hung inside rooms with open fires and cooking vapors.[41]

Recent petrographic analysis indicates that the Safavid-era ceramics found at Kubachi are of Iranian manufacture—as earlier scholars had already

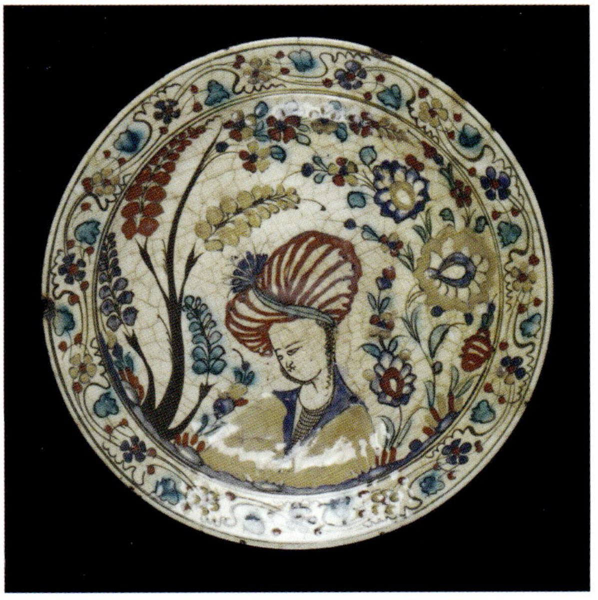

2.9. Dish, stonepaste with colors under clear glaze (so-called Kubachi ware). Attributed Iran, 17th century. Victoria and Albert Museum, C.58-1952.

surmised—and suggests that they may have been produced at multiple sites, including Nishapur, Mashhad, Tabriz, and Isfahan.[42] To date, however, no one has been able to explain how or why they came to be consolidated in the village, hundreds of miles away from even the closest of those production sites. Hypotheses include a caravan robbery, the migration of a collection formed somewhere else, or targeted trading for locally produced metalwork.[43] The first two of these, however, don't really account for the considerable presence in the village of medieval Iranian metalwares and ceramics as well as the more famous Safavid dishes, which together suggest longer and more complex patterns of trade rather than a one-off event. Targeted trading seems more likely, particularly in light of an oral history publication that describes Kubachi residents buying up collections of ceramics of "Isfahan type" from villages in Azerbaijan, for resale to Kelekian and other dealers.[44] But to date it is not even clear how long the Safavid ceramics had been in the village prior to the late-nineteenth-century arrival of the dealers.[45]

Unsurprisingly, the mystery surrounding this corpus was played up in the dealer literature. Kirkor Minassian, who would later claim to have been the first "modern traveller" to visit Kubachi, asserted in 1906 that he was "the only merchant who went looking for antiquities in this unknown corner, whose population is made up solely of shepherds living amongst their flocks."[46] Certainly, he was a major trader in "Kubachi ware" dishes: three undated photographs in the Minassian archives illustrate a total of thirty-four such dishes and these seem to represent only a part of his stock (fig. 2.10). In contrast to Minassian's story, however, a Scottish visitor to the Caucasus in the 1880s has given us an early eyewitness account of the Kubachi wares in situ, from which it is clear that dealers oriented toward the Russian market had been there long before Minassian arrived:

> The *yüzbashi* and at least three other men have collections of pottery, plates, dishes, &c., . . . I was shown one type of plate, of which I have not taken any note as I did not think anything of it, which seems to have attracted the

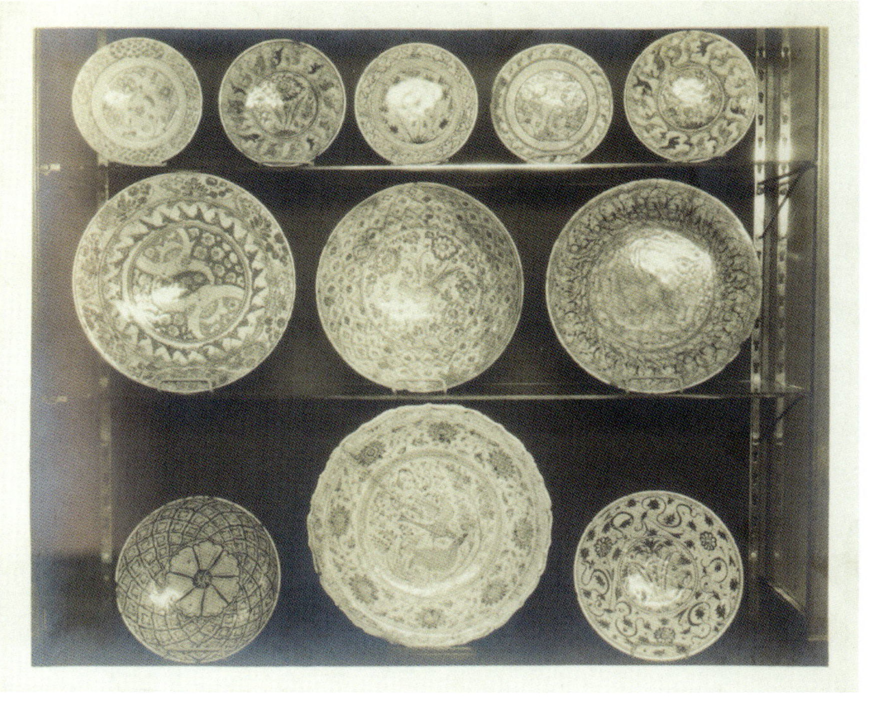

2.10. Photographic print. Early 20th century. Minassian Collection, Box 14, John Hay Library, Brown University.

> attention of some Russian collectors. They told me of a prince who had carried off to St Petersburg something like four hundred of these plates on his first visit, and about one hundred and fifty on his second visit.
>
> The *yüzbashi* told me an extraordinary yarn about the origin of these plates. The prince had told him he was interested in that particular kind of pottery, and bought it up because it came from a country now submerged by the sea, but which his ancestors had formerly inhabited. I naturally thought of Holland, and suggested that country, but my host went on to say that though he did not know the name of the land, it was somewhere in the neighbourhood of the Caspian.[47]

The strange, liquid fable of the drowned country reintroduces something that is often lost in histories of collecting. At the same time that dealers were romanticizing the sources of their wares for an eager paying clientele in Russia and Europe, those at the other end of the supply chain were being provided with—or perhaps generating for themselves—equally romantic hypotheses about where their things were going, and what they meant to their new owners. One of the acquisitive "Russian princes" may well have been the Georgian photographer Alexander S. Roinov [Roinashvili], who lived for several years in Temi-Khan-Shura in Daghestan. In Moscow in 1887 he sold the industrialist collector Pyotr Ivanovich Shchukin (1853–1912) a collection of Iranian ceramics he had acquired "from a village in Daghestan."[48]

Whatever stories might have circulated in the 1880s, by the beginning of the twentieth century (and probably much earlier), the residents of Kubachi were highly active and knowing participants in the antiquities trade. A book published in 1976 by the Hermitage Museum curator Anatoly Ivanov includes oral histories of the village as recounted by a jeweler of Kubachi, Rasul Alikhanov.

He tells of an entire early twentieth-century industry of imitation metalwork produced in the village, with Kubachi craftsmen copying old "Persian" metalwares and eventually creating their own historicizing inventions for sale to buyers who clearly believed—at least for a while—that they were purchasing genuine antiquities.[49] We also learn from Alikhanov that residents of Kubachi traveled to Paris many times in the early years of the twentieth century to sell their antiquities (real and imitation) to collectors and museums; in Paris, Armenian dealers—including Dikran Kelekian—acted as their translators, guides, and intermediaries.[50]

Within Kubachi, the Iranian ceramics had apparently functioned as a form of accumulated capital. Minassian asserted that collections of the dishes were used as dowries or bride-wealth, to be hung on the walls of the home as evidence of status, and the same idea is repeated in later Russian sources.[51] The dealer-cum-broker Arthur Upham Pope described a watercolor painting by a Russian artist that showed "the interior of the chieftain's house with the walls entirely covered by Kubachi plates."[52] Most illuminatingly, Alikhanov tells that the *kunatskaya* (the main formal social space) in Kubachi homes usually served as a "museum-room" (*komnatoy-muzeyem*) for the display of fine ceramics and metalwares, indicating a conscious relationship with modern institutional practices of collection and display.[53] In Paris, the men of Kubachi used some of the money they made by selling antiquities to acquire French porcelain, which was especially valued by the women of the village.[54] As the villagers liquidated their collections of Iranian ceramics, one wonders what such exchanges represented to them: a regrettable sacrifice of precious family collections, deliberated over at length? Or simply the transfer of one form of capital into another, with the additional benefit of an upgrade from old Persian stonepaste to new French porcelain?

Pope, writing in 1932, has given the most matter-of-fact summary of the story from the market end. "Kubachi has been visited at least six times by dealers, first in 1891, and again in 1893 by Mr. Cerof Filippo, who may be credited with the discovery of its commercial possibilities; twice by Mr. Varsharg, and still later by Kirkor Minassian, to say nothing of various Russian merchants and a number of scholars, including Prof. Josef Orbeli of the Hermitage."[55] Cerof Filippo (d. 1941) is an intriguing figure, an Italian-Romanian "musician and musical instrument maker" who was reportedly resident in Iran from 1894 to 1908. As well as associating with Pope, Filippo sold many Iranian ceramics to Friedrich Sarre that are now in the collection of the Museum für Islamische Kunst, Berlin.[56] The dealer Dikran Kelekian offers a story that aligns with Pope's timeline of dealer extraction at Kubachi. In 1909 Kelekian described his own first encounter with the Kubachi wares some years earlier (1905, according to a later Russian source) through the intermediary of "an Italian traveller returning from a voyage to the East."[57] This must surely be Filippo. After buying up the eight polychrome plates that the Italian traveler had to offer, Kelekian dispatched an agent to look for more such wares in Iran. His agent, however, turned up nothing until a chance encounter with "two Circassians, Hassan and Aumeratta, who had come in to a local fair" from the Caucasus, with another polychrome plate to sell. Contact made and pipeline established, Kelekian went on to sell a number of "Kubachi ware" ceramics to European and American collections over several decades, with Kubachi residents coming to Paris specifically to sell him their pieces.[58] A very large number of Kubachi wares were offered for sale at the Whitney auction in Paris in 1910, and this must have been around the peak of the market.[59]

Three remarkable early twentieth-century photographs capture the visits of Daghestani men to Paris, in the company (in person or by proxy) of the dealers Kelekian and Minassian. The first of these, published by Marilyn Jenkins-Madina, shows four men in North Caucasian dress outside Dikran Kelekian's antiquities shop in the Place Vendôme in Paris. She dates the image to circa 1912.[60] The second and third are undated prints held in the Minassian archives that show men in the same style of dress—some of whom may be identical with individuals in the Kelekian photograph—with Kirkor Minassian standing proprietorially beside them in one image and seated among them in another (figs. 2.11 and 2.12). In the latter, Minassian has dressed up in an astrakhan hat and holds a rifle, with a similarly hatted child in front of him. The striped wallpaper of a bourgeois room, hung with early modern dishes and Iznik-type tiles, suggests that the photograph was taken in Minassian's trading premises or home in Paris, likely around the same time as the photograph outside Kelekian's shop.[61] The existence of these photographs indicates that the villagers' visit was held by both Kelekian and Minassian to be worth recording, something that could add to their own mystique as dealers. The second half of the nineteenth century saw the displacement of approximately one million Muslim refugees from the North Caucasus to the Ottoman Empire, creating an image of the "Circassian Other" that would have appeared exotic in Istanbul, Moscow, or Cairo, let alone Paris.[62] The oral histories supplied by Alikhanov show full awareness of this among the villagers, who seem to have somewhat enjoyed their visibility abroad.[63]

Alikhanov's slew of stories describes a multifaceted engagement by the residents of Kubachi with the international antiquities trade. This included the strategic acquisition and resale of Afghan, Iranian, and Egyptian antiquities—the latter somewhat surprising to encounter in the Caucasus, but Egyptian and Roman antiquities (authentic and inauthentic) were reportedly also being sold in Russian Turkestan during the same period.[64] Kubachi was represented in the dealer reports as a remote cache with unwitting guardians, its treasures ripe for extraction by intrepid international adventurers. But in sharp contrast to this market mythology, Alikhanov's oral histories reveal that the residents of Kubachi were fully conscious agents who actively made their village into a significant node of the global antiquities trade in the first years of the twentieth century.

Finally, there are two published references to ceramics fabrication and forgery in relation to Kubachi, pointing in two different directions. The collector R.H.R. Brocklebank reported in 1931 that four Kubachi wares offered for sale at auction in Paris in 1927 were modern forgeries (fig. 2.13).[65] After firsthand examination of two of these pieces, which were withdrawn from the Paris sale but turned up a short time later in the hands of a dealer in Cairo, he concluded that "Suspicions would be aroused by their heavy weight, by their being so perfect, by the very fine crackle that covered them, and by the lack of any patches of the red 'varnish' [the grime layer] on the back." He concluded that they had probably been made in "some French ceramic works."[66] This is suggestive, and Paris appears again in chapter 4 as a possible site of Islamic ceramics forgery.

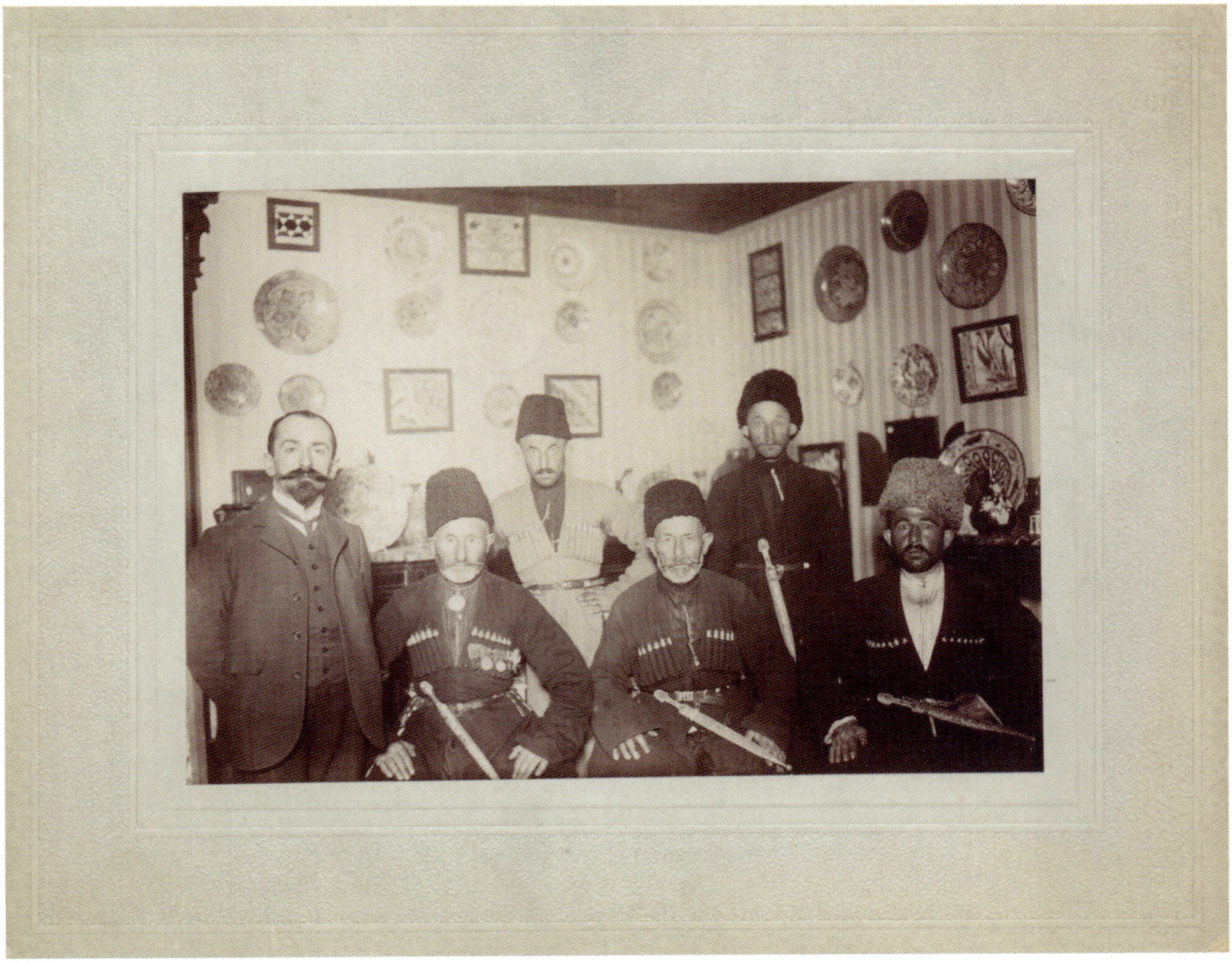

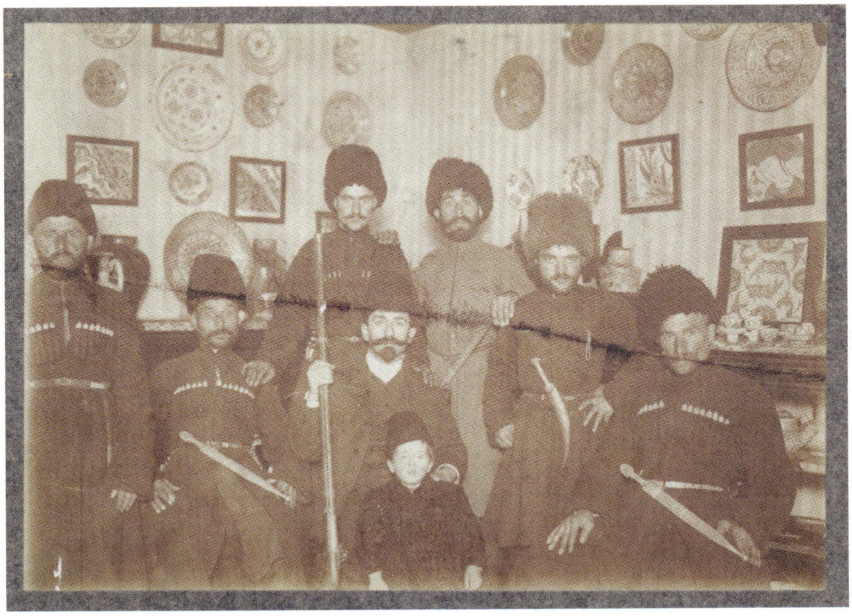

2.11. Photographic print. Early 20th century. Minassian Collection, Box 14, John Hay Library, Brown University.

2.12. Photographic print. Early 20th century. Minassian Collection, Box 14, John Hay Library, Brown University.

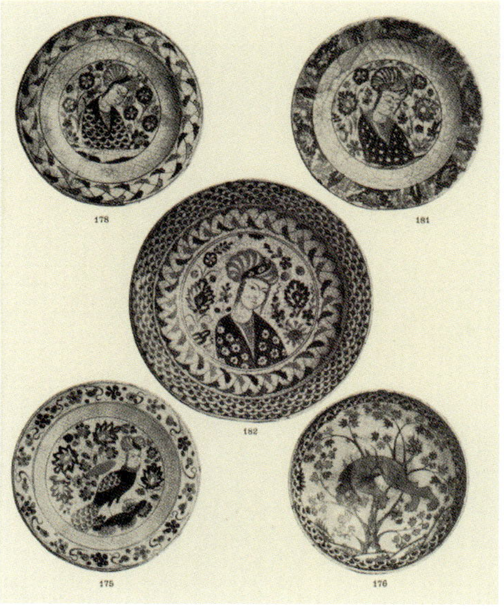

2.13. Hôtel Drouot catalogue, sale of the collection of M. S. Sevadjian, 1–3 June 1927, unnumbered plate.

The second reference to Kubachi ceramics fakery opens up a different avenue, for it implicates the villagers themselves in material fabulation. In 1947 the Soviet scholar E. K. Kverfel'dt claimed that the residents of Kubachi were known to have practiced a form of artificial aging on glazed ceramics by immersing and heating them in a fatty composition. This drew the color of the body underneath into the craquelure of the glaze, making the craquelure more pronounced and warmer in tone and creating an effect that enchanted collectors—especially, he noted, those from the west.[67] Chapter 3 introduces a more detailed account from Iran of modern glazed ceramics artificially aged with fatty liquids and other chemical preparations. Versions of this technique could easily have been reached independently by multiple groups of craftspeople at different nodal points of the antiquities market as they recognized the value that buyers accorded to the appearance of age, and Kverfel'dt's observation raises the tantalizing prospect of yet another highly knowing craft skill at Kubachi, aimed squarely at that market. Who knows what other mysteries of the antiquities market might eventually be traced to the village of Kubachi?

Tiles, Violently

Thus far, this history of extraction has looked at the circulation of early modern ceramics from above-ground domestic collections. The first *medieval* Islamic ceramic products to be traded at scale on the art market also came from above-ground sources, but of a very different kind. These were thirteenth- and fourteenth-century Iranian stonepaste tiles with overglaze luster decoration, ripped from the walls of shrines and other religious buildings. By the 1890s, wrote Sarre, "they found their way into the great European museums without really being noticed."[68] They were even appearing in American home decorating magazines.[69] More has been written about the stripping of medieval tiles from religious sites in Iran than about any other aspect of ceramics collecting from the region, but it is important here to restate the facts and set

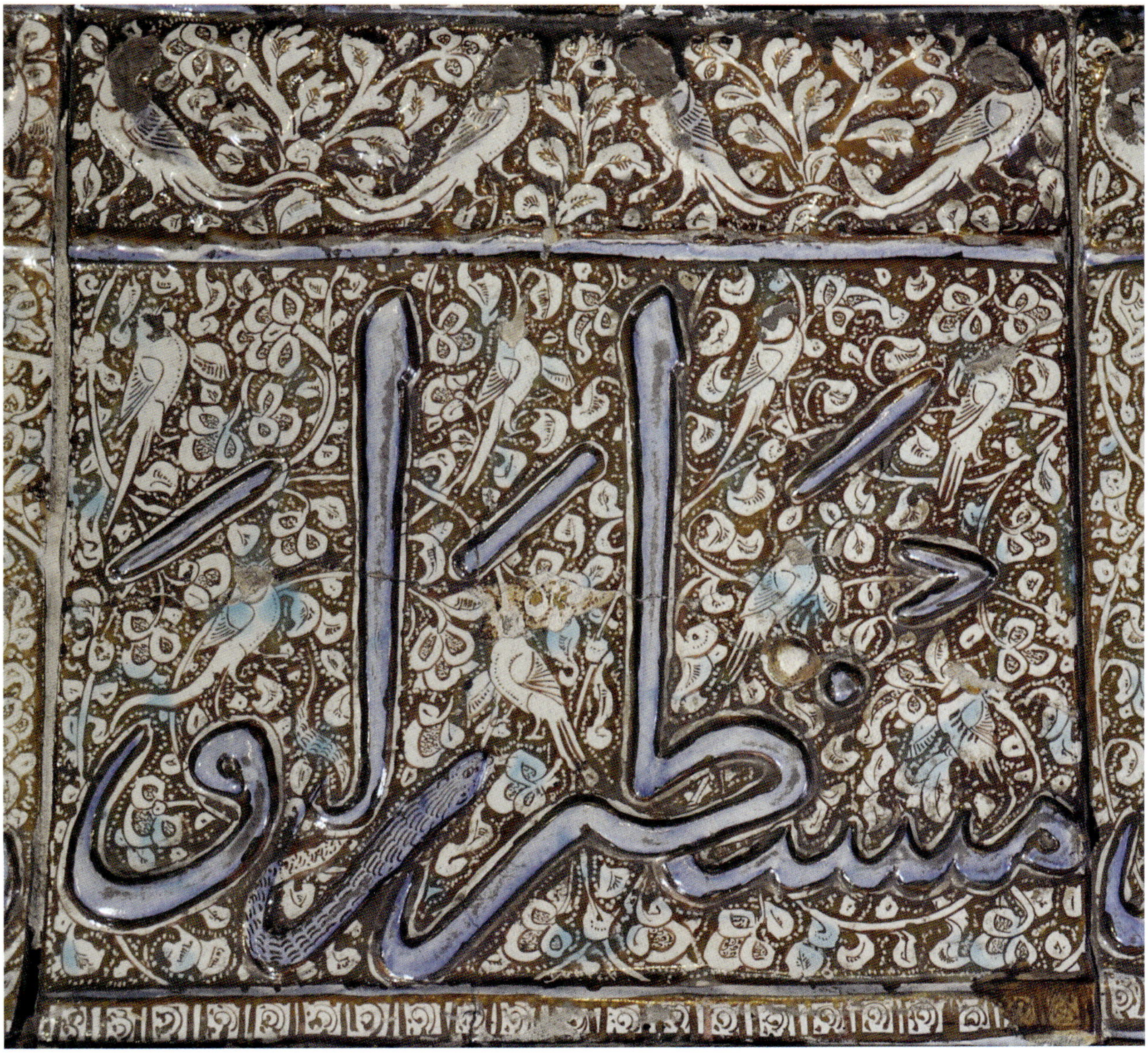

2.14. Tile, glazed stonepaste with luster overglaze. Iran, ca. 1308, from the shrine of shaykh ʿAbd al-Samad, Natanz. Length approx. 37.4 cm. Hetjens Museum, Düsseldorf.

the timeline alongside the trade in historic vessels, while also scrutinizing some overlooked aspects of this dismembered and scattered corpus.[70]

In fact, the medieval luster tiles of Iran had been attracting the covetous attention of European and Russian art collectors since at least the 1860s. C. J. Wills, a British physician resident in Iran, tells of seeing a large collection of Iranian antiquities in the Tehran home of the French dealer Jules Richard (1816–1891) circa 1866, including luster tiles "such as one seldom sees nowadays."[71] (Tellingly, Wills noted that at the time he was writing [ca. 1881], "in a hundred specimens [of antiquities] from Persia, be they what they will, ninety are shams.")[72] Similarly, in 1867 de Rochechouart devoted considerable space in his *Souvenirs d'un voyage en Perse* to the tiles from the tomb-shrine of the Sufi shaykh ʿAbd al-Samad at Natanz (tilework completed ca. 1308), which he regarded as the superlative examples of the tilemaker's art in Iran (fig. 2.14).[73]

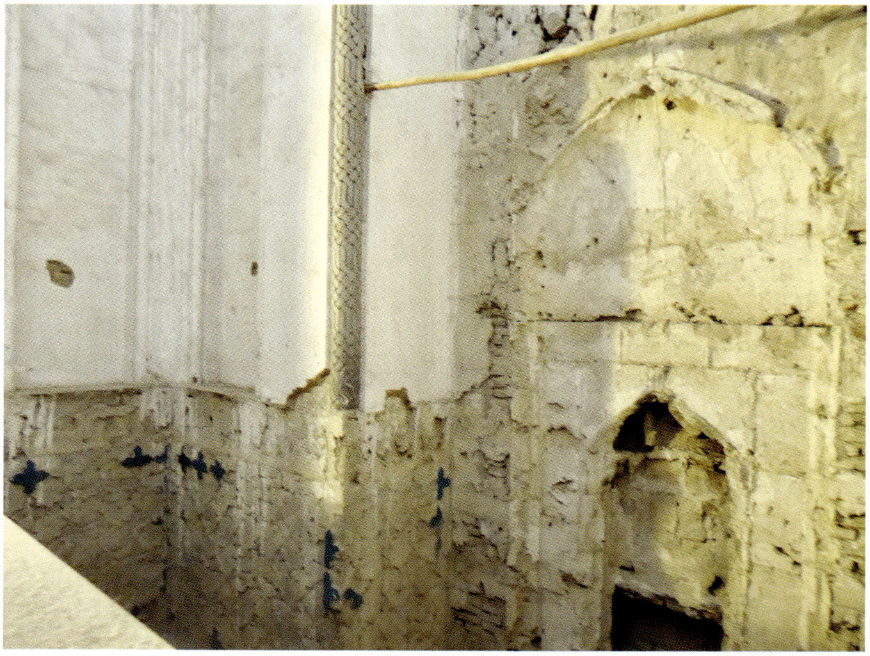

2.15. Interior, shrine of shaykh ʿAbd al-Samad at Natanz, photographed by Keelan Overton, 2018.

Tiles were being removed from the shrine at Natanz by 1862 and likely earlier, and most had been plundered by 1875. The scale of the looting was such that it reportedly prompted the Qajar ruling powers to issue an edict in 1876 against the despoliation of religious buildings, although if such an edict was issued, it clearly did not stop the problem.[74] The consequences of this despoliation are starkly evident in the shrine at Natanz today. The once spectacular mihrab is now a stark emptiness of mortar sockets and exposed brick where fifty or more tiles were prised off the walls (fig. 2.15). The lower walls are also a field of ghosts, with only a few fragments of the star-and-cross tile schema remaining, and an empty band above them where large dado tiles like the one illustrated in figure 2.14 once carried a frieze of Qur'anic inscriptions.[75] Only when faced with the physical scars of an eviscerated monument does it become possible to see the violence lying behind the celebrated medieval luster tiles that now glitter in museum vitrines all over the world.[76]

In his book, de Rochechouart also praised the tilework of the *chapelle* at Qum;[77] in another publication of 1867, Ferdinand Méchin commented favorably on the glazed bricks and tiles at Nayin.[78] Over the next two decades further reports from European travelers would add other sites to this treasure map of potential acquisition in Iran, including the shrine at Mashhad and the architectural remains at Sultaniya.[79] Tahvildar Isfahani, in the social geography of Isfahan that he completed in 1891, noted that "for three or four years now people have been coming from Russia to buy Iranian antique tiles ... in Isfahan there are many beautiful madrasas and mosques that are no longer in use. Because they are religious endowments nobody is responsible for them and nobody cares for their materials. These mosques have much marble stone and very good tiles. Some people have become thieves, who gradually steal these tiles, which they sell to Russian merchants for prices ranging from three *qrans* to 5,000 *dinars* and more for a single tile."[80]

As was so often the case in the nineteenth-century scramble to extract antiquities from the Middle East, the praise and mapping of sites of potential extraction was accompanied—practically simultaneously—by published laments about the spoliation of those same sites.[81] Jane Dieulafoy, who had visited Iran in 1881, noted in a book published in 1887 that the shrine of the Imamzadeh Yahya at Varamin, not far south of Tehran (and still very much in active devotional use today), had already suffered greatly, recording that "some parts of the tile revetment have been stripped and sold in Tehran for very high prices."[82] In her book she included an image of the partially stripped mihrab of the nearby shrine of the Imamzadeh Shah Hossein at Varamin, made after a photograph she took at the site (fig. 2.16). The image makes a stark point about the state of the monument while also perhaps stoking avaricious interest in the remaining sections of tilework visible in the picture.[83] Poignantly, Keelan Overton and Kimia Maleki have shown that printed copies of the images from Dieulafoy's book were displayed in the despoliated shrine of the Imamzadeh Yahya at Varamin as recently as 2018.[84] Framed and mounted, they were hung in a void once occupied by the spectacular fourteenth-century luster tile mihrab—which is now, after removal in the late nineteenth century and a period spent in Paris as security against a financial loan, in the collection of the Doris Duke Foundation in Honolulu, Hawaii (fig. 2.17).[85]

What drove this frenzy of despoliation? Why were collectors prepared to pay enough to incentivize such looting? The tiles themselves, as might be guessed from the foregoing discussion, are now scattered through museums

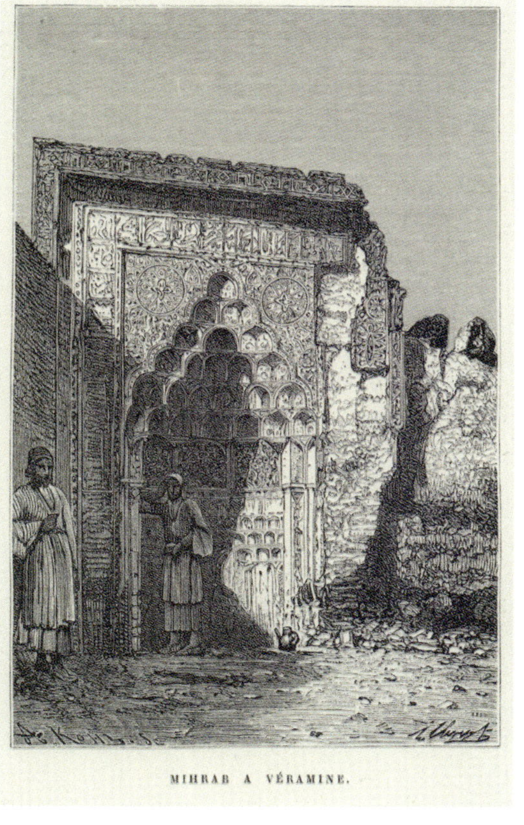

2.16. Jane Dieulafoy, *La Perse, la Chaldée et la Susiane: Relation de voyage* (Paris: Hachette, 1887), p. 149.

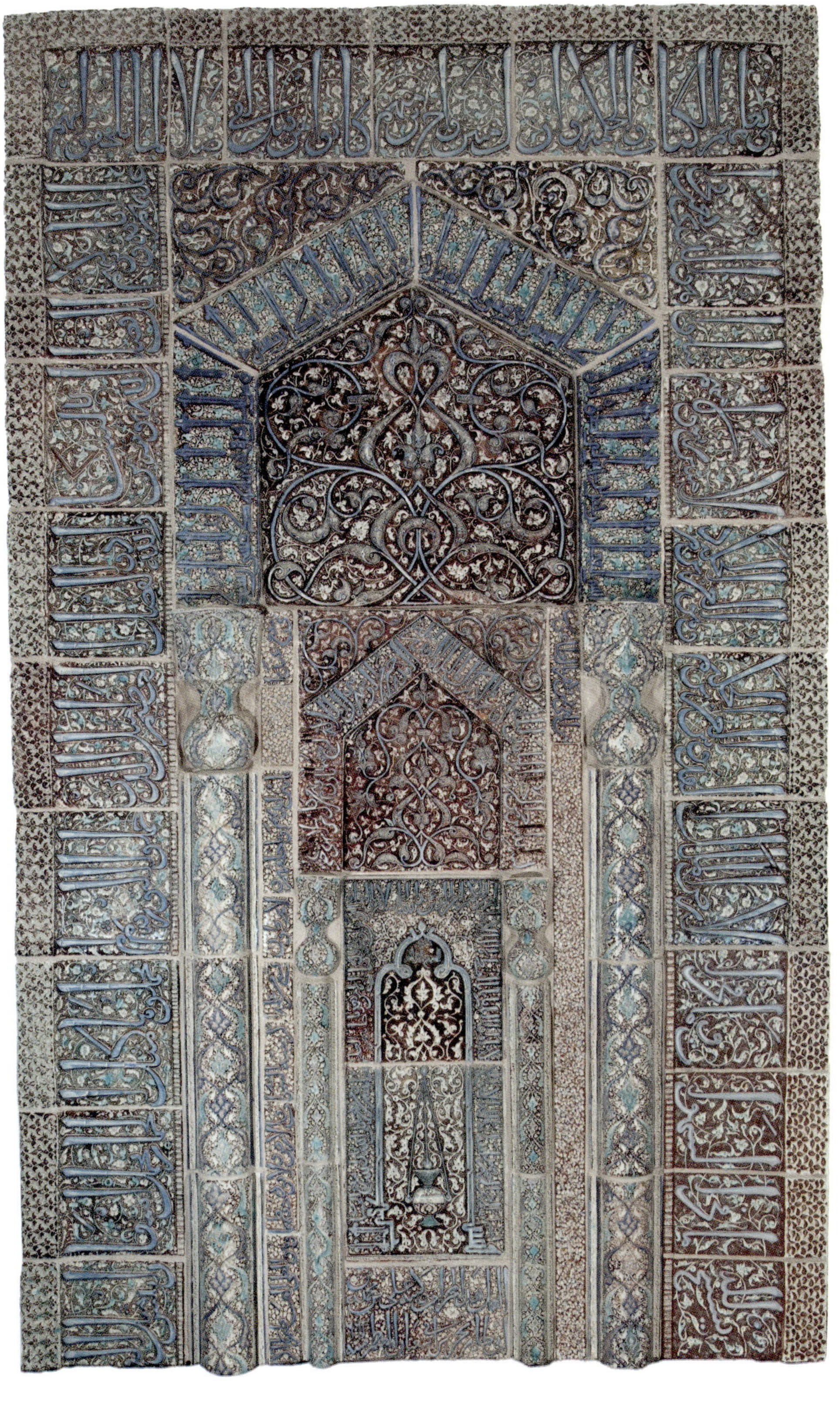

and private collections around the world. Their lure for collectors is best understood at close quarters. Here, the exemplar is one of three tiles from the Natanz shrine that are now in the collection of the Hetjens Museum in Düsseldorf, on the banks of the Rhine (see fig. 2.14). The tiles were moved to the Hetjens Museum in the late 1920s, following the dissolution of the Düsseldorf Kunstgewerbemuseum (Museum of Decorative Arts) in 1927.[86] From a tile frieze completed in 1308, these were once part of the dado of Qur'anic inscription running around the inner walls of the shrine.[87] The Hetjens example showcases the heft of these large-scale stonepaste tiles and their arresting tonal combination of inscriptions highlighted in cobalt, dots of turquoise, and dense, skillfully executed overglaze decoration in glittering luster.

Technologically, both stonepaste (the body of the tile) and luster decoration (the brown parts of the painted design) are important innovations that were refined and raised to uniquely celebrated heights in medieval Iran, although the full-blown technique of luster-decorated ceramics first emerged in ninth-century Iraq (see below) and there are ongoing debates about the origins of stonepaste.[88] Stonepaste was the body fabric of the most rarefied types of ceramic production in the medieval Middle East; it is made from ground quartz pebbles or quartz sand, along with smaller quantities of fine white clay and ground glaze frit.[89] What this produces is, at its most refined, a pale, stiff, and light ceramic body that can be used to make thinner walls and lighter slabs than are possible with common clay, enabling a great surge of experimentation in ceramic forms. The stiffness of stonepaste also works particularly well with molds, holding fine detail with crisp precision.[90] Here, the dado tile has been made from a thick sheet of stonepaste pressed into a mold to create the raised designs of the birds and plants in the upper band, while the elegant Qur'anic inscriptions in thuluth script were cut from a separate sheet of stonepaste and luted (attached with liquid clay) onto the main body before glazing and firing.

Within this tile, a possible textual confusion arose between the initial application of the inscription and the completion of luster painting, giving rise to a whimsical improvisation that reveals the ingenuity of the medieval luster painter. To follow this improvisation, one must first understand the multistage creation of lustered ceramics, which involves at least two firings. For this tile, the finished stonepaste form—complete with its luted-on inscription—would have been covered in a white glaze opacified with tin oxide, with the blue and turquoise colorants (made with cobalt and copper, respectively) painted onto that white glaze. The piece would then undergo its first firing, fixing the white glaze and the colors. After cooling, the luster designs were painted in a brown luster medium (a mixture of metal oxides held in a refractory medium like ocher) over the top of the fired glaze layer. The whole thing then underwent a carefully controlled second firing in oxygen-reducing conditions, bonding the metal oxides in the luster medium to the glaze and creating a microscopically thin, brown metallic layer with the lustrous sheen and iridescence so prized by medieval and modern audiences alike.

The word starting at the right of the Hetjens Museum's tile is *mustatira(an)*, meaning "widespreading." This unusual word appears only once in the Qur'an, in sura 76 verse 7. The letters *ya*ʾ (ي) and *ra*ʾ (ر), which appear next to

2.17. Mihrab of glazed stonepaste tiles with luster overglaze, made by ʿAli Ibn Muhammad Ibn Abi Tahir for the shrine of the Imamzadeh Yahya at Varamin. Iran, dated Shaʿban 663/May 1265. Height 385 cm. Doris Duke Foundation, Honolulu, 48.327.

each other in this word, have been written on the tile in such a similar manner that they initially appear as if they are simply the letter *ra'* repeated. This calligraphic idiosyncrasy might explain the curious actions of the luster painter, who has used a fine paintbrush to turn the letter *ra'* into a sinuous creature with scales or fur, its appearance somewhere between a snake and a polecat. It fixes one of the luster birds on the tile with a beady eye as it lunges forward, its tail twining upward behind the following letter *alif*. The *ra'*-creature of the Hetjens Museum's tile could be pure whimsy. In the absence of comparable animate letters elsewhere among the tiles from this frieze, however, it might be read as one luster painter's ingenious resolution of what they took to be an extraneous letter *ra'* already baked in at the first firing: adapting the "mistake" into a new design via luster decoration. At some point prior to the shrine's despoliation most of the birds in this tile frieze were decapitated, presumably by iconophobes, but the *ra'*-creature kept its head, hidden inside Qur'an 76:7 from 1308 until now.

Like many other medieval Iranian tiles that have traveled through the antiquities market, the three Natanz tiles now in the Hetjens Museum were enclosed at some point within a wooden frame, in this case bolting together three discontinuous fragments of Qur'anic inscription. The act of framing is, on the one hand, a straightforward way of making antique tiles easily wall-mountable while also isolating them to render them equivalent to paintings. It thus translates them into a familiar paradigm for collectible art and brackets them off from their original, aggregated contexts. On the other hand, there is something very reminiscent of the taxidermist's art in all of this. A page of framed and labeled Iranian luster tiles sold at auction in 1913 immediately brings to mind a wall full of hunting trophies, with dismembered architectural decoration taking the place of stuffed and mounted animal heads (fig. 2.18).[91]

Elsewhere, the violence of this marketplace is evident within the tiles themselves, however carefully it has been covered up prior to sale. Two tiles now in the Eskenazi Museum of Art at Indiana University (fig. 2.19), bought in 1961 from the New York dealer Hassan Khan Monif (1888–1964), appear at first glance to be relatively untroubled specimens.[92] They come from a now dispersed group of fourteenth-century Iranian palatial luster tiles with parrots and verse lines from the *Shahnama* (the Persian Book of Kings), recently studied by Yves Porter. These two bear verses from the Bihzan and Manizeh cycle (left) and the Khusraw cycle (right) that both invoke the poetic topos of hair as an agent of beauty: "All in a tall cypress with musk-scented hair" and "If the moon has two black curls," respectively.[93]

Close examination of the Eskenazi tiles reveals considerable overpainting, made very obvious when photographed under UV light that causes the modern overpaint to fluoresce yellow (fig. 2.20). One tile (left) shows overpainting everywhere that fragments have been pieced back together, revealing that it was shattered into at least nine pieces at some point—probably when it was ripped off the wall in the modern era. The reconstruction of the other tile is more suggestive. A single line of overpainting runs top to bottom in the dead center of the tile, covering a complete split between the two halves. CT scanning shows that the cut edges of the tile are beveled along this split, creating a V-shaped "valley" opening toward the back of the tile, now filled with what

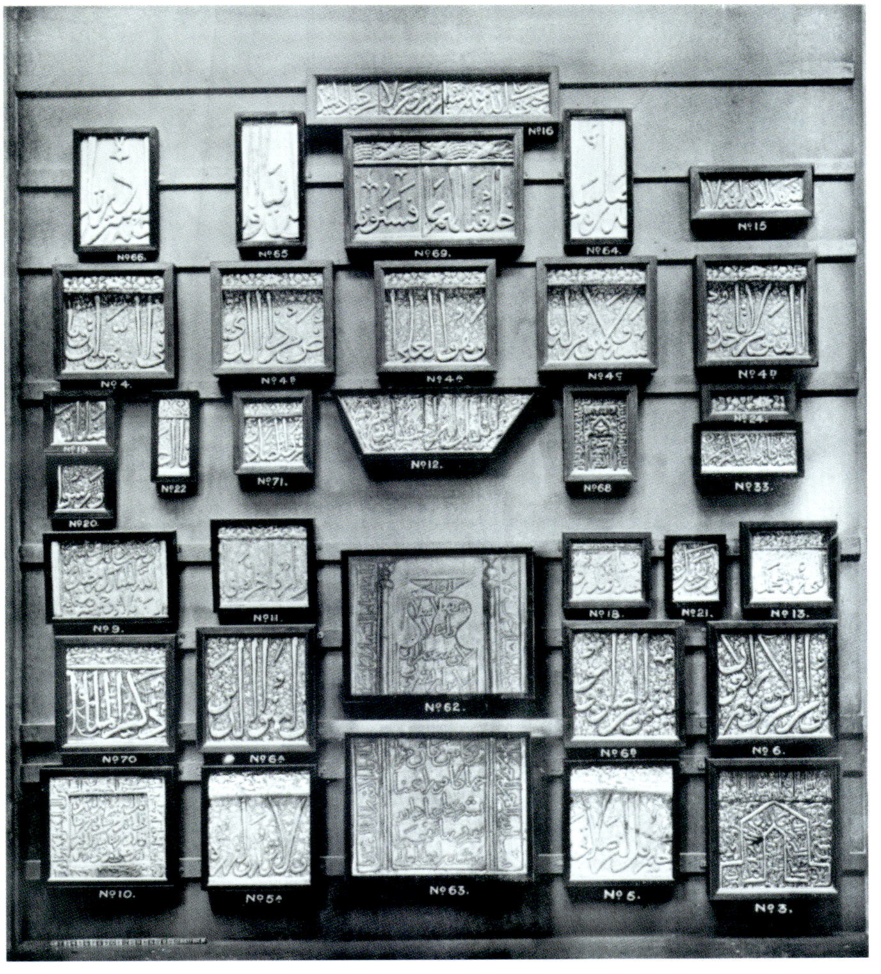

2.18. Vincent Robinson Galleries, *Exhibition of Persian Art & Curios, the Collection Formed by J.R. Preece Esq. C.M.G.* (London: Vincent Robinson Galleries, 1913), plate 1.

appears to be earthenware (a layer of reddish clay also covers the entire back surface of each tile, covering up the joins).[94] This means that the original tile was carefully cut in half after firing and the joining edges were beveled in order to fit them together as neatly as possible at a ninety-degree angle to each other. In other words, this piece was originally used to face a corner. Only when the two halves were stripped from their walls for the market were they flattened back out again into the more saleable single face of their original fired shape.

The violent despoliation of all these tiles and their dispersal on the market forestalls attempts to reconstruct not only decorative schema but even processes of production. And yet, there are traces of process to be found, if you can look at the backs that are so often hidden from view in museum displays. Many of the Mongol-era star tiles bear kiln shadows where the luster design of the next tile over in a tightly packed kiln has been transferred during the firing process onto its neighbor's unglazed back surface. This presumably occurred when the oxides in the luster medium vaporized (fig. 2.21). Such kiln shadows are strikingly prevalent among the large star tiles completed in 1262

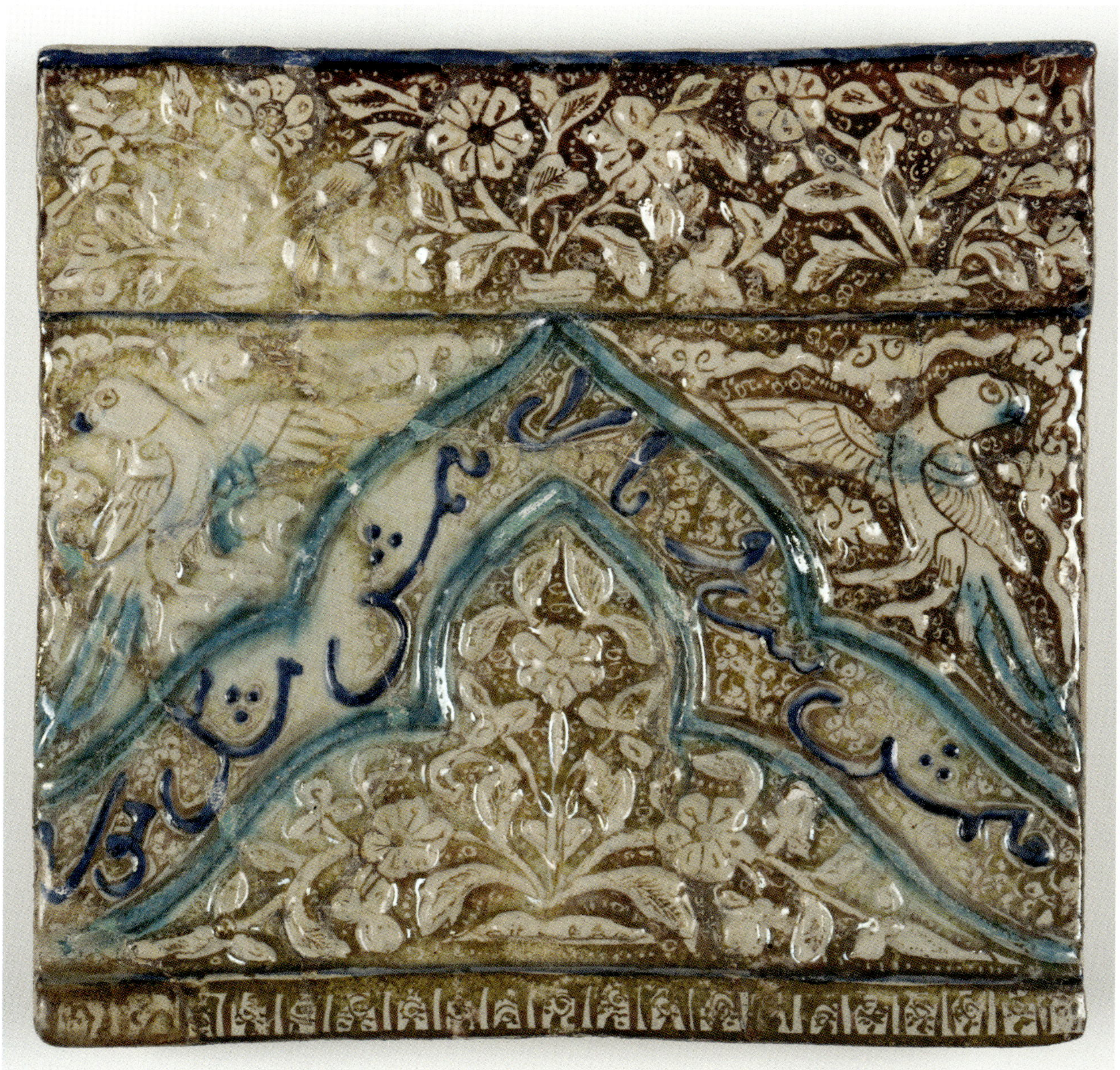

2.19. Two tiles, glazed stonepaste with overglaze luster. Attributed Iran, 14th century. Length of each approx. 27.3 cm. Eskenazi Museum of Art, Indiana University, 61.72 a and b.

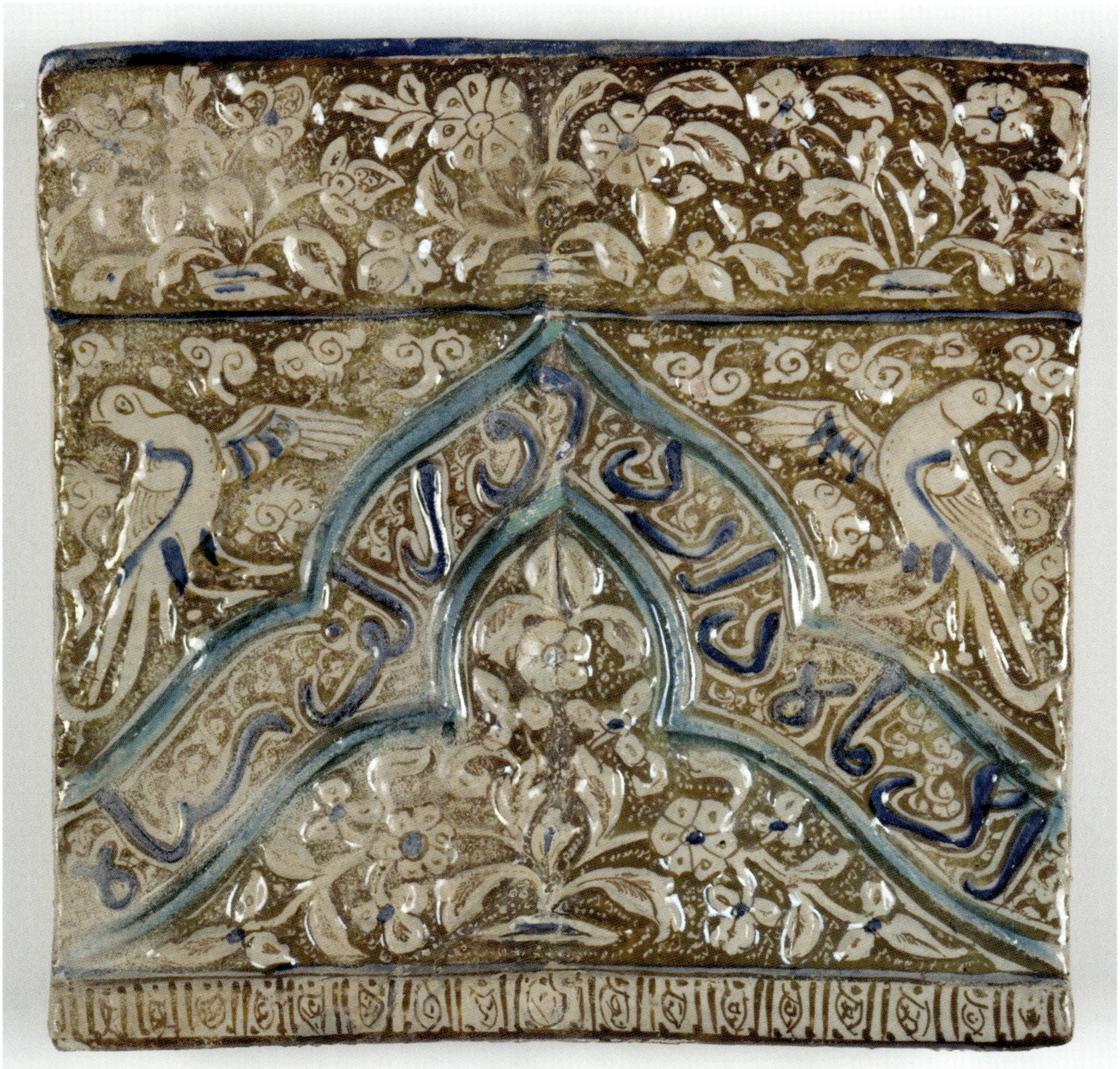

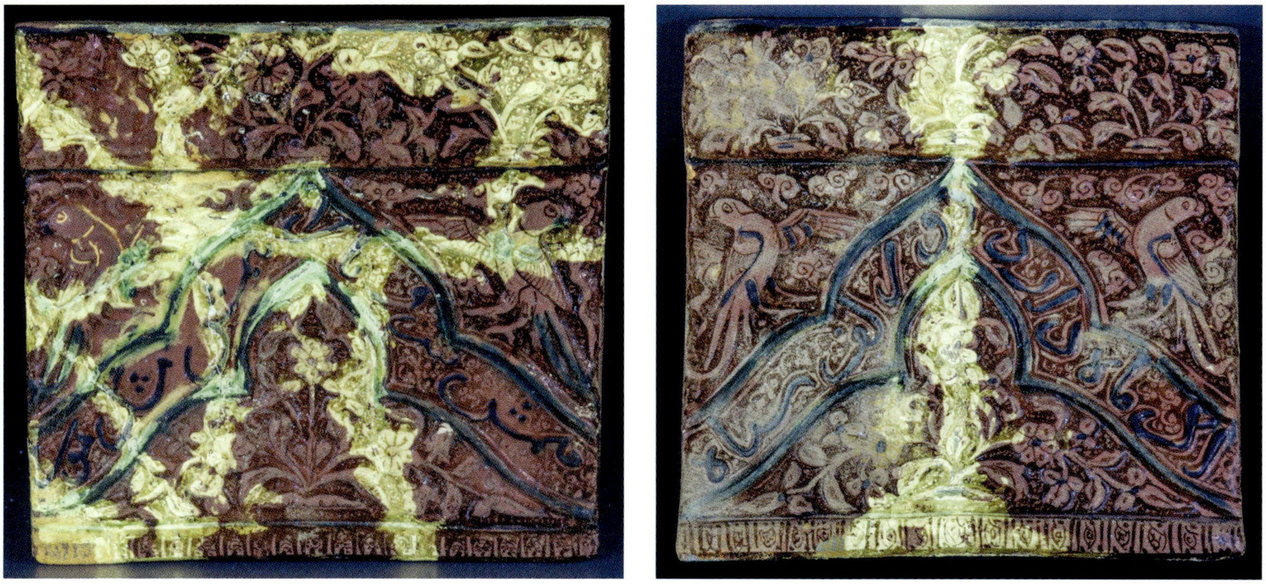

2.20. UV images of tiles illustrated in figure 2.19.

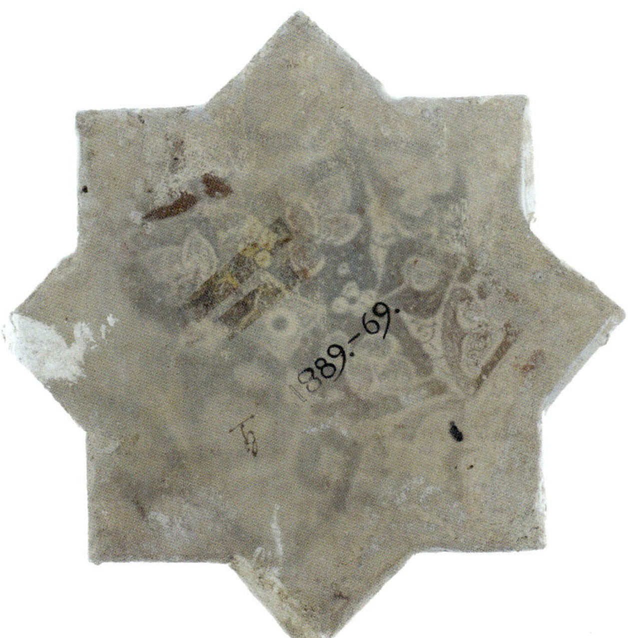

2.21. Star tile, glazed stonepaste with overglaze luster, reverse showing “kiln shadows.” Iran, ca. 1262, from the shrine of the Imamzadeh Yahya at Varamin. Height approx. 31 cm. National Museum of Scotland, 1889–69.

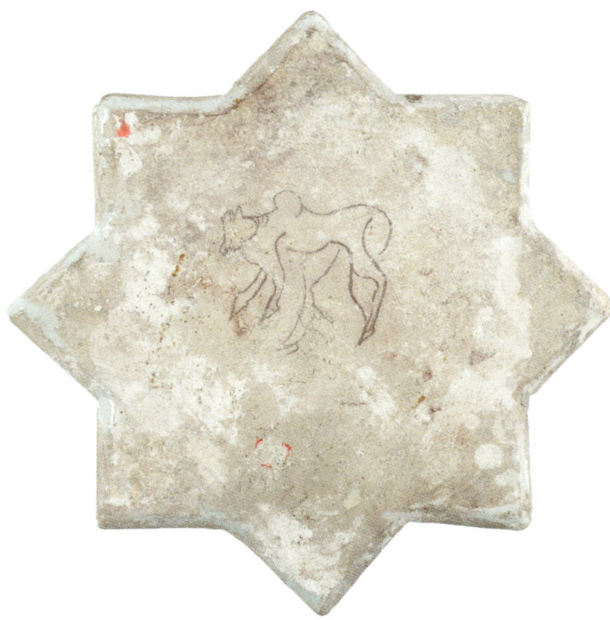

2.22. Star tile, glazed stonepaste with overglaze luster, reverse showing sketch of zebu. Iran, ca. 1262, from the shrine of the Imamzadeh Yahya at Varamin. Height approx. 31 cm. The Walters Art Museum, 48.1292.

for the shrine of the Imamzadeh Yahya at Varamin.[95] Even more intriguing are the traces of freehand outline painting on the backs of a handful of luster tiles, like the abortive depiction of a zebu on the back of a Varamin tile now in the Walters Art Museum (fig. 2.22).[96] These look like trial sketches, offering us an oblique but tantalizing window onto the workshop processes of making Ilkhanid luster tiles.[97] Currently there is no published archaeological evidence to document kiln practices for this material, and the problems of working from a corpus of tiles thrown all over the world by a rapacious market, without a scrap of documentation, are obvious.[98] But we may one day be able to piece together more of the processes of production of these extraordinary artworks, by looking closely and pooling information.

Below Ground: Harvesting a Disorderly Corpus

From the despoliation of tiled shrines in Iran, this chapter now hinges over to the extraction of ceramic material from below ground for sale on the open market, and the expansion of market interest beyond medieval tiles and into vessels.[99] It is widely recognized today that the scientific discipline of archaeology in the Islamic world developed out of European and Russian colonial interests in territorial control and knowledge production.[100] Less often acknowledged in the historiography of the discipline is the colossal role played by undocumented, market-driven digging for antiquities. Very frequently, reports of success by commercial diggers at a particular site acted as the prompt for starting a campaign of scientific excavation in the same spot or nearby. This meant that archaeologists were often coming to a site that had been picked over for years or even decades, its artifacts dispersed far and wide on the market, before any scientific campaigns were initiated. Such was the case at Rayy in Iran, Raqqa in Syria, Afrasiyab in Uzbekistan, Fustat in Egypt, and many other places.[101]

It would be impossible to disaggregate commercial and scientific digging in the region entirely from each other; the two developed in symbiosis. Consequently, the archaeological picture for much of the Middle Eastern ceramic corpus is far murkier than some museum labels and catalogue attributions might suggest. One should be especially skeptical about confident designations of single sites of origin that aren't accompanied by any information about excavation. Single-site attributions are sneaky. They make it sound as if Kashan, or Tell Minis, or Samarqand, was the definitive and verified findspot and/or production site for a particular object—when in fact the attribution has usually been made entirely on stylistic grounds *after* the object appeared on the market, without any verifiable information at all about (a) where it was found, or (b) where it might have been made.

These "zombie attributions," as I call them, usually originate in unverified information transmitted by middlemen. Such information, provided at the moment of transaction, might reflect a real findspot but might equally be a fiction based on whatever site was in vogue with collectors at the time. There is simply no way to be sure. Zombie attributions can also arise from the guesses made by early cataloguers, working in a time when archaeological knowledge about medieval Islamic ceramics was hesitant and speculative. As well as keeping market fictions afloat, they also contribute to overall opacity by continually conflating (putative) findspot with (speculated) production site, and they have a pronounced tendency to become received wisdom and generate their own echo chambers. I have seen many museum accession cards where the origin line for an Iranian ceramic object reads "~~Rayy~~ Kashan," an amendment made not because new information about that specific object had come to light but because a new site had come into scholarly ascendance as the preferred best guess.[102] Most problematically, zombie attributions can be—and are—used to lend a veneer of authoritative certainty, and thereby respectability, to taxonomies that are in reality built on very shaky foundations, often working in the service of the market.

The conditions of archaeological confusion are most pronounced in Iran, where the levels of commercial digging in the late nineteenth to early twentieth century were positively frenetic. But they obtain to a greater or lesser degree across much of the medieval Islamic ceramic corpus. Because of this confusion, the original production sites of some types of prized ceramic are the subjects of still-unresolved scholarly debates. Medieval Iranian lusterware is the most obvious case in point. To date, no site in Iran has yielded incontrovertible physical evidence for large-scale luster production in the form of scientifically excavated and published evidence of medieval kilns with luster wasters (pieces that went wrong in the kiln) documented in situ. And yet, great quantities of luster vessels and tiles were certainly produced in the region, and the historical textual evidence shows that Kashan, in north-central Iran, was undoubtedly a major site of production. But was it the only place where lustered ceramics were made in medieval Greater Iran? Gurgan and more recently Jiroft have also been proposed as sites of medieval luster production, alongside Kashan;[103] farther out in the Persianate cultural area, there have also been claims for luster production at Ani (Armenia) and Merv (Turkmenistan).[104]

If the archaeological picture of the Middle East has been churned to such confusion by decades of commercial excavation, what were all those diggers looking for? The answer is simple: antiquities, especially medieval ceramics in the form of sherds that could be built back up again into whole objects and sold. Islamic burial traditions do not normally include grave goods, so caches of medieval ceramics are not usually preserved at interment sites. Once in a very great while, medieval ceramics in the Middle East have been found intact because they were buried carefully not long after their production. The only securely documented and verified instance of this that I am aware of was uncovered at Ghazni, in Afghanistan, where a cache of eight Iranian lusterware vessels was found in excavations carried out in 1957.[105] The vessels were recovered mostly intact, hidden inside a vaulted niche in the wall of what is surmised to be an elite domestic residence from the Ghaznavid era (977–1186) (fig. 2.23). At the same site, a large jar was found to contain some intact small vessels of sgraffito earthenware.[106]

There are, of course, further unverified stories about buried caches of fine ceramics. A group of medieval lusterwares found at Gurgan in Iran in the 1940s (and dispersed on the market shortly thereafter) was reportedly buried inside large storage jars, although full documentation has never been published.[107] The deus ex machina of storage jar burials, group survival in caves, or miraculously preserved medieval potters' "shops" has also been invoked

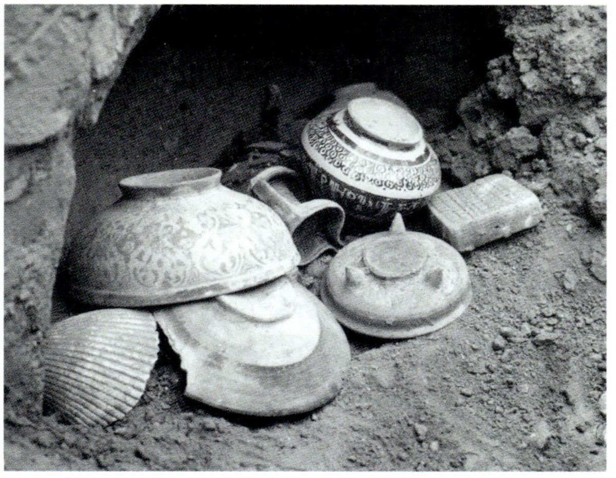

2.23. Repository with lusterwares and other objects excavated at Ghazni, Afghanistan, photographed 1957. Archives of the Italian Archaeological Mission in Afghanistan, 1957.

in dealer reports to explain the large numbers of medieval Syrian stonepaste vessels reportedly found at Raqqa and Tell Minis, the so-called Sultanabad wares of Mongol-era Iran, and the Harari silver hoard.[108] In those cases, however, there is nothing but hearsay and dealer reports to go on. None of the circumstances retailed in those stories are impossible, but dealer reports obviously cannot be taken as reliable sources without independent verification. Many puzzles remain: how to explain the undocumented, miraculous survival of an intact Iranian luster bowl that first appeared in scholarship in 1910 (fig. 2.24)? The bowl is distinguished not only by its incredible condition but also by an inscribed date of 668 H (1269–70 CE) in Arabic.[109] So determined was the dealer Dikran Kelekian that this hard-to-read date would be properly conveyed to prospective buyers that he actually wrote it himself onto the surface of the vessel in black ink, glossing the lustered inscription with his own inky superscript in text and numerals (fig. 2.25).[110]

Overwhelmingly, though, what diggers extracted were not whole objects, perfectly preserved in mysterious circumstances, but thousands upon thousands of fragments. As is shown in chapter 3, these were used to build up vessels of greater or lesser fidelity to the medieval originals. Sometimes nearly all parts of a vessel were located and painstakingly stuck back together; more often, however, there was improvisation with pieces from multiple objects—and sometimes new material as well, as we shall see in chapter 3—sutured together into a new whole. It is worth pausing for a moment over a paradigmatic piece that has survived in something close to its true original state (fig. 2.26). How were these objects of desire originally made, and why have they captivated audiences, past and present?

While modern collectors have usually been most interested in painted surface decoration, the stonepaste body is key to understanding what makes medieval Iranian ceramics so special. The fineness and delicacy of the medium is illustrated here by a reconstructed fluted bowl of the late twelfth or early thirteenth century, loaned by Kelekian to the V&A in 1912. The first appearance of this market antiquity is in a glass negative likely made in Sevruguin's photographic studio in Tehran, prior to 1910 (fig. 2.27). At the time the photograph was taken, the breaks between fragments were still visible, but

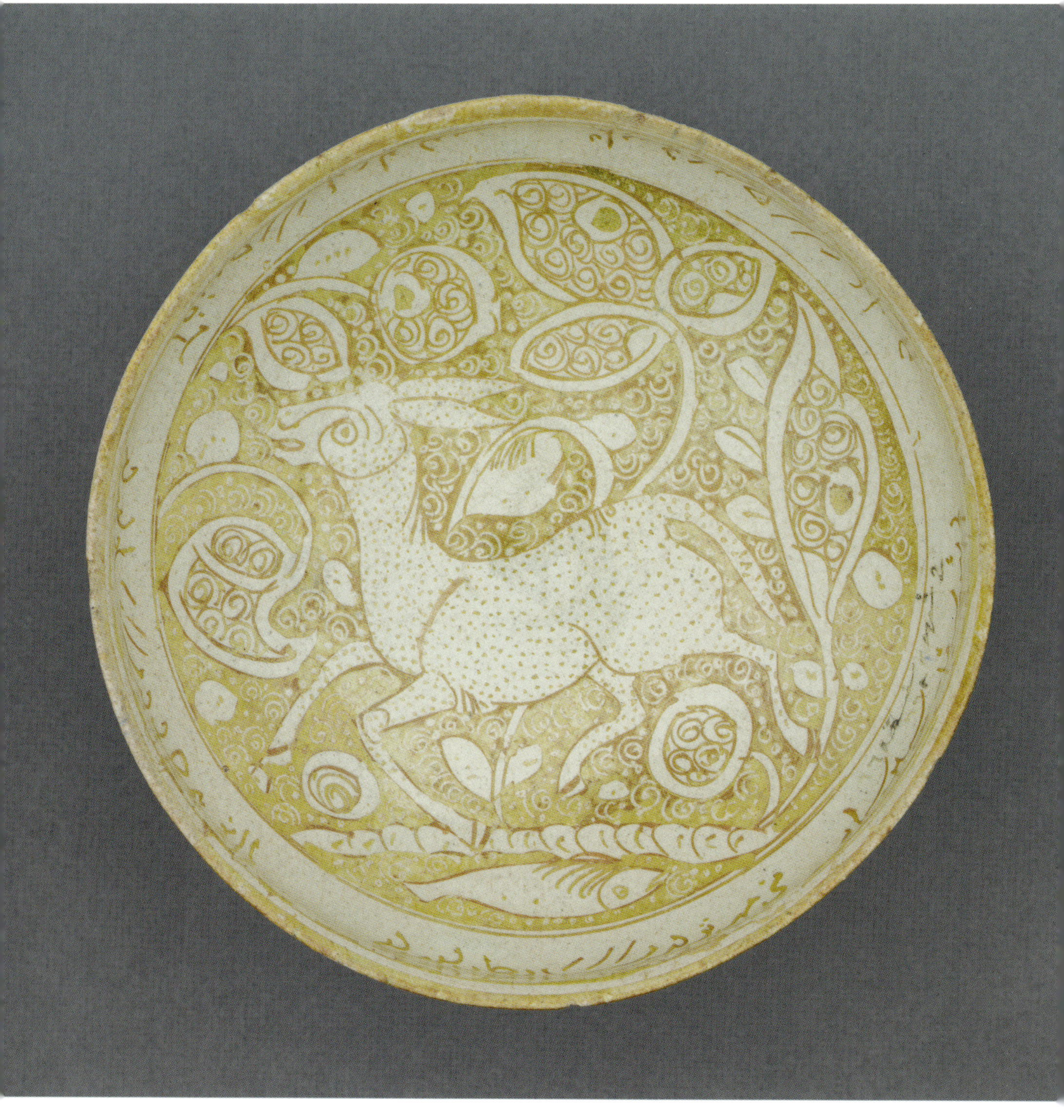

2.24. Bowl, glazed stonepaste with overglaze luster. Attributed Iran, inscribed date of 668 H (1269–70 CE). Diameter approx. 18 cm. Cincinnati Art Museum, Museum Purchase, 1952.259.

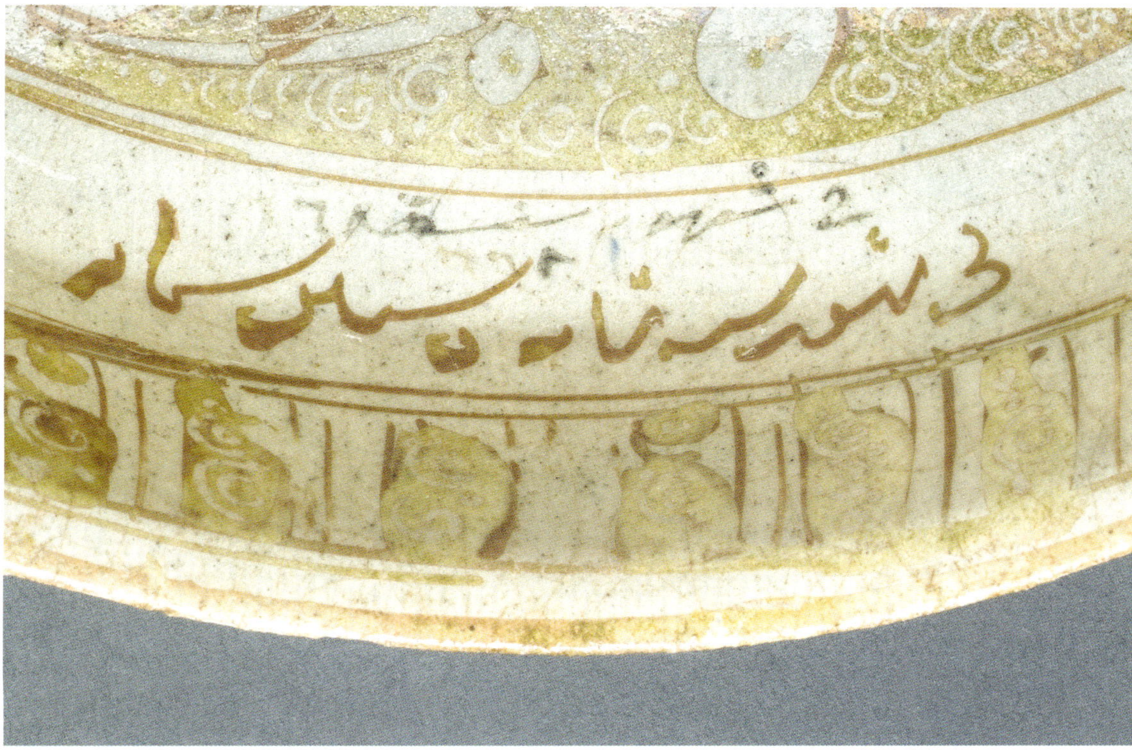

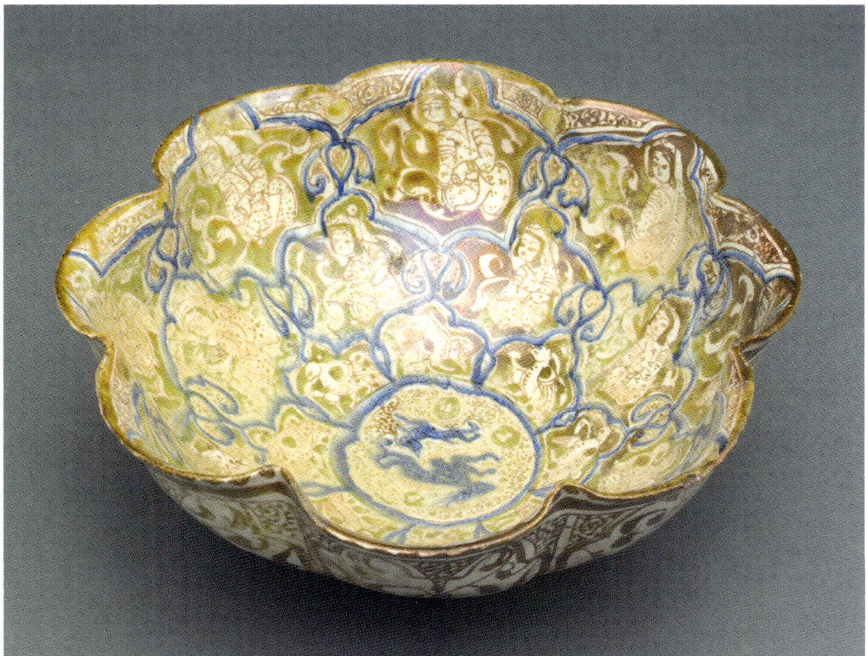

2.25. Detail of figure 2.4, showing inscribed date in luster, with faded glossing in ink added above.

2.26. Fluted bowl, glazed stonepaste with cobalt and overglaze luster. Attributed Iran, late 12th–early 13th century. Diameter approx. 19.5 cm. Cincinnati Art Museum, Museum Purchase, 1952.253.

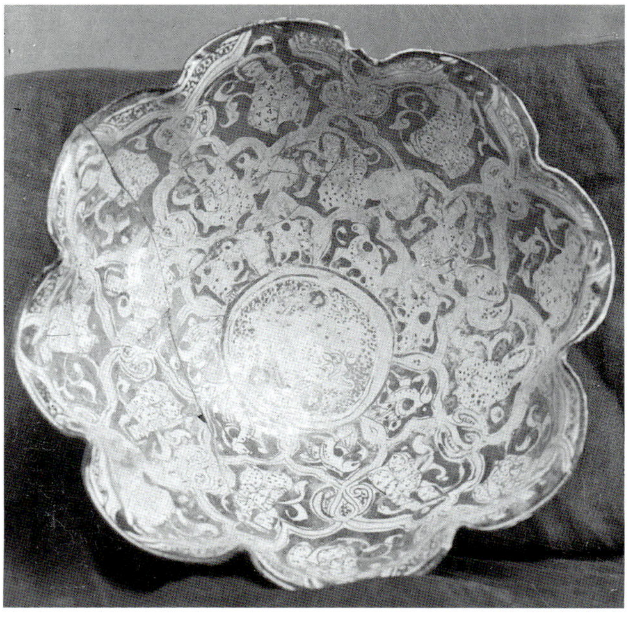

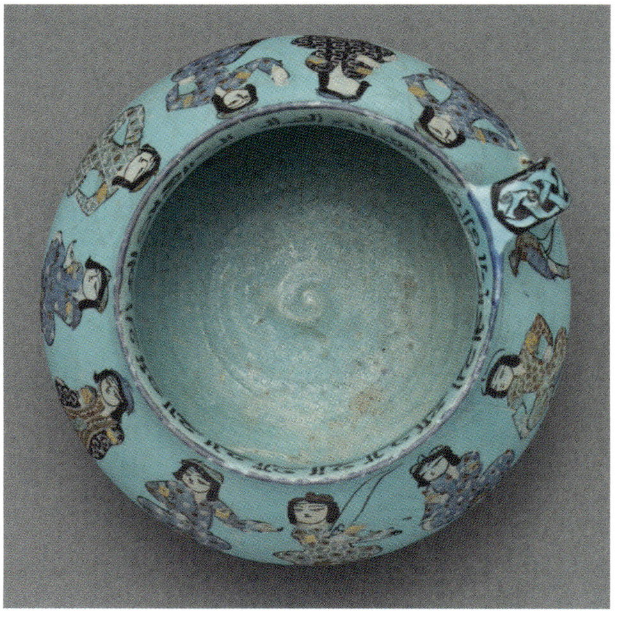

2.27. Bowl shown in figure 2.26. Positive image from glass plate negative, photographed before 1910, probably in Tehran. Antoin Sevruguin/National Museum of Asian Art Archives, Smithsonian Institution, Myron Bement Smith Collection, Gift of Katharine Dennis Smith, 1973–85, FSA_A.04_2.12.GN.10.08.

2.28. Handled jar, glazed stonepaste with in-glaze and overglaze colors and modern overpainting (so-called mina'i ware). Attributed Iran, late 12th–early 13th century. Height approx. 14 cm. Cincinnati Art Museum, Museum Purchase, 1952.256.

these would later disappear under fill and overpaint.[111] The delicate curves of the bowl's eight-lobed form recall medieval sheet-metal work, and the potter probably achieved this by draping a sheet of stonepaste over a specially shaped hump mold and working it to an even thinness before adding a high foot, turned on the wheel.[112] The stiffness and low plasticity of stonepaste present challenges for wheel-throwing: "closed" vessels (those with openings narrower than their widest points) were often thrown in two or even three pieces, which would then be joined together with wet paste before being smoothed with a turning tool.[113] In the bottom of a turquoise-glazed stonepaste jar (also loaned to the V&A in 1912), we can see the fingertip-trace of an umbilicus created by the lift of the potter's hand as he turned the piece on the wheel, many centuries ago (fig. 2.28).[114]

Once the footed form was complete and air-dried to leather-hardness, the undulations of the fluted bowl were enhanced with a layer of opaque white glaze. A remarkably complex pattern in cobalt colorant was painted onto this white glaze prior to firing. Cobalt lines divide the surface of the bowl into trilobed, radiating niches of graduated size, bracketed by ornate escutcheons; these must have been painted freehand and at speed, starting from the base and working outward and upward. Evenly mapping such a complex design onto the folds and troughs of a fluted bowl like this represents a considerable cognitive challenge and could only have been managed by a practiced painter. Finally, after the first firing to fix the white-and-cobalt glaze layer, the luster medium would be used to paint all the seated figures, birds, vegetal scrolls, and background fill, before a further firing in an oxygen-reduced kiln and a final cleaning.[115] Thus, every lustered stonepaste ceramic object represents not only a series of major technical achievements but also a multistage design process necessitating careful procedural thinking and visualization across several steps. The cognitive complexity of these objects is much greater than we sometimes give them credit for.

Iranian luster vessels were in ascendance on the antiquities market by the 1880s.[116] For modern collectors, the most desirable kind of lusterwares were those like the fluted bowl that bore images of humans and/or animals in their decoration. Such figural subject matter naturally piqued the interest of collectors raised on the western painting tradition. Perhaps unsurprisingly, the proprietorial literature on the medieval Iranian ceramics made in lustered and polychrome techniques sometimes took on an insidiously sexual tone that fused figural subjects with a sweaty-palmed Orientalism. Invocations of "feminine lovliness [*sic*]" and veiled harem beauties in a catalogue from 1891 merge the desirability of lusterware with the desirability of its youthful, often androgynous subjects (many of the figures depicted on lusterware and *mina'i* ware, a prized form of Iranian polychrome ceramic, can be identified from their clothing and attributes as beardless young men, but were read as women by early collectors).[117] The vessels themselves are praised in a 1907 publication with nudge-nudge innuendo for their "coyness that withholds the full sight of their charms until the owner has merited greater knowledge by long acquaintance."[118] More explicitly, Royall Tyler, friend and guide of collectors, fused a reviewer's fantasies of commodity possession with those of sexual possession when he wrote in 1910 that "[the painters] studied the fat, soft curve of a woman's wrist, the round, almost featureless moon-face of the maiden of blushing fifteen, and rendered them with a sense of character and a malicious delight in the roly-poly chubbiness of the little harem beauties that borders on caricature."[119]

Digging Up Rayy: From Fragment to (Reconstructed) Whole

Trays of lusterware sherds now held in the V&A give a sense of what it must have been like to harvest this strange crop (fig. 2.29). These represent only the largest fragments from a single batch of sherds that the museum bought in 1903, reportedly all "found in the ruins of Rhages [Rayy]," in northern Iran. They joined a few other luster sherds attributed to Rayy already acquired by the museum in 1868 and 1878 from two well-known French dealers based in Tehran, Ferdinand Méchin and Jules Richard.[120] The medieval site of Rayy, long identified as a key destination for the antiquities hunter, has particular importance in this history and stands in this section as an exemplar of the widespread archaeological extraction taking place at multiple sites in late nineteenth- and early twentieth-century Iran.

Rayy in the nineteenth century was a large, abandoned site with visible traces of ruined buildings, not far from the Qajar capital at Tehran; it has since been absorbed into the city suburbs of Greater Tehran. For western audiences it was also known as Rhages—a name that carried a Biblical thrill, for it is mentioned in the Apocrypha. The British artist and traveler Robert Ker Porter (1777–1842) quite literally put Rayy on the map for Anglophone audiences when, in 1821, he published his descriptions of the site and an accompanying plan (fig. 2.30).[121] In Porter's schematic image, the enclosed space of the ancient city is helpfully labeled as prime terra for the treasure hunter: there is almost nothing inside its walls but the legend, "the whole cover'd with remnants of Ruins, Tiles, Brick, &c."[122] Looking at the trays of sherds, one can start to imagine the massive scale of the harvest at Rayy, as well as the

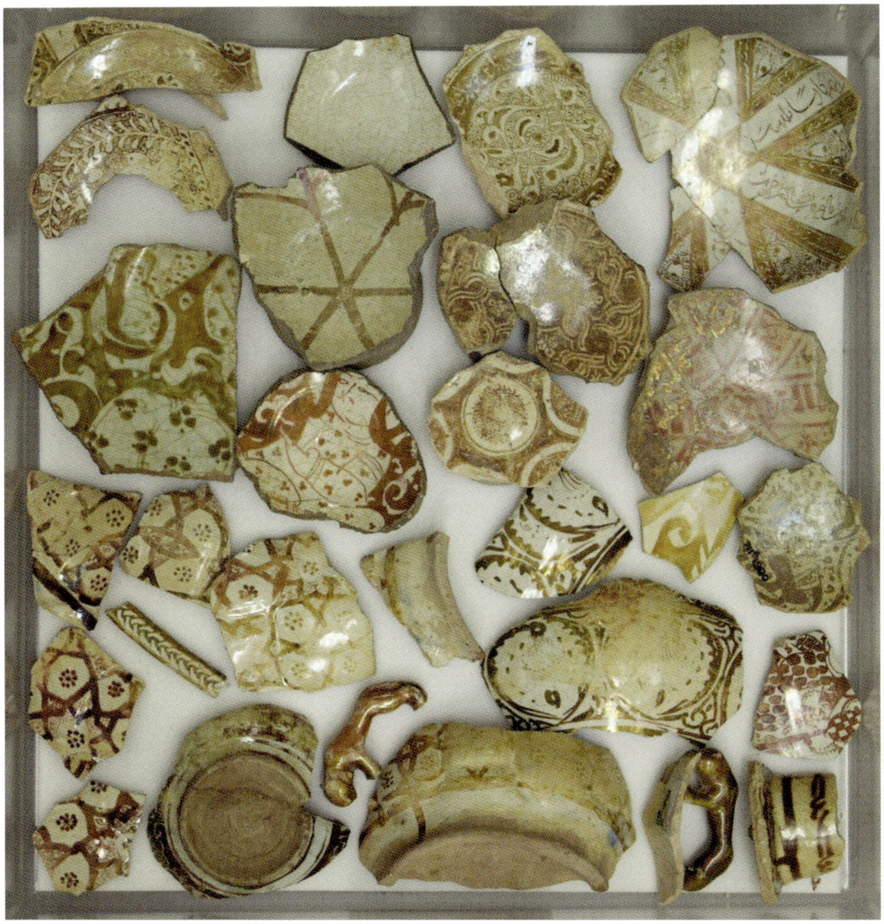

2.29. Tray of sherds, glazed stonepaste with overglaze luster. Attributed Iran, 12th and 13th centuries, reportedly found at Rayy. Victoria and Albert Museum, 1118:1–1903 and others.

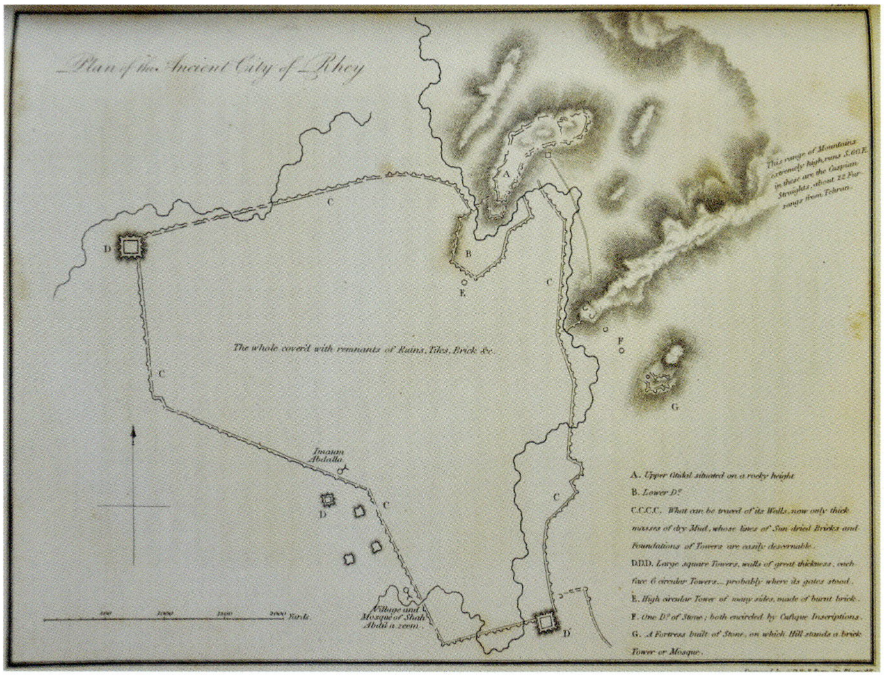

2.30. Robert Ker Porter, *Travels in Georgia, Persia, Armenia, Ancient Babylonia, &c. &c. During the Years 1817, 1818, 1819, and 1820* (London: Longman, Hurst, Rees, Orme, and Brown, 1821), vol. 1, p. 364.

intricate industry of reconstruction that arose as systematic sherd extraction got fully underway.

The scattered references to commercial digging at Rayy suggest a near-continuous operation of extraction at the site, extending over more than forty years.[123] The American diplomat Samuel Benjamin, resident in Iran between 1882 and 1885, reported that "Peasants from time to time discover old coins and bits of gold ornaments and iridescent tiles when turning up the soil of Rheï in the springtime. But no systematic exploration has yet been taken of the ruins of the fallen city."[124] Things would change very soon, however. Kelekian may have been engaged in commercial digging there as early as 1885.[125] Filippo was acquiring ceramic vessels from Rayy in the winter of 1897–98, which he sold to Friedrich Sarre.[126] Sarre also reports buying sherds at the site that same winter, from "illicit excavations by Armenian dealers."[127] The medieval material was dug up at Rayy by the residents of the adjacent settlement around the shrine of Shah Abdul Azim, and most of it was exported directly to Paris and London.[128] Reportedly, Hagop Kevorkian led digging at Rayy in 1904,[129] Alexandre Tabbagh in 1908,[130] and Émile Vignier (brother of the dealer Charles Vignier) in 1910–14,[131] followed by a number of French archaeologists and diplomats, from Georges Pézard and Georges Bondoux in 1909 to Maurice Dayet in 1924.[132] By the twentieth century, the trade was not primarily in sherds but in reconstructed whole vessels. The romance of the site was getting amplified in dealers' lore. When the Tabbagh Frères presented Rayy bowls and dishes to a New York clientele in 1911, the objects had their rarity value elevated by breathless stories of disinterment, "from under the tumuli of drifted sand which alone marks the site of the former city of 700,000 inhabitants."[133]

This was the era of formal French monopoly over Iranian archaeology, and international diplomacy was key. Iran first granted permission for Marcel and Jane Dieulafoy to excavate at Susa in 1884; in 1895, after years of French diplomatic persuasion and expenditure, Nasir al-Din Shah's government granted France exclusive rights to excavation in Iran. The agreement was strengthened under Mozaffar al-Din Shah in 1900.[134] Plainly, though, the French monopoly did not stop the seemingly incessant stream of commercial excavations by international traders. By 1931 there were an estimated two to three thousand people in Iran employed in commercial excavation and other activities related to antiquities export.[135] The French monopoly did, however, cause much perturbation among the other colonial powers. In 1907 the British Museum curator Charles H. Read called for what he named a "free trade" model of archaeology in Iran, underscoring the economic paradigm that shaped Middle Eastern archaeology.[136] The Americans and the Germans also agitated for the French monopoly to be lifted.[137] By the end of the 1920s, their calls were answered and a new Iranian antiquities law brought an end to French monopoly, leading to an expansion of American excavation at Rayy.[138]

The American excavations at Rayy in 1934–36 were led by Erich Schmidt and funded by the Museum of Fine Arts, Boston and the museum of the University of Pennsylvania (now known as the Penn Museum). The Schmidt excavations at Rayy are sometimes presented as a clean switch from commercial to scientific archaeology at the site, although the reality was not quite so straightforward.[139] One of the forerunners to Schmidt's large-scale mission was a small and previously overlooked but revealing excavation at Rayy led by Arthur Upham Pope and his associate, Khalil Rabenou, and funded by the Detroit Institute of Arts (DIA). A financial statement submitted by Pope to the DIA director outlines the arrangement: he was paid an advance of $7,500 in 1929 in exchange for the promise of excavating materials for the museum.[140] Other parts of the archived correspondence expand the details: the site of excavation is named as Rayy, the excavator as Rabenou, and the land as the property of "the Shoah es Sultaneh" (the governor of Pars and second son of Mozaffar al-Din Shah, although he had died several years earlier).[141] The expedition could hardly be called a success. Pope claimed that the pieces he and Rabenou excavated at Rayy in 1930 were not, in the end, good enough for museum display, forcing him to buy pieces from the market to make good his promise of display specimens for the museum.[142]

The torturous correspondence around this rather chaotic mission details Pope's complaints about his treatment by the Persian Council of Ministers and Export Department over export tax ("a sort of sabotage"), hold-ups caused by a rebellion in Shiraz, and the slowness of the ceramic restoration workshops in Paris—to which we return in chapter 4.[143] One can only sympathize with the financial director of the DIA when he eventually begged Pope to stop sending him long letters filled with jumbled excuses and confused accounting.[144] Unsurprisingly, the DIA did not attempt any other excavation projects with Pope, although he did go on to be involved in several other archaeological projects in Iran in the 1930s, some of them with commercial excavators.[145]

In the next, more significant round of American excavation at Rayy in 1934–36, Erich Schmidt started one of his excavation trenches at a site suggested to him by Pope and Rabenou, who had been digging there not long before.[146] Pope regarded Schmidt as his protégé, and the continuity of their excavations at Rayy is not surprising.[147] In the Schmidt excavations, half the finds were to be given to the Iranian government, under the terms of the new antiquities law. Though there was tolerance for fragments, complete or near-complete objects were the most desired type of ceramic for missions predicated, as Schmidt's was, on finding specimens for museum display.[148] Along with selected sherds, the ceramics taken from Rayy to the United States also include vessels that have borne experiments with very heavy reconstruction and in-painting. A photograph from the ceramics workshop of the 1936 excavations at Rayy shows a site worker—presumably one of "three expert restorers" described by Schmidt in 1935—piecing together objects from fragments and filling gaps with gypsum plaster, while the shelves behind him are filled with reconstructed objects, and children work next to him (fig. 2.31).[149] To modern eyes, it might seem more reminiscent of a shop than of the sherd tables one now expects to see at an excavation.

In this context, reassembly of vessels was more important than keeping fine-grained stratigraphic records. A beautiful series of watercolor paintings by an unknown artist spotlight what were clearly the prize objects of the Rayy excavations, including a remarkable glazed stonepaste figurine of an elephant now in the Museum of Fine Arts, Boston (depicted in fig. 2.32).[150] "With infinite patience our head restorer succeeded in fitting the pieces of this beautiful specimen which were scattered in many different pits and in the refuse of several different rooms. Finally, about four fifths of the unique specimen

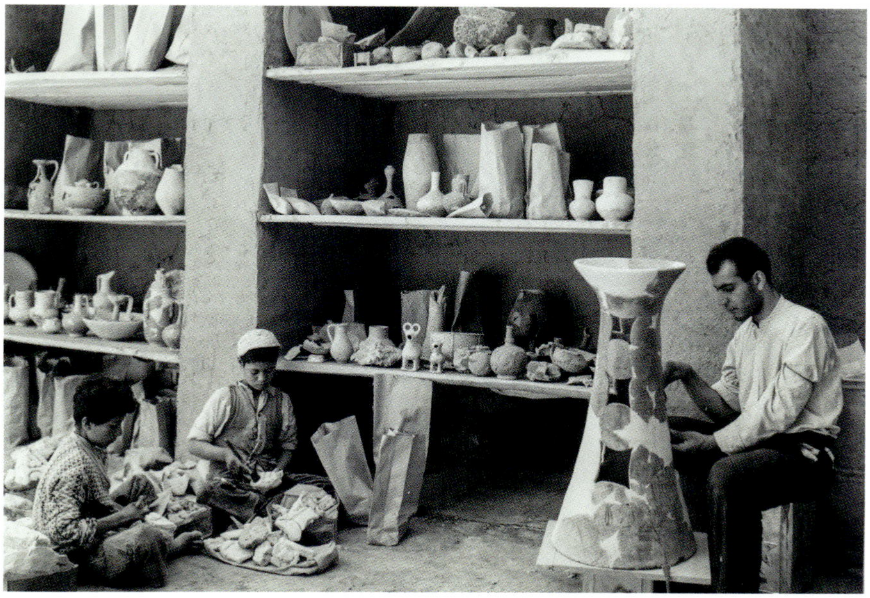

2.31. Ceramics workshop at excavation site in Rayy, Iran. Rayy Excavation Report, 1936. Museum of Fine Arts, Boston.

was assembled while the rest will be restored in gypsum."[151] The impression that emerges from Schmidt's brief reports of the excavations at Rayy is of a grand-scale sherd-sorting exercise. "Hundreds of thousands of fragments" were sifted and rebuilt into whole objects wherever possible, with the resulting reconstructions being more important than precise documentation of where each fragment was found, or any attempt at detailed stratigraphy.[152]

Rayy was by no means unique in being a tilling ground for commercial (and subsequently scientific) sherd extraction; the same story was repeated, albeit with even less documentation, at other sites across Iran. In Kerman in the 1890s the British diplomat Percy Sykes was buying fragments of luster tiles retrieved by the locals; some of those are now in the British Museum.[153] In the first years of the twentieth century, Kelekian and others were acquiring material dug up at Varamin; an eyewitness account by a Qajar official describes illegal excavation there by Jews (*kalimi*) who uncovered fragmentary luster ceramic vessels that were subsequently confiscated by the police.[154] Benjamin Mahboubian ran commercial digs at Hasanlu and Luristan in the 1920s and '30s,[155] while Pope tried from the late 1920s (with little success) to make the case that Saveh, a town about seventy-five miles southwest of Tehran, was the principal site of fine ceramics production in medieval Iran.[156] An aerial photograph from the 1930s shows the ground around the medieval mosque at Saveh completely riddled with holes from commercial digging, a circumstance repeated at many other sites in the Middle East (fig.2.33).[157]

Even more opaque is the case of Sultanabad, where Kevorkian and Kelekian were reportedly involved in commercial extraction in the early twentieth century.[158] The town of that name was in fact only founded in the early nineteenth century, and the fourteenth-century ceramics associated with it—often labeled in catalogues and collections as "Sultanabad ware"—probably come from as-yet-unidentified sites nearby.[159] Sultanabad seems simply to have been where those pieces first entered the international market, doubtless because the town became an important hub for international import

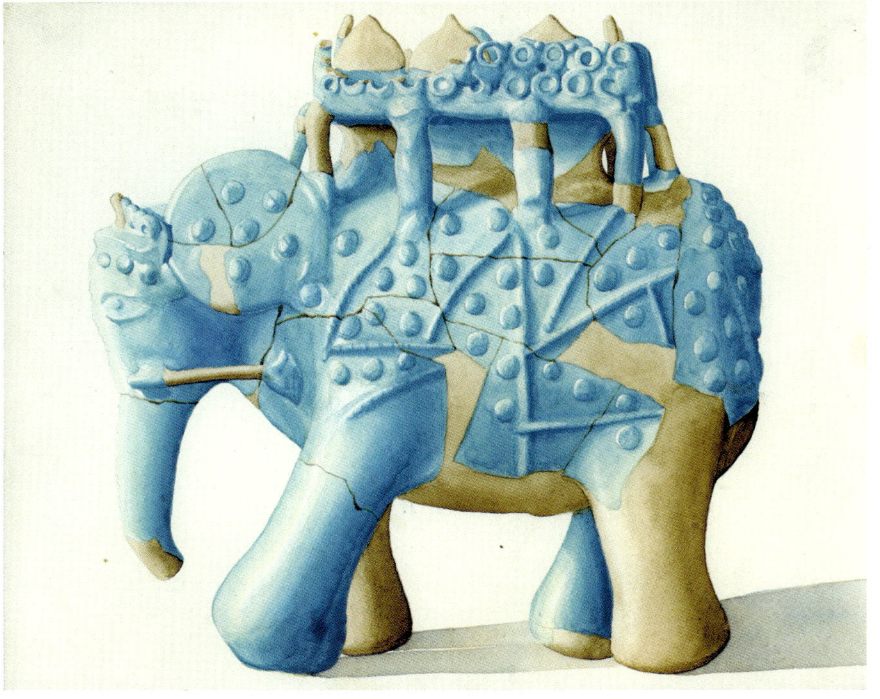

2.32. Unknown artist, reconstructed ceramic elephant excavated at Rayy. Watercolor on paper. 1930s. Institute for the Study of Ancient Cultures, University of Chicago, RH 6105.

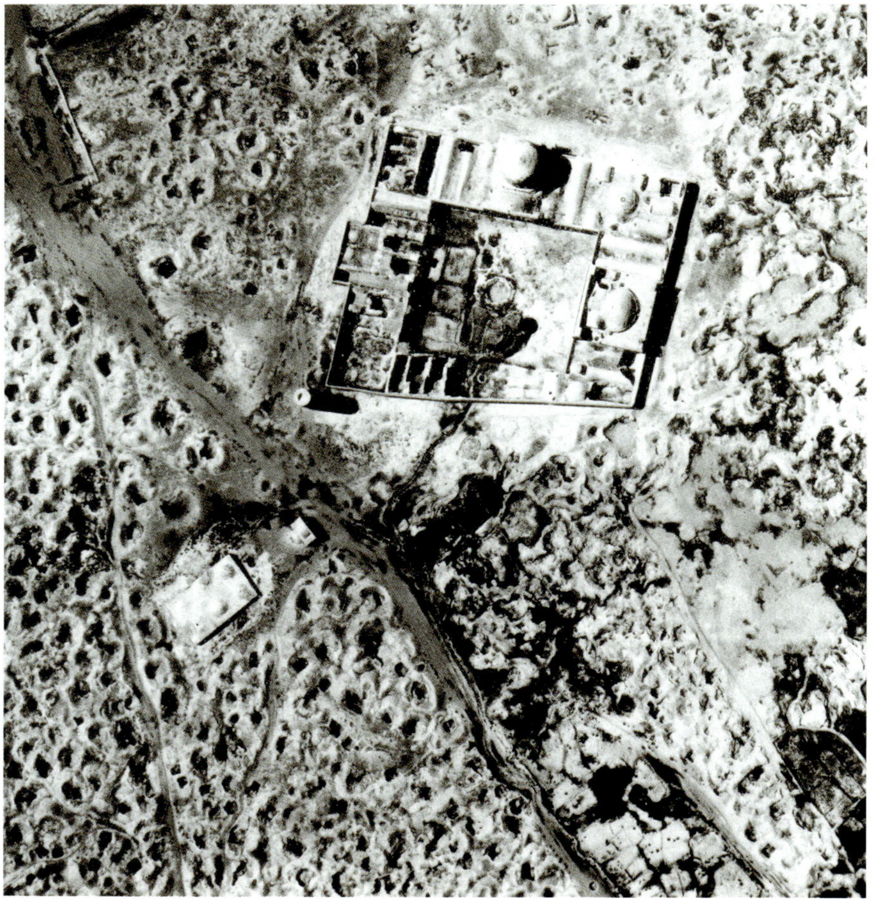

2.33. Erich F. Schmidt, *Flights over Ancient Cities of Iran* (Chicago: University of Chicago Press, 1940), plate 30.

and export of various kinds after the establishment there of internationally funded carpet manufactories in the 1870s and 1880s, including the British-Swiss Ziegler & Co. and its Dutch competitor, Hotz & Zoon.[160] The zombie attribution of Sultanabad still circulates, nonetheless.

As can be imagined, this decades-long frenzy of commercial earth-churning across Iran created the perfect conditions for faking, forgery, and sleight of hand. Sometimes this involved passing off historicizing objects as genuine antiquities. Ferdinand Méchin sold multiple late nineteenth-century historicizing tiles that he claimed to have excavated from the ruins of the Safavid-era Farahabad palace in Isfahan.[161] The porosity of the largely unregulated antiquities market also made space for full-blown forgeries, a practice certainly not limited to ceramics—as can be seen from the tidal wave of "Luristan bronzes" that hit the market from the late 1920s and included forgeries cast in molds taken from original pieces.[162] A letter written in 1931 from the dealer Hassan Khan Monif to the newly established curator of Islamic art at the DIA, Mehmet Ağa-Oğlu, reveals Pope's associates, the Rabenou brothers, making a name for themselves in an antiquities marketplace where even acknowledged forgeries could be rated in the terms of connoisseurship:

> As for antiques, it is terribly hard to find good pieces [in Persia], everything in the field of antiques is finished, except Luristan bronzes; when I was at Teheran, I saw about 5000 Luristan bronzes, some of them very rare and fine, but bought none, as I think within next few years they will excavate some 100000 pieces of bronzes. They are making lots of fake bronzes, some of them well done, Raben-nouh in Teheran and his brother in Paris has also large numbers of good fake pieces.[163]

The churning of the earth generated not just potsherds but all kinds of premodern—and modern—treasure that could be entered into an avaricious antiquities market. In chapter 3 I detail the techniques by which those hundreds of thousands of excavated sherds, along with other materials, became the raw material for making new whole objects that could be sold to an eager paying clientele.

Beyond Iran: Harvesting Central Asia

Thus far, this survey of extraction has focused on Iran, where a combination of three factors created a feeding frenzy: a truly remarkable medieval ceramics tradition, the pressures experienced by a state seeking to fend off simultaneous imperialist advances from both Europe and Russia, and early antiquities laws that seem to have been only partially or sporadically enforced. The extraction process unfolded somewhat differently in Russian Central Asia and the Ottoman Middle East, although the tendency for "scientific" excavation to follow after commercial extraction was common across all regions. Imperial Russia's conquest of Central Asia in the nineteenth century was accompanied by increasingly centralized, state-directed structures for financing and using archaeology, consolidating it as a base from which the imperial image of the Russian Empire could be constructed.[164] The Ottoman Empire, meanwhile, attempted to stem the flow of antiquities to Europe that had been going on since the seventeenth century (see chapter 1) by introducing a series of increasingly stringent antiquities laws and eventually undertaking its own excavations.[165] Across both empires, the harvest grounds of medieval ceramics dumps caught the attention of local treasure hunters, transregional commercial excavators, and state actors alike.

In the eastern reaches of the Islamic world, the most celebrated ceramics to emerge from Islamic Central Asia were glazed earthenware dishes of the ninth to twelfth centuries, decorated in a dazzling range of techniques. Another tray of sherds in the V&A gives some sense of the range and finesse of the decoration seen on these pieces, and the vivacity of their designs in red, brown, and white slip (liquid clay) (fig. 2.34). Most of these slipwares (as they are called) are covered with a transparent leaded glaze that can reflect the faintest of oil-slick sheens when the light is right (fig. 2.35).[166] The ruined site of Afrasiyab, near the city of Samarqand in modern-day Uzbekistan, was a major production center for such slipwares until it was sacked by the Mongols in the thirteenth century. Soviet excavations in the twentieth century uncovered Islamic-era potters' quarters, kilns, and wasters, leaving no doubt that most of the thousands of sherds at the site were from locally produced ceramics.[167]

Afrasiyab's plenitude of archaeological remains attracted treasure hunters and historians alike, and it has the distinction of being the first medie-

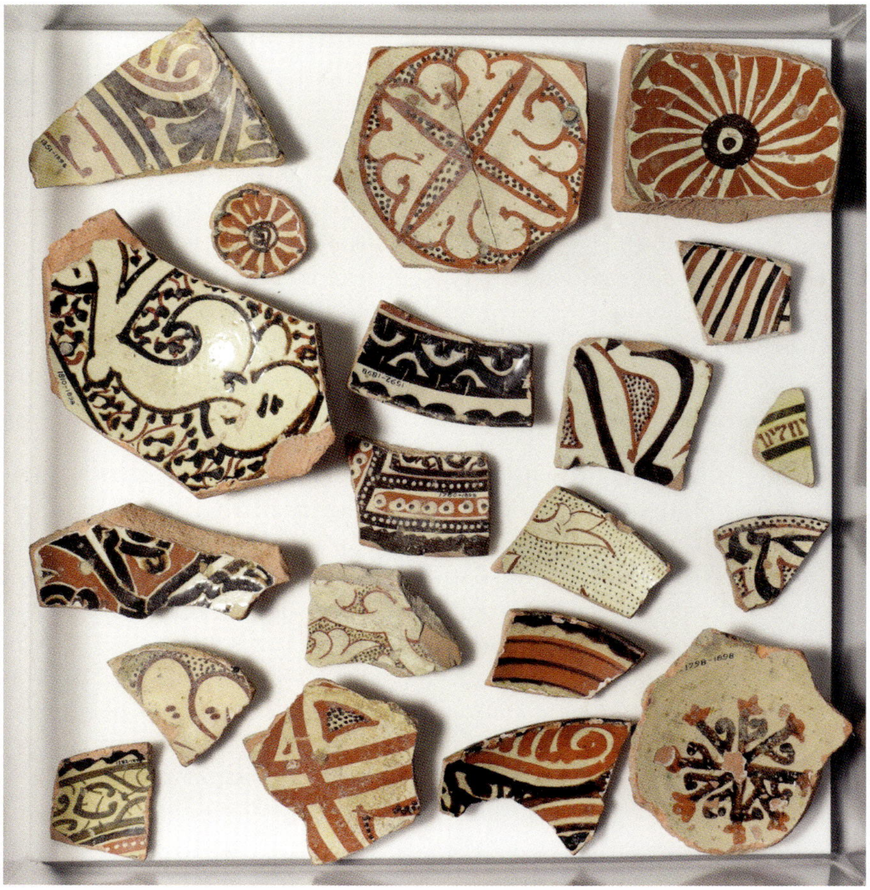

2.34. Tray of sherds, glazed earthenware with slip decoration. Attributed Afrasiyab, 10th–12th centuries. Victoria and Albert Museum, 1365–1898 and others.

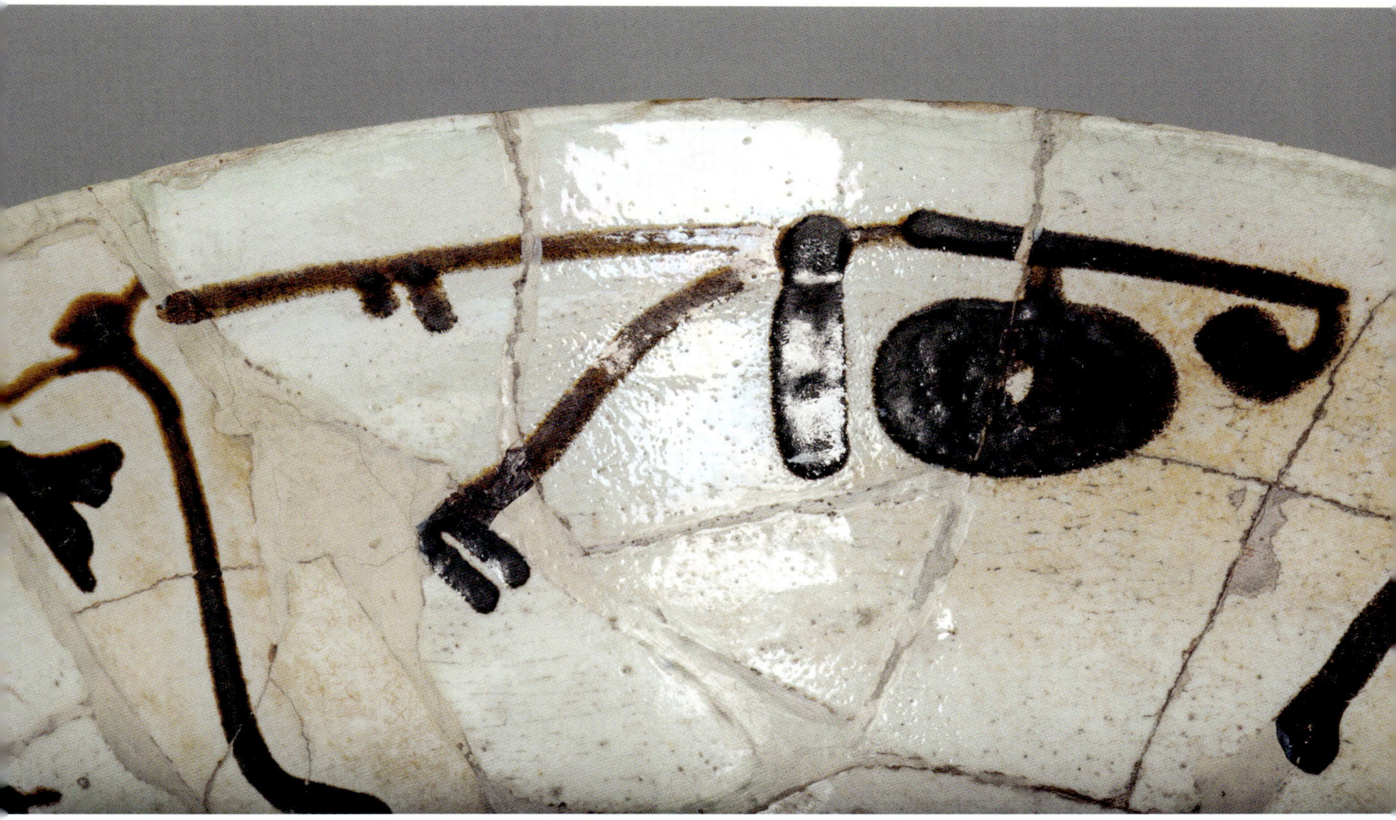

2.35. Detail of heavily restored dish, earthenware with slip decoration and clear leaded glaze. Medieval material attributed Greater Iran or Uzbekistan, 9th–11th century. Diameter 25.6 cm. Eskenazi Museum of Art, Indiana University, 61.64.

val Islamic site to be "systematically" excavated, an undertaking headed by Nikolai Ivanovich Veselovsky (1848–1918) in 1885. However, as Michael Rogers has noted of the Veselovsky excavations, "they were probably not very systematic—the adjective is Bartol'd's—but they did keep day books."[168] The Orientalist scholar Vasily Vladimirovich Bartol'd (1869–1930) would later make Afrasiyab the site of his one and only excavation season, in 1904, but he did not regard his dig as a success. In an article published the same year, he complained about illicit commercial excavation at the site and the growing market for fake Afrasiyab ceramics. "I heard not long ago that one of the local masters, after long practice, developed the skill of producing undetectable fake terracottas; they even called him by the name of The Forger; but the goods were sold at such low prices . . . that [the money] could hardly compensate his painstaking work."[169] Local men also amassed collections of antiquities from the site, some of which were eventually acquired by the Hermitage Museum and other metropolitan collectors.[170]

One of the most striking things to emerge from the piecemeal excavation history of the eastern Islamic world is how many very similar types of lead-glazed slipwares were excavated at multiple sites, sometimes very far apart. Nishapur is well known in western scholarship as a source of medieval ceramics because the Metropolitan Museum undertook a series of excavations there, from 1935 to 1940 (with a final postwar season in the winter of 1947–48). The division of finds meant that both the Tehran Bastan Museum and the Metropolitan Museum now have large holdings of ceramics excavated from Nishapur. Afrasiyab and Nishapur are more than 650 miles apart, and yet the archaeological ceramics from the two seem in some cases to be almost identical—so much so that slipwares surfacing through the market are often attributed to "Nishapur or Samarqand [i.e., Afrasiyab]." Once you also add in the related material found at Tashkent (equally impressive, but less widely known in western scholarship), it is quite possible to have an unresolved debate about the attribution of a celebrity object (fig. 2.36), bought from Khalil Rabenou in 1957 and known to scholars for more than sixty years, and whether it is to be attributed to Nishapur, Afrasiyab, Tashkent, or some other site in the eastern Islamic world.[171]

Some types of ceramic found at Nishapur were not common to the other sites, the most famous of them being the colorful so-called Nishapur buffwares (fig. 2.37). Hundreds of these transited through the twentieth-century market, especially after the Metropolitan Museum excavations gave them a profile, and collectors and scholars alike have been entranced by the vibrant figural designs found on some of them.[172] Their market popularity of course gave rise to countless rounds of reconstruction and fabulation; they also appear to have been a source of inspiration for the painters of the *Andarznama* manuscript forgery (see chapter 4).[173] The local economy was affected by the cessation of the MMA excavations, and later, by Iran's 1955 ban on domestic opium production (opium poppies being a crop in the region); local labor

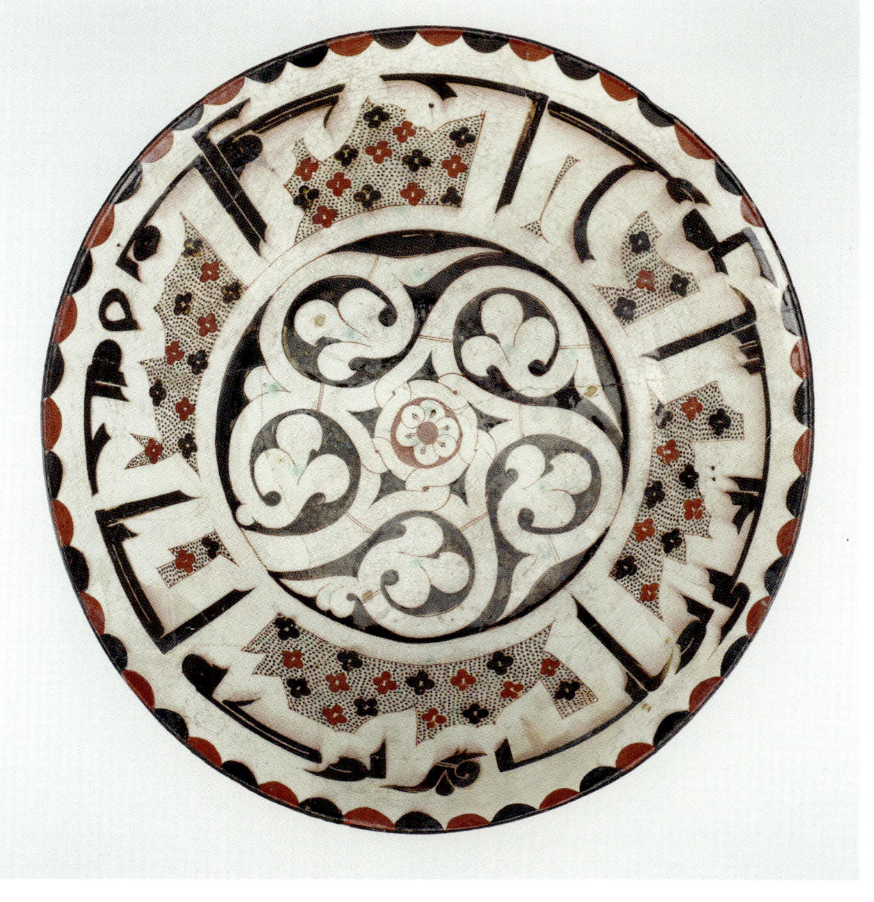

2.36. Bowl, earthenware with slip decoration under clear glaze. Attributed Greater Iran or Uzbekistan, 10th century. Diameter 39.3 cm. National Museum of Asian Art, F1957.24.

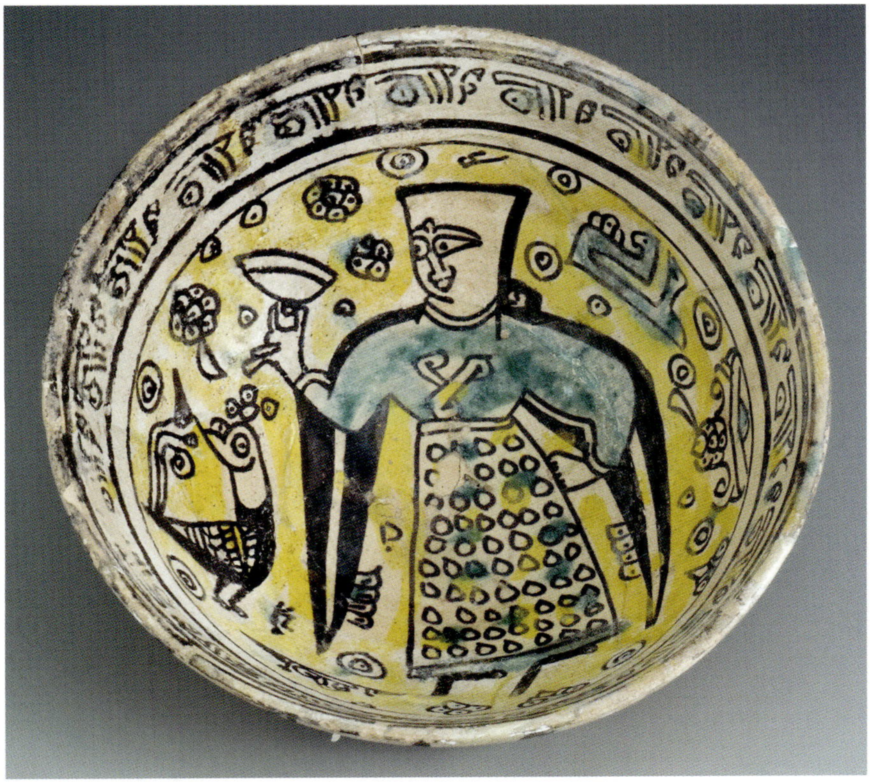

2.37. Bowl, earthenware with polychrome decoration under clear glaze. Attributed Iran, 9th or 10th century, with modern material. Diameter 18.7 cm. Eskenazi Museum of Art, Indiana University, 73.46.3.

was further rerouted into digging for antiquities to sell on to dealers.[174] I have not been able to trace much documentation on commercial excavation at the site but it certainly occurred: some postwar dealers from Iran, including the Frankfurt traders Saeed Motamed (1925–2013) and Mohammad Yeganeh (1932–2012), apparently held official licenses to excavate at Nishapur.[175]

From both Afrasiyab and Nishapur, the "types" that emerged to greatest acclaim on the antiquities market were epigraphic bowls of the tenth century. Decorated with crisp Arabic epigrams written in elongated Kufic script, these bowls make striking use of the stark tonal contrast created by dark brown slip on a cream slip background (fig. 2.38). One celebrated example was acquired by the Louvre in 1935, from the collector Alphonse Kann (1870–1948), who bought it from the Kiev collector A. Vassilieff—who reportedly bought it from a painter who had got it from the ruins at Afrasiyab.[176] It is easy to see the appeal of these austere epigraphic wares for early twentieth-century collectors whose tastes were inflected by modernism, and there was a bullish market for putting them together from fragments—sometimes with more fiction than reality in the finished product. A dish in the Eskenazi Museum, bought from Hassan Khan Monif in 1961, is revealed under UV light to be a pastiche of different objects with a program of modern overpainting that makes up most of the inscription (fig. 2.39). One sizable section of an original lead-glazed slipware dish—showing darker in the UV image—was apparently enough to make it financially worthwhile to build up the rest from unrelated material.

With tantalizing ruins and potsherds aplenty, lying only a short journey from the city of Samarqand, Afrasiyab was one of the prime sites for treasure

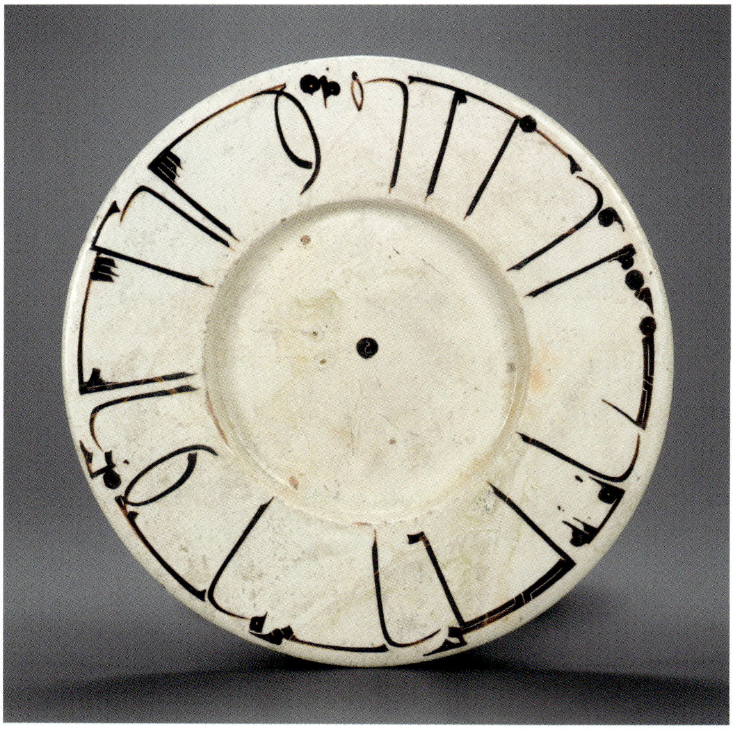

2.38. Dish, earthenware with slip decoration under clear glaze. Reportedly found at Afrasiyab, Uzbekistan, attributed 10th or 11th century. Diameter 37.6 cm. Musée du Louvre, AA96.

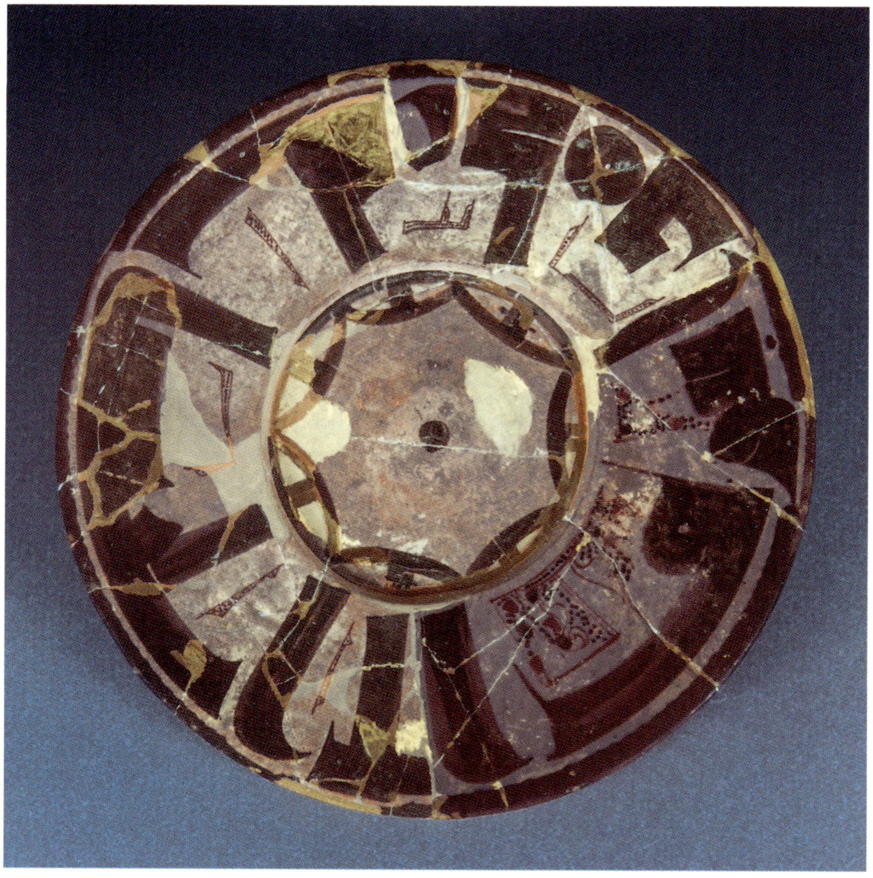

2.39. UV photograph of dish, earthenware with slip and clear glaze. Medieval and modern material. Diameter 34.3 cm. Eskenazi Museum of Art, Indiana University, 61.60.

hunters in the Great Game. The Russian administration of Turkestan reportedly tried to stem commercial excavations in the region with an 1871 edict, but to little effect.[177] Large quantities of antiquities, including some enormous sherd collections, were extracted from the site by military men, nobility, and adventurers, with one tranche of sherds now housed in the V&A (see fig. 2.34).[178] A further, vast collection of some twenty thousand sherds from Afrasiyab is now in the Museum für Islamische Kunst in Berlin, transferred there from the Königliche Museum für Völkerkunde (Royal Museum for Ethnology).[179] Comprehensive analysis and publication of those sherd collections might one day provide an important corpus for comparison with the wealth of material excavated at other sites in Uzbekistan, including Termez, Budrach, Bukhara, and Binkath (Tashkent), and more recently in Turkmenistan.[180] It may also provide some correctives for a group of startlingly perfect, colorful glazed bowls that have appeared on the market since the beginning of the twenty-first century. These last have been tentatively attributed by Jangar Ilyasov to late tenth- or early eleventh-century production in Afghanistan, although, as he acknowledges, at least some of them are known to be modern forgeries.[181]

Harvesting the Ottoman Territories

Around the same time that sherds from Afrasiyab were being transported en masse to Berlin, scholar-harvesters were also looking toward the Arabic-speaking regions of the Ottoman Empire. After a "reconnaissance mission" in the region in 1907–8, the German scholar and curator Friedrich Sarre and the archaeologist and sometime dealer Ernst Herzfeld (1879–1948) decided on Samarra (now in Iraq), the capital of the ʿAbbasid caliphate from 836 to 892, as their preferred medieval Islamic site for excavation.[182] Their choice was motivated in large part by the limited period of historical occupation at Samarra, which seemed to make it a tidier historical prospect than the more stratigraphically complex sites of Raqqa or Resafa (both in modern-day Syria).[183] After obtaining a license to excavate from the Ottoman authorities, Sarre and Herzfeld directed more extensive work at Samarra between 1911 and 1913. They were funded in this by the German state, private individuals, and the Deutsche Bank.[184]

Herzfeld photographed some of the ceramic finds excavated at Samarra in situ (fig. 2.40); these pieces were subsequently published in Sarre's 1925 volume, *Keramik von Samarra*.[185] The mass of high-quality glazed ceramics excavated in Sarre and Herzfeld's campaign at Samarra created an enduring narrative of the "Samarra horizon" of pottery production. This proposed that ninth-century Iraqi potters were inspired by imported Chinese vessels to take a great leap forward, kickstarting the entire high-level glazed ceramic tradition in the Islamic world.[186] Bowls decorated with splashes of green and yellow onto an opaque white tin-glaze were argued to be direct imitations of Chinese ware (fig. 2.40), while ninth-century Iraqi tin-glazed bowls with cobalt decoration—quite a few of which have since come up through the market—are now understood to have been part of a two-way mercantile dialogue with China (fig. 2.41).[187] The reality was probably not so simple as just the solitary catalyst of Chinese "inspiration" falling on fertile ground, but that narrative

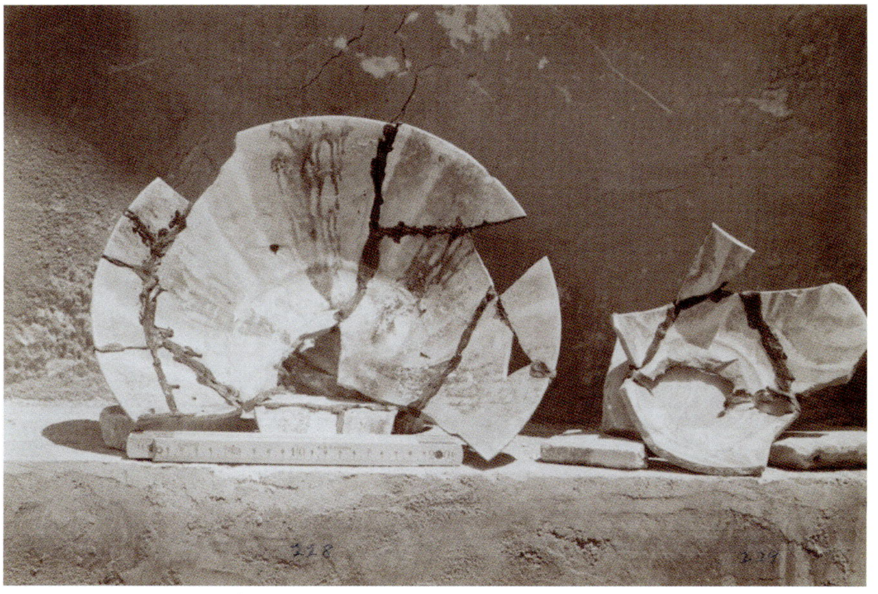

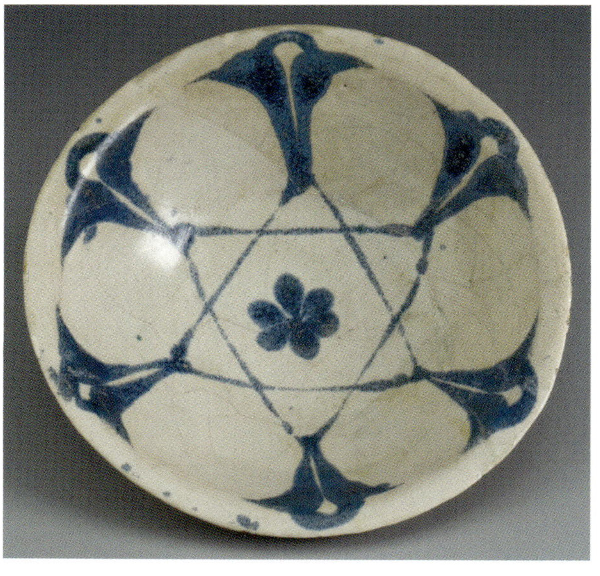

2.40. Fragments of ceramic vessel, found in al-Quraina, House II, Room 29, and al-Qatun, House XI. Photograph taken by Ernst Herzfeld at Samarra. Ernst Herzfeld/National Museum of Asian Art Archives, Smithsonian Institution, Ernst Herzfeld Papers, FSA A.06 04.PF.20.077.

2.41. Dish, glazed earthenware. Attributed Iraq, 9th century. Diameter 18.7 cm. Eskenazi Museum of Art, Indiana University, 73.46.3.

has nonetheless held fast through a hundred years of cataloguing and display.[188] After the disruption of World War I, the Iraqi Directorate General of Antiquities conducted excavations at Samarra between 1936 and 1939.[189]

It will come as no surprise to learn that the most celebrated ceramics found at Samarra were the lusterwares, especially those with figural designs.[190] Although there remains some scholarly debate about how the technology of luster was transmitted across regions, there is now a consensus that "true" lustered ceramics were first produced in the ninth and tenth centuries in Iraq, likely at Basra and possibly at other centers as well.[191] That these were highly valued in and beyond Iraq during their own time is quite clear from fragments excavated at multiple medieval sites around the western Indian Ocean and throughout the Middle East, North Africa, Central Asia, and the Cauca-

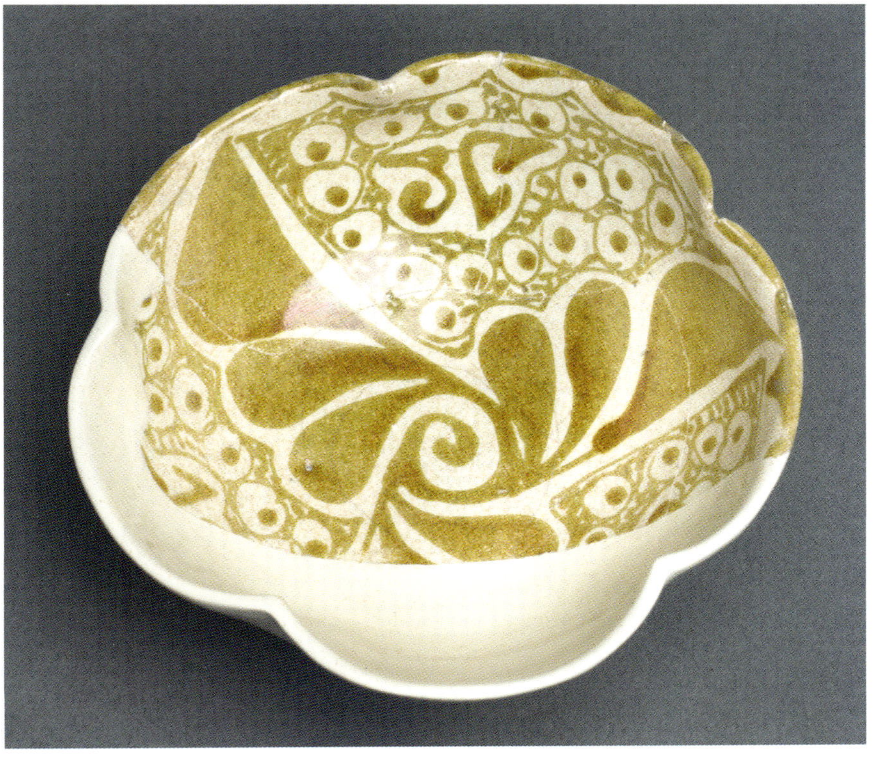

2.42. Lobed dish, glazed earthenware with overglaze luster. Attributed Iraq, 10th century. Diameter approx. 12 cm. Cincinnati Art Museum, Museum Purchase, 1952.246.

sus.[192] Matthew Saba has shown that there was even an Arabic word for the unique visual effects achieved by luster decoration: medieval authors used the words *abu qalamun* (sometimes contracted to *buqalamun*) or *talawwun* to denote the changeable colors of iridescent surfaces, including luster ceramics, peacock feathers, and shot silk.[193]

By the tenth century, Iraqi luster potters had shifted their energies from polychrome lusterwares to pieces decorated with only one shade of luster, usually using a silver-based oxide paint to create an olive-greenish or brownish golden color.[194] This enabled them to perfect the firing process for achieving maximum consistency in the metallic sheen of the golden color, using it to create bold designs like the extravagant palmettes seen on a lobed bowl first loaned to the V&A in 1922 and now in Cincinnati (fig. 2.42).[195] There are at least three other extant tenth-century Iraqi luster bowls of the same delicate five-lobed shape, which comes by descent from East Asian metalwork.[196] Recent conservation of this piece means that we are now able to see clearly the large, continuous, and well-preserved original fragment making up about two-thirds of the bowl. When it was first entered onto the early twentieth-century art market, the missing area had been made up from alien sherds and overpaint to complete the lobed form and the centripetal design of three whirling palmette fronds, inscription fragments in reserve, and fields of peacock-eye ground (fig. 2.43).[197] It was this early twentieth-century market restoration that launched the bowl on its trajectory as an asset, while its reproducible photographic portrait confirmed and broadcast its new identity as an intact and therefore desirable commodity. Iraqi luster remains one of the most sought-after types of medieval ceramic for collectors.

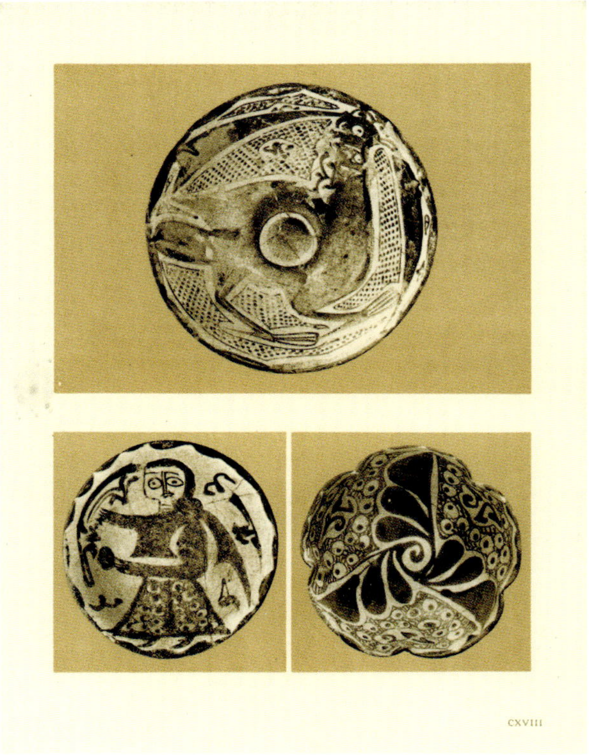

2.43. Maurice Pézard, *Le céramique archaïque de l'islam et ses origines* (Paris: Ernest Leroux, 1920), vol. 2, plate CXVIII.

Of course, the collectors' canon of medieval Islamic ceramics did not come only from the so-called eastern Islamic lands. Late Ottoman Syria and Egypt, too, were major fields of extraction. Controlled excavations of the medieval dumps at Fustat (medieval Cairo) began in 1912, under the direction of ʿAli Baghat (1858–1924) for the Cairo Museum of Arab Art, but the site had already been mined by commercial excavators for decades.[198] For example, thousands of sherds of all kinds were extracted from Fustat in 1896 by the notorious Swedish collector Fredrik R. Martin, many of them now in the Medelhavsmuseet in Stockholm (fig. 2.44).[199] Predictably, one of the most prized forms of medieval ceramic from Egypt, past and present, was lusterware. When Nasir-i Khusraw wrote in praise of Cairene ceramics in the eleventh century (quoted at the beginning of this chapter), he commented not only on their fineness but also on their iridescent, *buqalamun* qualities. Clearly, he was describing lusterwares.[200] A sherd of Egyptian earthenware with luster decoration, now in the DIA, demonstrates the medium's continuing powers of captivation in even the most modest fragments: its cruciform pattern shines brightly in a greenish-golden luster, applied in thick bands to maximize the visual impact of the luster itself (fig. 2.45).[201] There are quite a number of Egyptian luster bowl fragments around that show cruciform patterns like this one, suggesting it was originally a popular form of design and well represented in the Fustat dumps.[202] These afigural designs have not, however, been singled out for reconstruction, display, and publication nearly so often as have contemporaneous Egyptian luster bowls decorated with animal and human figures.[203] As ever with this material, the physical remnants of the

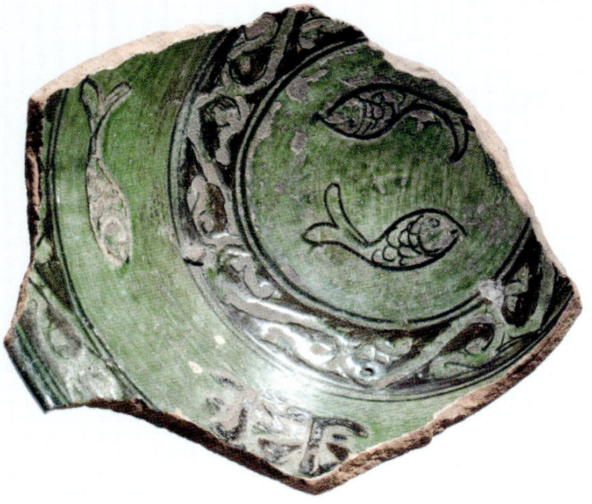

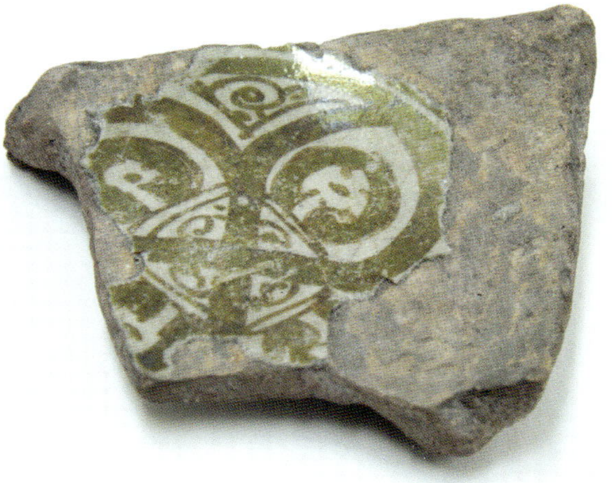

past have been filtered through a marketplace that skews heavily toward pictorial representation and figural subjects.

In Greater Syria, the most famous source of medieval ceramics valued by collectors—and a subsequent site of scientific excavation—was Raqqa, discussed in detail in chapter 5. But in spite of (perhaps because of) the dominance of the Raqqa "brand" in the antiquities market, fine ceramics production in Syria is quite hard to map. Even the various different forms of decorated stonepaste conventionally known as "Raqqa" wares were likely produced at multiple sites (see chapter 5). Most known examples of other celebrated types from medieval Syria, especially the so-called laqabi and Tell Minis wares, have surfaced for the most part through the market, their production sites open to speculation and their findspots completely obscure.

To take the first of those two types, so-called laqabi wares have cast a long spell over collectors (fig. 2.46). The name "laqabi" is a pseudo-Arabic term derived from *laqab*, meaning title or honorific, and was presumably attached to these wares by a plausible trader or ambitious collector in the modern era.[204] To make this type of ceramic, the design was carved into the clay body using a knife to create channels that would keep the different colorants in separate fields, almost like cloisonné, and prevent them from running into each other in the clear leaded glaze. On this dish in the Cincinnati Art Museum, the rather filleted appearance of the three fish, with their jaunty manganese purple, cobalt blue, and copper turquoise color fields, showcases the appeal of the technique and its capacity for creating intensely colored low-relief images of real and fabulous creatures.[205] Production of "laqabi" wares is now attributed to an unidentified site or sites in twelfth-century Syria on the basis of fragments found at multiple medieval sites in the region, and sherds have even been recovered from medieval sites as far afield as western Russia and Belarus, indicating the prestige of these ceramics in their own time.[206] The technique seems to have been somewhat experimental and even fragments of "laqabi" ware are fairly rare; museum specimens tend to have undergone very heavy reconstruction from many small fragments, as is visibly the case with the fish-dish.[207]

2.44. Bowl fragment, glazed earthenware with slip decoration. Attributed Egypt, 15th century, reportedly excavated at Fustat. Width 14 cm. Museum of Mediterranean and Near Eastern Antiquities, Stockholm, 207/1922.

2.45. Vessel fragment, glazed earthenware with luster overglaze. Attributed Egypt, late 11th or 12th century. Length 8.9 cm. Detroit Institute of Arts, 27.329, Gift of Dr. W. R. Valentiner.

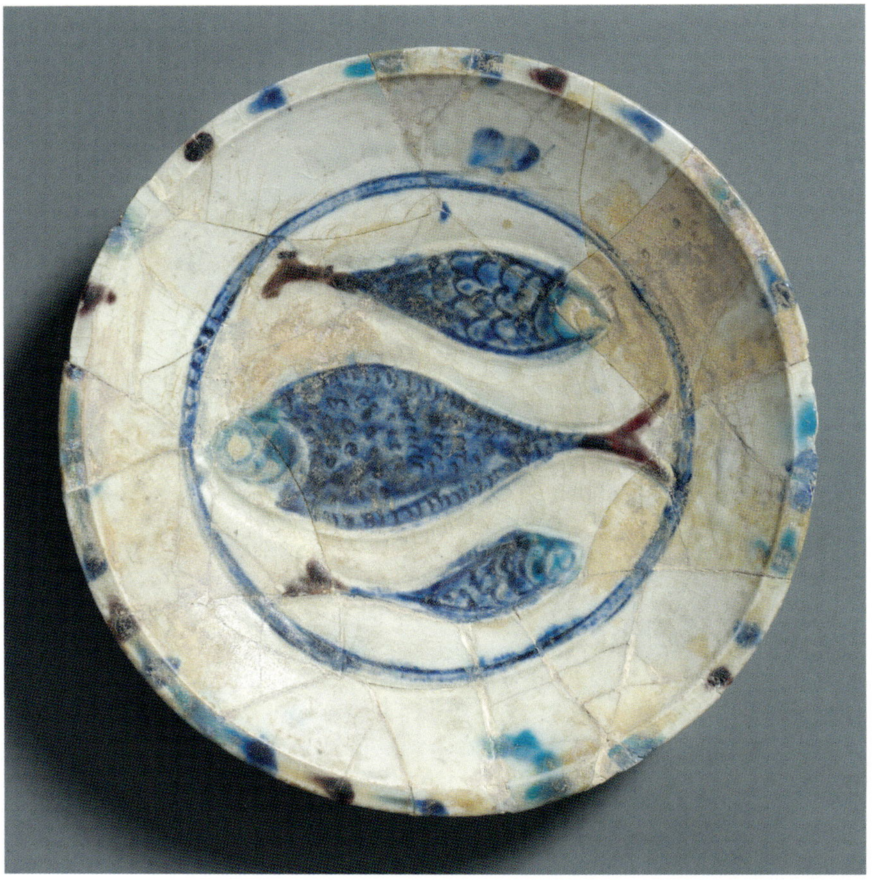

2.46. Dish, glazed stonepaste with carved design and in-glaze colors and modern restoration (so-called laqabi ware). Attributed Syria, 12th century. Diameter approx. 23 cm. Cincinnati Art Museum, Given in honor of Mr. and Mrs. Charles F. Williams by their children, 1948.99.

The last Syrian piece in this condensed tour through the canon is a striking—and long overlooked—bowl with luster decoration on a dark manganese purple glaze (fig. 2.47). The Toledo Museum of Art acquired it in 1941 from the dealer MacDermid Parish-Watson (d. 1941), who described it at the time as a "rare Resafa" bowl, relating it to the ancient city of Resafa in north-central Syria—another site with glamorous Biblical connotations.[208] It is a large and quite spectacular example of what is now known as Tell Minis ware, a group of eleventh- or twelfth-century Syrian stonepaste vessels, many of which have survived in remarkably good condition. The story of the Tell Minis wares was painstakingly excavated by Oliver Watson and Venetia Porter, who showed that a few bowls of this type had entered collections intermittently from 1840, with reported findspots in Syria.[209] However, the group only became a defined entity in collecting and scholarship in 1960 when the dealer Robert Hecht (1919–2012) approached the British Museum with thirteen such dishes and the story that they had been found altogether in 1959 in a cave at Tell Minis, a village not far from the town of Maʿarrat al-Nuʿman in north-central Syria.[210] Two further dealer reports, one of them from as early as 1905, also link these bowls to Maʿarrat al-Nuʿman and vicinity.[211] Interestingly, that town has come up already in this book: it was one of the proposed findspots of the Antioch chalice (see chapter 1), or at least, according to Leonard Woolley, the place where the chalice first exchanged hands for money. Somewhere in the swirls of hearsay,

Maʿarrat al-Nuʿman emerges as a significant point of entry for Syrian artifacts in the early twentieth-century antiquities trade.

It's also worth noting that Hecht, the American dealer who sold the 1959 Tell Minis group, is now quite notorious. Very soon after he offered the Tell Minis wares to the British Museum (who declined them) and subsequently sold them to the V&A and the David Collection in Copenhagen, he was accused in both Turkey and Italy of antiquities smuggling. Seemingly unrepentant, he ended his days embroiled in the scandal surrounding the Getty Museum's acquisition of looted antiquities in the 1990s.[212] The bowl in Toledo, however, was bought by the museum in 1941, and was never part of the group Hecht touted around northwestern Europe in 1960. How, when, and in what state the Toledo bowl left Syria is an open question, as it is for virtually all museum pieces of Tell Minis ware. A 1990 conservation report for the Toledo bowl suggests only small amounts of fill and limited overpainting were necessary to its reconstruction, implying that it was originally found in a fragmentary state but with little loss.[213]

The large size of the Toledo bowl distinguishes it within the overall group of Tell Minis wares, but the fabric (a fine, pale stonepaste) and the very distinctive cut of the foot ring (cut on the wheel at an angle so that the bowl stands on the sharp edge) align perfectly with the rest of the group.[214] It is clearly from the same medieval Syrian production site(s) as the rest of the Tell Minis wares, although we do not know exactly where that site is. Its decoration—especially the fish shapes with simple, scribbly designs incised with a sharp point into the luster—link it directly with a bowl excavated at Hama in northern Syria in the 1930s, now in the National Museum in Damascus.[215] More surprisingly, a fragment of another bowl like this, with the same greenish-golden luster on

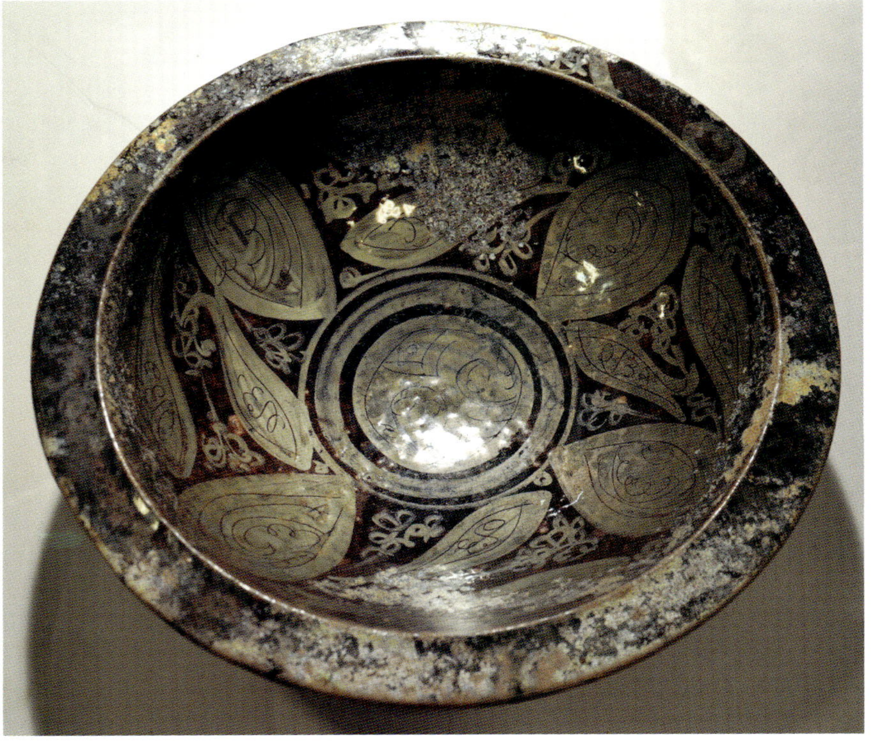

2.47. Bowl, glazed stonepaste with overglaze luster (so-called Tell Minis ware). Attributed Syria, 11th or 12th century. Diameter 35.9 cm. Toledo Museum of Art, 1941.9, purchased with funds from the Libbey Endowment, Gift of Edward Drummond Libbey.

purple glaze, was excavated from late twelfth-/early thirteenth- century layers at the ancient city of Novgorod in western Russia. Not only must the piece in Novgorod have traveled very far indeed within the first century or so of its existence, but it also bears traces of medieval repairs done with metal fasteners. A great deal of value was once placed upon that exotic object by a medieval audience who lived very far from its original place of production.[216]

The tour d'horizon of medieval ceramic extraction from the Islamic world that I have presented in this chapter has sought not to survey the entire medieval production of ceramics in the Islamic world, but rather to show how the collectors' canon has been shaped primarily by practices of extraction formed through modern political economies, in the space of a few decades across the late nineteenth and early twentieth centuries. This has wrought a canon of objects that require the researcher to shuttle back and forth continually between temporalities: no single historical ceramic can be responsibly studied without simultaneous consideration of its modern history of extraction and reconstruction as well as its speculated histories of production and earlier use. When set against the longue durée of ceramic as a medium, the epochs of other kinds of history—political, social, economic—come and go like the chapters of a book. Those histories also accumulate in the physical bodies of ceramics through production, breakage, burial, and repair. In preparation for the content of chapter 3, the last part of this chapter turns to a group of truly multitemporal ceramics to show how the subjects of this canon can physically aggregate the medieval and modern eras.

Fire Worship, Fired Again

By the end of the 1910s a curious group of earthenware bowls was starting to storm the antiquities market. These were characterized by stylized champlevé images of humans and animals, often quite fantastic, cut through a slip layer and covered with clear, green, or brown glaze (fig. 2.48).[217] In a publication of 1913—one of the earliest appearances of this type of ware in collecting literature—two such pieces were attributed to Egypt (although with a note that one of them had been found at Hamadan in Iran).[218] Now commonly known as Garrus or Guebri wares, word soon gathered that they came not from Egypt but from the northwest of Iran, near the southern edges of the Caspian Sea. The term "Garrus" was used rather loosely in older literature to denote the historically Kurdish district around the present-day cities of Zanjan and Bijar, south of Ardalan.[219] "Guebri" or "Gebri," on the other hand, was a designation for the dialect spoken by Zoroastrians, a religious group that held much fascination for European visitors to Iran.[220]

Associations between ancient Zoroastrian traditions and what I henceforth call "Garrus wares" were zealously promoted by collectors and dealers. These included the French sometime archaeologist Maurice Pézard, who published a number of these dishes in his trendsetting luxury two-volume book, *Le céramique archaïque de l'islam et ses origines* (1920). Perhaps the most prominent voice on the Garrus wares was the French dealer Arthur Sambon (1867–1947). He argued in two publications of 1925 and 1928 that the Garrus bowls then flowing through the Paris market were documents of an exotic history of fire worship and Avestan legend that had survived into the medi-

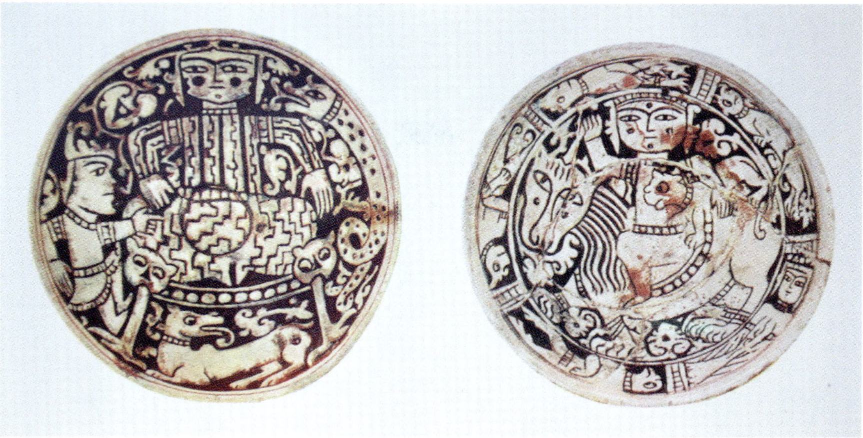

2.48. Arthur Sambon, *Images populaires de l'Avesta en Perse, aux XIIe et XIIIe siècles: Description d'une collection de faïences persanes à sujets nationalistes et d'une servie orvietane de style sassanide* (Paris: Bibliothèque du Musée, 1928), plate 1.

eval era, captured in the remote Iranian hinterlands like a fly in amber.[221] The most elaborate pieces in his collection carried images of men, animals, masked figures, serpents, and human-headed beasts (fig. 2.48).[222]

So far, so good. Doubts were quickly raised, however, about the exotic imagery on these objects. In 1938, Arthur Lane not only proposed that many of the Garrus wares were modern fabrications, but also outlined in general terms how he thought they had been made.[223] By the 1970s word had spread across not only the European museums but also the North American ones, and a veritable rash of thermoluminescence testing broke out in response to this infectious doubt. TL testing undertaken in the 1980s and 1990s showed that many Garrus ware bowls had been last fired within the preceding hundred years, condemning most such pieces to the perpetual darkness of museum storage.[224]

If we can move beyond the reductive binary of authentic versus inauthentic, what are these pieces? Fragments of authentic slipwares of this type, some of them decorated with animals or birds, have been recovered archaeologically at sites in Iran including Takht-i Sulayman (fig. 2.49) and, more recently, Aghche Rish.[225] The Takht-i Sulayman excavation materials now in Berlin reveal a range of decorative techniques on heavily potted dishes and bowls, made in a fairly coarse red earthenware body. It is not clear at present where the pieces excavated at Takht-i Sulayman and Aghche Rish were made, or if there were multiple sites of production.[226] The decoration on the archaeological pieces is dominated by designs that range from simple geometric borders and even scribbles to inscriptions, birds, and animals, and the archaeological material is attributed the eleventh to twelfth centuries.[227] Thus, there certainly were "real" Garrus wares made in medieval Iran, although to the best of my knowledge, none of them have so far presented with any human imagery of the type seen on Sambon's bowls and the more exotic market pieces.

The technique for producing "modern" Garrus wares with fetching figural imagery is rather elegantly simple. The process begins with genuine medieval slip-covered glazed bowls, either plain or with modest amounts of incised decoration in their original state. A largely complete example of this type of bowl was excavated at Takht-i Sulayman, along with countless smaller fragments of the same kind (fig. 2.50). A very similar plain bowl with a crosshatched

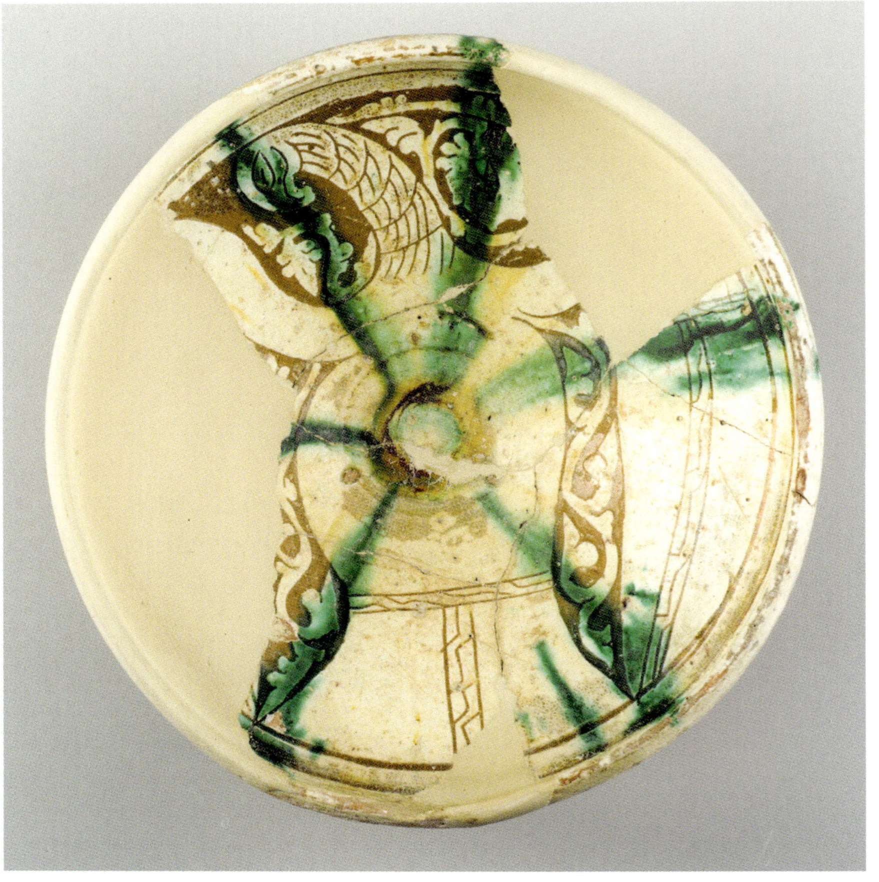

2.49. Bowl, glazed earthenware with slip decoration (so-called Garrus ware). Attributed Iran, 12th or 13th century, excavated at Takht-i Sulayman, Iran. Diameter 25.9 cm. Museum für Islamische Kunst, I.17/69.

band was included in Pézard's 1920 *Le céramique archaïque de l'islam et ses origines*, confirming the presence of such pieces on the early twentieth-century market.[228] These plain bowls, built back up from large and small fragments, formed the substrate of the new Garrus wares. Early twentieth-century craftspeople took those largely plain medieval bowls and cut into them with new, market-friendly designs, carving right through the old glaze and slip layers and down into the clay bodies. Handling the archaeological material makes this easier to understand: the original glaze layers have degraded from burial and are now thin and friable, so much so that it would be quite easy to cut through them to the clay body using a sharp tool. Once the new design was cut in, the modern craftsman then covered the inside face with a new layer of clear or colored transparent glaze, usually quite shiny and sometimes with splashes of green or brown added to mimic the originals, before firing the whole piece. Et voilà, a new-made medieval bowl, complete with valuable figural imagery and desirable connections to an exotic fire-worshipping past. A rather heavy-duty intervention, but an effective one.

Some of these modern reworkings speak more clearly about their processes of construction than others. One, acquired in 1925 by the Detroit Institute of Arts from Dikran Kelekian, raises immediate questions on the basis of style: the lion with a humanoid, bearded face does not look like the designs seen on excavated examples of this type of material (fig. 2.51).[229] TL testing of a sample from the foot of this piece in 1983 indicated that the sampled sec-

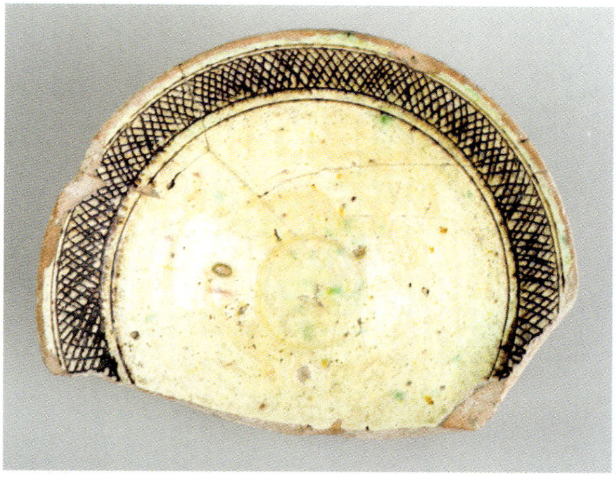

2.50. Bowl, glazed earthenware with slip decoration (so-called Garrus ware). Attributed Iran, 12th or 13th century, excavated at Takht-i Sulayman, Iran. Diameter 16.8 cm. Museum für Islamische Kunst, I.3/67.26.

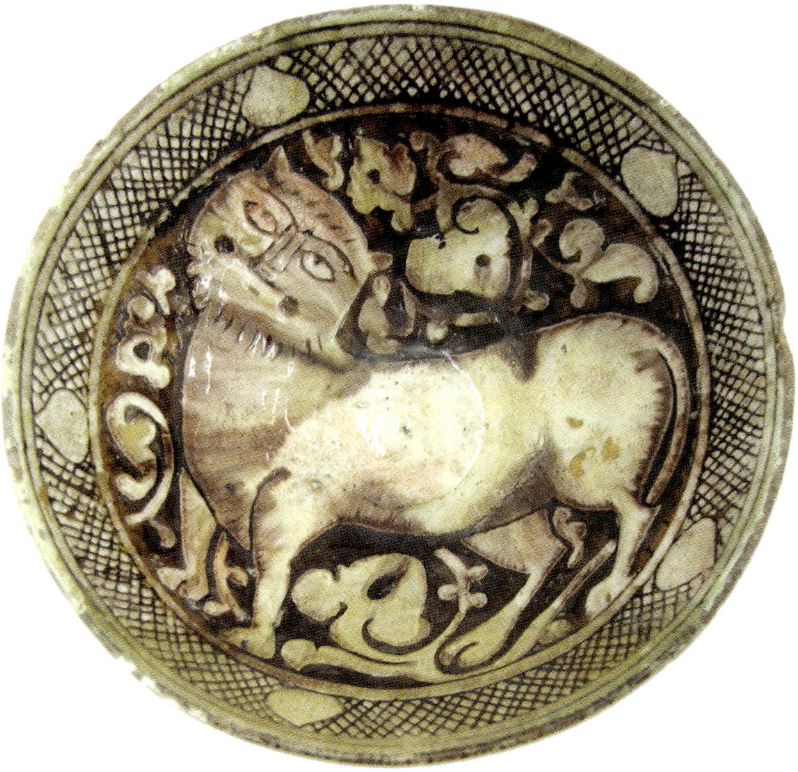

2.51. Bowl, glazed earthenware with slip decoration (so-called Garrus ware). Attributed Iran, 12th or 13th century, with 20th-century design and reglazing. Detroit Institute of Arts, 25.32.

tion had last been fired within the last one hundred years.[230] In this case, the cross-hatched design around the edge of the lion bowl is such a close match for that seen on the white bowl excavated at Takht-i Sulayman that the cross-hatched band probably represents the original design on the underlying medieval bowl.[231] The lion, on the other hand, was added in the modern era. Recent research by conservator Christina Bisulca confirms that the bowl has been reglazed and refired over its original glaze and slip, leaving material traces of this process upon the layered surface of the object. Microphotography shows an old staining pattern in the lion's forehead where the cracks in

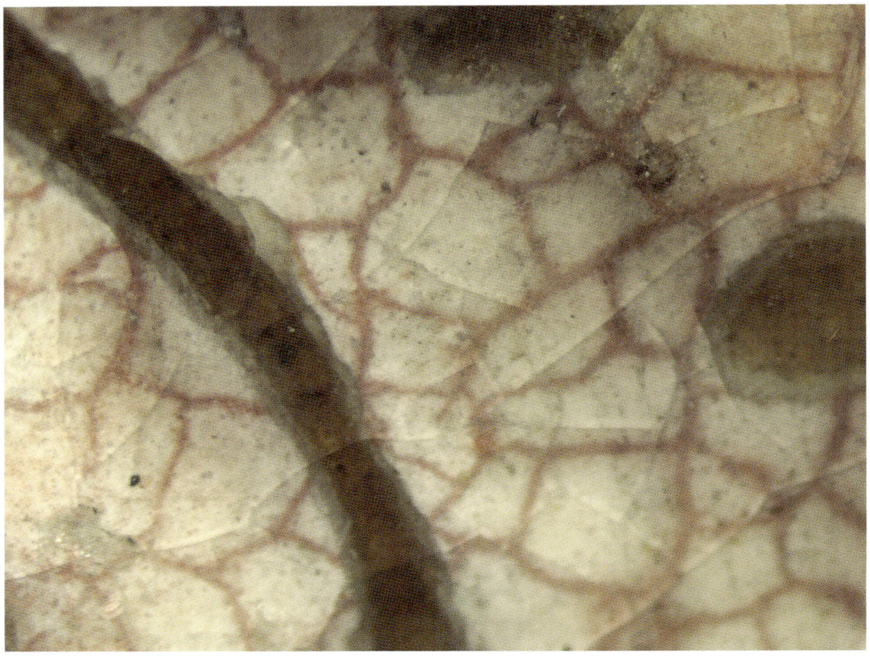

2.52. Detail of bowl illustrated in figure 2.51 showing separate layers of medieval and modern craquelure.

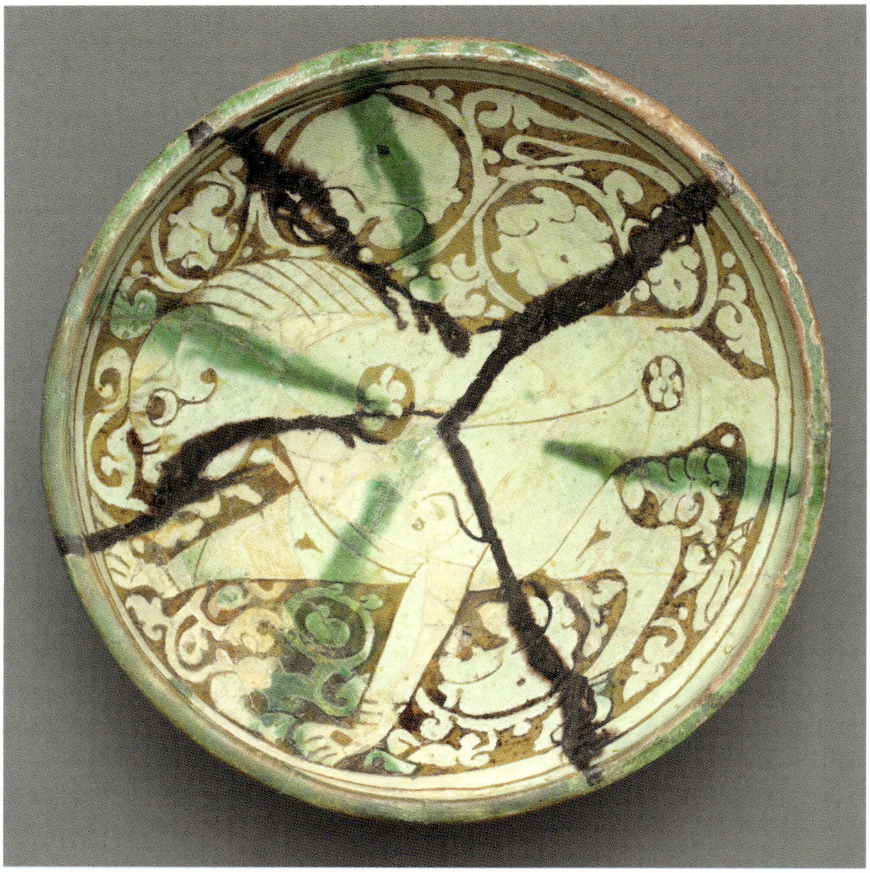

2.53. Bowl, glazed earthenware with slip decoration and some modern material (so-called Garrus ware). Original material attributed northern Iran, 12th or 13th century. Diameter approx. 30 cm. Cincinnati Art Museum, Museum Purchase, 1952.250.

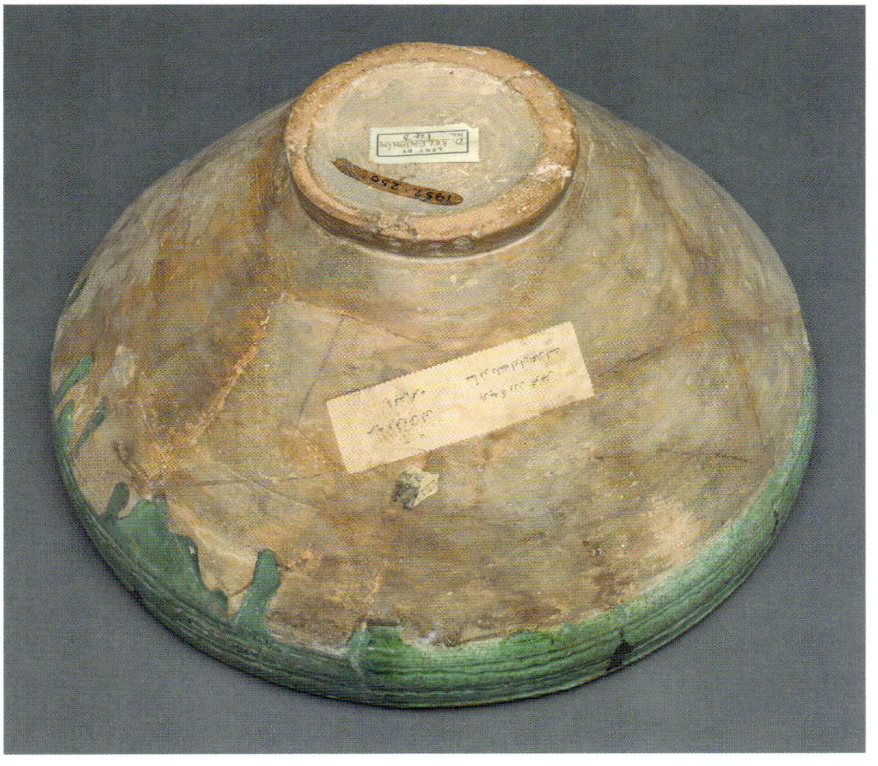

2.54. Underside of bowl illustrated in figure 2.53, showing export label.

the original glaze layer were penetrated by soluble materials, staining the slip layer beneath with a network of fine orange cracks—a common occurrence with archaeological ceramics that have been in the ground for centuries. This old craquelure pattern does not correspond to the pattern of the surface craquelure seen in the clear, shiny glaze layer that now lies over that same area (fig. 2.52).[232] Exactly as described above, an old, glazed slipware bowl has had a new champlevé design cut through the original glazed surface and the slip layer below, before receiving a new covering of clear glaze and another firing.

Diagnosis of these pieces is rarely straightforward. Many of the Garrus bowls now in museum collections have been reconstructed from multiple fragments and some have large amounts of modern overpainting, which one would not expect to find on reglazed and refired objects, yet the sampled parts of those same pieces sometimes return TL testing results indicating modern firing.[233] Others give medieval date ranges in TL testing but are confusingly constructed. A further Kelekian piece, this time in Cincinnati, was TL tested in 1984 using a sample taken from the foot (fig. 2.53).[234] The results indicated a date of last firing between the early eleventh and late fourteenth centuries, which would fit with the current proposed timeline for production of Garrus wares.[235] However, a conservation report written at the time of sampling also noted that the bowl contains several ceramic fragments not original to the object, as well as extensive overpainting, plaster fill, and a brownish substance mimicking glaze (possibly a form of wood varnish).[236] The bowl has an Iranian export permission label pasted over several repair lines, meaning that the restoration work must have been done before the piece left Iran and traveled to London via Paris, reaching the V&A in 1922 (fig. 2.54).[237] Without dismantling it, the best guess is that this is a composite of original and modern material with a design based largely on the original fragments and some modern-day window-dressing, but not the full treatment of reglazing and refiring. As a group, the Garrus wares represent such a thorough and complicated physical interweaving of medieval and modern production technologies, contexts, and desires, that they can only really be understood on a case-by-case basis.[238]

* * *

In the end, the extractivist history of Islamic ceramics presented in this chapter bears out a simple statement made long ago by Michael Rogers, a historian of Islamic art: "It has never been certain with commercially acquired pieces whether a given provenance is correct, or a guess, or camouflage."[239] Even collected sherds, which are sometimes erroneously assumed to be unproblematic archaeological material, can be much less secure than they first appear. Their site names frequently turn out to have been supplied by dealers rather than confirmed excavations and their designs have sometimes been enhanced for the market, for sherds too are objects of desire. In the late nineteenth- and early twentieth-century zenith of Islamic art collecting, thousands of medieval ceramics were dug out of the ground as fragments. Some of those fragments were attractive enough to be sold as they were (sometimes with some retouching or finessing), while others were built up into whole objects and entered into the rapidly globalizing art market, all without any real form of documentation. Early modern vessels and tiles were liquidated or stripped from above-ground repositories and loaded into the same circulatory routes. These pieces moved within an international network of diggers, brokers, dealers, and collectors who took advantage of a largely unregulated marketplace to exchange and amass objects that were fabulous—sometimes in every sense of the word.

As shown in this chapter, the canon of Islamic ceramics has tended to divide into one set of categories approaching the European idea of "fine art"—exemplified by the refinements of Iznik vessels and tiles and Iranian stonepaste vessels—and a smaller set of subjects that hold what could be termed "ethnographic interest," embodied by the Garrus wares. Other factors emerged to define the popularity of other kinds of material: the heraldic devices and inscriptions of Mamluk sgraffito earthenwares appealed to collectors of a historical bent, while proximity to East Asian traditions was more appealing for others, and so forth. The case of the Garrus wares is also emblematic of emerging national narratives of collecting among the most powerful western states. The Garrus wares seem to have been particularly popular with French collectors, perhaps in part because of their fitness for emerging French scholarly narratives of material ethnography. British institutions acquired them too but seemingly without quite the same degree of gusto; possibly they saw less in them that could be used in the great national project of industrial design reform. American institutions usually bought some when convinced to by influential dealers—especially Kelekian—but then never seem to have been very sure what to do with them after that. American collectors, both private and institutional, generally responded better to narratives of princely splendor than of remote cultural survival and preferred their Islamic ceramics to be more fancy than folksy.

There is a danger, however, that the surplus of information we hold from the demand side will keep blinding us to the input coming from the supply side. What might those modern-day Garrus ware designs of harpies, griffins, sphinxes, and Zahhak with snakes sprouting from his shoulders have meant to the craftspeople who cut them into medieval bowls in the workshops of the early twentieth century? And were they created in Iran, or in Paris? Were those artists in fact engaged in their own project of picturing an exotic, pre-Islamic past for the most distant regions of the country? They acted with awareness of the market, no doubt, but they must have had their own reveries too, and made their own projections into a national history that was actively under construction at the time they were working. Like the villagers of Kubachi, they likely had more creative agency in this landscape of extraction than we have tended to give them credit for. There is no doubt that the antiquities market tore through the Islamic world like a cyclone: tiles ripped from walls; diplomats and dealers squabbling over the shattered harvest of sherds; bowls pulled out of caves and fields and off the walls of houses; and everywhere, a chaos of churned earth and zombie attributions that keeps on marching into the present. Somewhere in the middle of it all, a craftsman cleans a bowl that has been pulled from the ground and carves into it the image of a man, a snake, a dog. Carefully etching the curved surface with his own imagined version of a distant history, he is as much a maker of modernity's dreams as any poet or painter. The composition of those dreams is the subject of the next chapter.

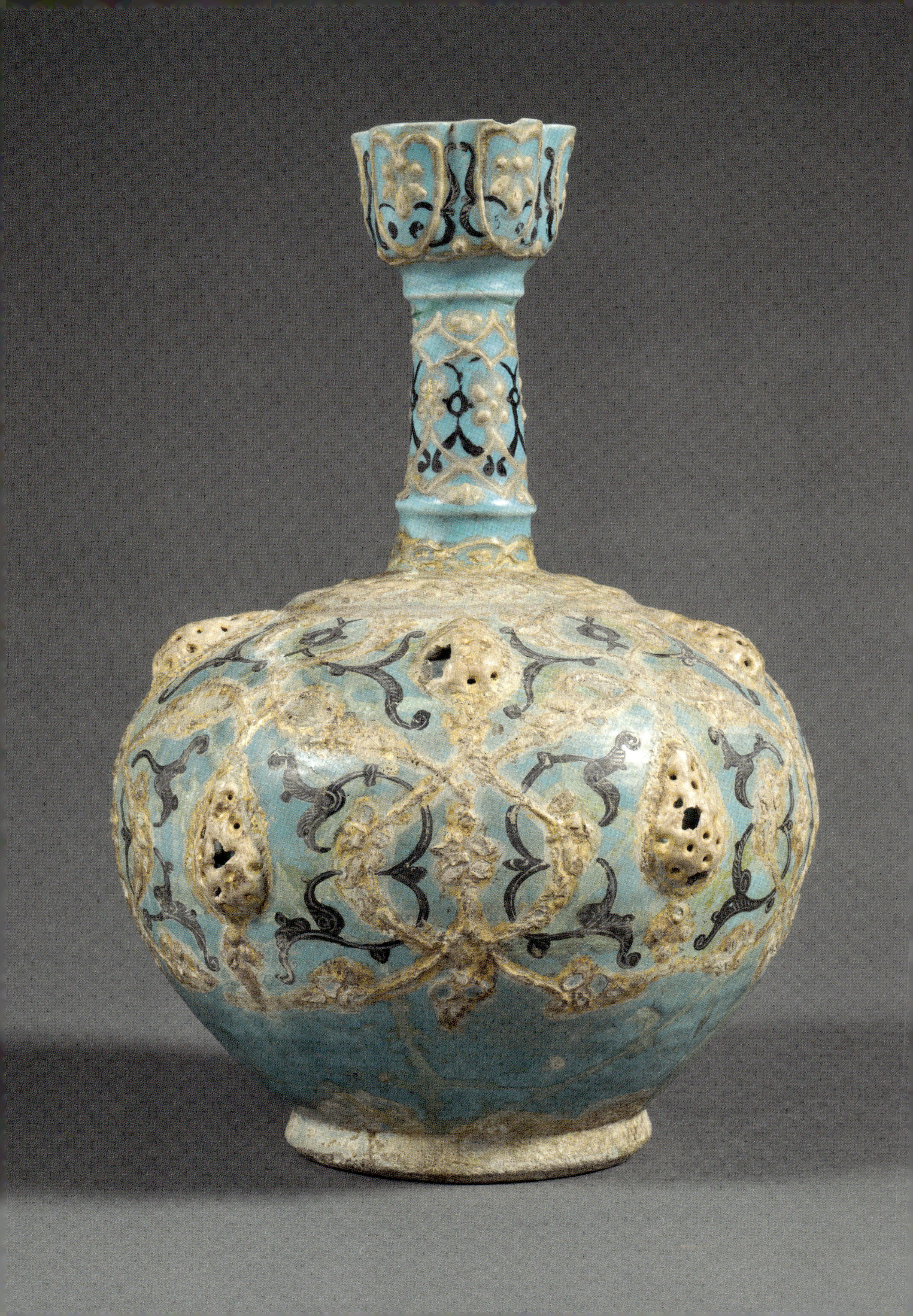

3 Making Gold from Base Matter

POTSHERDS, PAINT, AND PATIENCE

Labor pertinax omni vincit.
Un travail opiniâtre surmonte toutes les difficultés.
[Persistent work overcomes all obstacles.]

—OSCAR RIS-PAQUOT, *Manière de restaurer soi-même les faïences*, 1872

It is appropriate that the pleasure of the collector should be ennobled by some risk.

—CHARLES VIGNIER, "Sur les truquages des faïences persanes," 1928

Beyond the Label, Beyond the Vitrine

Museums display dazzling works of ceramic art, carefully curated on fabric-covered mounts with their attendant information laid out on labels that follow the institution's house rules. Maximum number of sentences; maximum syllable count per word; even the maximum assumed reading age of the audience. Education departments usually set the strictures, leaving curators to pare down the information they share to its pithiest form.[1] The competing imperatives of educators, curators, conservators, and others shape the information shared with the public about any given object in a museum, and the tensions between those different constituencies can sometimes become quite pronounced—to say nothing of what happens when donors, funders, and other higher-ups weigh in with their own agendas.

Within the museum, the fragile realities of material condition are primarily the domain of conservators rather than art historians. The investigation of condition takes place in specialist laboratories, out of the glare of the vitrine spotlight, and there is not always much opportunity for information about condition to make its way into label texts. I have heard museum staff refer wryly to the conservation department as the "object hospital," a place where broken things go to get better—or sometimes, a morgue from which the worst cases will never return. Most conservators, for their part, would prefer their work to be properly understood as a positive and deeply considered set of efforts toward the ethical stewardship of historical materials, rather than just the remedial steps taken to fix a failing join or cracking canvas.

The restoration practices of the past, the focus of this chapter, are precursors of the modern science of conservation. But much of the time, the intent of those early restorers was almost diametrically opposed to the work that institutional art conservators do today. The guiding principles of modern ceramics conservation vary by region and tradition, but there are some increasingly shared ideals: many professional conservators now hold that interventions on an object should be minimal, reversible, and to some degree identifiable to the naked eye.[2] By contrast, most of the art market restorations of Islamic ceramics explored in this chapter were commercial actions intended to complete and often to "improve" objects without revealing the restorer's hand. Those craftspeople aimed at the permanent, irreversible occlusion of loss and damage—and sometimes the ambitious creation of entirely new objects—and they dedicated untold hours of highly skilled labor toward the realization of these fictions. Pathbreaking studies by Oliver Watson, published in two overlapping articles in 1985 and 2004, first laid out some parameters for "fakes and forgeries" in Islamic ceramics.[3] In this chapter I expand some of the widespread phenomena described by Watson, using objects from other institutions—especially the extensive and often overlooked collections in the American Midwest—and new analysis, while framing new lines of inquiry into other techniques. My focus throughout this chapter lies on locating skill in the modern restoration workshop and the forger's kiln, questioning how we should best recognize a form of craftsmanship that depends for its success on effacing itself as thoroughly as possible.

Like other of the so-called decorative arts, ceramics have traditionally been treated as rather sedate staples of the art museum. The material stability of fired ceramics makes them ideal for filling out displays: they aren't damaged by light exposure and are relatively resistant to humidity and temperature variation, meaning they don't need to be rotated off display regularly the way works on paper or textiles do. But the seeming docility of ceramics has recently started to come under scrutiny. In line with larger discussions about the colonial-era acquisition practices that stocked the world's museums, many institutions are beginning to foreground the less decorous histories of the medium. These conversations range from questionable collecting practices to the historical role of fine porcelain in promoting consumable crops that are inextricably bound to the history of slavery, like sugar and coffee.[4] Market interventions, too, are gaining more and more exposure, even in the rarefied air of the ceramics gallery. In the last decade, select examples of recently conserved ceramics from the Islamic world at the Metropolitan Museum of Art, Cincinnati Art Museum, and Ashmolean Museum, for example, have been presented to viewers not as flawless simulacra of original objects but instead as more transparent records of their transformation en route to the display case.

We might think authenticity is a very modern concern, but early debates about how far ceramics restoration should go and where the lines should be drawn between restoration and falsification were already underway in the first half of the nineteenth century. Such questions were initially asked in relation to ancient Etruscan and Greek vessels, the first type of archaeological ceramics to be traded at scale through the modern art market.[5] By that time, ceramics restoration had become a highly skilled profession increasingly geared toward an international collectors' market, although its practitioners have left almost no written traces of their techniques or recipes behind them. The clandestine, often illicit nature of the craft in relation to the market, as well as the pressure to keep successful techniques secret from other practitioners, has precluded significant written records.[6] Instead, this chapter uses the objects themselves as the primary evidence base, opening up the material workshop of Islamic ceramics fabrication during the late nineteenth-

and twentieth-century peak of European colonial expansion in the region. Through close looking and laboratory analysis it lays out the spread of skills required to turn base matter—sherds, clay, glue, plaster, glaze, and paint—into an internationally tradeable commodity of great financial value: whole, beautiful vessels, seemingly beamed direct from the past.

What It Takes

With industrial arts like ceramics there is a triple requisite for successful deception. The workshop that undertakes ceramics doctoring must have, first and foremost, the technical knowledge required to create or modify objects successfully in the kiln or to produce convincing imitations of fired effects through other means. At the same time, its craftspeople must also boast sufficient skill in their production of form and their draftsmanship to persuasively imitate historic shapes of vessels and styles of decoration—including the most fleeting traces of the hand. In addition to all of this, there has to be a good understanding of the logic of design that was at work in the originals if that logic is to be successfully replicated on the new. Many ceramics that have been fabricated with the intention of deceiving buyers will reveal themselves through infidelities of design and/or draftsmanship before technical analysis is even begun. Compositions that don't sit convincingly on three-dimensional surfaces, labored drawing, color that stands proud of the surface when it shouldn't: such things tend to register quickly during firsthand examination once one has spent lots of time looking closely at historical objects. Connoisseurship has become a bit of a dirty word in art history, and not without reason: the field has not been helped by a history of elitism, unscholarly pronouncements, and conflicts of interest. Nonetheless, the knowledge that comes from close looking should never be discounted. The eye and the fingertip that have been trained to work together through years of focus are powerful instruments indeed.

In the case of premodern ceramics, there are three main routes toward a whole object that would meet most criteria for "inauthenticity." These are explored in turn, and in some detail, in this chapter. First—and most common among ceramics from the Islamic world now held in museums—is the art of bricolage. In practical terms, the ceramic art of bricolage involves suturing whole objects together from sherds derived from either the remains of multiple old objects or a mix of old and new-made fragments. The term has long been borrowed by literary theorists to designate a kind of intertextuality. Here, however, I use it to refer to a practice that resonates more directly with the word's earlier meanings of physical and material improvisation, while still carrying some of the weight it has accrued via Claude Lévi-Strauss's influential concept of bricolage in mythmaking. In Lévi-Strauss's terms, "the characteristic feature of mythical thought, as of 'bricolage' on the practical plane, is that it builds up structured sets, not directly with other structured sets but by using the remains and debris of events . . . fossilized evidence of the history of an individual or a society."[7] Read literally, this is a near-perfect description of the manual-cerebral skill of improvisation that can produce new objects from a discontiguous scattering of archaeological fragments. The ingenuity and dexterity that goes into this art is demonstrated below.

A second kind of ceramic fabrication, often undertaken in collaboration with bricolage, is to upgrade pieces by dressing them up in borrowed skins. This can be done in many different ways, all with the aim of adding appeal and financial value to plain, worn, damaged, or visibly reconstructed surfaces. Through painting, gilding, relief work, and other modifications—up to and including the extreme interventions of reglazing and refiring, already seen on the "Garrus wares" described in chapter 2—craftsmen put new skins upon old and broken bodies. By this means, they increase the market prestige and financial value of individual pieces while simultaneously creating surface interference that masks the realities of condition.

Finally, there is the coup de théâtre of true forgery, a completely new-made object that is successfully masqueraded on the market as an old one.[8] This phenomenon lies somewhat apart from the obfuscations of bricolage and skin swaps, which deliberately mislead and misdirect but are essentially improvisational and are normally contingent on the availability of at least some original material. By contrast, launching a completely new fabrication onto the market as an antiquity is a sleight of hand that calls for considerable technical and financial investment, ingenuity in the planning and production stages, and quite a bit of time—but it is certainly not, as we shall see, unheard of.

Most common, then, are modifications that start with at least some original ceramic material, either sticking together old and new fragments or "enhancing" them in some way. Such practices are found across ceramics from every tradition traded on the art market in the nineteenth and early twentieth centuries. Once again, the private pages of the hundred-year-old art forgery detection journal, the *Mitteilungen*, provide an instructive series of aperçus. Witness, for example, wheel-cut coats of arms added to plain early eighteenth-century German stoneware;[9] hydrofluoric acid used to strip certain types of vessel—ancient Greek wares and Italian majolica are both mentioned—back to neutral surfaces before finishing with new, more elaborate designs that could be glazed and fired if desired;[10] and bogus signatures or makers' marks added to previously glazed vessels through a second firing in a reduction kiln.[11] By these means, some celebrated works of pottery have turned out to be faulty foundations for scholarship.[12] As we shall see, however, doctored ceramics from the Islamic world represent something of a special case in the exceptional scale of their circulation and the multifarious means by which they were remade—many of which boil down to a combination of glue, plaster, paint, and patience.

The Patient Art of Bricolage

The desire to mend broken ceramics is far older than the modern antiquities market and has not always aimed at making pieces look like new. Lime plaster, animal glues, and leather or string bindings have been used to repair broken pots for millennia. The more elaborate practice of joining broken pieces of ceramic vessel back together using drilled holes and metal rivets is recorded in premodern contexts across the world and was already seen in chapter 2 on Syrian ceramic fragments excavated from medieval contexts at Novgorod. The widespread use of riveted ceramics mending and its professionalization as a craft may have originated in medieval China; in some re-

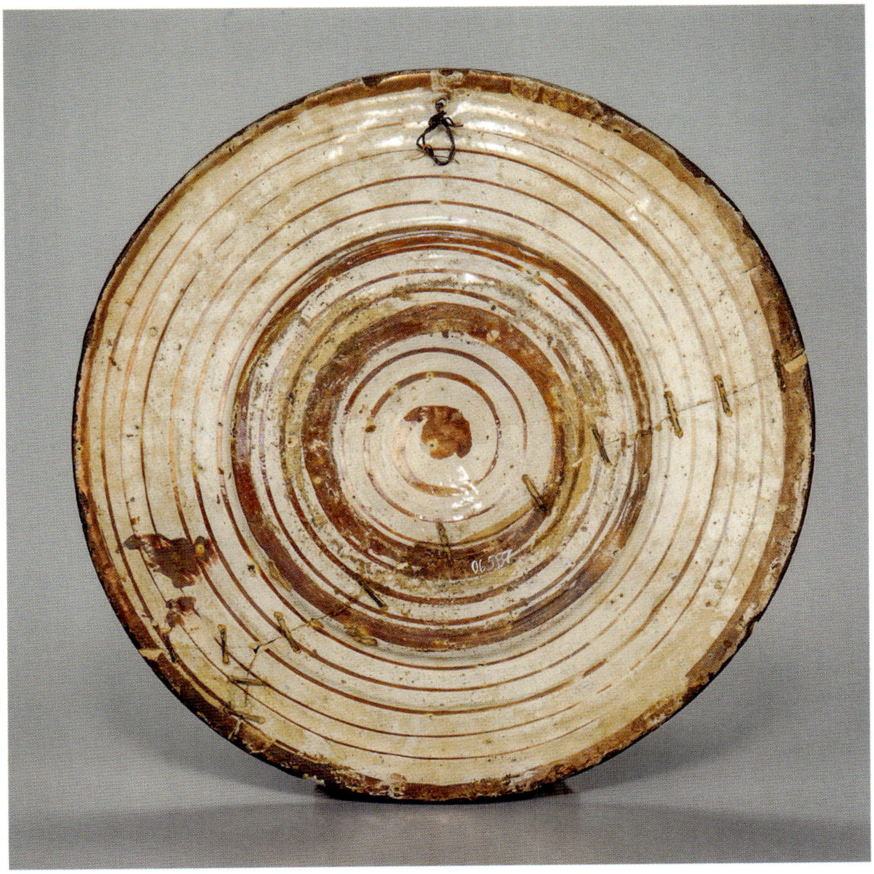

3.1. Reverse of molded dish, glazed earthenware with luster overglaze and riveted repair. Attributed Spain, probably Seville (Triana), first half 16th century. Diameter 34.3 cm. Morton and Marie Bradley Memorial Collection, Eskenazi Museum of Art, Indiana University, 2006.587.

gions, including rural Scotland, ceramics continued to be repaired in this way by itinerant tradesmen well into the twentieth century.[13] In early twentieth-century Damascus it was noted as a dying art.[14] Riveted repairs were primarily done for domestic ends, although they did come to be used in art market restorations too. Riveting would typically be sought if the value of the broken object—in terms of monetary replacement cost and/or practical use—was sufficient to justify it, and the breakage had resulted in only a few, reasonably large pieces for the mender to work on. Vessels that have shattered into dozens of tiny fragments are usually beyond riveting.[15]

Riveted repairs on ceramics can look quite brutal. Some, like the repair on the Iberian luster dish in figure 3.1, bring a staple gun to mind.[16] The practice is, however, a highly skilled one that demands considerable care and judgment. The mender must tie the broken pieces together so that they are in correct alignment, then use a drill to make fine holes into the brittle ceramic surface, angled slightly toward the fracture to aid the grip of the rivets. For maximum control a bow drill was commonly used, a method shown in the depiction of a Chinese ceramic mender at work from a late eighteenth-century suite of paintings of trades and occupations in Guangzhou (fig. 3.2).[17] Once the holes were drilled, metal rivets were inserted into them to bind the pieces together permanently, with the rivets sometimes heated immediately prior to insertion so that they would contract slightly as they cooled, gripping the

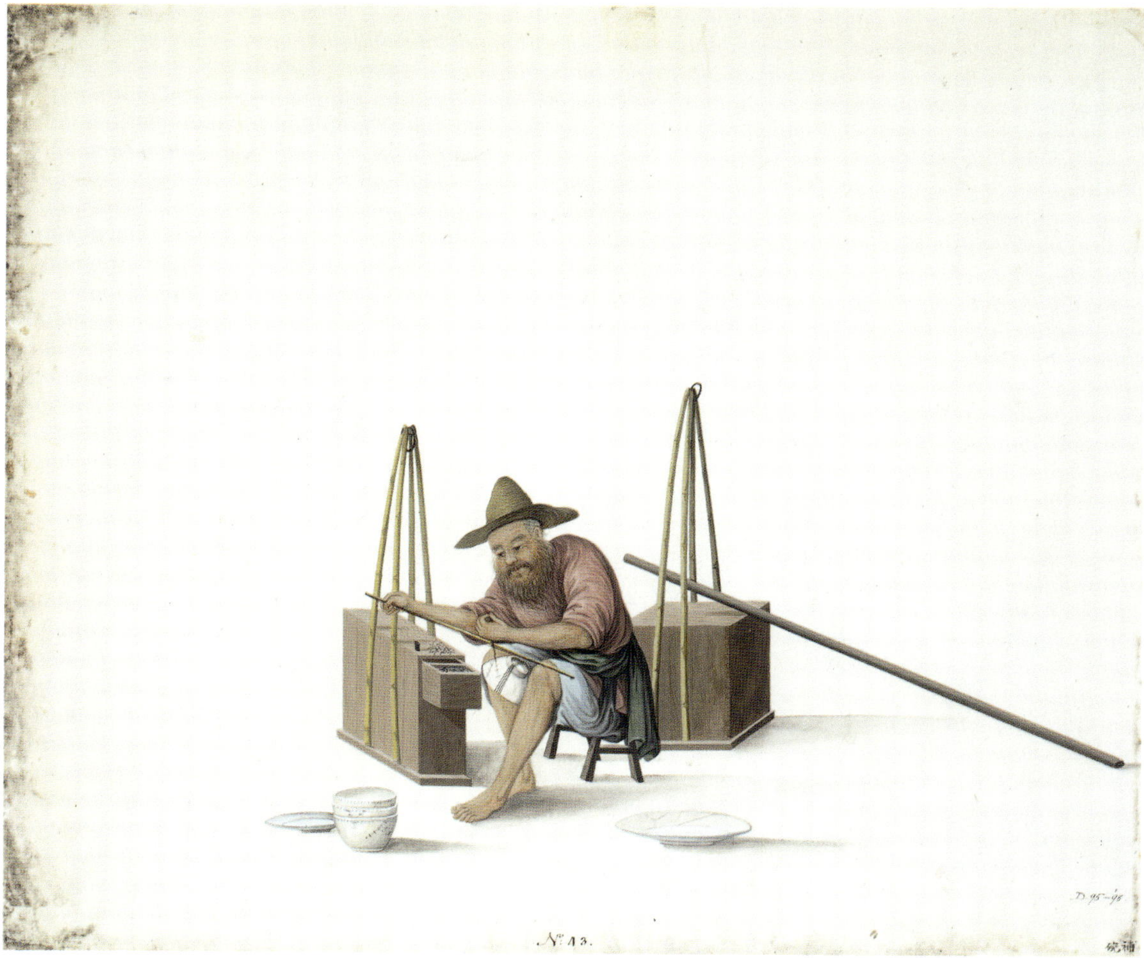

3.2. "A Porcelain Mender," from an album of trades and occupations in Canton. Watercolor and ink on paper. Guangzhou, China, ca. 1790. Victoria and Albert Museum, D.95-1898.

two pieces of the surface together. In a thick earthenware body like that of the slump-molded Iberian luster plate shown here, the drill holes do not need to go all the way through to the other side of the ceramic surface and U-shaped rivets can be used, making the mend much less visible on the front (fig. 3.3). Alternatively, with thin-walled fabrics or on areas of heavy use, the "through-and-through" method is often necessary for a strong join; this entails drilling all the way through and lacing wire completely through the holes. Despite centuries of respected use, riveting came to be viewed negatively by ceramics collectors in the nineteenth century. The paradigm was shifting from repair to restoration, and the market in historic ceramics was coming to prize the appearance of unbroken completeness above all else.[18]

The patient art of ceramic bricolage emerged in response to this commercial desire for intact objects. It is one of the most self-effacing of all craft skills, and often requires special imaging equipment to be seen clearly. To explore this ideal within museum ceramics, let us look closely at an instructive piece that appears to be an unbroken and continuous entity when it is, in fact, anything but. Our object lesson is a small pouring vessel in the form of a bovine creature—a cow, bull, or ox—with luster painting over an opaque white glaze, consistent in style with Iranian luster ceramics of the late twelfth century (fig. 3.4).[19] It has been in the Eskenazi Museum of Art since it was purchased from the dealer Susette Khayat (1898–1980, daughter of the dealer Azeez Khayat, 1875–1943) in New York in 1960.[20] There are quite a number of these Iranian ceramic bovine pouring vessels, in various sizes and techniques of decoration, held in collections around the world, and their medieval popularity has been linked to the growth of cattle husbandry in Iran between the twelfth and fourteenth centuries.[21] The appeal they hold for modern collectors is easy to understand: animal figurines have a perennial charm, and these aquamanile creatures can be finely decorated and even rather winsome. The large eyes and long eyelashes of the Eskenazi Museum's example resonate with early poetic topoi of beauty (fig. 3.5): the Qur'anic term *hurʿin*, meaning "black-eyed" or "great-eyed," comes from the large black pupils of the wild cow.[22] They also give the piece an adorably daft gaze above its cylindrical spout-mouth. How these pieces were used remains something of an open question. An eleventh-century Persian lexicography designates pouring vessels in the form of bulls by the name *takuk*, documenting the medieval existence of such things and recalling the pre-Islamic tradition of the rhyton (a wine vessel of animal form).[23] However, many of the extant ceramic pouring vessels of this type, including this one, are too small to make much sense as vessels for pouring wine or water.

The restoration on this vessel is highly skilled, but on close inspection it is possible to see with the naked eye that there is quite a bit of matte overpaint-

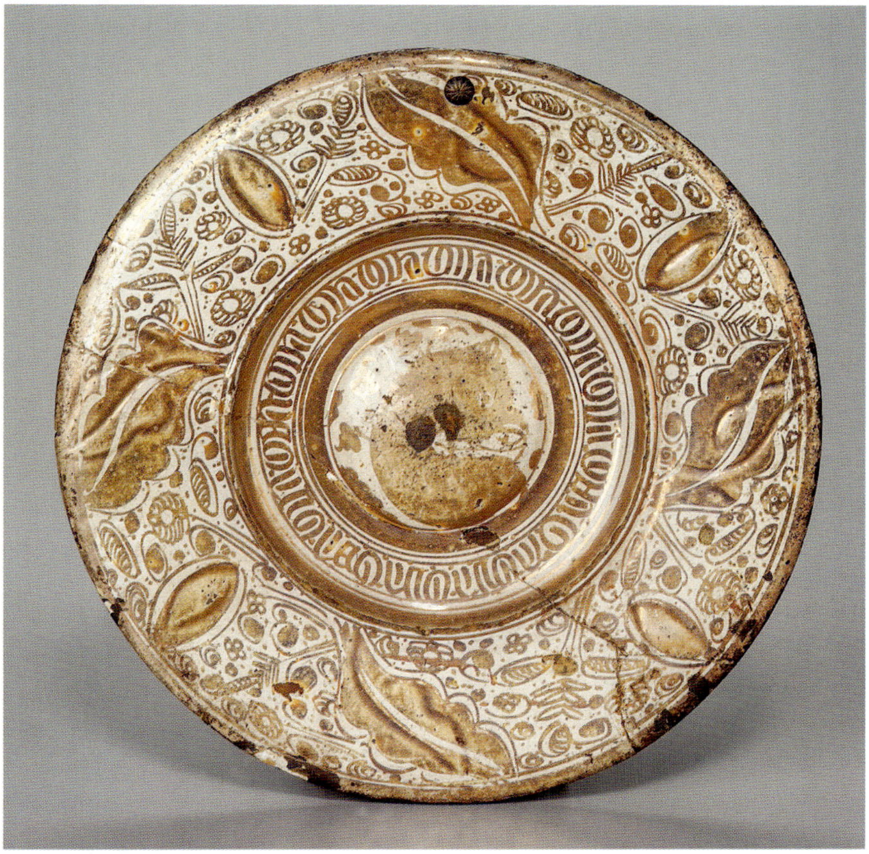

3.3. Front view of molded dish illustrated in figure 3.1.

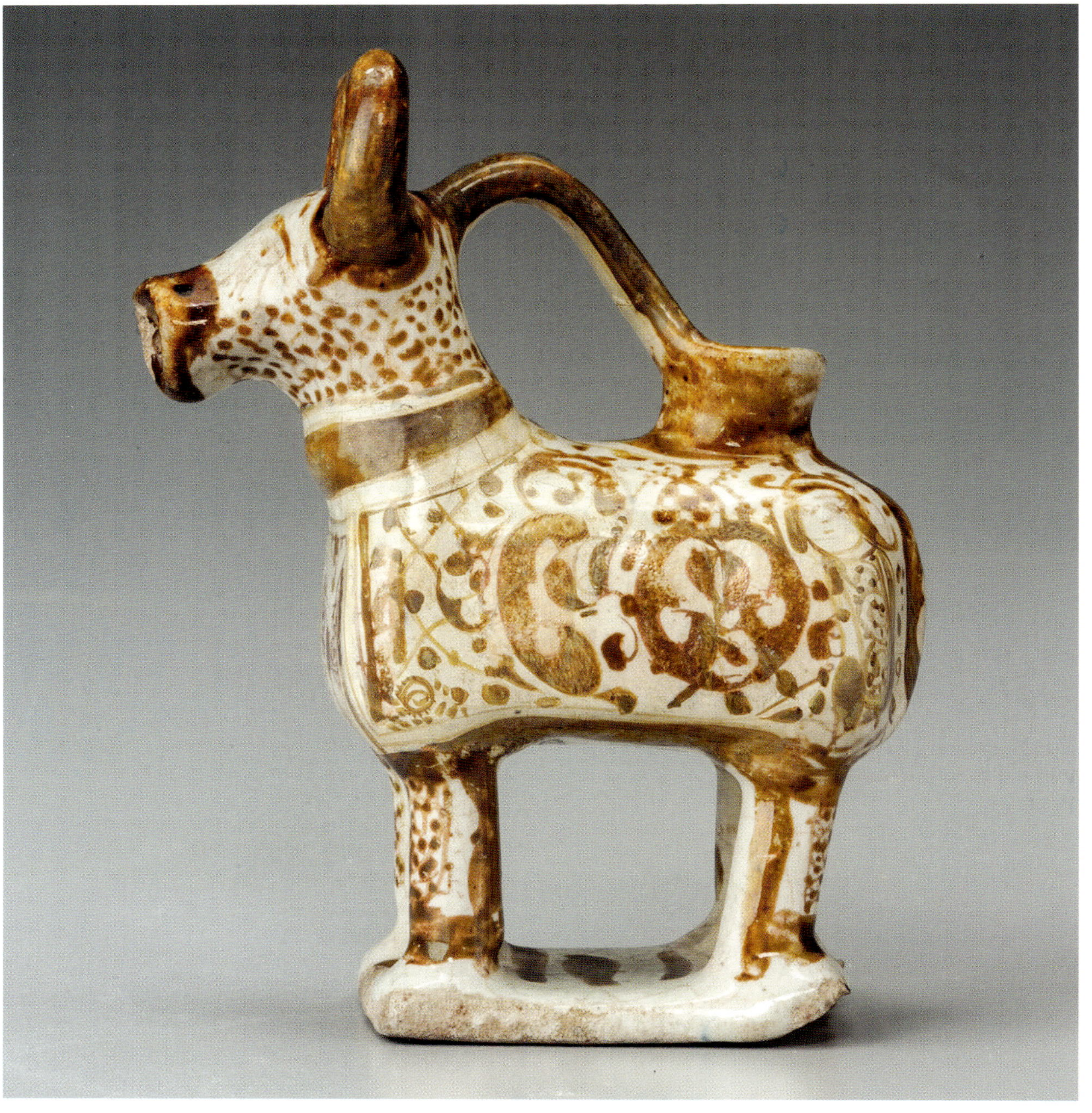

3.4. Aquamanile, glazed stonepaste with overglaze luster and modern material. Original material attributed Iran, late 12th/13th century. Height 14.6 cm. Eskenazi Museum of Art, Indiana University, 60.58.

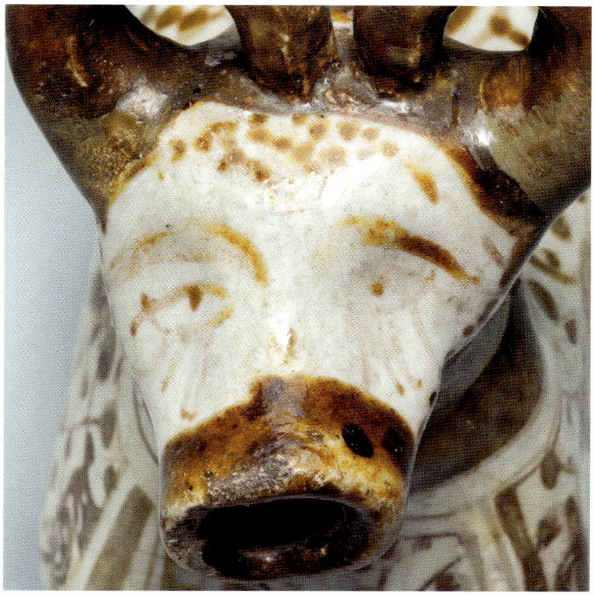

3.5. Detail of aquamanile illustrated in figure 3.4.

ing that is not original to the object. In the detail of the face shown in figure 3.5, layers can be traced where overpaint has been applied over the original luster, like the small lustered dots at the top of the creature's forehead that are partly obscured by the brown overpaint covering the joint of the horns. What cannot be shown in photographs is the feel of "seams" on the body of the object. Fingertips sense what the eye does not; ridges in the topography of the surface, most apparent near the turning point from the creature's front to its flanks, are more readily sensed through touch than sight. In a complete vessel, smoothed into a continuous surface before firing, there should not be such tangible seams on the exterior.

Laboratory imaging was necessary to establish precisely how the piece has been reconstructed. Ultraviolet (UV) light requires a completely dark room but is cheap, easy to use, doesn't damage ceramics, and can usually give a lot of immediate information about condition. Most modern adhesives, varnishes, fills, and paint binders will fluoresce under UV light, making it a good first line of inquiry for ceramics investigation.[24] In this case, longwave UV light immediately shows very extensive overpainting over more than a third of the object, all of which fluoresces a bright yellowish white (fig. 3.6). In some places the UV light reveals fine mend lines where fragments of the original object have been glued back together with almost no loss, like the line running across the rump in figure 3.6. In other areas like the animal's chest, by contrast, overpaint has been used to obscure large margins around little "islands" of glazed surface, as on the chest of the creature. This strongly suggests a full-blown form of bricolage with alien sherds, in which gaps left by lost material have been supplemented with fragments from other glazed ceramics of approximately the same date, origin, and technique, cut to fit and matched as well as possible to the surface designs of their new host with overpainting. The art of the ceramics bricoleur can reach remarkable heights, but it can never create a perfect fit between sherds that don't come from the same break or even the same object. It will always require some fudging at the joins with filler and paint to mask the disjunctions between parts.

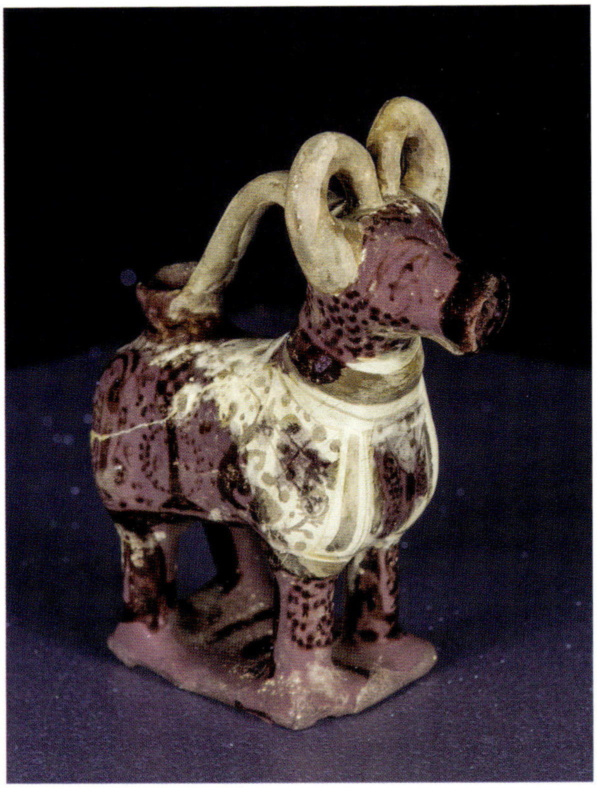

3.6. UV photograph of aquamanile illustrated in figure 3.4.

In this case, it is computed tomography (CT) scanning that gives the most complete picture of the pouring vessel's remarkable restoration. The same machines that scan human beings can be used to produce sectional X-ray imaging of complete ceramic objects, revealing just how complex the work of the bricoleur can be. With the aquamanile, section views showed that some parts of the body are glazed on both the inside and the outside—impossible for a closed vessel like this—while other parts are not. This means that some of the reconstruction work uses sherds glazed on both sides, probably fragments from plates or bowls. Three-dimensional reconstruction from CT imaging is even more illuminating (fig. 3.7). CT imaging works by passing X-ray photons through an object and using them to measure density, which is imaged in shades of gray, with greater density showing on the image as greater whiteness. This means that glazed and fired ceramic shows up light in color on the CT image because glaze is much denser than clay, while the unglazed edges of the base plate and the unglazed, new-made and painted horns and handle and the painted modern fills in the body all appear darker.

There are several published examples of medieval Iranian bowls and dishes put together from mixed sherds in this way.[25] An early twentieth-century glass negative in the Sevruguin photographic archive even illustrates a partially reconstructed luster bowl, likely on its way to a parallel state of modern completion, that gives some sense of the difficulty of this kind of work (fig. 3.8). One of the outcomes of this practice is that truly stunning medieval objects that have survived only in fragments are now often obscured by overpaint and confusion in their new, bricolaged settings. At the peak of their skills in the late twelfth to early thirteenth centuries, the luster painters of medieval Iran

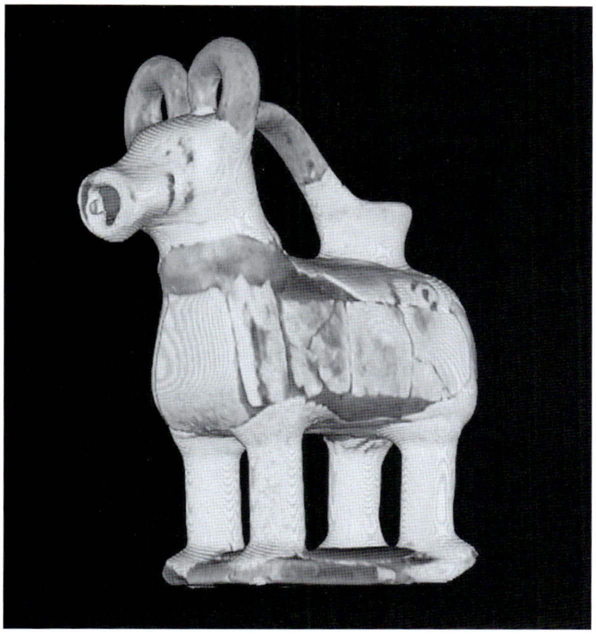

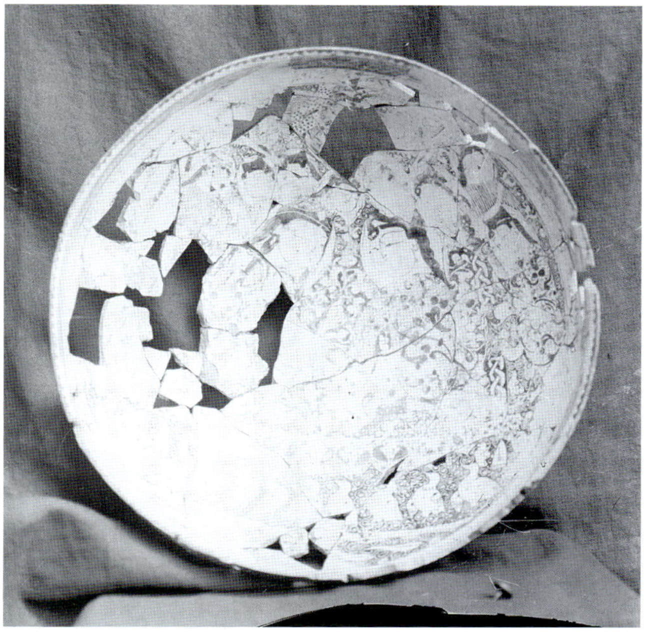

3.7. CT scan of aquamanile illustrated in figure 3.4, showing composition from fragments of multiple ceramic objects and modern material.

3.8. Studio photograph of Iranian luster dish, partially reconstructed. Positive image from glass plate negative, probably taken in Tehran before 1910. Antoin Sevruguin/ National Museum of Asian Art Archives, Smithsonian Institution, Myron Bement Smith Collection, Gift of Katharine Dennis Smith, 1973–85, FSA_A.04_2.12. GN.05.05.

produced works of staggeringly fine execution and compositional complexity (fig. 3.9). By way of example, surviving fragments from a very large luster bowl are decorated with roundels representing the signs of the zodiac (Cancer is visible in the upper left) and the planets (Mercury, personified as a scribe, can be seen below). Between those celestial girdles, a frieze of interlocking dancers sway rhythmically to an aphonic beat.[26] The remaining fragments of this dish have today been cleaned of their twentieth-century overpainting and can now be seen in their true glory, however fractured, as a testament to the superlative skill of medieval Iranian luster painters and potters.[27] The complex form and diminutive scale of the Eskenazi aquamanile, however, showcases a different set of skills: those of the modern bricoleur. To manufacture half a miniature, cylindrical body from mismatched rectilinear fragments is a special kind of three-dimensional challenge of visualization and manipulation, even more complex than constructing a flat plate in the same way.

What we see in the CT scan is a fairly large proportion of one original zoomorphic vessel, with base plate, all four legs, and a chunk of the left side and back end of the body coming from the same original object. These parts all fit together without loss.[28] Thermoluminescence (TL) testing of a sample taken from the base in 2016, prior to the CT scan, gave a date range for the piece's last firing between 600 and 1100 years ago.[29] This would accord with the stylistic attribution of the original material to late twelfth- or early thirteenth-century Iran. The head (minus the horns) is likely also original to the same object as the base, even though it was at one point completely detached from it, because the luster-painted surface of the head matches that of the legs when viewed in both regular light and UV, and its proportions fit well with the body. But the front and right side of the object have been built up from fragments of unrelated glazed vessels. Three square cut sections make up the flat part of the right flank, and a slightly curved fragment that looks like it came from the edge of a dish acts as a kind of breastplate at the front.

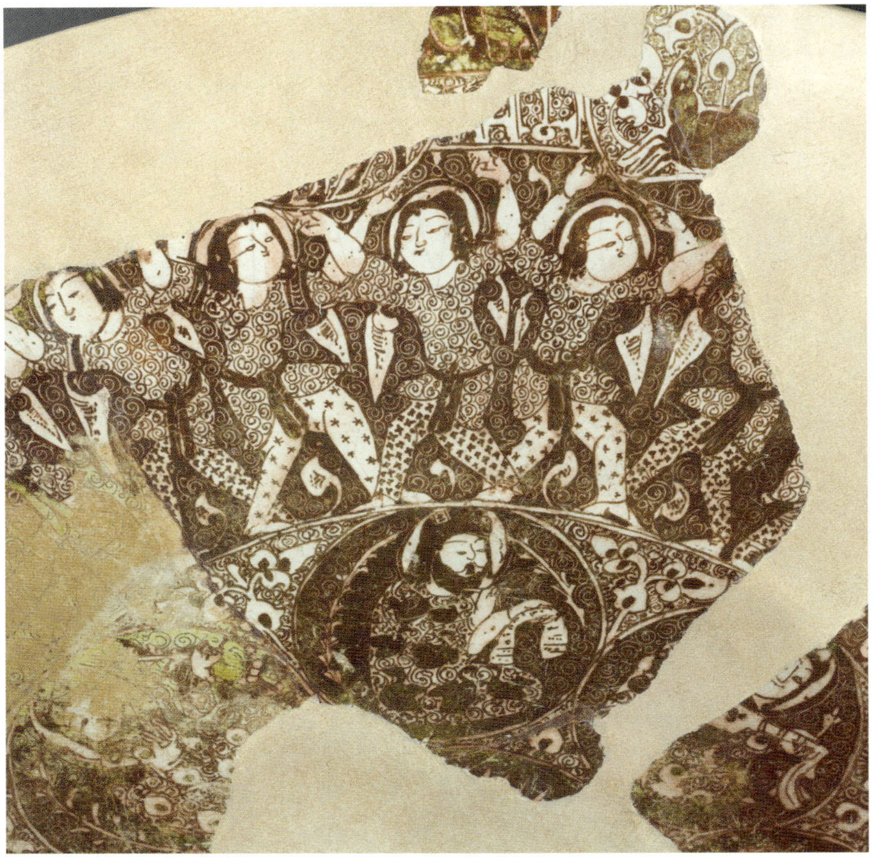

3.9. Fragments from a large bowl with zodiac symbols and dancers, glazed stonepaste with overglaze luster. Attributed Iran, early 13th century. Cincinnati Art Museum, Given in honor of Mr. and Mrs. Charles F. Williams by their children, 1948.113.

Glue and Sandwiches

A different kind of three-dimensional challenge is furnished by vessels that have been built up like mosaics from literally hundreds of fragments, a craft that has as much in common with intarsia or *khatam-kari* (an Iranian tradition of marquetry inlay with tiny pieces of wood, bone, and sometimes metal) as it does with ceramic-making. A bowl of this type was acquired by the Toledo Museum of Art in Ohio, who bought it from the dealer MacDermid Parish-Watson in 1941 along with eighteen other pieces.[30] A photograph that came with it at the time of acquisition—its official "portrait shot" from Parish-Watson—shows a pictorial arrangement of two large figures with curiously amorphous robes of dense patterning (fig. 3.10). Notable iconographic oddities in the composition are two miniature seated humans, one on the inner knee of each figure, and the tiny human-headed, footless harpy hovering above the hand of the left figure. The bowl has pedigree: it appeared in a major exhibition of Persian art held in New York in 1940, shortly before the museum acquired it.[31] When it was selected for conservation treatment in 1992, however, the curator and conservator agreed partway through the process to stop the work and leave it in a partially disassembled state (fig. 3.11).[32]

Looking at the piece today, it is easy to see why they reached this decision. Once the overpaint had been cleaned off and the first round of fragments detached from the rim, the true condition of the object was visible to all. It was made by sandwiching together tiny pieces of ceramic from an untold number

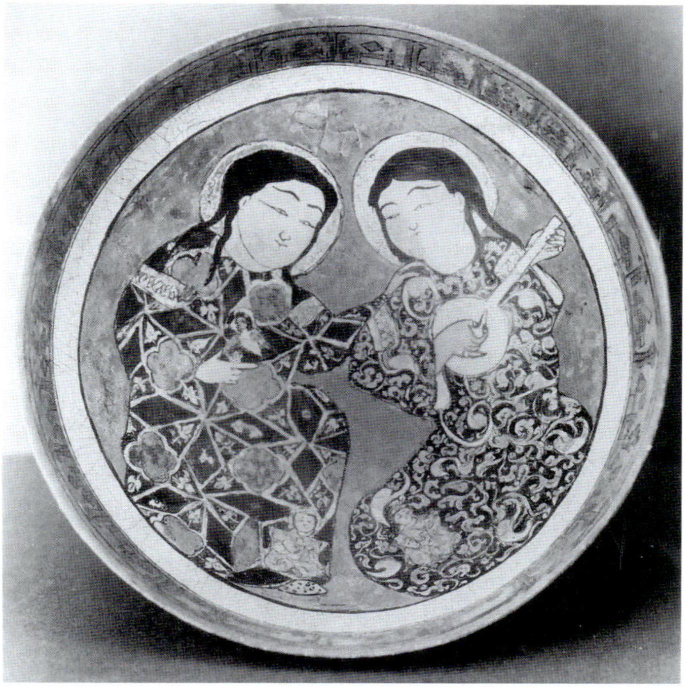

3.10. Undated photograph of so-called mina'i ware bowl prior to conservation, Toledo Museum of Art, curatorial files for object 1941.16.

3.11. Bowl composed of fragments from multiple ceramic objects, partially disassembled. Some material attributed Iran, 12th and 13th centuries. Toledo Museum of Art, 1941.16.

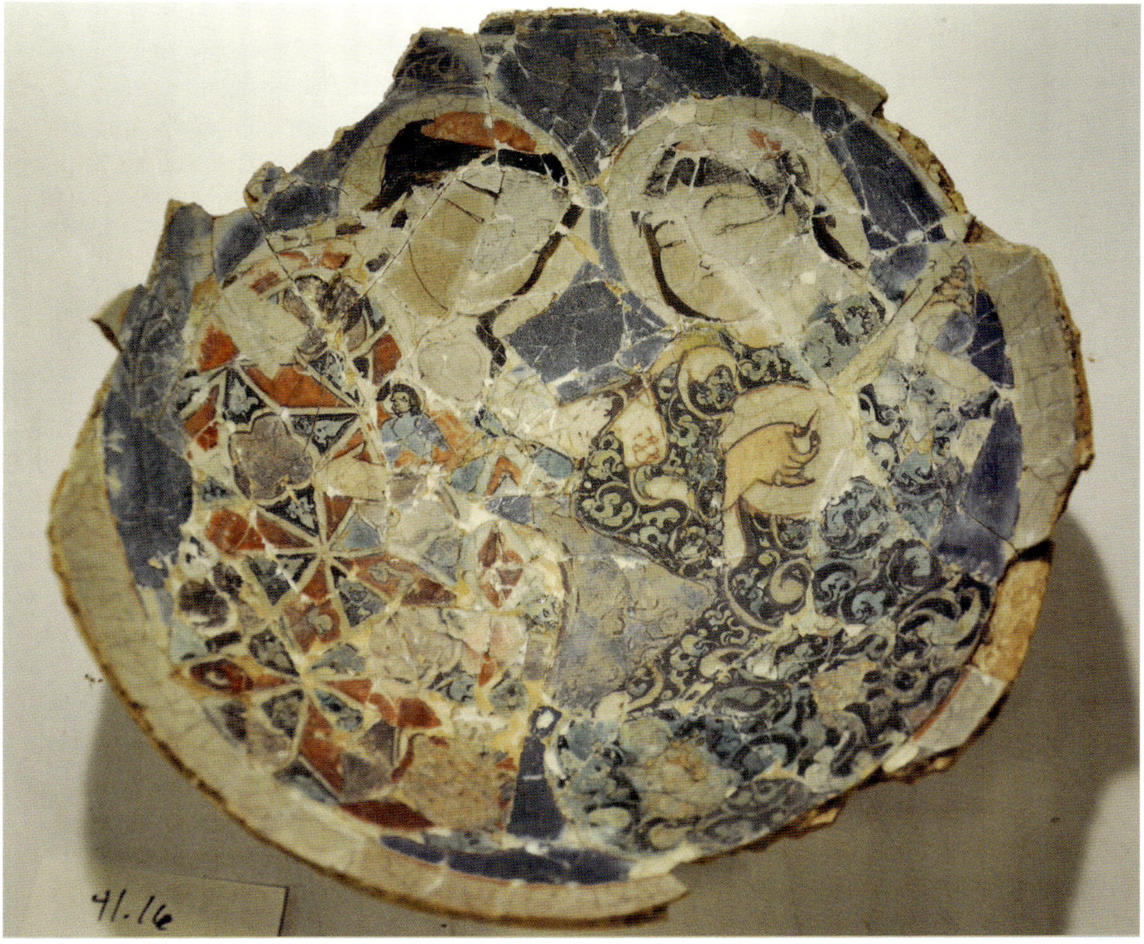

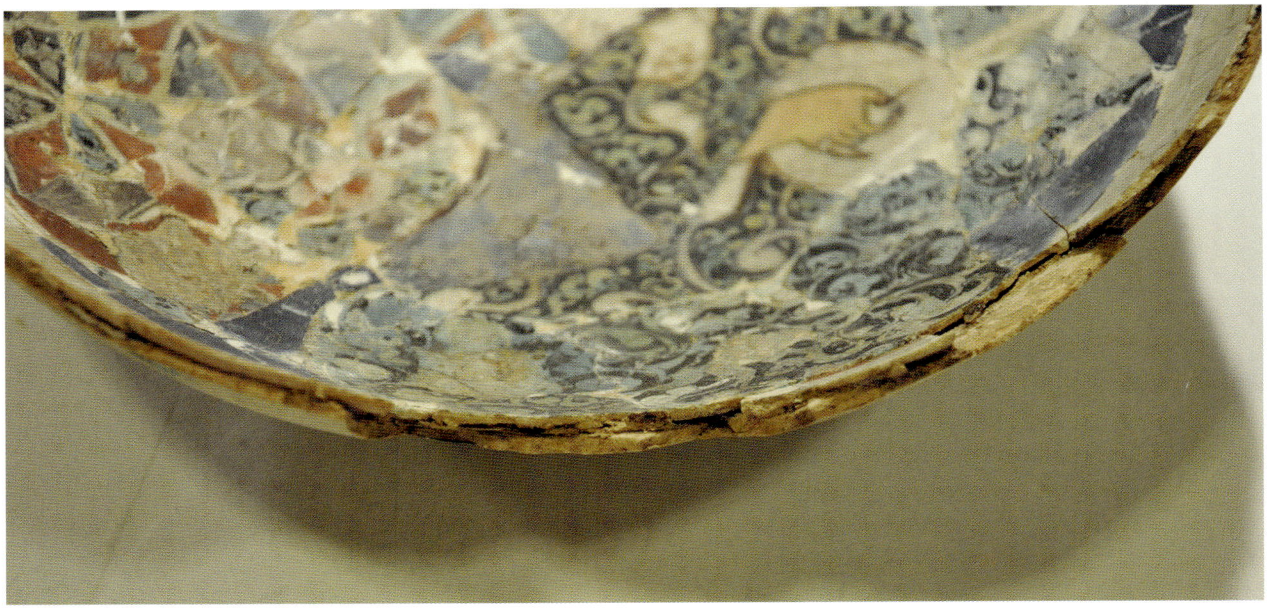

3.12. Detail showing edge of object illustrated in figure 3.11, with sandwiching of sanded-down sherds visible.

of different objects. Most of the sherds in the piece had one face filed off before being stuck together, exposed side to exposed side, to produce a simulacrum of a glazed surface inside and out. This is easiest to understand by looking at the disassembled edges, where the two layers of the "sandwich" are exposed (fig. 3.12). The lower part of the outer surface is made up of somewhat larger pieces, while the all-important decorated inner surface has been painstakingly assembled from dozens and dozens of tiny pieces. The extreme fragmentation of this surface comes from cutting already broken pieces in order to build up an image from unrelated parts, while also fracturing flat sherds in order to fit them to the curved surface of the new bowl—essentially crushing them into the curve before covering up the crack map with overpainting.

The practice is familiar to ceramics conservators who work on this material, but the Toledo bowl is an extreme case by any standards.[33] In 1928 the Paris dealer Charles Vignier (1863–1934) described a slightly simpler version of this technique, reporting that it had first been practiced in Aleppo before being refined in the bazaars of Tehran.[34] Another bowl reconstructed using the same "sandwich method" as seen on the Toledo bowl, now in the Fitzwilliam Museum in Cambridge, confirms the development of a full-blown "sandwich method" of this type within Iran—almost certainly at Tehran, the center of the Iranian antiquities market (fig. 3.13). Although its various paper labels were removed during conservation in 2010, at the time of its 1935 accession to the Fitzwilliam Museum a pink Iranian export slip was still glued onto the bowl (and therefore on top of all the restoration work), demonstrating that the construction of the bowl from mosaiced and sandwiched fragments must have been completed in Iran, prior to export.[35] I am yet to see a full-blown sandwich technique like this on any ceramic vessel originating from outside Iran, reinforcing the likelihood that it was, as Vignier suggested, a particular specialization of Iranian workshops.

The decision to stop the investigation on the Toledo bowl, rather than continue disassembly until only a pile of disparate tiny pieces remained, has left

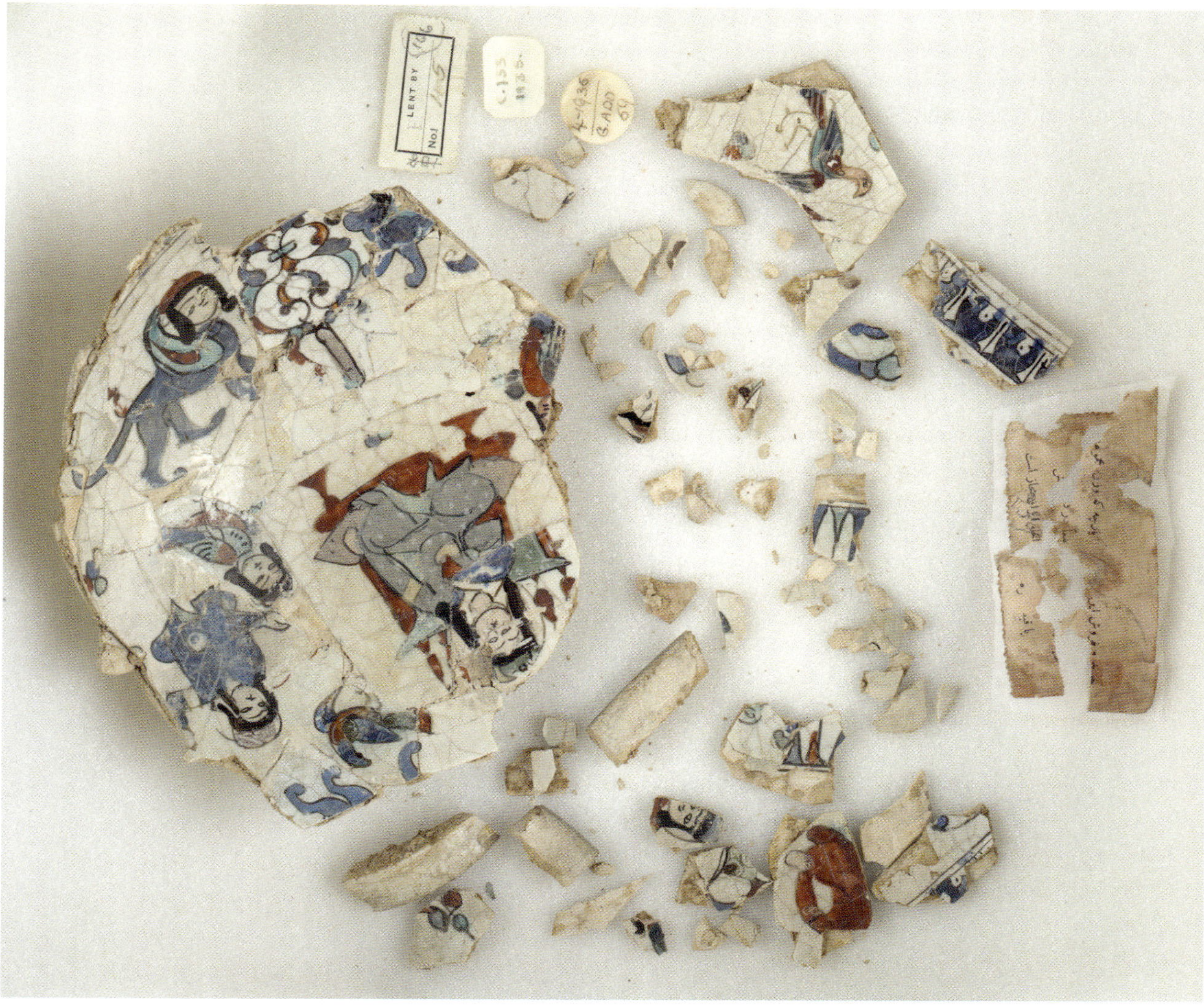

3.13. Fragments of disassembled so-called mina'i ware bowl composed of fragments from multiple objects, with Iranian export label. Most remaining material attributed to Iran, 12th and 13th centuries. Fitzwilliam Museum C.133-1935.

us with an instructive artifact that illuminates a very particularized form of manual skill while also exposing the metacondition of the museum object itself. The commodity system of art and antiquities requires there to be something we can point to as the proper subject of acquisition, ownership, and display; after a certain point of fragmentation, that proper subject disappears. With the Toledo bowl, investigation revealed that it had transgressed the parameters of the marketplace and the museum by appearing to be a "proper" subject when it wasn't one. It was made up from fragments too small, too disordered, and carrying too many traces of modern hands to be considered a coherent exemplar of any medieval ceramic tradition. As a composite that fuses together multiple temporalities (like the Garrus wares in chapter 2), it could not, in the end, deliver on its promise to act as conduit to a singular historical moment in the way that its assumed identity in the marketplace had claimed it could. Accordingly, its trajectory as objet d'art was arrested, and the mosaiced "sandwich" bowl dropped into the stasis of perpetual storage.

A highly complex undertaking, mosaiced "sandwiches" like the Toledo bowl are possible only when the correct resources are available: archaeological sherds, knowledge, time, dexterity, and adhesive. Plaster and slip formed one kind of adhesive in these confections, but more specialized sticking power was needed as well. Prosper Thiaucourt's handbook for the ceramics restorer, published in Paris in 1865, lists a wide range of adhesives recommended for use in ceramics restoration: animal glues, fish glue, potash silicate, gum arabic, shellac, glazier's mastic, and various waxes.[36] Most if not all of these were available internationally in the late nineteenth century and can be encountered in ceramic restorations of the era. Animal and fish glues were used on many Syrian and Iranian ceramics traded through the early twentieth-century market, sometimes bulked with fillers or pigments to make a kind of "glue putty" that could then be used to fill gaps as well as join fragments.[37] For example, a jar bought by Charles Lang Freer from the Aleppo antiquities trader Vincenzo Marcopoli in 1911 was stripped of its overpaint in a conservation campaign undertaken in the 1990s, revealing a veritable mosaic of fragments set into a bed of animal glue fill.[38] Perhaps this is the type of Syrian ceramic Vignier was referring to when he wrote that the technique of filling gaps with sanded-down alien sherds was pioneered in Aleppo.[39] Ayşin Yoltar-Yıldırım's research in the Ottoman archives has even identified an Irish brand of fish glue, Seccotine, that was used by the excavator Théodore Macridy to glue together fragments of ceramics he uncovered in the excavations of 1905–6 at Raqqa before sending them to the imperial collections in Istanbul.[40] That a fish glue manufactured in Belfast should be the adhesive of choice for an Ottoman-Greek excavator in northern Syria during the first years of the twentieth century gives some sense of the interconnected, transregional marketplace in which all of these activities were taking place.

New-Made Glazed Fragments

Finally, as well as all the variations on patching and filling around old fragments, there is a topmost level of ceramic bricolage that we have not yet explored. That is, the creation of new-made, glazed and fired ceramic fragments to fill losses in vessels. Examples of this technique have been identified on a host of different objects traded through the art market since the early nineteenth century: ancient Greek vases, medieval Iranian bowls decorated in the mina'i technique (see below), Italian majolica, and sixteenth-century Iznik dishes have all been found to contain modern fired and glazed replacement parts made in the nineteenth or twentieth century.[41] Vignier again furnishes useful, if unsubstantiated, information about this in his 1928 article, describing a practice that he claims was invented by Parisian restorers for use in the reconstruction of ceramics from medieval Iran. A vessel would be rebuilt from sherds with new parts made from pliant clay to fill in major losses. The clay parts were then left to dry leather hard, detached from the piece, glazed and fired, and finally glued back in.[42]

Manufacturing replacement parts in this way would have been far harder than Vignier's rather blasé description makes it sound. Clay shrinks as it dries and can easily distort in the kiln, necessitating careful calculations in scale simultaneous with getting outline, curvature, and thickness just right—to say nothing of the challenges of convincingly matching localized and historically specific body fabrics, glazes, and pigments. A successful outcome would be a replacement part that looks and feels more or less continuous with the origi-

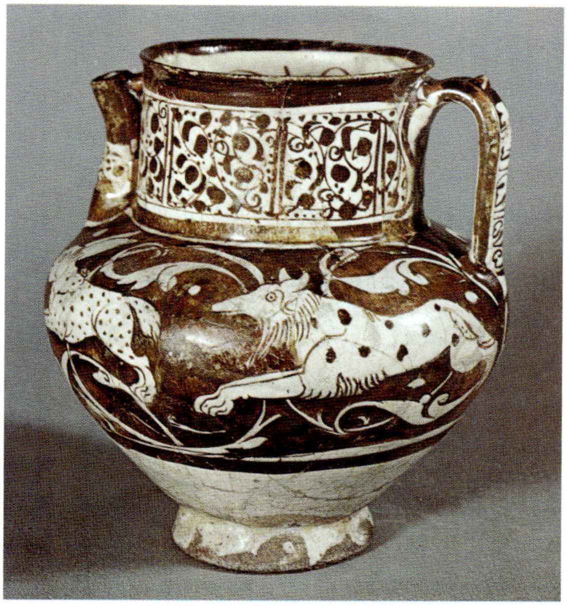

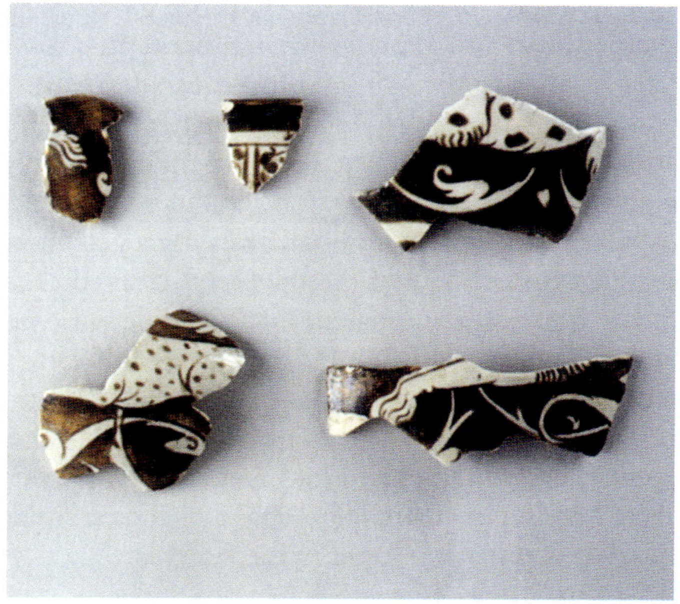

nal and can "pass" without immediately registering as an interloper. Surface abrasion, paint, and dirt could then be used to play down the difference between a new section and its older neighbors.

The creation of new glazed and fired fragments to fit losses precisely must be difficult in any technique, but the technical demands of creating such pieces with overglaze luster decoration—one of the most unpredictable techniques in ceramics manufacture—are truly daunting to contemplate. The potential financial rewards were huge, though, in a market where extraordinary sums were being paid for medieval luster vessels. To date, only a handful of examples of this superlative skill have been identified among Iranian lusterwares, but there are doubtless more instances out there that have not yet been recognized; workshops that were capable of pulling off this feat would surely not have stopped at only one or two pieces.

One of these rare instances is a pitcher acquired by Charles Lang Freer in 1909 from T. J. Larkin, an Irish dealer trading in primarily East Asian art through his gallery in London. It is shown here as it appeared before it was disassembled in conservation in the 1990s (fig. 3.14).[43] In his meticulous conservation work, Stephen Koob revealed that this medieval Iranian luster vessel contained a substantial number of modern, custom-made fired fragments, complete with perfectly executed luster overglaze decoration (fig. 3.15). These modern fragments were manufactured with such skill and matched so well to the original vessel that they had gone undetected for nearly a century.[44] The presence of chromium on the glazed inner surfaces of the new-made pieces puts their date of manufacture somewhere between the 1820s—when the discovery of chromium mines in France and the Shetland Isles initiated the element's widespread use as an industrial colorant—and Freer's acquisition of the piece in 1909. The likely time of production is the late nineteenth or early twentieth century, in light of the trade in luster vessels on the antiquities market by that point. Francesca Leoni and her colleagues recently published an Iranian luster dish in the Ashmolean Museum with similarly successful

3.14. Spouted jug, glazed stonepaste with overglaze luster and modern material, prior to conservation. Original material attributed Iran, late 12th to early 13th century. Height 17.9 cm. National Museum of Asian Art, F1909.370.

3.15. Fragments of new-made replacement fragments used in market restoration of jug illustrated in figure 3.14, stonepaste with overglaze luster. Made early 20th century, location unknown.

(albeit less three-dimensionally complex) new-made luster replacement fragments.[45] The Ashmolean team did not commit to a date of production for the modern fragments but tentatively suggested that they might be linked with the dealer Khalil Rabenou (1906–1961; see chapters 2 and 4), from whom Sir Alan Barlow seems to have bought the Ashmolean bowl at an unknown date, possibly in the early 1930s.

If the Ashmolean team's timeline of new-made luster fragments produced close to the early 1930s is correct, it would mean that the highly specialized craft of manufacturing luster fragments for ceramic restoration was still going strong more than two decades after the Freer pitcher had left the market. These two rare, documented instances of the technique might have been judged unthinkable had the evidence not been painstakingly analyzed and published, and they show how seriously the field of Islamic ceramics studies has previously tended to underestimate the skills of the craftspeople working in the early twentieth-century restoration market. Completing a fragmentary object with new-made luster-decorated pieces represents the apex of the ceramics fabricator's art, a feat even more technically impressive than manufacturing a whole new vessel in the technique—although getting the latter to "pass" on the market is a whole other story.

The Hidden Violence of Artificial Limbs

One of the most dramatic interventions on reconstructed ceramics, usually only visible through X-ray or CT imaging, is the use of metal armatures or wires for restoration. The commonest place to encounter this is in the handle of a vessel, when a missing handle has been replaced with a new-made one built around a wire armature or an old one has been reattached using wires. This method was apparently in wide restoration use on a range of ceramics by the late nineteenth century, if the "how-to" manuals for ceramics restorers are anything to go by.[46] An illustration from a manual published by Oscar Edmond Ris-Paquot in Paris in 1872 shows a jug prepared with wire for a replacement handle of this type (fig. 3.16).[47] Interestingly, the design on the jug signals that it is to be understood as either Turkish Iznik ware or an imitation of it, and it is the only ceramic object from any Middle Eastern tradition illustrated in the manual.

The accompanying text in the manual describes, step by step, how to prepare the site of the broken handle by drilling a hole using a bow drill. Once this is complete, you insert a piece of copper wire (not iron, because of the risk of rust damage and discoloration) into the holes drilled at top and bottom, to form the desired shape of the handle. Next, you attach a curved strip of cardboard to shape the underside of the handle as you construct it around the wire using a mixture of blanc d'Espagne (a powdered form of calcium carbonate, also known as whiting) and potash silicate, mixing the two to form a putty-like substance that sets hard.[48] The technique requires the craftsman to work quickly as well as accurately, for the whiting and potash mixture passes rapidly through the malleable stage.

Some Islamic ceramics that have come through the market reveal a measured practice of carefully building up new handles around metal armatures, exactly as shown in Ris-Paquot's manual. On a lobed cup of "Raqqa" ware from medieval Syria in the Brooklyn Museum, bought in New York from the

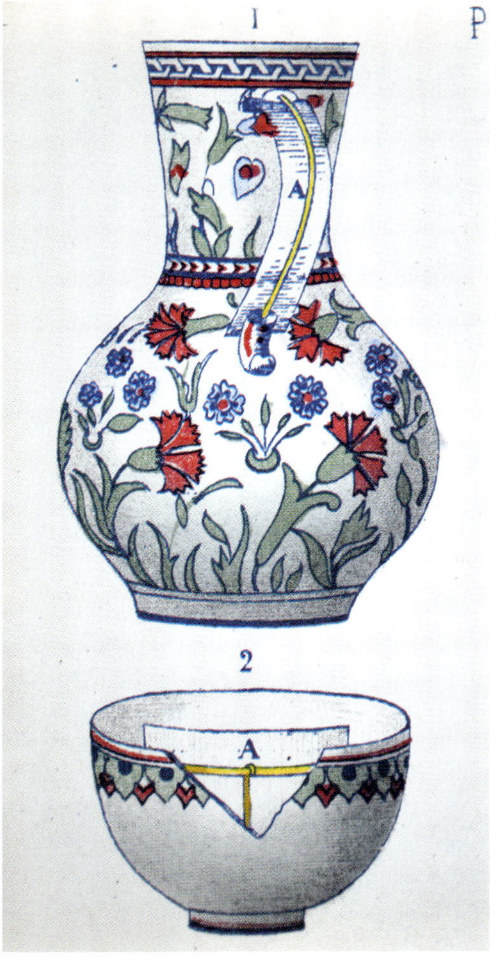

3.16. Oscar Edmond Ris-Paquot, *Manière de restaurer soi-même les faïences, porcelaines, cristaux, marbres, terres cuites, grès, biscuits, émaux, etc.* (Paris: Librairie Eugène Delaroque, 1872), plate 3.

dealer Azeez Khayat in 1908, X-ray images show a curved piece of twisted wire inside the handle (fig. 3.17).[49] The tight curvature of the wire means that the handle must have been built up around it after the wire was driven into the exposed areas where the original handle had broken off. Another Raqqa vessel acquired around the same time by the Brooklyn Museum, either direct from Khayat or via a donor who bought it from him, shows the same kind of twisted wire inside the handles when X-rayed—used this time as anchoring "pins" rather than a complete armature. From the X-rays, it looks as if the armature material on both could be a double twist of industrial copper wire, a product manufactured on a massive scale for the telegraphic and electrical industries by the end of the nineteenth century.[50] A third vessel in the same group has a handle built around two curved pieces of plain wire (fig. 3.18).[51] Conservators at the Brooklyn Museum also report the use of plaster, paint, applied flakes of glaze, and metal leaf, all used to disguise the restoration work and mimic the effects of the degraded glaze, across multiple pieces in this batch of Syrian wares acquired from Khayat.[52]

The material evidence of similar restoration practices, especially the telltale use of the same twisted wire in handle reconstructions on two of the pieces, is the strongest indication one can have that the group now in the Brooklyn Museum was restored in the same workshop prior to its accession

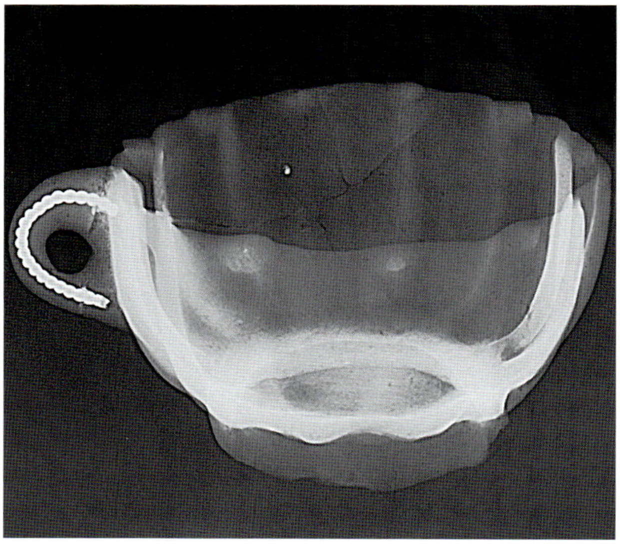

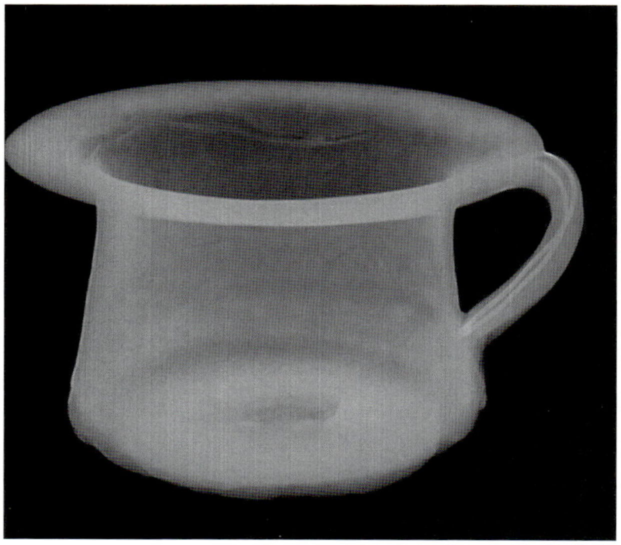

3.17. X-ray of "Raqqa ware" cup showing modern twisted wire armature in restored handle. Brooklyn Museum, 08.21.

3.18. X-ray of "Raqqa ware" cup showing modern wire armature in restored handle. Brooklyn Museum, 08.23.

to the collection in 1906 and 1908. The dates at which these pieces entered the Brooklyn Museum are significant. As is discussed in more detail in chapter 5, 1906 and 1908 saw official excavations at Raqqa sponsored by the Ottoman authorities. These followed years of reports about ceramics being illicitly excavated there by local people and Aleppo dealers, for sale on the international antiquities market.[53] Khayat's stock of Raqqa wares in New York was part of a flow of ceramic material from the site that had been going on for some years, peaking in the second half of the first decade of the twentieth century. The scattered evidence points to workshops in Aleppo as a major site of reconstruction for these and related pieces that were traded onto the international market from Ottoman Syria, often traveling via Paris to enter the United States at New York.

The forced insertion of metal wires, rivets, and rods into medieval ceramics can be quite shocking when it is revealed on an X-ray image, showing up in hard white lines where only the ghostly grays of glazed ceramic were expected. In terms of apparent violence to the medium, however, the neat wire armatures on the Brooklyn pieces are surpassed by what is concealed within the handle of a Syrian pitcher in the Eskenazi Museum (fig. 3.19). Two pointed screws of nineteenth- or twentieth-century manufacture, their threads clearly visible on a CT cross section, have been driven into the glazed, fired body of the jar to attach a new-made handle (fig. 3.20). The space around the tip of the lower screw in figure 3.20 shows that a drill bit must have been used to make the holes into which they have been driven. The material used for the new-made handle is also quite distinct from that of the body, showing up on CT imaging denser and without the inclusions seen in the main body of the vessel. The lower part of this jar has been stuck together from many fragments, most of which fit neatly and seem to belong together, with a long crack running down from the lower joint of the handle that may be a stress fracture sustained when the piece was drilled to take the screws. Yellowed overpaint that fluoresces brightly under UV light is clearly visible on the whole of the handle and several parts of the belly, underneath a shiny varnish that has been used to cover the whole object. Once one has seen these hidden screws,

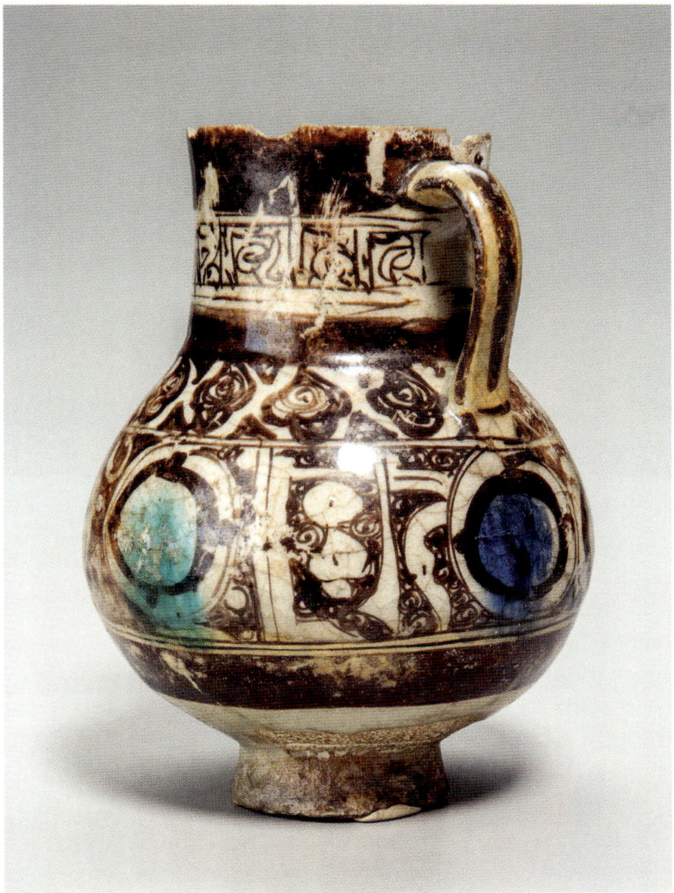

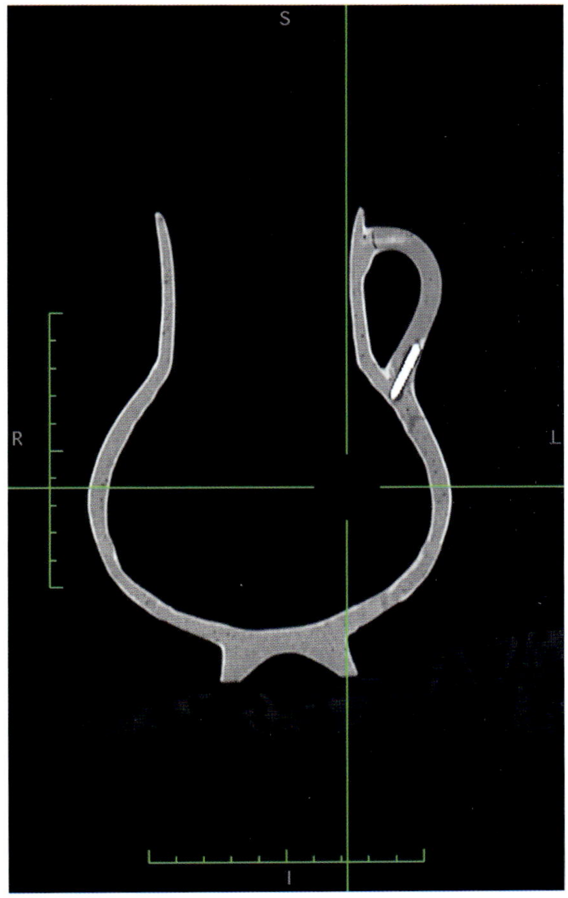

3.19. Handled jar, glazed stonepaste with overglaze luster and modern material (so-called Raqqa ware). Original material attributed Syria, late 12th or 13th century. Height 17.5 cm. Eskenazi Museum of Art, Indiana University, 72.6.11.

3.20. CT scan of handled jar illustrated in figure 3.19, showing modern screws in restored handle.

it is hard to imagine a more visceral embodiment of the antiquities market as an inanimate extension of the colonial program, with all its hidden violence and its history of disfigurements inflicted in the name of improvement.

And yet, even as we balk at the brutality of driving screws into friable ceramic walls, there are traces of more discernment in this intervention than we might at first imagine. The handle is elegantly shaped and has been made by a trained ceramist who knew what they were doing; moreover, the CT scan and the interior surface of the jar show that the two screws have been driven in until they just, *just* touch the back of the glazed inner surface—the point of one has created the tiniest imaginable hole in the glaze, so minute I only noticed it on a second inspection. The new-made handle is slightly torqued to coordinate with the not-quite-straight alignment of the original handle's attachment points, and the inflexible straightness of the screws has required the modern craftsman to work with great care to build a curved form that completely covers them without appearing awkward or distended.[54] The heavy-handedness of the materials chosen to act as armatures in this restoration—screws!—is belied by the care taken in its execution.

The pitcher in the Eskenazi Museum was acquired in 1972 from Fahim Kouchakji, whose trade in Raqqa wares is further discussed in chapter 5. Kouchakji probably bought it at the auction of Dikran Kelekian's remaindered collection, sold off in 1953 after his death (see chapter 4). A photograph in that auction catalogue shows it with the modern handle in situ, meaning that the screws and the rest of the restoration work predate the 1953 sale.[55] Given its likely arrival in the Kelekian collection considerably earlier, quite possibly in the first decade or two of the twentieth century when the Raqqa wares were flowing freely through the art market and Kelekian was doing a good trade in them, the unusual restoration on this pitcher may well be from the early years of the twentieth century. This is the first and only time I have seen screws used as integral components of a ceramic restoration, but who knows what X-ray and CT imaging might reveal in the future?

All of the forms of ceramic bricolage I have discussed here create objects that appear to be whole and singular when they are in fact combinatory assemblages. These assemblages do many things, including a confusing metaphysical achievement: they suture together multiple historical moments. In a marketplace that requires individual commodities to be both discrete and unitary, and to speak from one temporal period only, this raises problems. But if we depart from the category anxieties of the market and the museum, there are other ways to think about what these objects are doing. As Paul Losensky has recently observed in relation to the unique aesthetics of Persian poetry, the idea of "unity" in literary and artistic production has been used since the European Enlightenment to mean "organic unity." But, he asks, what about other types of unity? Assemblage theory proposes wholes that emerge from the interrelations of constituent parts (rather like Lévi-Strauss's concept of bricolage), creating the possibility of unities that are not necessarily *unified*.[56] These assemblages compose their own parameters of coherence, with component parts that could in theory be extracted and plugged into a different assemblage.[57] The "whole made of wholes" of assemblage theory resonates strongly with the aesthetics of the Persian album or *muraqqaʿ*, a word descended from the Arabic *raqaʿa*, meaning "to patch, mend, or piece together."[58]

Thus, while the bricolaged ceramics in this chapter were certainly intended to pass as unities in an "organic," Enlightenment sense—their raison d'être being the accumulation of financial value in a marketplace predicated on the idea of the artifact as a discrete commodity—they arose in an environment that had its own longstanding theories of artistic assemblage and its own combinatory aesthetic traditions. Pausing with those traditions allows us to sidestep, even if only for a moment, the tyrannical desire of the market-museum complex for a unitary "authenticity." By looking beyond those desires, it becomes possible to see the bricolaged ceramic as a unique—and satisfyingly complex—material assemblage, arranged by skilled fingers working through three dimensions, multiple media, and staggered temporalities.

Borrowed Skins

Thus far this chapter has lingered on the structural idiosyncrasies of various forms of bricolage, repeatedly burrowing down into questions of technique to show how pieces were put together, why they were done that way, and what kinds of skill were involved. But there is also a vast expanse of surface to consider. All those thousands of pieces of broken and reconstructed ceramic have surfaces that offer themselves up for enhancement, their market value increasing when new skins are put on old bodies. The possibilities are virtually endless: completing missing imagery and inscriptions or painting

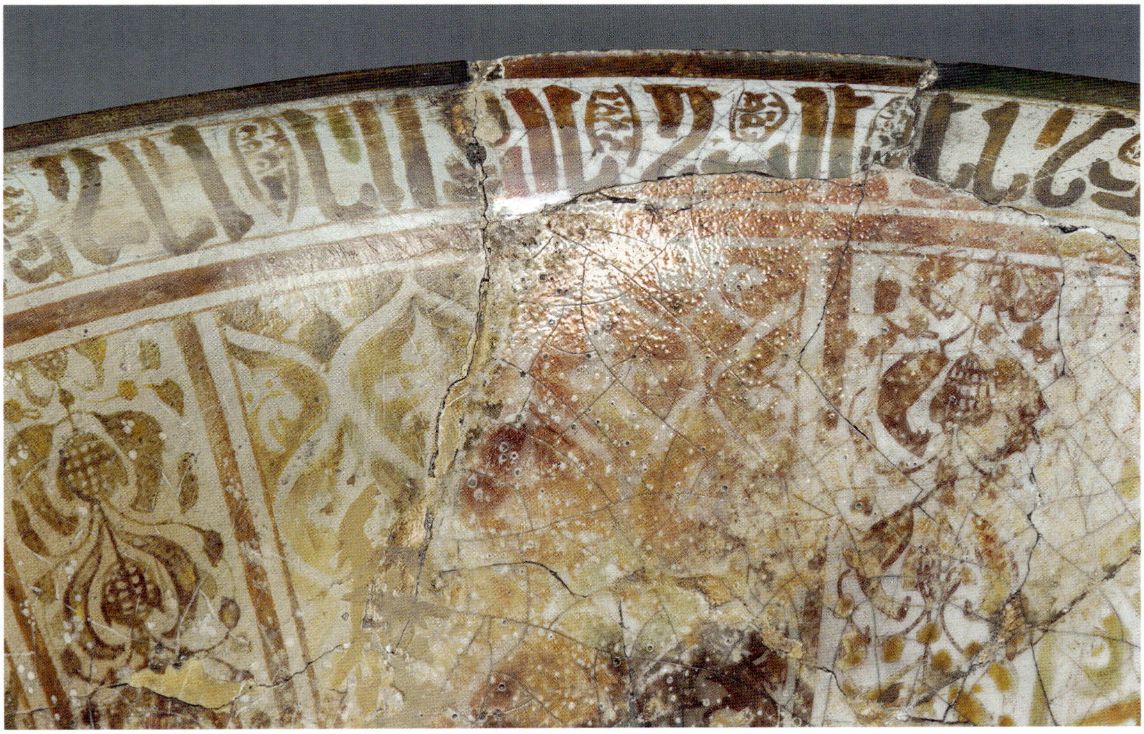

3.21. Detail of basin, glazed stonepaste with overglaze luster (right) and large areas of modern fill with overpaint (left). Medieval material attributed Iran, late 12th or early 13th century. Diameter 31.9 cm. Eskenazi Museum of Art, Indiana University, 61.68.

on new, adding gilding, encrusting with new textures, even creating entirely new designs and glazing and refiring whole pieces, as was already seen on the Garrus wares of chapter 2. Some techniques of medieval ceramic decoration lend themselves particularly well to modern augmentation and imitation, while others have proved much trickier to mimic. As in all arenas of craftsmanship, a wide spectrum of artistic and technical skill is on display if you know where to look.

Some of the most compelling modern upgrades to medieval Islamic ceramics—if not necessarily the most successfully deceptive—have been effected through the simplest of means: brush painting, done with care and finesse. Passages of painting that simulate qualities of slip and glaze through illusionistic brushwork do not usually fool the eye up close: paint does not resemble glaze, however carefully it is used. It can, however, provide its own kind of delight. A reconstructed Iranian basin with luster decoration, bought from the New York dealer Hassan Khan Monif in 1961 and now in the Eskenazi Museum, shows how quietly captivating modern overpainting can be (fig. 3.21).[59] In the right half of the detail image is a large fragment of original medieval material, its crackled surface decorated with a rich, bronze-colored luster over a pitted, tin-glazed white ground. To the left, a large piece of modern fill material has been painted to continue the design across an area of major loss. The twentieth-century painter has simulated the changeable tones of luster in flat, lusterless paint by blending and shading from one color to the next through a muted rainbow of ochers, olives, and browns. At the far left of this modern section, speckles of white paint have even been used to mimic the pitting of the glaze in the original fragment, where tiny expulsions from the ceramic body disrupted the glaze and luster in firing.

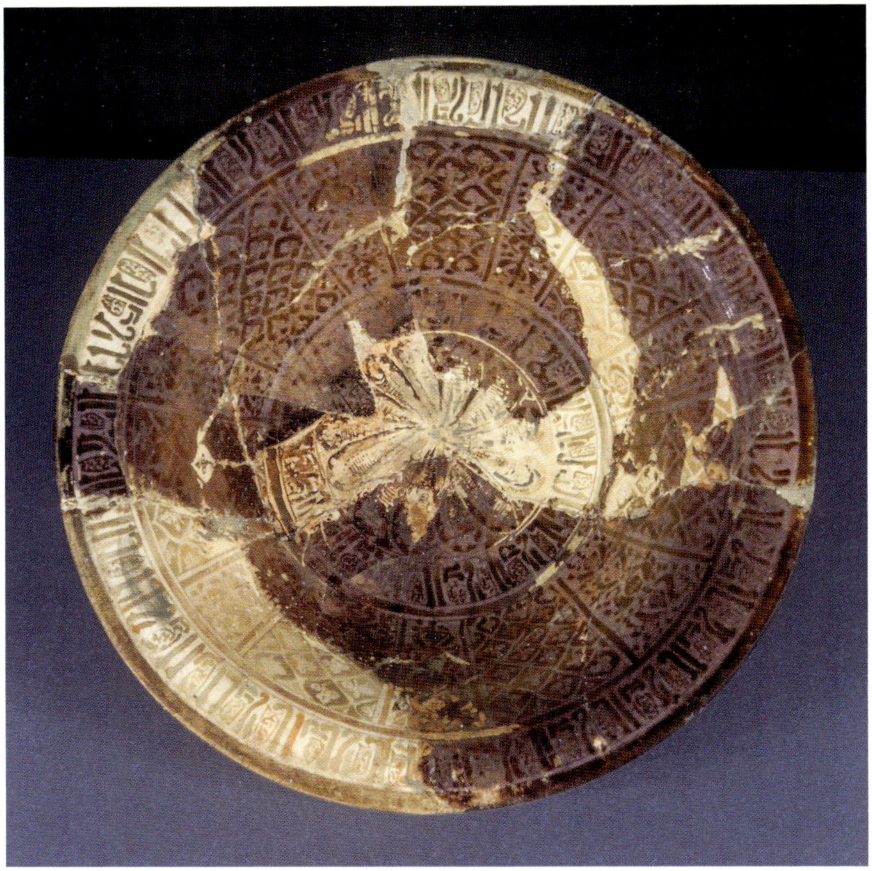

3.22. UV photograph of basin illustrated in figure 3.21. Eskenazi Museum of Art, Indiana University, 61.68.

A UV photograph of the whole basin shows all the overpainted sections fluorescing yellow, with touch-ups done on small sections of damage as well as large portions of new material replacing substantial missing sections (fig. 3.22). All of this work was probably intended to harmonize the parts with the whole more than it was to convince potential buyers that the piece was complete and unmodified, for it is hard to see how anyone used to handling and scrutinizing ceramics would fail to notice the differences in surface and finish between the original, glazed and luster-painted sections and the modern parts (although it is true that buyers have not always looked as closely as one might expect).[60] Perhaps for this very reason of tacit self-disclosure, the whole effect of the modern painting is curiously lovely. It makes visible both the care taken in the modern painting's execution and the impossibility of the painter's task, as he or she labored to make complete what cannot be completed.

In other instances, the painstaking painted mimicry of glaze evinces a desire to deceive that was demonstrably sufficient to play the market, even if it doesn't stand up to close attention. A very large slipware bowl with dark brown epigraphy on white was sold to the Cincinnati Art Museum (CAM) in 1958 by the broker Arthur Upham Pope, who, in the inflationary language so typical of his correspondence, called it a "superlative" example "from almost the peak of this great art" (fig. 3.23).[61] Things start to register as slightly off

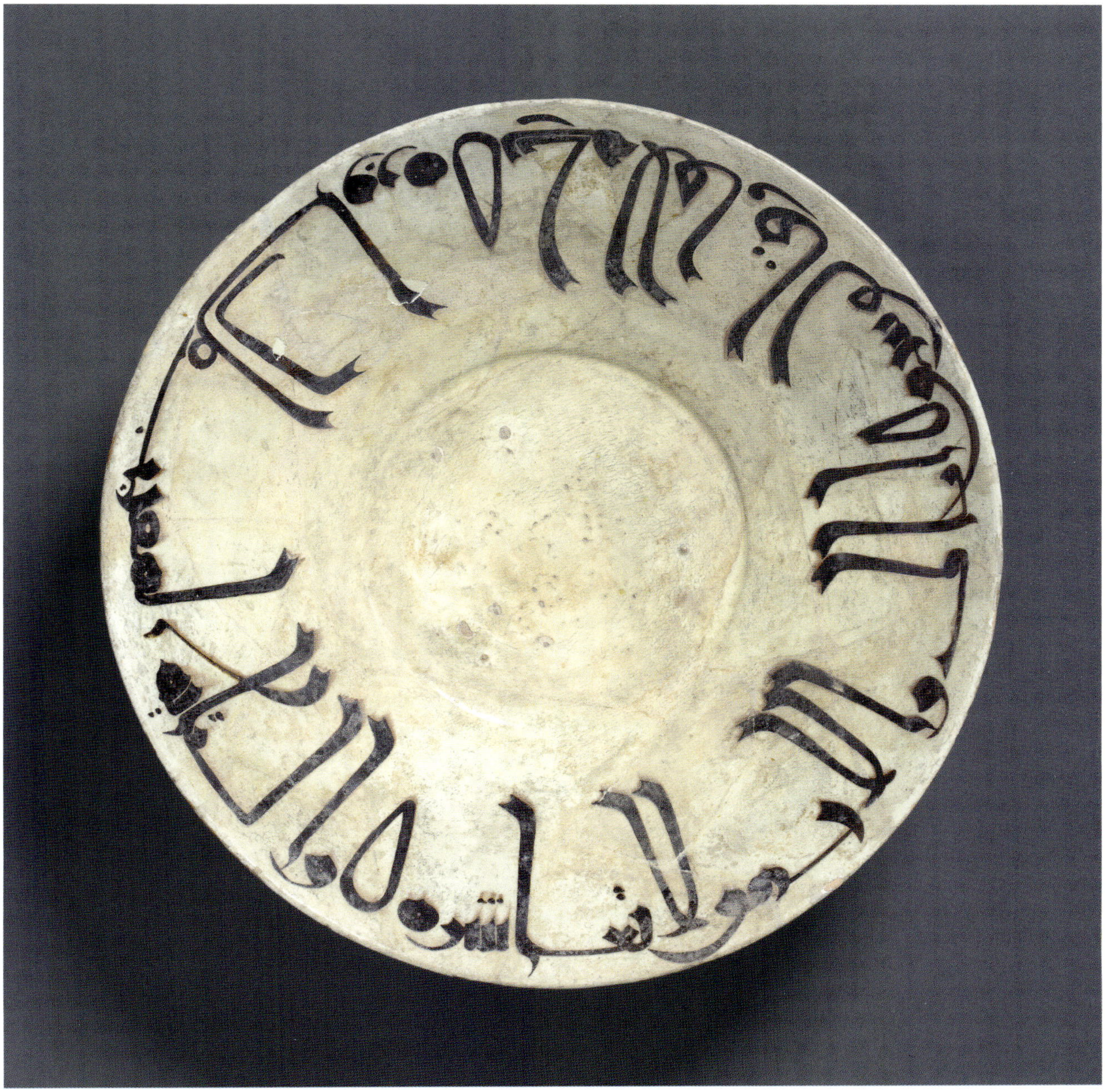

after a moment's attention. The epigraphy is similar to that seen on other examples, but the letter forms are erratic: the shafts of the uprights are more curved in some parts than others, the letter *waw* (و) is sometimes in line with the rest of the inscription but sometimes tucked under, and one truly bizarre conjunction of "letters" follows no known conventions of Arabic orthography even in the wildest reaches of this particularly difficult form of script. It is, in fact, not script at all but meaningless shapes, possibly a scrambling of the word *al-mulk* made up by someone without knowledge of Arabic (fig.3.24).[62] The matte appearance of parts of the epigraphy further signals that a significant part of the design is modern overpaint.[63] A composite X-ray of the piece

3.23. Large dish, earthenware with slip decoration under clear glaze and modern materials. Older material attributed to Central Asia, 9th or 10th century. Diameter approx. 46 cm. Cincinnati Art Museum, Museum Purchase, 1958.86.

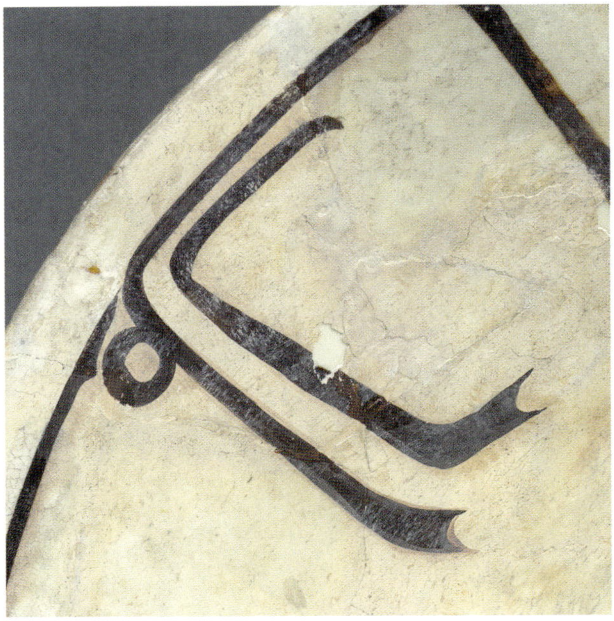

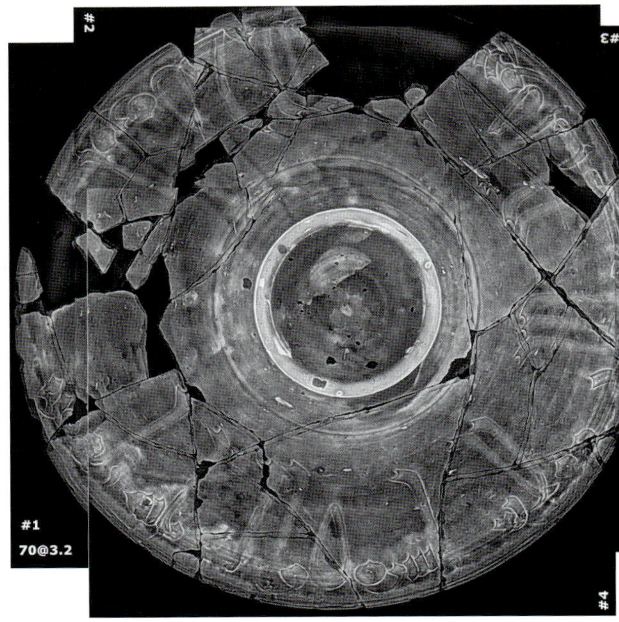

3.24. Detail of dish illustrated in figure 3.23.

3.25. X-ray of dish illustrated in figure 3.23.

reveals the fragmentary state of the underlying ceramic object, areas of modern fill showing as black spaces next to the more dense glazed and fired material, with the high-density mineral slip of the original inscription partially legible in X-ray (fig. 3.25). The inscription is not one of the more common phrases found on plates of this type and the reconstruction has garbled what is there; thus far what can be made out is likely a rhyming phrase, with sections ending *taʿasharah* and [. . .]*awara*.[64]

Despite the oddities in the epigraphy, the twentieth-century painting has been done with a skilled artist's care. In real slipware of this type, the iron and manganese oxides acting as colorants in the dark slip will bleed slightly into the clear glaze fired over the top, creating a faint "shadow" or halo around the letters that can be seen on some of the genuine parts of this dish (fig. 3.26). Compare the staining of the brown colorant into the glaze, as seen around the letters on the right of this detail, with the painted imitation of that staining seen around the fabricated letters on the left, with its slightly paler color and harder outlines.[65] In the pursuit of trompe l'oeil, the modern painter has painstakingly aped the bleed at the edges of the letters with carefully blended paintwork.[66] Meticulous attention to color and judicious sponging and speckling of the painted surface have done much to superficially blend away disjunctions between the real lead-glazed slipware fragments and the painted modern fills. Nevertheless, the material differences between these two types of surface are too great to be overcome by visual camouflage alone. Moreover, the damning inclusion of nonsensical characters shows not only that this has been heavily restored in a modern workshop, but also that it was most likely done not in Iran but in the west. It is quite possible it was restored in Paris, where Pope worked with specialists in ceramics reconstruction before shipping pieces on to the United States (see chapter 4). The sheer theatricality of this miscarried attempt to deceive the eye is a kind of heroic failure—and yet, it succeeded in floating the piece on the market in the mid twentieth century.

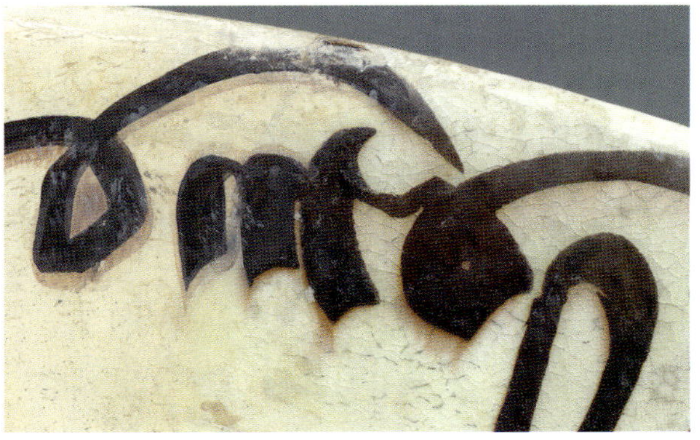

3.26. Detail of dish illustrated in figure 3.23.

Mimicking Mina'i and Populating Pots

Of all the surface upgrades encountered on medieval Islamic ceramics, the most ubiquitous are touched-up or entirely invented designs on the stonepaste mina'i wares of twelfth- to thirteenth-century Iran. Mina'i vessels are typified by a high frequency of figural imagery and a small-scale pictorial aesthetic that relates them to the contemporary arts of the illustrated manuscript.[67] (The Persian word *mina'i*, referring to the technique of enameling, is a modern label rather than a medieval term.)[68] Like lusterware, mina'i ware requires multiple firings and careful temperature control. Several colors in the original mina'i palette, including the blues, are painted into the base glaze before the first firing. After the first firing is complete, other colors—including the black used for outlining—are painted on top of the glaze and then fixed on top in another firing, this time at a lower temperature.[69] Because they sit on top of the glazed surface, the enameled colors of mina'i ware are extremely easy to mimic by painting directly onto the glazed surface of the object, with no need for a covering of varnish or resin to mimic glaze over the top. Enhanced or invented mina'i painting is certainly the best-documented and most easily identifiable mode of fabrication in all of Islamic ceramics collecting and is often used in conjunction with various forms of bricolage—including, for example, the extraordinary mosaic "sandwich" of figure 3.11.[70] Mina'i ceramics have been subject to more overpainting and invention than any other kind of ceramic in the medieval Islamic canon, and no one should ever take the iconography, design, or inscriptions of any mina'i vessel at face value without carefully examining the piece in person—and ideally, in the company of a specialized conservator.[71]

With so much of the mina'i corpus so heavily reworked, it is rare to find a piece that we can be confident represents the unmediated design practices of medieval mina'i painters. However, a relatively modest bowl in Cincinnati does just that, following a recent round of conservation that showed it was made up of many fragments from the same object, with very little loss (fig. 3.27).[72] The painting is not of the highest caliber and few of the rich overglaze colors have been used, but for once we can be sure we are looking at something very like the original appearance of the whole object. The arrangement of the compositional elements across the concave surface has a rhythmic lightness often lacking in the overpainted pieces; here there is enough

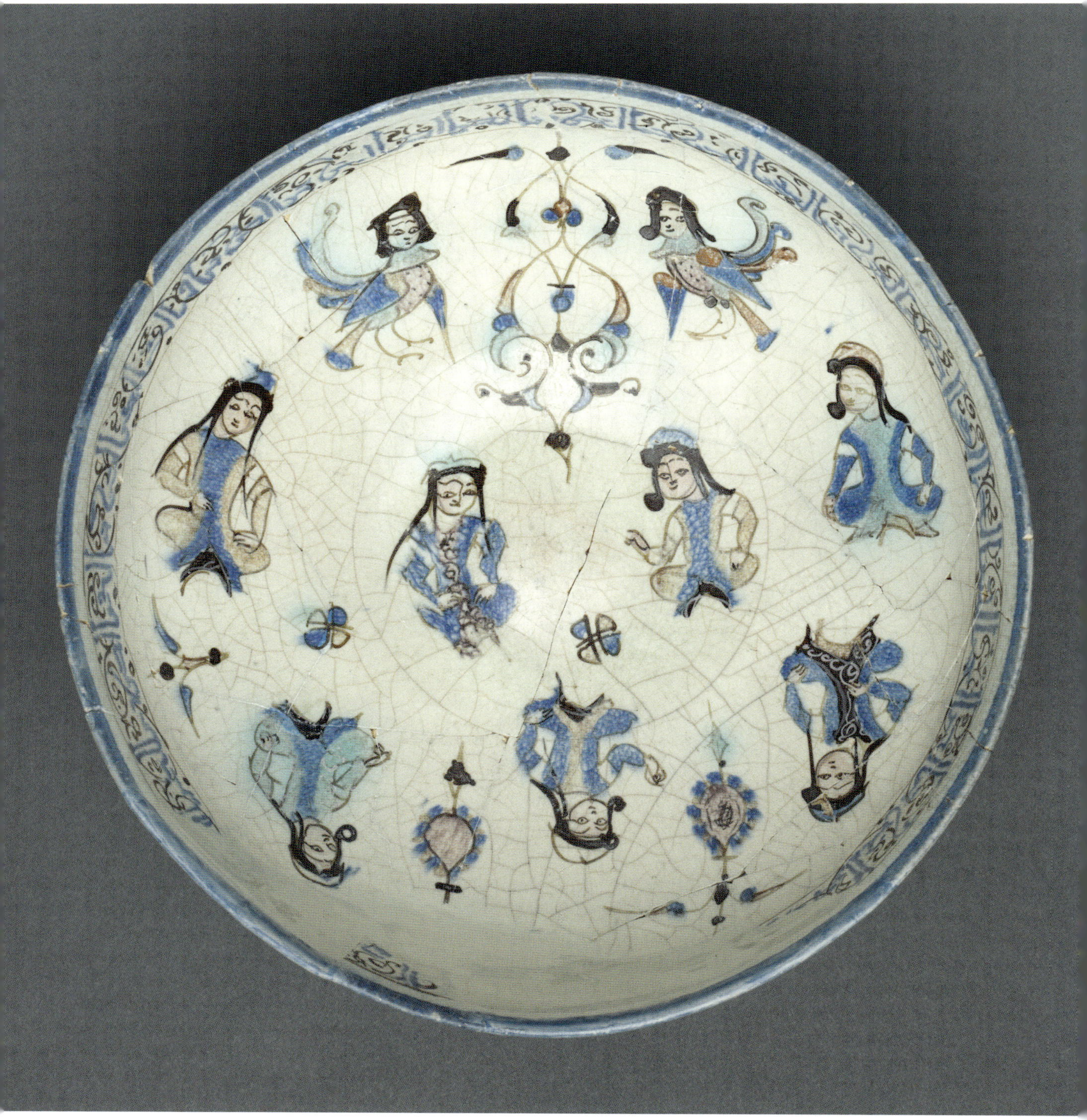

3.27. Bowl, glazed stonepaste with in-glaze and overglaze colors (so-called mina'i ware), after recent conservation. Attributed Iran, second half of the 12th century or early 13th century. Cincinnati Art Museum, Given in honor of Mr. and Mrs. Charles F. Williams by their children, 1948.109.

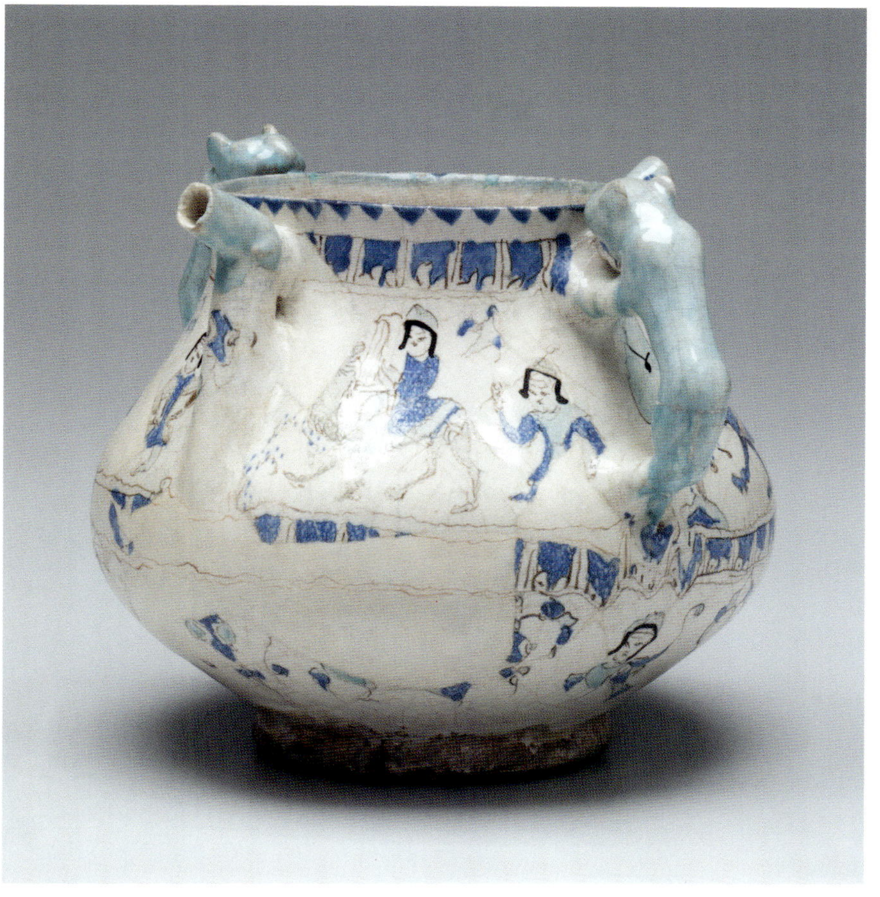

3.28. Spouted pot, glazed stonepaste with in-glaze and overglaze colors (so-called minaʾi ware); the blank areas are modern conservation work where the original material was absent. Attributed Iran, second half of the 12th century or early 13th century. Height 20.3 cm. Toledo Museum of Art, 1941.14.

space between the individual figures and elements to create balance, and a comfort with the idea of rotation and figures in multiple orientations. Sometimes, however, things didn't go to plan even for the medieval potters. A handled jar in the Toledo Museum of Art, now cleaned of its twentieth-century overpainting, is an object lesson in the challenges of kiln control that faced the original minaʾi potters (fig. 3.28).[73] Here, the second firing must have been at slightly too high a temperature: the glaze has started to melt in the kiln, pulling the painted designs down with it.

Rare pieces like the Cincinnati bowl give a true sense of the scale and artistry of what Vignier described as the "endless little figures in *décalcomanie*" of minaʾi, those repeating figural types that are so fungible and therefore lend themselves so well to bricolaging together unrelated sherds to make new wholes.[74] To do an upgrade in the style of minaʾi painting, the modern painter could improvise upon various well-worn themes seen on the original fragments—horsemen, musicians, harpies, sphinxes, trees, couples, and endless seated drinkers—or launch more ambitious programs of copying and invention drawn from published vessels or other sources.[75] There is a full spectrum of ability evident across all the modern minaʾi overpainting now in museum collections and in truth, it is hard to ever be sure precisely what you are looking at, even on the collected sherds. Most collected minaʾi wares are confusing composites of multiple vessels and old and new painting that

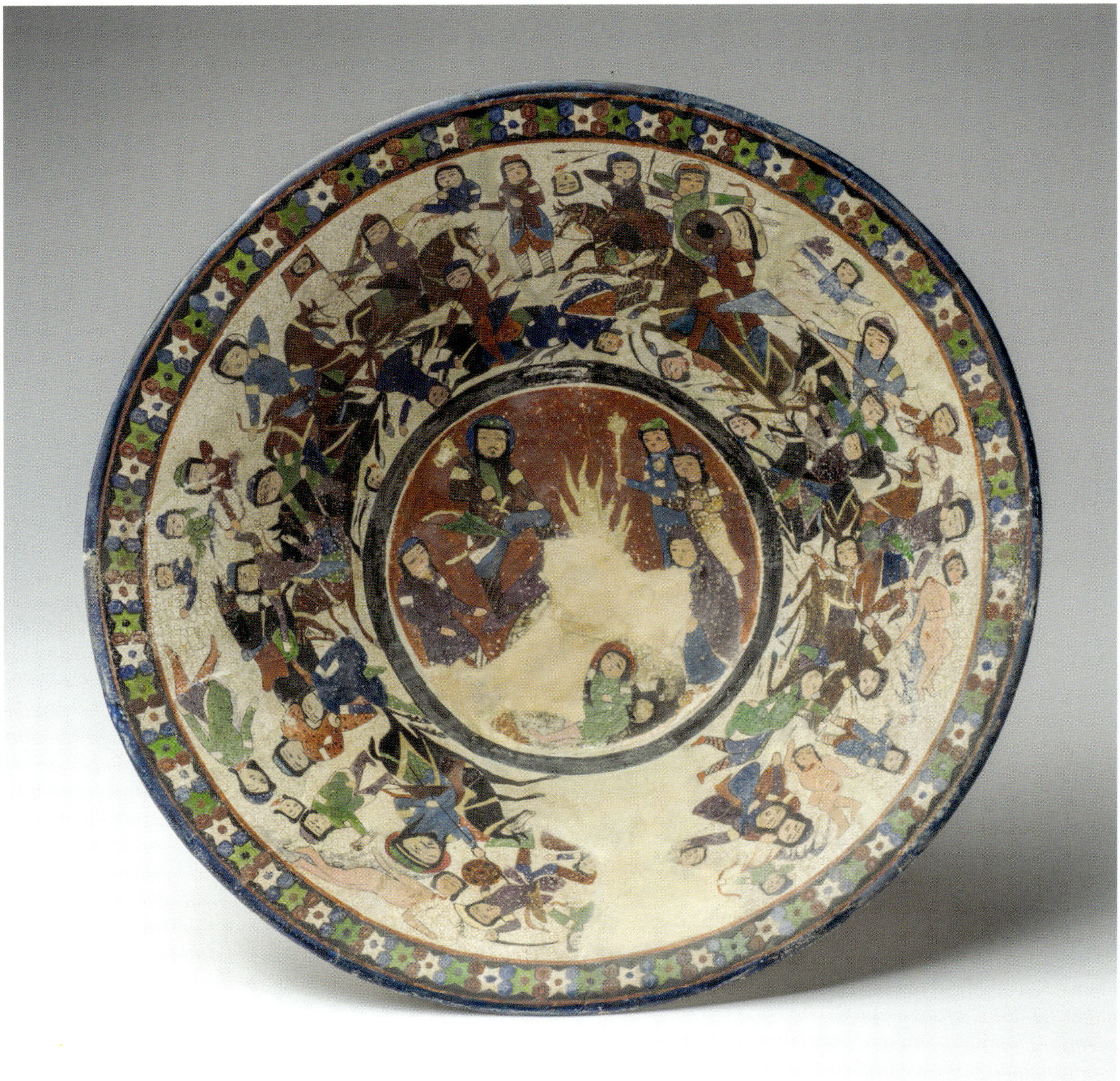

3.29. Bowl with modern imitation of so-called mina'i ware designs. Diameter 40 cm. Museum für Islamische Kunst, I. 14/64.

require laboratory imaging for their techniques of reinvention to be properly understood.

The wholesale fabrication of entire decorative schema is rare but not unheard of, with a large bowl in the Museum für Islamische Kunst in Berlin apparently representing just that (fig. 3.29). Acquired in 1964 from "R. Schnyder" in Zurich (this must be Rudolf Schnyder, curator at the Swiss National Museum and president of the Académie Internationale de la Céramique), it has an extraordinarily dense interior scheme of pictorial decoration.[76] A battle scene rages around the interior walls, with severed heads rolling into every available space like marbles. Its closest cognate in design is the heavily restored "siege plate" acquired by the Freer Gallery from Dikran Kelekian in

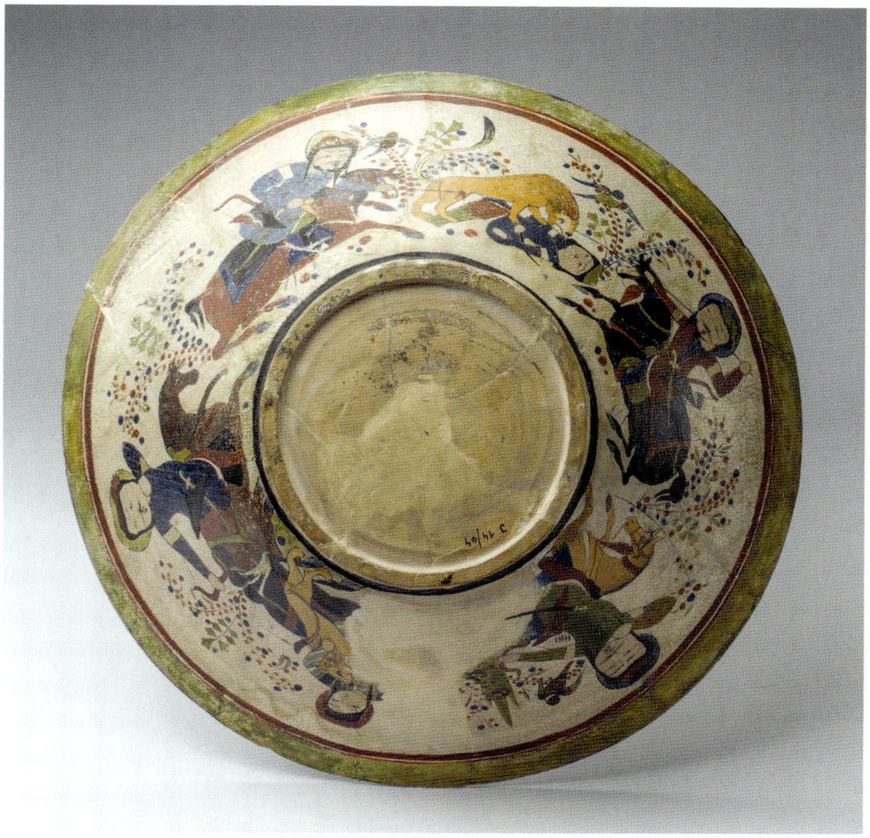

3.30. Underside of bowl illustrated in figure 3.29.

1943, but the Berlin bowl has a much greater density of overlapping among the riders on its crowded walls.[77] The copyist's model here seems to be manuscript painting, primarily, rather than ceramic arts. At the base of the bowl, surrounded by all this violence, is a damaged narrative roundel on a red background that illustrates the *Shahnama* story of the princess Manizeh lighting a fire to guide the hero Rustam (here holding a rather broken-necked ox-headed mace) so he can rescue her love Bizhan from an underground pit.[78] This depiction resembles paintings of the scene found in manuscripts from the fifteenth century onward much more than it resembles anything from the late twelfth- to early thirteenth-century era of mina'i painting.[79]

The outside of the Berlin bowl departs even further from the norms of mina'i decoration, with oversize figures riding and hunting, while a lion mauls a felled man (fig. 3.30).[80] There are some semiprecedents for such figures—the exterior walls of the Freer "siege plate," with large-scale hunting men, animals, and trees, are again the closest point of comparison—but the drawing and palette of the Berlin bowl, with its lime greens, harsh reds, and buttercup yellows, leave little doubt that the design is a modern concoction.[81] The paints show every bump, pit, and crackle of the surface underneath, rather than forming their own discrete surfaces the way enameled glaze colors do in a second firing. Furthermore, blue colors that would normally be fixed into the glaze in the first firing have here been painted over the fired surface, and the entire palette runs completely out of sync with the chromatic range of genuine medieval mina'i painting.[82] Oddly, accession notes record that the bowl was reconstructed from fragments by a Herr Karl in 1963–64, prior to its accession to the museum.[83] Everything about this piece indicates that it is a modern design painted onto an old, reconstructed bowl.

The disjunctive modern pictorial program of the Berlin bowl, conjoining a chaotic, continuous battle scene with a self-contained *Shahnama* episode and large-scale images of the hunt, suggests the painter was drawing on a range of published sources to generate a composite schema oriented toward a market primed on manuscript paintings. This would fit with its possible execution toward the middle of the twentieth century, by which point a wide range of Islamic art publications were available as source material. Most published images at that date were in black and white, however, and the color images available were often chromatically quite askew from reality, which might explain the off-kilter palette of virtually all the painting on the Berlin bowl. The coloration throughout the whole design suggests it was painted by someone whose familiarity with real mina'i ceramic material was limited—or at least, they didn't have real examples in front of them during execution, only bookplates of manuscript illustrations and ceramics. In this way, the oft-noted close relationship between mina'i painting and book illustration in the medieval period has redounded all the way into the twentieth century.[84]

Most cases of fabrication on mina'i wares are not as simple as painting on a whole new scene. The last mina'i piece to be discussed in this section is one of the most fascinating and perplexing artifacts of this marketplace: a handled cup, now in the CAM and formerly part of the Kelekian collection at the V&A (fig. 3.31). It is a finely potted stonepaste vessel, with beautiful fingertip traces inside from turning on the wheel (see fig. 2.28). It has been rebuilt from fragments that seem to come mostly from one original object, with much of the lower section complete. The cup entered the V&A in 1912, and its entry in the loan records was accompanied, quite unusually, by a thumbnail sketch (fig. 3.32). The decoration of the upper part of the cup is quite standard, with the usual little beardless seated figures in patterned robes and caps, one of whom plays a harp that has not been completed with strings.[85] As we would expect, the overglaze decoration was enhanced for the market prior to its arrival at the V&A. A 1989 conservation report in Cincinnati notes that the white designs on the robes, the gold leaf squares on the armbands, and at least some of the black outlining have all been touched up and strengthened in the modern era, with very good draftsmanship. The same report observes that the black substance used for retouching the outlining is remarkably similar to the original black overglaze painting, even under magnification, but is slowly soluble in ethanol.[86]

So far it's business as usual for collected mina'i wares, but things get stranger below. The thumbnail sketch does not include them but the 1912 loan entry notes that "[r]ound the lower part of the body are two figures in black outline."[87] In fact, as well as two complete figures in outline (fig. 3.33), there are also traces of the outlined head of another figure and the feet of a walking animal (which would have been upside down when the cup was right way up); these have been almost entirely cleaned off the surface (fig. 3.34). The erasure of the animal and the third figure must have occurred prior to 1912, since they aren't mentioned on the loan entry at the V&A. The black substance used to paint the surviving outline figures is rather thick and stands proud of the

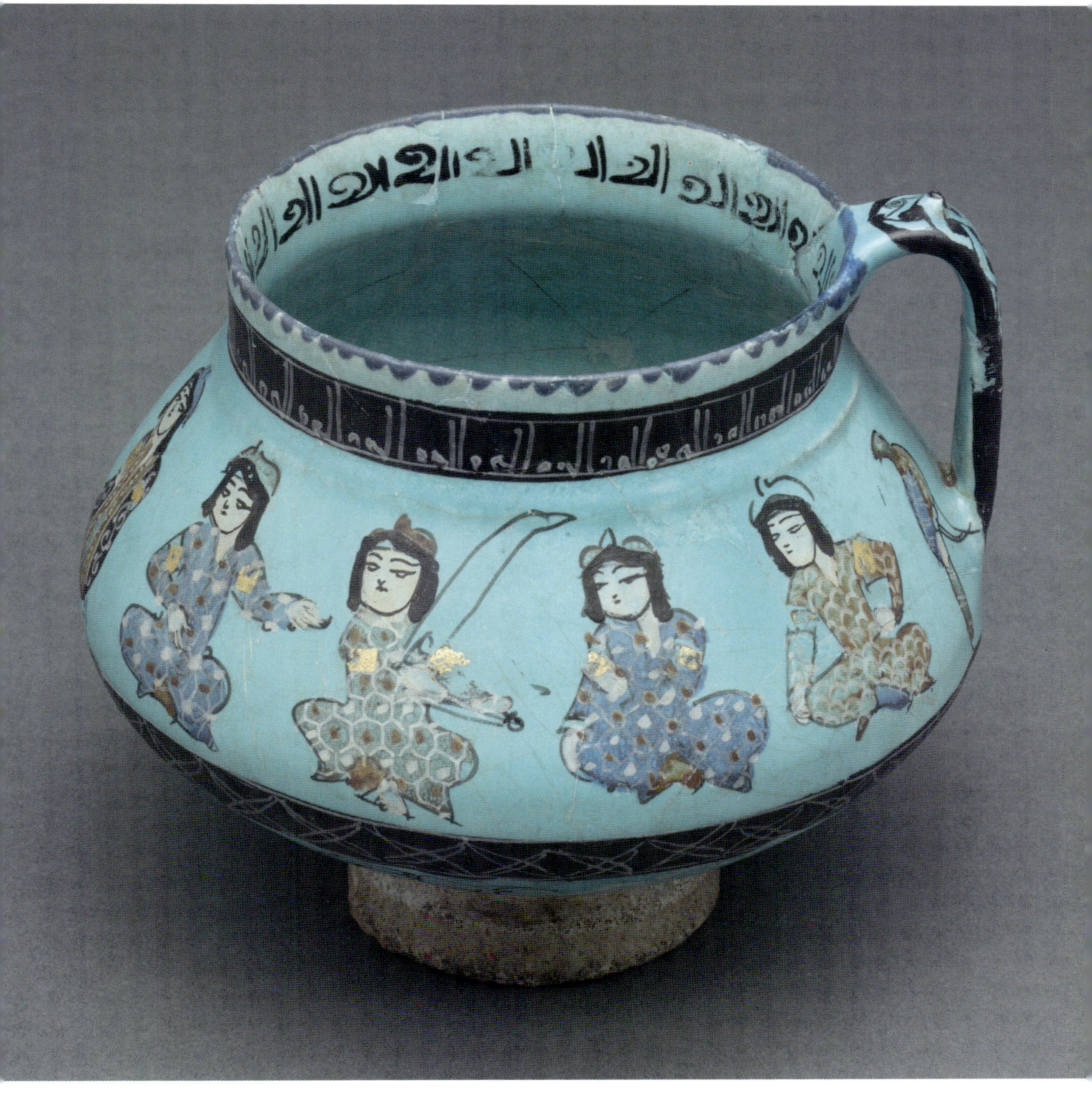

3.31. Handled jar, glazed stonepaste with in-glaze and overglaze colors and modern over-painting (so-called mina'i ware). Attributed Iran, late 12th–early 13th century. Height approx. 14 cm. Cincinnati Art Museum, Museum Purchase, 1952.256.

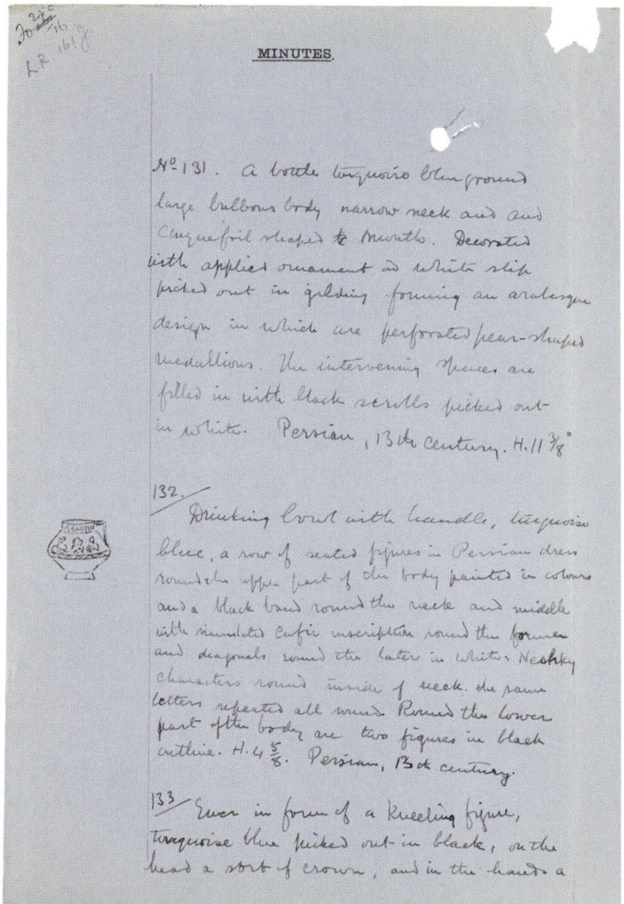

MINUTES.

No. 131. A bottle turquoise blue ground large bulbous body narrow neck and and cinquefoil shaped the mouth. Decorated with applied ornament in white slip picked out in gilding forming an arabesque design in which are perforated pear-shaped medallions. The intervening spaces are filled in with black scrolls picked out in white. Persian, 13th century. H. 11 3/8"

132. Drinking bowl with handle, turquoise blue, a row of seated figures in Persian dress round the upper part of the body painted in colours and a black band round the neck and middle with simulated Cufic inscription round the former and diagonals round the latter in white. Neskhy characters round inside of neck. the same letters repeated all round. Round the lower part of the body are two figures in black outline. H. 4 5/8. Persian, 13th century.

133 Ewer in form of a kneeling figure, turquoise blue picked out in black, on the head a sort of crown, and in the hands a

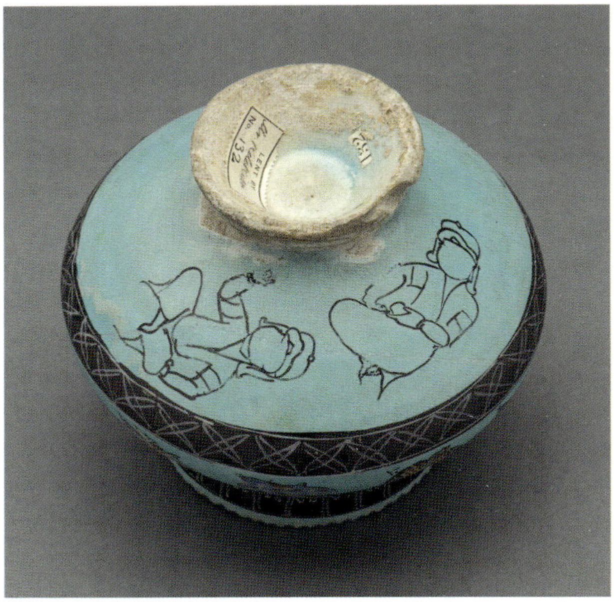

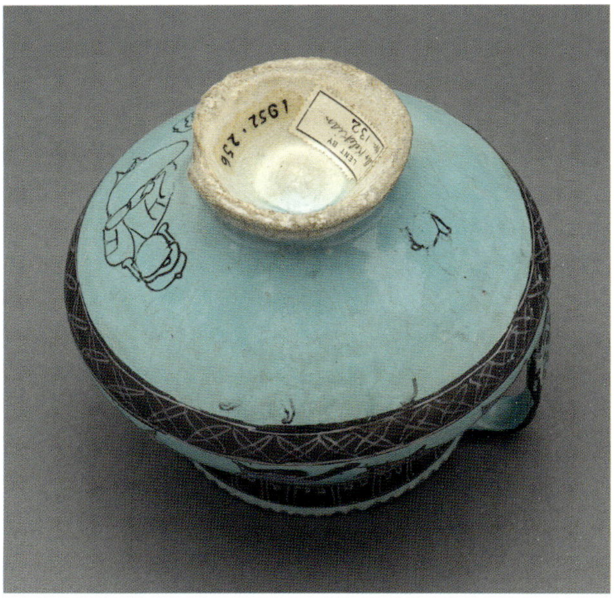

3.32. Loan approval form dated 16 July 1912, showing thumbnail sketch of handled jar illustrated in figure 3.31. V&A archive, Nominal File: Kelekian 1892–1912.

3.33. Detail of handled jar illustrated in figure 3.31.

3.34. Detail of handled jar illustrated in figure 3.31.

surface, with a shinier, more textured appearance than the usual chromium oxide blacks used in minaʾi overglaze outlining.[88] Black overglaze components are the last stage of minaʾi painting, not the first, and here the black outlines continue right over a long, overpainted join running across the lower body of the cup. Their origins therefore must lie in modernity rather than medieval manufacture. But why are they there at all?

The two surviving outline figures on the lower part of the cup carefully mimic the standard figural types seen on medieval minaʾi, including the characteristic caps and bobbed hair. Although they are out of scale and orientation with the figures above, they are nonetheless well observed and very practiced imitations of the minaʾi figural type. It seems that someone in the modern era, prior to 1912, started the work of adding more figural decoration to the mina'i object. This was presumably intended to enhance its value by upping the figural content. A second possible interpretation is that this piece was used as a practice surface by a modern painter, but given the object's saleability, this seems less likely. For some unknown reason, at any rate, the painter did not try to finish their work, and indeed some of it was deliberately obliterated. Perhaps the painters of the unknown workshop lost confidence as they realized the out-of-orientation and out-of-scale figures were going to look rather implausible, however good the draftsmanship. How and why one human figure and an animal were largely erased, while the other two figures were not, remains a mystery. Nonetheless, two things are particularly striking here. One is the notably high level of skill evident in these imitations of mina'i figures, and the other is the early date at which this work was done.

Watson has shown that European collectors were slower to develop a taste for mina'i wares than for Iranian luster vessels, which were being excavated from the same sites as mina'i wares. Luster vessels as well as tiles were being quite assiduously collected by private individuals by the 1880s, and subsequently entering museum collections.[89] The V&A's first acquisition of a mina'i vessel, on the other hand, was not until 1909 (as opposed to mina'i sherds, which were making their way into institutional collections by the 1880s and 1890s).[90] No further mina'i vessels were purchased by the museum until the end of World War I, after which a steadier flow started to come in. Watson traced a similar pattern in the British Museum's acquisition records for medieval Iranian ceramics.[91] This assessment of institutional mina'i acquisition, however, doesn't include the mina'i pieces that entered the V&A through the Kelekian loan, including this cup in 1912. Being a loan rather than a purchase, it doesn't show up in the purchase ledgers, but Kelekian's Islamic ceramics collection and its loan to the V&A represent an important public display of medieval Islamic ceramics and indeed played a major role in the formation of a scholarly and commercial canon for this material (see chapter 4).[92] In a market that was rapidly expanding when this cup was moving through it in the run-up to 1912, skilled copyists were already perfecting—with a quite startling degree of finesse—their imitations of the "endless little figures in *décalcomanie*" with which they would populate a whole world of reconstituted mina'i vessels for sale to eager collectors.

New Skins, New Topographies

Modern overpaint on top of an original glazed and fired piece is the most obvious kind of surface upgrade on ceramics that have been through the antiquities market, and mina'i wares are the paradigmatic example of such painted embellishment. But all sorts of other skins have also been applied to reconstructed ceramics, including all the glossy resurfacing provided by varnishes and waxes. Mixed with colors, varnishes could be used to paint a shiny design onto an area of new-made fill; when left clear, they were used to cover entire restored objects, blending away cracks and masking variations between original glazed surfaces and matte, porous new ones.[93] Any form of varnish used to simulate glaze poses major challenges for the craftsman, though. Spirit varnishes made with alcohol dry quickly and set hard and clear but are difficult to

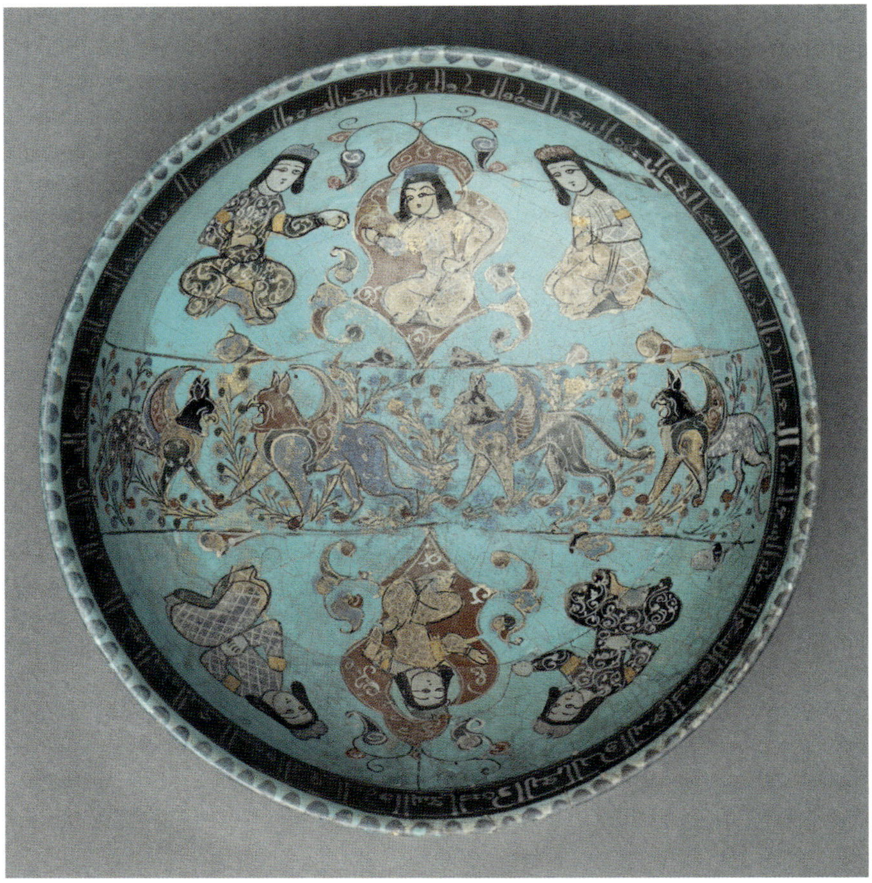

3.35. Bowl, glazed stonepaste with in-glaze and overglaze colors and modern material (so-called mina'i ware). Central section attributed Iran, late 12th or early 13th century. Diameter approx. 15.5 cm. Cincinnati Art Museum, Given in honor of Mr. and Mrs. Charles F. Williams by their children, 1948.104.

work with and have an annoying tendency to retain brushstrokes, thus making them easily identifiable as varnish rather than vitrified glaze. Oil-based copal (tree resin) varnish and shellac (made from insect secretions) can be built up in thin layers and worked with a brush, but they veer toward yellowish or brown tints and are rarely completely colorless.[94] Many kinds of varnish were in widespread manufacture by the late nineteenth century, including proprietorial brands sometimes named in ceramic restoration manuals, such as those manufactured by the Soehnée Frères.[95]

Moreover, all varnishes behave very differently from glaze as they age. Where a varnish once presented a shiny, clear surface, it might, decades later, have become yellowed, opacified, or even partially detached from the object. A turquoise mina'i dish in Cincinnati, bought from Dikran Kelekian in 1948, gives a case in point (fig. 3.35). The base of the object is one large continuous central well of medieval turquoise glazed stonepaste, but the upper sides and rim—almost the entire upper third or so of the bowl—are new-made, with the designs on the original fragment skillfully continued into the new areas by a modern hand.[96] In the original section of the bowl, a layer of gum arabic or some other kind of organic varnish seems to have been painted with precision over every part of the original painted design. Over time this shiny substance has become iridescent and yellowed, almost like an onion skin, forming a visible layer that is now lifting away from the painted design. What once presumably blended old and new surfaces harmoniously by putting an artificial gloss on the old enamels to match the sheen of the new paint, giving pleasure to a delighted purchaser, now makes a conservator's hair stand on end.

Along with all the shiny accretions of varnish, modeled relief work provides yet another means of resurfacing fractured objects, very often going hand in hand with modern gilding and shiny finishes. In real mina'i sherds bearing genuine medieval relief work, the raised designs were made from a paste that is compositionally very similar to the stonepaste of the underlying ceramic body. They were formed from a malleable slip made by adding some liquid to the paste used for making the vessel, which was then piped onto the surface of the vessel (a technique known as barbotine or slip trailing). In those genuine examples, the relief work is modeled fairly low to create subtle raised designs and is applied over the base glaze on the body before being covered in glaze itself.[97] Obviously, simulating the raised designs of relief work creates yet another opportunity for the modern fabricator to cover cracks and disjunctions while adding glamour to the object. As a result, the surfaces of medieval Iranian vessels have been built up with modern relief work ranging from the modest to the very extravagant.

At the relatively restrained end of the spectrum, images taken before and after the 1991–92 conservation of a pitcher in the Toledo Museum show how an unusual vessel with some low relief work and partial glazing was glammed up in the early twentieth-century restoration workshop.[98] Prior to its first publication in the Parish-Watson catalogue of 1922 (fig. 3.36), the pitcher had been reconstructed from fragments and overlaid with additional projecting bosses (probably skimmed from other medieval fragments), squares of gilding, and overpainting, the whole thing then being covered with a resinous

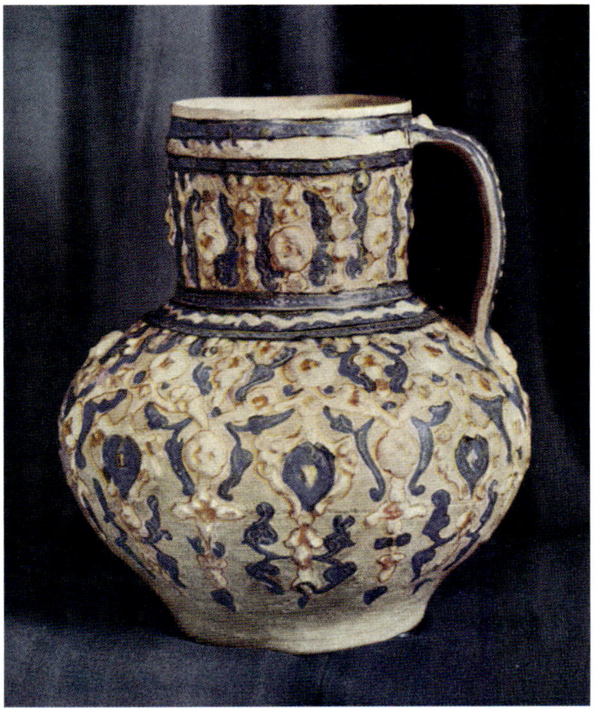

3.36. Handled jar now in Toledo, shown prior to conservation. After Rudolf Meyer Riefstahl, *The Parish-Watson Collection of Mohammadan Potteries* (New York: E. Weyhe, 1922), p. 183.

varnish. Fast-forward to the 1990s, when much of the modern material was removed in a conservation campaign. What was left after the modern restorations were removed is a more modest—if still very unusual and interesting—vessel, highly fractured and with some parts missing (fig. 3.37). Postconservation, the piece provides us with a rare window onto an unusual medieval decorative technique of partial glazing, where a design has been painted onto the bare surface of the vessel using glaze as if it were paint—in this case in white and cobalt blue—while leaving the rest of the surface unglazed before firing.[99] In its early twentieth-century incarnation, prior to the 1990s conservation work, it must have been a tour de force of modern resurfacing.[100]

Similar modern relief work has also been identified on Iranian vessels in the Metropolitan Museum, the most elaborate being a basin with pierced bosses, gilding, and mina'i-style painting formerly in the Robert Lehmann collection (fig. 3.38).[101] A sample taken from the handle of this last proved it to be made of earthenware rather than stonepaste and TL testing in 2009

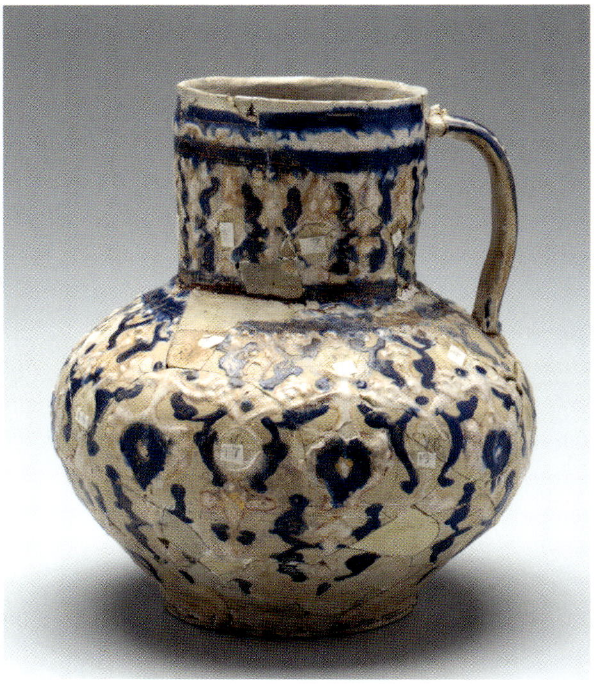

3.37. Handled jar, partially glazed stonepaste with barbotine decoration, after conservation. Attributed Iran, possibly 12th century. Height 16.5 cm. Toledo Museum of Art, 1941.15.

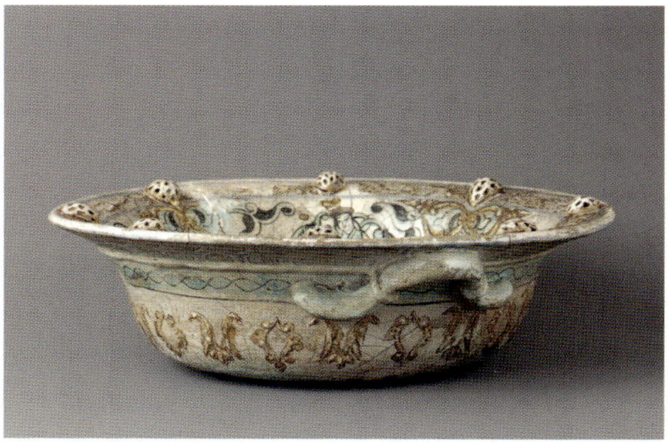

3.38. Basin, glazed with gilding and enameling. Attributed early 20th century. Diameter 28.5 cm. The Metropolitan Museum of Art, Robert Lehman Collection, 1975.1.1641.

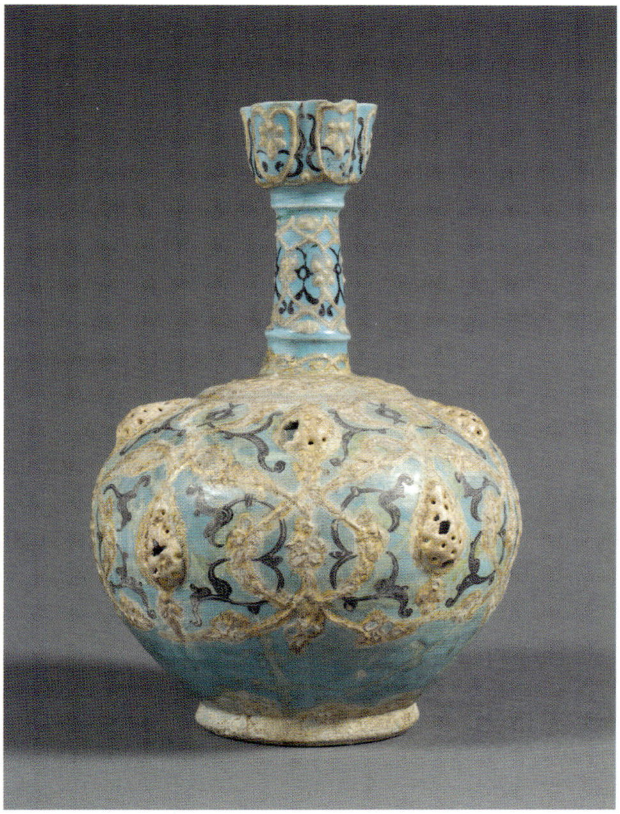

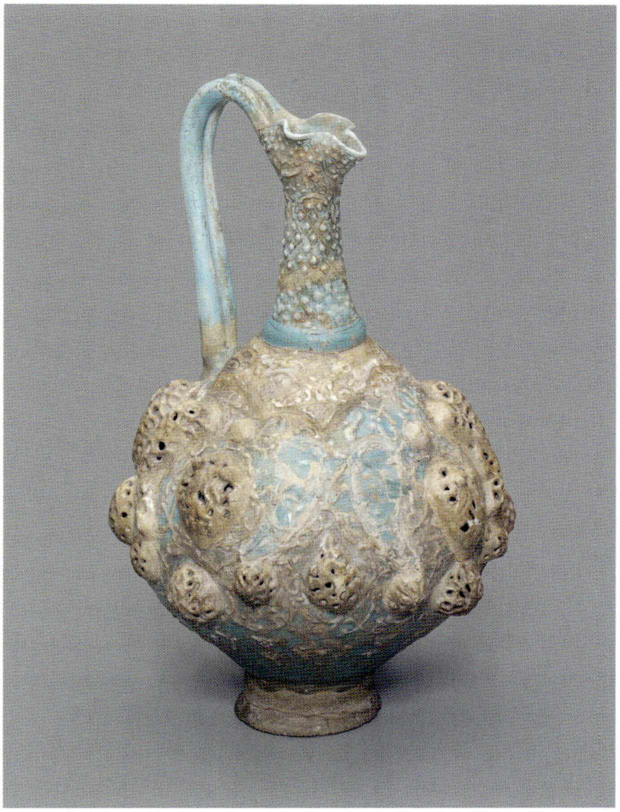

gave a date of last firing within the last hundred years, suggesting some or all of the piece could be a modern fabrication (depending on whether or not the rest of the body was made from the same material as the sampled handle).[102] Elaborate pierced projecting bosses like those seen on the basin are yet to be attested on archaeological material, as far as I am aware. And yet, they appear not only on this basin but also across a group of extraordinarily elaborate bottles and spouted cups held in various collections, encrusting them with perforated projections like egg cases or tumorous growths.[103] One bottle of this type was lodged at the V&A by Dikran Kelekian in 1912 (fig. 3.39), eventually making its way to Cincinnati.[104] Examination under UV light reveals a fluorescing substance running along many joins and visible around the edges of all the perforated bosses, strongly suggesting that the latter were all glued on in the modern era. It's quite possible that none of the bosses are original to the object. The entire neck is also made from a different material and seems to be a modern attachment. A related piece gifted to the Yale University Art Gallery in 1953, reportedly from the Parish-Watson holdings, also seems to have a modern neck, and moreover exhibits particularly extreme symptoms of this type of resurfacing. A rash of gilded accretions completely obscures the condition of the underlying bottle, with its bumpy neck and faux-riveted handle (fig. 3.40).[105] The decoration of the Kelekian bottle is rather simpler than that of the Yale piece, and probably represents an earlier experiment with this particular type of market-oriented upgrade.[106]

Those two are by no means the only examples: a third such bottle is illustrated in the catalogue for the famous exhibition of Islamic art held in Munich

3.39. Bottle, glazed stonepaste(?) with modern materials and gilding. Height approx. 28 cm. Cincinnati Art Museum, Museum Purchase, 1952.257.

3.40. Bottle, glazed stonepaste(?) with modern materials and gilding. Height 27.94 cm. Yale University Art Gallery, 1953.24.5, Gift of Wilson P. Foss, Jr., Ph.B. 1913.

in 1910 (it was in the possession of Fritz Gans in Frankfurt at the time); a fourth entered the Parish-Watson collection by 1922; and a fifth was acquired by the Berlin museums in 1935 from the collection of the Dresdner Bank.[107] Clearly there was a strong flow of such pieces through the early twentieth-century market, and the ingenuity of modern restorers had successfully created a new class of ceramic. The point of all the gilded excrescences on these bottles is, presumably, to dazzle the eye and cover up all the joins and fill. However glitzy the effects, it is not so very different from the time-honored tactic of gluing the dirt and muck of a theatricalized "excavation" to bricolaged vessels to conceal their mismatched parts.[108]

Reglazing and Refiring

Without doubt, the most extreme form of resurfacing found on collected ceramics from the Islamic world is the heavy-duty intervention of reglazing and refiring to put more elaborate new designs onto plainer, original ceramics. In chapter 2 we already saw the ingenuity with which the so-called Garrus wares were cut with new designs, glazed and fired anew to be launched onto the market as exotic documents of a fire-worshipping past on the shores of the Caspian. It has been possible in that case to reconstruct in some detail how the modern work was done through conservation analysis and comparison with archaeological materials. However, other interventions of this type are often much harder to parse. Without completely dismantling the object, it is sometimes impossible to tell how a modern upgrade was done—even when it is quite clear that something *has* been done.

A bowl of a different sort presents an odd set of puzzles to close this section (figs. 3.41 and 3.42). It has a checkered history on the art market. At one point it was in the Dumbarton Oaks collection in Washington, DC, having been bought by collectors Mildred and Robert Woods Bliss from Dikran Kelekian in 1932, but they sold it back to Kelekian in 1946—who then sold it on to Cincinnati as part of a large group the museum acquired in 1948.[109] Perched

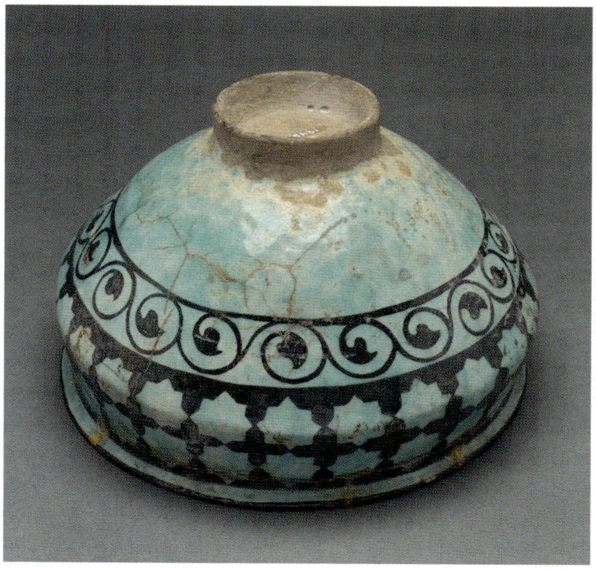

3.41. Bowl imitating so-called black-under-turquoise ware. Possibly medieval ceramic fragments with modern glazing, painted design early 20th century. Diameter approx. 24 cm. Cincinnati Art Museum, Given in honor of Mr. and Mrs. Charles F. Williams by their children, 1948.98.

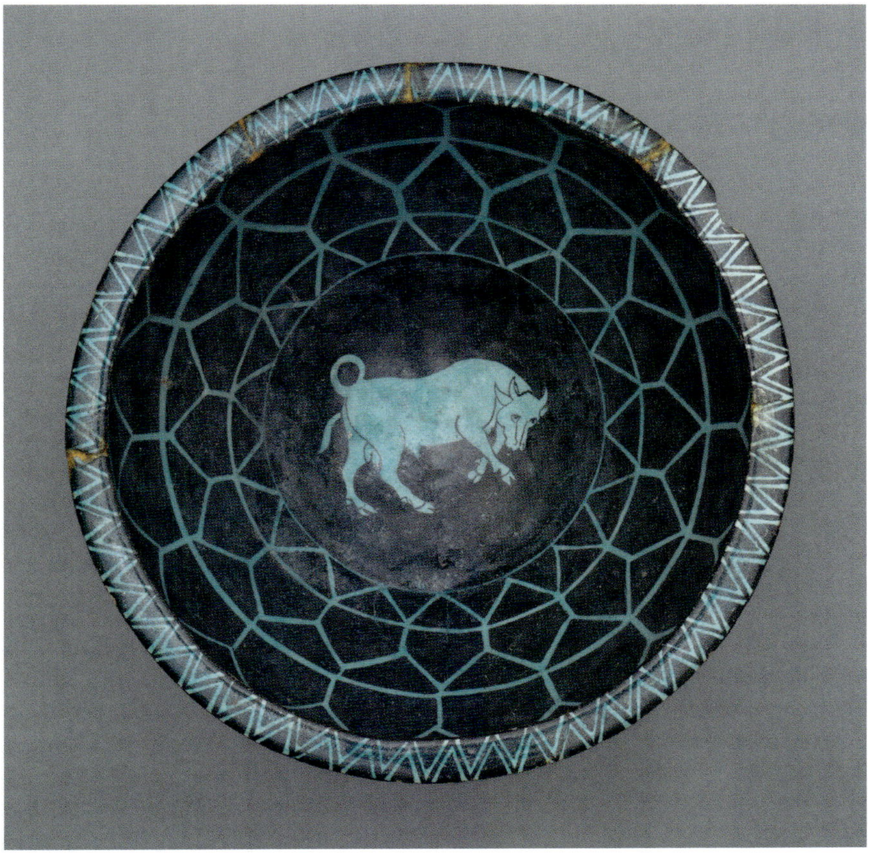

3.42. Interior view of bowl illustrated in figure 3.41.

on an awkwardly small foot, the whole bowl has an extremely strange surface, superficially smooth but full of unevennesses below the outer layer, like a lumpy bedspread. To the touch, it feels as if it has been put together from fragments, then covered in a thick coating of strange, fondant-like glaze that has crawled and split in places. TL testing in the 1970s gave inconclusive results; another TL sample taken in the 1980s indicated that the foot was last fired between 120 and 190 years prior.[110] With the object seemingly composed of fragments, it is hard to draw many conclusions from TL testing. There is a possibility that the odd effects of the glaze have been produced through glazing and refiring at a low temperature, which can also lead to ambiguous results in TL testing.

The oddities of the surface decoration on this bowl provide more scope for speculation. The black and turquoise design is presumably supposed to ape the so-called silhouette wares of twelfth-century Iran. In real silhouette wares, the unglazed vessel was covered in a black slip layer that the artist then cut designs through, down to the light surface of the stonepaste body, thereby creating white-against-black motifs before the whole piece was covered with a transparent turquoise glaze and fired, rendering the white parts of the design turquoise in the finished piece.[111] Here, though, all of the black components of the design have been painted *on top of* the opaque, sugar-pasty turquoise layer, before it was fired. The design on the outside of the bowl looks strikingly modernist, a solid/void pattern derived from "star-and-cross" tile

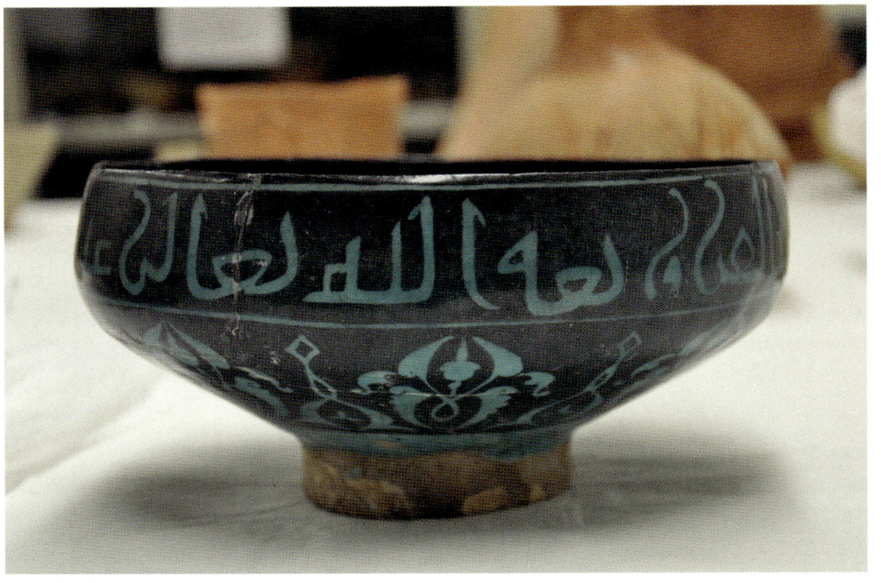

3.43. Bowl imitating so-called black-under-turquoise ware. Possibly medieval ceramic fragments with modern glazing, painted design early 20th century. Museum für Islamische Kunst, I.4643.

friezes of Mongol Iran but stripped down to the simplest graphic elements in black and reserve, over a very even, very slowly executed rinceau (fig. 3.41).[112] The inside, meanwhile, is decorated with a line drawing of an elegant bull in reserve who would be at home on the pages of a 1920s issue of *The New Yorker*, set inside concentric rings of geometric shapes in decreasing scale.[113] The net result is a schema that now signals not so much "medieval Iran" as "skilled early twentieth-century design trying to signal medieval Iran."

I have found one other bowl that seems to have been produced in the same technique, bought by Friedrich Sarre from Hassan Khan Monif in 1925 and now in the Museum für Islamische Kunst in Berlin (fig. 3.43). Like the bull bowl in Cincinnati, the black design of the piece in Berlin has been painted on top of a fondant-like turquoise glaze with a somewhat weighty and distinctively modern graphic elegance. The impression of careful modern copying is especially evident in the external band of epigraphy that includes, very unusually, the name of Allah, along with other words and fragments copied from an as-yet unidentified source. The stylized Kufic script, proportions of the letters, and inclusion of "Allah" suggest the copyist was probably working from reproductions of early architectural inscriptions, ponderously transplanting their monumentality to a ceramic context.

Like the forged "Botticelli" Madonna that passed muster in the early 1930s but now seems laughable, with its Jean Harlow eyebrows and sulky starlet pout from the silent movie era (fig. 3.44), the bowls in Berlin and Cincinnati attest to the stubborn persistence of the early twentieth century present in the artifacts of a fabricated past.[114] The aesthetics of the era in which a deception was produced will often be manifest in the product of that deception in ways that are apparently invisible at the time but become increasingly obvious decades—or sometimes even just years—later. As Emil Hannover noted in his observations on ceramics forgery in the 1920s, "no one can copy a historical style without unconsciously adulterating it more or less with the idea of that style current in his own time."[115] The same has been observed

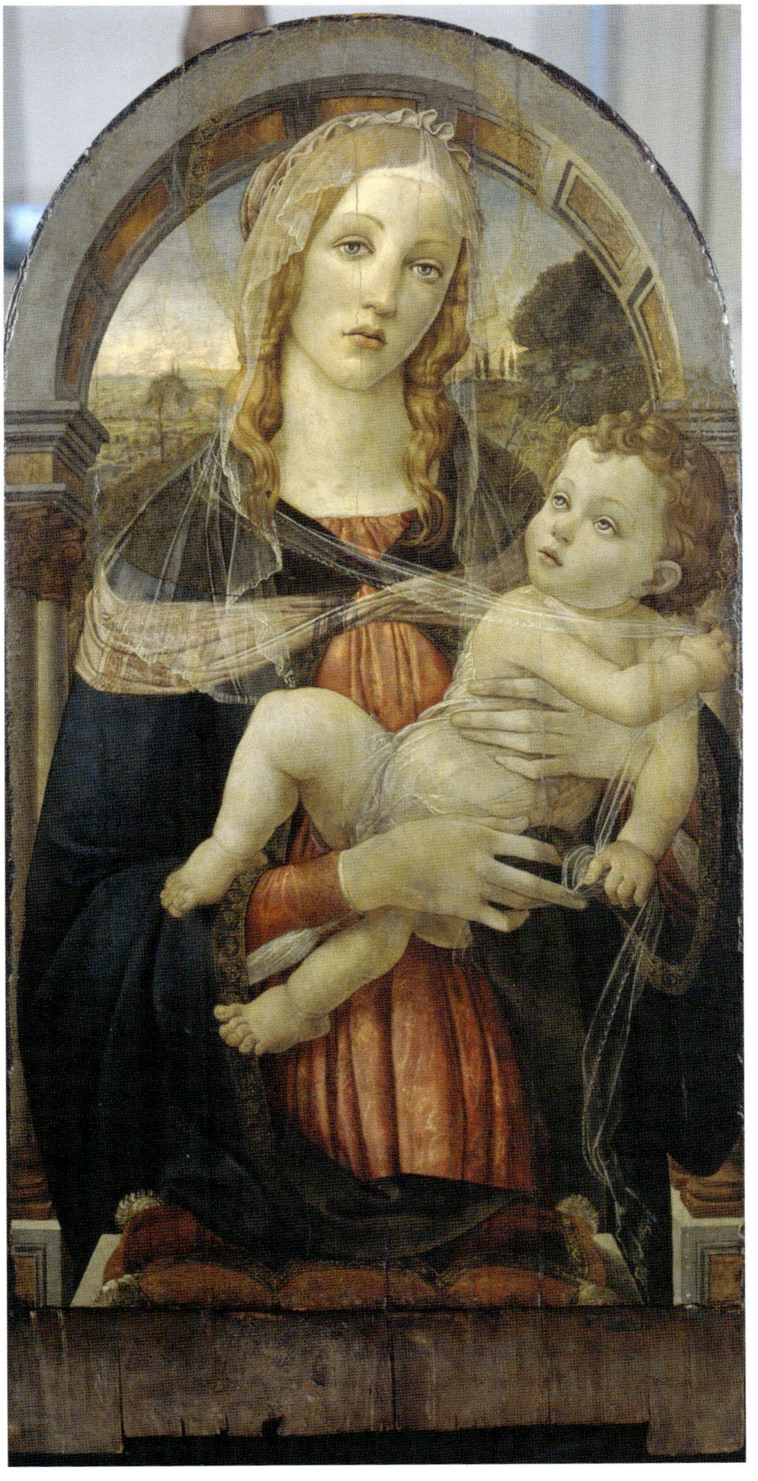

3.44. Umberto Guinti (1886–1970), *Virgin and Child* (in imitation of Botticelli). Tempera painting on panel, 1920s. Length 88.2 cm. The Courtauld, London (Samuel Courtauld Trust), P.1947.LF.40.

in many archaeological reconstructions, perhaps most famously the Minoan fresco paintings at Knossos, "reconstituted" in the early 1900s by the painter Émile Gilliéron and his son—who have also been implicated in the creation of Minoan forgeries for the antiquities market of the 1920s and '30s. Of the frescoes at the site, which were commissioned by the archaeologist Arthur Evans, Evelyn Waugh observed, "It is impossible to disregard the suspicion that their painters have tempered their zeal for accurate reconstruction with a somewhat inappropriate predilection for covers of Vogue."[116] Every surface upgrade, every attempt to put new skin onto old bones, brings the paintbrush of the present to bear on the past and risks exposing the hand that wields it.

The Many Roads to Luster

Bridging the way, finally, from surface upgrades to the new-made object of true forgery, this section looks at the extraordinary inventiveness with which craftsmen have tried to capture the financial value of the most consistently celebrated technique in collected ceramics from the Islamic world: luster decoration. Experiments in luster imitation run from superficial interventions with paint to the technological challenges of creating an entirely modern antiquity. A true, successful luster surface in ceramic is almost impossible to fake convincingly. The specular reflectivity and iridescent sheen of the microscopically thin metallic layer cannot be truly replicated with paint or foil, both of which will always stand somewhat proud of the surface and can never match the unique optical qualities of a true luster.

This has not stopped anyone from trying, though. One aid to the modern fabricator is the fact that lots of medieval luster is not fully lustrous. If luster gets overfired, it comes out looking "burnt," matte, and monochromatic rather than reflective and iridescent. If it is underfired, it doesn't bond properly with the glaze and can look anemic, just a weak stain on the glaze rather than an iridescent metallic surface. It can also become abraded over time. These problems for the medieval potter have been turned into a boon by the modern painter, who can always mix an appropriate brown or ocher to match the base tone of a luster even when they cannot ape the iridescence of the real thing.

At its simplest, overpainting that seeks to pass as luster is easy to detect. It turns up everywhere in reconstructed Iranian lusterwares, sometimes in limited areas of retouching, at other times much more comprehensively changing or creating a design. An example in the Eskenazi Museum, acquired in 1973 from Peter Marks (d. 2010)—a New York dealer of dubious reputation—shows quite clearly how layers of overpaint can be built up to generate a largely new design, purportedly executed in the prized technique of luster (fig. 3.45).[117] From a distance, the dish is an attractive lobed shape with cobalt and turquoise colors in the glaze, a brown luster overglaze image of a harpy in the central roundel, and luster vegetal designs in the lobes. There are pieces with similar designs in several well-known collections, including a luster bowl decorated with a harpy that was excavated by Schmidt at Rayy in the 1930s.[118] Here, the obvious modern reconstruction on two of the lobes doesn't really interfere with the overall appeal of a piece that would work well in a museum display on, say, fantastic creatures across cultures. Close looking in raking light at the profile of the harpy, however, reveals that much

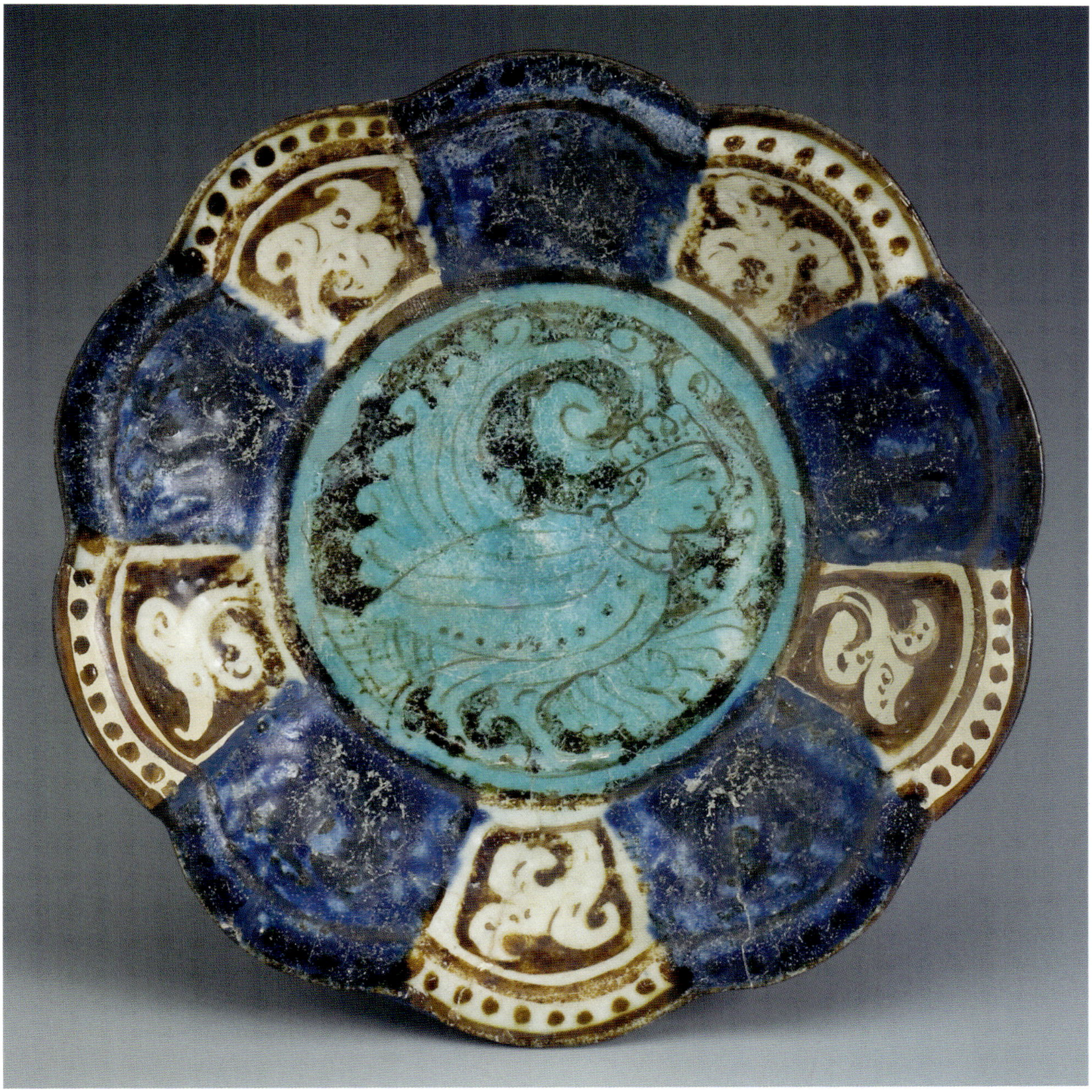

3.45. Dish, glazed stonepaste with luster overglaze and modern material. Medieval material attributed Iran, 13th century. Diameter 19.1 cm. Eskenazi Museum of Art, Indiana University, 73.46.6.

of it has been painted in with a rather dilute brown paint that stands proud of the surface (fig. 3.46).[119] Under a magnifying lens, the glazed surface under the modern brown paint is revealed to be heavily abraded. Someone has sanded away the remains of an earlier design in a dark brown luster, leaving scratches all over the surface and especially in the areas of the original luster. The original design was probably considered too damaged or inchoate to attract buyers, and so the ground was prepared for an enhanced or possibly entirely new image, with proven market appeal.

In this instance, the modern painter has even left an unintentional trace of him or herself behind (fig. 3.47). A close detail from the edge of the turquoise

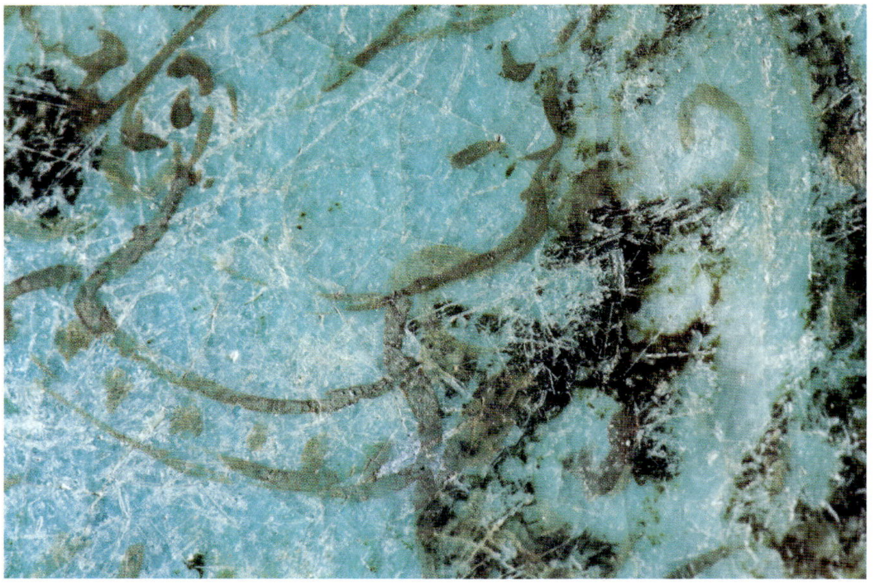

3.46. Detail of dish illustrated in figure 3.45 showing abraded surface and modern overpainting.

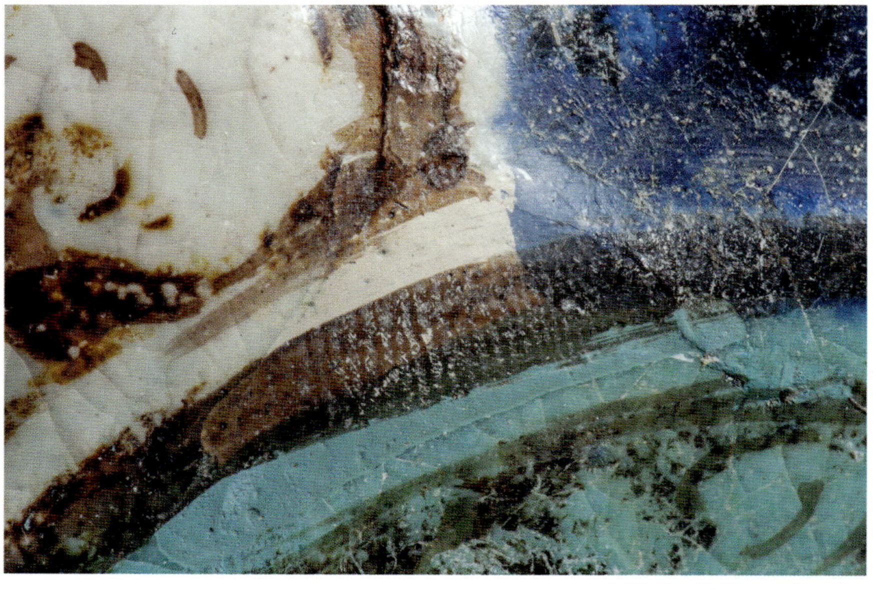

3.47. Detail of dish illustrated in figure 3.45 showing a fingerprint in the overpaint.

roundel shows the stratigraphy of the overpaint layers, brown on top of the cream, cobalt, and turquoise used to neaten the edges of the different color fields. At the very center of the image, light ridges are clearly visible where a fingertip has picked up some of the cream overpaint and transferred it to the brown. The indexical trace of a long-vanished living person, left behind in clay or paint, always delivers a jolt. Here, a fingerprint in the overpaint takes us startlingly close to the invisible hands of the reconstruction workshop, a tantalizing moment of unintended proximity via the most individualized of human traces. It is as if a little wormhole had opened up in time, transporting us through our uniquely human powers of haptic sympathy to the moment a contact trace was created.[120]

As with all techniques that put new skins onto old ceramics, the use of brown paint as ersatz "luster" was sometimes taken to the extreme, beyond

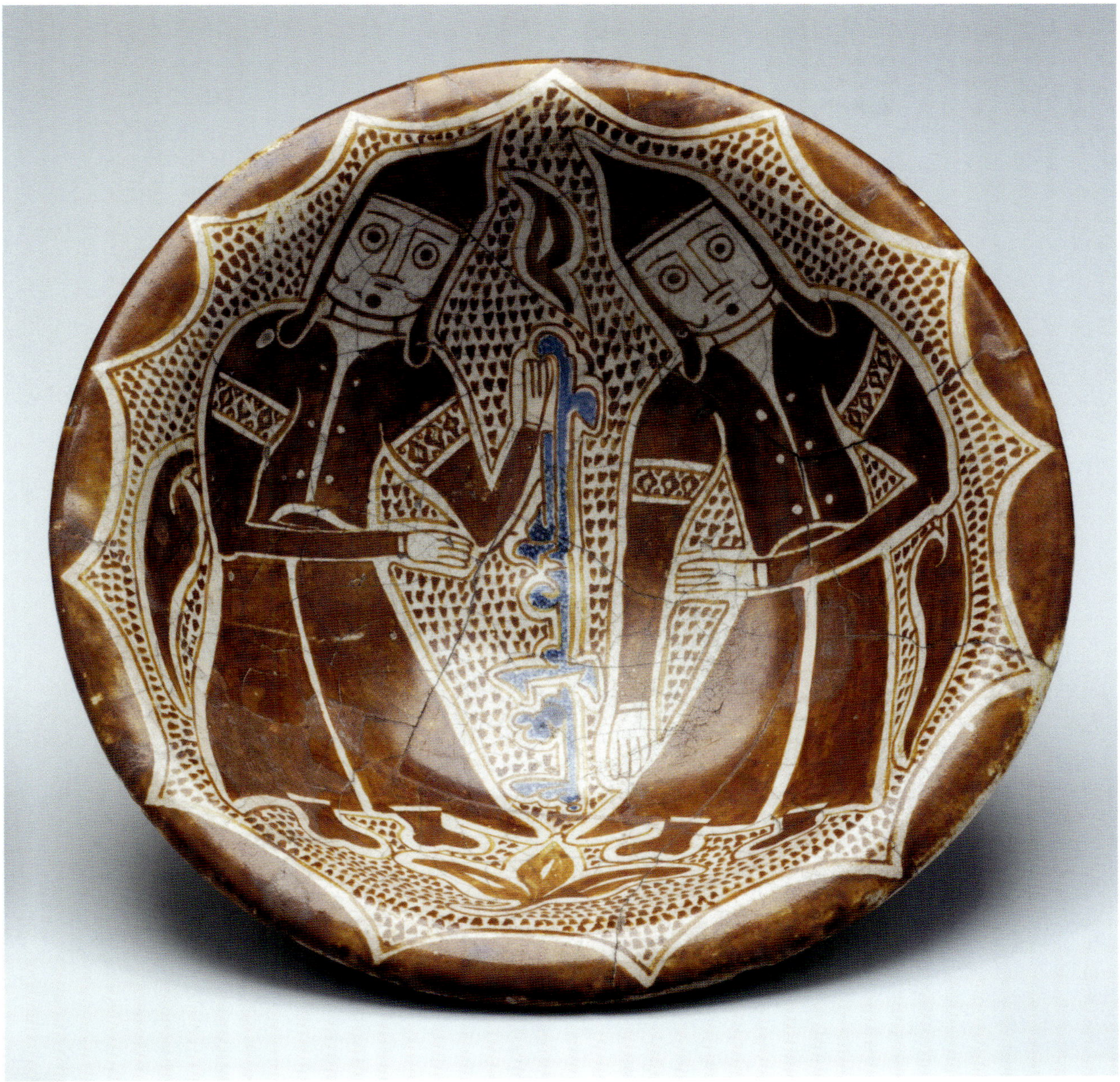

3.48. Bowl, glazed earthenware with cobalt in-glaze and modern overpainting imitating luster. Original material attributed Iraq, 9th or 10th century. Diameter 21.6 cm. Toledo Museum of Art, 1941.23.

mere enhancements. The seemingly simple, vivacious designs of early Iraqi lusterware bowls seduced some workshop painters into making their own attempts at the type. Sometimes these went as far as completely inventing entire programs of decoration. There is already at least one published instance of a bowl that was once believed to be a tenth-century Iraqi lusterware but has proved, upon investigation, to be a modern design painted in brown on top of a fragmentary and reconstructed plain white bowl—probably a genuine ninth- or tenth-century Iraqi monochrome vessel.[121] That bowl, in the Freer collection at the National Museum of Asian Art, was bought from Parish-Watson in 1925. To it can now be added another, even more spectacular example in the Toledo Museum of Art, bought from Parish-Watson very shortly before his death in 1941 (fig. 3.48).[122] Its first appearance in the public record was in 1936, in the catalogue for the posthumous auction of the collection of dealer Émile Tabbagh (1879–1933).[123]

Like its confrère in the Freer collection, the bowl in the Toledo Museum seems to represent the superimposition of a modern design in brown paint onto an original ninth- or tenth-century Iraqi tin-glazed vessel. In this case the underlying bowl is white with a cobalt inscription fired in the glaze, which includes the word *ʿamal* ("work"; when followed by a name it becomes a statement of authorship, "work of . . ."').[124] The initial clues that the "luster" part of the design is modern lie in the painting: it is too neat, regular, and matte when seen alongside genuine Iraqi lusterwares of this type that have been recovered through reliably documented excavation.[125] More particular infelicities quickly disclose themselves. The overprecise facial features, perfectly circular little beards, labored outlining, and completely flat, even tone of the "luster"—as well as the painstakingly regulated design on the exterior—all suggest careful copying from books rather than the rapid execution one sees on the genuine article.[126] When viewed alongside excavated Iraqi luster bowls and sherds, the Toledo bowl looks like a prop from a film set. Initial examination suggests the entire "luster" design has been painted on using a fine brush and two shades of orangey-brown paint, before the whole bowl was coated with some kind of varnish or lacquer.[127]

On the Toledo Iraqi bowl, the original inscription on the bowl in cobalt blue posed something of a challenge for the modern painter.[128] The solution is audacious: rotating the inscription ninety degrees counterclockwise to take up a vertical rather than horizontal orientation in the new composition. The rotation allows it to serve as a secondary design element, becoming a central axis for the paired figures. Of course, this adaptation also greatly reduces its epigraphic role. What was conceived by the ninth-century potter as a singular, central statement of authorship has been moved into a supporting role within an early twentieth-century composition intended for consumers who cared more for figural designs than for austere and difficult-to-read Arabic inscriptions. The care taken over this new composition, though, deserves recognition not just for its success on the market but also for the labor of love involved in copying and adapting designs from real Iraqi lusterwares, whether objects or their published images. As every art student knows, only when you have copied out a design or drawing yourself do you come to know it completely, and to appreciate all the intricacies and oddities of its construction even as you fail to emulate them perfectly.

Reviving Luster for the Modern Era

The quest for a simulation of luster certainly did not stop at brown paint. One French handbook for ceramics restoration, from 1865, includes instructions for making imitation luster (*reflets métalliques*) on repaired and filled ceramics by applying gold powder sparingly over a background color, mixing in some silver if the tone needs lightening.[129] This technique sounds like it would be quite easy to identify, but I am yet to encounter it knowingly on restored ceramics from the Islamic world. A much more extreme solution would be to reluster a historic object, applying a carefully prepared luster paint of metal oxide and refractory medium over an original glazed surface and attempting a second firing in a reducing kiln to fix it, or possibly even reglazing and re-

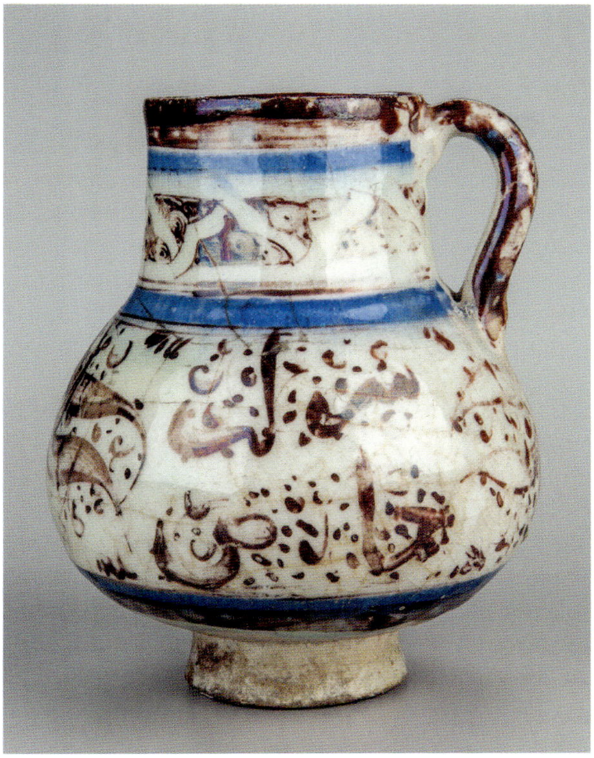

3.49. Jar, glazed stonepaste with overglaze luster. Height 16.5 cm. Eskenazi Museum of Art, Indiana University, 72.6.10.

firing first and then doing the second luster firing. This would undoubtedly require a lot of skill, but there is no reason it wouldn't be possible. Indeed, very recent anecdotal reports from the market suggest that the skill of ceramics lustering is even now in demand for precisely those reasons. Medieval glazed white vessels recovered illicitly have reportedly prompted a search for potters with sufficient skill in the luster technique to add new, medievalizing designs onto their surfaces so that antiquities vendors can sell them as masterpieces of early lusterware, thereby commanding a much higher market price than the pieces ever could in their true identity as plain white bowls, no matter how old.

Modern relustering may well be what has happened to a handled cup in the Eskenazi Museum, one of the "Raqqa ware" cobalt-and-luster group bought from Fahim Kouchakji in 1972 (fig. 3.49). The cup is part of a corpus usually attributed to late twelfth- or early thirteenth-century Syria. TL testing of the cup in 2016 indicated the piece was last fired within the last 150 years.[130] I discuss this group and its dating further in chapter 5, but this particular cup stands out among the Eskenazi Museum's group of "Raqqa" wares for the stylistic oddity of the inscriptions and decorations on the belly, and its unusually streaky and bright reddish luster. The script style, the thick and clumsy painting with a scraggy brush, and the clouds of heavy dots all depart radically from what is usually found on other examples of this ware, both excavated fragments and art market objects alike.[131] Are we looking at a layer of modern luster medium fired onto a medieval glazed jar? Under magnification, the luster on the jar certainly looks like it is bonded to the surface of the glaze rather than sitting on top of it the way paint would, and parts of it have a true iridescent sheen. But the fixing of the luster has not been a roaring success overall. In some places, notably the vessel's lip, a stronger layer of luster seems to lie over a much weaker one.[132] It is very possible that the jar was first found with an unsuccessful or largely lost original luster layer, which then received a modern makeover.

For the moment, this piece in the Eskenazi Museum remains somewhat mysterious, although we will return to it and its fellow travelers in chapter 5. At any rate, we should at least entertain the possibility that craftspeople in the modern era could have fired new luster designs onto old ceramics. While the documentation for Syria is lacking, the late nineteenth century certainly did see the successful revival of lusterware production in Iran, after a seeming hiatus that had followed the large-scale lusterware production of the late seventeenth century.[133]

ʿAli Muhammad Isfahani (fl. 1870s–1890s) is the figure most associated in art historical scholarship with revivalist ceramics—including lusterware—in Iran.[134] He ran a successful ceramics workshop in Tehran in the late nineteenth century, where his work caught the attention of the V&A's agent in Iran (and subsequent director of the Edinburgh museum), Robert Murdoch Smith.[135] Surviving luster pieces from ʿAli Muhammad's workshop include at least one inscribed with a medieval date, raising questions about whether it was intended to deceive viewers into thinking it was a medieval artifact—which it certainly did on at least one occasion (fig. 3.50).[136]

ʿAli Muhammad Isfahani does not seem to have been the only one with the know-how. A luster tile bought by Friedrich Sarre in the bazaar in Tehran in 1899 and now in the Museum für Islamische Kunst in Berlin (fig. 3.51) is signed ʿAli bin Ahmad al-Husseini (or possibly al-Hassani). When Sarre gifted it to the museum, it was recorded in the inventory books as an example of modern

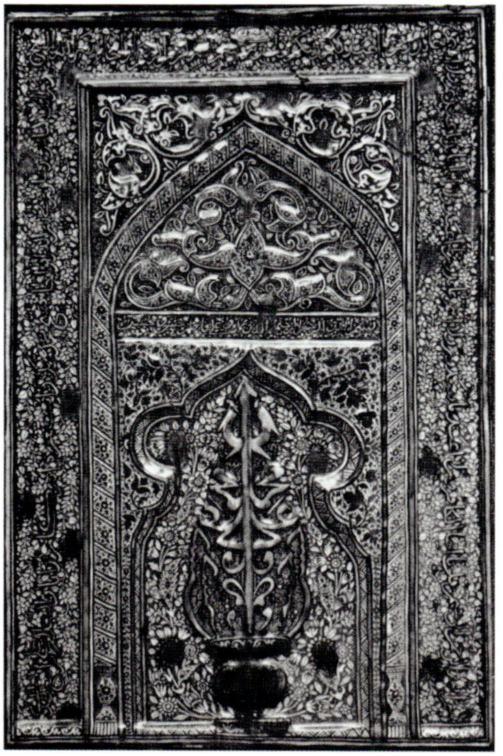

3.50. Glazed tile with overglaze luster and inscribed false date of 751 H/1350–51 CE. Iran, late 19th or early 20th century. Length 70 cm. Current whereabouts unknown.

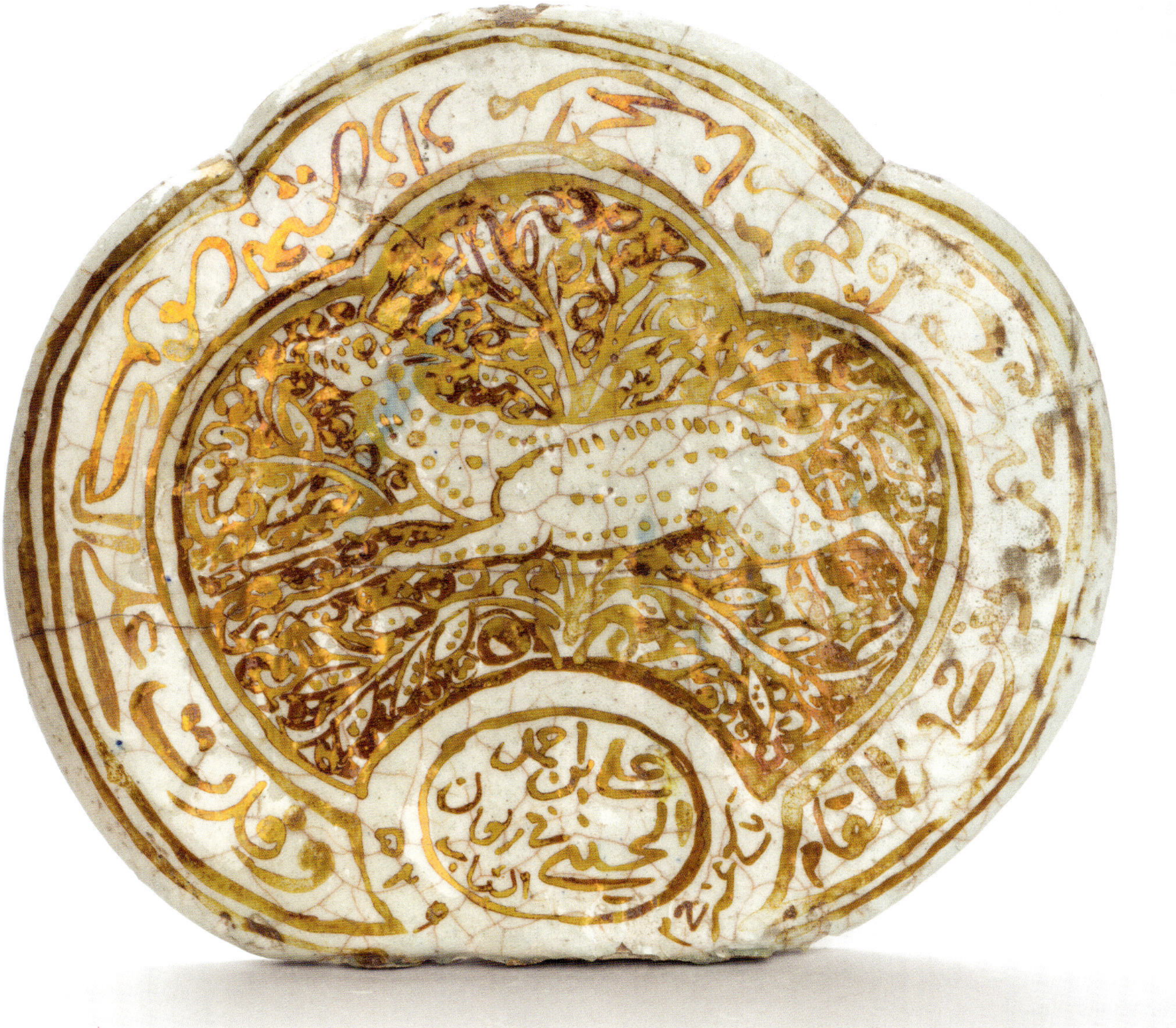

3.51. Tile, glazed stone-paste with overglaze luster and inscribed false date of 529 H/1135 CE. Iran, late 19th century, bought in Tehran in 1899. Width 29.8 cm. Museum für Islamische Kunst, I.3937.

work (*Persien, moderne Arbeit*), although it bears the date of 19 [Jumada?] 2, 529 H (12 April 1135 CE) written in a combination of words and numerals.[137] Everything about the paste, glaze, and brushwork of the luster design announces the tile as a modern production, which Sarre recognized when he bought it. Moreover, the leaping, spotted deer on the tile clearly attempts to mimic animals seen on medieval Persian bowls, like that shown in figure 2.24, and the fictive date is too early for Iranian luster production—the earliest dated object currently known is from 575 (1179–80 CE).[138] Evidently, Iranian potters were making historicizing luster ceramics, complete with false dates, by the late 1890s. Some similar modern imitations of medieval lustered tiles and bowls have also turned up recently in auction houses, where they are sold as nineteenth- or twentieth-century objets d'art, and in less salubrious online sites where they are sold as medieval.[139]

Friedrich Sarre, writing in the *Mitteilungen* about some modern forgeries of medieval Persian luster that he saw in 1906 in the possession of the dealers Siegfried Bing and the Tabbagh Frères, mentioned that there was "in Tehran in 1899/1900 an Armenian potter who knew how to do excellent lustre painting, but the forms and the drawing never left any doubts that they were modern."[140] This "Armenian potter" might possibly be Ali Mohammed Sabbak Barseghian, who is named in another issue of the journal, along with his Iranian confrère Hussein Ghouli Khan, in a note on the luster ceramics shown in the Persian pavilion of the Paris Exposition of 1900. "Both have the genuine old recipe (siliceous) and glaze, and if their work at the exhibition was not yet very convincing, it could soon become so."[141] Perhaps this might be the outfit who made the Berlin tile, or perhaps there were multiple ateliers reviving luster in Iran at the turn of the century. Oliver Watson has speculated that the pair might be linked with yet another report in the *Mitteilungen*, this time from the director of the Victoria and Albert Museum, who warned in 1901 of Persian lusterware forgeries being sold by Armenian dealers.[142]

These glimpses and flashes of modern lustered ceramics making their way through the antiquities market are as evanescent as the material itself. As can be seen from this very brief survey, the consistently high value placed on medieval lusterwares in the collectors' market generated an uncounted number of modern pathways toward luster and its simulations. In terms of technological skill, these run the gamut from the simplest of low-tech solutions—the artistry of a brush and brown paint—to the successful revival of the technique in tiles and vessels and the incredible feats achieved by the unknown creator of the modern lustered fragments used to complete the jar bought by Freer in London in 1909 (see fig. 3.15). As more analysis is done and more questions are asked about the hundreds of Middle Eastern lusterwares that circulate today without any verifiable archaeological record, we will continue to learn from the modern craftspeople who went to such lengths to simulate and recreate this most capricious and demanding technique.

Coup de Théâtre: Forgery from Whole Cloth?

Finally, the third branch of fabrication among the Islamic ceramics that traveled on the art market is what we could call true forgery. This is an object that has been made from scratch with express intention to deceive, rather than improvised through bricolage or the surface upgrades of skin swapping. The lustered tile in Berlin discussed above might be classed as such: the falsified date suggests a real intention by the maker to deceive buyers into thinking they were getting a medieval artifact, even if the product would not pass expert examination. Whole-cloth forgery is less common than the other types of intervention discussed thus far and if done with skill can be very hard to identify definitively. Currently, the only real scientific test of age in ceramics is TL testing, which can give an indication of how long ago a piece was last fired (see chapter 5). It is expensive, invasive, works better with some ceramic bodies than others, and if the object is not intact it will of course only give a date estimate for the fragment from which the sample has been taken. Never-

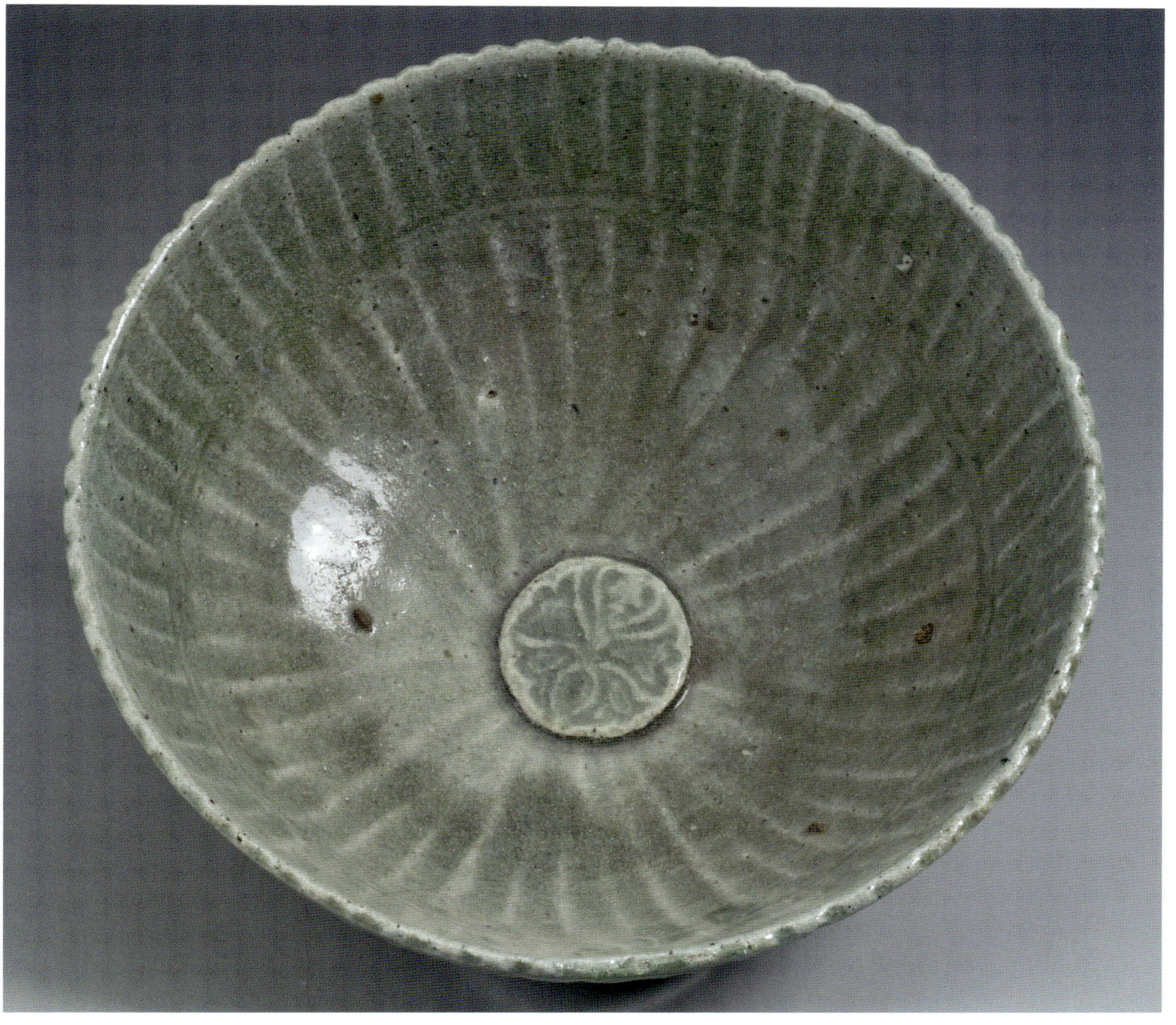

theless, it can be very useful as a blunt instrument in cases like that of a purportedly medieval bowl in the Eskenazi Museum (fig. 3.52).

3.52. Bowl, glazed stonepaste (so-called imitation celadon ware). TL testing in 2016 indicates it was last fired less than 200 years earlier. Diameter 25.4 cm. Eskenazi Museum of Art, Indiana University, 73.46.5.

In this instance, a suspiciously perfect, completely intact object, of a type normally known only from fragments, was bought from the dealer Peter Marks in 1973 with no provenance information recorded. It was sold to the museum as a twelfth-century Egyptian imitation of Chinese celadon ware. In fact, the reddish-bodied, green-glazed bowl with a pronounced crackle in the glaze closely resembles fourteenth- and fifteenth-century imitation celadon bowls made in Mamluk Egypt. Imitation celadon was a surprisingly common type of glazed ware produced in late medieval Egypt, to judge from the large number of fragments recovered from the excavations at Fustat and elsewhere.[143] The detailing on the Eskenazi bowl is extremely well done. Like this piece, sherds of medieval Egyptian imitation celadon excavated at Fustat and Alexandria have molded "chrysanthemum" discs covering a hole in the

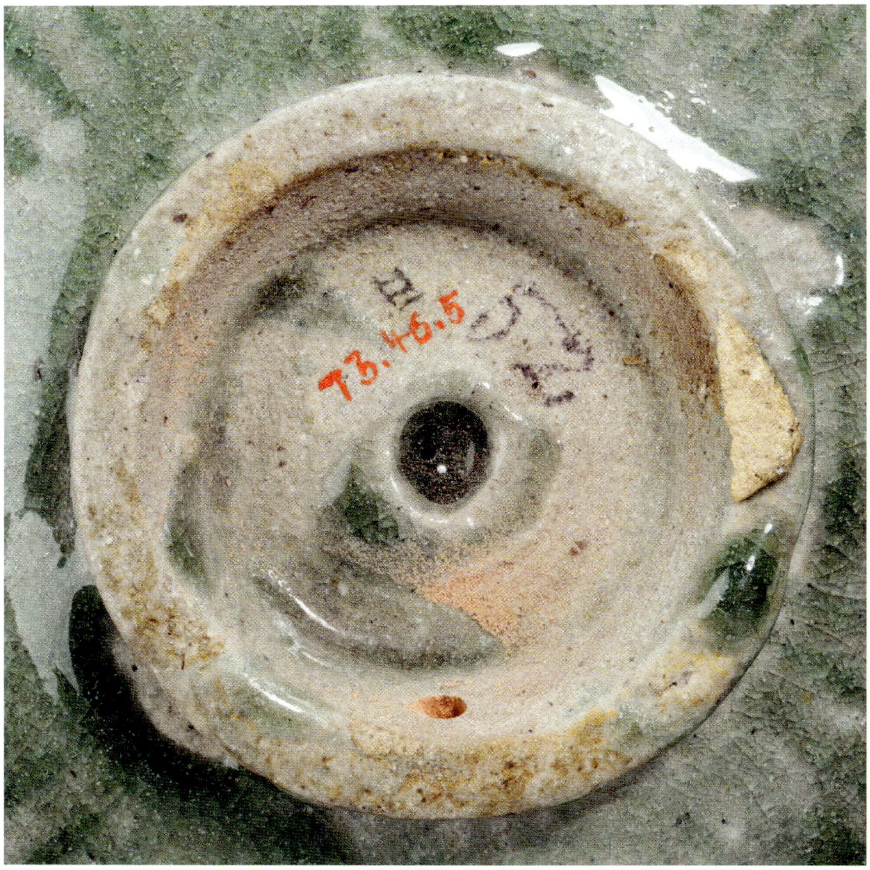

3.53. Base of bowl illustrated in figure 3.52.

base (fig.3.53), closely imitating the structure of the imported Ming Chinese porcelanous celadon bowls after which they are modeled.[144] In the Egyptian examples (fig. 3.54)—as in the Chinese originals—the bowl and the little disc were separately covered in glaze before the disc was carefully stuck over the hole prior to firing. In the kiln, glaze would fuse the disc to the bowl, with the excess running out of the hole below.[145] All of this has been replicated on the Eskenazi bowl, using a disc ornamented with a bilaterally symmetrical floral motif comparable with some seen on foot-ring sherds of imitation celadon reportedly excavated at Fustat.[146] The whole piece is in incredible condition, especially for such a large vessel, without a break or even a scratch on it. The transparent, finely crackled glaze looks like it was fired yesterday. Too good to be true, it seems. TL testing in 2016 gave results indicating it was last fired less than two hundred years prior.[147]

As far as I am aware, there are no other recorded cases of forged Mamluk imitation celadon, and indeed I know of no other examples of Mamluk imitation celadon, authentic or inauthentic, that purport to be intact. This raises the question of motivation, as well as sources: what would be the market for a highly skilled forgery of this type, if there are no other complete vessels of Mamluk imitation celadon in known collections? And where did the makers even find their model? The lack of an obvious collectors' market for Egyptian imitation celadon bowls makes all the more mysterious an object that already

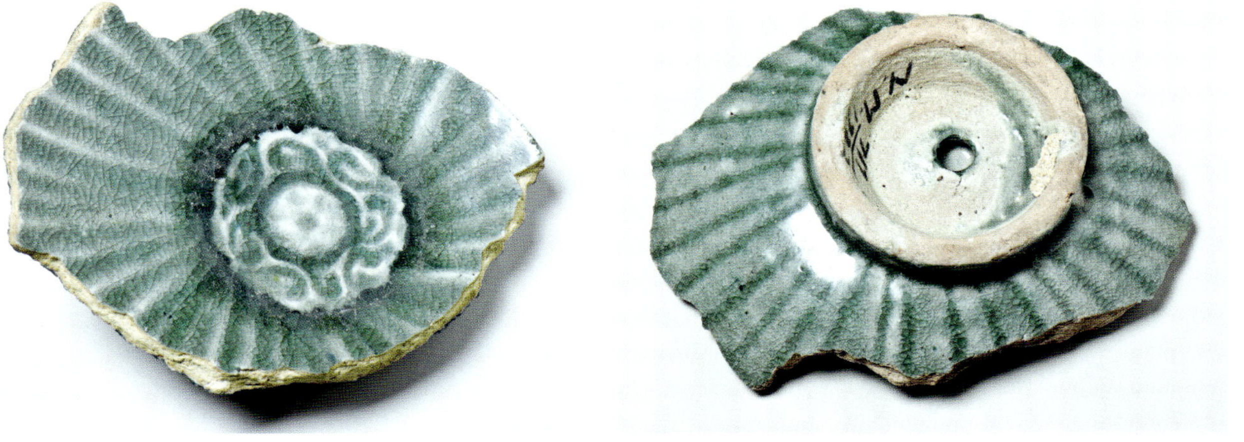

3.54. Fragment of bowl, glazed stonepaste (so-called imitation celadon ware). Attributed Egypt, 14th or 15th century. Width 19.4 cm. Museum of Mediterranean and Near Eastern Antiquities, 0717/1922.

transits the confusing realm of the copy twice over; as best we can tell, it is a modern imitation of a late medieval Egyptian imitation of a late medieval Chinese bowl. Further analysis of the body fabric and glaze might eventually clarify the circumstances of production through comparison with known paste and glaze types.

The Shadowland of Copies

Could the Eskenazi "imitation celadon" bowl be the work of a recent copyist, not intended to "pass" as a medieval object but somehow undergoing a transformation of identity on the market? The phenomenon of true ceramics forgery is always entangled with the shadowland of imitations and copies. Trade networks have long produced ceramic mimicry when one culture tries to emulate the prized wares of another, and later copies of earlier ceramics have been made for all sorts of reasons, not all of them intentionally deceptive.[148] Time and again, however, objects surface on the market that may not have been intended to "pass" as historical material when they were created but have ended up being coopted into deceptive transactions as they circulate between owners, as was already briefly discussed in chapter 2.[149] Individual dealers were sometimes named in the *Mitteilungen*—including Dikran Kelekian in 1907—for unscrupulous practices of intentionally removing or altering accurate dates of creation inscribed on modern historicizing objects by their makers, or knowingly trying to pass off imitation wares as genuine antiquities.[150] Later in the twentieth century, ceramics seemingly made by revivalist potters working in Iran sometimes made their way onto the international market in the post–World War II era, where they passed into circulation as genuine antiquities.[151] Glazed mid-twentieth-century "medieval" ceramics can carry some of the same traits described for the bull bowl in Cincinnati, especially the careful, labored drawing and the sometimes clumsy forms in potting.[152] Another trait, not obviously evident in the bull bowl, is a reliance on published images of historical material.[153] It is not always possible, however, to make clear determinations about intention in the shadowland of the copy.

European copyists of Islamic ceramics focused their attentions primarily on the famous ceramics of the Ottoman imperial kilns at Iznik, as well as the ceramics of Safavid Iran and Ottoman Kütahya.[154] Of all ceramics copyists, the French company founded in 1845 by Edmé Samson was by far the most notorious in the nineteenth and early twentieth centuries. The company comes up again and again in the pages of the *Mitteilungen*, manufacturing copies of a whole range of ceramic traditions and, it is repeatedly claimed, complicit in passing them off as originals.[155] Unlike other well-known copyists who signed their imitation wares with identifiable maker's marks, Samson et Cie often added no marks, or sometimes included a pseudo-Arabic mark, based on the letter *sin*, on their imitations of Islamic ceramics. Their pieces were thus primed to deceive while the company stayed on the right side of the limited legislation that existed at the time: they eventually even registered a rather stylized version of their pseudo-Arabic maker's mark.[156] Copying at Samson et Cie was focused, logically enough, on ceramic types that were popular, well researched, represented in major collections, and available in photographic reproductions. The company also bought historic pieces to serve as models, which, once successfully copied, would be sold on again, with the proceeds used to buy more historic pieces of a different type, which would then be copied before being sold, and so on. The modern antiquities market is very accommodating of pieces that jump on and off the carousel in this way.[157]

By the late nineteenth century, the gathering international craze for Islamic ceramics was also generating experiments within Iran in the modern manufacture of "antique" ceramics. Benjamin noted in 1887 that modern attempts to imitate the highly valued medieval tiles of Iranian monuments could be identified by the relative softness of their fired paste.[158] Twenty-one years later, Louis-Joseph Olmer, a professor of physics and chemistry at the Collège impérial polytechnique de Téhéran (the Dar al-Funun, founded in 1851) described in a detailed technical report of 1908 how Tehran potters would mimic older pastes and glazes in their quest to simulate antique ceramics for the antiquities market. He identifies a fine clay from Aliabad, mixed with ground glass frit, that was used to create a convincing stonepaste body for imitations of old wares.[159] It was presumably the presence of this clay that prompted the celebrated Qajar-era merchant banker and businessman Amin al-Zarb (1834–1898), described by one scholar as "Iran's leading entrepreneur," to open a fine ceramics manufactory near Aliabad in the 1880s.[160] Regardless of whether Amin al-Zarb's factory might have produced imitations of older wares, his involvement in ceramics manufacturing during the same period that he was custodian of the state mint and advocating for a Persian national bank dangles yet another intriguing point of contact between the emerging world of international banking and the rapidly changing landscapes of craft production in the late nineteenth-century Middle East.[161]

Time's Shadow, Time's Capital

At the very end of the process of fabrication is time itself. To pass off a new-made object as an antique, it is not enough just to fire a convincing imitation of an old ceramic type. In spite of its striking appearance of material "correctness," the Eskenazi imitation celadon bowl first raised questions precisely because it looked too complete and too perfect to be a plausible example of a type otherwise recovered only in fragments. Accordingly, after firing is finished, the work of artificial aging begins. This is usually the last set of physical acts in any sequence of antiquities forgery, and every medium can be subjected to the finesse of temporal camouflage. The methods of artificial aging being used on the antiquities market before World War II were varied and ingenious. In the pages of the *Mitteilungen* and elsewhere in the early twentieth-century literature, one reads of silver being aged through burial in sand soaked in nitric acid;[162] oil paint used to mimic the patina of prehistoric bronzes or, more ambitiously, mixed with turpentine, copper acetate, clay, and cupreous oxide to imitate the patina of Tang dynasty silver;[163] freshly made ceramics intentionally broken, mended, and abraded to lend them the aura of antiquity;[164] and modern glazed vessels rubbed with muck collected from gutters and mixed with glue, or buried in manure.[165]

The snapshots provided by the *Mitteilungen* are necessarily brief, but the processes of artificial aging for ceramics forgery had in fact developed to an extraordinary level in Iran by the first years of the twentieth century. The 1908 eyewitness report of Olmer describes an astonishingly complex and carefully worked out technique for artificially aging ceramics that must have been preceded by hundreds of hours of dedicated experimentation:

> After firing, you chip the rim and base [of the glazed and fired piece]. Next, you fill it with sand. The piece is then placed in a stone crucible [*creuset*] and surrounded with the same fine sand. Next, you apply very strong pressure to the whole thing for several days. The glaze comes out of it with fine cracks.
>
> You then fill it with fatty oil and leave it like that for some weeks. The piece is then dipped, without drying, in a very light slip of litharge [lead monoxide],[166] silica, soda and white lead. Then it is fired.
>
> I don't know what sort of reactions take place between this new covering and the fatty oil, but the vase comes out with *reflets métalliques* in certain spots only.
>
> All that now remains is to make some new nicks, leave the thick oil for a few weeks, then leave it to ferment in some grape juice, which gives the *reflets* different colours. Next, the vase is left on top of the kiln at a temperature of 60 to 80 degrees, exposed to soot and smoke.
>
> It then sells, depending on how successful it is, for 10 to 100 francs, through the intermediaries of Jews and dellahs.[167]

A more laconic reference to these practices is found in a report published by Charles Vignier in 1914, who observes in a footnote that "Nowadays the globe-trotter is sure to buy in the bazaar of Teheran the latest make of antique on which superficial iridization has just been produced by a process wherein, as it seems, mutton fat and a second baking play important parts."[168]

These descriptions raise many questions about what the results of this process look like, and how one could identify them. Certainly, there is a lot of iridescence on medieval Iranian ceramics that looks suspiciously cosmetic, sometimes as if it has been sponged on. On occasion, these strange iridescences attain their own kind of beauty: an atypical example, a black-under-turquoise bowl in Cincinnati, first published in 1910 and housed at the V&A from 1911 as part of the Kelekian collection, has long ridges of gold drifting

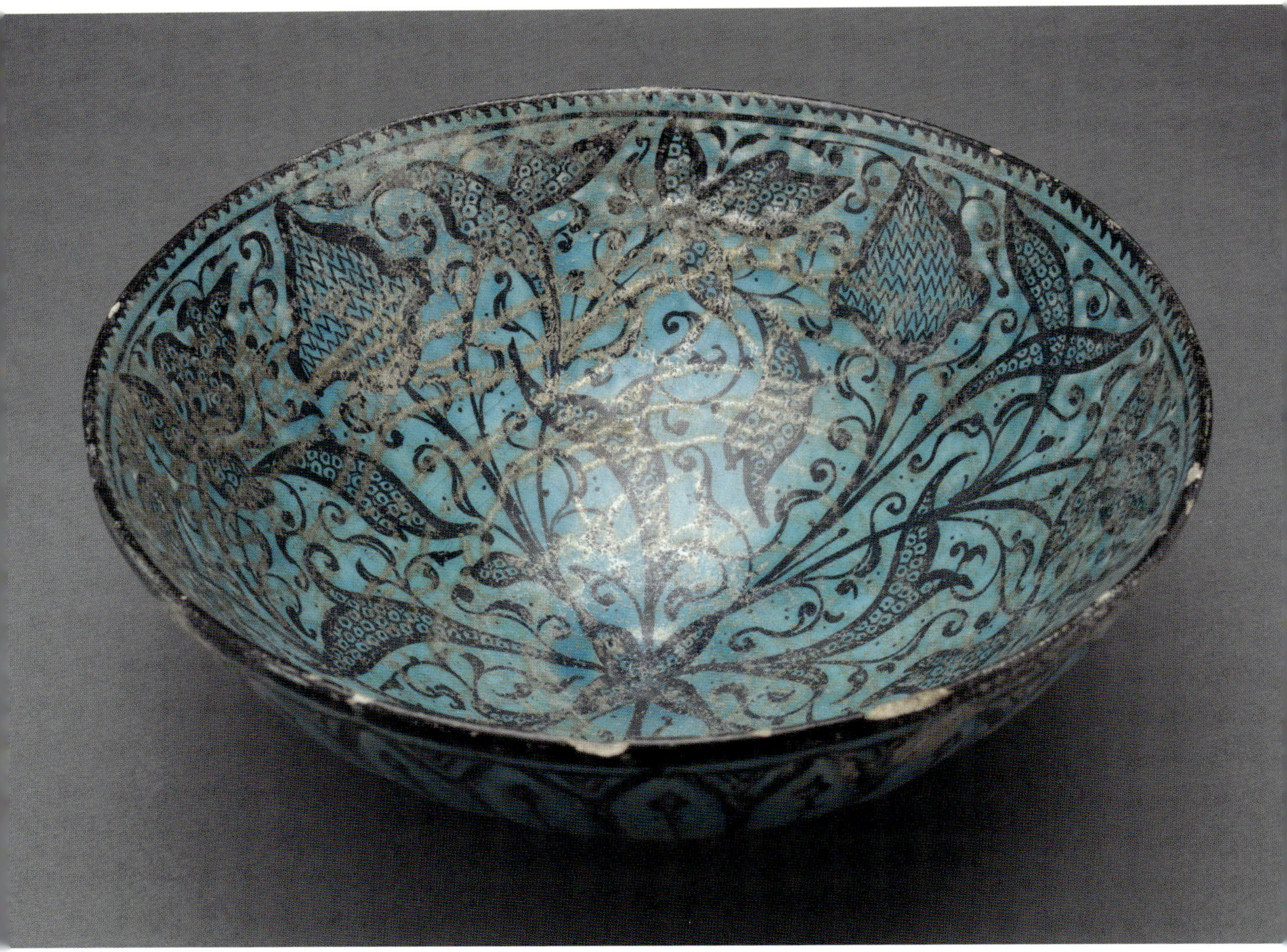

3.55. Bowl, glazed stonepaste. Attributed Iran. Diameter approx. 22 cm. Cincinnati Art Museum, Museum Purchase, 1952.263.

across the surface (fig. 3.55).[169] The bowl seems intact and in extraordinary condition, one of a group of black-under-turquoise wares with decoration typified by fields of tiny zigzags. Pieces with this design have been variously attributed to both Syria and Iran.[170] A fragment decorated with the same type of design is among the sherds reportedly found at Rayy that were acquired in 1878 from Jules Richard (1816–1891) by the V&A (fig. 3.56), and it also appears on sherds excavated from medieval sites at Hasanlu (northwestern Iran), Rostov (northern coast of the Black Sea), and Tver (on the Volga).[171] This strongly suggests historical wares of this type were produced in Mongol-era Iran and exported via the Mongol trade networks of Eurasia to the lands of the Golden Horde. To complicate things, however, a sherd bearing a similar field of slightly thicker black-under-turquoise zigzags was excavated at the Damascus citadel and is attributed by Stephen McPhillips to Damascene production between the second half of the twelfth century and the early thirteenth.[172] Perhaps a taste for this particular design spread with the export of stonepaste wares across the Middle East.

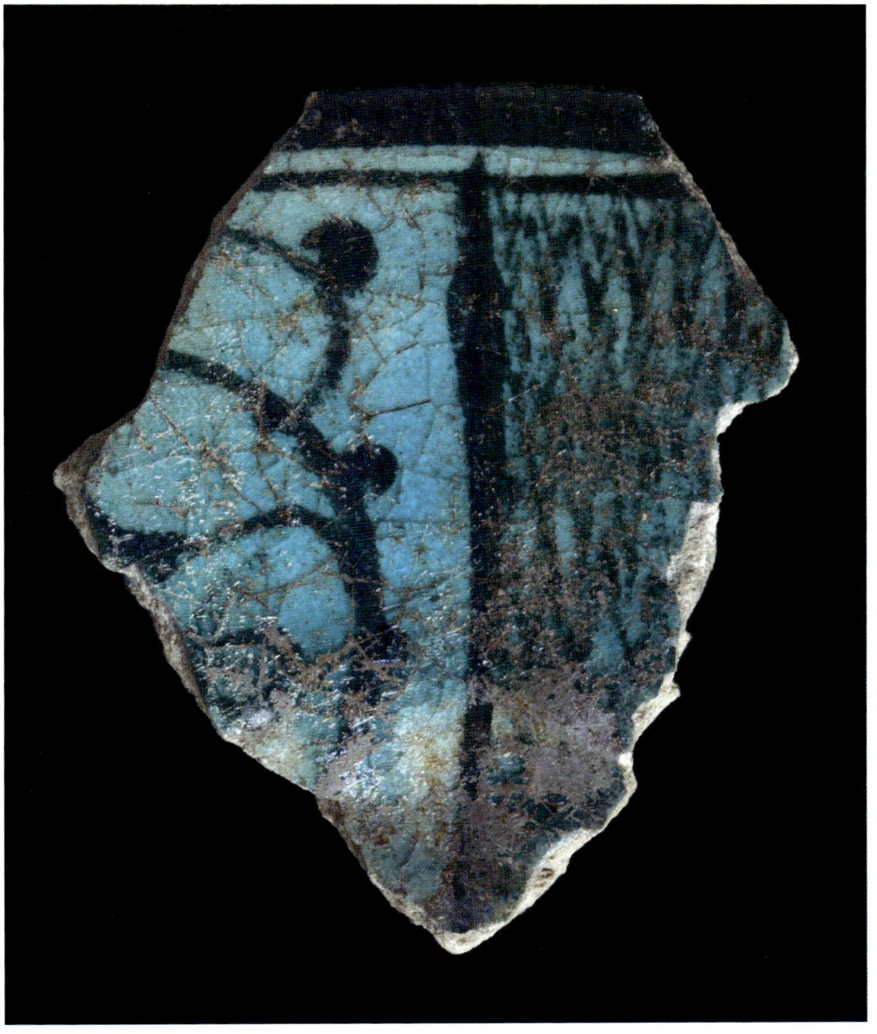

3.56. Sherd, glazed stonepaste. Reportedly found at Rayy. Victoria and Albert Museum, 619:54-1878.

But what of the bowl in Cincinnati, which is not an archaeological sherd but a complete vessel in seemingly perfect condition? Are the fine seams of gold, which have settled across it like windblown snow across a hillside, the result of a process like the one described by Olmer, or something even more particular? Do they seek to disguise a new-made object meticulously painted in a mode copied from historic fragments? Only close material analysis of this bowl and the other pieces of the same type, now in museums across the world, could eventually answer these questions.

Every technique of artificial aging is intended to induce a kind of temporal vertigo in the beholder. Painted patinas, smoked surfaces, and glued-on dirt serve to blur the distance between a prospective buyer's eyes and the true position of the object in time, manufacturing temporal shadows where real ones have not yet fallen. The alchemy of these transformations was manipulated in economic earnest by highly skilled and dedicated early twentieth-century craftspeople working to project the illusion of centuries of existence onto the surfaces of new-made objects. In a marketplace predicated on the idea that physical antiquities can sublimate time into a new form of capital, artificial aging is a technology of pure capitalist enchantment. It imprints the shadow of age where it has no temporal right to be, deliberately inflaming a market hungry to grasp the physical past. Time's shadow becomes time's capital.

* * *

All the techniques of transformation that I have outlined in this chapter exert a bewitching power over audiences and investors who want to see, touch, and possess the glamorous survivals of history. The craftspeople of the restoration workshops were latter-day enchanters, modern masters of extraordinary skill and dexterous ingenuity who could make the new old and the broken whole again. Ceramic objects of vertu, some of them made for elites in the first place, have been fractured by time, remade, fabricated, exaggerated, improved, and sometimes entirely invented for an eager paying clientele, creating new objects of pleasure for a global elite. All of this was brought about by the hands of an unknown number of unrecorded artisans, leaving little beyond the occasional fingerprint behind them. Who were they? The archives remain, for the most part, obdurately silent about those who labored within this industry, although the next chapter teases out what can be told about these hidden workshops and the people who might have populated them.[173] Journeying across the collecting landscape of the twentieth century, it charts the networks of the market-museum complex keeping all these objects afloat, especially in the new Babylon of the United States.

The ironies of the antiquities market's processes of commodification and its incredible powers of physical and psychological distortion have not been lost on contemporary artists. The magical fictions of Walid Raad have created skin-swapping objects from the Islamic art department of the Louvre, hybrid pieces that the artist tells us have merged and dissimulated in their long passage to the Louvre Abu Dhabi. In Raad's narrative, these pieces not only swapped their skins and organs but also lost their shadows inside their packing cases; when they emerged, they had to have prosthetic shadows painted on in the gallery (fig. 3.57).[174] Wrapping the profile of a medieval spouted ewer in the skin of an outsized *cuerda seca* tile design from Safavid Iran, *Preface to the Third Edition: Acknowledgements (Fragment II)* shows the objects of Islamic art history going quietly and completely rogue at the very moment they were supposed to acquiesce to their role as chips in a game of global geopolitics. In transit from one megamuseum to another, they shed and swap their identities as commodities, withdrawing themselves from the taxonomies that were intended to keep those identities afloat. Their prosthetic shadows on the gallery wall are doubled and redoubled by the real shadows of the gallery spotlight, trompe l'oeil merging with physical presence to create uncanny new possibilities for those who choose to suspend disbelief. Like the bricolaged bovine pouring vessel in the Eskenazi Museum, Raad's hybrids are fictions of surface and form that will, nonetheless, come to sustain themselves as commodities, floating within a market that keeps spinning the imaginary gold of capital from base matter and time.

3.57. Walid Raad, *Preface to the Third Edition: Acknowledgments (Fragment II)*, 2017. 3D printed plaster composite, paint, wood. Height 31.8 cm.

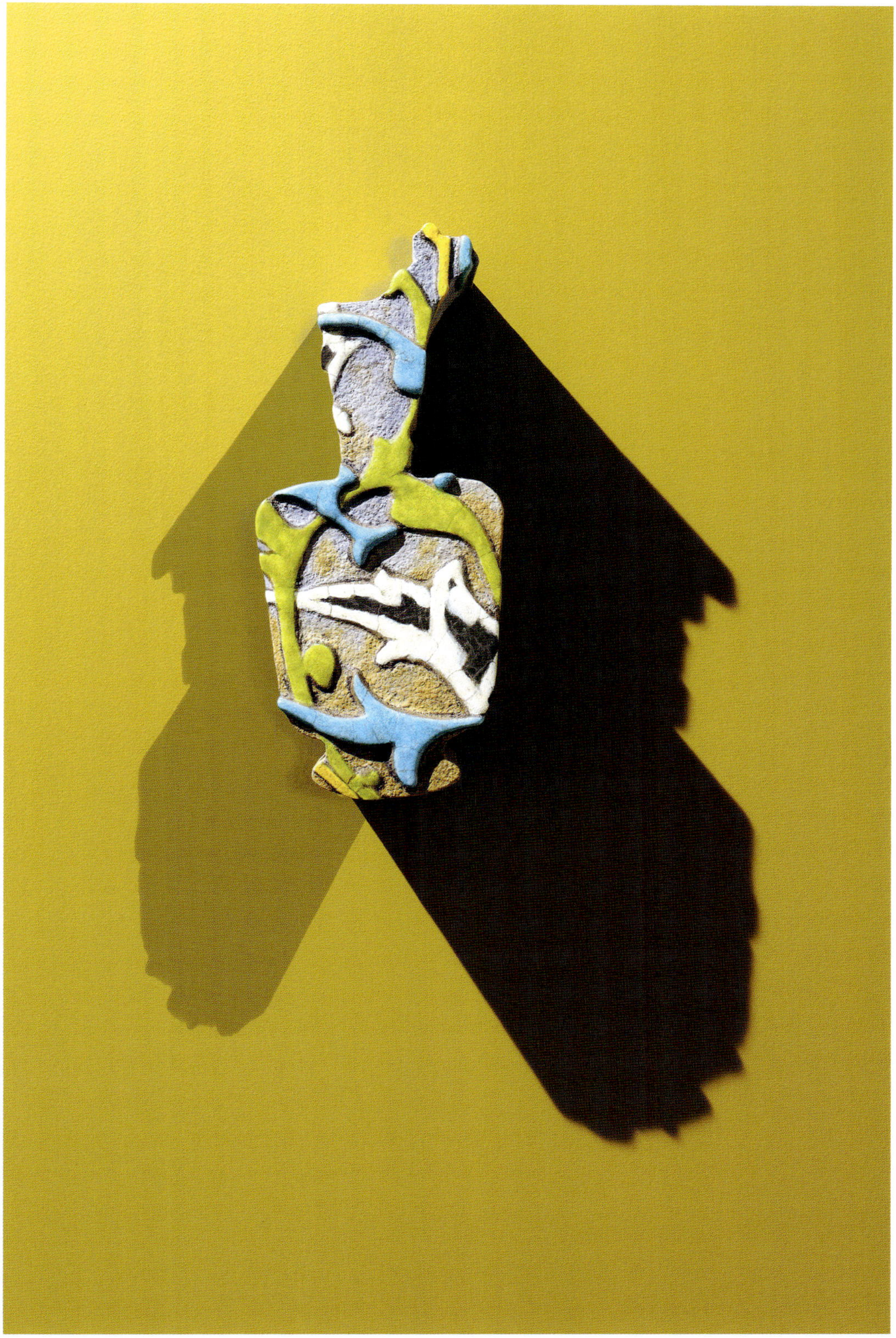

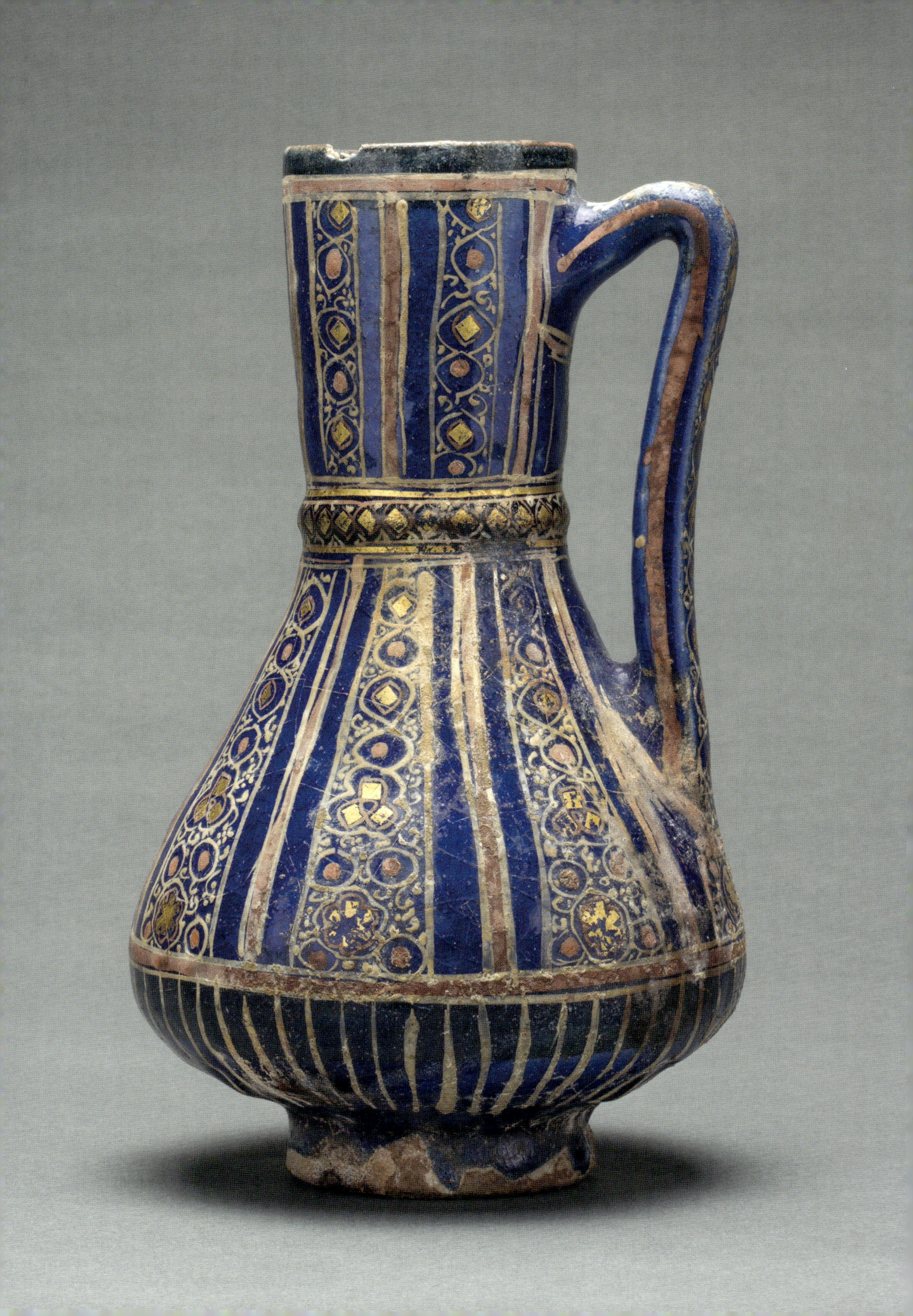

4 The New Babylon

DEALING IN AN AMERICAN CENTURY

There was money in the air, ever so much money—that was, grossly expressed, the sense of the whole intimation. And the money was to be all for the most exquisite things—for all the most exquisite except creation, which was to be off the scene altogether; for art, selection, criticism, for knowledge, piety, taste.

—HENRY JAMES, *The American Scene*, 1907

Chapter 2 of this book showed how, in just a few decades spanning the turn of the twentieth century, the growth of a collectors' market for Islamic ceramics liquidated most of the older holdings and accessible archaeological sites in the Middle East. While it was still possible in the early 1890s for collectors to acquire historic Islamic ceramics direct from local sources or even pick up surface finds themselves in the region, by World War I they depended largely on the stock of a number of dealers who traded in the metropoles of the Middle East and Europe or, increasingly, New York.[1] The market was becoming more organized, and with it, enterprises of fabrication became more sophisticated. Anxieties about authenticity grew, and chapter 3 has shown us that these anxieties were well founded. In particular, the splendor of the exhibition *Meisterwerke muhammedanischer Kunst*, held in Munich in 1910, sowed seeds of doubt. The English painter and collector Henry Wallis, whose close watercolor studies of Islamic ceramic fragments in multiple collections show his deep understanding of the material (fig. 4.1), was one of those who decried many of the pieces shown at Munich as inauthentic. As Friedrich Sarre wrote, "People began to doubt the authenticity of this new pottery, which had appeared so suddenly on the art market."[2] Across the Atlantic, however, the market was growing at an extraordinary rate.

Writing in 1928, the Parisian dealer Charles Vignier characterized American collectors of Islamic ceramics with waspish acerbity. "The forger's craft would not put food on the table if he were only to target a French clientele—but America is there, gaping, like the maw of Grandgousier."[3] Clichéd as it is, there is a grain of truth in Vignier's withering assessment. One of the seismic shifts accelerated by the Great War was the transfer of global financial firepower from Europe to the United States. The European market for Islamic art never completely recovered after World War I, but in the United States the market expanded apace, with collectors and institutions buying hand over fist as the American century progressed.[4] By the second quarter of the twentieth century—and even more so after World War II—some of the civic museums

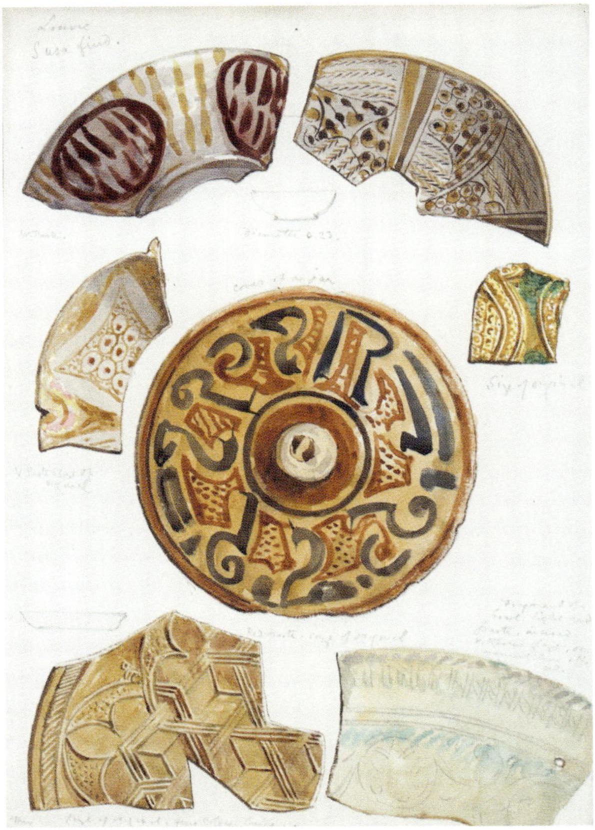

4.1. Henry Wallis, *Islamic Ceramics in the Louvre Collection,* found at Susa. Watercolor and pencil on paper, ca. 1891. Victoria and Albert Museum, E.472-1918.

of the Midwestern United States had more buying power than the most venerable institutions of Europe.[5] They did not, however, always have trained experts assessing what was on offer, and some of the US dealers seem to have specialized in selling ritzy, overrestored Islamic ceramics to a clientele that was sometimes more eager than it was experienced. Notable for this among the American vendors was MacDermid Parish-Watson, several of whose pieces we have seen in chapter 3.

This chapter looks at the activities of the people who made up the supply chain for historic Islamic ceramics during that period of social and economic transformation, from diggers to fabricators to dealers. An economic history refracted through archival documents, it seeks to understand how the market for Islamic ceramics worked. What were the economic conditions that gave rise to the industries of fabrication explored in chapter 3? Where did this work take place, and when, and who might have been doing it? How did these objects travel? And in a marketplace of networked dealers, brokers, and scholars, how were these pieces framed and presented as they underwent the translation from artifact to asset? Finally, what becomes of collected objects when they have completed that transition? The documentation that can answer these questions gets progressively more concrete as one moves closer to the demand end of the chain, starting from very occasional mentions of diggers, menders, and local traders, and ending with the plentiful correspondence in museum archives between dealers and buyers that reveals some—although not all—tricks of the trade.

Shifting Centers, Archival Voices

As the poles of early twentieth-century capitalism shifted from Europe to the United States, the most successful international operators in the market for Middle Eastern antiquities were those who established salerooms in both Paris and New York. Chief among these was Dikran Kelekian (fig. 4.2), who was trading at scale between the Middle East, Europe, and the United States earlier than almost any other dealer. He became one of the most important tastemakers in American collecting of Islamic art.[6] Kelekian is of special significance for this book not only as a major dealer in diverse types of "Islamic art," but also as the owner of a now dispersed group of more than 180 glazed ceramic vessels, loaned to the V&A from 1910, that played a significant part in establishing a collecting canon for Islamic ceramics. Objects from Kelekian's V&A loan group have already been illustrated and discussed at several points in this book. The eventual fate of those pieces, detailed in the last part of this chapter, emblematizes the dramatic changes in the global economic order that had taken place between Kelekian's initial deposit of his ceramics in London in 1910 and his death in New York in 1951. Only by triangulating between the correspondence from competing institutions engaged in a semiblind international bidding war has it been possible to reconstruct what happened to the Kelekian ceramics collection after his death, and why.

Inevitably, one of the things to emerge from the archives is the personalities of the most voluble letter writers. After encountering the correspondence of the same individuals repeatedly across multiple repositories, it is impossible not to have some personal feelings about the individuals one keeps encountering in this voyeuristic way—whether those feelings be expressed in a wry smile or an eye roll. Within the United States, no one person looms larger

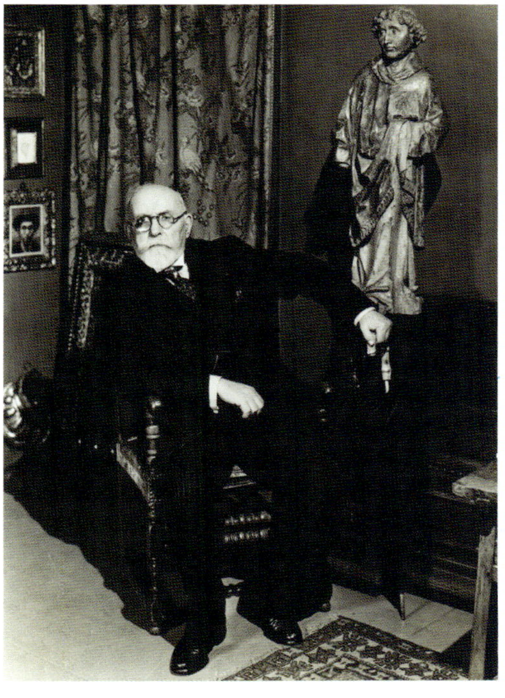

4.2. *Dikran Kelekian*, ca. 1938. Photography by Alfredo Valente. Alfredo Valente papers, 1941–1978. Archives of American Art, Smithsonian Institution.

in the collecting of Islamic (specifically Iranian) art than Arthur Upham Pope (1881–1969). By the early 1920s this broker-cum-showman of Iranian antiquities seems to pop up in every museum archive in the country. At first his correspondence looks like it will be a treat in comparison with the stringent bureaucratic prose of busy museum administrators, his formidably long letters usually an admixture of the oily and the petulant. How much gossip there must be in here, one thinks, rubbing one's hands together in glee; what a full picture of the collecting ecology this will provide! But after a while the rich fare becomes a blue-cheese nightmare and one begins almost to dread the sight of his letterhead. Pope oozily peddling an epigraphic bowl, "milk white with superlative monumental Kufic in velvety black" (in fact heavily reconstructed and overpainted with nonsense characters, as shown in chapter 3);[7] Pope toadying to museum directors;[8] Pope self-righteously briefing against his rivals when his suspect artifacts are called into question.[9] Every problem, delay, and mistake is always someone else's fault, and his labors and his genius never receive sufficient recognition for his liking.

Yet even as one reels from Pope's unctuousness, there are other things in the paper trail that make him seem quite benign. The archives of the Detroit Institute of Arts (DIA) hold letters from the Vienna School art historian Josef Strzygowski (1862–1941) to one of his former students, the DIA curator of textiles Adèle Weibel (1880–1963). Strzygowski is an important but deeply problematic figure in the history of art, who interrogated the supremacy of "classical art" and the European tradition at a time when few other art historians were asking such questions. His championing of late antique and medieval artistic traditions in western Asia, Egypt, Armenia, Russia, and Iran provided the nascent discipline with some much-needed counterweight to the hegemony of the Greek and Roman past and he played a significant role in launching the study of West Asian art as a serious scholarly endeavor.[10] Don't be too quick to applaud, though. As the storm clouds of Aryanism gathered across his writings and across Europe, Strzygowski's polemical promotion of his preferred West Asian traditions was increasingly accompanied by invective against the "Semitic races" that he came to view as responsible for degenerating European art.[11]

Strzygowski's eventual embrace of Hitler's National Socialism is well known, but it was startling nonetheless to encounter the virulent anti-Semitism scattered within his earlier correspondence. I read his letters to Weibel in the hope that they might shed light on the antiquities trade, but mostly what I found was endless Great Man complaints about his treatment by various of his peers and the world at large. In among them, however, was a phrase that stood out like a bile stain on the page. *[D]ie kleine jüdische Laus* ("the little Jewish louse"), he wrote in 1923 of his own former student, Maurice Dimand (1892–1986). At the time, Dimand had recently joined the staff of the Metropolitan Museum, where he would eventually become curator of Near Eastern Art. In the same letter, Strzygowski refers to Dimand as a "parasite" (*Schmarotzer*), and in another, as a "clever little Jew."[12] While Strzygowski's slurs toward his own student are among the most personal and vicious I came across, explicit or implicit disparagements of Turks, Persians, Arabs, Jews, Armenians, and Syrians appear in various contexts throughout the archives and published sources that make up this history. Museum archives contain more than just circumscribed information about collected objects: they reflect the whole history of the modern era, including its worst forces. Sometimes one leaves a day in the archives feeling quite sick of the world of men.

Craft and the Colonial Economy

Before moving to the American end of the chain, everything must start in the region of supply. Between the mid nineteenth and early twentieth centuries, the changing economies of the new world order had dramatic effects on local systems of artisanal production and exchange across the Middle East and Central Asia. The extensive business archive of the important Iranian merchant banker and businessman Mohammad Hasan Amin al-Zarb, and his son Mohammad Husayn Aqa Amin al-Zarb (1872–1932), runs from 1865 to 1910 and opens a window onto shifting global trade patterns in precisely this period. The early years of the archive, observes Ashgar Mahdavi, attest to internal, localized trade flows for the products of local artisanry. By the early twentieth century, however, those were gone. In a shift paralleled across the region, local systems of exchange for craft products were replaced by new trade routes for consumer goods imported from Europe and Russia and materials destined solely for export. During the same period, Amin al-Zarb's business grew from one with an initial focus on local markets to, by the early 1870s, a firm with representation in all the major cities of Iran and the Russian Caspian port cities, as well as Moscow, Istanbul, Trebizond, Marseilles, and Manchester.[13]

Through these expanding international networks, merchants like Amin al-Zarb acted as links not only between geographic hubs but also between modes of production.[14] One outcome of the shifting economies and labor structures of late colonialism is that craft trades which had once produced both luxury and quotidian products, like metalworking or pottery, increasingly targeted only the lower end of the market.[15] In some places, specific local industries of quotidian pottery production, like the unglazed earthenware storage jars, irrigation and sewage pipes, and such produced at Isfahan in the late nineteenth century or Gaza into the twentieth century, continued as relatively strong industries that met local needs.[16] Elsewhere, glazed ceramic production struggled in marketplaces that were increasingly flooded with foreign ceramics and porcelain, to say nothing of imported vessels in other media, like enameled tin or glass. The particular case of ceramics was also affected by the prestige that had long been attached within the Islamic world to certain types of foreign luxury production, such as East Asian or European porcelain: think of the Kubachi traders encountered in chapter 2, who liquidated their collections of historic Iranian ceramics in order to acquire modern French porcelain. In some places, like Fez in Morocco, established but ailing ceramics industries would be reoriented toward growing tourist markets through colonial programs of craft reform (fig.4.3). Local markets for fine ceramics production dwindled away and the costs of artisanal production became largely unsustainable in a market flooded with cheap goods manufactured in Europe.[17] While some traditional crafts—notably carpet production in Iran—were successfully reoriented toward new markets and underwent something of a revival in the later decades of the nineteenth century, fine ceramics were not among them.[18]

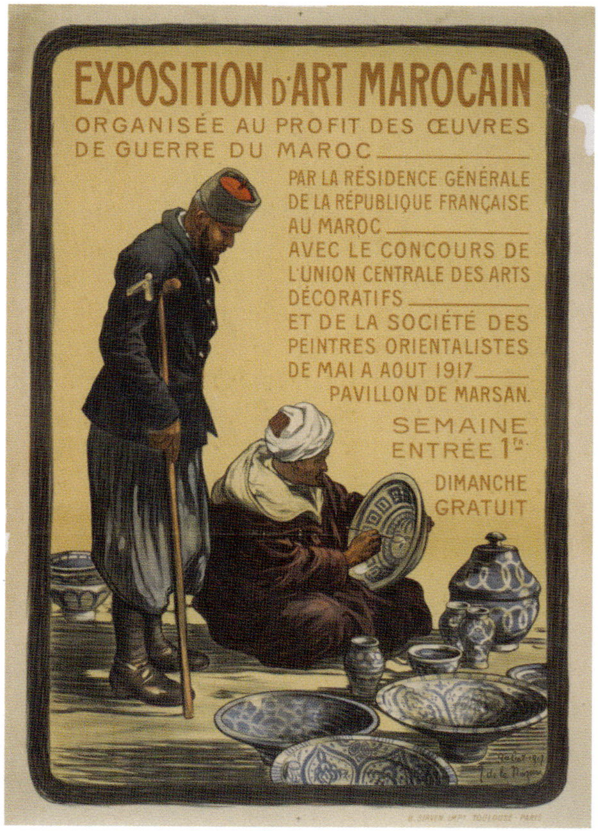

4.3. Joseph de la Nézière, *Exposition d'art marocain*, 1917 (Paris: B. Sirven, Imp). French World War I posters collection, Library of Congress, Prints and Photographs Division, POS - Fr.N49, no. 1 (C size) [P&P].

At the same time that craft production was being squeezed in this way, the dramatic expansion of antiquities vending as a trade opened new opportunities for wealth. In such an economic environment, it is entirely in keeping with capitalist logic that craft specialists would turn away from collapsing artisanal markets and toward production for a closely related, rising asset class: antiquities. As we have seen in chapter 3, the objects themselves provide ample evidence for the redirection of skilled craft toward new areas of fabrication and fabulation. The direct relationship between the antiquities trade as a new vector of commerce and the rise of new industries of imitation is attested by the authors of the remarkable *Qamus al-sinaʿat al-shamiyya* (Dictionary of Damascene Crafts), studied in depth by Marcus Milwright. This early twentieth-century text, completed circa 1908 and written from within a society undergoing radical transformation, sought to capture all aspects of craft production in the city of Damascus during the last decades of Ottoman rule, a time of heightened anxieties about the disappearance of craft.[19]

The authors of the *Qamus*—who included the notable reformist legal scholar Jamal al-Din al-Qasimi—do not give specific details about the types of antiquity that were being imitated at the time they wrote their entry on the craft of the *antakji* (antiquities vendor).[20] Their description hints, however, at multiple forms of imitation, as well as the coalescence of old and new within emergent categories of consumer desire:

> In our city of Damascus there are now many shops dealing in this craft [i.e., the antiquities trade], full of these antiquities [*al-athar*, lit. "traces (of the past)"]. Some [of these *athar*] are old, and some of them are imitations of old things [*taqlid al-qadima*], and some of them are new handiworks [*al-ashgal al-jadida*], with wonderful designs and beautiful forms, and they are all desirable to Franks [i.e., Europeans]. Some people have made it a trade [*tijara*] and have appointed an agent [*ʿamila*] to send these things to the lands of the Franks.[21]

Earlier in the entry on the *antakji* the authors name some things being traded in this burgeoning industry, referring to the overarching category as *al-athar al-qadima* (literally, "the ancient traces [of the past]") and *qitaʿa qadima min ʾay nawʿ wa shakl* ("ancient pieces of any nature or shape").[22] The particular artifacts of the past cited as being of potential interest to European tourists are an old garment, like a robe (*malbas*); coverings, including rug (*busut*) and carpet (*sajjada*), even if they are torn; "stone" (here presumably meaning pottery), especially glazed ceramics and/or tiles (*hajar sima al-qishani*); copper/brasswork (or possibly copper coins: *qitʿa nuhas*); and the weaponry of sword (*sayf*) and gun (*bunduqiyya*).[23] Local observers were well aware of the layered valuations systems of the antiquities market and of the expanding financial capital embodied in objects as they were removed farther and farther from their original point of discovery. The authors of the *Qamus* illustrate this phenomenon with the story of a man who bought an ancient copper bowl (*tasa nuhas qadima*) at Mecca for one rupee (which they state as equivalent to half a *riyal*); in Beirut he sold it to an antique dealer for thirteen gold coins (*faransawiyya*, i.e., the French gold coins also known as Napoleons); then the antique dealer sold it to a European tourist for 150 gold coins.

The growth of a prosperous antiquities trade in Damascus—where, as the authors of the *Qamus* observe, it had previously been nonexistent—reflects the new economic conditions of modernity traced throughout the book. In keeping with the interest in interconnected economies of labor seen across the entire text, the trade of the *antakji* is shown to be populated by multiple agents, locally and internationally: "Other people make a living from that craft [*hirfa*], such as the shopper [*al-mutasawiq*], who is the first buyer [*al-mushtari al-ʾawwal*], and the vendor [*al-baʾiʿu*], and the broker [*al-simsar*], and the agent [*al-wasita*], the dragoman [*al-turjuman*], and the [final] buyer [*al-mushtarin*], who is a Frank, who might sell it in his country at a great profit."[24]

The authors of the *Qamus* could see very clearly that the emerging antiquities trade was closely connected with international speculative trades like merchant banking. Within the economic landscape outlined in the *Qamus*, antiquities serve for the most part as another type of extracted resource, moving within a trade that had its own criteria for excellence but essentially operated in a similar manner to the markets in minerals or crops. Indeed, a diplomatic report sent from Iran to the United States in 1884 drew a direct line between the decline of local mineral industries and the rise of antiquities forgery. After discussing the slowdown of the turquoise mines and pearl fisheries, S.G.W. Benjamin observed that "What has been lost by Persia in the pearl fishery she seems likely, however, to make up in part by the new industry of manufacturing imitations of ancient Persian armor and coins to meet the extensive demands of European collectors."[25] A small but crucial point observable in the *Qamus*, though, was the authors' awareness of an overlap between three different temporal categories of object moving within this new market: "ancient traces of the past," imitations of those ancient traces, and new-made objects of vertu. The authors of the *Qamus* recognized that these three "types" all traveled through the same routes, and they regarded them as constituting one category or continuum of desire for European audiences.[26] The potential fungibility of those three "types" is, of course, at the heart of this book. The *Qamus* gives no further information about those who worked in the present to fabricate the pieces in this category; for that we must look elsewhere.

The task of tracing the self-effacing craft skills of faking and forgery through institutional archives faces some fundamental problems. Naturally, vendors of luxury goods like antiquities tend not to advertise the compromised condition of their stock, nor to be forthcoming about what was done to their pieces, where, when, and by whom. Moreover, the fallacy of native incapacity is one of the most distinctive tropes in the history of antiquities forgery and adds another layer of misdirection. Over and over again one encounters the incredulity of Europeans, Russians, and North Americans when faced with the suggestion that indigenous populations of the Islamic world could possibly perpetrate masterful fabrication or forgeries—or even convey accurate information or possess archaeological expertise beyond brute strength in digging.[27] In the introduction to this book we already encountered the example of Salim al-Kari, whose successful large-scale forgery of Biblical terracottas was wrongly judged by some contemporary European audiences to be beyond the capabilities of any Arab. Similarly, the confidence of the archaeologist Nikolai Ivanovich Veselovsky was matched only by his naiveté when he declared in 1886 that counterfeit antiquities could not possibly exist in Central Asia, because the local populations were too thoroughly lacking in taste and skill.[28] (Needless to say, history has proven him wrong about that.) And Islam Akhun and his workshop managed to create and sell forgeries for several years, aided by the initial belief of European agents that such an ambitious operation of manuscript forgery was beyond the imagination and capacity of a Uyghur man from Khotan "and his comparatively illiterate confederates."[29]

Nor did Iranians always fare better, in spite of well-documented European and North American biases within Islamic art scholarship and collecting toward Persian products.[30] The rapid rise and fall of the *Andarznama* manuscript provides a compelling example of presumed native incompetence within the Iranian context (fig. 4.4). With 109 paintings and a false date of 483 H/1090 CE, the wholly bogus *Andarznama* manuscript was sold in the United States in the middle of the twentieth century, in two parts, with the involvement of Arthur Upham Pope and (initially, at least), the scholar Richard Frye (1920–2014).[31] It ended up split between the Cincinnati Art Museum and the collection of the dealer Hagop Kevorkian. The full story of this infamous artifact must wait for another day, but the archives pertaining to the section now in Cincinnati furnish a most revealing line from the German curator of Islamic art, Ernst Kühnel (1882–1964). Speaking in defense of the manuscript at a conference in 1960, he opined that "I cannot imagine a Persian inventing this style. The genius, perhaps [of] a European painter, Picasso perhaps,

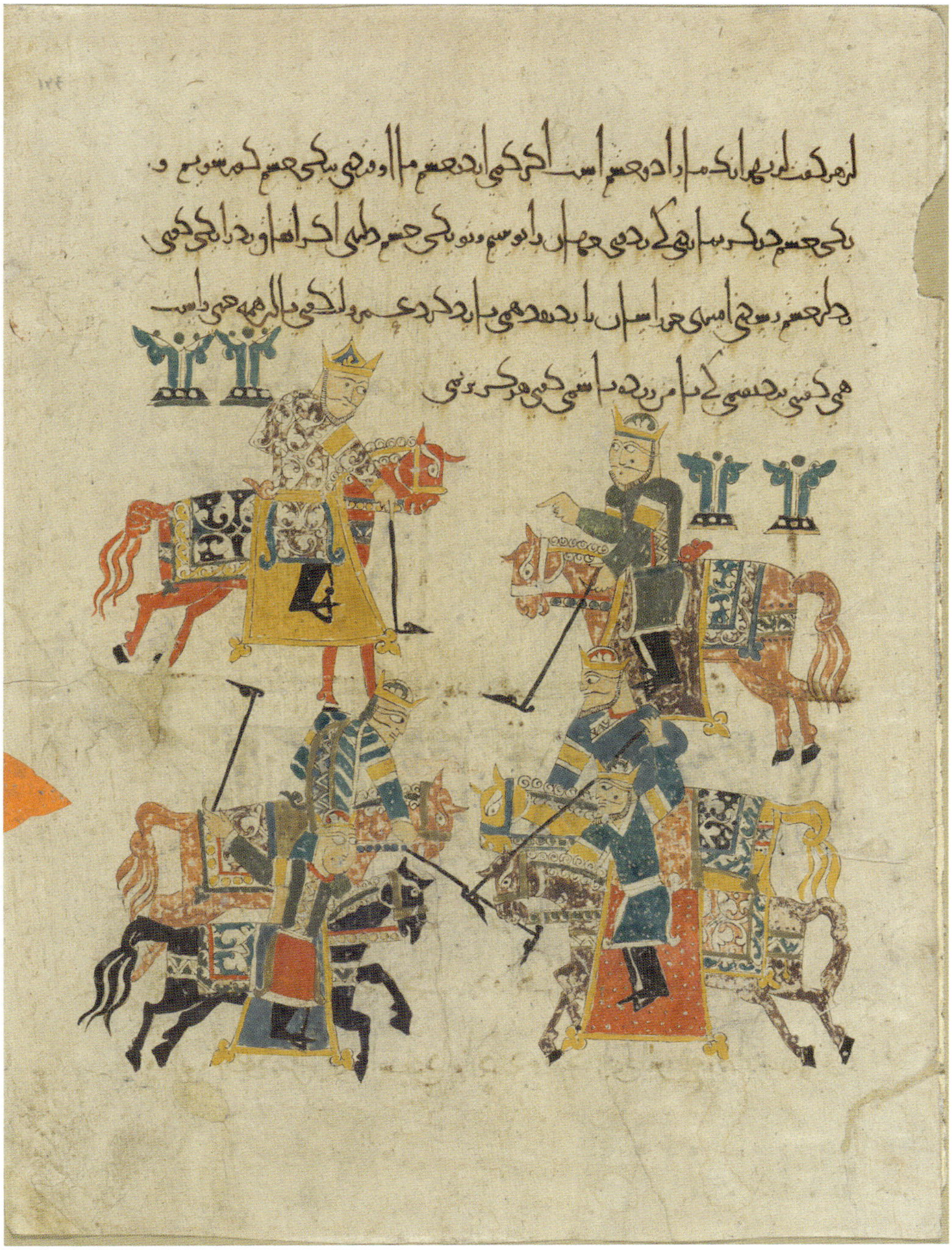

could have invented this style."[32] Hindsight is a wonderful thing, of course; we know now that these paintings were created in Iran in the middle of the twentieth century. Their colorful, frenetic synthesis of imagery drawn from multiple sources (including the buffware vessels made famous by the then recent excavations of the Metropolitan Museum team at Nishapur) attests neither to the genius of eleventh-century manuscript painters nor to that of any European master modernist, but to the invisible hands of twentieth-century Iranian artists.

4.4. Page from the *Andarznama* manuscript forgery. Iran, created between 1942 and 1950, inscribed with a false date of 483 H/1090 CE. Cincinnati Art Museum, 1954.412.

Mapping a New Category of Craft

Turning to the specific craft of ceramics fabrication, and particularly the skills that went into bricolaging ceramics together as explored in chapter 3, the first question is one of mapping. Where was this work done? And where might the more elaborate procedures of resurfacing and whole-cloth forgery have taken place? The evidence in the archives and published sources points to at least three principal locations of ceramics fabrication that fed the international antiquities market: Aleppo, Tehran, and Paris. Later, some work was also being done in the United States, probably in or near New York. We should assume, however, that other centers of activity will emerge as the historical picture for this illicit craft skill is gradually brought into greater focus by future researchers.

Early mentions of ceramics fabrication are tantalizing but tend to be too cursory for us to glean much information. For instance, the British physician Charles James Wills, writing about his life in Isfahan in the late 1860s–1870s, described his time spent with "Houssein Khari, who has a factory for false antiquities." Wills does not describe the types of objects he saw there, although his reference to a "jade teapot"—jade usually referring to a glaze color rather than a material in this context—suggests that Khari traded in ceramics.[33] The name Khari might simply be the word *kari*, denoting Houssein as a craftsman.

It is only in the twentieth century that more information about who, where, and how starts to filter through. Charles Vignier's 1928 article on ceramics forgery has already been mentioned in chapter 3; his rather blasé tone notwithstanding, many of his assertions in that article seem to be borne out by the evidence of the objects. He proposed that the more sophisticated forms of bricolage were first practiced in Aleppo and subsequently refined in Tehran.[34] Corroborating this, Charles Lang Freer reported that medieval ceramics were being brought from Raqqa and repaired for him in Aleppo in 1908, and Friedrich Sarre reported ceramics being "skilfully completed in Aleppo" in the same year.[35] Certainly, a number of the pieces Freer acquired in Aleppo have clearly been bricolaged together from fragments of multiple objects (see chapter 5). In a book published posthumously in 1925, Emil Hannover attributed the restoration of Persian and Syrian ceramics to workshops run by Armenian traders, although it is unclear if he believed these workshops were located in Paris and London—where the pieces were being sold—or somewhere else:

> The Armenians are masters of *restoration* in the widest meaning of the word. In most cases there is more plaster than earthenware in the botched-up pieces they offer for sale, a fact which they understand all too well how to conceal by means of painting, including very deceptive patches of silica with the glitter of gold or silver, which they have no difficulty in procuring from the iridescence on worthless potsherds. Their skill in this province is so extensive that from the bottom of one piece and some fragments from the sides of another they will make up a bowl that to all appearance is entire.[36]

From Iran, there are eyewitness accounts of ceramics bricolage in Tehran in the middle decades of the twentieth century. The Harvard professor Rich-

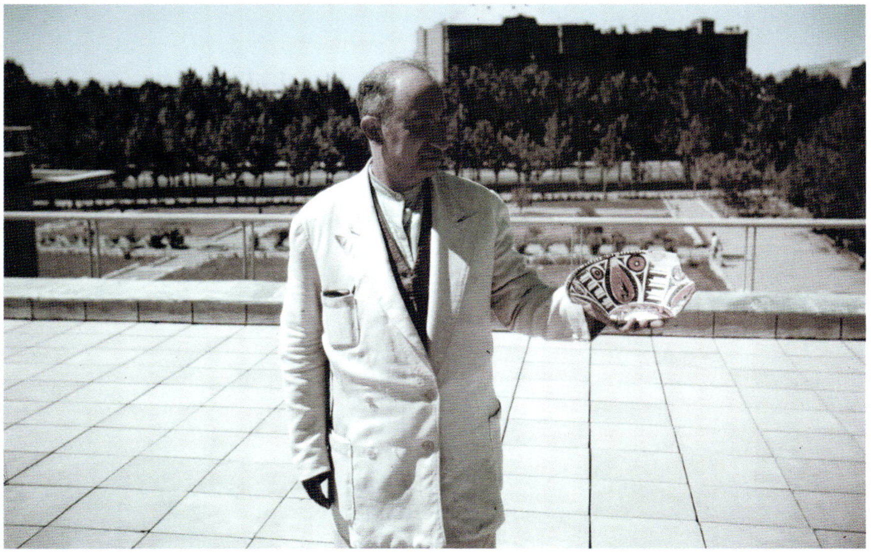

4.5. Manager of a "restoration factory" holding a slip painted bowl fragment prior to reconstruction. Photographed by Richard Frye, Tehran, 1953. Harvard Art Museums Archives.

ard Frye, mentioned above in connection with the *Andarznama*, toyed early in his career with a sideline as a Pope-style antiquities broker. This led him to visit an antiquities restoration workshop in Tehran in 1953 (fig. 4.5). His account, published by Mary McWilliams, is very revealing. As he describes it, the ceramics operations of the workshop were built on the use of archaeological sherds supplied by vendors all over the country. Across separate rooms dedicated to pre-Islamic, early Islamic, and later Islamic ceramics, sherds were sorted by type, color, and shape. These were then assembled into whole objects by the factory's craftsmen, with plaster fills and overpaint used to conceal gaps and mask the differences between unrelated sherds. The workshop also held libraries of technical literature to aid the craftsmen in their work.[37] Two decades later Oliver Watson witnessed the same practice firsthand in the early 1970s, when he "chanced into the back room of a dealer's shop in Tehran, where laid out on ranges of trestle tables were cardboard boxes filled with sherds of different types of ware—all acquired from around Iran and sorted by type, waiting to fill *lacunae* in more complete pieces, or to be used to reconstruct entirely new objects when stock was low."[38] The evidence of Iranian export labels pasted over extremely complex bricolage work (see figs. 2.54 and 3.13) proves incontrovertibly that this art was practiced to a high degree in Iran at an earlier point, in the 1920s and 1930s. Whether this was always completed in Tehran, or if there might have been workshops located elsewhere—perhaps closer to the sites of excavation for Garrus wares, for example—remains an open question.[39]

Who did this work? Hannover has already mentioned Armenian involvement, but there were undoubtedly craftsmen of other backgrounds too. Interestingly, Frye noted that although the manager of the Tehran workshop he visited in 1953 never revealed his name, he mentioned that he was a Zoroastrian.[40] The persecution of Zoroastrians in nineteenth-century Iran meant that at the time of Frye's visit there was still a significant rural Zoroastrian community living in deprivation.[41] This might have contributed to the success of this Tehran factory, which must have depended on a steady supply of sherds from remote rural sites and would therefore have been aided by community networks of individuals and families ready to undertake the menial work of sifting sites for pottery fragments. At least one extended Jewish family, too, was active in the trade. The future director of the Bezalel Museum, Karl Katz, recalls visiting the home of the Mahboubian family of dealers in Tehran in the winter of 1956–57, where he saw a great mound of pottery sherds in the backyard, brought from the family's rural estates. According to Katz, "Iran's still antiquated laws decreed that if you owned the water supply for a village, all the land that relied on that water was also yours. And not only did you own the soil, but you also had a claim on all the antiquities found therein."[42] The eighty-eight-year-old Benjamin Mahboubian (1868–1968) used this mound of sherds to give Katz lessons in the different types of pottery found in the fields of Iran, cracking fragments to show him their fabric and glaze in cross section.[43] Although Katz reported that the Mahboubians were interested only in complete pieces, this massive sherd collection likely represented some of the raw material for bricolage work.

Beyond group identities, there is also the relationship with "scientific" archaeology to consider. Frye's host in the restoration workshop was quite right when he said, "We get sherds and we put them together. We're not doing anything the museums don't do."[44] The antiquities trade grew in tandem with archaeology, where bricolage was not an illicit skill but a licit one. As already mentioned in chapter 2, most archaeological missions were underwritten by institutions that expected to receive some display objects as returns on their investment.[45] The photograph from the restoration workshop of the Schmidt excavations at Rayy in the 1930s shows a young man, wearing a button-down shirt and pinstripe trousers, at work on the skilled craft of painstaking reconstruction with glue and plaster (see fig. 2.31). We should consider the likelihood that such a craftsman, engaged during excavation season in the intricate jigsaw-puzzle of archaeological reconstruction, could have turned his skills toward the market in the off-seasons. While archaeology in the first half of the twentieth century was slowly becoming professionalized and turned into an academic discipline, commercial excavation went on regardless and provided seasonal employment in places that had often fared very poorly in the modern economic order.[46]

Although much of the work of ceramics fabrication appears to have taken place in urban centers within the Middle East, Paris was also an important site. In an exchange between Pope and the DIA in 1931–32, Pope asserted that Paris was the place to get Iranian ceramics reconstructed.[47] He describes in 1932 "the confusion and congestion in Paris, resulting from the sudden arrival of thousands of pieces of Persian pottery, the necessities of the London exhibition [of 1931] and the reduction through death, old age and retirement of about half the repairers in Paris that were at work two years ago."[48] Pope was no stranger to hyperbole, so we may want to take the thousands of objects and the mass dying-off of craftsmen with a pinch of salt. Nonetheless, there is every reason to believe that Paris really was a site of Islamic ceramics fabrication. Vignier corroborates it, other sources allude to it, and there is even a momentary glimpse of a named individual within the Pope archives. In a letter of 1934 to his close associate, the dealer Ayoub Rabenou, Pope names "David Zadeh" as a restorer in Paris who was at that time working on the restoration of a bowl that Pope wished to include in his monumental *Survey of Persian Art*.[49]

The surname Zadeh, meaning "descendant of," is a Persian patronymic; together with his first name of David, this suggests that Pope's restorer might have been from an Iranian Jewish background, as was the Rabenou family. Nothing more is known about Zadeh, but the Rabenous have a higher profile. Hailing from an extended family of landowners and related to the Mahboubian family mentioned above, the Rabenou brothers Ayoub (1902–1984) and Khalil (1905–1961) were based in Paris and Tehran respectively, before Ayoub shifted operations to New York. They worked closely with Pope from the 1920s to the mid twentieth century, acquiring objects in Iran that Pope then brokered on to North American buyers.[50] Pope in his turn introduced Ayoub to collectors such as George Eumorfopoulos (1863–1939).[51] Several of the women in the family, including Khalil's wife Elsa, as well as Louise and Yris Rabenou, were also active in the antiquities trade.[52]

The name of Rabenou has come up repeatedly in association with the forgery of Iranian antiquities. A "Monsieur Rabenou" (no first name given) was reported in the *Mitteilungen* in 1938 for trying to sell forged medieval Iranian tiles in The Hague, together with an associate called Habibollah Kazemy, and in chapter 2 we have already heard mention of the Rabenou brothers in connection with some "good fake pieces" of Luristan bronze.[53] Even more explicitly, the recently published memoirs of the London dealer Oliver Hoare (1945–2018) allege that Ayoub Rabenou, after financing archaeological digs on his property, had copies made of the best excavated ceramics "on an industrial scale." Hoare claims that Ayoub used "expert traditional craftsmen who were still available and capable of copying in almost any material and style. Since nobody had seen the originals to compare, his copies passed muster everywhere." Other traders followed suit, "but without the back-up and expertise of the academics and archaeologists upon which Rabenou could call," they were not always as successful.[54] By teaming up together, Pope and the Rabenou brothers formed a transcontinental chain that was quite successful in moving antiquities—sometimes of very doubtful vintage—from Iran to New York.

The Shifting Sites of Aghkand Wares

With Pope and Rabenou already starting to assert themselves here, I want to return briefly to the question of locations before turning the floor over completely to the dealer network in the next section. To understand how the locus of fabrication might change over time, it is helpful to look at the case of one particular type of ceramic. So-called Aghkand wares, named after the village in the northwest of Iran where they were purportedly found, are earthenware, slip-decorated bowls with incised designs painted with brown and green under a clear glaze. Looking at an example in the CAM, photographed prior to a recent campaign of conservation, one can see why these boldly designed bowls enjoyed some popularity, especially when they were decorated with ever-appealing animal imagery (fig. 4.6). This piece is one of the former Kelekian V&A group and arrived at the V&A in 1922 in the condition in which it appears in figure 4.6.[55] A more recent photograph shows the same piece after alien fragments and modern material were removed during conservation (fig. 4.7), revealing a much more modest but nonetheless striking fragment.

A letter from Ayoub Rabenou to Pope, written in 1934, lays out the multitemporal and multilocational history of this object class.[56] Rabenou was writing

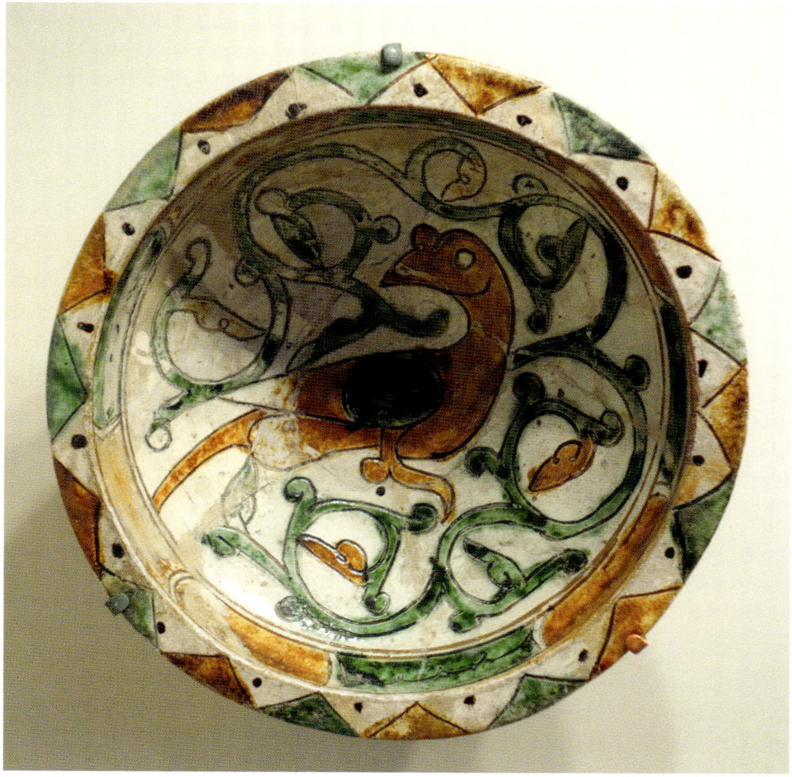

4.6. Bowl, earthenware with carved decoration and slip under a clear glaze (so-called Aghkand ware), prior to conservation. Attributed Azerbaijan or Georgia, possibly 12th or 13th century. Diameter approx. 25 cm. Cincinnati Art Museum, Museum Purchase, 1952.251.

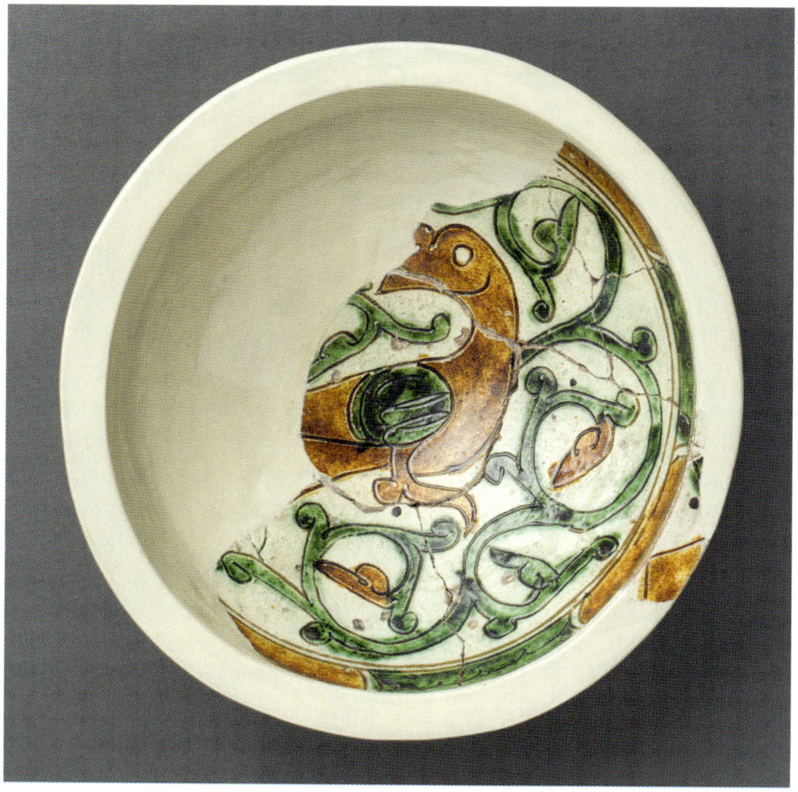

4.7. Bowl illustrated in figure 4.6, shown after conservation.

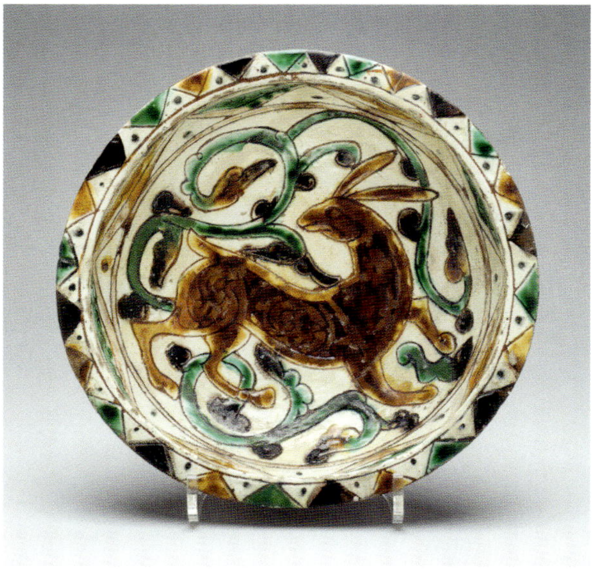

4.8. Bowl, glazed earthenware with carved decoration and slip under a clear glaze (so-called Aghkand ware). Diameter 25.4 cm. Fitzwilliam Museum, OC. 153–1946, Oscar Raphael Bequest.

in response to a query from Pope about an "Aghkand" bowl connected with "Mr Raphael," who must be the British collector Oscar Raphael (1874–1941). Pope had apparently sent Rabenou a photograph of Raphael's bowl; Rabenou, after studying the image, wrote to Pope that he thought Raphael's piece was not authentic. The bowl in question is likely the one published by Pope in 1931 and now in the Fitzwilliam Museum (fig. 4.8).[57] The backstory of the so-called Aghkand wares, as retailed by Rabenou, is that in 1912 a representative of Benjamin Mahboubian spent six months excavating at Aghkand.[58] (Rabenou's close familial relationship to Mahboubian presumably gave him access to the inside story.) At Aghkand, Mahboubian's agent found a few pieces of what is now known as Aghkand ware. These met with little regard in the market of the time and Mahboubian sold them cheaply. In 1919 and 1920 further digging at the site by others turned up some more pieces, this time with animal subjects like the bird seen on the CAM example. By Rabenou's reckoning no more than twelve to fifteen pieces of this type of ware were ever found at Aghkand; all the rest that appeared on the market were inauthentic. He further specifies that falsifications of "Aghkand wares" were produced in Paris from 1923 or 1924 onward.

"Aghkand ware" bowls that look like complete forgeries can certainly be seen in collection databases and at recent auctions, although as Rabenou himself noted, one always needs to examine a piece in person to be sure.[59] Such pieces may one day turn out to confirm Rabenou's assertion of French production, perhaps even involving the infamous Samson et Cie. The ambiguity of Rabenou's wording in his letter to Pope leaves open the question of whether the bricolaging of the Kelekian/CAM bowl would have been done in Iran or in Paris, but the former is much more likely. Not only did the Parisian "falsification" of Aghkand wares begin (according to Rabenou) after this piece had arrived at the V&A in 1922, but there is also highly skilled bricolaging, definitely performed in Iran, to be seen on a "Garrus ware" bowl that reached the V&A in the same batch as this bowl (see figs. 2.53 and 2.54). Thus, in terms of fabrication techniques and locations, bricolage in Iran may have given way to whole-cloth forgeries in France as the market profile of these pieces rose. On the other hand, Rabenou's entire story to Pope may simply have been intended as misdirection away from his own enterprises of ceramics copying.

In an ironic coda, the purported rarity of these bowls and their association with Aghkand have both turned out to be red herrings. In reality, the "Aghkand wares" only appeared to be rarities when they were first uncovered in Iran because they were probably not actually made there but were instead produced at sites farther north in Azerbaijan and Georgia—where many more have since been excavated.[60]

After all this activity in Aleppo, Tehran, and Paris, there is also evidence of some ceramics bricolaging within the United States. In 1927 Pope wrote to the Parish-Watson dealership asking them to take charge of repairing a "little Rhages ewer" for him after it arrived at their New York offices. "It was almost intact when I got it but it was badly smashed in transit, and it was only patched together temporarily in the [Chicago] Art Institute. Would you be good enough to turn it over to your repairer, and ask him to make it as fine as possible."[61] He later mentions that he only wants it "worked over so as not to be conspicuous."[62] This was perhaps a wise choice, in light of the extreme fabrication and fabulation that seems to have characterized the Islamic ceramics traded through Parish-Watson. No name or location is given for the repairer, who was presumably based in or near New York City.

Practicalities and Pitches

In a century of movement, how did such fragile objects travel? Long-distance communication and transportation technologies, including telegraph, steamships, trains, and eventually gasoline-powered vehicles, enabled the rise of the antiquities market. The route taken by the ceramics Pope sent to Detroit from his chaotic 1929/30 excavations at Rayy for the DIA (see chapter 2) seems quite typical for the time. The pieces appear to have been transported from Tehran to Baghdad by the Persia Export Company, from Baghdad to Paris with the involvement of the art packers and handlers Maison Lérondelle, by steamship passage (arranged by Ayoub Rabenou) from Paris to New York, then by railroad to Detroit.[63] The hazards of earlier passage were giving way to more and faster routes of connectivity. Gone were the times when collectors like Freer could have a crate of Syrian sculptures smuggled in 1908 from Aleppo to Damascus to Haifa, only to be seized by the Ottoman authorities at Haifa before it could be shipped across the Mediterranean and onto London and New York.[64]

Transport infrastructure may have changed but in this maelstrom of movement, ceramics still got broken in shipping. In 1910 Freer complained to the Marcopolis about their poor packing of a ceramic shipment from Aleppo, which resulted in most of the pieces arriving in Detroit damaged and broken; in 1934 Pope was remonstrating with Rabenou about the very same problems of inadequate packing in shipments sent from Paris to New York, Chicago, and Kansas City.[65] Scattered across the archives are various acknowledgments of the fragmentary condition of these pieces and the vulnerability of old animal glue joins, especially to the humidity created by packing and shipping in excelsior (a packing material made from wood fibers). There are quite a few tense exchanges over pieces that arrived broken.[66]

Financially, money moved internationally via telegraphic transfer between banks. Telegraphically transferred credit advances ("wire transfers") and currency exchange were necessary if an agent sought to make purchases in the region, rather than via invoices from established dealers. For example, from Tehran in 1929, Pope asked the DIA to wire advance credit to him at the Guaranty Trust in Paris: "I will transfer by wire the exact amount of notes issued to my account in the Imperial Bank of Persia here; the balance I will keep for one or two purchases I think that I can make in Russia."[67] Financial institutions also provided other services necessary to the antiquities trade. As noted in chapter 1, these included not only the financial instruments of credit and mortgaging, but also secure physical storage for the objects. Banks also had an important social function for international travelers: the use of banks as international "care of" addresses and recommenders of personal standing appears across all sorts of professional correspondence in the first decades of the twentieth century.[68]

Once the objects were looking presentable and had arrived in the country of final destination, what happened next? They would be put on display in the dealer's premises, of course, but the most ambitious dealers did not restrict their objects to the shop window. Exhibitions at museums became arguably the most important route by which commercially available antiquities were circulated, exposed to buyers, and raised in value. Many early exhibitions of Islamic art were made up largely of objects loaned from dealers, especially in the United States where there were fewer established private collectors of Islamic art than in Europe. Dealers had the stock, after all, before collectors or museums did. They were also usually willing to cover the transportation and insurance costs of lending their objects, rather than requiring the host institution to cover those costs as it normally would if seeking loans from another institution. In return for the outlay on shipping and insurance, dealers might expect to make a sale of some of their pieces to the host institution after the exhibition was over. They also got the publicity and pedigree that their objects accrued through such exposure, which they knew would translate into increased financial value. This model enabled many museums to put on exhibitions of Islamic art in the first half of the twentieth century without significant collections of their own.[69] The loan exhibition of Islamic art held at the Cleveland Museum of Art in 1944, for example, included loans from "17 museums, 10 collectors, and 12 dealers" (fig. 4.9).[70] Sometimes the dealers themselves instigated exhibitions: for example, the *Special Exhibition of Persian Art* held at Toledo Museum of Art in 1935 appears to have been initiated by a suggestion from Hagop Kevorkian that he send the museum some of his pieces for display (fig. 4.10).[71]

In such an ecology, dealers anticipated sales to result directly from exhibitions and were disappointed if they didn't occur. An exchange between Arthur Upham Pope and Dikran Kelekian in 1927 shows Kelekian displeased at the outcome of the Persian exhibit arranged by Pope at the 1926 Philadelphia Sesquicentennial—an event that had caused great friction between the two men before it closed, with Kelekian threatening at one point to withdraw his entire

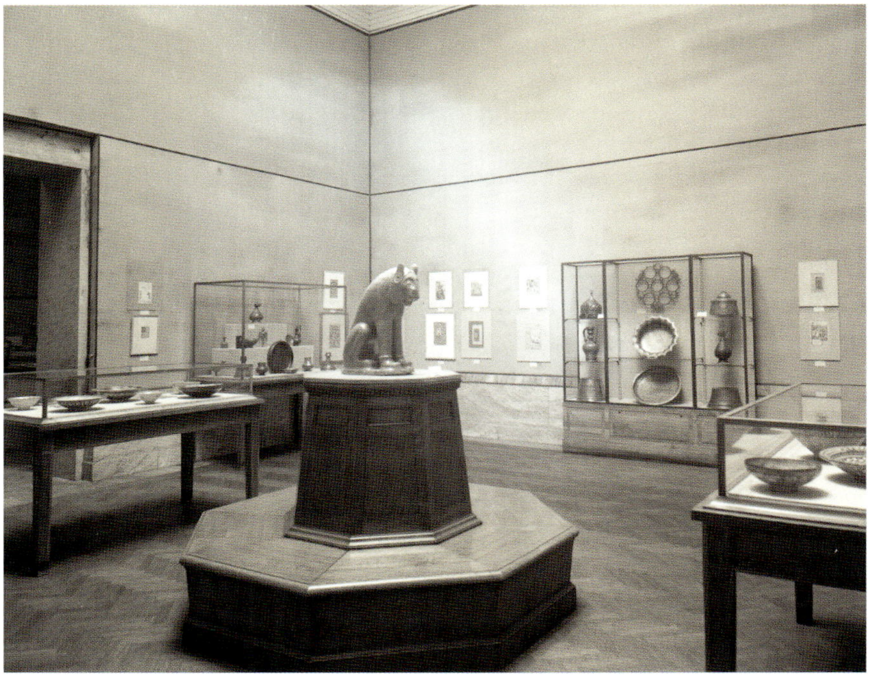

4.9. Installation view of exhibition *Islamic Art*, 3 November 1944–4 February 1945. Cleveland Museum of Art Archives, negative no. 21123A.

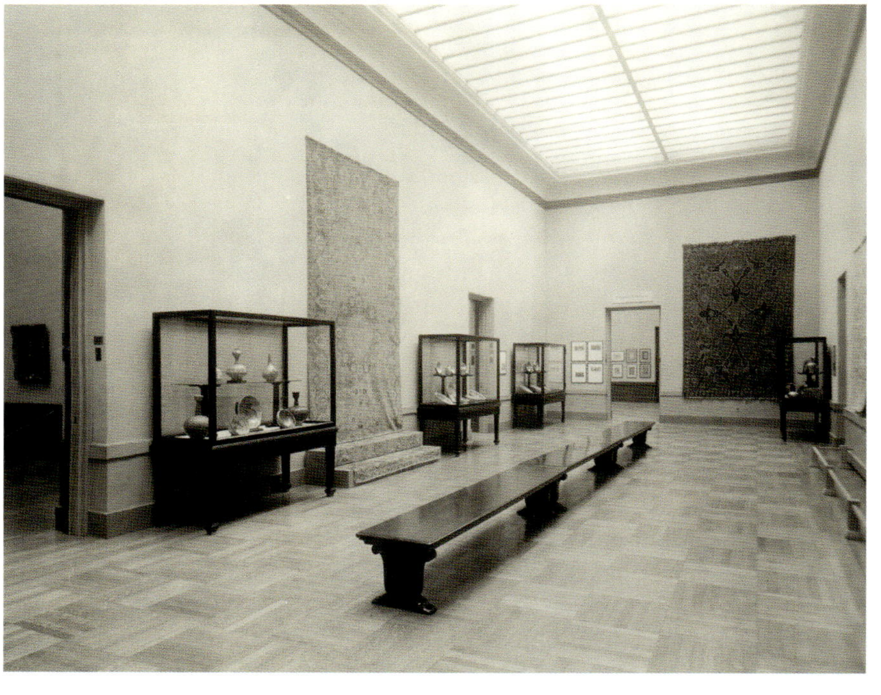

4.10. Installation view of exhibition *Persian Art*, 1935. Toledo Museum of Art curatorial files.

textile collection from display in the pavilion Pope had designed (fig. 4.11).[72] Pope, replying to complaints from Kelekian, wrote, "As for the Philadelphia exhibit, you say you 'got no benefit whatsoever out of it.' As a result of that exhibit you sold the basin for $5,000, the Rhodian textile for $750, a couple of Persian miniatures for nearly $2,000, and a door.... I know just how disappointing it was to you, but don't forget that it cost me nearly $6,000 and nearly put me in my grave. Between $50,000 and $60,000 worth of things were

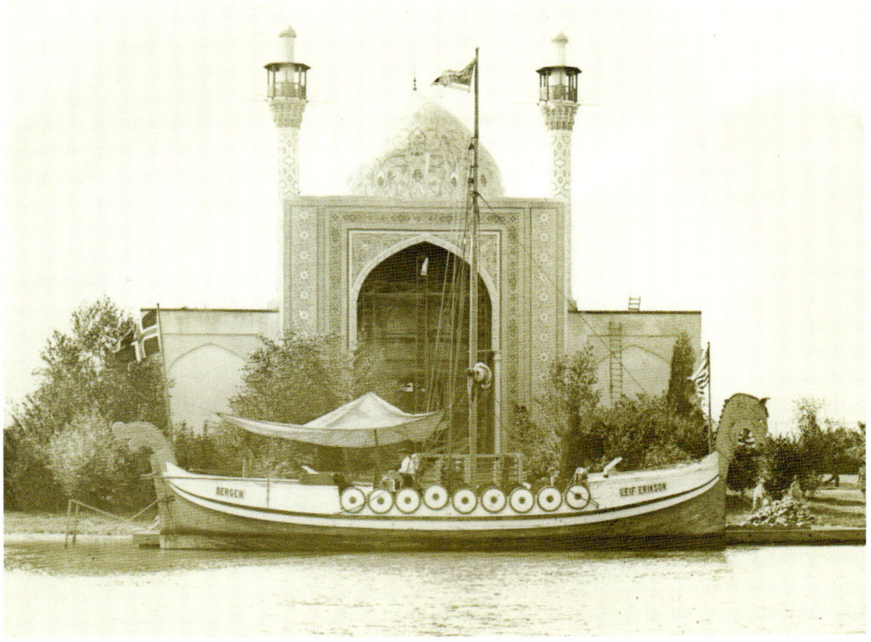

4.11. *The Leif Erikson in Front of the Persian Pavilion, Philadelphia Sesqui-Centennial Exposition,* 1926. Photographic print.

sold."[73] Exhibitions were a business. In spite of his protests to Kelekian, Pope received a fee from the organizing committee for his role in the pavilion and presumably further money from the government of Reza Shah, who selected him for the task. He also took a 10 percent cut from all exhibits sold.[74] But even for individuals as savvy as Kelekian or Pope, things did not always go to plan. When all else failed, lower-value items that were proving hard to shift were sometimes sold off at Collector's Corner, or batch resold to other dealers.[75]

These, then, were the mechanics by which Islamic ceramics were moved around in the antiquities market. But what was the language that accompanied all that movement? Sales pitches were many and varied, but the trope of scarcity was the most prevalent. This was not new; anxieties about antiquities as a finite resource had been going on for a long time. Already in 1875 Robert Murdoch Smith was urging the V&A authorities to move fast on buying up Jules Richard's collection of Iranian art in Tehran, arguing that "[Isfahan] has however been so much ransacked of late years by European Collectors and their Persian Agents that articles of value and interest such as those in M. Richard's collection are now only rarely to be found."[76] Unsurprisingly, by the early twentieth century one encounters everywhere dealer reports of scarcity and dwindling supplies, almost invariably attached to a "buy now while stocks last" pitch for a specific object. In a related maneuver, forgeries were sometimes even presented as stolen property, wanted by the authorities in their country of origin, as a tactic to increase their scarcity value, market mystique, and perceived verisimilitude.[77]

As well as talking up individual pieces, dealers sometimes threw in sweeteners, gifting a piece or two to a museum that was making a significant purchase. This created a network of personal obligations, as well as positioning dealers within the socially elevated class of donors and institutional patrons.[78] Sometimes these sweeteners were felt to raise awkwardness: a letter from Kirkor Minassian in 1925 to the director of the DIA references a request made by the latter to pay for something that Minassian had offered as a gift. Minassian surrendered the point, writing, "I shall accept $300 in payment for it since it puts you at ease in the matter. I did not, however, intend the gift to influence your attitude in the purchase of my objects, at present or in the future."[79]

More complex tactics seen in the archives included playing institutions off against each other—a process that proved very successful in the case of the Kelekian ceramics collection, detailed below. The usual line was to tell institution A that certain pieces have already been offered to institution B at such-and-such a price, but that the dealer would be willing to offer them to institution A at a discount in view of the dealer's long relationship with institution A, or out of an earnest desire to have such pieces better known to the people of Detroit, or Toledo, or wherever.[80] Some of the most oozy buttering-up came, inevitably, from Pope. "I did not wish to make any money on Detroit, but sincerely did wish to make a contribution to the institution. I think it is one of the most perfectly planned and executed of any small museum in the world."[81] This is part of a classic one-two punch by Pope: you're awfully good, but I could make you better. Similarly, he wrote to Philip Adams, director of the Cincinnati Art Museum, in 1954, "Your faience collection is one of the best outside the three or four greatest museums—but its foundation is weak and doesn't give quite a fair picture of the art as Persia developed it. What would you think of a history of music that couldn't find room for Bach or a collection of Hi Fi records that couldn't afford a collection of Vivaldis?"[82] The "Bach" in this case was the heavily restored Central Asian epigraphic bowl seen in chapter 3 (see fig. 3.23).

Of course, authenticity was also a recurring theme in dealer correspondence with buyers. Dealers frequently delivered warnings to curators and collectors about forgeries, generally with the implication that they and they alone could be trusted to distinguish and deliver the real thing. In correspondence with brokers like Pope they sometimes reported directly on who was inserting forgeries into the supply chain. Thus Khan Monif wrote to Pope in 1927, "I am not able to find any really antique doors [in Persia], they are making lots of fakes, especially painted doors, all the painted doors Kevorkian has are fakes."[83] But in letters to final-end consumers, norms of business meant that written warnings were most often given without naming names. Hence Dikran Kelekian wrote in December 1934 to J. Arthur MacLean, curator of the Toledo Museum of Art, as the latter prepared his exhibition of Iranian art,

> I am sorry to have to draw your attention to the fact that in recent years many very cleverly made forgeries of textiles and potteries have appeared on the market and that dealers and experts have been fooled by them and even sold them, although honestly, as genuine, through lack of experience. I wish therefore to warn you, confidentially, to be careful while making your selection from the pieces submitted to you...[84]

Later the very same month, Hagop Kevorkian wrote to the same curator,

> There is another piece of private information which I feel I ought to give you at this time as it might serve useful purpose. I refer to frequency of forgery which appeared, in recent years, in Persia and European and American markets concerning mostly done to pottery and Miniatures. Some of these are

> very skillfully done. In many cases, which fell under my notice, old material has been used which makes their detection extremely difficult; Some, otherwise respectable dealers are involved though in good faith.[85]

It is hard to tell at this distance in time if these twinned warnings were coincidental, or briefing against each other, or deliberately coordinated to keep MacLean on his guard against an unnamed third party. The forgeries using "old material" that Kevorkian mentions could certainly apply to the techniques of ceramics bricolage and resurfacing discussed in chapter 3, many of which were in very wide circulation by the mid 1930s.

Finally, if there is one word that emblematizes the language of dealers, it is "fine." Everywhere it is repeated as a term of praise, as if it has almost talismanic powers. Fine potteries, fine miniatures, fine manuscripts: everything is "fine." Along with "masterpiece," the word "fine" was and is so entrenched in dealer lexicon that its appearance within the description of an artwork can function as a tell of commercial authorship. At times "fineness" is invoked almost as if it were a legally binding category. Writing in 1927, Khan Monif declared to Pope, "Referring to the miniatures left with Mrs Drum and you, once more I assure you that every one of them is fine and I guaranty them in every way and at any time I guaranty to refund the money if any one of them which you found is not fine enough."[86]

Conflicts of Interest: Dealers, Brokers, Scholars

It is clear that many dealers were sensitive about how their trade was named and framed. Operating in an elite social world where there were inhibitions about acknowledging profit as a direct motive, and often coming from ethnic or religious groups that were perceived as outsiders to that world, dealers frequently took pains to represent what they were doing as a form of expertise born out of the love of art. There are frequent claims in dealer correspondence of pieces being sold at cost price or less in order that such-and-such object should have the perfect institutional home, painting antiquities dealing as "principally a labor of love."[87] In a 1964 witness testimony concerning the sale of an antiquity, Fahim Kouchakji, then late in his career, described himself in the opening questions as an art dealer, semiretired (he was in fact still dealing at this point; see chapter 5), as well as a collector. He was keen, however, to represent himself as a collector and independent expert rather than a vendor or a broker, per se:

> Mr. Sutter: Q. Well, I take it from your answers that you have been dealing with antiquities for some 50 odd years? Do you purchase and resell Hellenistic-Syrian antiquities?
>
> The Witness: A. I used to. Now, if I find something suitable for my private collection, I purchase it for my own.
>
> [. . .]
>
> Q. I would like to ask you whether you have participated in the sale of any antiquities which you either purchased and resold or just acted as a broker and a dealer.
>
> A. Oh, no, I never act as a broker. I buy things and so did my family. We never acted as brokers. We would buy things for our own and resell them.[88]

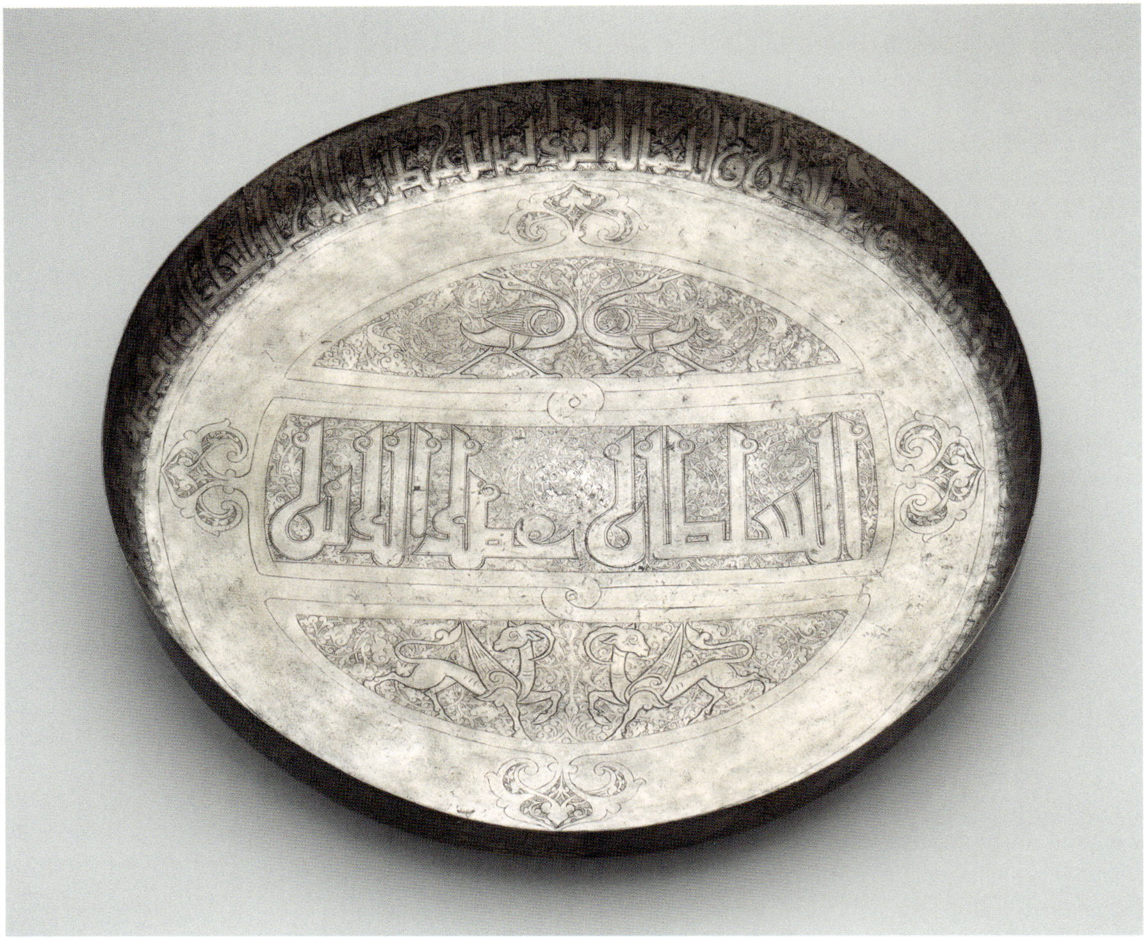

4.12. Salver, hammered and chased silver, with inscribed dedication to Alp Arslan (ruled 1063–1072) and date H. 459 (1066–67 CE). Iran, probably early twentieth century. Diameter 41 cm. Museum of Fine Arts, Boston, Martha Silsbee Fund, 34.68.

In related rhetoric, Pope set himself up as a "museum's agent" as opposed to a dealer or broker.[89] In his long and checkered career as not-quite-scholar, not-quite-archaeologist, and not-quite-curator, Pope worked hand-in-glove with several dealers. Essentially, he served as their broker, in a manner not dissimilar to the institution of the *dallal* mentioned in chapter 2.[90] As noted above, Pope worked most extensively with Rabenou, but he also brokered deals for Kelekian, Khan Monif, Nazare-Aga, Demotte, and others, carrying news of their objects to museums and collectors, arranging terms, setting dealer and buyer up with each other, and receiving a cut of the final sale price.[91] This made his employment by a collecting institution untenable, hence his eventual departure from the position of advisory curator at the Art Institute of Chicago after antiquities he had brokered for Rabenou failed to materialize for years and the institution grew tired of his modus operandi.[92] Serious question marks remain around some of the pieces whose sales he zealously promoted, like the Alp Arslan silver salver now regarded by many specialists as a twentieth-century object rather than an eleventh-century one (fig. 4.12). Moreover, there are several proven forgeries brokered by Pope, most famously the *Andarznama* manuscript (see fig. 4.4) and the artificially aged "Buyid silk" forgeries that he circulated and published with his wife, Phyllis Ackerman.[93]

There have long been questions about how aware Pope was that some of the pieces he promoted were optimistic fabrications or outright forgeries. Certainly, his desire to believe in—and promote—objects that attested to the greatness of what Judith Lerner has called a "nearly immutable Persian artistic sensibility" seems genuine, if somewhat messianic.[94] From the archives of his correspondence in the New York Public Library, it appears his lack of knowledge about the origins of the pieces he brokered was at times quite startling. For example, in unguarded correspondence of 1934 about some woodcarvings, he asked Ayoub Rabenou, "Is it possible to find out from what monument your carved wooden doors came from? It would be the greatest triumph possible for me if I could find that building. If I could get a trace of it, I would send Farajollah to photograph it."[95] (Rabenou avoided answering the question in his letter of reply.) Such lack of awareness is not out of step with the standards of the time, when collectors generally accepted what they were told (or not told) about provenience by dealers, but it is a little surprising that someone so deeply embroiled in the supply end of the chain—and who boasted so much of his insider knowledge—could be so clueless as to the origins of the pieces he promoted.

The kickbacks and percentages Pope received do not appear to have made him colossally rich. Whatever one thinks of him, his drive to create a commercial and institutional profile for Iranian art had a missionary zeal to it that suggests other motivations in addition to money. The same can perhaps be said for all successful antiquities dealers, to a greater or lesser extent. It would be very naïve to lose sight of the fact that everyone working in the antiquities trade was there principally to make money, but it was also quite a strange and risky line of work. Those who succeeded in it and were able to convince collectors to buy their wares must have been compelled by the artifacts they traded—and perhaps also by less tangible things, like social ambition and posterity—in ways that went beyond the bottom line.[96]

Outsiders might well ask where, if anywhere, was the regulation of this market? How could a trade that depended so heavily on the authenticity of historical objects have so few mechanisms for guaranteeing that authenticity? In fact, there were systems of a sort, but they were fundamentally flawed. There existed a form of certification within the Paris market, described by Brocklebank in 1931 in relation to some Kubachi wares he believed to be forgeries, withdrawn from a 1927 auction after appearing in the sale catalogue (see fig. 2.13).[97] "When objets d'art are sent for sale by auction in Paris, they have to pass through expert hands and bear a certificate of genuineness if described as let us say 'ancien faïence de Koubatcha' in the catalogue."[98] To avoid conflicts of interest, however, such a system would obviously require a complete and insurmountable firewall between those who perform authentication and those who stand to benefit from it financially, professionally, or socially. Self-evidently, no such firewall was, is, or ever will be possible. In illustration of the problems this raises, Charles Vignier appears to have operated as an authenticator on the Paris market, as well as a dealer—leading, inevitably, to questions about the authenticity of objects he validated. In a revealing exchange in 1930 over a set of supposedly antique doors from Hamadan, Mehmet Ağa-Oğlu wrote with strained politeness to the dealers Arnold Seligmann, Rey and Co., "I fully believe that you and Mr. [Joseph] Brummer bought them under guaranty from Mr. Vignier. I am well aware that Mr. Vignier is an 'expert assermenté', but nevertheless the doors are of a later period."[99]

Informal versions of this system existed elsewhere in Europe and the United States, with dealers often serving as the experts who pronounced on authenticity. Fahim Kouchakji, in his 1964 witness statement, described himself as fulfilling this role for private individuals, and he seems to have been asked to provide such an assessment of the National Museum of Asian Art's Raqqa ceramics in the early 1940s (see chapter 5).[100] The fundamental conflicts of interest inherent in this model have never really been surmounted, and the same problems dog the antiquities market today.

As the twentieth century went on, the gradual professionalization of scholarly archaeology and art history started to draw a dotted line between scholars and dealers. Things were anything but sharply defined, though. Some academics with positions at exalted universities brokered or directly sold antiquities to museums, or wrote commercial catalogues of objects for sale, paid for their expertise by dealers. This is one form of the value-boosting "scholarly transactions" discussed in the introduction to this book. To take one example among many, Rudolf Meyer Riefstahl (1880–1936), Professor of Fine Arts at New York University from 1924, worked prior to his appointment at NYU as a dealer and professional writer for the market, first in Europe and then in the United States.[101] He wrote commercial catalogues for Anderson Galleries, as well as dealers and collectors including Parish-Watson, P. Jackson Higgs, and Phoebe Hearst—in fact, he cut his teeth in the United States on the 1917 Hearst catalogue that he prepared with none other than Arthur Upham Pope and Phyllis Ackerman.[102] Riefstahl's bona fides as a scholar and later a university professor now gives his commercial writing the appearance of disinterested scholarship when it was in fact paid for (much, although not all, of it was undertaken prior to his appointment to NYU, it should be noted). An example of this is discussed in chapter 5, a small but luxuriously produced and privately published catalogue of so-called Raqqa wares, belonging to an unnamed owner (actually the dealer P. Jackson Higgs), that Riefstahl authored circa 1926 (fig. 4.13).

In Riefstahl's time there was considerable slippage between the emerging career paths in professional art history: scholar, dealer, curator. The conflicts of interest that ensued, however, can no longer be judged as lightly as they once were. One egregious example is the career of Ralph Van Deman Magoffin (1874–1942), a professor of classics at NYU from 1923 to 1930. In 1927 he wrote to the DIA to offer the complete contents of a Palestinian tomb:

> While in Palestine last spring, I attended the excavations of five tombs near the Syrian border. The contents of all five were practically alike so far as the twenty or twenty-five pieces of pottery went. I brought back the pottery contents of two of the tombs. When one of the tombs had been cleaned out supposedly, it was decided just for fun to dig on below the floor, and about two feet down were found two skeletons and with them some beads and rings and four pairs of earrings.[103]

The DIA did not buy Magoffin's wares, but records of what he was offering are preserved in the museum's archives and document his direct involve-

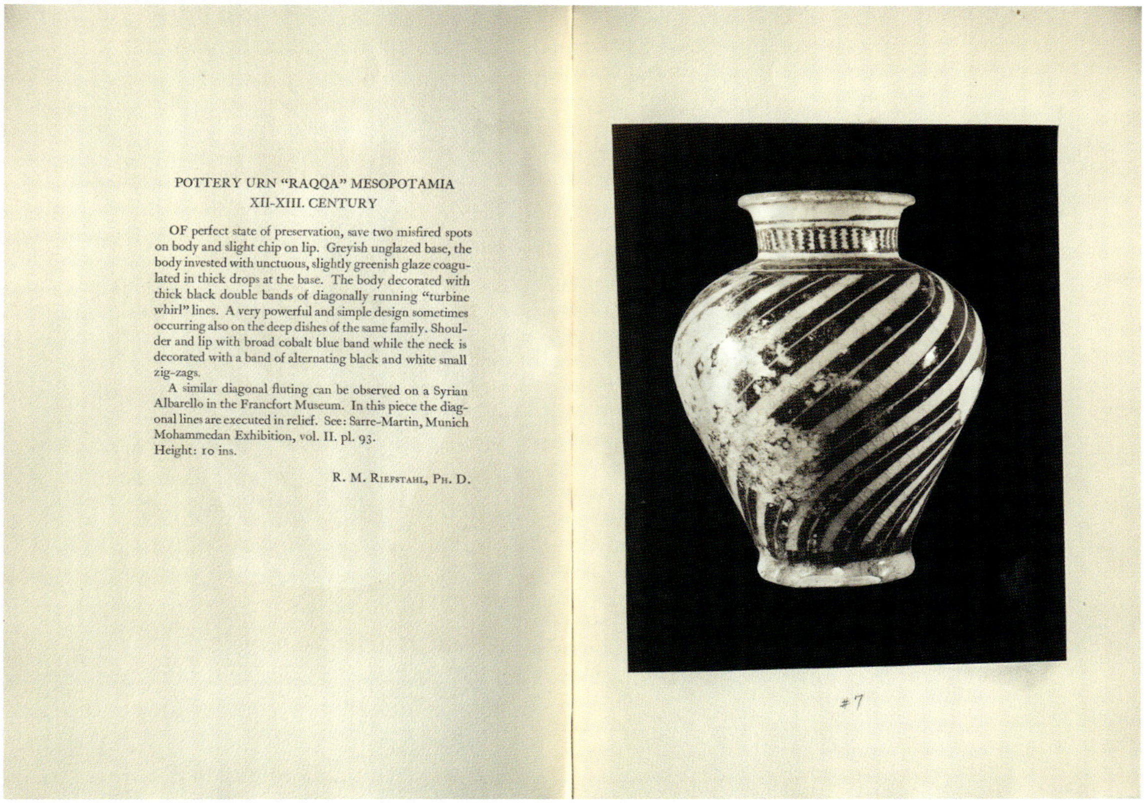

POTTERY URN "RAQQA" MESOPOTAMIA
XII-XIII. CENTURY

OF perfect state of preservation, save two misfired spots on body and slight chip on lip. Greyish unglazed base, the body invested with unctuous, slightly greenish glaze coagulated in thick drops at the base. The body decorated with thick black double bands of diagonally running "turbine whirl" lines. A very powerful and simple design sometimes occurring also on the deep dishes of the same family. Shoulder and lip with broad cobalt blue band while the neck is decorated with a band of alternating black and white small zig-zags.

A similar diagonal fluting can be observed on a Syrian Albarello in the Francfort Museum. In this piece the diagonal lines are executed in relief. See: Sarre-Martin, Munich Mohammedan Exhibition, vol. II. pl. 93.
Height: 10 ins.

R. M. RIEFSTAHL, PH. D.

#7

4.13. Rudolf Meyer Riefstahl, *A Collection of Ancient Raqqa Pottery* [1926], unnumbered plate [7]. Object now Cincinnati Art Museum, 1948.117.

ment in tomb-robbing within the former Ottoman Empire to obtain antiquities, which he then offered for sale:

> 9. 2 pairs solid gold earrings of 8th or 10th century B.C. (1 pair 1½ inches long) dug from tomb in Palestine above the sea of Galilee, close to the border of Syria, obtained by R.V.D. Magoffin on the spot of the excavation.
>
> 10. Seal of white jade with running deer in intaglio on bevel. Obtained by friend from a dig in Mesopotamia.
>
> 11. 4 pairs gold earrings, one extra, from tomb in Syria, dug up in 1926. Beautiful things.
>
> [. . .]
>
> 17. 1 box Phoenician beads (66 of them), splendid assortment, from tomb R.V.D.M. saw excavated in Upper Palestine in 1926.[104]

At the same time that university professors were peddling their archaeological finds, fully market-facing figures like Pope and Ackerman premised their personal authority upon research credentials they were at pains to assert. Alert buyers, however, were very well aware that Pope was not a disinterested scholarly advisor. As Royall Tyler wrote in 1931 to his friend, the collector Mildred Bliss,

> I spent a week in London and had a good look at the Persian Exhibition [the International Exhibition of Persian Art held at the Royal Academy of Arts in

> 1931]. It was a fine show, but not quite as good as I had expected. The pottery might have been much better, had the organizers asked for Kelekian's collection, at present deposited at the Victoria and Albert, which Kelekian would have been glad to lend. Instead of this, there were a great many rather inferior pieces belonging to Messrs Parish Watson and their clients. One was thus forcibly reminded of the fact that the animateur of the exhibition [i.e., Pope] is a business associate of certain dealers, an observation which one could not help making in other connections besides that of pottery.[105]

As the fault lines widened, tensions between commercial and academic attitudes to art objects increased. A letter from Phyllis Ackerman to the director of the DIA, William Valentiner, illustrates the increasing incommensurability of knowledge industries in the divided world order of the twentieth century. As a commercial operator based in the United States, Ackerman was nonplussed and apparently frustrated by the standards of scientific archaeology emerging in the Soviet bloc. Writing from France in 1929, following a trip to the Soviet Union with Pope and a solo return through Europe, she complained, "Poland was beastly and all the kunsthistorikers standing around moaning about their limited opportunities and yet not doing any decent work on what they have got. And arguing for an hour, without any evidence, whether a filthy rag of a rug came from one bank or the other of some damned river, when the thing may just as well have come from a dump heap and should be sent back at once."[106] The free marketeers of the west saw stringent scientific research as a threat to the beauty and glamour of their trade, while archaeology in the Communist world—which had its own narratives to promote—had little time for the fictions of the western market.

Kelekian's Ceramics at the V&A

The last part of this chapter turns to the revealing case of Dikran Kelekian's ceramics. This group of 182 premodern Islamic ceramic objects entered the sphere of stable documentation relatively early, between 1910 and 1926, making some of them extremely important exemplars for this book. Kelekian's collection consolidated an embryonic canon of Islamic ceramics, with a pronounced emphasis on glazed Iranian stonepaste, and was formed during a period when there were some largely complete original pieces still moving through the market—along with increasing numbers of pastiches, confections, and reglazed and refired pieces.[107] The eventual fate of Kelekian's collection illustrates both the global transfer of financial might from Europe to the United States, and the final translation of physical artifact into virtual asset.

In August 1909 Dikran Kelekian and the Victoria and Albert Museum began negotiations over what was initially proposed as a loan of approximately fifty "of the most remarkable pieces of antique Persian pottery" in Kelekian's collection. These were to be loaned from the dealer's collection in Paris to the museum in London, freeing them from storage in the vaults of the Crédit Lyonnais to enjoy public view for what was initially agreed to be a period of two years.

It is hard to tell from the surviving correspondence who made the first approach, but both sides were keen, and the number of ceramics in the proposed

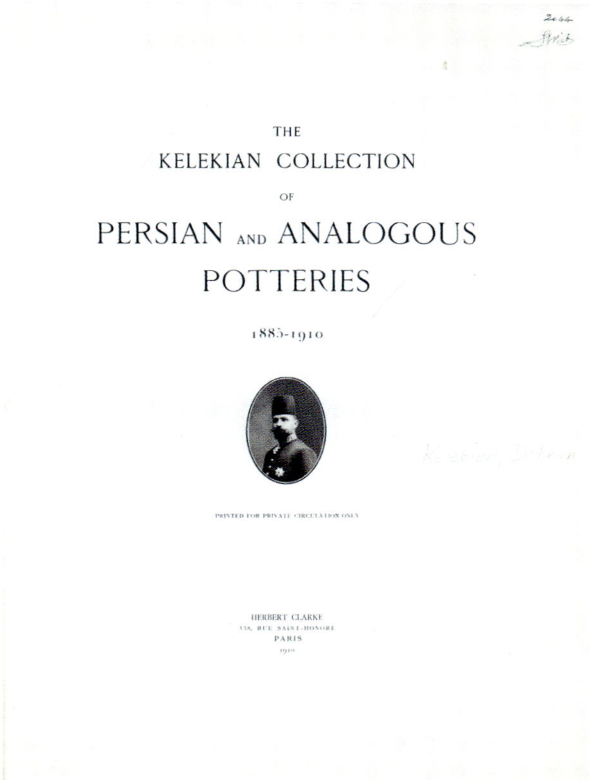

THE
KELEKIAN COLLECTION
OF
PERSIAN AND ANALOGOUS
POTTERIES
1885-1910

PRINTED FOR PRIVATE CIRCULATION ONLY

HERBERT CLARKE
338, RUE SAINT-HONORÉ
PARIS
1910

4.14. Dikran Kelekian, *The Kelekian Collection of Persian and Analogous Potteries, 1885–1910* (Paris: Herbert Clarke, 1910), title page.

loan increased along the way. The initial loan of what was by then 127 pieces was received by the V&A in December 1910. The first 112 of these objects had been published in 1910 in a luxurious privately issued volume, *The Kelekian Collection of Persian and Analogous Potteries, 1885–1910* (fig. 4.14).[108] Prepared as a limited print run, Kelekian sent copies of this promotional volume to museum directors and connoisseurs across Europe and the United States, sometimes with personal inscriptions and compliments on the title page. For the V&A, the Kelekian ceramics loan represented an excellent group of objects, in an area in which they had only recently begun serious collecting, that they could have for free to put on public display. A major point of appeal for the museum was the loan's potential to expand the museum's educational mission, at a moment when the medieval ceramics of the Middle East (especially lusterwares) were beginning to be recognized as exemplars for industrial design in their own right.[109] For Kelekian, who had already forged some advantageous connections in the United States, it was an opportunity to exhibit some of his wares at a most prestigious venue in London, a much shorter and safer journey from Paris than sending them across the Atlantic.[110]

The director of the V&A noted from the outset that there were potential issues in accepting a loan of this kind from a dealer. Namely, "[i]t is obvious that should Mr. Kelekian ultimately desire to sell his collection, the very fact that they have been exhibited in this Museum must inevitably increase their value."[111] This was an astute observation on the part of the museum authorities, who were aware how the market worked. In particular, the V&A had recently learned from its dealings with J. P. Morgan's enormous collection of medieval art, which included objects of doubtful worth as well as high-quality pieces, that collectors and dealers sought the scholarly transaction of display in a prestigious museum because it gave them free access to expertise and increased the value of their pieces.[112] In the case of Kelekian's ceramics, the V&A certainly had an eye to their own possible purchase, somewhere down the line, of the collection or parts thereof. However, they were also quite sensibly concerned about creating a precedent whereby dealers could start lodging pieces with them as a way of raising the profile, pedigree, and market value of their stock, and the damage this could do to the institution's public and academic reputation.

Accordingly, the loan agreement with Kelekian was drawn up with several provisos intended to forestall, as far as possible, use of the museum as a machine for boosting the pedigree of his ceramics prior to selling them.[113] As to value, Kelekian requested that the loan collection—which stood at 125 pieces by the time the agreement was being settled in late 1910—be valued at £125,000. This was an utterly extraordinary valuation by the standards of the time and completely out of step with the market. The V&A authorities noted as much, remarking that this "absolutely prohibitive" valuation "has the advantage that it makes it practically not for sale," thereby apparently removing any likelihood that Kelekian would attempt to sell the collection onward during the period of the loan. With the loan initially thought to be only for two years' duration, the museum moved forward with this fantastic valuation in place. Those in charge trusted that if, at the end of two years, they wanted to buy the collection and Kelekian was interested in selling it, they would probably be able to negotiate a more realistic price based on current market rates.[114] This was a decision that their successors would come to regret, several decades later.

Two years passed and the collection continued its stay in the V&A. A request to extend the loan for another two years was granted in December 1912, and another was sent to Paris in December 1914 but the disruptions of World War I meant it never received an answer. In 1919 Kelekian wrote of possibly ending the loan in 1920, but he did not follow up on this and continued to add pieces to it.[115] His last additions to the V&A loan group were made in the 1920s, including the "Garrus ware" bowl (see fig. 2.51) and the "Aghkand ware" bowl (see figs. 4.6 and 4.7).[116] The final piece was added to the group in 1926, bringing the total number of ceramics in the Kelekian loan at the V&A to 182.[117]

From that point onward an intermittent, cordial correspondence continued between the V&A and Kelekian over matters relating to the publication of the collection, but the terms of the loan were not revisited. Meanwhile, Kelekian had expanded his business in the United States from his New York premises. He had many eager buyers of other Islamic ceramics, one of the most important of whom was Philip Adams (1908–1993), director of the Cincinnati Art Museum from 1945 to 1973. In 1948 the CAM finalized a long-orchestrated purchase of "seventy-two pieces of Near Eastern pottery" from Dikran Kelekian's stock (not in the V&A loan), several of them illustrated in this book. The purchase of these pieces for the museum by an anonymous donor was organized through extensive negotiation by Adams, who wrote in a letter to Kelekian that the purchase was "the fulfillment and monument to one of the most cherished friendships of my life."[118] Kelekian, for his part, seems to have regarded Adams as an ally and a friend. This relationship culminated in an enigmatic series of letters, now in the CAM archives, written during the last weeks of Kelekian's life.

When Artworks Become Assets: Kelekian's Will

Dikran Kelekian died by suicide on 30 January 1951, at the age of eighty-three. At seven that morning he fell to his death from the window of his suite on the twenty-third floor of the Hotel St. Moritz in New York, his slippers left side by side under the windowsill. According to a report in the *New York Times*, his vision and mobility were impaired and a nurse was tending him during the daytime, although he was alone at the time of his death.[119]

The archived correspondence sent from Dikran Kelekian to Philip Adams in the fortnight leading up to Kelekian's death is painful and confused. There is a telegram from Kelekian asking that the CAM pay him as soon as possible for his last shipment to them because he needed cash urgently, which Adams arranged for him. Harder to read, both literally and figuratively, are the handwritten letters on hotel notepaper that beat an anxious refrain of deep financial worries, people seeking money from him, and unhappiness with his family over the management of the business.[120] The last letter in the file from Kelekian to Adams was sent on 29 January, the day before his death. It is a comparatively cheerful note, repeating some gossip about the export of a Sasanian plate from Iran—information that he had already sent to Adams in another letter, three days earlier. There was, however, another letter seemingly sent to Adams the same day, which is no longer in the CAM archive. The now absent letter was marked "personal" and was returned to Kelekian's son Charles, at the latter's request, after Kelekian's death.[121]

It is not a secret that there was a conflict between Kelekian father and son in the period leading up to Kelekian senior's death. This much was reported in the *New York Times* a few days after Dikran's death, when the recently merged Bank of New York and Fifth Avenue Bank, one of three executors of the will, was appointed temporary administrator to resolve the estate. Reportedly, tensions at the Kelekian antiquities business were running so high that Charles barred Dikran's employees and associates from the business premises within days of his father's death.[122] Dikran Kelekian's wife had died in 1948 and at the time of his death he had recently revised his will. The new terms did not pass his residuary estate to his two adult children, Charles and Adine, but instead put the estate in trust, with the principal to pass upon their deaths to the Armenian General Benevolent Union (AGBU) and other charitable causes.[123] Kelekian had been a very active fundraiser and philanthropist for Armenian causes during the aftermath of the genocide and beyond, working with the AGBU and other organizations.[124] In addition to the bank, the two other executors of the will were Haik Kavookjian, a campaigner for charitable causes related to the Armenian church, and Hagop Andonian, representative of the AGBU.

The legal convolutions of the estate in 1951 and 1952 can be traced through the memos and correspondence from the bank, attorneys, and family members that piled up in the museums that held loans from Kelekian's collection at the time of his death, especially the V&A. In a copy of part of the will, now held in the V&A archives, it is written that Charles and Adine were to receive annuities of $7,500 a year each from the trust (equivalent to about $85,000 per annum in 2023), and Adine was also the sole beneficiary of a life insurance policy taken out by her father, less the value of outstanding loans against this policy.[125] Additionally, the will named Adine alone in a codicil that requested everything should be done to avoid selling the business and its assets at a sacrifice, "insofar as said procedure can be followed without depriving my daughter, Adine Kelekian, of the funds necessary for her maintenance and support."[126] Court rulings of 1952 and 1953 designate Adine "an Incompetent" living in Switzerland and represented by a guardian. It is not clear what this means, but it may explain her father's concerns about making sure she was provided for after his death.[127] Charles, meanwhile, seems to have been deliberately and pointedly excluded by his father from inheriting the business (where he had been serving as vice president for some years) and its assets, which were immediately taken under the control of the executors. The terms of the will evidently created confusion and surprise in many quarters. Charles's wife, Beatrice Kelekian, strongly implied in two letters to the director of the V&A that her father-in-law was not of sound mind when he changed his will in his last, unhappy weeks.[128]

We will never know Kelekian's inner state in his last days of life, nor what took place between father and son. Rereading Kelekian's last letters to Philip Adams only a few months after my own father's death, I recalled viscerally the shattering sadness of the notes I found around my father's house—my childhood home—in my last visits to him. On slips of paper, with names and instructions and questions written out over and over again in mounting confusion, I saw my father's intermittent terror at his own diminishing comprehension, his fear of a world that was no longer making sense, the anguish of searching in vain for a lost wife through a house he no longer always recognized as his own. The final stages of a mind being unstrung by illness, grief, and fear are terrible to witness. It can be dangerous to project one's own experiences onto the historical archive, but in their anxieties and confusions, Kelekian's last letters to Adams seemed to me to have the confused contours of a darkening and fragmenting mental state, with dangers sensed or imagined and drawing closer.

The legal processing of Kelekian's estate carried on throughout 1951, driven by the attorneys acting for the bank and the other two executors of the estate. Plainly, the executors all had good reason to seek to liquidate the collection as fast as possible, especially when the threat of a legal challenge from Charles and Beatrice Kelekian over the legitimacy of the will was clearly in the air. Letters went out to museums that held parts of the collection on loan, requesting complete inventories of all property owned by Kelekian: the one sent to the V&A was dated 2 February, three days after Kelekian's death. These were followed by recall notices as the bank sought to consolidate the collection in New York and get valuations prior to sale, or in some cases, letters of inquiry to the holding institutions about whether they wanted to buy the pieces Kelekian had loaned them. Somewhere along the line, however, differences between Charles Kelekian and the executors must have been settled, for by the spring of 1952 they were working together.

The letters sent from Beatrice Kelekian to the director of the V&A during the initial fallout from the will state unequivocally that Dikran Kelekian always intended to bequeath his ceramics collection to the V&A and had said so on many occasions to many people.[129] Beatrice and Charles Kelekian may have had their own motivations at that stage for seeking to demonstrate that the final will was the product of an unsound mind. There is no obvious reason, however, to doubt the sincerity of Beatrice's assertion. Kelekian had deposited the first tranche of the collection at the V&A over forty years earlier, and had he wanted to retrieve any or all of it at any point prior to his death, he could have. In effect, the V&A had served as a premium storehouse that both cared for his collection and gave its enormous public audience the opportunity to see his pieces and associate them with his name within a prestigious setting. It is not unusual for loans left with public institutions for such a great length of time to be converted to gift bequests after death by the prior arrangement of their owners, or sold to the holding institution en bloc at a favorable rate. There is more than just the immediate cash value of antiquities at stake in these transactions: considerable cultural capital inheres in having one's name live on through a renowned piece or collection displayed in a world-famous institution.

Kelekian's revised will made no specific mention of the V&A ceramics. Without a written gift agreement in place the ceramics were of course subject to the same conditions as the rest of the stock of the business. They were to be returned to New York and liquidated by whatever means the executors chose. The V&A naturally hoped the executors would honor Kelekian's promise of first refusal on the collection or parts thereof if it should be sold, which was written into his agreement with them in 1910. The executors' lawyers, however, did all they could to evade that commitment, claiming that their clients wanted to keep the entire Kelekian collection whole so they could sell it altogether.[130] This was a partial truth at best: rather than concerns about selling the entire collection whole (which would not have made any market sense), the executors undoubtedly preferred to get as many pieces as possible out of the UK and onto the New York market to avoid the risk of incurring UK duties and international currency exchange complications, and to maximize their chances of selling to financially healthy US institutions rather than cash-strapped European ones.[131]

It quickly became obvious that the V&A was not going to get to keep the collection unless it could pay for it. The question was, how much? The estate's lawyers tried to hold the museum to an en bloc purchase at the £125,000 valuation listed in the 1910 loan agreement, which was completely unrealistic in 1910 and even in 1951.[132] Estimates prepared by Sotheby's for probate valued the collection in 1951 at a fraction of that amount. However, the lawyers were not budging: the £125,000 valuation was in the original agreement, and that was what they would hold to. Meanwhile, the V&A curator and Islamic ceramics expert Arthur Lane set to work preparing detailed notes and prioritization groups for the whole collection, grouping them into "A" (most desirable), "B," and "C" (fig. 4.15). These lists were sent to the lawyers for the estate in January 1952, who then sent copies on to the executors in New York.[133] The V&A then submitted a formal proposal, dated 9 May 1952, to buy the pieces on

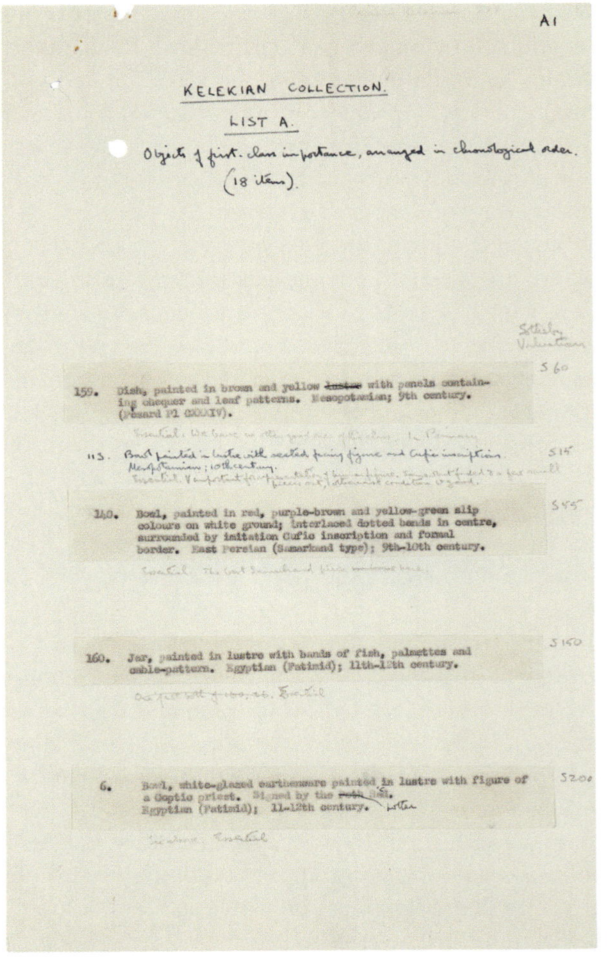

A1

KELEKIAN COLLECTION.

LIST A.

Objects of first-class importance, arranged in chronological order.
(18 items).

Sotheby Valuation

159. Dish, painted in brown and yellow ~~lustre~~ with panels containing chequer and leaf patterns. Mesopotamian; 9th century. (Pézard Pl CXXXIV). $60

113. Bowl painted in lustre with seated facing figure and Cufic inscriptions. Mesopotamian; 10th century. $15

140. Bowl, painted in red, purple-brown and yellow-green slip colours on white ground; interlaced dotted bands in centre, surrounded by imitation Cufic inscription and formal border. East Persian (Samarkand type); 9th-10th century. $45

160. Jar, painted in lustre with bands of fish, palmettes and cable-pattern. Egyptian (Fatimid); 11th-12th century. $150

6. Bowl, white-glazed earthenware painted in lustre with figure of a Coptic priest. Signed by the ~~potter~~ Sa'd. Egyptian (Fatimid); 11-12th century. $200

4.15. List of the Kelekian ceramics prepared by Arthur Lane and sent to the executors for Kelekian's estate, January 1952. Nominal File: Kelekian, Dikran, 1912–1954, Victoria and Albert Museum archives.

Lane's final A and B lists (forty-seven objects total) for £12,000, or failing that, a premium list of the fifteen pieces they most desired for £5,000.[134]

Eschewing the offer for the forty-seven pieces, the lawyers for the estate accepted the V&A's smaller offer of £5,000 for their top fifteen pieces. This left a handpicked list of thirty-two pieces still in play from Lane's initial forty-seven-object selection. Charles Kelekian took that list straight to Philip Adams at the CAM, offering him a set of objects selected from his father's famous collection by the world's leading expert on Islamic ceramics and asking what the CAM would be willing to pay for those pieces. Undated notes that must be from a telephone call between Philip Adams and Charles Kelekian, now held in the CAM archives, show the workings of the deal. Adams proposed an initial offer of $16,000 for the thirty-two pieces (i.e., $500 per object). Countering this, Charles Kelekian subtracted the V&A's accepted offer for the fifteen pieces (£5,000) from their initial offer for all forty-seven pieces (£12,000) to get £7,000, which he converted to a dollar equivalent of $19,600. He then asked Adams if the CAM would be prepared to pay a total of $20,300 for the thirty-two pieces, outbidding the V&A by $700.[135] Adams, despite originally offering him a considerably lower amount, was apparently happy to close the deal at $20,300. Charles Kelekian and the executors did not offer the V&A the chance to rebid and the group went to the CAM. By 22 May, Charles Kelekian confirmed that CAM's formal offer had been received and accepted by the executors and the deal was done.[136]

It is clear that in this case there was a preexisting desire to sell the pieces to Cincinnati rather than the V&A, and that this was not just about the money to be made in the immediate sale. As a business decision, it made good sense for Charles Kelekian and the estate's executors to continue the Kelekian family's longstanding relationship with the then-flush museum at Cincinnati. The Midwestern museums of the United States had been booming for some time and the CAM was far more likely to yield dividends in the form of future sales than was the cash-strapped and bureaucratic V&A. While everything involved was perfectly legal and reflects nothing more or less than the economic realpolitik of mid-twentieth-century museums, it is difficult not to feel a bit sorry for the V&A, or at least for Arthur Lane.[137] The V&A had stored, displayed, protected, conserved, and published the collection for four decades and through two world wars, and Lane—the foremost scholar of such material in his generation—had been a most careful custodian of it. But in the end the CAM, which at that time had no expert in Islamic art on its staff, reaped the benefits of Lane's expertise after being given two opportunities to top the V&A's initial offer. Kelekian's ceramics had completed their transubstantiation from artifacts to assets.

* * *

This chapter has sought to portray the supply chain for Islamic ceramics with as much clarity as possible, from the early impressions of the Syrian antiquities trade recorded in the *Qamus* to the flickering views of sherd sorters and bricolagers glimpsed through time, and the clamoring network of transnational dealers writing endless letters. Over time, more information might emerge from other sources that can sharpen our picture of the first stages of that chain, perhaps eventually providing more details about the men and women who worked as diggers, transporters, fabricators, and intermediaries within the great web that moved the objects of Islamic art history all around the world. The major dealers are much easier to hear, their words written out, filed, and carefully stored. Yet even as the archival mass of their writings threatens to overwhelm researchers, it remains difficult to know what some of them really thought about the work they did and the objects they sold.

The conclusion of the Kelekian ceramics affair reveals a mid-century museumscape that would have been unrecognizable in the first decade of the twentieth century, when Kelekian first entered into talks with the V&A about the loan of his collection. Gone were the days when the institutions of Paris and London could expect to have first word of the latest antiquities arriving from the Middle East. The trade was now focused on the American market, and the Cincinnati Art Museum was a more important buyer than the Victoria and Albert Museum.

In trying to grasp the large-scale histories of global knowledge economies and asset accumulation, it is easy to lose sight of the objects themselves. After the mid-century flurry of legal activity that removed most of Kelekian's ceramics from London to the United States, some of the pieces traveled onward

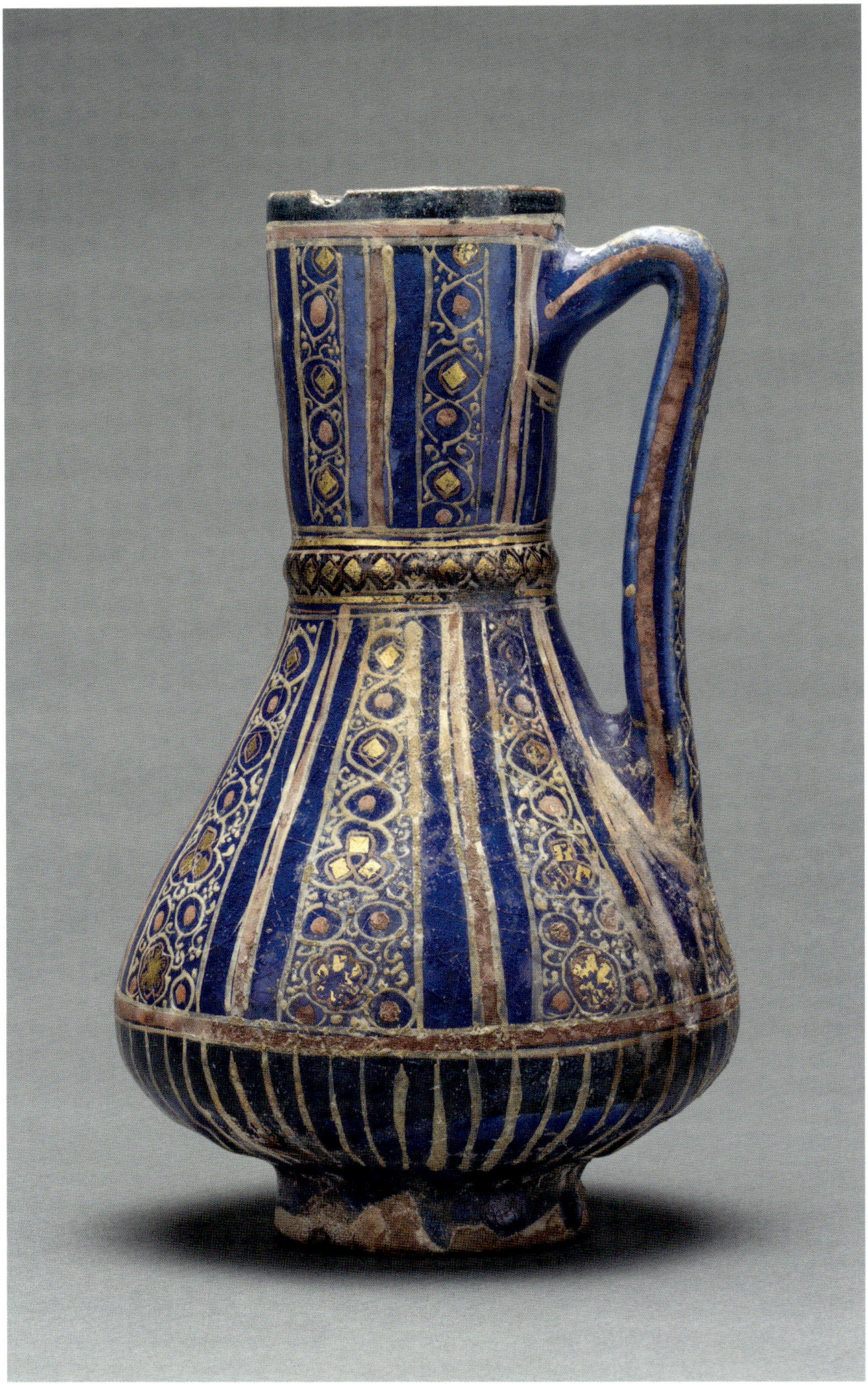

through the market to new locations, eventually landing in such collecting centers as Tokyo, Kuwait City, Rome, Los Angeles, and Bloomington, Indiana (see next chapter). The biggest tranche, however, came to rest in Cincinnati. And there those pieces remain, carefully cared for by a succession of curators and conservators for more than seventy years now (fig. 4.16). But what is seventy years in the life of a ceramic vessel? We like to believe that we can write the biographies of objects, but our anthropocentric presumptions only end with us realizing how short our own lives are in comparison with the existence of even the humblest potsherd. To the fragments that make up Kelekian's blue pitcher, with its enameling and little squares of gilding glued on in the early twentieth century, we are just the latest in a long line of human handlers who have come and gone.[138]

4.16. Handled jug, glazed stonepaste with overglaze colors and gilding (so-called lajvardina ware). Original material attributed Iran, second half of 13th or 14th century. Height approx. 22 cm. Cincinnati Art Museum, Museum Purchase, 1952.258.

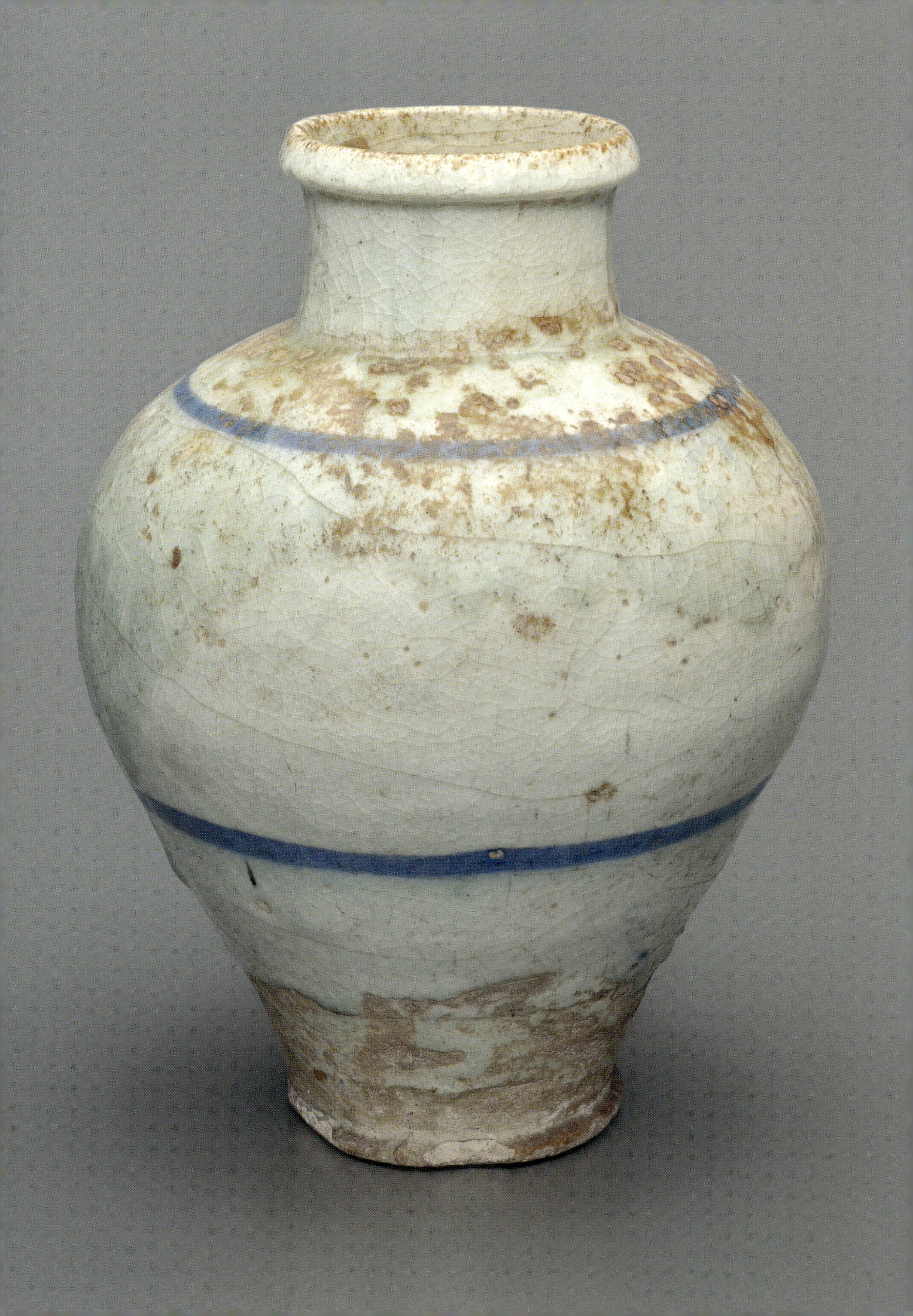

5 The Riddle of Raqqa

Time will talk.

—DIKRAN KELEKIAN TO CHARLES LANG FREER, 28 March 1905

The final chapter of this book presents a case study in the possibilities of ceramics fabrication within the frenetic first decade of the twentieth century. Its subjects are the "Raqqa wares" of medieval Syria, star attractions in the nascent canon of Islamic art that sold for extraordinary sums in the years before World War I.[1] The central objects of this chapter are now held in the Eskenazi Museum of Art at Indiana University, a group of previously unpublished pieces that reached the United States via similar routes to those taken by more celebrated Raqqa wares in other collections. In this chapter, three separate temporal episodes trace the story of the Indiana pieces back to Syria: first, the 1970s arrival of the pieces into the Indiana University collections; second, analysis conducted on campus between 2016 and 2021; and third, the first years of the famous ceramics of Raqqa on the international market, between the end of the nineteenth century and the interwar years. This anachronic investigation into an overlooked collection of Raqqa wares questions both the intact and perfect condition of some of these medieval survivals, and the stories used to explain their seemingly miraculous passage into the present.

Bloomington, Indiana: *Islamic Art Across the World*

In 1970 the campus of Indiana University in Bloomington hosted a loan exhibition titled *Islamic Art Across the World*. With over three hundred pieces, covering territory "as far as Ghana to the West and the Philippines to the East," the exhibition was a diverse and, judging from the installation photographs, rather crowded affair (figs. 5.1 and 5.2).[2] The driving force behind this venture was Theodore Bowie (1905–1995). A self-declared "jack-of-several-trades," Bowie was a professor in the university's Fine Arts School as well as a librarian, administrator, and sometime curator of Asian art in the Indiana University Art Museum (now the Eskenazi Museum of Art).[3] He staged exhibitions on many facets of Asian art throughout his career, including one of North America's first major exhibitions of the arts of Thailand in 1960. The 1970 show, however, was his only significant professional venture into the Islamic world.[4]

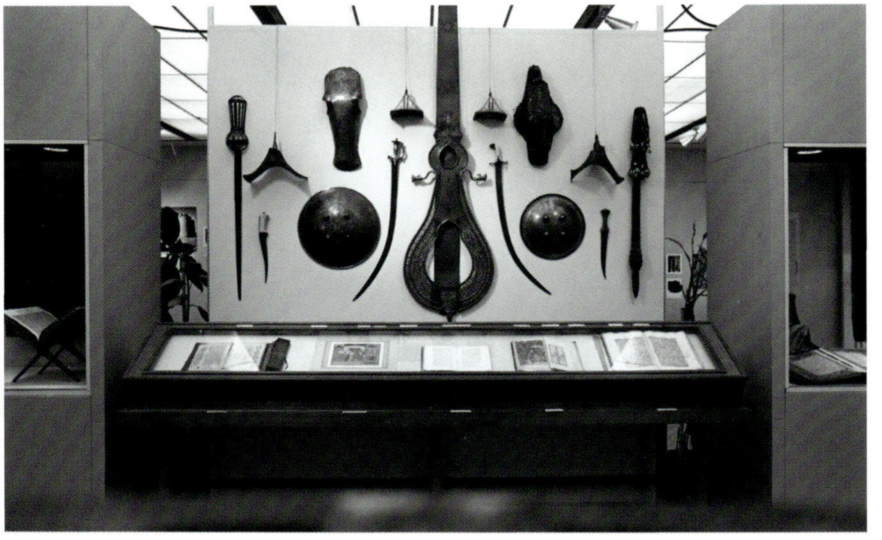

5.1. Installation view, *Islamic Art Across the World,* Indiana University, 1970. Eskenazi Museum of Art archives.

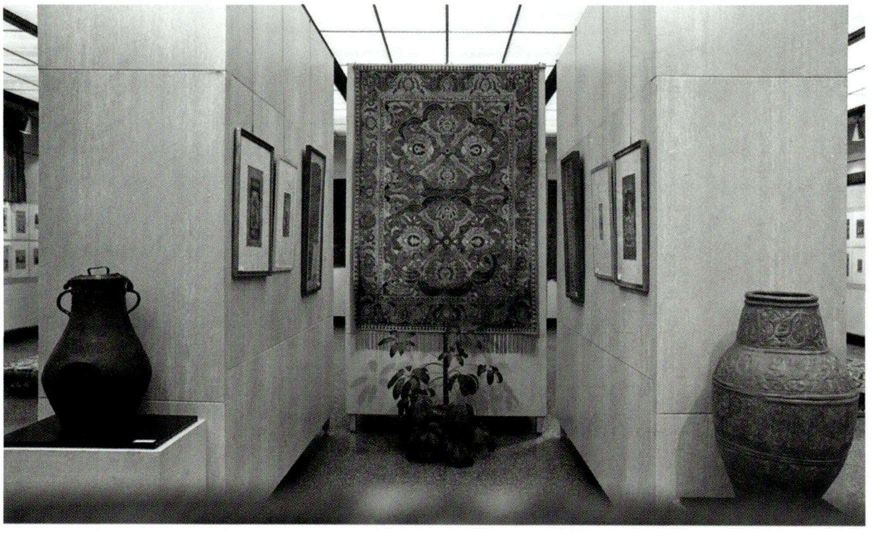

5.2. Installation view, *Islamic Art Across the World,* Indiana University, 1970. Eskenazi Museum of Art archives.

Whether the exhibition really lived up to its claim to be "probably the most comprehensive show of Islamic art ever attempted in this country," or if it could truly be said that "the only precedent comparable in scope to the I.U. show was the one which took place in Germany in 1910," are debatable points. The exhibition held in Munich in 1910, with over 3,600 objects on display, was more than ten times the size of Ted Bowie's venture.[5] Hubris aside, the Indiana exhibition was certainly noteworthy for its unusually broad geographical conception of Islamic art. Indeed, it was rather visionary in this respect, a reflection of Indiana University's remarkable diversity of area studies specializations (themselves the outcome of astute institutional stewardship during the Cold War era).

In 1969, early in the planning process for the exhibition, Bowie made contact with Ernst Grube (1933–2011), a notable scholar of Islamic art who was then curator at the Metropolitan Museum of Art. Grube became the major scholarly advisor to the Indiana exhibition, giving Bowie detailed information on the characteristic products of various regions and time periods, suggesting the names of individuals and institutions to ask for loans, lending some of his own pieces, and acting as go-between for a number of anonymous lenders.[6] He also contributed an introductory essay to the catalogue.[7] The two largest lenders to the show were the collector Edwin Binney III (1925–1986), who loaned more than ninety pieces, and the MMA, which loaned seventy pieces. Following Grube's departure from the MMA later in 1969, the incoming curator Richard Ettinghausen honored the loan agreement put in place by Grube and seems to have visited Bloomington to give a lecture to accompany the exhibition.[8] Among the private lenders for the exhibition was the New York art dealer Fahim Kouchakji (1886–1976), who has already appeared in chapter 1 and is central to the story that follows here.

The Kouchakji Frères—Constaki, Salim, Georges, and Habib—began trading antiquities in the fevered marketplace of late nineteenth-century Aleppo. By the end of the twentieth century's first decade, they had established an international family enterprise that we have already encountered in connection with the (in)famous Antioch chalice. Georges ran a branch of the Kouchakji antiquities business in Paris from at least 1908 but probably earlier, while Habib and his nephew Fahim (eldest son of Georges) traveled to New York a few years before the outbreak of World War I and established a saleroom there.[9]

The fortunes of the business can be glimpsed in the pages of the trade publication *American Art News*. The name of Kouchakji Frères appears in it from 1908 onward, in the listings of Paris salerooms.[10] The New York saleroom, initially located at East 40th Street, is mentioned for the first time in an issue dated 2 April 1910.[11] The firm's classified advert ran regularly for several years from 1910, illustrated with a Raqqa ware pitcher that was photographed in Aleppo circa 1909 and possibly offered to Gertrude Bell for sale by the Marcopoli family, before it entered the Havemeyer collection and subsequently the MMA (fig. 5.3).[12] In 1914 the gallery announced its move to 719 Fifth Avenue, with "an interesting exhibition of recently imported Arabic enameled glass, and Rakka and Persian potteries."[13] From 1929, following liquidation sales at the Anderson Galleries and the American Art Galleries in New York in 1927 and 1928, Fahim was the sole proprietor of the Kouchakji antiquities business in New York.[14] He later claimed a close friendship with Dikran Kelekian, which is quite possible; among other connections, both men were first-class passengers on the SS *Leviathan* during one of its passages from Southampton and Cherbourg to New York in 1927.[15] The two of them may have arranged to travel together on some of the many transatlantic trips they both undertook for the business of gathering antiquities in the Middle East.

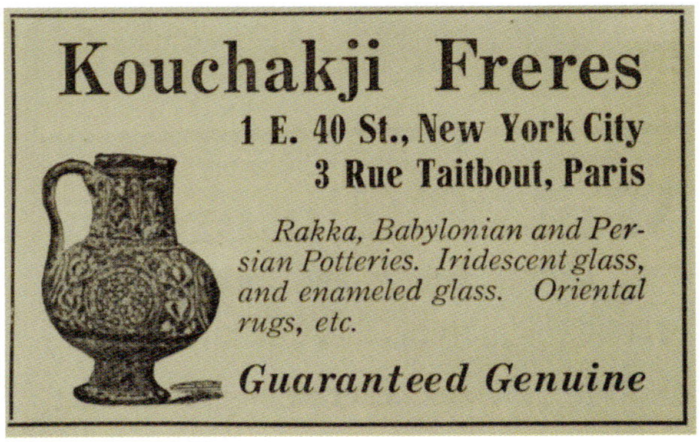

5.3. Advert for Kouchakji Frères showing a jug now in the MMA (48.113.16), *American Art News*, 28 October 1911. Museum of Fine Arts, Boston library.

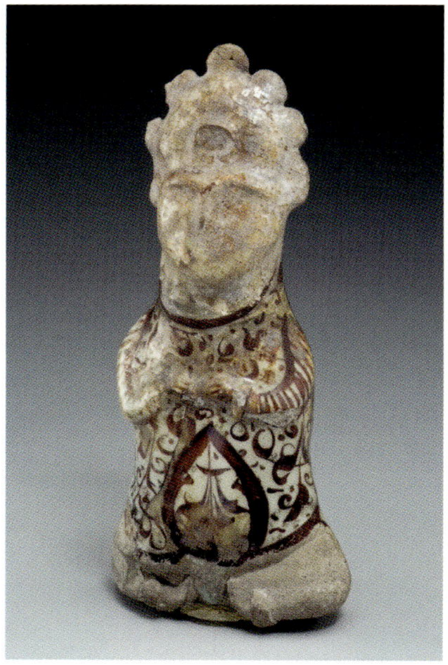

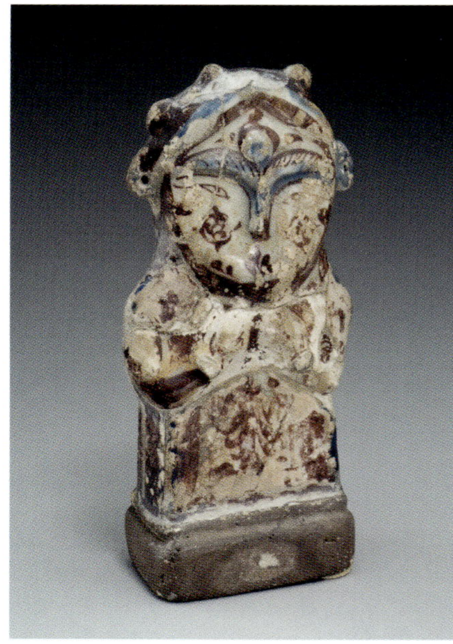

5.4. Figurine, glazed stonepaste with overglaze luster and modern material (so-called Raqqa ware). Height 22.5 cm. Eskenazi Museum of Art, Indiana University, 72.6.16.

5.5. Figurine, glazed stonepaste with overglaze luster and modern material (so-called Raqqa ware). Height 18.1 cm. Eskenazi Museum of Art, Indiana University, 72.6.17.

Bowie's initial contact with Kouchakji for the Indiana exhibition was made through Grube, whose twenty-two-page typewritten document of suggestions for the exhibition included the note "Rakka Pottery—best coll. MMA. But Fahim Kouchakji, a New York dealer who brought most of these things to the US has still soem [*sic*] very fine pieces and I am sure would lend. . . . If you wish I can talk to him."[16] Kouchakji was indeed happy to lend. In response to Bowie's initial request, he sent a folio of photographs of pieces in his collection for Bowie to choose from. In a further letter Kouchakji also sent Bowie drawings of a pair of "Rakkah 'dolls' . . . glazed and with some iridescence, 12 century. They have interested Dr. Gruber [*sic*], and actually, according to the late Professor Pijoan, author of Summa del Arte, they are fertility figures intended to be placed in the bedroom to encourage reproduction."[17] This interpretation may have added to their appeal for Bowie, who was deeply interested in erotic art and was at that time publishing a book on the subject, illustrated with artworks from Indiana University's Kinsey Institute for Sex Research.[18] Kouchakji's "dolls" (figs. 5.4 and 5.5), a pair of figurines of a type also found in fragmentary form in other collections, were illustrated in an article Grube had published in 1966.[19] Grube encouraged Bowie to take the figurines for the show and they were added to the Indiana loan.[20] In total six ceramic objects, all attributed in the loan documents to twelfth-century Raqqa or Syria, were loaned from Kouchakji for the exhibition, along with a metal candlestick and an ivory plaque.

The original group of ceramics Kouchakji loaned to Bloomington for the 1970 exhibition were an albarello (a jar of distinctive, waisted shape; fig. 5.6), a small jar (fig. 5.7), an ovoid bowl (fig. 5.8), a small dish (fig. 5.9), and the two figurines.[21] The four vessels are all notable for their incredible condition: intact, pristine, and virtually without iridescence, they stand in sharp contrast to the very obviously fragmentary figurines, both of which have clearly been reconstructed using pieces from multiple objects and new material. One of the figurines is mounted on a modern oblong "plinth" of a concrete-like

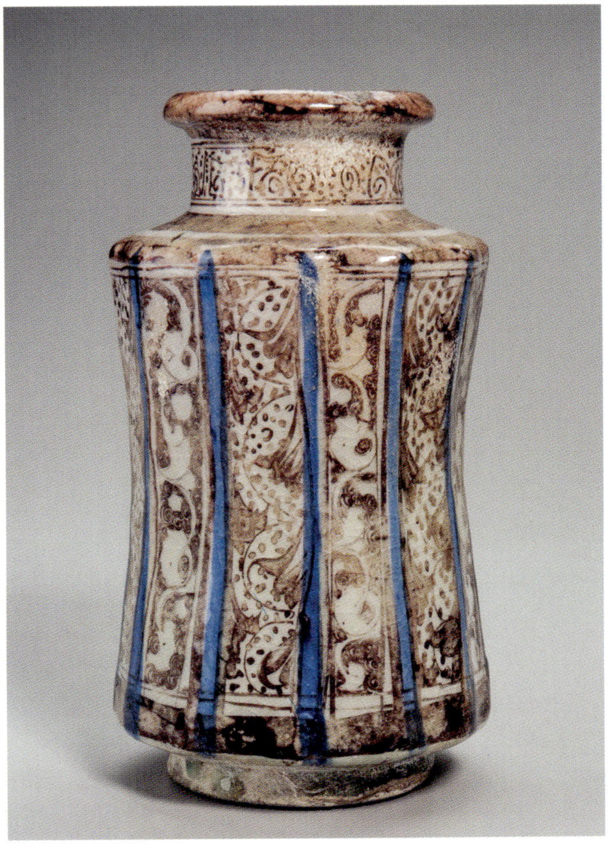

5.6. Albarello, glazed stonepaste with overglaze luster (so-called Raqqa ware). Height 25.4 cm. Eskenazi Museum of Art, Indiana University, 72.6.5.

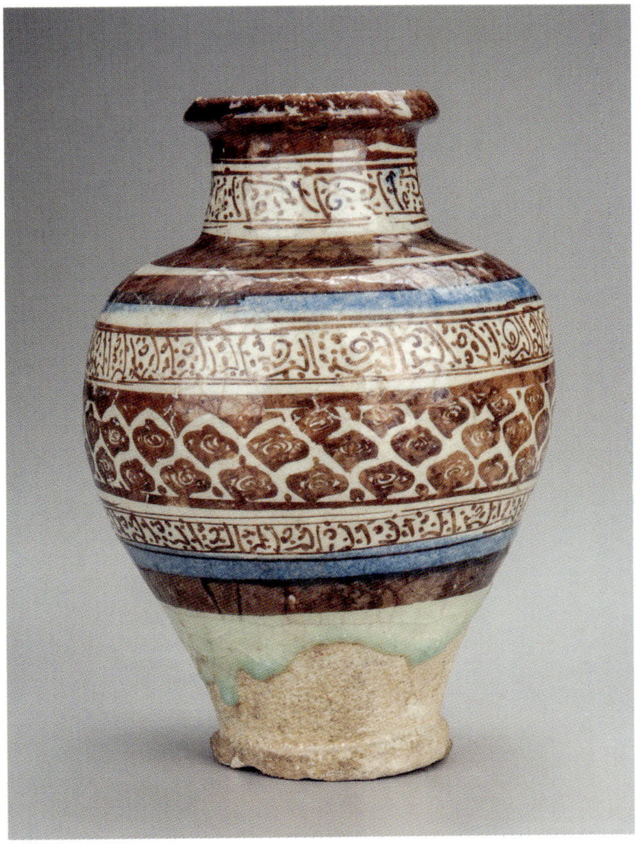

5.7. Jar, glazed stonepaste with overglaze luster (so-called Raqqa ware). Height 24.1 cm. Eskenazi Museum of Art, Indiana University, 72.6.6.

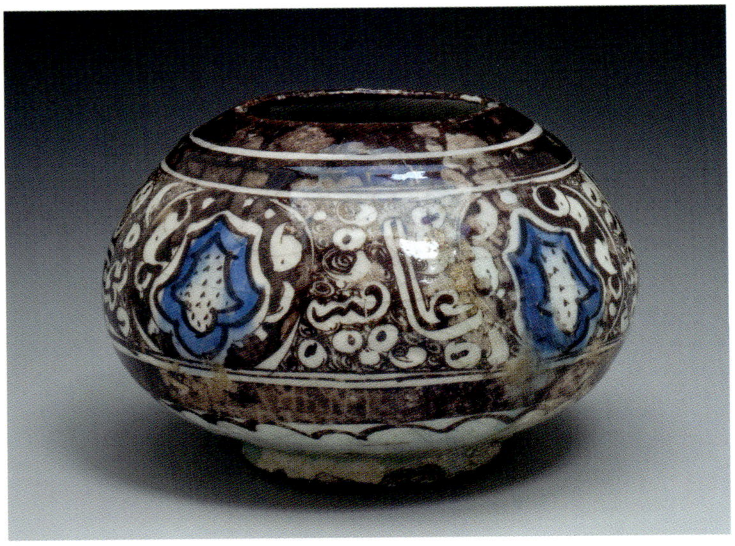

5.8. Globular bowl, glazed stonepaste with overglaze luster (so-called Raqqa ware). Height 12.7 cm. Eskenazi Museum of Art, Indiana University, 72.6.7.

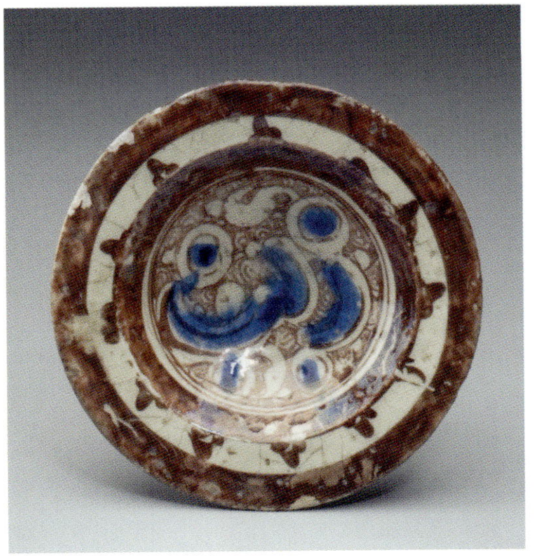

5.9. Dish, glazed stonepaste with overglaze luster (so-called Raqqa ware). Diameter 14.8 cm. Eskenazi Museum of Art, Indiana University, 72.6.13.

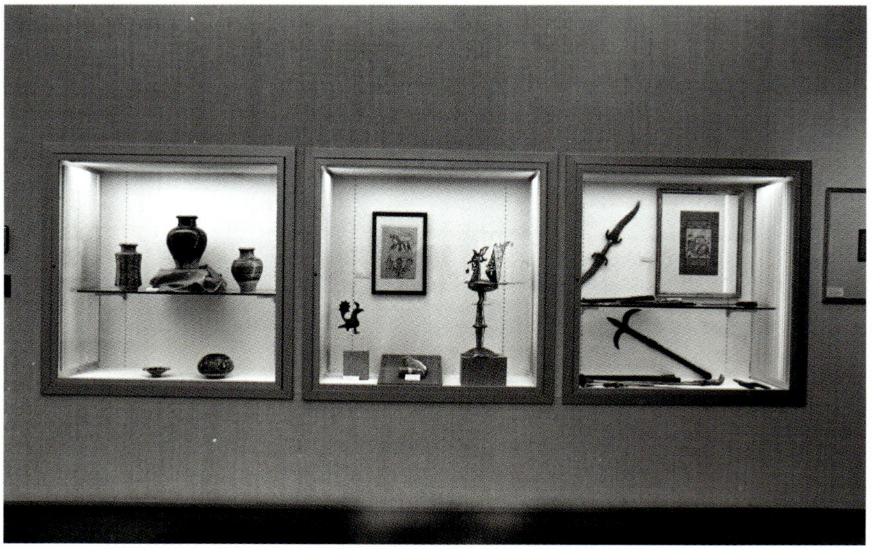

5.10. Installation view, *Islamic Art Across the World*, Indiana University, 1970. Eskenazi Museum of Art archives.

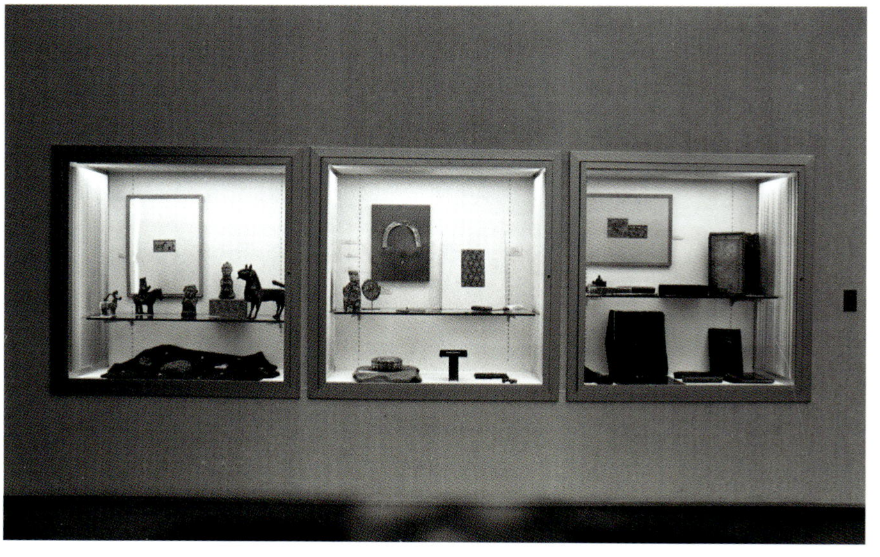

5.11. Installation view, *Islamic Art Across the World*, Indiana University, 1970. Eskenazi Museum of Art archives.

substance. Installation shots from the 1970 exhibition show the vessels displayed in one vitrine in a group, arranged around a large underglaze-painted turquoise jar, also attributed to Raqqa, that was loaned from the Metropolitan Museum (fig. 5.10), while the figurines were placed alongside a ceramic mounted figurine from the collection of Ernst Grube (fig. 5.11).[22] All of Kouchakji's loaned objects were returned to him in New York in November 1970, shortly after the show was dismounted.[23]

Fahim Kouchakji and the Coda to a Collection

From the 1970 exhibition until his death in 1976 at the age of ninety, Kouchakji maintained a correspondence with the director of what is now the EMA, Thomas Solley (d. 2006). Solley, who hailed from a branch of Indiana's Lilly pharmaceutical empire, bought many pieces for the EMA with his own money

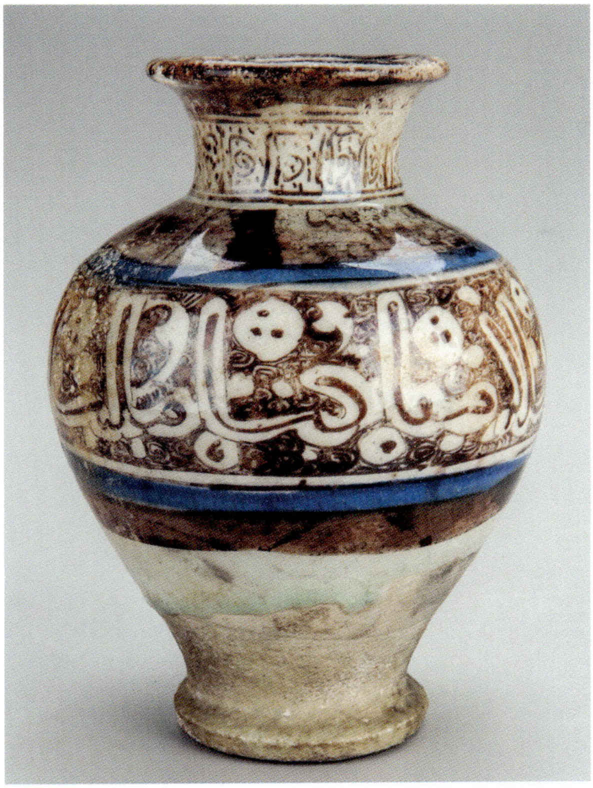

5.12. Epigraphic jar, glazed stonepaste with overglaze luster (so-called Raqqa ware). Height 16.5 cm. Eskenazi Museum of Art, Indiana University, 72.6.8.

during his tenure as director from 1971 to 1986. Archived letters show that he had bought some pieces from Kouchakji at an earlier date, and the loan for the Islamic exhibition seems to have restarted a relationship that eventually saw Solley visiting Kouchakji and his wife Evelyn "Peggy" Kouchakji (1905–1980) in New York on several occasions in the first half of the 1970s.[24] For the EMA collections, the most important outcomes of this relationship were the purchase of a turquoise-glazed "Parthian" vase and, critically for our story, a group of seventeen pieces of so-called Raqqa ware, including all six of the pieces that had been loaned for the 1970 exhibition.[25] All of the pieces of Raqqa ware bought from Kouchakji are still in the EMA collection today, and all bar three of them are decorated in the celebrated "cobalt-and-luster" style.

While the four vessels loaned for the exhibition are notable for their pristine condition, and the figurines are clearly reconstructed, the other pieces of Kouchakji's Raqqa ware in the EMA are a rather mixed bag in terms of condition. An epigraphic jar (fig. 5.12) and a hemispherical footed bowl (fig. 5.13) are every bit as incredible in condition and decoration as the albarello or the ovoid jar. These two, together with the four other pristine vessels loaned for the 1970 exhibition, are remarkably similar in glaze, body, form, and decoration to some much better-known pieces held in other institutions, notably the Metropolitan Museum of Art and the National Museum of Asian Art. Furthermore, as shown below, at least some of them arrived in the United States via the same routes as their more famous siblings in those collections.

Other pieces in the Indiana group are less breathtaking. At first glance one of the handled ewers merely looks a bit beaten-up; this is the one with

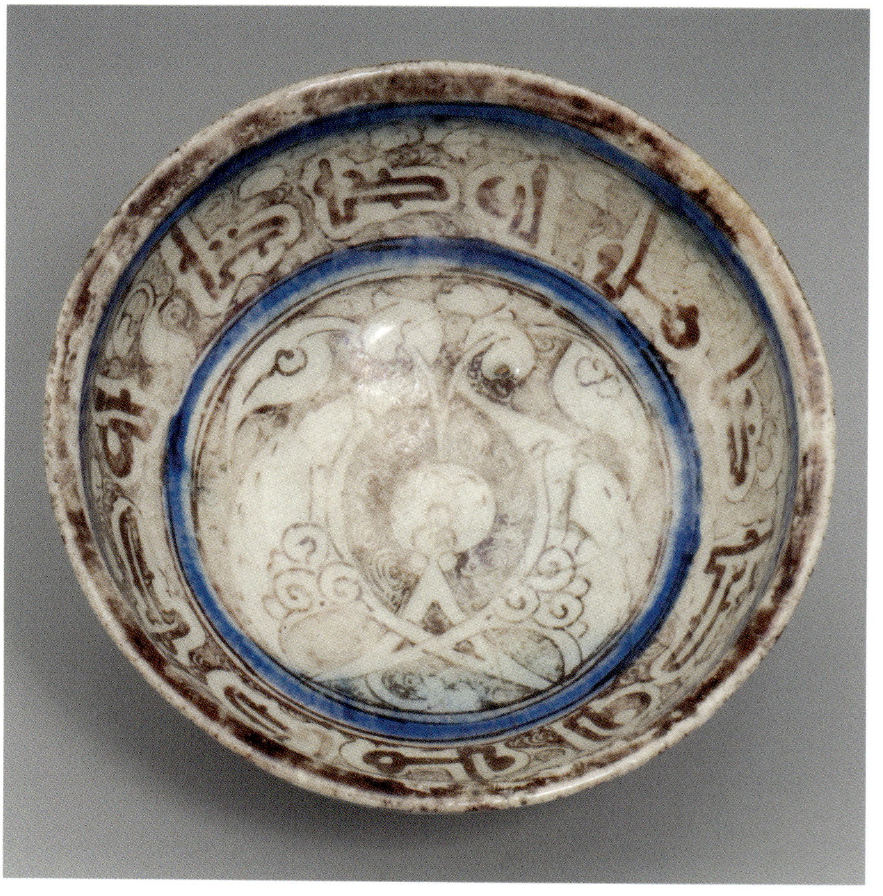

5.13. Footed bowl, glazed stonepaste with overglaze luster (so-called Raqqa ware). Diameter 13 cm. Eskenazi Museum of Art, Indiana University, 72.6.15.

screws holding on the handle that we already encountered in chapter 3 (see fig. 3.19). Another handled ewer with distinctly strange epigraphy was also seen in chapter 3 (see fig. 3.49). A further footed dish is intact but not so spectacular (fig. 5.14), while three large ovoid jars are made up of many fragments (figs. 5.15–17)—although all three, and especially the cobalt-and-luster jar in figure 5.17, attest to the remarkable skill of the craftspeople who undertook their early twentieth-century restoration (to which I return below). Some of the other vessels (figs. 5.18 and 5.19) present enough oddities of form, epigraphy, and overpainting to raise immediate questions. The remaining piece is a fragmentary polychrome bowl painted with the image of a camel.[26]

The seventeen Raqqa ware ceramics were shipped to Bloomington in February 1972. The memo sent from Solley to the university's president gives some of the background to the purchase and sees the museum director deliberately invoking the Raqqa wares in the MMA in an attempt to loosen the president's purse strings:

> We have just received a collection of 17 superb faience vessels known as Rakka ware dating from the 12th century from Mr. and Mrs. Fahim Kouchakji on extended loan. This is one of the most important groups of this type of pottery in any Museum in this country and may, according to Ted Bowie exceed the important holdings of the Metropolitan Museum.

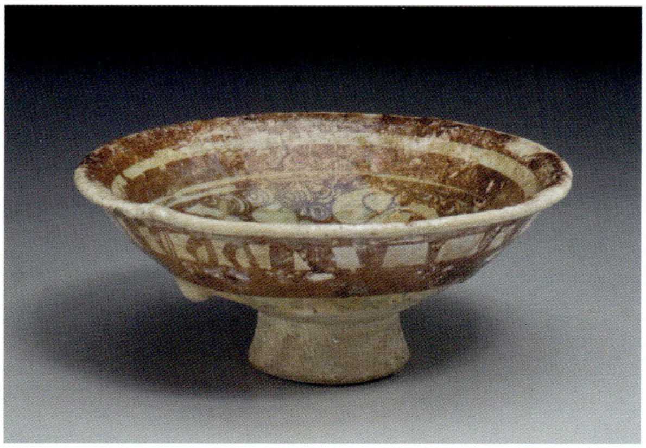

5.14. Dish, glazed stonepaste with overglaze luster (so-called Raqqa ware). Diameter 13.2 cm. Eskenazi Museum of Art, Indiana University, 72.6.14.

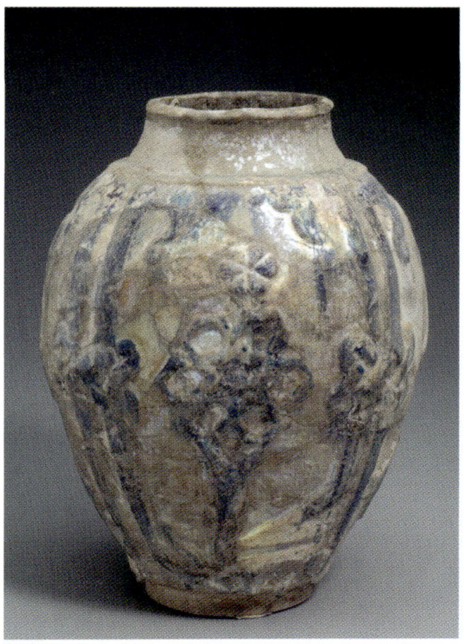

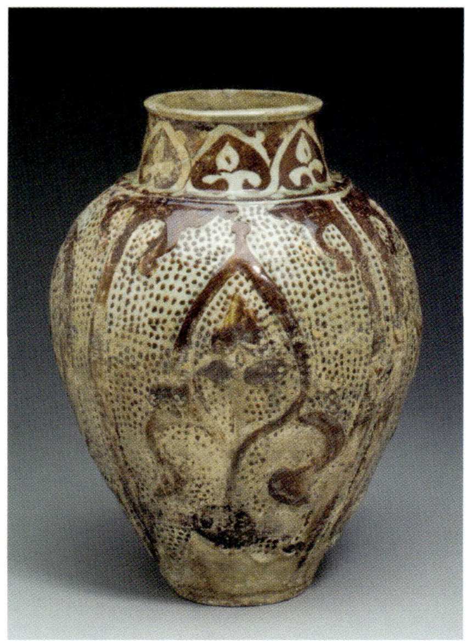

5.15. Large reconstructed jar, glazed stonepaste and modern material (so-called Raqqa ware). Height 46 cm. Eskenazi Museum of Art, Indiana University, 72.6.2.

5.16. Large reconstructed jar, glazed stonepaste with overglaze luster and modern material (so-called Raqqa ware). Height 42.2 cm. Eskenazi Museum of Art, Indiana University, 72.6.3.

Mr. Kouchakji who is in his 80's was the son and nephew of two of the most celebrated antiquities dealers in Aleppo and Paris before World War I. Mr. Kouchakji was caught in the United States at the outbreak of the first War and stayed on to open the New York branch of Kouchakji Freres. He was largely responsible for the extensive collection of antiquities assembled by Mrs. C. H. Moore and the former owner of the celebrated Chalice of Antioch now in the Cloisters....

Mr. Kouchakji is anxious to arrange the dispositions of his collections in order to protect his wife in the event of his death.[27]

Indiana University agreed to purchase the Raqqa ceramics from Kouchakji, paying in installments.

Solley continued to correspond and visit with the Kouchakjis, but the 1972 purchase of the Raqqa wares was the last acquisition that the museum made from Fahim Kouchakji. The letters between the Kouchakjis and Solley become rather painful reading after that point. The health of both Fahim and

5.17 (*overleaf*). Large reconstructed jar, glazed stonepaste with overglaze luster and modern material (so-called Raqqa ware). Height 42.5 cm. Eskenazi Museum of Art, Indiana University, 72.6.4.

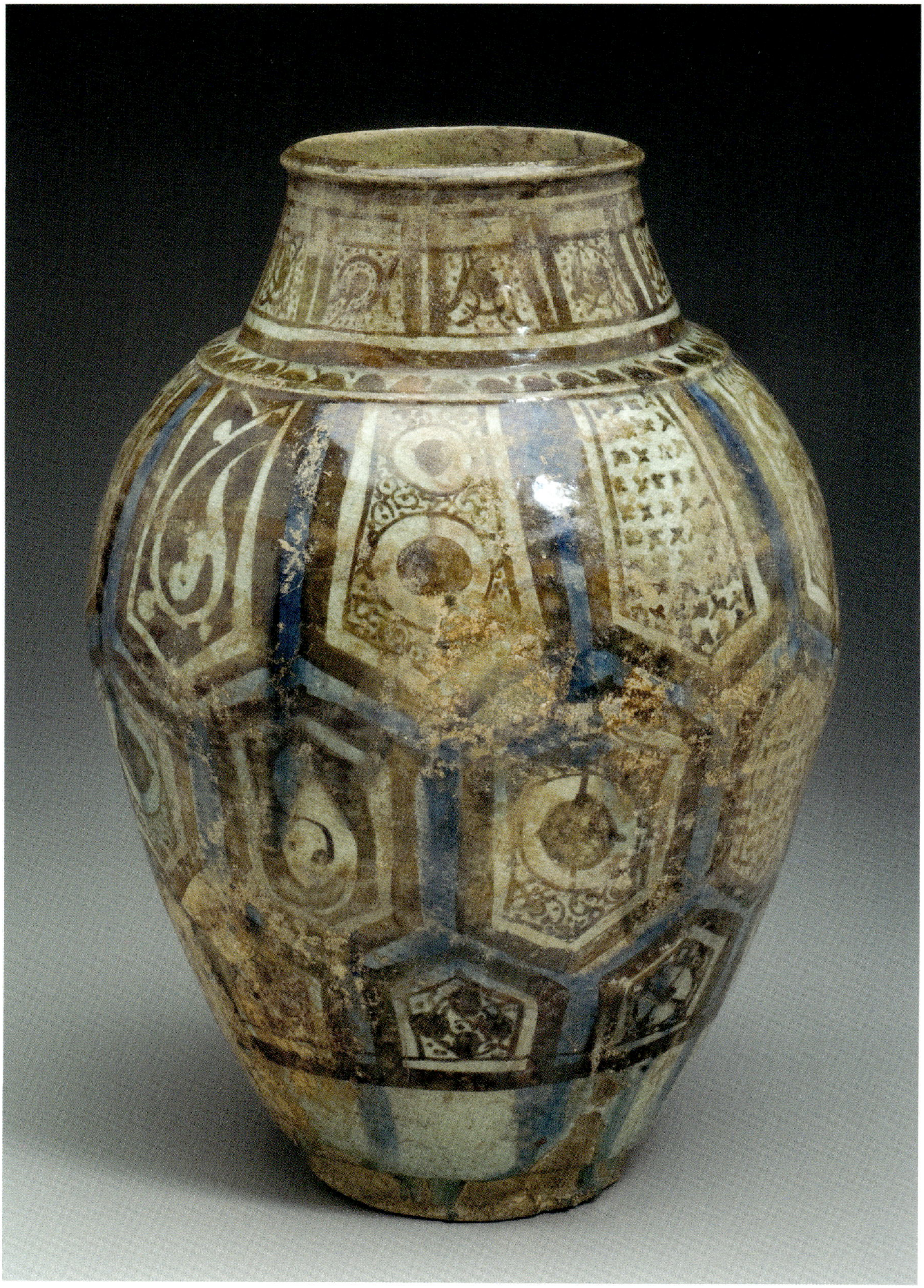

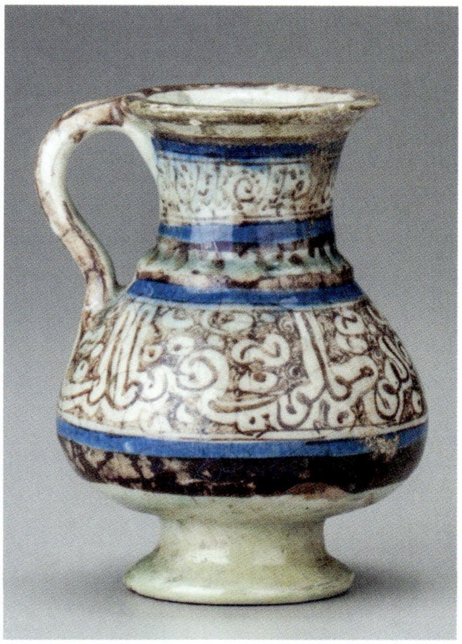

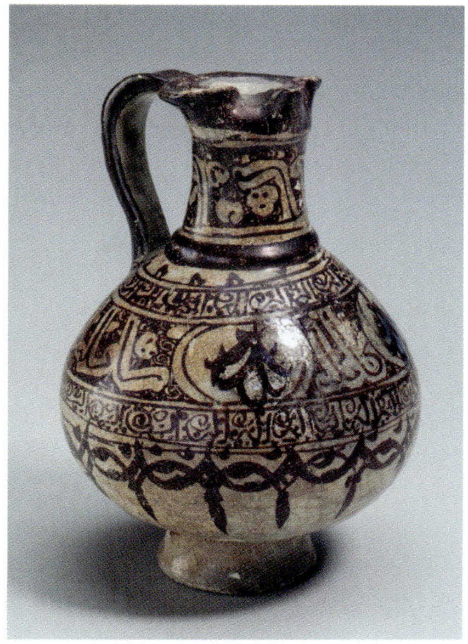

5.18. Handled jar, glazed stonepaste with overglaze luster (so-called Raqqa ware) and some modern material. Height 14.9 cm. Eskenazi Museum of Art, Indiana University, 72.6.9.

5.19. Handled pitcher, glazed stonepaste (so-called Raqqa ware). Height 18.1 cm. Eskenazi Museum of Art, Indiana University, 72.6.12.

Peggy Kouchakji was deteriorating, and a further acquisition of some other pieces for the Indiana University collections (a group referred to in a later document as "Roman Treasure")[28] stalled and ultimately fell through when Solley decided, on the advice of unnamed experts, to have the pieces sent for examination and testing at various institutions and laboratories before committing to purchase them.[29] It is clear from the correspondence that there were doubts about the authenticity of pieces in Kouchakji's collection. Solley may have informed Kouchakji in person or over the phone about the decision to send the pieces for testing, for there is no written record of this communication in the archive. However, the written response from Kouchakji was politely dismayed: in a letter of 9 May 1975, he cites the various respected authorities who had already examined the pieces, continuing:

> But it is difficult to respond to criticism from an unknown source. In all the years, since 1909 in fact, that I have been active in this field, I have never passed along a spurious object, and always I've tried to solve any problems involved.[30]

A letter from Peggy Kouchakji dated 10 December 1975, indicates the true extent of Kouchakji's anxieties about Solley's decision to have the pieces tested:

> We are sorry that the work on the objects is being so complicated as [Fahim] had an idea that the work could be done in the laboratory of your museum. Also knowing that practically all of them had had extensive "expertise" by well known and reliable authorities in their various fields. But as you doubtless know nothing is really "fool-proof", there being always some "doubting Thomases" plus those [who] just don't know or are doubtfull [*sic*]. For this was something which Fahim struggled with for many years during the "Chalice days".

> Hopefully the ghosts will all be laid by your kind and able efforts and that this has not been too hard on you. The sooner you can conveniently finish with them the happier you will be, and Fahim too. I am hoping he will have the spirit to shake off his depression and be able to come to the office, as there is so much he worries about doing here. He asked me to tell you how really deeply he appreciates your friendship and the trouble you are taking.[31]

Kouchakji's "Chalice days," which revealed his flair for showmanship, have already been detailed in chapter 1.

One senses in Solley's rather evasive replies to the Kouchakjis that he was probably making excuses about delays to the testing processes in order to avoid relaying the results to the couple, both of whom were by this point in poor health. In March of 1976 both Kouchakjis were hospitalized, and after visiting them in the hospital Solley wrote to their accountant of his concerns about the care Peggy would require when she returned home, and the couple's need for help with management of their collection. During Solley's visit to the hospital, the Kouchakjis asked him to assist a family member with the inventory and appraisal of their library and "the objects," presumably meaning the residue of the stock from Fahim's antiquities business.[32] In August 1976 Fahim Kouchakji died. The next month Solley received a letter from a firm of New York attorneys informing him that he was named in Fahim Kouchakji's will as coexecutor of his estate—a position he does not seem to have anticipated, and one that he felt unable to accept.[33]

The last document in the file is a copy, dated 7 December 1977, of a letter sent at an unknown date after Fahim Kouchakji's death, from Solley to Peggy Kouchakji. Curiously, unlike the rest of Solley's letters in the file, this document is not a "true" copy in the form of a photostat but seems instead to be a typed transcript of a letter that must have been sent to Peggy at some earlier point after Fahim's death. After admitting that he has been avoiding writing the letter and stating that he felt he could not act as coexecutor, Solley delivers the bad news:

> this raises the other matter which I have delayed as long as possible conveying to you because I know it will come as a rather unpleasant surprise. As you know, when Fahim asked me to serve him in this capacity [as advisor on disposal of his collections] late last year, I told both of you that colleagues whose opinions I respected had expressed over the years reservations about certain things in the collections and that these matters would have to be clarified for me to best serve your interests and protect my professional standing. We have been conducting the tests that I wished to undertake for many months now and have most of the responses. Some of the objects have fulfilled our expectations, but a number of others produced results which are difficult to resolve or have in fact proven to be nineteenth century works. Specifically, the two Minoan maidens proved to be about 100 years old through thermoluminescence tests. The millefiori glass plate which was supposed to be Roman is, in fact, in the opinion of the Corning Museum of Glass, nineteenth-century. It is nonetheless, in their opinion, a very desirable object.
>
> Rather than run through item by item, I am enclosing a list with the results that we have found.[34]

Neither a copy of the test results nor a list of objects tested was included in the archive and it is impossible to guess how many pieces might have been involved, although ceramics, metalwares, and glass are all mentioned at points in the correspondence concerning this group. It is certain, however, that neither the Bloomington "Raqqa wares" nor the turquoise "Parthian" vase were among the tested objects. After this point the Raqqa wares in Indiana largely disappeared from view, and most of them have spent the last five decades in storage.

The Cult of Raqqa Ware

Seeing and handling the unpublished Raqqa wares for the first time in the EMA's storage rooms was a thrilling experience. The ceramic vessels attributed to medieval Raqqa, especially the cobalt-and-luster type that makes up the bulk of the EMA group, are celebrity objects. The Indian art historian Ordhendra Coomar Gangoly, writing in 1925, summed up the almost mythical status attained by the Raqqa wares in the rapidly expanding antiquities market of the preceding decades: "In 1890 a call for a new cult came from the Near East. It came in the shape of a few fragments of pottery from the ruins of a Syrian village. It at once roused the interest of a few connoisseurs, and turned the gaze of those who until then would not look at anything but Attic Kylix and Beotian Amphora."[35]

In reality, it is very unlikely that all of the medieval ceramics now conventionally known as Raqqa ware were actually made at Raqqa in north-central Syria. Raqqa is a site of long habitation on the banks of the Euphrates, about one hundred miles east of Aleppo. Ceramics were certainly produced there prior to the Mongol conquests of the thirteenth century, and medieval potters' quarters and glassworks at Raqqa have been excavated and published.[36] However, most archaeology scholars now argue that some of the most prized types of "Raqqa ware" that have circulated on the antiquities market—including ceramics decorated in black under a turquoise glaze, as well as the famous cobalt-and-luster wares—were in fact produced at multiple locations in Syria, including not only Raqqa itself but also the various kiln sites along the banks of the Euphrates and related production as far south as Damascus.[37] There is general agreement that the objects now known as Raqqa wares were produced in the later twelfth century or the first half of the thirteenth.[38] Further archaeological research, including the forthcoming publication of excavated kilns at the site of Balis in Syria, should eventually help clarify our understanding of medieval Syrian ceramics production.[39]

If the archaeological landscape of Islamic Syria is still somewhat hazy today, this is in no small part because of the confusions generated by the antiquities market throughout the twentieth century. At the start of the century, that archaeological landscape was almost completely obscure. When the objects that are now known as Raqqa wares first started to enter the market in the final years of the nineteenth century, there was not yet an associated site or name for them. The first formal identification of these ceramics with Raqqa appeared in a publication of 1901 by Gaston Migeon, who reported that ceramics from the site, reconstructed from fragments, had started appearing en masse in Paris just three years earlier. They were, he reported, being sold by Armenian dealers who sought to conceal the site of extraction.[40]

A note on a purchase record from August 1902 suggests Dikran Kelekian was at that point telling prospective buyers that they came from "Nineveh," a location mentioned in the Bible and therefore holding obvious market appeal. He would, however, attach the name of Raqqa to them very shortly thereafter.[41] With the site name in circulation and increasingly romanticized, Raqqa wares became, for a time, the sine qua non of Middle Eastern ceramics.

Recent studies by Marilyn Jenkins-Madina, Ayşin Yoltar-Yıldırım, and Filiz Tütüncü Çağlar have illuminated the intricate routes traveled in the modern era by some of the Raqqa wares now in collections all over the world, as well as the market frenzy that followed their discovery in late nineteenth-century Syria.[42] In particular, those recent publications have exposed the vexed status of Raqqa ceramics as extractable resources at a moment when the Ottoman Empire was trying on the one hand to stem the flow of illegally extracted antiquities into the international market, and on the other to articulate its own vision of imperial patrimony through the establishment of museums and archaeological missions. The Raqqa wares in Indiana are thoroughly entangled with those same narratives; at the same time, they also have their own secrets to add to the enduring riddle of Raqqa. Most pressingly, technical analysis of the EMA pieces raises questions about their authenticity, as seen in the next section.

First, though, what created the cult? The Raqqa wares certainly arrived on the market at the perfect moment. As shown in chapter 2, their initial extraction in the 1890s was part of a much larger gold rush for historical ceramics taking place across the Islamic world, with prospectors plowing their way through every site that had ever yielded accidental or surface finds. But what was the particular appeal of the Raqqa wares, beyond their apparent plenitude? To understand this, one must look to the objects themselves.

Across many collections there are a great number of Raqqa ware vessels that look exactly as one would expect archaeological ceramics to look; that is, degraded from burial and reconstructed from many fragments. Then there are a smaller number of pieces that are as perfect as the most arresting pieces in the EMA, like the albarello: intact, unblemished, and with pristine shiny glazes. A notable feature of the Raqqa wares that have clearly been in the ground is the tendency for their vitreous, alkaline glazes to develop a striking and sometimes rather beautiful opacity and iridescence as they degrade, the sodium in the glaze seemingly reacting to the saline soil of burial.[43] It was this quality, perhaps more than anything else, that first attracted the attention of the wealthy collector and patron of the Aesthetic Movement Charles Lang Freer. He was so besotted with the opalescent effects of the degraded glazes on these wares that he traveled to Syria in 1908 to buy them as close to the source as possible, sending some forty-plus Raqqa wares back home to his collection in the United States.[44] A curious comment in a letter sent in 1908 suggests he may even have believed this iridescence could be nourished by sunlight.[45] Interestingly, this glittering degradation does not appear as frequently on archaeologically excavated assemblages of "Raqqa ware" as does a less optically exciting white patina. This inconsistency between the archaeologically recovered material and the market pieces raises the possibility that dealers were somehow cultivating or "forcing" the iridescence of the degraded glazes through chemical processes, precisely because the effect was known to hold great appeal for buyers. Dealers certainly recognized the

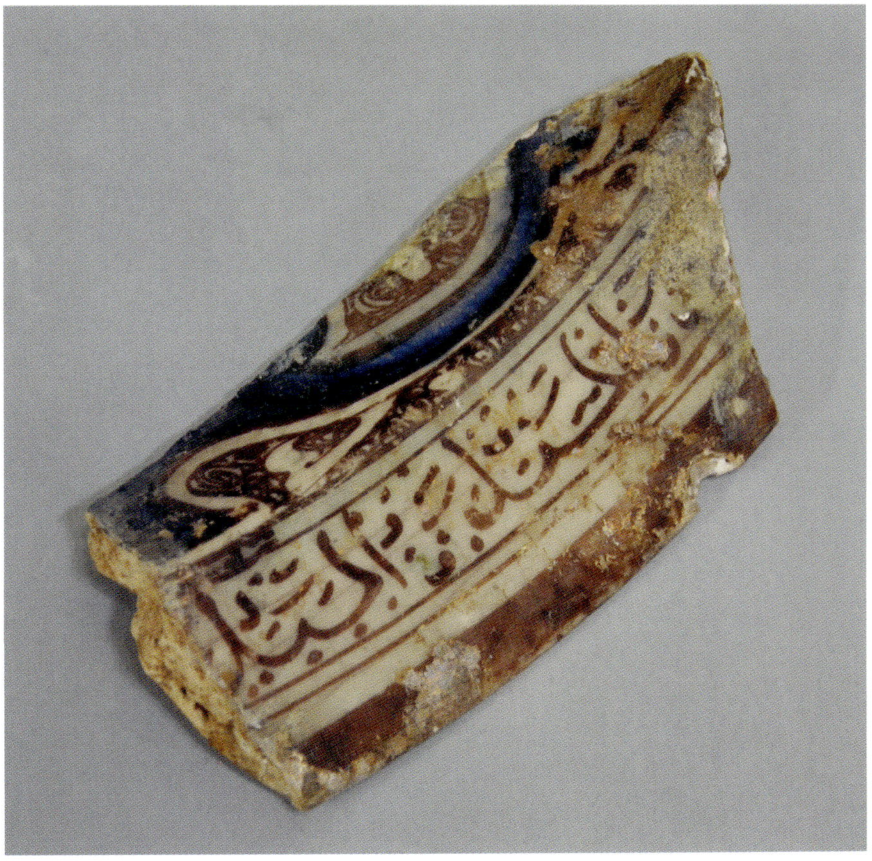

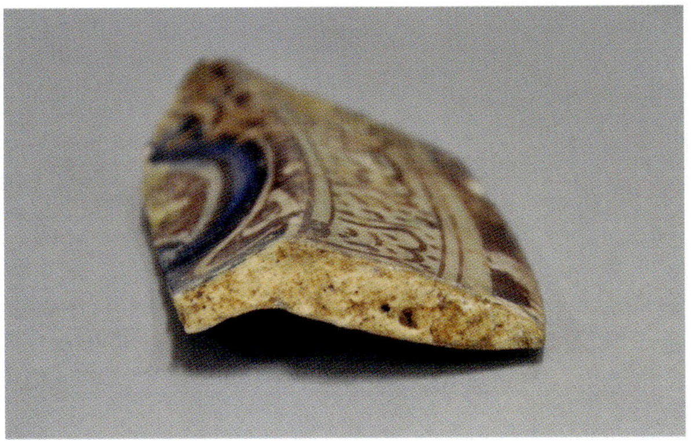

5.20. Fragment from a disassembled vessel, glazed stonepaste with overglaze luster (so-called Raqqa ware). Attributed Syria, late 12th or 13th century. Detroit Institute of Arts, 54.504.

5.21. End view of fragment illustrated in figure 5.20, showing coarse and sandy stonepaste body.

charm that these degraded glazes held for Freer and other collectors of an Aestheticist bent and repeatedly stressed the extent and beauty of the iridescence on their wares in sale catalogues and private correspondence alike, as if it were an intrinsic design element or mark of material quality.

In terms of production, there are qualities that can be generalized across the rather ill-defined corpus of "Raqqa wares." The paste is usually a coarse and gritty, pale-colored stonepaste. A fragment from a now disassembled bowl acquired on the market shows the sandy siliceous body in cross section, yellowed from old adhesive (figs. 5.20 and 5.21). The low plasticity of the paste means that the closed vessels in the Raqqa ware group—fragmentary and pristine pieces alike—have usually been created by throwing sections

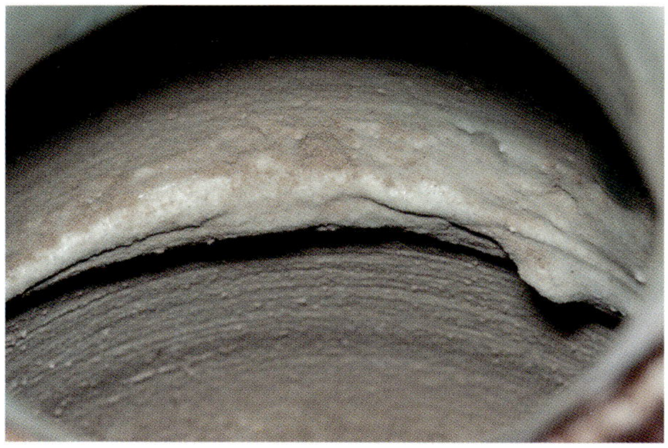

5.22. Interior of albarello illustrated in figure 5.6. Eskenazi Museum of Art, Indiana University, 72.6.5.

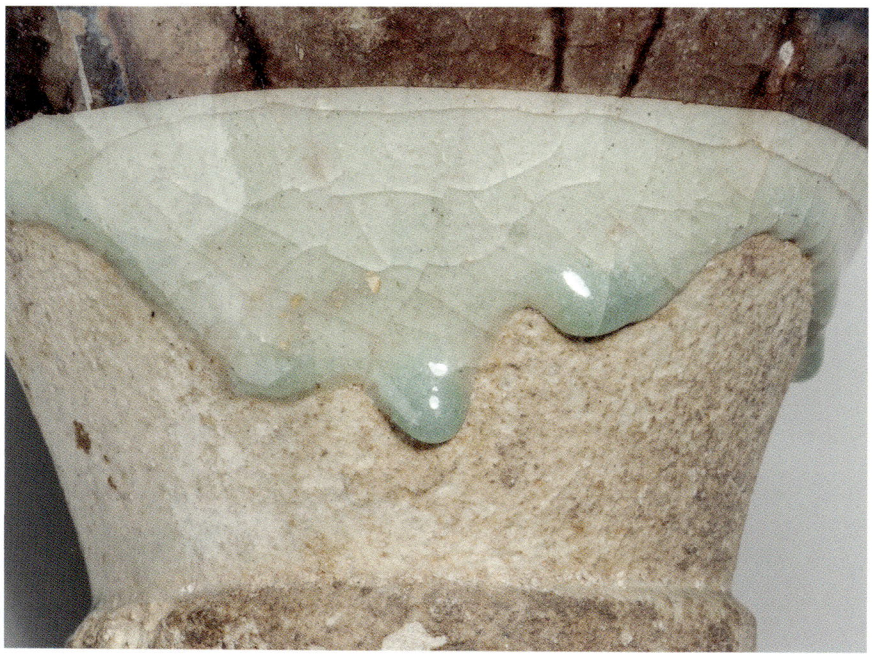

5.23. Glaze at foot of jar illustrated in figure 5.7, Eskenazi Museum of Art, Indiana University, 72.6.6.

separately on the wheel and then joining them together. The inside of the albarello shows this clearly in the join seam visible around the middle of the vessel (fig. 5.22): to make this form the potter would have turned the top and bottom halves of the albarello separately, joined them together to create a thick-walled, cylindrical vessel, then cut the facets down the waisted body with a knife.[46]

After forming, the "cobalt-and-luster" Raqqa wares were often covered before glazing with a layer of white slip that was sometimes decorated with touches of cobalt and/or turquoise colorant.[47] The viscous transparent glaze that covered all this has a greenish hue from its iron content, usually most visible where it has pooled at the feet of vessels (fig. 5.23).[48] Some of the pristine dishes have holes for suspension that were pierced in the feet at this stage, prior to first firing (fig. 5.24).[49] Surviving wasters show cobalt-and-luster pieces arrested at an intermediary stage in production, after the first firing and before the luster layer was added. Here, the wall of a bowl now in the Hetjens

Museum split in the kiln during its first firing, so it was discarded by the potter and never received its luster decoration and second firing (fig. 5.25).[50] With some other pieces it is not clear why they were abandoned at this intermediate stage (fig. 5.26).

Finally, the luster seen on Raqqa wares is usually a dark, chocolate-colored, copper-rich brown, often without very much metallic reflectivity.[51] Patches of true *reflet métallique* can sometimes be seen, for example, on the neck of the EMA albarello, but here and elsewhere much of the luster medium has merely stained the glaze without forming a true luster (fig. 5.27). This could be from the luster wearing off over time but more likely it was never really bonded to the glaze in the first place; luster is a notoriously difficult technique, especially on an alkaline glaze without lead, and on the Raqqa wares it

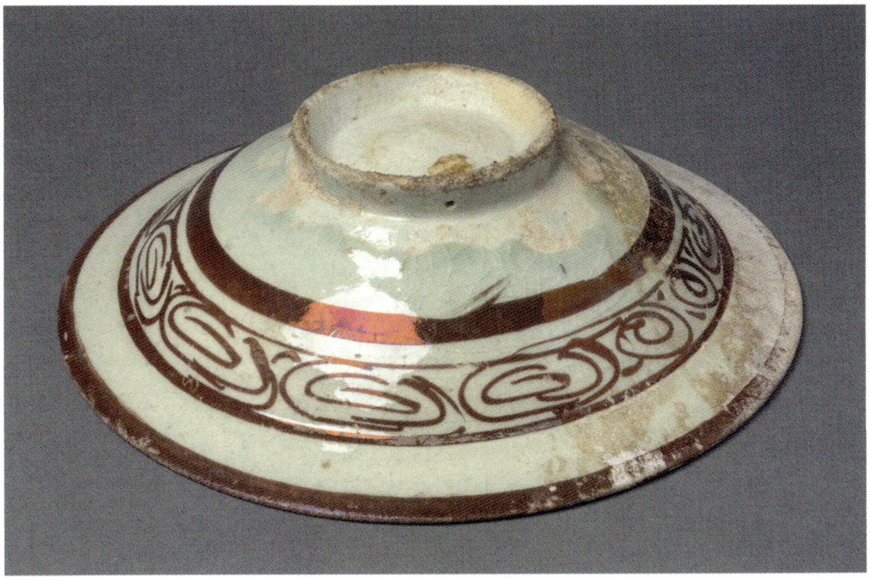

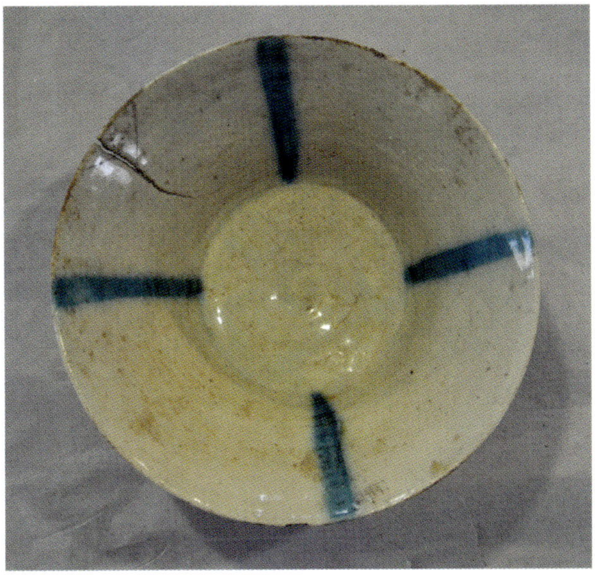

5.24. Underside of dish, glazed stonepaste with luster overglaze (so-called Raqqa ware). Diameter approx. 25.5 cm. Given in honor of Mr. and Mrs. Charles F. Williams by their children, Cincinnati Art Museum, 1948.118.

5.25. Bowl (waster), glazed stonepaste. Attributed Syria, late 12th or 13th century. Diameter 19.5 cm. Hetjens Museum, Düsseldorf.

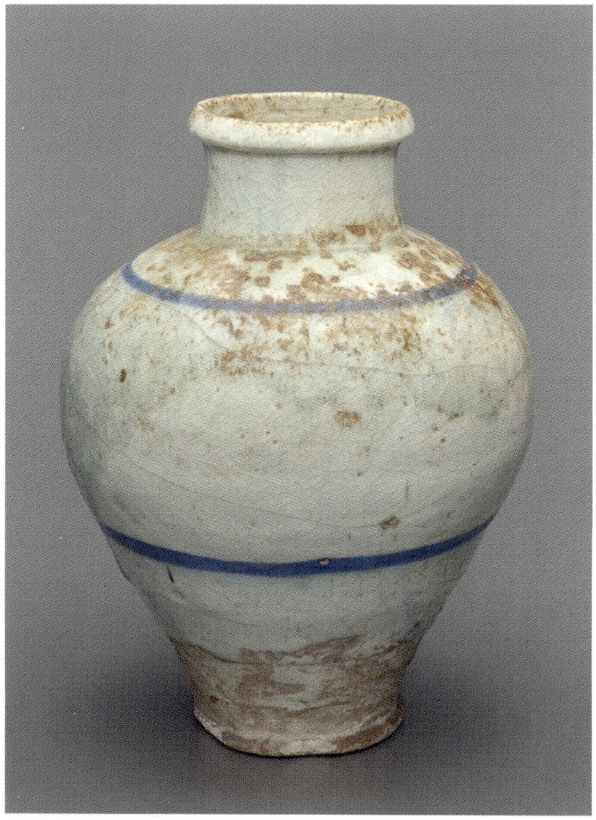

5.26. Jar, glazed stonepaste. Attributed Syria, late 12th or 13th century. Height 31.8 cm. Yale University Art Gallery, 1958.63.25, Gift of David M. Levitt.

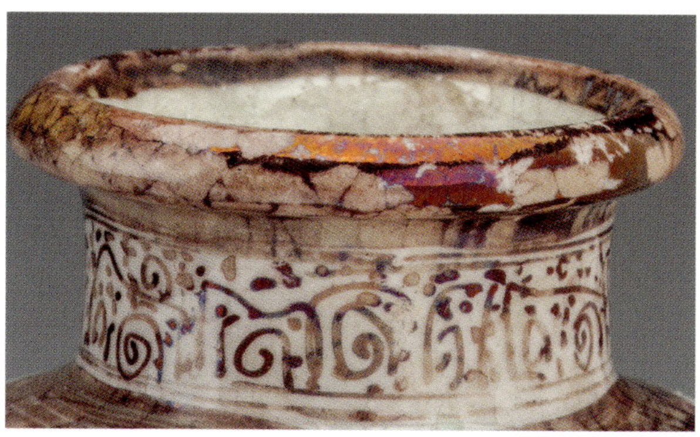

5.27. Neck of albarello illustrated in figure 5.6, Eskenazi Museum of Art, Indiana University, 72.6.5.

seems it was usually only partially successful at best. Nevertheless, the dark brown luster designs of the Raqqa "cobalt-and-luster" pieces constituted a major part of their appeal for early twentieth-century buyers. The designs were dense, usually banded, and sometimes with supplicatory phrases written in cursive or Kufic scripts within reserve bubbles (see fig. 5.12), as well as strips of pseudoinscriptive motifs and dots, foliate designs, and cloud-scroll patterns.

After studying all of the EMA Raqqa wares firsthand, I traveled to examine their sister objects in storage at the MMA and the Freer Gallery (now the National Museum of Asian Art). As I handled and photographed dozens of these objects, the incredible condition of the intact pieces—and the dealers' lore that purported to explain that condition—increasingly gave me pause. The story of the so-called Great Find is analyzed in more detail below, but in brief, it proposes that the intact and perfectly preserved pieces of Raqqa ware now dispersed across multiple collections have come down to us in such remarkable condition because they were buried inside large storage jars, shortly after their production in the medieval period. In these storage jars they lay undisturbed and protected from soil degradation and breakage until they were uncovered in the early twentieth century, some of them apparently looking as if they had just come out of the kiln moments earlier. As already noted in chapter 2, similar stories have been told about other groups of fine ceramics that appeared on the antiquities market in the twentieth century, but I know of only one verifiable instance of such a cache of luster ceramics recovered in a documented archaeological context—and in that case, it was not storage jars but a niche built into the lower wall of a house that preserved the Iranian luster bowls found at Ghazni.[52]

Examining dozens of pieces of commercially acquired Raqqa ware in person, I found the material differences between the intact objects and the reconstructed ones too striking to pass over without question. The layers of confusion added by the overpaint, fill, and degraded glazes on the reconstructed pieces, however, made it hard to compare paste, glaze, and decoration by eye and hand alone. Curiosity led me to ask staff members at the Freer Gallery and the MMA, when I examined their pieces in 2014 and 2016 respectively, if there were records of any of their Raqqa cobalt-and-luster wares undergoing thermoluminescence testing to establish the dates of last firing. Both replied in the negative.[53]

Storage, Science, Surprises

Once you start wondering about the true condition of canonical artworks, it is hard to stop. In Indiana I collaborated with the EMA's curator of Asian art, Judy Stubbs, to begin a technical investigation of the museum's collection of premodern Islamic ceramics—including the Raqqa ware group. There is early market documentation for a few of the EMA Raqqa pieces: the albarello and the "cloud-scroll" jar were both published by Dikran Kelekian in his collection catalogue of 1910, and were therefore part of the group housed at the V&A between 1910 and the dispersal of that collection in 1952 (see chapter 4).[54] The albarello and another piece, the epigraphic jar, are visible in a photograph held in the travel archives of the English explorer and archaeologist Gertrude Bell, who was probably given the photo by the Aleppo dealer Vincenzo Marcopoli (or possibly the Kouchakjis) in 1909 (fig. 5.28).[55] And the epigraphic jar and the footed bowl came to the EMA with a story that they had been exhibited at the MMA and were previously in the collection of Horace O. Havemeyer, who bequeathed many of the most famous Raqqa ceramics in existence to the MMA, although it has not been possible to confirm this.[56] The connections between the Havemeyer collection of Raqqa ceramics and the Kouchakjis have been discussed by Jenkins-Madina.[57]

Our project submitted every piece in the EMA Islamic ceramics collection to three procedures: first, condition assessment by a specialized object conservator; second, thermoluminescence (TL) testing to determine the date of

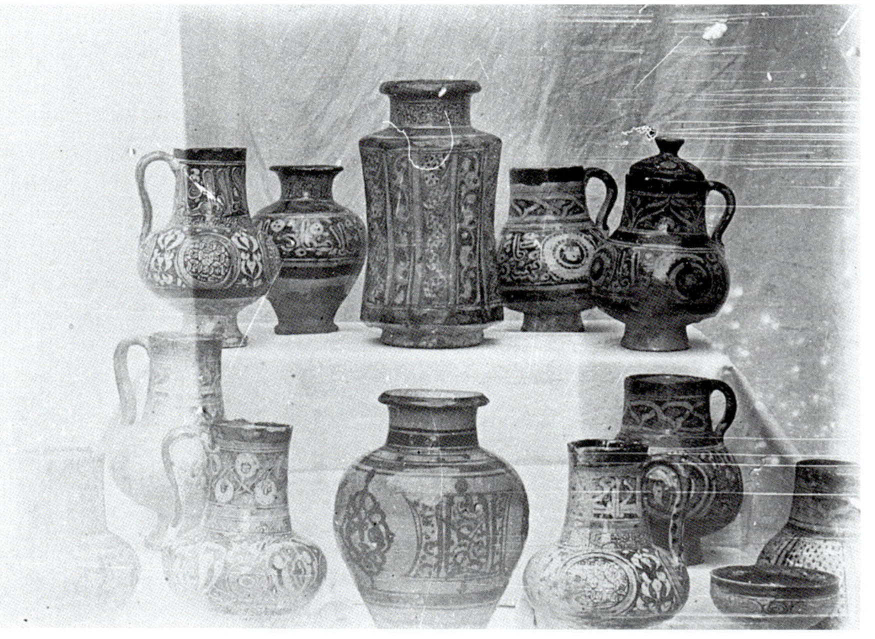

5.28. Photograph of Syrian ceramics (so-called Raqqa wares) taken ca. 1909, probably offered for sale by the Marcopoli Brothers, Aleppo, and including objects now in the Eskenazi Museum of Art and Metropolitan Museum of Art. Gertrude Bell Archive, Newcastle University Library, O_224.

last firing; and third, computed tomography (CT) scanning to assess the extent of breakage and repair on each object.[58]

TL testing, already mentioned at various points in this book, is a well-established tool for dating ceramics. Acting on mineral components of ceramic bodies, it measures how much radiation has been accumulated by a ceramic body since it was last fired. This makes it possible to determine a date range for the time that has elapsed since it last left the kiln. The date ranges returned from TL testing are typically quite broad; in analytic terms it is a blunt instrument, most useful for distinguishing ancient and medieval ceramics from modern production. Hence, its main commercial application is in determining whether a purportedly premodern piece is actually as old as it is alleged to be, or if it is of more recent manufacture—like Islam Akhun's earthenware Zahhak sculpture or the "Asiatic Terracotta" forgeries described in the introduction to this book. TL testing is an invasive and expensive procedure that involves drilling a small hole into the body of the object, usually in the foot of a vessel or the back of a tile, and it won't work without a sufficient concentration of feldspar and quartz in the sample.[59] Its limitations notwithstanding, it is a widely accepted method for the analysis of ceramics that have circulated on the antiquities market. Oxford Authentication, who performed the TL testing for the EMA objects, is one the few laboratories that do TL testing commercially for museums and private collections. In an article published in 2010 they reported that their database holds tens of thousands of TL analyses completed.[60]

The results of the TL testing for the EMA Raqqa cobalt-and-luster group are laid out in table 1.

Bearing in mind that the Raqqa wares are supposed to have been produced in the twelfth or early thirteenth century, the TL results are, to say the least, suggestive. On the one hand, there are two large jars that returned medieval date ranges of last firing (between 700 and 1,100, or 600 and 1,000 years ago, i.e., 916–1316 or 1016–1416 CE). This is in line with the late twelfth-/early thirteenth-century scholarly consensus for dating Raqqa wares. Both of those jars have been reconstructed from fragments. The only other published record of TL testing on a Raqqa cobalt-and-luster vessel was performed on the base fragment of a heavily reconstructed dish, and, like the two reconstructed jars in the EMA, also returned a medieval date range for last firing.[61] On the other hand, every single one of the intact Raqqa ware vessels in the EMA returned date ranges consistent with a last firing in the modern era. The only contradiction from the verifiable documentation of the objects is that one of them (the epigraphic jar, 72.6.8) returned a date of last firing "less than 100 years ago," when it is in fact visible in a photograph thought to have been taken circa 1909 (i.e., 107 years before the TL sample was taken), but that seven-year difference lies within a reasonable margin of error. Questions have sometimes been raised about the accuracy of TL testing and the possibility of error always remains.[62] I do not know, however, of any published cases with this level of internal consistency where TL test results have been shown to be at fault.

Assuming the TL results for the EMA Raqqa wares are accurate, then, they point to one of two possibilities for the intact wares returning modern dates of last firing. Either the intact wares were made in the modern era, or they are old ceramics that underwent refiring in the modern era. This would mean that they are either extraordinarily accomplished forgeries or old wares successfully upgraded with new skins and new decorative programs. In either case, the levels of skill involved would be staggering.

With such an eyebrow-raising set of TL results, it was imperative to determine if the pieces returning modern dates were truly intact: if they weren't, samples could have been unwittingly taken from modern material inserted during reconstruction. CT scanning after the TL testing was complete confirmed that all the vessels that appeared to be intact were indeed so, and the state of each object—intact or reconstructed from fragments—is noted in table 1.[63] The CT scans also gave a great deal more information about the state of the pieces reconstructed from fragments and revealed some startling surprises, like the threaded screws holding on the handle of the jug discussed in chapter 3.

Reviewing the CT information alongside the TL results, the EMA Raqqa wares can be separated into three groups. The first group comprises the two fragmentary jars that returned medieval date ranges from their sampled fragments. The second group includes the ten intact or near-intact vessels that returned modern date ranges. The third group is made up of four pieces that did not fit easily into either group because there was reason to believe that the samples could have been taken from modern material used in their reconstruction (the two figurines; the jug with screws in the handle; and a fragmentary large jar with modern material in the base). This third group was excluded from further analysis.

Finally, several types of chemical analysis were performed to determine if there were material characteristics that would suggest a difference in paste makeup between group one (the two fragmentary jars returning medieval date ranges) and group two (the ten intact or near-intact pieces returning

TABLE 1. Table of Thermoluminescence (TL) Testing Results for "Raqqa ware" Vessels in the Eskenazi Museum of Art

EMA acc. no.	*Thumbnail image*	*Condition assessment based on examination in regular light and UV, and CT scanning*	*TL results from analysis performed by Oxford Authentication, 2016: date of last firing*	*Documentation prior to entering EMA in 1972*
72.6.2	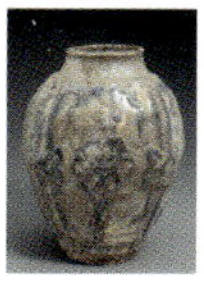	Fragmentary. Assembled from numerous fragments, with a foot ring that appears to be a restoration. TL sample taken from fragment in base.	Less than 300 years ago	
72.6.3	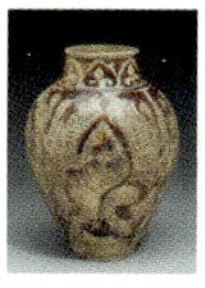	Fragmentary. Assembled from numerous fragments, with broad areas of overpaint. Two TL samples taken from fragments in base, one of which was taken from a site with evidence of plaster fill, the other from a fragment of glazed stonepaste.	Between 700 and 1,100 years ago	
72.6.4	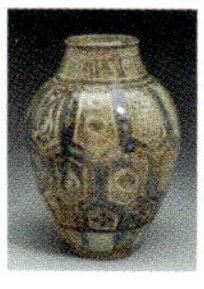	Fragmentary, with many join lines along the upper body, and the perimeter of the lip restored. More polished restoration work than 72.6.2 or 72.6.3. TL sample taken from large stonepaste fragment in base.	Between 600 and 1,000 years ago	Published in Kouchakji sale catalogues, 1918 and 1927 (ill.).
72.6.5	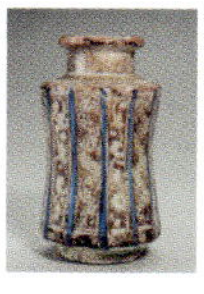	Intact. TL sample taken from base.	Less than 200 years ago	Visible in photograph taken Aleppo, ca. 1909 (Gertrude Bell Archive O_224). Published in Kelekian 1910 (ill.).
72.6.6	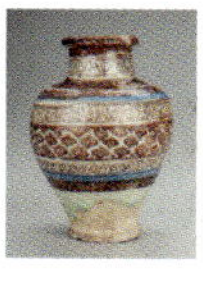	Intact. TL sample taken from base.	Less than 200 years ago	Published in Kelekian 1910 (ill.).
72.6.7	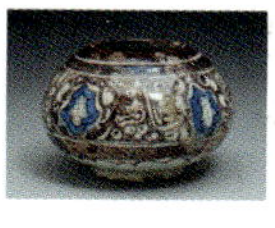	Intact. TL sample taken from base.	Less than 100 years ago	
72.6.8	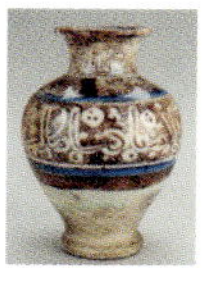	Intact. TL sample taken from base.	Less than 100 years ago	Visible in photograph taken Aleppo, ca. 1909 (Gertrude Bell archive O_224). Reported by Kouchakji to be ex-Havemeyer collection; seemingly spurious MMA acc. no. on base.
72.6.9	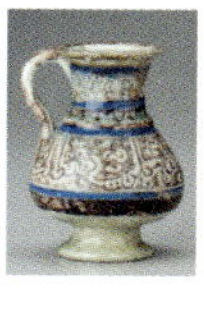	Largely intact. Edges of foot and lip restored, as well as handle; rest appears on CT to be intact. TL sample taken from elevated inner surface of foot that is continuous with the body of the object and distinct from the restored sections.	Less than 150 years ago	Published in Kelekian collection sale, Sotheby Parke Bernet, 1953, lot no. 330 (ill.)

EMA acc. no.	*Thumbnail image*	*Condition assessment based on examination in regular light and UV, and CT scanning*	*TL results from analysis performed by Oxford Authentication, 2016: date of last firing*	*Documentation prior to entering EMA in 1972*
72.6.10	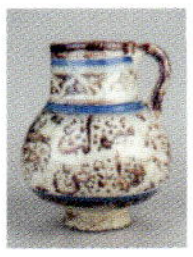	Intact, with minor chips to rim and foot. TL sample taken from base.	Less than 150 years ago	
72.6.11	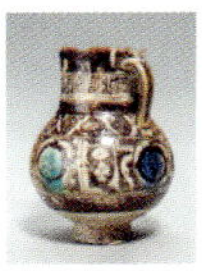	Fragmentary. Modern handle fixed with screws top and bottom (see chapter 3), belly a mix of fragments and lower part of object may not be original. TL sample taken from foot that could be a later addition.	Less than 350 years ago	Published in Kelekian collection sale, Sotheby Parke Bernet, 1953, lot no. 332 (ill.).
72.6.12	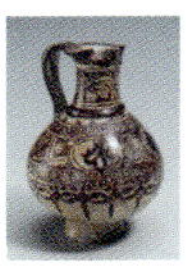	Body intact; handle a replacement; some infills on rim. Large inclusions in paste; fissure in base that occurred during firing, with glaze in it. Brown "luster" is entirely matte, appears to stand slightly proud of the surface in places. TL sample taken from base.	Less than 150 years ago	
72.6.13	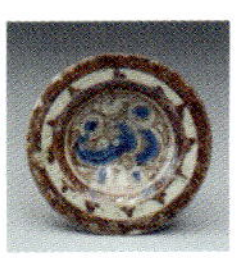	Intact. TL sample taken from base.	Less than 300 years ago	
72.6.14	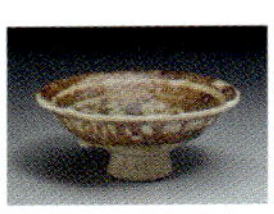	Intact. TL sample taken from base.	Less than 100 years ago	
72.6.15	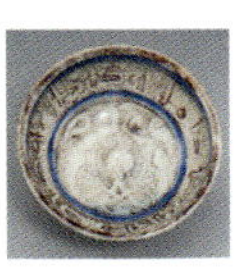	Intact. TL sample taken from base.	Less than 200 years ago	Reported by Kouchakji to be ex-Havemeyer collection; seemingly spurious MMA acc. no. on base.
72.6.16	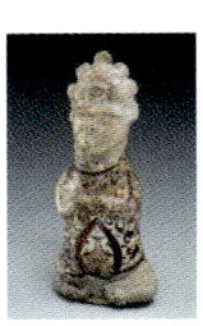	Fragmentary. Head distinct from multiple fragments making up body. A fragment that can be seen in CT scan to be glazed front and back at bottom front of body is probably a sherd from a dish. TL samples taken from left and right side of base; both yielded same result.	Less than 200 years ago	Published in Grube 1966 (ill.).
72.6.17	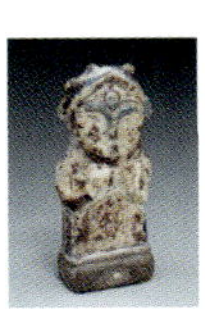	Fragmentary. Mounted on modern pediment; back is a piece of unglazed material planed or sanded to shape and unrelated to the head; front upper body and head composed of fragments. TL sample taken from lower left part of unglazed material on the back.	Between 600 and 1,000 years ago (sample taken from fragment that is not part of original object)	Published in Grube 1966 (ill.).

modern date ranges). If the two groups were made in completely different historical epochs, they would be unlikely to have been made with the same stonepaste recipe or materials, and therefore one would expect to find observable chemical differences in the composition of paste or glaze. The results of the analytical testing are detailed in a separate study, and the conclusions are summarized here only briefly, to avoid trying the patience of readers who don't engage regularly with the periodic table.[64]

First, the intact pieces with the modern TL dates all have alkaline glazes without lead, which is consistent with archaeologically recovered sherds of "Raqqa ware" type. The two fragmentary jars with medieval dates, on the other hand, have leaded glazes like those found on other types of archaeologically recovered medieval Syrian ceramics, such as sherds of "Tell Minis" ware type and some medieval Syrian pieces that have been presented as intermediaries between "Tell Minis" and "Raqqa" production.[65] Second, bulk element analysis of the pastes did not signal major or obvious differences between the two groups, and neither group appeared to be strongly out of range with the Syrian stonepastes that have been analyzed in other studies. However, the very small data sets—especially for the medieval group of only two objects—make it impossible to draw hard comparative conclusions. To make matters even more complicated, many of the published analytical studies of Raqqa ware pastes have drawn their samples from unprovenienced pieces acquired through the antiquities market, or sometimes a confusing mix of unprovenienced objects and archaeologically recovered ones.[66] Until more archaeologically excavated sherds are analyzed to provide control data, and other institutions perform TL testing and paste analysis on the Raqqa wares in their collections, the most plausible hypothesis at present is that the EMA's intact pieces of Raqqa ware are old objects that were refired in the modern era, or, less likely, whole-cloth modern forgeries made with a paste recipe similar to the original. In either event, the levels of skill involved are breathtaking—so much so that they necessitate a total rethink of the craftsmanship available for ceramics fabrication in the early twentieth century.

Material Riddles

If the intact Raqqa wares are of wholly or partially modern manufacture, what material evidence is there within the larger corpus of Raqqa wares for refiring, or indeed for other forms of modern fabrication? And how might such a process have worked? One possibility is that luster decoration could have been added in the modern era to ceramics that had undergone glazing and first firing complete with cobalt designs, like figures 5.25 and 5.26, but had never received their luster layers. Although many of the Raqqa wares that have been recovered in an unlustered state are wasters, there are some unfinished Raqqa "cobalt-and-would-be-luster" wares that have made their way onto the antiquities market without any obvious sign of something having gone wrong in firing (fig. 5.26). Could someone in the early twentieth century have come across a cache of extremely well preserved but unfinished pieces, and decided to raise their financial value by finishing them off with the prized designs in luster? Reportedly, this has happened with other types of medieval Islamic ceramic in recent years.

The possibility of relustering old ceramics was raised in chapter 3, with the example of the EMA Raqqa ware handled jar that has very odd epigraphy, scratchy brushwork, and possibly more than one round of luster decoration (see fig. 3.49). To do this would be technically demanding but there is no reason it should be impossible, on the face of it. Luster is fired at a temperature of around 600 degrees Celsius (1112 Fahrenheit), which is also the approximate threshold firing temperature for "resetting" a ceramic's TL signal.[67] This means that a medieval ceramic that undergoes a successful luster firing in the modern era would likely be reset to year zero in terms of radiation, and hence would return a TL date that started from the time of its refiring.

Documentation for modern luster production seems thus far to be lacking for the Syrian context, but of course, absence of evidence is not evidence of absence. The late nineteenth-/early twentieth-century frenzy on the antiquities market for medieval Middle Eastern lusterwares would have provided a powerful stimulus for potters to experiment with such techniques. As noted in chapter 4, the *Qamus al-sinaʿat al-shamiyya* (Dictionary of Damascene Crafts), completed circa 1908, shows that antiquities vendors in turn-of-the-century Damascus were very alert to the movements of the antiquities market and adept at providing western buyers with what they were looking for, including *taqlid al-qadima*, "imitations of ancient things."[68] When the gold rush for the medieval ceramics of Raqqa and other north Syrian sites was at its peak in the early years of the twentieth century, with medieval lusterwares emerging as a prime commodity on the global antiquities market, it would be entirely logical for enterprising vendors and potters to try recreating the technique of luster to add value to old, plain wares—and we do have known examples of medieval "Raqqa ware" vessels that were found partially completed, without having undergone the application of luster and a second firing (see fig. 5.26).[69]

It is also possible to imagine a scenario where incomplete medieval pieces could be covered in the modern era with a new layer of clear glaze, fired, then lustered and fired again—which would also reset TL to zero. Possibly pertinent to this is an unusual feature of the glazing seen on several of the intact Raqqa wares. That is, they seem to have two distinct and separate layers of greenish clear glaze, a thinner one underneath and a much thicker and more vitreous one over the top (see fig. 5.24). This is visible where the thicker glaze stops short of the foot of the object. It's an oddity of glazing seen across many—although not all—of the most perfect pieces and was noted as early as circa 1926 by Rudolf Meyer Riefstahl, who repeatedly described two layers of glaze on intact Raqqa wares of both cobalt-and-luster and turquoise-and-black type.[70] This is not a common phenomenon among medieval ceramics, and Tonghini's excavation report from the medieval Syrian site of Qalʿat Jaʿbar states unequivocally that the feet of the Raqqa-type vessels excavated there were unglazed.[71] However, one of the pieces excavated by Macridy at Raqqa in 1905 might have the same "double glaze" effect.[72] It's hard to know what this means without examining the piece firsthand: if the two glaze layers are indeed present on an object excavated at Raqqa by Macridy, then it must be an outcome of the original medieval production process. If not, it could be evidence of more recent reglazing.

A further peculiarity of the intact Raqqa wares is the existence of several otherwise perfect dishes in collections in the United States that look as if they

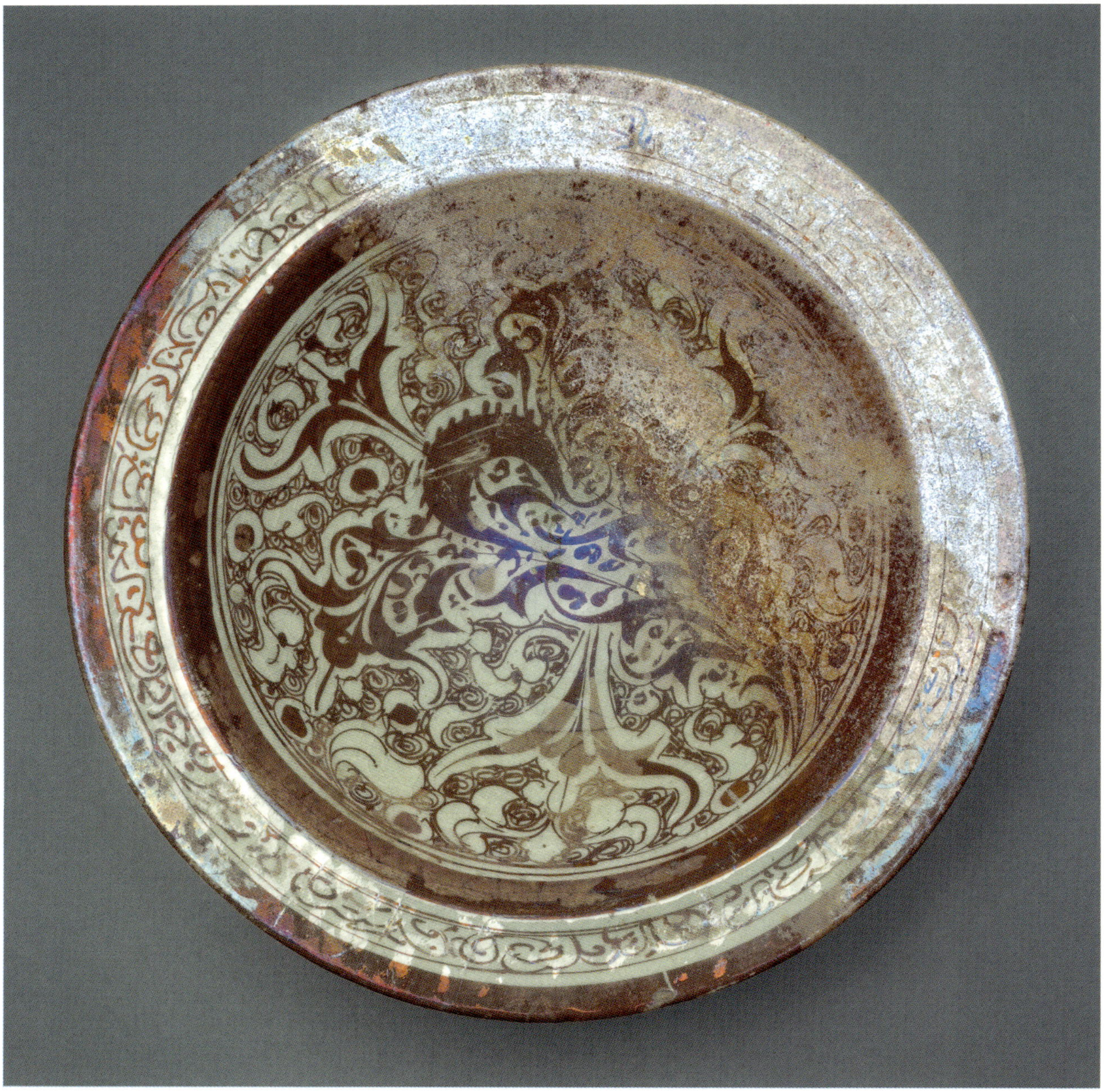

5.29. Top view of dish illustrated in figure 5.24, showing segment of iridesced glaze.

have been partially dipped in something that has iridesced one neat segment of the glazed surface while leaving the rest immaculate (fig. 5.29).[73] Presumably, the explanation offered for this on the market would have been that such bowls were found partially submerged in sand or soil within the storage jar that protected them; hence the degraded glaze occurs only on the part that rested in contact with the dirt for centuries. That this deterioration has occurred so neatly, and without sacrificing the overall attractiveness of the design, gives it a distinctly cosmetic appearance. Indeed, in a marketplace where a certain amount of picturesque aging was desirable and Raqqa wares in particular were prized for the iridescence of their degraded glazes, it would

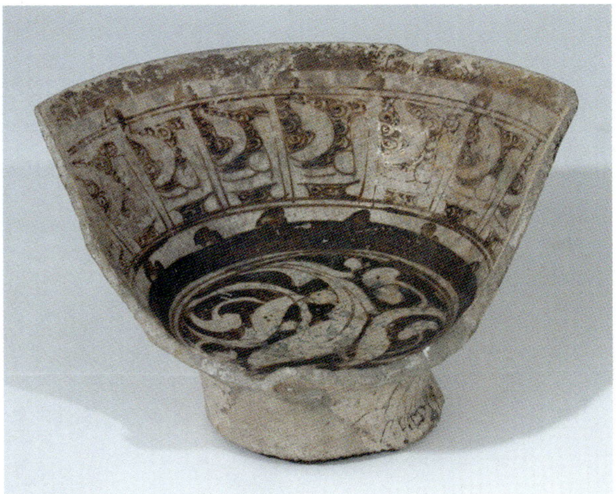

5.30. Fragment of bowl, glazed stonepaste with overglaze luster(?) and modern overpainting. Attributed Syria, late 12th or 13th century. Height 9 cm. Metropolitan Museum of Art, Rogers Fund, 1907, 07.212.3.

likely have enhanced their appeal. It immediately brings to mind the artificial aging processes witnessed in Iran by Olmer and Vignier (chapter 3) and the similar processes imputed to the craftsmen of Kubachi by Kverfeldt (chapter 2). Those techniques of artificial aging sought to degrade modern glazes in attractive ways through complex procedures involving the application of fatty and acidic liquids and additional firing.

The other Raqqa wares that should be put under the spotlight are those that bear modern painting in brown paint that seeks to enhance or entirely invent luster designs. Some pieces look like they might have been touched up with the aim of making a faint design stronger. This is evident in the very first piece of Raqqa ware that the Metropolitan Museum acquired on the market (fig. 5.30). The museum bought it in 1907 from one "A. Filippo" in London. (Could this be the dealer Cerof Filippo, encountered in chapter 2?) In particular, the scrolling vegetal design at the base of the fragment looks like it has been enhanced with modern brown watercolor that lies on top of the degraded glaze, rather than being bonded to the glaze itself the way a true luster would be. Similar enhancement—or in some places, pure invention in brown paint—is visible on some of the bowls Freer bought from Vincenzo Marcopoli in Aleppo in 1908.[74]

A bowl in the NMAA, also acquired by Freer from Marcopoli during his 1908 trip to Aleppo, reveals a more systematic attempt at putting a new skin onto an old Raqqa ware bowl in the early twentieth century (fig. 5.31). The underlying piece is a flaring bowl of the classic "biconical" type so strongly associated with Raqqa. It looks to have undergone the first stage of glazing and firing, with cobalt and turquoise circles fired under the glaze. Someone has then sought to enhance it in the modern era with two rounds of linear painting in brown. In one round of modern upgrading, an outline design has been painted with great skill by a practiced draftsman, creating a taut, springy curvilinear schema across the whole inner surface. The very thin, cleanly executed lines of this design lie with equal visibility across iridesced and non-iridesced areas of the glaze alike, which would be highly unlikely if such a design were original to the object.[75] Whatever the medium is that has been used for this round of painting, it seems it could only really work in outline,

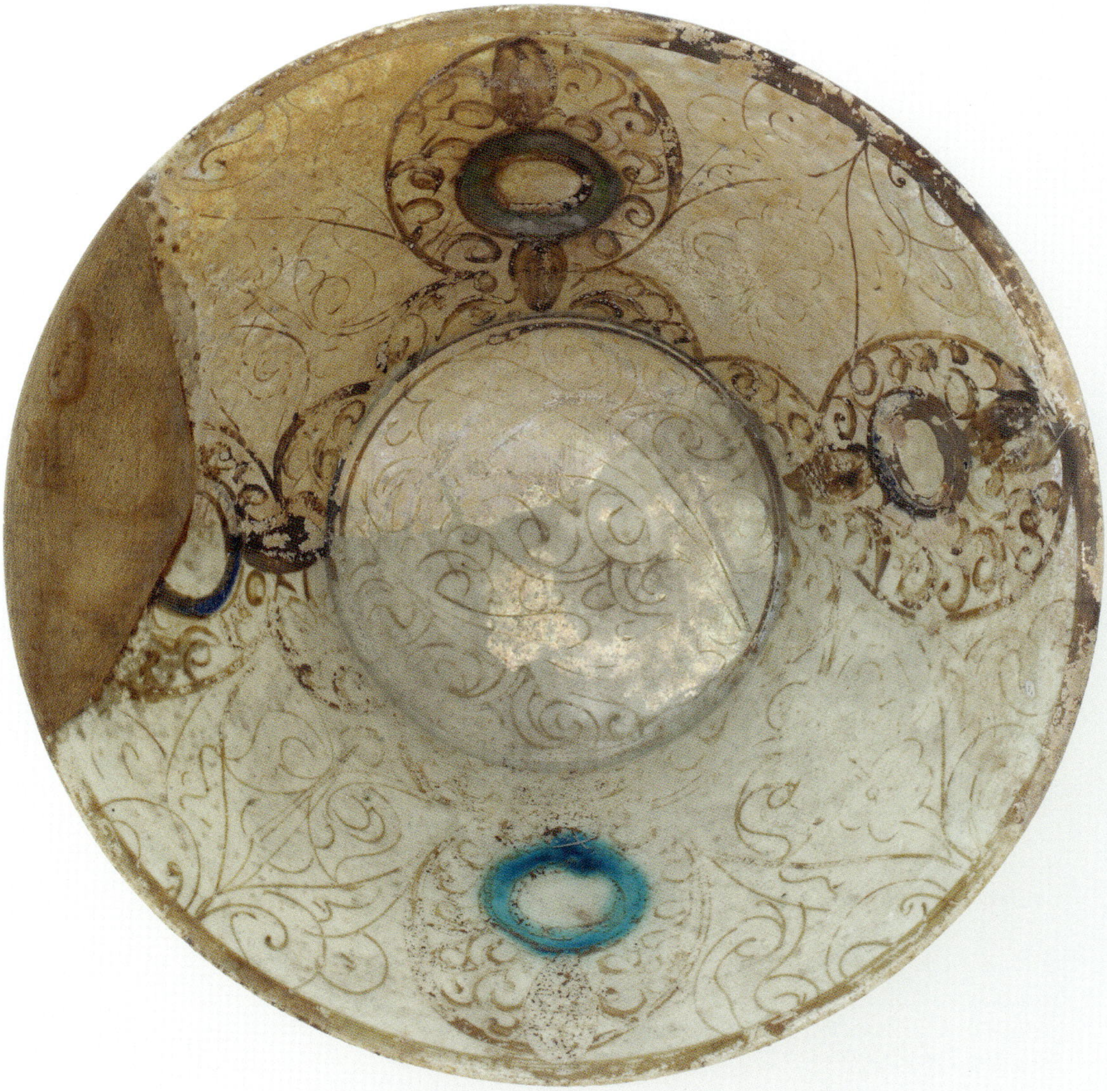

5.31. Bowl, glazed stonepaste with modern overpainting. Attributed Syria, late 12th or 13th century. Diameter 24.5 cm. National Museum of Asian Art, Gift of Charles Lang Freer, F1908.145.

without solid blocks of brown color that would perhaps give too much away. Against this outlining there has been a much less successful second round of modern painting in darker brown using what appears to be a watercolor paint. The darker painting attempts to deepen the design around the colored circles and add some of the density that a real medieval luster design would have, but instead descends into a mess of thick lines and curlicues. Moreover, the shiny areas of the glaze have visibly resisted this dark brown paint, leaving a speckled residue familiar to anyone who has ever tried to paint with watercolors onto plastic or waxed surfaces.

The outlined design on this bowl looks like the practice ground of a highly skilled painter developing his or her ability to imitate not just individual motifs but entire design schema, using original Raqqa ware cobalt-and-luster designs as source material. The coherence, confidence, and ingenuity of the outlined schema puts it in a different league from the sometimes clumsy touch-ups with a paintbrush seen elsewhere. One wonders if a strange, accomplished but partial piece of calligraphy in brown outline on the unglazed base of an immaculate cobalt-and-luster basin, sold to Gulbenkian by the Kouchakjis in 1908, might be by the same hand.[76] In considering practice pieces, we should also return to the handled jug discussed in chapter 3, with its poorly executed luster inscription in a very modern-looking script. That jug seems to represent an applied layer of modern luster design, executed with unconvincing draftsmanship but successfully fired onto a medieval glazed object. It too may have been a kind of tryout, or an attempt by a not-so-skilled painter to turn his hand to a new kind of commission.

Naturally, the many Raqqa wares that have been stuck together from fragments are sometimes also heavily reworked, and the skill involved can be remarkable. The existence of workshops in Aleppo dedicated to reconstructing Raqqa ware ceramics from sherds was reported as early as 1908 in a letter from Friedrich Sarre to the *Burlington Magazine* and in a letter sent from Aleppo by Freer in the same year.[77] Vignier, we recall, asserted in the late 1920s that methods of reconstruction from disparate sherds had been pioneered first in Aleppo, before they were taken to new heights in Tehran, and in chapter 3 we already encountered a Syrian jar bought by Freer from Marcopoli in Aleppo in 1911 that proved in conservation to be made of fragments set into a mortar of thickened fish glue.[78]

An excellent example of the technique is one of the large jars in the EMA that returned a medieval date range (see fig. 5.17). The jar is first documented on the antiquities market in a slightly doctored image in the Kouchakji sale catalogue of 1918 (fig. 5.32).[79] As can be seen from the CT imagery, this massive

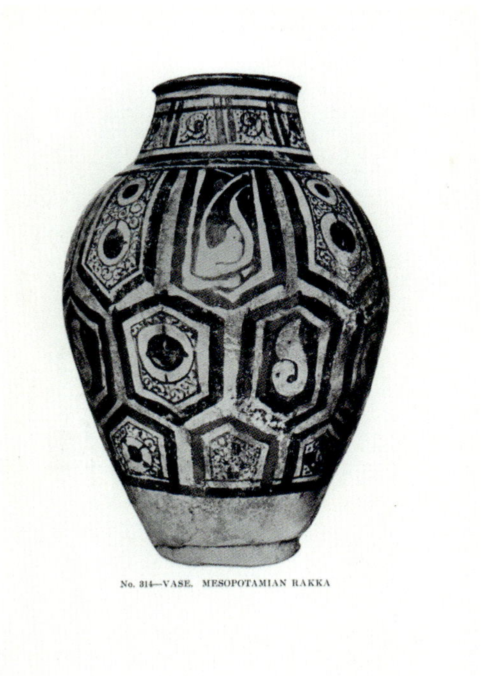

5.32. American Art Galleries, *The Kouchakji Frères Collection of Graeco-Roman, Rakka, Persian, Hispano-Moresque Faiences, Italian Majolicas, Persian and Indian Miniatures and Rugs, Egyptian, Ptolemaic, Sidonian, Roman and Arabic Glass, Greek and Roman Bronzes*. American Art Galleries, NY, March 1918, no. 314.

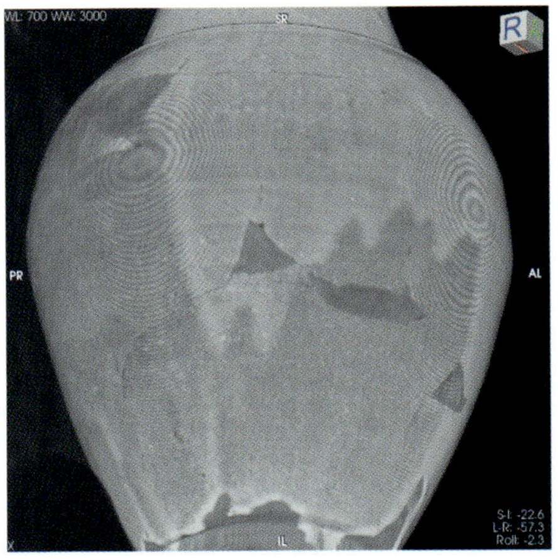

5.33. CT image of large reconstructed jar shown in figure 5.17.

5.34. UV image of large reconstructed jar shown in figure 5.17.

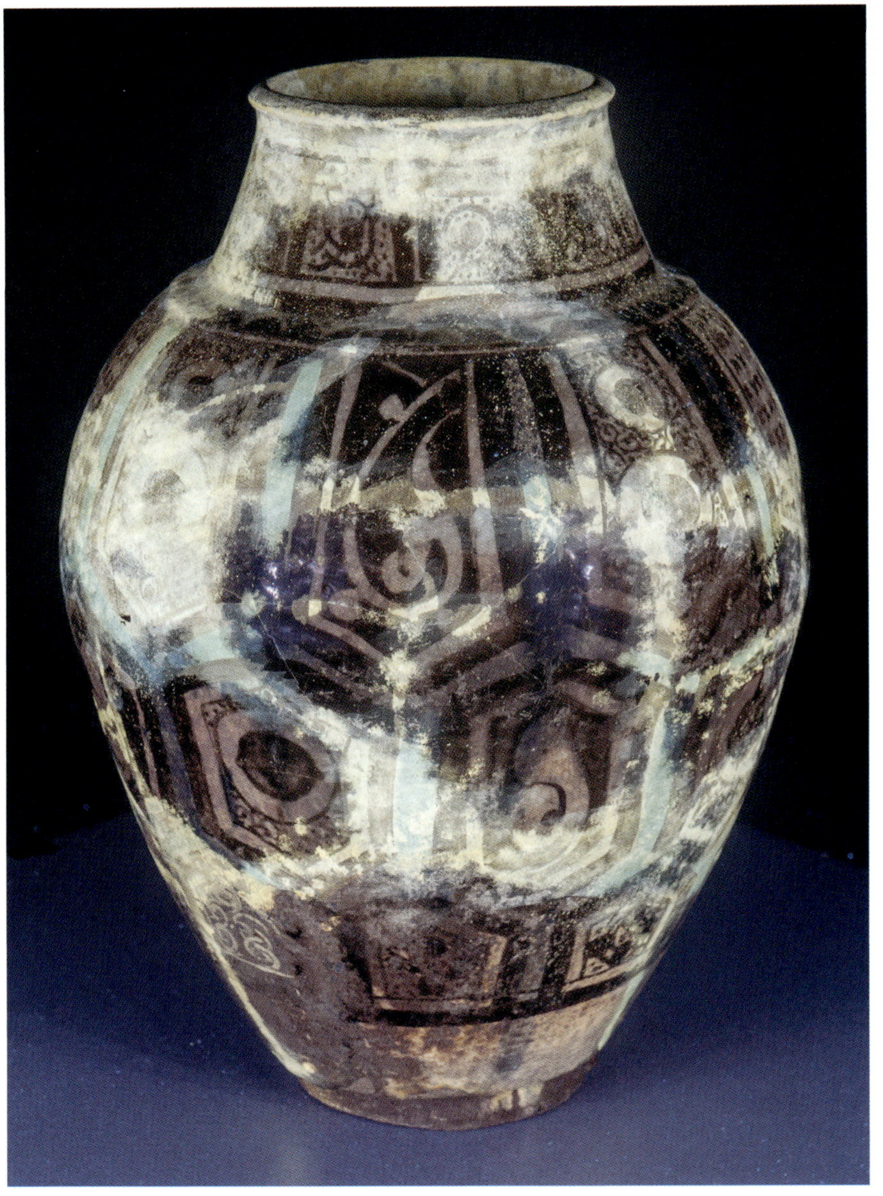

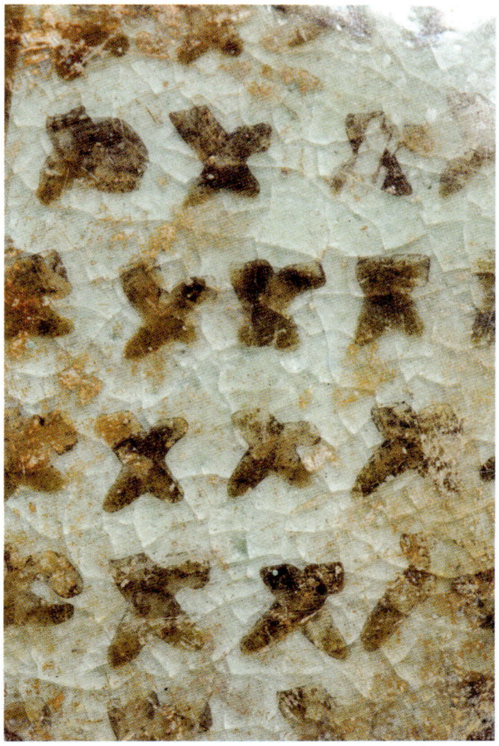

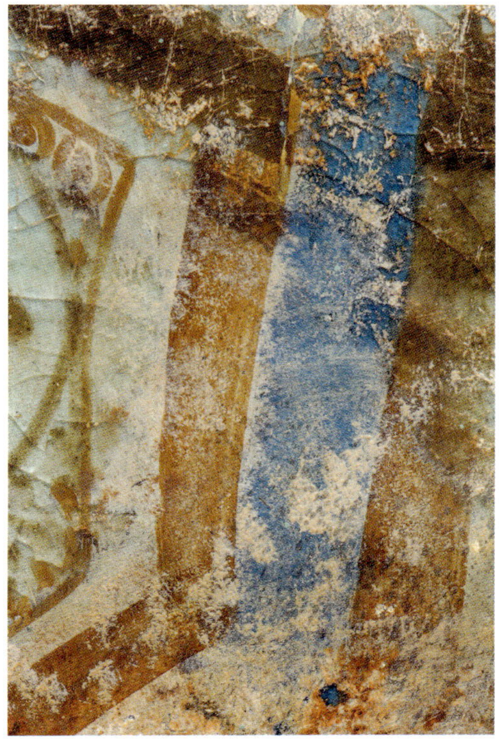

5.35. Detail of large reconstructed jar shown in figure 5.17.

5.36. Detail of large reconstructed jar shown in figure 5.17.

jar was skillfully put back together in the early twentieth century from pieces, much of the body seemingly originating from a single original object (fig. 5.33). The drips of its glaze layers track across fragments, while darker areas represent interstitial bits of fill material, possibly glue putty. Only UV light shows how much overpainting has been used to stage-manage the image of unbroken completeness (fig. 5.34). Up close, the incredible intricacy of the surface layers overwhelm the eye, from the sharp brown edges of the medieval luster medium in a field of little crosses (fig. 5.35), to the layering of brown and blue overpaint next to original designs, with sponged-on muddy coloring speckled everywhere to blur the distinctions between old and new surfaces (fig. 5.36). Many of the original motifs seen on this jar—the kite-shaped fields of little crosses, circles within circles, and palmette designs that curve back on themselves—match those seen on a bowl excavated at Hama, thus anchoring the jar within the medieval Syrian stonepaste corpus despite all its modern upgrading.[80]

This section has explored an odd set of material puzzles. The painted touch-ups to worn-out luster designs are an uncomplicated form of window dressing, and the large jar is an assemblage of fragments and overpaint, put together with remarkable skill but using techniques that are by now familiar. The others, though, are much harder to parse. Doubled glazes, cosmetically degraded segments, synthesizing designs practiced in outline, and above all the possibility of modern luster designs fired onto old objects: these all point to the likelihood of person or persons unknown honing their skills and putting new skins on old pots. Having taken the material proof as far as it can go, the rest of this chapter turns to the circumstantial evidence surrounding the Raqqa wares and their oblique passage from the Middle East to the Midwest.

Raqqa Ware on the Market: The First Decades

It is time to spool back to the start of the aboveground story. When and how did Raqqa ware first surface as an international commodity in the antiquities market? Dealer lore locates this event in the 1890s, with the Tabbagh Frères (Émile and Georges Tabbagh) claiming that their father Joseph first introduced Raqqa wares to the European market around 1891.[81] Gangoly, as we have already heard, placed the first discovery in 1890. Jenkins-Madina has shown, however, that a ceramic lantern decorated with cobalt-and-luster designs, now in the MMA, was offered for sale at the 1888 auction of the collection of Albert Goupil (1840–1884). This is, thus far, the earliest known appearance of a piece of "Raqqa ware" on the modern antiquities market, although it was not recognized as such at the time. It is possible that Goupil acquired it during his five-month trip to the Middle East in 1868, made in the company of the painter Jean-Léon Gérôme (Goupil's brother-in-law) and others. More likely, however, it was acquired on the Paris art market after his return, in his years as a tastemaker with a notable private collection of "Oriental" artworks at the Goupil family home on the rue Chaptal.[82] Three years after it went up for sale at the Goupil auction, the Raqqa lantern was given to the MMA in 1891 by the silver magnate and art collector Edward C. Moore, along with some other, less spectacular ceramics now also attributed to Raqqa.[83]

The year 1891 saw another sign of Raqqa ware's coming ascendance. In that year, one of the high priests of ceramics collecting in Britain, Henry Wallis, published the first illustration of an identifiable piece of Raqqa ware (fig. 5.37). The handled cobalt-and-luster cup appears in a painting by Wallis published in a catalogue of Persian luster ceramics from the collection of Frederick DuCane Godman (1834–1919).[84] Wallis's excellent draftsmanship leaves no doubt that we are looking at what would now be called Raqqa ware. Specifically, it is a handled jug with the classic vitreous glaze, cobalt underglaze circles, and cursive luster inscriptions executed in reserve around the belly, as well as a characteristic band of rather scribbly pseudoinscription around the neck. (Wallis's caption correctly identifies the neck band as "fictitious Arabic characters." The same designs would be proclaimed "Nashki inscriptions" by twentieth-century dealers, including Kouchakji, who invoked the gravitas of legible content and the Arabic calligraphic tradition for audiences who usually wouldn't know the difference.)[85] The object itself is now in the British Museum, where it can be seen to be missing a fragment from the neck that Wallis had imagined back into existence in his painting (fig. 5.38).[86] In the 1891 catalogue, the handled jug is reported to have been brought to Istanbul by a merchant who claimed it had been "found in the ground at Mosul."[87] This unnamed merchant could have been any one of a number of candidates: the Tabbagh family, for example, or the Kelekian brothers, who were trading antiquities in Istanbul by 1892.[88] But the jug could easily have traveled from Ottoman Upper Mesopotamia to the imperial capital via another, less well-known trader.

At any rate, the first documented appearances—the lantern in 1888, a fragmentary bowl accessioned to the Princeton University Art Museum in 1890, the jug illustrated in 1891—seem to represent the early vanguard.[89] By the late 1890s, the floodgates had well and truly opened and Raqqa wares were flow-

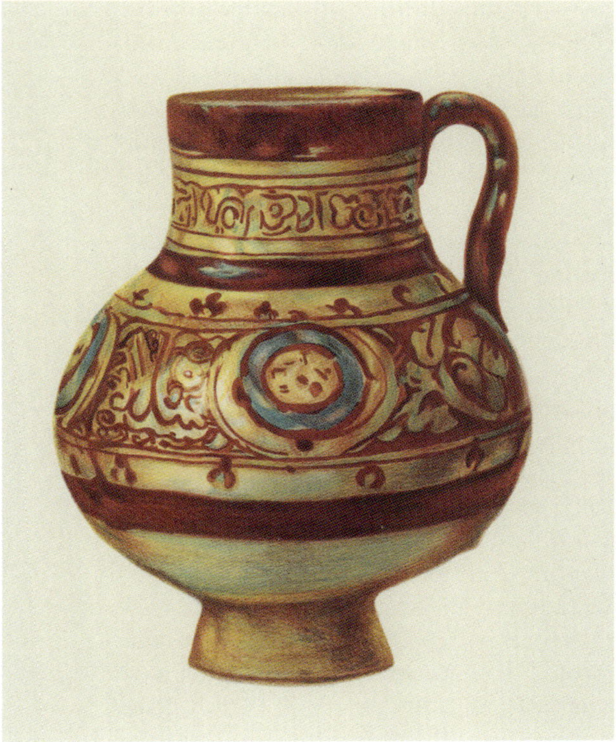

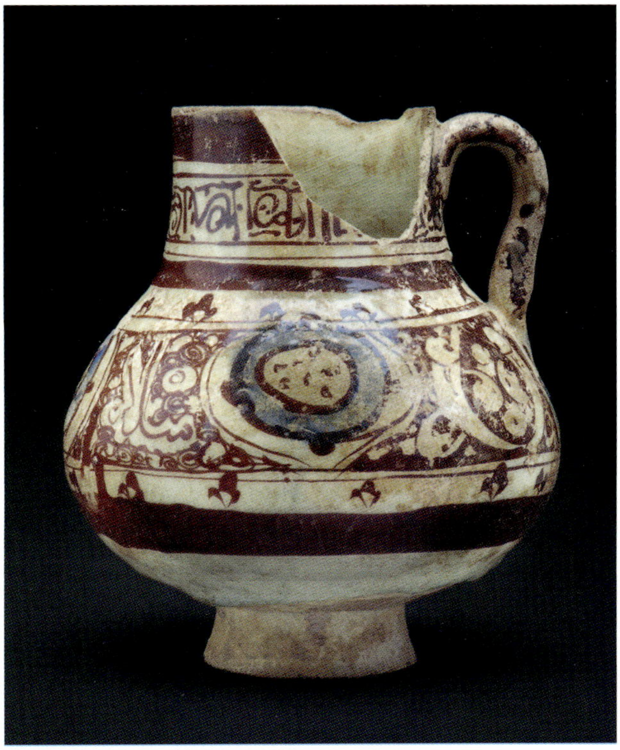

ing through the market. Yoltar-Yıldırım's meticulous research in the Ottoman archives has shown that by 1899 local administrators were sending reports to Istanbul about illegal excavation at Raqqa, urging the empire's central authorities to take charge of the situation and initiate their own excavations.[90] According to a letter sent in 1900, pieces of "antique pottery, including colored and figural vases," were being dug out of the ground by local men working for dealers. In 1904 a teacher in Raqqa named Kazim Efendi even provided specific information about where to dig at the site in order to conduct a scientific excavation of the pottery sellers' quarters of the medieval city; these details, along with proposed manpower needs and costings for such an excavation, were sent to the Imperial Museum in Istanbul with a plea to get the work started.[91] In spite of all this, however, Istanbul did not initiate excavations until the end of the next year. When the Ottoman authorities finally sent in Théodore Macridy to start official excavations on 31 December 1905, he dug out a trench and sent some kiln furniture to Istanbul along with objects he reconstructed from fragments. Further Ottoman excavations in 1908 led by Haydar Bey yielded more pieces for the imperial collections in Istanbul but in poorer condition, with little potential for museum display.[92]

While these excavations would not meet modern scientific standards, they have given us some pieces of Raqqa ware excavated in the early twentieth century that can be incontrovertibly identified with the site.[93] None of the materials unearthed in either of the Ottoman excavations is in the fabulous, pristine condition of the best-known pieces traded on the art market. But somewhere in between those two rounds of Ottoman excavation at Raqqa lies the portentously titled legend of the "Great Find," a cache of pristine and immaculate

5.37. Henry Wallis, *The Godman Collection: Persian Ceramic Art in the Collection of Mr. F. DuCane Godman, F.R.S., The Thirteenth Century Lustred Vases* (London: privately printed, 1891), plate XXIII.

5.38. Jug, glazed stonepaste with overglaze luster (so-called Raqqa ware). Attributed Syria, late 12th or early 13th century. Height 15.2 cm. British Museum, G.268.

ceramics supposedly found inside larger storage jars unearthed at the site. On the evidence of Yoltar-Yıldırım's archival research and the romanticized origin story promoted by Fahim Kouchakji, Jenkins-Madina has proposed that the "Great Find" likely occurred after the documented relocation of Circassian refugees from Aleppo to Raqqa in the week of 2 April 1906.[94] The fable of that cache is extremely important to this chapter, not least because it included, by Fahim Kouchakji's account, the albarello and possibly other objects now in the EMA (see fig. 5.6). I return to the question of the "Great Find" below, after building upon the timeline of the early twentieth-century trade in Raqqa wares laid out by earlier scholars, with particular emphasis on the condition of the objects moving through the early market and the rise of the Kouchakji family.

After the first pieces of Raqqa ware appeared on the market in the late 1880s and early 1890s, the collecting picture is somewhat opaque until the end of the 1890s. By 1902, there starts to be much more solid documentation in museum and collection archives.[95] In that year, Charles Lang Freer—an early collector of Raqqa ceramics—acquired his first pieces of what we would now class as Raqqa ware. Luckily for future art historians, Freer kept unusually complete and careful documentation of his art purchases. By late 1902 purchases start to appear in Freer's records with Raqqa as their stated origin, sometimes attributed thus by the dealers, sometimes by Freer. Between 1903 and 1905 he bought multiple "Raqqa" ceramics in Paris from Dikran Kelekian (from whom he also bought in New York), Siegfried Bing, Onnik Kalebdjian (whose letterhead identifies him as a restorer of all types of ceramic, "Françaises & orientales"), and the Kalebdjian Frères.[96] This marks phase one of the full flow of Raqqa wares through the European market. The craze was accompanied by the inevitable dealer warnings that the supply might dry up at any moment, with Kelekian writing to Freer in 1904 and 1905 to warn of increasing scarcity in the Raqqa supply chain and competition among dealers over the available pieces.[97] Dealer concerns about Ottoman restrictions on supply were based on political realities, however much they might have been tuned up to heighten buyer interest. By 1906, the year of the revised Ottoman antiquities law, the Ottoman central powers were making more structured efforts to stop the smuggling of antiquities from the site: approximately 208 confiscated objects from Raqqa had arrived at the Ottoman Imperial Museum in Istanbul by that date.[98]

The trade went on regardless, shaped by the geopolitics of the early twentieth century. The documented relocation to Raqqa of Muslim refugees arriving from the Russian North Caucasus, beginning in the 1880s, may or may not have given rise in the spring of 1906 to a find of perfectly preserved wares (see below). There is, however, no reason to doubt the story that it was North Caucasian refugees digging at the site for building materials (an action initially authorized by the Ottoman authorities) that brought the first finds to light and set off the frenzied harvesting of Raqqa by antiquities dealers and their agents.[99] The international financial crisis of 1907, plus poor harvests and crop failure across much of the Ottoman Empire in that year, can only have fueled further digging at the site as local people sought to stay afloat in desperate times and looked to the mine of globally tradeable resources on their doorstep.

In 1908, just before the Young Turk Revolution started to unfold in the west of the Ottoman Empire, Freer decided to go to the source. In a buying spree that cut across Europe and the Middle East through the summer months, he bought Raqqa wares from Tabbagh Frères, Paris; Murad Baroody, Beirut; Au Musée Oriental (Moussa Arouani & Co.), Istanbul; Elias Hatoun, Cairo; Maurice Nahman, Cairo; Vincenzo Marcopoli, Aleppo; "a street dealer in Aleppo"; and "an Arab at Aleppo."[100] These last two give some indication of the quantities of Raqqa ware that must have been moving through the region, if unidentified street vendors were handling them. Later in the same year Freer also bought Raqqa wares in New York from Dikran Kelekian and Azeez Khayat, as well as further pieces shipped from Aleppo to the US by Vincenzo Marcopoli.[101]

Writing on 19 June 1908, Freer described his delight with the Aleppo leg of his journey:

> Aleppo is a charming surprise—a beautiful ancient city, and in every way more attractive than I had fancied. It is the nearest city to Racca, an old-time caravan town filled with artistic treasure! The store house from which Kelekian, Kalebdjian and Noorian have drawn their supplies for years. Tourists have as yet never been here—the railroad only recently finished—and the dreaded Aleppo boil a menace to even all of the dealers, excepting Tabbagh, who was born here and who first recognized the artistic quality of Racca pottery. Not more than half a dozen Americans have as yet visited this locality. I am in the best of hands here and in direct contact with the original discovere[r]s of the arts of Racca. There's more than pottery—and all is beautiful; I am now more than ever satisfied with every piece of Racca pottery purchased for my collection from the beginning. I have, since coming, secured twenty additional pieces which we hope to ship to England—a dangerous business, but if confiscation by the Turkish officials is avoided, my collection will be greatly enriched—made absolutely the finest extant.... I must return sometime in March or October to see Racca proper, but Aleppo is Racca for all but romantic purposes. Still, I should like to see the deserted old ruins from which this matchless pottery is being rescued. The finest specimens come from Racca proper. Inferior specimens and other fine examples as well, are being found in other localities on the Euphrates, in and near Mesopotamia. Tomorrow, I shall leave for the mountains for change of air.[102]

Freer was very pleased with the pieces shown to him in Aleppo by Vincenzo Marcopoli and he bought twenty-four of them, arranging for their shipment back to the United States—which involved smuggling them out of Ottoman territory.[103] This marked the start of further purchases by Freer from Marcopoli. As Jenkins-Madina has shown, however, the Marcopoli firm does not seem to have been ready for the complexities of trading antiquities across international borders, and they frustrated Freer with some unrequested and badly packed shipments they subsequently sent to him in Detroit (although he did end up buying those pieces). The Marcopoli family's rather messy handling of the relationship with Freer contrasts with the increasingly internationally mobile Kouchakjis and their rise to become major vendors of Raqqa wares—perhaps, as Jenkins-Madina has suggested, working in tandem at first with the Marcopolis.[104] Freer's comments in his 1908 Aleppo diary, however, foretold neither the rise of the Kouchakjis in the international antiquities market nor the retreat of the Marcopolis into relative obscurity. Quite the opposite, in fact. "17-Jun. Aleppo. 2 brokers homes. . . . Marcopoli and co. Fine collection. Koushakzy Bros. did not show good."[105]

Despite their failure to impress Freer, 1908 was in other respects a banner year for the Kouchakji family firm. Marlia Mango has convincingly argued that the silver hoard that would make up the Hama, Stuma, Riha, and Antioch "treasures" was found in its entirety near Stuma in 1908 and the Kouchakji family spent the next couple of years engaged in acquisition, misdirection, and financial leveraging so as to enter the hoard into the market in tranches with putative "find dates" of 1910.[106] In January and March of 1908, the Kouchakjis sold two perfect, intact and pristine pieces of cobalt-and-luster Raqqa ware—an albarello and a basin—to another extremely wealthy collector of Middle Eastern antiquities (and former sometime dealer), Calouste Gulbenkian.[107] This seems to mark the Kouchakjis' full-fledged entry into the Raqqa ware trade and the beginnings of their long association with the material. It also marks 1908 as year zero for the entry of intact and pristine Raqqa vessels into western collections. Alongside the perfect pieces the Kouchakjis sold to Gulbenkian that year, Freer acquired five intact pieces in the batch he bought from Marcopoli in Aleppo, although not all of those five had quite the gloss of the pieces Gulbenkian bought from the Kouchakjis.[108] Over the next few years, Raqqa wares would start to appear in influential publications with the Kouchakji name attached to them.[109] One wonders what Freer objected to among the Raqqa wares he saw at the Kouchakjis' salesroom in Aleppo in June of 1908. Had they sold their best pieces to Gulbenkian, leaving nothing impressive in their Aleppo stock at that time? Or was Freer suspicious of perfectly pristine medieval ceramics?

By 1909 Freer was starting to move on from Raqqa ware, although he was still acquiring.[110] In 1910, an eyewitness account from Raqqa reported that digging had increased at the site and was taking place in broad daylight.[111] In some quarters there were rumors of a market slowdown in Raqqa ware, but the US museums were starting to jump in, feet first.[112] The MMA, the Museum of Fine Arts, Boston, and the Philadelphia Museum of Art all publicized their acquisitions of Raqqa wares between 1907 and 1910.[113] Phase two of the Raqqa ware trade had begun, and it was focused on New York. Paris was gradually becoming secondary in the Middle Eastern antiquities trade, although the major dealers—which now included the Kouchakjis—were all still selling there.[114]

As shown in chapter 4, World War I would change everything. By the end of the war extraordinary quantities of Raqqa ware had been offered for sale at the American Art Galleries in New York, in the Kouchakji sales of 1916 and 1918 and the 1917 sale of art dealer Thomas B. Clarke's huge ceramics collection.[115] Indeed, by 1917 the sale of Raqqa ware through North American vendors had reached the point where the interior decorating and collectibles magazine *Arts & Decoration* was discussing Raqqa ceramics in a column titled "Your Home and Its Decoration."[116] But in the same years, Raqqa itself became part of a much darker episode in twentieth-century history. From 1915 Raqqa and the surrounding area became a site of deportation camps during the genocide of the Armenian people by the Ottoman authorities. Recently published documents from the German Foreign Office tell of hundreds of thousands of Armenians deported by train, boat, and forced marches to sites in modern-day Syria and Jordan, especially Raqqa, Deir ez-Zor, and the plains of the Hawran.[117] For those who survived the death marches through the desert, there was no respite at the end. In 1916 a Swiss observer reported that "In Rakka [alone] there are 15,000 deported in tents. The camp is situated on both the banks of the Euphrates but these people are not allowed to enter the city. Rich people are paying from Lt. 30–40 to get permission from those in authority to live for a length of time in the city. Everywhere the same lamentable pictures repeat themselves."[118] Death from starvation, exposure, exhaustion, and disease was everywhere. After decades of using the area around Raqqa as an outpost for depositing Caucasian refugees, the Ottoman Empire was now using it as a wasteground for the lives of its Armenian subjects. It is even possible that Armenians who survived the genocide ended up providing the next rounds of extraction labor at Raqqa. The market certainly slowed down, but the quantities of Raqqa ware offered for sale by the Kouchakjis alone in the 1920s suggest that the supply line was active into the interwar years.

The Great Find: A Study in Spin?

With the timeline established and the authenticity of the EMA's collection of immaculate cobalt-and-luster Raqqa wares in doubt, it is time to revisit the story of the so-called Great Find of perfect ceramics found inside giant storage jars in the ruins of Raqqa. This event was circulated in early twentieth-century dealer literature as a means of explaining the condition of some of the most celebrated pieces of Raqqa ware. It was then revisited by Jenkins-Madina in her 2006 book on Raqqa wares, where she proposed that something of this nature could really have occurred in 1906, and might be accepted as the origin story for the immaculate Raqqa wares now around the world today.

The scholarly argument for the Great Find has been built on three different forms of written evidence, but it must be stressed from the outset that none of these contain direct or eyewitness accounts of such a find. The first body of evidence comes from Yoltar-Yıldırım's research in the Ottoman archives; the second is hearsay reports from the archaeologists Gertrude Bell and Friedrich Sarre; and the third is dealer literature. The first of these provides important proof that huge amounts of commercial digging were underway at Raqqa by 1900, that potters' quarters had been identified at the site by local people by 1904, and that a new wave of North Caucasian refugees were settled in Raqqa in the week of 2 April 1906.[119] The published Ottoman archives do not, however, make reference to anything that could be interpreted as the Great Find.[120]

The earliest hearsay report of a special find at Raqqa occurs in Gertrude Bell's description of her travels in Mesopotamia in 1909, published in her 1911 book *Amurath to Amurath*. She notes a find of unbroken pieces, although without mention of it being protected inside storage jars:

> The whole of the two areas of ruin are strewn with potsherds of the Mohammadan period, and over the greater part of the walled city the ground is honeycombed with irregular holes and trenches, the excavations of peasants

> in search of the now celebrated Raḳḳah ware. A few years ago their labours were rewarded by a large find of unbroken pieces, many of which made their way through the hands of Aleppo dealers to Europe, and though such a stroke of good fortune is rare, I saw a considerable number, together with one or two fragments of exquisite glass embossed with gold, during the two days I spent at Raḳḳah. In some instances the original factories and kilns have been brought to light, and it is not unusual to see bowls or jars which have been spoilt in the baking and thrown away by the potter. No exhaustive study of Raḳḳah ware has yet been made, though it is of the utmost importance in the history of the arts of Islâm.[121]

Curiously, although she included this story of the unbroken Raqqa finds in her 1911 book, she doesn't mention it in her letters or diaries from the 1909 trip.[122] It is possible that she only heard about it after she had left the region. Something similar was mentioned briefly in a letter of May 1911 by a decidedly interested party—the dealer Vincenzo Marcopoli, who wrote from Aleppo to Charles Lang Freer that "Our attention has been drawn to the discovery at Raqqa of many new pieces, interesting and in perfect condition."[123] Marcopoli, however, seems in his pitch to Freer to be representing something that had supposedly happened recently.

Returning to more disinterested commentary, the other archaeologist who reported this story was Friedrich Sarre, in a book first published in 1920:

> The fact that the pottery that has come to light in Raqqa is, for the most part, not imported from abroad but made on the spot is proven by the many vessels that failed during firing and were discarded by potters, which have come to light in the district of the potters' shops, where large unglazed pots have occasionally been found which were filled with smaller, well-preserved glazed vessels. The rich collection of beautiful Raqqa ceramics belonging to Mr. Charles F. [sic] Freer in Detroit, U.S.A., can be traced in large part to one such find, brought to the art market by an Aleppo antiquarian.[124]

This last sentence must refer to Freer's acquisitions from Marcopoli. As noted above, only five of the seventy-plus pieces of Raqqa ware Freer bought from Marcopoli have the unbroken forms that would come to be associated with the Great Find, and of those, only three have the completely pristine appearance claimed for the cache. All of those five were bought in Aleppo in 1908.

Bell's and Sarre's reports are suggestive. However, they are both based on hearsay and refer to events supposed to have occurred "a few years" prior to publication, in the case of Bell, and well over a decade earlier in that of Sarre. Bell doesn't mention any storage jars. Neither author lays claim to a singular event accounting for the appearance of sixty or more perfect pieces on the market. And critically, Sarre was writing after the first commercial versions of the Great Find narrative had already started to circulate and appears to be referring to those rather than to any more reliable source.

For the full-blown story of the Great Find, then, we must look to the people with a vested financial and social interest in Raqqa wares: dealers, collectors, and auctioneers. The story is, of course, an advantageous one for those with Raqqa wares to sell. It is dramatic, romantic, and neatly explains the huge disparities in condition clearly visible across the known corpus of Raqqa wares. It started to gain momentum sometime between Bell's testimony and Sarre's, first appearing in print in the sale catalogue for the auction of some of Thomas B. Clarke's collection at the American Art Galleries in New York in 1917. This sale included a number of pristine and perfect Raqqa ware jars and bowls, mostly of the black-under-turquoise type but also some cobalt-and-luster pieces.[125] The versatile cataloguer Dana H. Carroll references an embryonic version of the story in the catalogue's introduction:

> A number of the Rakka pieces which are in their original coloring, wholly or mainly free from iridescence, were found within one large vase or receptacle in the cellar of a house in Rakka, according to information brought by the seller to Mr. Clarke, about ten years ago, the manner of their protection accounting for the preservation of the glaze. Few other specimens from that find are known either in Europe or America.[126]

Without knowing the name of the dealer who sold the pieces to Clarke, we cannot know the source of the story. The Kouchakji Frères are the most likely contenders, though, in light of the hold they apparently had on the Raqqa trade from 1908 and their successful establishment in Paris and New York by 1910.

The "Great Find" gained its portentously capitalized title and much of its traction in an essay published in *International Studio* by Fahim Kouchakji himself in 1923, perhaps encouraged by the story's circulation from so great an authority as Sarre in 1920. "Glories of Er-Rakka Pottery," illustrated with nineteen ceramic pieces from Kouchakji's stock, disperses the story of the Great Find between two paragraphs on the first and last pages of the article. The crux of the story is that Circassian refugees digging in the ruins of Raqqa for building materials circa 1905 (conveniently, one year before the 1906 Ottoman antiquities law came into effect) turned up "some sixty unbroken articles" inside "a series of huge jars, each of which contained perfectly preserved specimens of the finest Er Rakka pottery."[127] The greater part of the article is taken up with arguments for a ninth-century date for the ceramics and attempts to establish a direct association with the illustrious person of Harun al-Rashid—one of the very few figures from Islamic history well-known to western audiences of the time, via his role in the *One Thousand and One Nights*. In his efforts to persuade the reader of the Harun al-Rashid association and the palatial mystique of his wares, and to explain the "Great Find" itself, Kouchakji launches into an extraordinary pseudodocumentary description of a palace interior. Into this fevered passage he manages to squeeze virtually every form of Raqqa ware that had emerged onto the art market to date—tiles, jars, flasks, bowls, and so forth. The text then climaxes in a dramatic explanation for the survival of intact pieces that will be offered for sale on the international art market:

> There is a sudden commotion. Arriving guests turn, and they and servants flee. Messages have been received that the enemy is near the city's gates. The gates outside the palace, the shops in the market are closed as if by magic and those who have foreseen such a fate scurry to hide the most valuable

parts of their stock in trade. In this manner were specimens saved, to be revealed to the excavators of our day.[128]

Unsurprisingly, the story of the Great Find was taken up eagerly by the market. The next sale of Thomas Clarke's Raqqa wares, held at the American Art Galleries in 1925 with a catalogue introduction again from Dana H. Carroll, made use of the newly available name and amplified the story: "Most important perhaps of all these are the Rakka potteries of supreme quality first revealed in the 'Great Find', an historic occasion which has been written of, and of which mention is made in the catalogue; there can never be anything like them again."[129] Later in the catalogue an anonymous author, probably also Carroll, introduces ten objects purportedly from the "Great Find" with a blurb that cribs all its assertions directly from Kouchakji's 1923 article, although without acknowledging its source. The author thus strengthened the story's power by appearing to provide independent confirmation of its claims while actually just repeating it—a phenomenon familiar to us all in the internet age. In this regard, Kouchakji had produced a perfect piece of dealer literature. One of the primary purposes of that genre is to give prospective collectors a crib sheet, providing them with memorable tidbits of history and correct terminology that can, if the incantation is performed correctly, make the reciter appear urbane, sophisticated, and deeply knowledgeable.

Further cannibalization and amplification in Raqqa ware collectors' literature reveals the role played by scholars within this collecting ecology. One of the early scholarly publications of Raqqa ware is an undated and privately printed booklet, briefly mentioned in chapter 4, titled *A Collection of Ancient Raqqa Pottery* (see fig. 4.13). This was published circa 1926 by Rudolf Meyer Riefstahl, then a professor at NYU.[130] With only seven objects in attractive individual plates and accompanying descriptive comments, plus a short introductory text, the luxurious booklet does not name the owner of the group. However, five of the seven pieces in it were loaned to Detroit in 1930 by the New York dealer P. Jackson Higgs, and Higgs is named as the owner of the group in a typed document signed by Ernst Kühnel, which was inserted in the front of a copy now in the Toledo Museum of Art library.[131] The absence of any owner's name in the publication suggests that Higgs intended the little book to serve as marketing material with a scholarly flavor, ready to be adopted as a personal catalogue by the next purchaser of the group. Riefstahl's text and its images were subsequently cannibalized by a staff writer at the *International Studio* for a 1927 article titled "Ancient Potteries from the Site of Rakka," showing how an ostensibly scholarly publication, commissioned and paid for by a dealer, could function as a press release.[132]

The Riefstahl book does not mention the Great Find or anything relating to the circumstances of discovery. Higgs did, however, complain in a letter to the curator of the 1930 exhibition in Detroit that he was "very disappointed that my Raqqas were separated [in the exhibition], for inasmuch as they were found together in one cache and most likely made at the same time by the same hand, they have always been regarded as a complete group, and now that they have become officially separated, I feel that it harms their sale as a group."[133] This quote is quite revealing of the cachet of a cache, and its potential financial value.

Finally, yet another version of the Great Find mythos appears from Paris, in a footnote to Charles Vignier's 1928 article on forgery in Persian ceramics. Vignier accepts the explanation, stating that the find took place about twenty years previously, and mentions that pieces from it can be seen in the Doucet and Gulbenkian collections (the latter presumably referring to the intact pieces bought from the Kouchakjis).[134] However, Vignier limits the cache to about twenty objects rather than the sixty or more that Kouchakji claimed had been in the Great Find.[135]

Having seen the story circulate successfully for decades, it is not surprising that Kouchakji leaned into it during his later years in the trade. A note in the files in the National Museum of Asian Art, dated 1941, says that Fahim Kouchakji had examined the museum's Raqqa wares and reported that some of them came from the Great Find.[136] And in the end we circle back to Indiana, where notes received from Fahim Kouchakji during the initial negotiations of the loan for the 1970 exhibition demonstrate his enthusiastic, if unreliable, embrace of the Great Find legend.[137] The copies of Kouchakji's notes for the Raqqa ceramics begin at object number 9 of Kouchakji's portfolio, the globular bowl (now EMA 72.6.7), under the entry for which is written the following:

> There is a complete absence of iridescence, due to the fact that it [was] with some other Rakka objects which when excavated were found, contained in larger vessels and thus protected from the earth. Others of this "find" are part of the H. O. Havemeyer collection, now in the Metropolitan Museum.[138]

However, a subsequent hand has lightly struck through this paragraph in pen.[139] Later notes that must have been provided by Kouchakji, probably received by the EMA when the pieces were purchased in 1972, contain no mention of the "Great Find" for any object save the albarello: "The albarello is in perfect condition and was part of the 'Great Find.'"[140] All this inconsistency is hard to interpret, but it is clear that Fahim Kouchakji's statements on the so-called Great Find should not be treated as either stable or reliable.

Might the Great Find have been a Great Fabrication? Quite possibly. As has been shown, the references to this cache in the scholarly literature all refer to hearsay, dealer's lore, and spin; nowhere is a direct eyewitness account recorded, let alone corroborated. On the other hand, not everything Fahim Kouchakji said was untrue: Yoltar-Yıldırım has shown that North Caucasian refugees really were sent to Raqqa, and huge amounts of commercial digging certainly went on there for years. It's not impossible that there was, at some point, a find of well-preserved ceramics at Raqqa, whether stored inside bigger containers or encached in some other way, and that these pieces were sold on the antiquities market. But if such an event occurred, is it a plausible explanation for dozens of objects in perfect condition, with shiny, immaculate glazes and attractive luster designs, especially in light of the TL testing results seen on the intact pieces in Indiana? The conditions surrounding excavation at Raqqa could hardly be more conducive to the insertion of fabrications and forgeries into the corpus. Illicit digging was carried out night and day at the site, engendering a vast body of objects that moved without documentation to Aleppo and then onward to the international antiquities market.

The story of the "Great Find" shows how marketplace lore that may be grounded in a partial truth can be puffed up by the hot air of salesmanship. The danger of such a story is that once it is accepted, it stops being questioned and can make us blind to the questions raised by the material itself—which is, after all, exactly what it is supposed to do. The very fact that we are still debating the Great Find, more than a century after it supposedly occurred, demonstrates both the power of a romantic narrative and the paucity of verifiable sources in the modern history of Islamic ceramics. The whole episode brings into sharp focus a major problem of art history, or at least of the large parts of the discipline that deal with objects traded through the international market: the entanglement of art history and the commercial sphere, and the potential conflicts of interest that inevitably arise in such a milieu. Dealers like Kouchakji may have important information to tell us, but, self-evidently, they cannot be treated as disinterested sources or reliable narrators.

* * *

This chapter has inevitably skewed toward the question of authenticity. Scientific testing tends to be something of a black box in art historical studies; most readers without advanced scientific training prefer to be presented with a clear conclusion that tells us whether we can proceed with something as a piece of historical evidence or not. But for all its marvelous appearance of objectivity and certainty, laboratory analysis requires a great deal of careful interpretation and often raises more questions than it answers—especially when it necessitates careful triangulation between archaeology, art history, and material science. The TL test results from the EMA Raqqa wares leave a question mark for the time being over the whole corpus of intact Raqqa wares. Further testing and analysis of pieces in other collections and of securely excavated archaeological material are now necessary to confirm or disprove what the EMA group's TL test results strongly suggest: that these immaculate objects are at least partial products of the modern era, fired for the second time—if not the first—in the early twentieth century.

To move beyond the on/off switch of "authenticity," I would like to close by returning to the central claim of this book: that the fabrication and fabulation of historic ceramics for the antiquities market represents a locus of extraordinary craft skill in the late nineteenth- and early twentieth-century Middle East, hidden in plain sight for well over a century. For evidence that skills in this marketplace might lie far beyond what was previously thought possible, we can recall from chapter 3 the Iranian luster pitcher that Freer bought in London in 1909, with its new-made glazed and fired replacement fragments of perfectly executed luster decoration. If, as seems likely, the intact Raqqa wares have indeed had new skins put on them through refiring to add luster decoration, they represent a level of technical skill and artistic finesse that dramatically exceeds our assumptions to date about the abilities of late nineteenth- and early twentieth-century craftspeople. Think of the manual and cerebral dexterity it would take to convincingly mimic the luster designs found on fragmentary remains of ceramics from the twelfth or thirteenth century. Think of the practice it would take to get to a point of such convincing confidence in execution that those designs could go unquestioned over more than a century of public display. Think of the technical expertise necessary to fire new luster designs onto old skins. And if the intact EMA Raqqa wares are complete forgeries, with new-made bodies and glazes as well as new-made luster designs, then those skills are even more extraordinary.

In the case of the Raqqa wares, whatever was done to them must have been done in or near Aleppo, from the evidence of the photographs Marcopoli was sending out from Aleppo in 1909. Therefore, if these pieces represent modern craft skills, those skills were located within a region undergoing rapid and violent harvesting of antiquities at a moment when contemporary markets for locally produced fine pottery had recently disappeared.[141] How, and where, knowledge of the difficult technique of luster could have survived in the region is an open question. Could Syrian glassmaking have served as a vector of transmission? Might Iranian potters of the time, who were shown in chapter 3 to have successfully recreated luster technology by the late nineteenth century, have been involved? In light of everything else we have seen, we must at least consider these possibilities. The economic incentives were certainly there, in abundance, for anyone who could assemble craftsmen with the requisite technical knowledge and artistic abilities.

While much remains unknown, the spell cast by these ceramics has endured for more than a century and will continue to endure. Perhaps the last word should go to Fahim Kouchakji, a figure who remains, after all this time, something of an enigma himself. How much did he know, and how much did he conceal? In the catalogue for the family's 1927 sale, he writes an introduction that now raises more questions than it answers:

> For over thirty years the name of KOUCHAKJI FRERES has been known throughout the world for its facility to acquire the finest objects of the Near East. It has concentrated its entire resources and experience in the discovery and the bringing to America of the most important examples of Near Eastern art. In the entire thirty years' history of this firm not a single counterfeit object or imitation has ever passed its rigid inspection. Rakka pottery was introduced to America by Kouchakji Freres. It was a member of this firm who discovered the famous Chalice of Antioch, the most priceless individual art object in existence today.[142]

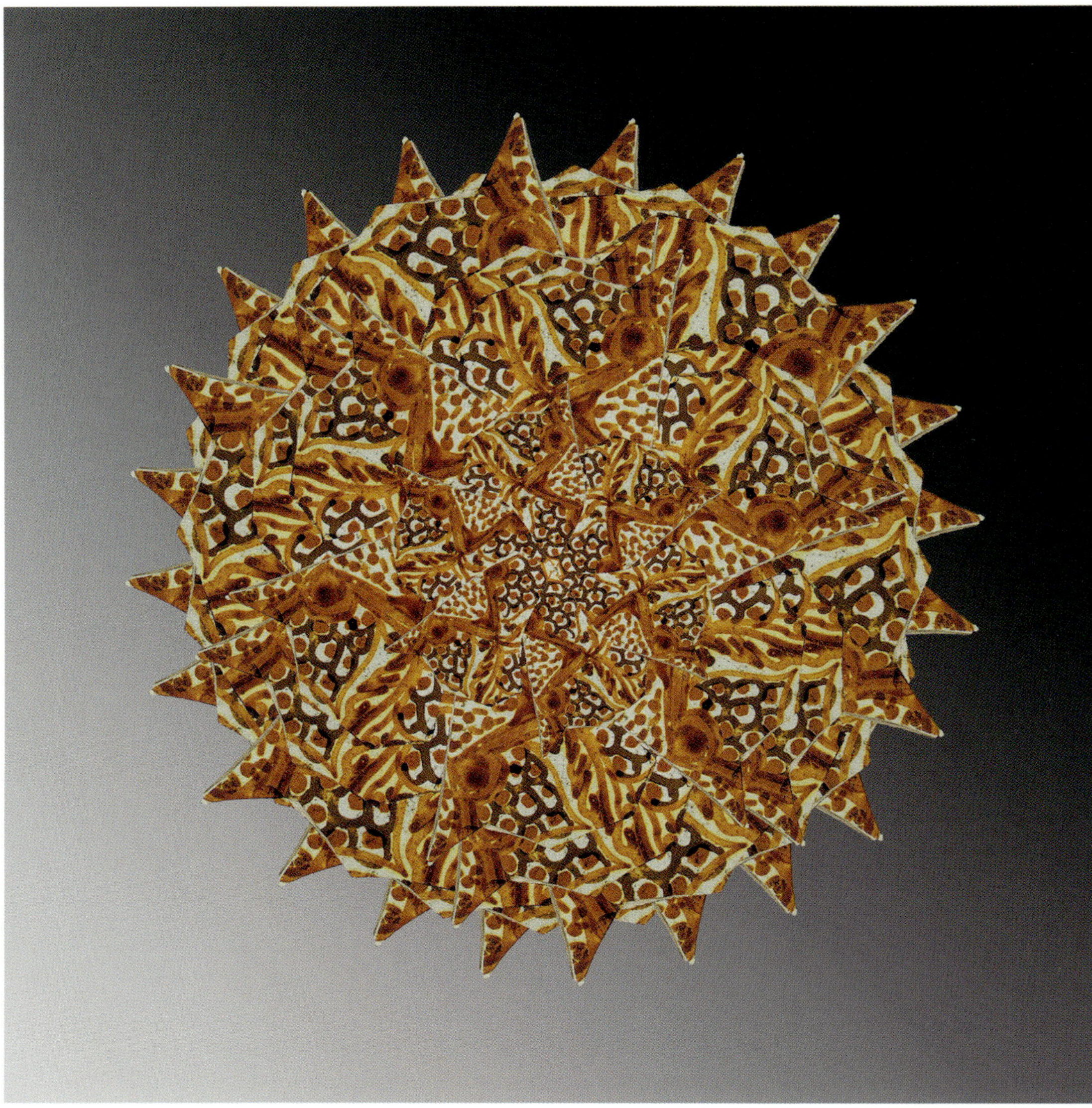

Epilogue

FRAGILE THINGS

As we have no immediate experience of what other men feel, we can form no idea of the manner in which they are affected, but by conceiving what we ourselves should feel in the like situation. Though our brother is upon the rack, as long as we ourselves are at our ease, our senses will never inform us of what he suffers. They never did, and never can, carry us beyond our own person, and it is by the imagination only that we can form any conception of what are his sensations.

—ADAM SMITH, *The Theory of Moral Sentiments*, 2nd ed., 1761

Now we have reached the end, there are so many pieces of broken pottery littering the stage that it is hard to know what to do with them all. Desublimating and reckoning with the material, social, and economic truths embodied in the collected canon of Islamic ceramics has left us not with a tidy singular narrative but with many fractured histories. It has also made visible a staggeringly sophisticated set of craft skills that blossomed as a rapacious antiquities market churned its way through the Islamic world in the late nineteenth to early twentieth centuries, from the patient art of bricolage to the virtuosic making anew of lustered designs and whole objects. What should we do with those histories, and how should we honor the skills of all those unrecorded and invisible hands?

As well as ceramics, craft skills, and colonial economies, this book is about museums. The research you have just finished reading was made possible through the cooperation and collaboration of many museum professionals across several countries and was informed by countless hours of discussion with curators and conservators, often conducted while examining objects together in storage or in the lab. This epilogue, then, is addressed partly to the institution of the museum as it considers what it might mean to tell the real, messy, multitemporal histories of these collected ceramics.

Museums, like the discipline of history, are structured around the telling of time. History retrieves the shattered debris of the past and puts it into an order that can be told with words; museums do the same thing with physical matter, arranged through space. Both can convince us that it is possible not just to understand but somehow also to access the past itself through facts and matter, reaching out through them to the lives that have gone before ours. But, as Adam Smith noted long ago in the *Theory of Moral Sentiments*, it is ultimately through our imaginations that we create the fibers of empathy, that essential human quality that underpins any functional society and makes us feel, sometimes quite viscerally, that we can access and even momentarily inhabit the experiences of others. To pose an analogy for the imagined encounter enabled by the museum object, think of the spiral seashell that you were once invited to hold to your ear when a teacher or a grandparent urged you to listen to it for the sound of the sea. In the same way, the museum invites you to pause before a vessel and imagine that through looking at it, you can connect yourself to the past and palpate the contours of a historical moment, somehow creating a portal between yourself and another moment in time the same way that the shell was supposed to connect you aurally to the shores of a distant sea. But what you heard inside the shell was actually the ambient sound around you, resonating at different frequencies through complex cavities. The object in the vitrine can help you to imagine other worlds and other lives, but it does not connect you to anything farther away than yourself. Perhaps what remains most remarkable about museums is that it does not need to.

Once upon a time, then, all the things in the museum were to be subordinated to the orderly ticking of imaginary clocks. They would progress from the deep past toward the present, case by case and room by room. Islamic ceramics were no exception and usually found themselves arranged in a chronological sequence from ninth-century experiments with tin glazing to the early modern glories of Iznik ware. Increasingly, however, and not just with material from the Middle East, the tidy chronologies of the museum are being disrupted by arrhythmic temporal explosions coming from the objects themselves. The eternal present tense of trauma and the modern histories of collecting are being felt more and more in the exhibition space, as audiences become increasingly attentive to the frenetic and sometimes violent harvesting that stocked metropolitan museums and shaped systems of knowledge.[1]

For the subjects of this book, reaped in that whirlwind, the question has so far not been one of repatriation except for certain cases of tilework stripped from religious monuments in Iran and Turkey (see chapter 2). These have given rise to some demands for the return of tiles and tile panels that can be identified with specific buildings. At the time of writing, however, I am not aware of any calls for the return of Islamic-era ceramic vessels to countries of production in the Middle East.

What, then, are the possible futures for all these fabricated and collected bowls, cups, pitchers, and dishes? As this book has sought to demonstrate, they have the potential to illuminate not just medieval ceramic techniques but also the workings of modern skilled labor economies and the place of artifacts within regimes of knowledge and acquisition. They show how thoroughly Orientalism and its modes of intellectual mastery have always been laced into the larger machinery of capitalism, and how that machinery has transformed the physical remains of the past in order to make it saleable. Harvested, processed, and launched into an accelerating economy of physical history, the subjects of this book have been jostled and shaped by political events both gradual—like Aleppo's incorporation into an international economy outside of Ottoman control—and seismic, like the Iranian Constitutional Revolution of 1906–1911 and the flood of artifacts it released onto the market.[2] Writers and collectors of the era often wrote in moralizing tones about fabrication and forgery and the extractivism that they were themselves fueling; to many it seemed obvious to blame Persian, Arab, Armenian, Turkish, or Jewish intermediaries and craftsmen for responding to the asymmetric conditions of modernity, rather than to consider what and who had created those

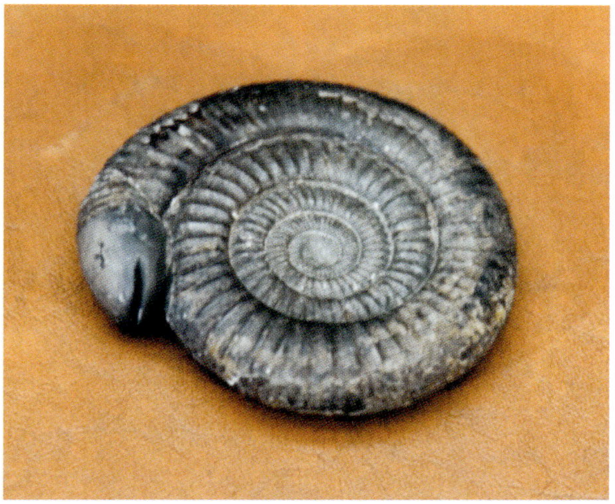

6.1. Yto Barrada, *Untitled (St. Hilda ammonite)*, 2014. Part of the series *The Lying Stones of Dr. Beringer*, 2014–15. C-print. 30 x 30 cm.

conditions. After all this time, we have never really shaken off those moralizing narratives that work in the service of the market.

Meanwhile the collecting industry has continued to grow, with all its fictions, collusions, and polite amnesia, and art historians are not the only ones who have pondered its eerie fabrications and sleights of hand. Contemporary artists have been working for some time now with the taxonomies of the museum and the detritus of the Middle Eastern antiquities market to produce new objects of encounter, and perhaps this is where we should start looking if we want to imagine new frameworks of display for Islamic ceramics. In *Faux Guide* Yto Barrada has even revisited the episode of Beringer's Lügensteine, reencountered through a passage into the modern-day industry of fossil hunting and fabrication in the Moroccan Sahara desert via the long history of fossil forgery (fig. 6.1). Inside some of Barrada's *Lying Stones* are false trilobites, ammonites, or scorpions, delicate fictions of time and geology that emerge like invertebrate valentines from the generative spaces of the collecting cabinet. Ali Cherri's hybrid creatures, on the other hand, stake out a more overtly confrontational position as composites of the collecting industry. Sutured together from disparate parts often acquired through the market, Cherri's guardians and gatekeepers merge zoological, geological, and cultural specimens into new figurations, becoming watchmen and apotropaia with the capacity to ward off the threats posed by our avarice. *Staring at a Thousand Splendid Suns* looks at first glance like any Egyptian antiquity for sale in a private gallery: wall-mounted and spotlit, it is suspended in the blank space and time of commodification (fig. 6.2). From its kohl-rimmed eye sockets, however, a pair of eerily realistic glass eyes stare out, jarring the anticipated encounter with the past by returning our gaze back to us.

Most explicit in its reckoning with Islamic antiquities collecting is Walid Raad's multiyear, multipart project, *Scratching on Things I Could Disavow*, already mentioned at the end of chapter 3. Within the universe Raad presents, which is almost—but not quite—indistinguishable from the Islamic art collecting circuit in our own, strange and disturbing events keep exposing the fictions of capital. Canonical artworks mutate and interbreed out of sight; reflections and shadows depart from the laws of physics and attach themselves instead

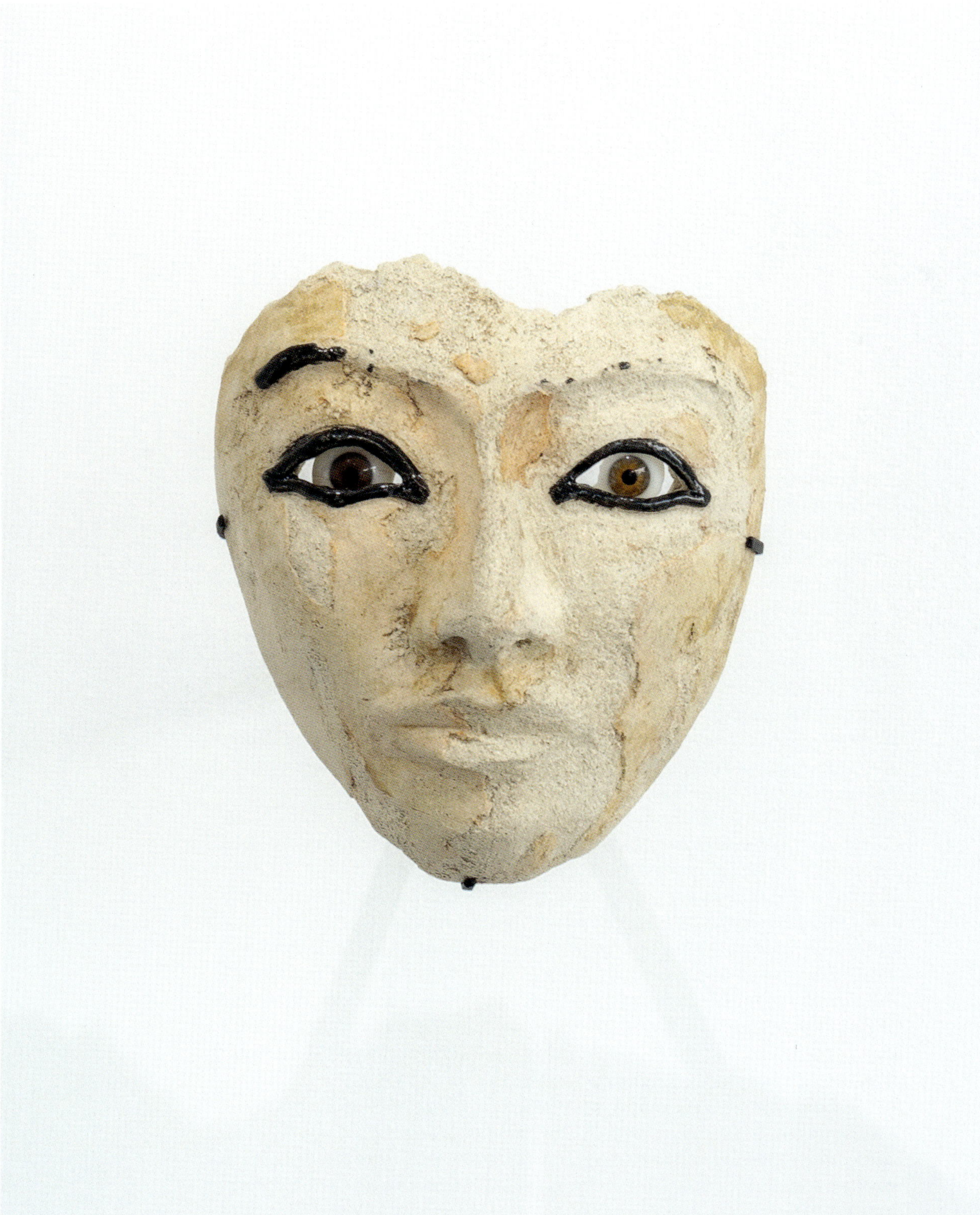

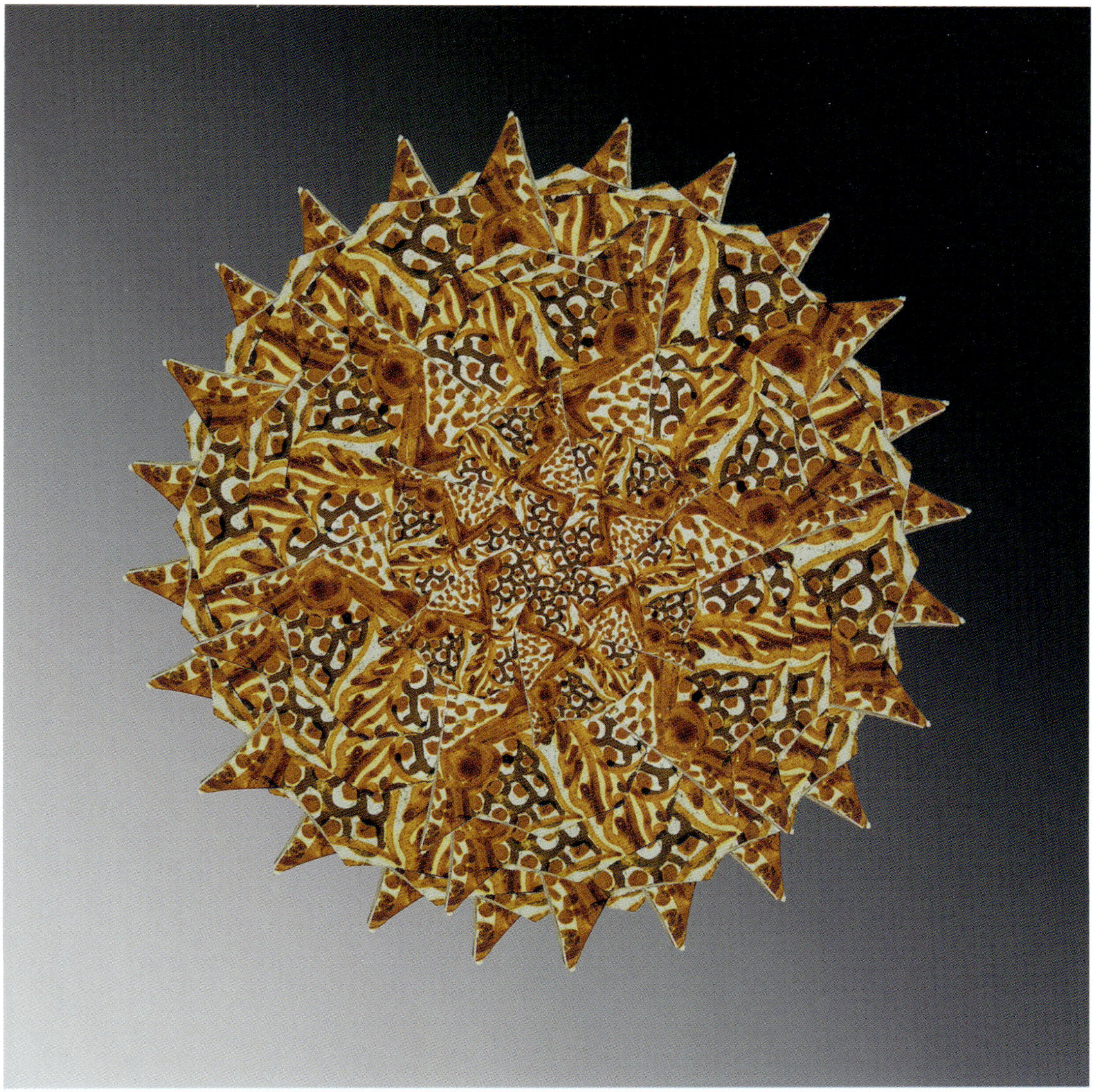

6.2. Ali Cherri, *Staring at a Thousand Splendid Suns*, 2021. Molding in glazed sandstone, glass ocular prosthesis. Height 21 cm.

6.3. Walid Raad, *Footnote 257_XIV*, 2003–23. Pigmented inkjet print.

to the trajectories of global modernism; motifs painted on ceramics break loose and eat their way through organic matter; and galleries, packing cases, and the backs of paintings become sites of morbid metaphysical transference. The generative power of mutation in this alternate universe gives rise to crystalline new entities. Witness what seems to be a shard of early luster-painted glass (or is it ceramic?) in the photo-montage *Footnote 257_XIV*, tiling itself outward like a barbed mandala (fig. 6.3). An orphaned fragment on a quest for completion, it will never find its lost "parent" object. Instead, it begins to self-replicate with a centripetal force that is both beautiful and disturbingly carcinomic. The work of Barrada, Cherri, Raad, and others is generating new worlds out of the wreckage left by decades of antiquities extraction, worlds that go beyond anything art historical analysis can achieve.

Before the curtain comes down, one last invisible hand gestures for us to look at something almost beyond sight. Let us not forget that Adam Smith's

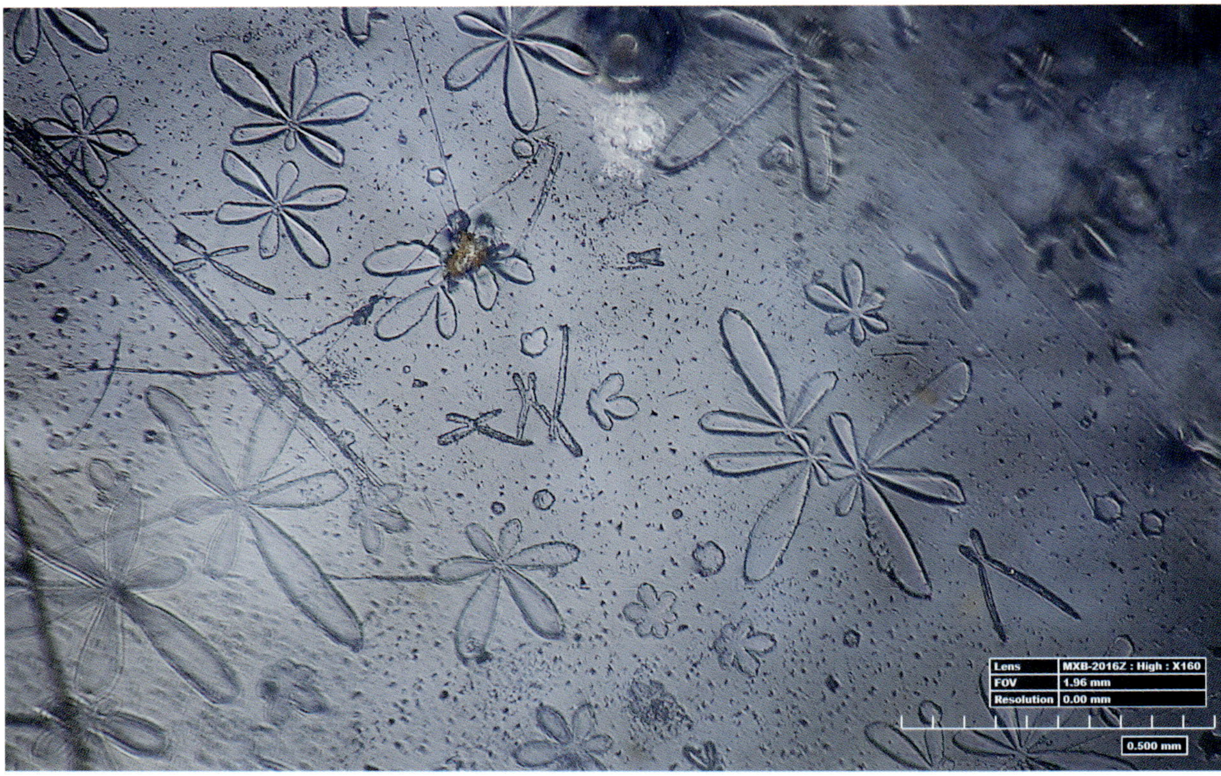

6.4. Microphotograph showing glazed surface of Eskenazi Museum of Art 72.6.4. Eskenazi Museum of Art, Indiana University, 72.6.4.

famous phrase was conceptualized by him to mean something rather different from the unfettered free market that it has come to emblematize in modern economic thought, however important a role that market has played in this book. The invisible hand, in Smith's *Moral Sentiments*, was the agent of Divine Providence; really, it was the Hand of God that would keep society in balance.[3] This book closes with a view that takes us as close to the divine as a book about decidedly earthly subjects can go, via the physical chemistry of glazed ceramics. In the EMA conservation lab, my collaborator put one of Fahim Kouchakji's fragmentary large jars (see fig. 5.17) under the microscope so that she and I could hunt for particles of ground cobalt in the streaks of blue in the medieval glaze. Increasing the magnification showed what looked at first like a tiny scattering of snowflakes indented across the surface. Zooming in even further revealed a breathtaking world of microscopic six-petaled flowers in the vastly magnified surface of the glaze, interspersed with forms that look like chromosomes (fig. 6.4). Perhaps for a physical chemist this microcrafted design would be quite prosaic, just the traces left by an intermediate stage of nucleation that somehow got arrested in a cooling glaze. But for the two of us in the lab that day, it was a moment of true wonder, a primordial garden suddenly revealed in a minuscule field of fused silica and flux. Every one of the objects in this book contains an infinite number of worlds. Depending on what you prefer to believe, the last invisible hand on stage is the hand of chemistry, or the Hand of God.

Acknowledgments

A very long time ago, before the global financial crisis, I had a job where I investigated suspected cases of money laundering for a large banking corporation. I credit that job with teaching me several important things—not least, how to follow the movements and transformations of money—that have underpinned this book in mostly invisible ways.

More recently, the years I spent researching and writing this book about fabrications and forgeries have seen the role of the fact in public life spin right off its axis. It seems important, in its own small way, to set down this record of the many individuals who helped in the pursuit of historical and material truth. This all began with an unpublished collection of Islamic ceramics in the Eskenazi Museum of Art at Indiana University. The museum's director David Brenneman and curator of Asian art Judy Stubbs were wholeheartedly supportive when I proposed a project about condition and modern markets that would see me subject their pieces to closer scrutiny than some institutions might have welcomed. Some of the most important work was done in collaboration with the EMA's conservator, Julie Ribits. I am deeply grateful to all three of them, and to my other colleagues at the EMA, especially Leila Reichert, Juliet Graver Istrabadi, Pete Nelson, Heather Hales, Mariah Keller, and the late Kevin Montague. Cheri Stoute and Diana Stewart of IU Health gamely undertook our request to put pots through the Bloomington hospital's CT scanner at five in the morning, Malcolm Mobutu Smith illuminated many aspects of production when we examined some of the pieces together, and Erika Elswick and Shelby Rader performed further laboratory analysis on the Bloomington campus.

Over time, this project grew to take in many institutions. In particular, the scale and richness of the relatively understudied collections of Islamic ceramics in the American Midwest have astounded me since I first arrived in the United States in 2012, and their stories have ended up at the heart of this book. The final list of curators, conservators, registrars, archivists, and photographers to whom I owe thanks is formidable, and I apologize to anyone I have missed: Greg Smith, Newfields; Ainsley Cameron, Trudy Gaba, Rose Milnes, Kelly Rectenwald, and Rob Deslongchamps, Cincinnati Art Museum; Katherine Kasdorf, James Hanks, and Christina Bisulca, Detroit Institute of Arts; Sophie Ong and Ahmad Rafiei, Toledo Museum of Art; Helen McDonald and Susan Allison, Institute for the Study of Ancient Cultures, University of Chicago; Massumeh Farhad, Simon Rettig, David Hogge, Julian Raby, and Blythe McCarthy, National Museum of Asian Art; John Hanson and Anatole Tchikine, Dumbarton Oaks; Joan Cummins, Lisa Bruno, and Maribel Cosme-Vitagliani, Brooklyn Museum; Martina Rugiadi, Sheila Canby, Annick des Roches, Jean-François de Lapérouse, and Marilyn Jenkins-Madina, Metropolitan Museum of Art; Denise Leidy, Yale University Art Gallery; Laura Weinstein, Museum of Fine Arts, Boston; Ayşin Yoltar-Yıldırım, Janet O'Brien, and Mary McWilliams, Harvard Art Museums; Andrew Scherer and Amy Gerhard, Joukowsky Institute for Archaeology and the Ancient World, Brown University; Wai-Yee Chiong, RISD Museum; Fahmida Suleman, Royal Ontario Museum; Mariam Rosser-Owen and Moya Carey, Victoria and Albert Museum; Venetia Porter, British Museum; Francesca Leoni, Ashmolean Museum; Flavia Ravaioli and Michael Jones, Fitzwilliam Museum; Deniz Erduman, Martina Müller-Wiener, and Stefan Weber, Museum für Islamische Kunst; Janine Ruffing and Daniela Antonin, Hetjens Museum.

Beyond the collections, I offer my sincere thanks to Indiana University for a New Frontiers grant that funded laboratory analysis and a College Arts and Humanities Institute fellowship for Fall 2020, and the Clark Art Institute and Florence Gould Foundation for a 2022–23 academic year fellowship. Departmental colleagues have helped me think through the project and made working life enjoyable, and at IU I thank Sarah Bassett, Melody Deusner, Faye Gleisser, Cordula Grewe, Giles Knox, Chaeri Lee, Bárbaro Martínez-Ruiz, Hoda Nedaeifar, Diane Reilly, Bret Rothstein, Jeffrey Saletnik, Liz Tuggle, and Julie Van Voorhis; at Brown, Sheila Bonde, Evie Lincoln, Jeff Moser, Jeff Muller, Doug Nickel, Itohan Osayimwese, Gretel Rodríguez, and Holly Shaffer. From my year in Williamstown, I thank Lucia Bay, Alex Bevilacqua, Olivier Bonfait, Holly Edwards, Jonathan Flatley, Turry Flucker, Caro Fowler, Sarah Grandin, Guy Hedreen, Sara Houghteling, Kathryn Howley, Tsedaye Makonnen, Jeremy Melius, Murad Mumtaz, Will Schmenner, Shawn Smith, and Shundana Yusaf. The book has been improved by questions and suggestions from audiences at the Detroit Institute of Arts, the Clark Art Institute, New York University, Brown University, Stanford University, Princeton University, and the University of Wisconsin–Madison. In addition, I thank Nader El-Bizri, Shireen Mahdavi, Wheeler Thackston, and Joanna Turnbull for granting me permission to use excerpts from their translations as epigraphs, and Yto Barrada, Ali Cherri, and Walid Raad for permitting me to reproduce their artworks.

I also owe special thanks to those who have answered my sudden queries, talked through critical aspects of this book with me, or read and commented on parts of it. These include Abbas Akbari, Ladan Akbarnia, Manijeh Bayani, Omniya Abdel Barr, Gardner Bovingdon, Moya Carey, Michael Chagnon, Deniz Erduman, Agnese Fusaro, Paul Losensky, Leslee Michelsen, Keelan Overton, Jennifer Pruitt, Walid Raad, Mariam Rosser-Owen, Leila Reichert, Yael Rice, Felipe Rojas, Marianna Shreve Simpson, Nancy Um, Tim Waters,

Ittai Weinryb, and Alyson Wharton. The anonymous peer reviewers of the manuscript provided extremely helpful suggestions for revisions, and the editorial oversight of Michelle Komie, Sara Lerner, and Kim Hastings has improved the final text. Above all, I thank Oliver Watson, the scholar who put this subject on the map. He was unfailingly generous in his responses to the questions I sent him over the years and always gratifyingly interested when I sent him a new oddity I had found. I did not realize during our last exchange in 2023 that he could possibly be gone so soon, and I wish I had been able to thank him in person.

My sister, my brothers and their families, and my husband's family have buoyed the many years of research and writing. Above all, Alexander and Adelina have given me their love and support through difficult times as well as happy ones, and I thank them from the bottom of my heart.

My father, Jeff Graves, was very curious about this book, in which the only one of his children who didn't pursue the sciences finally found herself in the laboratory. He taught me to look closely at the world, and to wonder. I dedicate this book to his memory, with love.

Archives Consulted

Cincinnati Art Museum (CAM), Dealer/Donor Records
Cincinnati Art Museum (CAM), Islamic Near East Object Files
Cincinnati Art Museum (CAM), Registrar Archives
Detroit Institute of Arts (DIA), Curatorial Records
Detroit Institute of Arts (DIA) Archives: William R. Valentiner Records; Clyde H. Burroughs Records; Islamic/Near Eastern Records; Weibel Correspondence
Detroit Institute of Arts (DIA) Registration Dept., Dealer/Donor Files
Dumbarton Oaks, Curatorial Records
Eskenazi Museum of Art (EMA), Curatorial Records
Freer, Charles Lang. Papers, National Museum of Asian Art (NMAA)
Gertrude Bell Archive, Newcastle University
Gertrude Bell Collection, Royal Geographical Society
Hetjens Museum, Curatorial Records
Indiana University (IU) Archives
Kelekian Archives, Metropolitan Museum of Art (MMA)
Minassian Archives, Brown University
Museum für Islamische Kunst, Curatorial Records
Museum für Islamische Kunst, Inventory Books
Pope, Arthur Upham. Papers, New York Public Library (NYPL)
Toledo Museum of Art, Curatorial Records
Victoria and Albert Museum (V&A), Nominal Files

Notes

Introduction. Fictions of Capital

1 Reilly 2001, 78.
2 Reilly 1987, 159.
3 Important projects include the Metropolitan Museum of Art's conservation project (de Lapérouse n.d.); *Transformed: Medieval Syrian and Iranian Art in the Early 20th Century*, curated by Martina Rugiadi at the Metropolitan Museum of Art in 2016; and recent permanent displays at the Cincinnati Art Museum, the Walters Art Museum, and the Ashmolean Museum.
4 Watson 1985; Watson 2004; Watson 2013.
5 Fields and Seddon 2002, 34. See also the slightly different inflection given in Hay 2008, which also explores forgery's challenge to conceptions of authorship.
6 For example, Bayard 1914.
7 Ginzburg 1979; Ginzburg and Davin 1980.
8 Wakeling 1912.
9 An interesting crossover text is Eudel 1907, translated into German as *Fälscherkünste* (1909). For early exhibitions, Stedelijk Museum 1952; Stedelijk Museum and Corning Museum 1953; Prisco 2019. The landmark exhibition to date is the blockbuster *Fake? The Art of Deception*, curated by Mark Jones at the British Museum in 1990 (Jones 1990).
10 For example, Ostapkowicz and Hanna 2021; Turner and O'Neil 2024.
11 Batres 1910; see also Achim and Olmeda Vera 2021; Jennings et al. 2022.
12 Radnóti 1999; Braudeau 2006.
13 On Beltracchi: Keazor and Öcal 2014. On Qian: Nir, Cohen, and Rashbaum 2013.
14 Beringer 1726, 4–6; Jahn 1963, 139.
15 Edmonds and Powell 1974, 550–551; Stafford 1984.
16 Lepper and Gill 2000, 25. On Layard's career, see Malley 2011, and for his role at the first Ottoman Bank, Eldem 1999, 32–33.
17 Whittlesey 1872; Whittlesey 1881.
18 Lepper and Gill 2000.
19 For examples, Ménant 1887.
20 See also the fabricated ancient Iranian animal and human figurines published as an appendix, "Forgeries and Pastiches," in Kawami 1992, 228–229.
21 Reinach 1888; Hannover 1925, 46–48; Lapatin 2002, 42–43.
22 Goedicke 1994, 81; Kriseleit 1994.
23 Frelinghuysen et al. 1993, 106–107.
24 Reinach 1888a.
25 Lapatin 2002, 153–175, details this in the case of Minoan antiquities.
26 Muscarella 2008, 17.
27 Hannover 1925, 47.
28 A recently documented forgery partnership, producing Cycladic figures in 1980s and 1990s Greece, began when a dealer teamed up with "a guy who painted Greek Orthodox icons and at the same time he was restoring old ones too." Tsirogiannis, Gill, and Chippindale 2022, 372.
29 Clermont-Ganneau 1885, 153; Press 2023.
30 Clermont-Ganneau 1885, 117–118, 121–128. The debate played out via publications and letters in various scholarly publications, some of which were gathered together in Anonymous 1874; Anonymous 1878.
31 Clermont-Ganneau 1885, 105; Anonymous 1874.
32 Conder's caption for the most striking object in this suite reads, "1. Female organ. N.B. Hole of Anus beneath, hollow throughout." See also Anonymous 1873.
33 For example, the rendering of the inscriptions on the objects are reminiscent of prints done from line drawings of early Islamic clay lamps: Clermont-Ganneau 1896; Clermont-Ganneau 1896a; Clermont-Ganneau 1899.
34 Michael Press notes that an ancient plaque figurine found in 1870 at Tel Gezer (Abu Shusha) on land belonging to the Bergheims, a Jerusalem banking family, might also have been a direct source of inspiration. Press 2023, 238; Clermont-Ganneau 1896b, 242.
35 Press 2021.
36 Clermont-Ganneau 1885, 151.
37 Salmon 2000, especially Be'er 2000; Shanks 2002.
38 Elikhina, Lurje, and Khavrin 2021.
39 Sims-Williams 2000, 116.

40 Stein 1903, 447–459; Sims-Williams 2000; Hopkirk 2006, 98–110; Whitfield 2002, 5–8.

41 Hoernle first reported in 1901 that pieces of pottery had also been attempted by the forgery workshop of Islam Akhun and his collaborators. "The result [of the attempt], however, was too grotesque to deceive": Hoernle 1901, 3.

42 Bartol'd 1966, 127; Gorshenina 2004, 35–37.

43 Elikhina, Lurje, and Khavrin 2021.

44 Elikhina, Lurje, and Khavrin 2021, 383.

45 At least three of the ceramics pictured in this group of negatives were in the possession of Dikran Kelekian by 1910 and 1912, and another was owned by Hagop Kevorkian by 1910. Two are illustrated in Kelekian 1910, nos. 37 (a lustered albarello with flying birds) and 69 (a "Sultanabad" bowl with two figures in central roundel). These are now, respectively, al-Sabah Collection LNS 302 C, and V&A C.55-1922. The third Kelekian piece (the lobed bowl with cobalt and luster, illustrated in fig. 2.26) is documented in a loan approval form in the V&A archive (nominal file Kelekian, Dikran, 1892–1912), dated 16 July 1912, and is now Cincinnati Art Museum, 1952.253. A fourth piece (an indented "sweetmeat dish") was published in the three-volume catalogue that followed the Munich 1910 exhibition, with the owner listed as Hagop Kevorkian: Martin and Sarre 1912, vol. 2, plate 102, no. 5.

46 It might relate to some molded, turquoise-glazed jars that Oliver Watson has identified as late nineteenth-century Iranian forgeries of thirteenth- and fourteenth-century Iranian wares, although it is less competently executed. Watson 1985, 39, fig. 2; Watson 2004, 524–525 and fig. 12; Watson 2013, 59–61, figs. 1–2.

47 Lee 2025.

48 Katz 2020; Thompson 2021; Sanderson 2020.

49 El Shamsy 2021.

50 On theologically motivated philological forgeries in the Arabic manuscript corpus, see El Shamsy 2020, 208–217.

51 Batchen 2002, 105.

52 Talbot 1844, plate III, "Articles of China."

53 Talbot even suggests later in *The Pencil of Nature* that photographic prints might be of use in inventorying not only the china collections of the English elite but also the nobility themselves. Talbot 1844, plate XIV, "The Ladder."

54 For an alternative interpretation of these images, Maimon 2008.

55 Anonymous 1845, 202. See also Anonymous 1844; Anonymous 1844a.

56 On print, see examples in Ménant 1887, 17–19; on photography, Fuchsgraber 2020, 111–112.

57 Wilson 2009/2010; Kirsch 2015; Fuchsgraber 2020.

58 Watson 1985, 42; Watson 2006, 345–346; Watson 2013, 61, n. 8.

59 *Mitteilungen des Museen-Verbandes als Manuskript für die Mitglieder* (July 1903), 1.

60 See also the copies of Native American woodcarving made in Indonesia and of Mimbres bowls made in Nicaragua, all copied from identifiable publications, cited in Berlo 2023, 36, 163–168.

61 Sarre 1929, 12–13. The other examples included a 40 cm high female bust in gold promoted by the London dealers Spink and Son as a medieval portrait of the Georgian queen Tamara; its appearance is strikingly similar to that of the various "Seljuq" stucco sculptures offered on the market around the same time (see Rugiadi 2016; Heidemann, de Lapérouse, and Parry 2014, 35, 57–62). Arthur Upham Pope claimed in 1929 to have been "the first to discover and disclose the false gold work that appeared in 1925" (Arthur Upham Pope to William Valentiner, 7 February 1929, Box VAL 13, Folder 8, William R. Valentiner Records, DIA). However, in 1927 he enthusiastically hailed the gold bust as "an extremely important piece" and "one of the most important pieces of gold work from the near east" (Arthur Upham Pope to Spink & Son, 29 August 1927, Box 1: General Correspondence 1926–29, Pope Papers, NYPL.

62 Sarre 1922; Sarre 1929, 12–13. The same relief section had circulated earlier in print imagery, appearing, for example, in Porter 1821, vol. 1, facing 598.

63 For example, Marianna Shreve Simpson has published a group of early twentieth-century Iranian manuscript paintings created using "reproductions published in 1912 and 1914 to make paintings that were available for sale six to eight years later." Simpson 2008, 386; see also Langer 2020.

64 Troelenberg 2014; Graves 2018, 113.

65 The expanding role of the photograph in the antiquities market invites comparison with Timothy Mitchell's "exhibitionary order," wherein nineteenth-century regimes of display and knowledge production sought to render the world as an endless series of images of itself. Mitchell 1991; Mitchell 1992.

66 Soudavar 2008, 253.

67 Angas 1937, 20.

68 Carney 2023; Graeber 2014, 36–41.

69 In this sense, the antiquities market operates in ways that are disconcertingly analogous not only with markets in other types of resource, such as minerals, but also with historical slave markets, which require human beings to be shorn of their original social contexts (and thus rendered socially dead) so that they can be entered into circulation as commodities: Patterson 1982; Kopytoff 1986, 64–65; Graeber 2014.

70 Shaer 2019.

71 Another extreme example of this is discussed in Nelson 2024. See also Kopytoff 1986, 82–83, on the movement between commoditization and singularity.

72 A point raised by several observers of the black market in so-called blood antiquities: see, for example, Brodie 2011.

73 See also Chippindale and Gill 2000.

74 Shaer 2019.

75 See the recent cases reviewed in Moaveni 2023.

76 As was the case with the Banque de Constantinople, one of the precursors to the Ottoman bank. Eldem 1999, 95–96.

77 Eldem 1999, 279–280.

Chapter 1. Middle Eastern Antiquities: The Making of a Modern Marketplace

1 Mahoney 2019; Kákosy 1989; Blakesley 2016.

2 de Voogt and Francigny 2012, 60–61; Vernus 2003, chapter 1; Blakesley 2016.

3 El Shamsy 2020, 10–19.

4 Damen 2012, 165.

5 Damen 2012; Christian 2010, 93–103.

6 Belozerskaya 2012.

7 The drawing bears an attribution to Muhammad Khayyam, an enigmatic figure to whom are credited several Timurid-era calligraphic samples and drawings. Roxburgh 2005, 1–6; Weis 2016.

8 Damen 2012, 109. On coin forgeries, see Beauvais 1741; Burnett 1992; Williams 2018; Holt 2021, 79–81. Coin forgery for the antiquities market is usually distinct from counterfeiting coins to use as specie: Saccocci 2019.

9 For recent literature on Renaissance-era art faking and forgery in Europe, Gregory and Hickson 2012; Catterson 2014; Hylkema 2019.

10 Furlotti 2019, 83–116.

11 Furlotti 2017, 147.

12 Furlotti 2019, 94; Furlotti 2010.

13 Guilding 2014, 22–65.

14 Allen and Carey 2021, 280–282; Volmert 2017.

15 Vickers 2006, 6; Angelicoussis 2004.

16 Allen and Carey 2021, 280.

17 Mack 2002, 73–93.

18 Volmert 2017, 100 n. 4.

19 First suggested in Hess 1950, 197. Arundel joined the Church of England shortly after his trip to Italy, on Christmas Day 1616.

20 Furlotti 2019, 9.

21 Dudley 2004, 55–56; Howarth 1985, 162–163.

22 Vickers 2006, 14.

23 Dudley 2004, 56; Motz 2024.

24 Hervey 1969, 266–267.

25 Hervey 1969, 268. See also Marchand 2017, 58.

26 Bahrani, Çelik, and Eldem 2011.

27 Thomasson 2010; Hamilakis 2011; Anderson 2015; Potts and Basello 2022.

28 Reinach 1883, 154–166; Reinach 1891, 57–61; Reinach 1882. See also Eldem 2011; Bahrani, Çelik, and Eldem, 2011a, 38. The 1906 Ottoman antiquities law made the first provisions for regional museums: Shaw 2003, 169–171.

29 On Petty's ultimately unsuccessful attempts to take the relief sculptures from the Golden Gate (Porta Aurea) in Istanbul (now surviving as a few fragments in the Istanbul Archaeological Museum), see Hervey 1969, 270–277. Some of the material Petty collected for Arundel in Smyrna was published in Selden 1628.

30 [Petty] 1938, 261. The attribution to William Petty is made in Chaney 1993, 720.

31 [Petty] 1938, 258.

32 Ferrier 1970, 51; Allen and Carey 2021, 328–333; Hervey 1969, 400–401.

33 These were in Thomas Herbert's *A Relation of Some Yeares Travaile . . . into Afrique and the greater part of Asia, especially the territories of the Persian Monarchie*. Allen and Carey 2021, 329–331; Vickers 1991.

34 Smith 2015, 283–287; see also Gilman 2002.

35 Hervey 1969, 273–274.

36 Potts 2020. Another loss, this time of sixty-three boxes of Cypriot antiquities acquired by Luigi Palma di Cesnola, occurred when the ship carrying them caught fire at sea and sank off the coast of Lebanon or Syria in 1872: Merrillees 2017, 74.

37 Hervey 1969, 275–276.

38 Bevilacqua 2018.

39 Gigante 2020; Karl 2011.

40 Flood 2006; Cooperson 2010; Cooperson 2014; Mulder 2022; Flood and Fricke 2024, 220–227.

41 Lee 2025; Capezzone 2020; Shafir 2022; Niyazioğlu 2022, 13–34.

42 Aghaie 2023, 6–7, 12.

43 Roxburgh 2003; Allen and Carey 2021. Moya Carey (personal correspondence) has suggested that antiquarianism in early seventeenth-century Iran might be linked to interests in tenth-century philosophy as part of the reinterpretation of Twelver Shi'ism, a fundamental part of the Safavid political project.

44 Matthee 2013, 19, citing documents in the Dutch National Archives in The Hague.

45 Antoine Galland, 1685 manuscript, BnF, Ms. Français 6130, fols. 3v-4r, quoted in Bevilacqua 2018, 24.

46 Bevilacqua 2018, 17–43; El Shamsy 2020, 11–19, 22–23.

47 El Shamsy 2020, 19–24.

48 Bahrami 2013; Nasiri-Moghaddam 2003; Nasiri-Moghaddam n.d.

49 El Shamsy 2020, 21–22, 26.

50 El Shamsy 2020, 16.

51 Enea Vico of Parma, *Discorsi . . . sopra le medaglie degli antichi* (1555). See Burnett 1992, 16, 18.

52 García-Arenal 2009; Colini 2020; van Koningsveld, Sjoerd, and Wiegers 2023.

53 See Maqrizi 1387 [1967]; Ibn Khaldun 1969, vol. 2, 54–60. Elsewhere Ibn Khaldun comments negatively (from his Sunni Maliki perspective) on the Ilkhanid Sultan Öljeitü, noting that "he had the names of the twelve imams engraved on coins": Ibn Khaldun, *Kitab al-ʿibar*, vol. 5, 549, quoted in van den Bent 2016, n. 86. See also Toll 1970/71; Meloy 2003.

54 Holt 2021, 75–88. Portrait designs on coins were described in the language of connoisseurship, sometimes shading later into the full-blown racist pseudoscience of phrenology.

55 Miller 2008; Diyab 2022, 15, 326–327.

56 The enlightenment-era scholarship of Georg Jacob Kehr (1692–1740), librarian to the Academy of Sciences in St. Petersburg, foreshadowed the eighteenth-century "scientific" study of Islamic numismatics in the works of Johann Jakob Reiske (1716–1774), the Abbé Jean-Jacques Barthélemy (1716–1795), and Peter Forsskål (1732–1763). See Ilisch 2015; Heidemann 2005.

57 *Das Neueste aus der anmuthigen Gelehrsamkeit* 6 (1752), editorial note on p. 480 and cover plate. See also Ilisch 2015.

58 Türker 2022.

59 Türker 2022, 217; G. C. Watson 2020.

60 For just a fraction of the literature on these topics in the nineteenth-century context, Adjemian and Nichanian 2018; Rogan 2024; Cohen 2014; Sahim 2005.

61 Reilly 2002, 60; Wallerstein 1979, 390.

62 Matthee 2013, 14.

63 Aslanian 2011, 121–165; Reilly 2001, 77.

64 Aslanian 2011, 66–85; see also Kévonian 1975; Osipian 2022.

65 Melkite Catholics, recognized as an official religious community under Sultan Abdülmecid I in 1848, made up the majority of Aleppo's Christian population: Masters 2010, 297. On Jewish traders as intermediaries for sixteenth-century Venetian-Ottoman trade in Greater Syria, Tracy 2009, 166–167.

66 Masters 2010, 301–302; Momdjian 2020, 113. On the role of language among non-Muslim elites navigating the structures of Ottoman governance, Shafir 2021.

67 Masters 2010, 301.

68 Diyab 2022, 158.

69 Panzac 1992, 204.

70 Masters 2010, 292–293; Momdjian 2017.

71 Masters 2010; Sluglett 2002; Klein 1999; Reilly 1992.

72 Masters 2010, 301–302.

73 Momdjian 2017, 99 n. 141.

74 Der Matossian 2013, 197–198.

75 Mairs and Muratov 2015, 91–104.

76 See the photograph that appears to show the tall, bearded William Hayes Ward wearing a pith helmet

near Baghdad (https://digital.library.cornell.edu/catalog/ss:12513155).

77 On the square tile in this group, which appears to come from the same frieze as a sequence of four bought by the Metropolitan Museum of Art from Hassan Khan Monif in 1912 (MMA 12.34.3), see Peck 1997.

78 Hallett and Chavak 2019, 57. See also the discussion of trade languages in Wagner and Beinhoff 2017.

79 French had been established as the lingua franca of the intellectual elite within the Ottoman Empire since at least the 1850s. Uslu 2017, 92.

80 A manuscript in the National Library in Tehran on the practice of photography, dedicated to the crown prince Muzaffar al-Din in 1878 by “Antoin Khan” (likely Antoin Sevruguin), was written in Persian but based on French photography manuals: Schwerda 2017, 85.

81 Wills 1891, 79. See also de Rochechouart 1867, 8–9; Benjamin 1887, 83–84.

82 Ménant 1887, 26–28.

83 On the problematic invocation of forgery, deception, and copying in relation to Jewish dealers in particular, see Briefel 2006, 116–145, and Westgarth 2020, 31–35, who primarily consider the appearance of such stereotypes within English and French literature.

84 Reilly 2001, 71–73.

85 Clay 1994, 590.

86 Eldem 1999, 43–44; Clay 1994, 591–592. The bank brought in more credit facilities, at a much lower rate of interest, than the traditional institution of local *sarraf*s (moneylenders/ moneychangers) had ever made available.

87 The complicated prehistory of this institution lies in the “Reuter concession” of 1872, which granted the naturalized British citizen Baron Julius de Reuter a railway concession in Iran and, in “an obscure article,” the right to establish a state bank. Floor 2009a, 64–67; Jones 1987, 70.

88 Jones 1987; Mahdavi 1976–77, 206–207; Enayat n.d. The British Albert Houtum Schindler, who held various positions under Nasir al-Din Shah and played a significant role in the establishment of the bank, exemplifies the combination of interests so often encountered in these colonial-financial contexts: as well as serving as general manager of the bank, he promoted British interests in Iran’s mineral resources (especially iron, copper, and coal mines), and collected and published premodern coins. Potts 2023.

89 Jones 1986, 47, 97, 133–134.

90 Eldem 1999, 422–432. See also the employee profiles drawn from the personnel files of the Ottoman Bank in Eldem 1998, 263–295.

91 Jones 1987, 77; Jones 1986, 156–157. This is paralleled in the stratification of labor within the Anglo-Persian Oil Company: see Floor 2009, 54.

92 Eldem 1999, 296–298.

93 Jenkins-Madina 2000, n. 18; Hallett and Chavak 2019, 56. Kirkor Minassian is sometimes reported to have been born in Kayseri, but the name Minassian does not appear in Alboyajian 1937, a history of the Armenian families of Kayseri. This might mean he was not actually from Kayseri or alternatively might simply mean he was not from a particularly illustrious or notable family. I thank Alyson Wharton for supplying this information (personal communication, January and June 2024).

94 Simpson 2000, 95; on Kayseri, see Der Matossian 2013.

95 Payaslian 2013, 285.

96 Wharton-Durgaryon 2020; Vernoit 2000, 31; Seraphin Abdullah and Macler 1909, 4–5.

97 Watenpaugh 2019.

98 Klein 1999, 353.

99 Tracy 2009, n. 45; Sluglett 2002a, paragraph 15.

100 Sluglett 2002a, paragraph 15; Masters 2010, 310.

101 David and Grandin 1994, 92.

102 Abdou 1910, 456.

103 Mango 1986, 21; Charles Lang Freer, diary vol. 18, entries for 17, 18, and 19 June 1908, Box 54, Folder 5, Freer Papers, NMAA; Gertrude Bell, diary entry for 7 February 1909, GB/2/11/7, Gertrude Bell Archive, Newcastle University, https://gertrudebell.ncl.ac.uk/d/gb-2-11-2-7.

104 This is presumably the same André/Andrea Marcopoli who is described by Peter Sluglett as a “banker, commission agent, importer of European goods, wool and leather merchant and consul of Portugal in Aleppo since 1866.” Sluglett 2002a, paragraph 15. On the Marcopolis’ residence in the Khan al-ʿUlabiyya, David and Grandin 1994, 95–97; on the khans of Aleppo more generally, see Lamprakos 2017.

105 Eldem 1999, 279–280.

106 Carswell 2000, 138–139.

107 The Harari silver is now held in the L. A. Mayer Museum for Islamic Art in Jerusalem. Allan 1976/77; Harari 1939. On the discovery and attribution of this group, Pope 1930.

108 Grunwald 1972, 20–21; Kupferschmidt 1995.

109 Guerin 1995; Anonymous n.d.; Rustow 2020, 47, 248–249, 460 n. 89, 495 nn. 4–5; Jefferson 2022, 184–187.

110 Volait n.d.; Çelik and Kinney 1990; Çelik 1992, 75–58; Mitchell 1991, 1–12. On Muhammad Amin Fikri’s description of the rue du Caire, see also Sabry 2018.

111 Saul 2013; Cannon 2001.

112 Abdulfattah 2020, 109; Talalay and Root 2015, 161–163; Volait 2021, 57; Jefferson 2022, 62.

113 Deniz Türker notes the meaning of the name, although without connecting it with the Kouchakji family: Türker 2014, 280. I thank Rita Koryan and Kaya Şahin for discussing the name and possible background of the Kouchakjis with me.

114 Jenkins-Madina 2006, 14–16.

115 Diehl 1926, 105.

116 Labrusse 2018; Lovino 2020, 514–515.

117 See the summary in Arnason 1941/1942.

118 See, for example, a letter from Charles Lang Freer to Frank Hecker, 27 June 1908, Freer Papers, NMAA, https://edan.si.edu/transcription/pdf_files/9459.pdf.

119 de Jerphanion 1926; for more recent publication, see Cormack and Vassilaki 2008, 382–383.

120 Mango 1986, 183–185.

121 Radcliffe n.d. In addition to his publications, Eisen had by 1902 assembled an important collection of Guatemalan textiles now in the Hearst Museum of Anthropology, University of California, Berkeley (Schevill 1993). He also published a three-volume catalogue of portraits of George Washington (Eisen 1932).

122 Gustavus Eisen is listed in the 1940 US census as the lodger of Fahim and Evelyn Kouchakji at their residence in Manhattan: 1940 US Federal Population Census, http://www.archives.com/1940-census/fahim-kouchakji-ny-57580050, accessed August 2019. In the census Eisen is recorded as being resident at the same address with the Kouchakjis five years previously. Schevill’s biography states that he moved

into the Kouchakjis' apartment in 1938, after breaking his leg in a car accident (Schevill 1993, 42). Sjöberg's account, on the other hand, states that Eisen lived with the Kouchakjis for the last two decades of his life: Sjöberg 2016, 533.

123 Eisen 1926, 41.

124 Eisen 1916; Eisen 1918.

125 Eisen and Kouchakji 1927. On the sandwich-glass forgeries, see Pillinger 1984, 15–26; Whitehouse 1994.

126 Eisen 1916a; Eisen 1917; Eisen 1917a; Eisen 1923; Eisen 1926; Eisen 1933.

127 Eisen 1916a, 426.

128 Eisen 1923, vol. 1, 3.

129 "After due deliberation as to some method for cleaning the objects of their oxidation which almost completely hid all the minor and finer details, Mr. George Kouchakji intrusted [*sic*] this work to Alfred André, the most skilful artist in his specialty known." Eisen 1923, vol. 1, vii.

130 Eisen 1926, 40.

131 Anonymous 1931, 38.

132 Eisen 1933, 6.

133 Thurber 1936.

134 Holcomb 2008, 13.

135 Fahim Kouchakji was buried with a funeral mass at a Roman Catholic church in New York, according to his obituary (Anonymous 1976). Reminiscences from his younger brother Henri, published online by Emile's granddaughter, state that both of Fahim and Henri's parents were Catholic: "Ma vie—4," kouchakji .blogspot.com, accessed 15 October 2022.

136 Levenson and Huff 1977, 15.

137 *Oxford English Dictionary* online (accessed 30 August 2019), which gives an earliest usage of 1865, in the *Pall Mall Gazette*.

138 Mango 1986, 33.

139 McDaniel 1925, 124. For parallel problems within Islamic art history, Ettinghausen 1955 and Hoffman 2008. For a different approach to the same issue in Minoan art, Gere 2009.

140 Anonymous 1924, 283.

141 Eisen 1923, vol. 1, 131.

142 For example, McDaniel 1925, 123–127; less sympathetically, Casson 1937; and with outright fury, Conway 1924.

143 [Kouchakji] n.d. For contrasting viewpoints, Strzygowski 1924 and Wilpert 1926.

144 Woolley 1924; Diehl 1926; Mouterde 1926. The site of Ma'arrat al-Nu'man was denied by Kouchakji, and a write-up of the debate in the *Proceedings of the Society for the Promotion of Roman Studies* in 1924 included the dismissal of Ma'arrat because it was "based merely on Arab information." Anonymous 1924, 282.

145 Woolley 1924.

146 Mango 1986, 20–34; see also Mango 1992, xxv.

147 Mango 1986, 25–34.

148 Henri Kouchakji to Emile Kouchakji, 14 February 1924, published on http://kouchakji .blogspot.com.

149 For example, Murphy 1925.

150 Levenson and Huff 1977, 17.

151 Abucasem, wittingly or unwittingly, was instrumental in furthering the obfuscation around the origins of the Hama treasure. He eventually sold the pieces on to the dealer Joseph Brummer, who sold them to Henry Walters. That part of the group is now in the collection of the Walters Art Museum. Mango 1986, 26; Diehl 1926.

152 Morgan's buyer, Belle da Costa Greene, reported that she viewed the piece in New York in 1912 before it was sent to Paris for restoration: Rorimer 1954.

153 United States Court of Appeals, *Chester D. Tripp v. Commissioner of Internal Revenue, 1964*, Petitioner's appendix, 120. The name of the bank has been rendered "Cradie Leonae" by the court stenographer.

154 It was also a training ground for financial figures like Joseph Rabino, who in 1889 moved from the Cairo branch of the Crédit to become the chief executive of the Imperial Bank of Persia in Tehran. Potts 2023, 177–179, n. 68.

155 Dikran Kelekian to Charles Lang Freer, 10 November 1905, Vouchers: Art, 1905, December, Freer Papers, NMAA; minute paper memo signed C. H. Wylde, 17 September 1909, Nominal File: Kelekian, Dikran, 1892–1912, V&A.

156 Saul 2003.

157 Eldem 1999, 171; Clay 1994, 598.

158 The name of Kouchakji Frères is mentioned in *American Art News* in the listings of Paris salerooms from 1908 onward. The New York saleroom, initially located at East 40th Street, is mentioned for the first time in an issue dated 2 April 1910. "Exhibitions," *American Art News* 6:23 (1908), 1; "Exhibitions," *American Art News* 8:25 (1910), 1.

159 A letter offering the Antioch hoard for sale to Morgan, dated 28 September 1912, is held in the Morgan Collections Correspondence, Metropolitan Museum of Art: Holcomb 2008, 6.

160 Gennari-Santori 2015.

Chapter 2. Objects of Desire, In and Out of Time: An Extractivist History of Islamic Ceramics

1 Watson 2014, 123.

2 Nasir-i Khusraw 2001, 70.

3 Rougelle 2023, 66; Donabédian and Porter 2017; Valiulina 2021; Boldyreva 2014; Nedashkovsky 2012, fig. 10; Kravchenko 2017, 549.

4 Vanke 1999. Ancient ceramics were collected in Italy as early as the fifteenth century: Damen 2012, 175–188.

5 Vanke 1999, 219; Gadoin 2022, 63–65; Sarre 1923, 80; Erduman-Çalış 2020, 22–24. Karabacek 1884 is an important early study in German.

6 On the "classic sequence," Watson 1999.

7 Sarre 1923, 78–79.

8 de Rochechouart 1867, 298–299.

9 Sarre 1939; Watson 1981; Atasoy and Raby 1989, 264–268; Yenişehirlioğlu 2004, 379–380.

10 Crowe 2002, 21–23.

11 Carey 2017, 15–17, 91–97; Reilly 2001, 77–78; Floor 2009a, 36–37, 190; Goldberg 2025, 107–108; see also al-Qasimi, al-Qasimi, and al-'Azm 1960, vol. 1, 147–148, vol. 2, 319–320 and 371, on the brokerage and commissioning activities of the *dallal*, *'amil*, and *qumisiyunji*.

12 Some collections were eventually incorporated into museums: Shaw 2003; Çelik 2016; Türker 2022.

13 For example, Robert Murdoch Smith purchased in Iran from brokers acting on behalf of financially embarrassed families: Vernoit 2000, 11; Carey 2017.

14 Atasoy 1989, 18.

15 Raby 1989, 269; Carswell 2006, 100.

16 Vanke 1999; Gadoin 2022, 47–49; Erduman-Çalış 2020, 24–29.

17 Slitine 1998; Watson 1985, 41; Tornier 2019; St. Laurent 1986.

18 Slitine 1998; Anonymous 1900, 4; Falke 1902.

19 Watson 1981; see also Barakat and Khademi 2019, 146–147.

20 Golombek et al. 2014, 25, 40–41; Emami 2016, 204–205; Um forthcoming.

21 Carey 2017, 75. Several similar examples were presented to the Ashmolean Museum in Oxford by Fortnum, who probably acquired them in Italy in the 1850s. Vanke 1999, 220–221. For examples in the Ashmolean, nos. EAX.3084-6.

22 Gadoin 2022, 47–50; Golombek et al. 2014, 404–405, 408–409. For a Gombroon ware vessel circulated as a product of twelfth-century Sultanabad, Kelekian 1910, plate 20.

23 Denny 2004, 149–151; Maury 2012; Anonymous 2021.

24 Bohrer 2018, 140–141. See also Eldem 2011; Çelik 2011.

25 Escalating problems of looting during World War I led to the creation of the Permanent Council for the Protection of Ancient Artefacts in 1917: Yildirim and Öztep 2019, 603.

26 Eldem 2016, 135–137.

27 Denny 2004; Willis 1987.

28 Yenişehirlioğlu 2013.

29 Denny 2004, 152; Denny 2006. A panel of these tiles was acquired in Alexandria by Alexandros Benakis before 1922: Carswell, Moraitou, and Gibson 2023, 192–193.

30 Lisa Golombek recently stated that the "Kubachi wares" first entered the market in the 1870s, although the source of this information is not given: Golombek et al. 2014, 169. Arthur Lane mentions examples of "Kubachi ware" ceramics acquired by the V&A in 1877 from Iran: Lane 1939, 156–161. The only piece I can find on the V&A database that would fit this is a tile panel (not a vessel) acquired in Iran by Caspar Purdon Clark, no. 9-1877.

31 Mammaev 2021.

32 Alikhanov and Ivanov 1976, 199–201, 203.

33 Astvatsaturian 1979.

34 Lane 1939, 156; Abercromby 1889, 274–282.

35 Hermitage Museum no. VC-118. Alikhanov and Ivanov 1976, 46–52.

36 Graves 2011; Chenciner, Ismailov, and Magomedkhanov 2006, 57. I thank Marcus Fraser for his help in solving this puzzle.

37 Medieval Iranian ceramic material, including a remarkable lusterware taboret, was also bought from the village: Giuzal'ian 1960, 318; Adamova et al. 2007, 49–52, 102; Graves 2018, 101–105.

38 Joukowsky holdings, Brown University, M039. Compare with two examples in Golombek et al. 2014, 384–387.

39 Golombek et al. 2014, 174–175.

40 Golombek et al. 2014, 169–171; Brocklebank 1931, 220.

41 Brocklebank 1931, 220.

42 Golombek et al. 2014, 169–174; Lane 1939.

43 Golombek et al. 2014, 172; Golombek 1999, 416; Hillenbrand 1999, 221.

44 Alikhanov and Ivanov 1976, 58–59.

45 Golombek et al. 2014, 171.

46 Anonymous 1906; Wadsworth Athenaeum 1925, 2.

47 Abercromby 1889, 287–288.

48 Shchukin 1907, 4–5, plate XVII. Roinashvili took one of the earliest known photographs of Kubachi, in the 1880s: Magomedov 2016.

49 Alikhanov and Ivanov 1976, 46–52.

50 Alikhanov and Ivanov 1976, 56.

51 Anonymous 1906; Alikhanov and Ivanov 1976, 19; Kverfel'dt 1947, 124.

52 Pope 1932, 375–376.

53 Alikhanov and Ivanov 1976, 48.

54 Alikhanov and Ivanov 1976, 52–53.

55 Pope 1932, 375.

56 American Art Galleries 1918; Sarre 1923, 79.

57 Kelekian 1909, 26–27; Kverfel'dt 1947, 124.

58 Alikhanov and Ivanov 1976, 56.

59 Whitney 1910, nos. 74–118.

60 Jenkins-Madina 2000, 76.

61 Minassian was listed under "Paris" in the lenders for the 1910 Munich exhibition of Islamic art. Anonymous 1910, 46.

62 Hamed-Troyansky 2024, 1–16. The "Othering" of North Caucasians is attested not only in Minassian's dressing up in this photograph, but also in a late nineteenth- or early twentieth-century studio photograph made in Cairo that shows an Egyptian man dressed up "in Circassian dress": Sheehi 2016, 115.

63 Alikhanov and Ivanov 1976, 52.

64 Alikhanov and Ivanov 1976, 57; Gorshenina 2004, 35–37.

65 Brocklebank 1931, 220; Hôtel Drouot 1927, nos. 169–182. Brocklebank bequeathed his collection of Islamic ceramics to Magdalen College, Oxford University: Carswell 2011.

66 Brocklebank 1931, 220.

67 Kverfel'dt 1947, 26.

68 Sarre 1923, 78–79.

69 Anonymous 1889; Lamprey 1890.

70 Masuya 2000; Overton and Maleki 2021; Overton 2022; Floor 2003, 80–82.

71 Wills 1891, 37.

72 Wills 1891, 37.

73 de Rochechouart 1867, 314–316; Blair 1986; Leone 2021.

74 Masuya 2000, 41–44, 50.

75 Overton and Maleki 2021, 123–124. I have seen many collected tiles that bear the scars of the crowbars used to prise them away from their mortar beds.

76 Several recent studies have sought to reconstruct the medieval tile schemata of despoliated buildings in Iran: McClary 2018, and especially Leone 2021, Grbanovic 2023.

77 de Rochechouart 1867, 314–316.

78 Méchin 1867, 4.

79 Benjamin 1887, 285–286.

80 Mirza Hoseyn Khan Tahvildar, *Joghrafiya-ye Esfahan*, translated in Floor 2009a, 163–164.

81 For example, Benjamin 1887, 285; Wills 1891, 191.

82 Dieulafoy 1887, 148.

83 The print is after a photograph taken by Dieulafoy in Varamin in 1881. Overton 2022; Overton 2024.

84 Overton and Maleki 2021.

85 Overton 2022; Blair 2014. A six-page typed document sent from Hagop Kevorkian to Charles Lang Freer (to whom he hoped to sell the mihrab) in 1913 details the history of the mihrab's removal from Iran, including a supposed offer made for it by the French banker Octave Homberg: Correspondence: Kevorkian, Hagop, 25 August 1913–12 February 1914, Freer Papers, NMAA.

86 Information supplied by Janine Ruffing, November 2024.

87 A separate tile from the same sequence, now in the Metropolitan Museum of Art, includes the date. MMA 12.44, Gift of Emile Ray. Blair 1986, 39 and plate 53; Leone 2021, 336.

88 Rugiadi 2011; McPhillips 2012; Rugiadi 2016a; Matin and Ownby 2023.

89 A surviving recipe in Persian from 700 H/1301 CE

attests to the high silica content: Allan 1973; Matin 2020.

90 Rugiadi 2011.

91 This 1913 sale also included the luster mihrab from the Maydan Mosque at Kashan, now in the Museum für Islamische Kunst, Berlin.

92 Hassan Khan Monif was the son of the Iranian dealer Reza Khan Monif (d. before 1923), "of an ancient and distinguished Persian family": Riefstahl 1923.

93 With thanks to Yves Porter (personal correspondence, 23 April 2019). The Eskenazi tiles are included in Porter 2021. Others in this group are in the Reza Abbasi Museum, Tehran, no. 1739, seen by the author in 2009 and illustrated in Porter 2021, 107; Harvard Art Museums, no. 1958-47, acquired from the Tehran dealer Soleiman Aaron (personal correspondence with Mary McWilliams, 19 April 2019), ill. Porter 2021, 141; and the Deniz and Pierre Darier Collection, Geneva, ill. Melville 2018, 324. See also Porter 2023, 110.

94 TL testing for both of these tiles was inconclusive, the results suggesting that the tiles might have undergone low-fire reheating at some point. Thermoluminescence analysis report dated 24 August 2016, and personal correspondence with Helen Mason and Doreen Stoneham, 16 November 2016.

95 Ghouchani 1371/1992, 32–34. Examples: Ashmolean Museum EAX.289.c, Allan 1971, 36; British Museum G.476, Porter 1996, 16; and National Museum of Scotland 1889-69, on display in 2021.

96 Walters Art Museum 48.1292, acquired from Dikran Kelekian in 1931. See also a bird on the back of a Varamin star tile, British Museum G.477; a "bear" on back of a Varamin cross tile, Sèvres, MNC 7826-1 (Porter 2023, 126); a non-Varamin star tile with both a kiln shadow and a drawing of a figure on the reverse, and the date Ramadan 663 H/June 1265 CE in the inscription on the front, in the MMA, 91.1.105 (Carboni and Masuya 1993, 16); and a sketched figure on horseback on the back of a non-Varamin star tile, British Museum G.487 (Akbarnia et al. 2018, 21, and Porter 1996, 47). This last tile was formerly owned by Frederick DuCane Godman, who acquired several tiles from Varamin: Masuya 2000; Carey 2017, 102–105.

97 Carboni and Masuya 1993, 16, state that the sketch on MMA 91.1.105 was not made using the luster medium.

98 See, however, Abbas Akbari's recent publication of a kiln found in the grounds of a nineteenth-century house of Kashan, and his references to the unpublished excavation of three damaged kilns found in the lower levels of the Seljuq-era Friday Mosque of that city: Akbari n.d.

99 Sarre 1923, 79.

100 Vernoit 1997; Rogers 1974.

101 For example, **F. R.** Martin at Fustat in the winter of 1896: Martin 1899, 4–5, plates II–V.

102 "Seljuk Plate, 1948.113," Islamic Near East Object File 1948.113, CAM.

103 Oliver Watson proposed that Kashan was the sole site of medieval Iranian luster production, while Mehdi Bahrami and other Iranian scholars have argued for Gurgan as a major production site. See Graves 2014. To this debate can be added new research proposing medieval luster production at Jiroft and/or other sites near Kerman: Choubak 2012, 94; Amirhajloo, Agha-Aligol, and Emami 2020; Amirhajloo et al. 2020. On luster production at Kashan after the Mongol conquest, see Kanda 2017.

104 On production at Ani, Babajanyan 2017, 276. More recent finds at Ani include fragments of what appear to be Iranian lusterware: Daily Sabah 2019. On an unpublished luster waster found at Merv, Gascoigne and Bridgman 2010, 118.

105 Fusaro and Allegranzi 2023.

106 Scerrato 1959.

107 Bahrami 1949, 13, shows a photograph of a man holding a spade in front of a storage jar, but gives no other information. On kilns excavated at Gurgan, Kiyani 1984, 37–38, plates 30–32, 34–35; Kiyani 1973. See also Watson 2006a.

108 Raqqa: see chapter 5. Tell Minis: Porter and Watson 1987, 175. Sultanabad: Pope 1932, 375. Harari hoard: Pope 1930.

109 Kelekian states that the piece was found at Sultanabad, in the "domain of Sadik-i-Houmayun" (Kelekian 1910, n.p. and no. 51). Lane noted the similarity of this bowl to those found at Gurgan in the 1940s. Arthur Lane, "Kelekian Collection, List B", Nominal File: Kelekian, Dikran, 1912–1954, V&A. The luster date is written في شهور سنة ثمانية ستون ستمائة. I thank Moya Carey for her help with this inscription.

110 Included in lists of dated Iranian lusterwares prepared by Kühnel 1931, 223, 224, 227; Ettinghausen 1981, 1674; Watson 1985a, 200. Kelekian's ink inscription is much more legible in the black-and-white photograph published in Butler 1926, plate XLIX. Kelekian (1910, no. 51) mistakenly wrote that 668 H is equivalent to 1290 CE, but this error in date conversion was not repeated in subsequent scholarship.

111 By 1912, loaned to the V&A by Kelekian. Loan approval, 16 July 1912, Nominal File: Kelekian, Dikran, 1912–1954, V&A.

112 Compare with a lobed master mold for the production of negative molds that would be used to make ten-lobed bowls with complex three-dimensional designs: Watson 2004a, 140–141.

113 Wulff 1966, 165–166.

114 Similar traces can be seen in the base fragments of eleventh- or twelfth-century Syrian stonepaste vessels excavated at Baalbek: Daiber 2006, tafel 5.

115 For medieval Persian potters' recipes for luster, Allan 1973; Porter 2011, 98–106, 227–259; Matin 2020.

116 Watson 1999, 426–427.

117 Wallis 1891, 27. See also Pope 1940, 8.

118 Read 1907, xiv.

119 Tyler 1910, 641.

120 The V&A also acquired siteless sherds from Ferdinand Méchin in 1868, including three in luster, that were subsequently attributed to Rayy in 1873 by Fortnum (Carey 2017, 76).

121 Porter 1821.

122 Porter 1821, vol. 1, 364. See also Carey 2017, 76–77; Rante 2015, 26–27.

123 Pope 1942, 186.

124 Benjamin 1887, 59, 286–287.

125 Hallett and Chavak 2019, 60. The authors do not give the source of this information.

126 Sarre 1923a, 40.

127 In what is now the Museum Fünf Kontinente in Munich, since 1932. Wallner 2022, 105.

128 Sarre 1923, 79.

129 Hallett and Chavak 2019, 57; Jenkins-Madina 2000, 73.

130 American Art Galleries 1911, no. 180.

131 Rante n.d.; Vernoit 1997, 5; Fry and Vignier 1914, 212; Nasiri-Moghaddam 2004, 275–276.

132 Nasiri-Moghaddam 2004, 182–184, 211–213; Fazeli, Coningham, and Blatt 2004, 13.

133 American Art Galleries 1911, no. 180.
134 Anonymous n.d.-a; Vernoit 1997, 4; Gasche n.d.; Grigor 2018, 124–126; Fazeli, Coningham, and Blatt 2004, 13. Jacques de Morgan and Roland de Mecquenem, successive heads of the Délégation scientifique française en Perse (responsible for archaeological research and extraction), were trained as mining engineers: Boucharlat 2005, 430.
135 Boucharlat 2005, 440; Ghiasian 2015, 893.
136 Read 1907, xi.
137 Mousavi 2005, 451; Arthur Upham Pope to George Eumorfopoulos, 5 April 1926, Box 18: Addition, Pope Papers, NYPL.
138 Vernoit 1997, 7; Mousavi 2005, 452–457; Majd 2003, 29-87.
139 The finds were divided between the National Museum in Tehran, the University of Pennsylvania Museum of Archaeology and Anthropology, and the Museum of Fine Arts, Boston. Schmidt's subsequent appointment to the faculty of the Oriental Institute of the University of Chicago means there are also archive material and sherds from the Rayy excavations there.
140 "Appropriation for Purchases to Mr. Arthur Upham Pope," 18 March 1929, Folder: Pope, Arthur Upham, Dealer/Donor Files, DIA Registration Dept.
141 Arthur Upham Pope to Clyde Burroughs, 15 August 1931, Folder: Pope, Arthur Upham, Dealer/Donor Files, DIA Registration Dept.
142 Arthur Upham Pope to Clyde Burroughs, 15 August 1931, Folder: Pope, Arthur Upham, Dealer/Donor Files, DIA Registration Dept.
143 Arthur Upham Pope to Clyde Burroughs, 21 July 1931, Folder: Pope, Arthur Upham, Dealer/Donor Files, DIA Registration Dept.
144 Clyde Burroughs to Arthur Upham Pope, 7 March 1932, Folder: Pope, Arthur Upham, Dealer/Donor Files, DIA Registration Dept.
145 Whitcomb 2016, 98. Pope also tried in 1929 to secure Ernst Herzfeld's collaboration in a German-American archaeological mission to Iran that he claimed would be underwritten by the University of Pennsylvania and the Philadelphia Museum of Art. Arthur Upham Pope to Ernst Herzfeld, 9 October 1929, Box 1: General Correspondence 1926–29, Pope Papers, NYPL.
146 Schmidt 1936, 79–80.
147 Kröger 2005, 68 n. 76; Whitcomb 2012.
148 Yoltar-Yıldırım 2013, 81, n. 62; Tütüncü Çağlar 2017, 122, 151–152.
149 Schmidt 1935, 48.
150 Treptow 2007, 29.
151 MFA Boston, acc. no. 39.430, excavated at Rayy in 1936. Schmidt 1936, 87.
152 Schmidt 1936, 80; Whitcomb 2012.
153 Sykes 1902, 190–191. British Museum, accession numbers starting at 1897,1216.1.
154 Kelekian 1910, n.p.; Bahrami 2013, 299.
155 Benjamin Mahboubian (1868–1968) was father of the dealers Houshang and Mehdi Mahboubian and uncle of the dealers Ayoub and Khalil Rabenou. British Museum, "M. Mahboubian," https://www.britishmuseum.org/collection/term/BIOG62576, accessed 19 May 2024.
156 Arthur Upham Pope to Ralph Booth, 4 June 1929, Folder: Pope, Arthur Upham, Dealer/Donor Files, DIA Registration Dept.
157 Schmidt 1940, plate 30, comments that "many beautiful polychrome vessels of the Seljuk period were found here." A description of the ground at Raqqa, similarly honeycombed by treasure hunters, is given in Bell 1911, 59–60.
158 Kelekian 1910, n.p; Vernoit 2000, 31. Vernoit does not cite the source of his information.
159 One report says excavation began there in 1905: Tyler 1910, 640.
160 Ettinghausen 1936, 11; Pope 1932, 375; Floor 2009, 7–8.
161 Carey 2017, 78–79. The governor of Isfahan, Zill al-Sultan, reportedly permitted the destruction of a number of historic palaces and the sale or reuse of their architectural elements: Vernoit 2000, 12; but see also Emami 2019, 74–75.
162 Muscarella n.d.
163 Hassan Khan Monif to Mehmet Ağa-Oğlu, 7 November 1931, Box *ISL 2: Curatorial Correspondence, Folder *ISL 2/6, Islamic/Near Eastern Records, DIA.
164 Smirnov 2013.
165 Bahrani, Çelik, and Eldem 2011a; Çelik 2016, 23–26; Yoltar-Yıldırım 2013; Tütüncü Çağlar 2017.
166 Lead isotope analysis has recently revealed that glazed slipwares excavated in Kazakhstan use lead from the Tianshan mountains and even, in some cases, from a particular site in Xinjiang. Klesner et al. 2021.
167 Tashkhodzhaev 1967. On imported Chinese ceramics excavated at Afrasiyab, Sokolovskaia and Rougeulle 1992.
168 Rogers 1974, 51. See also Shishkin 1969, 25–31; Gorshenina 1999, 366.
169 Bartol'd 1966, 127. I thank Gardner Bovingdon for translating this passage. See also Rogers 2000, 63–64; Shishkin 1969, 38, n. 95.
170 Shishkin 1969, 35–37, names men called Mirza Abdullah Bukharin (owner of a silk-weaving factory), Ghafiz, Mirza Barat, and Akram Askarov.
171 Ilyasov 2016; Blair 2014a, 11–56. For the fullest documentation of ceramics excavated from Tashkent, Ilyasova et al. 2016.
172 Samavaki 2021; Bulliet 1992; Pancaroğlu 2013.
173 Wilkinson 1973, 4–5. For archaeologically recovered sherds of Nishapur buffware with figural designs, Wilkinson 1973, 43–53; Rante and Collinet 2013, 68.
174 Ziaii-Bigdeli 2017, 48–51.
175 Erduman-Çalış 2020, 539–543.
176 Collinet 2022, 193; Juvin 2012. For a translation of the inscription, Ghouchani 1986, no. 59.
177 Shishkin 1969, 7–9.
178 The V&A received hundreds of sherds from Afrasiyab in 1898 (Hannover 1925, 549, n. 6). These are presumably the sherds attributed in the V&A's online database to Samarqand and received from Major William Joseph Myers (1858–1899).
179 Erdmann 1942; Erdmann 1946; Martina Müller-Wiener, personal communication, November 2024. A forthcoming publication by Ute Frank, Martina Müller-Wiener, and Pierre Simeon will hopefully clarify some of these questions.
180 Ilyasova et al. 2016; Ting, Rugiadi, and Wordsworth 2023.
181 Ilyasov 2014, 67, 72.
182 Kröger 2005; Dunn-Vaturi and Rugiadi, 2023, 433–436.
183 Canby 2000, 132. The occupation of Samarra was not quite as discrete as Sarre and Herzfeld believed: see Northedge and Kennet 1994.
184 Kröger 2005, 53; Phillip 2011, 387; Cooper 2013. In between the German reconnaissance in 1907–8 and their excavations in 1911–13, Henri Viollet excavated on a smaller scale at Samarra: Rose 2017.

185 Sarre 1925. Some of the material excavated at Samarra was sent to Berlin in 1913, a few pieces were sent to Istanbul, and a large amount of material was taken to London by the British after they captured Baghdad in 1917, and subsequently disbursed to museums in Europe, the United States, and the Middle East. Phillip 2011, 391.

186 Kühnel 1934; Lane 1947, 10–11.

187 Hallett 2012; Wen 2021. Acquired by the Eskenazi Museum of Art at Indiana University in 1973 from the New York dealer Peter Marks.

188 Northedge and Kennet 1994; Watson 2014.

189 Canby 2000, 132–134; Directorate General of Antiquities 1940.

190 Some dealers and scholars have tried to argue that these bowls were produced in Iran, but this has never been widely received: Vignier 1925; Melikian-Chirvani 1985, 20.

191 Hallett 2021. It should be noted that the case for Basra hinges in part on analysis of a kiln assemblage that wasn't archaeologically retrieved and is only linked with Basra by the unsubstantiated report of a former owner: see Priestman 2011.

192 Hallett 2012; Waagé 1948, 89–91, figs. 45–49; Grabar et al. 1978, vol. 2, 246–249; Stark 2023; Kalantaryan et al. 2009, plate 33; Amelia, Azhari, and Purnamasari 2023.

193 Saba 2012.

194 Pradell et al. 2008; Molina et al. 2014; Bobin, Schvoerer, and Ney 2003.

195 An Iraqi luster bowl in the V&A (C1323–1921), reportedly found at Fustat in Egypt, has similarly extravagant palmette fronds.

196 Croisier Collection, Mouliérac 1999, 93; Oscar Raphael bequest, former Eumorfopoulos Collection, Fitzwilliam Museum, OC.172-1946, https://data.fitzmuseum.cam.ac.uk/id/image/media-50381, accessed 19 May 2024; Benaki Museum, no. 306, Philon 1980, 154. See also Hallet 2012, 355.

197 Published in Pézard 1920, plate CXVIII; Pope and Ackerman 1981, vol. 9, 575 D. An archive print is held in the V&A from the time when the object was loaned to the museum (1912–52). Prints and drawings study room, level F, case BOX, shelf B.

198 Vernoit 2000, 30. Karl Katz (2016, 64) describes digging there himself in the 1950s and enlisting local children as paid diggers.

199 Martin 1899. On Martin's thefts from the Topkapı Library, Roxburgh 1998; Hillenbrand 2010.

200 Nasir-i Khusraw 2001, 70.

201 Acquired from the museum's director **W. R.** Valentiner in 1927. Compare with the very similar designs on two lusterware stonepaste sherds in the collections of the Musée du Louvre (OA 7513 and K 3492), acquired in 1889 and 1932 (the latter from Raymond Koechlin), and a third example in the Medelhavsmuseet, Stockholm (NM 0548/1921).

202 Butler 1926, plate XXXV.

203 On the figural material, Suleman 2003.

204 Cf. Tonghini 1998, n. 216.

205 A similar laqabi fish-dish was excavated at Hama. Riis and Poulsen (1957, 146) suggested the fish motif came from Chinese ceramics.

206 Including Balis, Aleppo, Hama, and Qalʿat Jaʿbar. Haddon 2012, 678–679; Riis and Poulsen 1957, 146–148; Tonghini 1998, 44, plate 50; Stephennie Mulder, personal communication, May 2024. On the Russian finds, Koval' 2010, 61–62, plate 18, nos. 2–6.

207 A reconstructed laqabi dish in the al-Sabah collection, Kuwait, proved in conservation to have been made up of literally hundreds of fragments, cut, filed, and "sandwiched" together (see chapter 3). Norman 2004, 78–80.

208 Toledo Museum of Art, 1941.9. The bowl was owned by Parish-Watson and sold by him to V. Everit Macy in 1926; in 1938 Parish-Watson bought it back again. American Art Association 1938, lot 493, 130–131.

209 Porter and Watson 1987; Tonghini 1994, 249.

210 Porter and Watson 1987, 175.

211 A "Tell Minis" bowl that entered the Louvre in 1905 (Louvre OA 6044) was reported to have come from ruins at "Maʿarrah près d'Alep," and a large group of illicitly excavated sherds, now in the Ashmolean Museum, reportedly came from a single spot near Tell Minis and Maʿarrat al-Nuʿman. Porter and Watson 1987, 176, 192–205.

212 Felch 2012.

213 Daedalus, Inc., "Record of Treatment," dated August 1990, Folder 41.9, Curatorial Records, Toledo Museum of Art.

214 Porter and Watson 1987, 179–180. See also Tonghini 1998, 38–42, for "fritware 1."

215 Riis and Poulsen 1957, 136–137. It is also very similar to Ashmolean Museum EA1978.2289, gift of Gerald Reitlinger. Porter 1981, 5.

216 Koval' 2010, 61–62, plate 13, no. 1.

217 Rivière and Migeon 1913, vol. 1, plates 25 and 26; Fiedley 1915, 216; undated glass negative in the Sevruguin archive (probably prior to 1910), FS-FSA_A.4_2.12.GN.10.06.

218 Rivière and Migeon 1913, vol. 1, plates 25 and 26.

219 Field 1939, 153. Pézard and Sambon, both writing in the 1920s, say the Garrus wares were being found at Hamadan and Zanjan; Pézard also identified them with a town called Garous, between Zanjan and Tehran. This information was repeated by Parish-Watson. Pézard 1920, vol. 1, 97; Sambon 1928, 3; Parish-Watson & Co. Inc., *Memorandum: Detroit Institute of Arts*, 23 September 1930, Box *ISL 2: Curatorial Correspondence, Folder 10: Parish-Watson & Co. 1929–1933, Islamic/Near Eastern Records, DIA. Hobson, Pope, and Lane state the source was a place called Yasskand or Yasukand, where Pope claimed to have seen kiln evidence of medieval production. Hobson 1932, 25; Pope 1932, 377; Lane 1937–38, 42.

220 Ferdinand Méchin published a protoethnography of Zoroastrians in Iran, written during a trip on which he was charged with collecting ceramic samples for the French national manufactory in Sèvres. Méchin 1867, 2.

221 Sambon 1925; Sambon 1928.

222 A Garrus ware of the same type as Sambon's pieces is now in the MMA, 64.274.3, donated to the museum by Fahim Kouchakji in 1964. There seem to have been quite a number of these bowls in the collection of one U. Cénani, a figure I have not been able to trace: Rozantal 1948.

223 Lane 1937–38, 42. Watson (1985) raised the point again, with more detail about possible technique. See also Ayoub Rabenou to Arthur Upham Pope, detailing objects selected for purchase from Rabenou by Maurice Demand and Eustache de Lorey: "4. A Metallic luster Guebri bowl, as document with Animal subject (falsified): 600 Fr." Ayoub Rabenou to Arthur Upham Pope, 30 August 1934, Box 2: General Correspondence 1930–34, Pope Papers, NYPL.

224 Esin Atıl to Dan Walker, 12 October 1984, Folder 1952.50, Islamic Near East Object Files, CAM. Folders 25.31, 25.32, 25.33, 29.35, 30.422, Curatorial Records, DIA. Daybreak report for 41.8, dated 25 March 1991, Folder 41.8, Curatorial Records, Toledo Museum of Art.

225 Schnyder 1972, 194–195; Schnyder 1974, plate II figs. 10–12; Kazempour 2023.

226 Analysis shows that the Aghche Rish sherds of this type were likely all from one workshop, not local to the site: Waksman 2023.

227 See, for example, the "Garrus ware" bowl decorated with two birds excavated at Takht-i Sulayman: Naumann 1961, plate 48.

228 Pézard 1920, vol. 2, plate LXI.

229 DIA 25.32. Dikran Kelekian to William Valentiner, 26 February 1925, Folder: Kelekian, Dikran G, Dealer/Donor Files, DIA Registration Dept.

230 TL testing performed by Gary W. Carriveau in the research laboratory at the DIA, report dated 4 December 1983, Folder 25.32, Curatorial Records, DIA.

231 See also a fragment of a similar champlevé bowl with a band of cross-hatching, excavated at Antioch and attributed to local production: Waagé 1948, 99–100, fig. 84.

232 I thank Christina Bisulca for sharing her research on this and other pieces of Garrus ware in the DIA during my visit in 2022.

233 For example, DIA 25.31. TL testing performed by Gary W. Carriveau in the research laboratory at the DIA, report dated 4 December 1983, Folder 25.31, Curatorial Records, DIA.

234 CAM 1952.250. No. 143 in the Kelekian V&A ceramics collection. Arthur Lane included this piece in the "A" list he prepared for the V&A (see chapter 4), annotating it "Essential. V large and powerful design, excellent condition. Far better than any other known piece of this class & beyond doubt genuine." Lists prepared for Kelekian estate, Nominal File: Kelekian, Dikran, 1912–1954, V&A. Lane 1947, plate 33B.

235 TL testing done at the Detroit Institute of Arts in 1984. CAM Conservation Lab Report of Treatment, 29 November 1984, Folder 1952.250, Curatorial Records, CAM.

236 CAM Conservation Lab Report of Treatment, 29 November 1984, Folder 1952.250, Curatorial Records, CAM.

237 Loan approval, 24 March 1922, Nominal File: Kelekian, Dikran, 1912–1954, V&A.

238 Norman 2004, 86–87.

239 Rogers 1973/74, 170.

Chapter 3. Making Gold from Base Matter: Potsherds, Paint, and Patience

1 McWilliams 2012.

2 Parry 2023; Venice Charter 1964; Code of Ethics of the American Institute of Conservation, https://www.culturalheritage.org/about-conservation/code-of-ethics, accessed 23 March 2023.

3 Watson 1985; Watson 2004.

4 See also You 2016; Martin 2020.

5 Milanese 2007; Milanese 2010, 20–23.

6 Raffaele Gargiulo (1785–after 1870), attached for over fifty years to what is now the National Archaeological Museum of Naples, left no direct records of his techniques or recipes: Svobodo 2013, 208. Andrew Oddy noted in the 1990s that "Even as late as the 1960s, those restorers who had been trained before the Second World War often had their own secret way of doing jobs, and their own secret recipes for sticking, colouring, or patinating." Oddy 1992, 11.

7 Lévi-Strauss 1966, 21–22.

8 See the definition in Watson 1985, 39: "an article made newly and wholely for the purposes of deception."

9 [Brinckmann] 1902; [Brinckmann] 1903. Brinckmann was founding director of the Museum für Kunst und Gewerbe Hamburg, acquiring for the museum between 1873 and his death in 1915: Dolezalek et al. 2022.

10 Zahn 1911; Rackham 1931, 20; von Bothmer 1998, 13–14.

11 Pazaurek 1929.

12 One Greek vase now in the State Hermitage Museum was formerly in the celebrated collection of the Marquis Gian Pietro Campana (1808–1880), who used his antiquities as collateral for loans before his imprisonment for fraud in 1857. The Campana krater was admired in the nineteenth century for its portrayal of Telephos; disassembly in 1912 revealed only fragments of original material against a large amount of new-made design painted on plaster—including several of the inscribed names of the figures. R. S. 1913; Bukina, Petrakova, and Phillips 2013, 105–125, 151–152.

13 Milwright 2001, 75–77; Milwright 2021, 142–144; Garachon 2010; Hsieh 2016; Dági 2003; Baseman n.d.

14 Milwright 2014, 212–213.

15 See, however, an Iberian luster plate in the collection of the National Gallery of Victoria with thirty-three fragments held together by rivets and plaster fill: Strohschnieder 2021. On the corporation of ceramic and porcelain gluers in late nineteenth-century Isfahan, see Floor 2009a, 210.

16 Attributed to the kilns at Triana in Seville, second quarter of the sixteenth century, by analogy with the pieces catalogued in Ray 2000, 141–149.

17 Jones et al. 2003, 179.

18 Garachon 2010, 48; Thiaucourt 1865, 5.

19 On stylistic dating of Persian lusterware, Watson 1985a, 68–85; Watson 2020, 201.

20 EMA curatorial record for 60.58. Azeez Khayat, a Melkite Christian born in Tyre (Sur) in what is now Lebanon, moved to the US in 1893 and traded antiquities, especially ancient glass, in Manhattan: Bergman 1974; Hilel 2021, 144.

21 Gibson 2010, vol. 2, nos. 173–218; Gibson 2008–9; Canby et al. 2016, 217–218, cat. nos. 134 and 135.

22 Neuwirth 2022, 434.

23 Melikian-Chirvani 1982, 276; Melikian-Chirvani 1991, 102–103.

24 Measday, Walker, and Pemberton 2017.

25 Pease 1958; Watson 1985, 42–43; Koob 1999; Norman 2004; Watson 2004, 521–522; de Lapérouse, Stamm, and Parry 2007; Sigel and McWilliams 2013; Michelsen and Olafsdotter 2014; Masteller 2016, 276–281; Graves 2018; Leoni et al. 2019; Norris and Watson 2021; Fischer 2022; de Lapérouse n.d.; McCarthy and Holod n.d.

26 Acquired by the Cincinnati Art Museum from Kelekian in 1948. Pope and Ackerman 1981, vol. 9, plate 712; Melikian-Chirvani 1967, fig 8.

27 It is closely comparable with a restored Iranian luster bowl with astrological symbols, a half meter in diameter, that Kelekian sold to the MFA Boston in 1909 (MFA 09.103).

28 A base and three legs from a similar zoomorphic figurine or vessel, with cobalt blue glaze, were

excavated at Rayy in the 1930s: Oriental Institute Museum A115161 and A115162, Treptow 2007, 30.

29 Thermoluminescence analysis performed by Oxford Authentication Ltd., using sample taken on 27 May 2016 by Helen Mason.

30 Toledo Museum of Art, nos. 41.8–41.25. Anonymous 1941.

31 Ackerman 1940, 48, no. 11B (not illustrated); de Batz and Pope 1940, no. 90 (not illustrated); Anonymous 1941. Curatorial records at the Toledo Museum of Art state that this bowl also appeared in the 1931 *International Exhibition of Persian Art* at Burlington House in London, but no number is given and it doesn't match any of the descriptions for the Parish-Watson ceramics in the catalogue of that exhibition.

32 Treatment report from Daedalus Inc., dated March 1992. Toledo Museum of Art, curatorial file for 1941.16.

33 Norman 2004, 78–80 and 83–86; Watson 2004, 522; Watson 2020, 22.

34 Vignier 1928, 84–85.

35 Fitzwilliam Museum C.133-1935, one of 136 pieces from the Frank Brangwyn collection acquired by the museum in 1935. I thank Oliver Watson for sharing a photograph of this object after I sent him images of the Toledo bowl in 2021, and Flavia Ravaioli for the provenance information she shared when I contacted the museum about this piece in April 2023.

36 Thiaucourt 1865.

37 Such mixtures could also be used as a finish layer over a coarser fill, since they are amenable to sanding and carving if required. Koob 1998, 53; Sigel and McWilliams 2013, 40.

38 Koob 1998, 53. This seems to be similar to the technique used in reconstructing a Raqqa ware jar in the Metropolitan Museum, MMA 17.74.2, bought from Tabbagh Frères in 1917.

39 Vignier 1928, 84–85.

40 Yoltar-Yıldırım 2013, 81, n. 62. On Macridy, Grigoriadis 2023.

41 Snow 1986; Oddy 1992, 11–12; Hogan et al. 1996, 833; Svobodo 2013, 211–212; Garachon 2017, 381; Koob 1998, 59–61; Pease 1958; Masteller 2016, 276–281.

42 Vignier 1928, 87–88.

43 Illustrated in Pope and Ackerman 1981, vol. 9, plate 637; Lane 1947, plate 53B; Ettinghausen 1960, 23; Atıl 1973, no. 32.

44 Koob 1999, 156–166; see also Portell 2003, 373–374.

45 Leoni et al. 2019.

46 Garachon 2010, 48.

47 Ris-Paquot 1872. This book was in the library of the Brummer brothers, major antiquities dealers in New York: see Force, Biro, and Brennan 2023, n. 49.

48 Ris-Paquot 1872, 30–36.

49 I thank Joan Cummins, Lisa Bruno, and Maribel Cosme-Vitagliani for sharing the X-ray images and conservation reports with me.

50 Blake-Coleman 1981, i.

51 Harry DeBauche, untitled blog post for *Brooklyn Museum* on tumblr, https://brooklynmuseum.tumblr.com/post/179214508435/in-the-early-20th-century-the-ruined-medieval-city, accessed 8 December 2022.

52 DeBauche, untitled blog posts for *Brooklyn Museum* on tumblr, https://brooklynmuseum.tumblr.com/post/179214508435/in-the-early-20th-century-the-ruined-medieval-city and https://brooklynmuseum.tumblr.com/post/180176048416/in-the-early-20th-century-dealers-who-handled-the, both accessed 8 December 2022. Brooklyn Museum acc. nos. 06.3; 08.19; 08.21; 08.23; 08.24; 08.32; 08.36 (08.18 and 08.35 do not say on the online database that they came via Azeez Khayat, but they appear to be from the same group).

53 Jenkins-Madina 2006, 21–35; Yoltar-Yıldırım 2013; Tütüncü Çağlar 2017.

54 It may have been made from unfired clay, perhaps mixed with shellac or animal glue for added strength. Koob 1998, 57–58.

55 Parke-Bernet 1953, no. 332.

56 Losensky 2023.

57 See DeLanda 2016, 10. DeLanda explicitly builds upon Deleuze and Guattari 2006.

58 See Roxburgh 2005, especially chapter 3, and Roxburgh 2001.

59 EMA accession record for 61.68, purchased from the Persian Antique Gallery, New York (prop. Hassan Khan Monif).

60 The EMA accession card for this piece makes no mention of the object's reconstructed state.

61 Arthur Upham Pope to Philip R. Adams, 12 November 1957, Calligraphic plate 1958.86, Islamic Near East Object Files, CAM. At just over 45 cm in diameter, the CAM dish matches the dimensions of a similar epigraphic bowl in the Sarikhani Collection (I.CE.2139), formerly in the possession of "US media tycoon" John W. Kluge and before that reportedly in the possession of the Pahlavi family (Anonymous n.d.-b; Watson 2020, 66–67). It also matches the dimensions of a more famous example in the MMA (65.106.2) bought from the New York dealer Edward Safani in 1965.

62 Compare with British Museum 1958,1218.1, acquired by the BM in the same year the CAM acquired theirs from Pope. The vendor of the BM bowl is listed on the online database as "H. Khan Moruf," likely a misreading of H[assan] Khan Monif. A jug in the Keir Collection (Dallas Museum of Art, K.1.2014.985) has similar calligraphy, and uses the same narrow teardrop form to indicate the end of a phrase.

63 This could be done within institutions as well as on the market. Abdullah Ghouchani, during his employment at the Iran Bastan Museum in Tehran, noted that he had painted in more than half of the inscription when reconstructing a bowl in that collection, copying the text from another, more complete bowl in the same museum. Ghouchani 1986, no. 120.

64 I thank Manijeh Bayani for her efforts to read this difficult and damaged inscription.

65 Henshaw 2020, 161–162.

66 The same painted trompe l'oeil might be in play on a slipware jug in the Sarikhani Collection (I.CE.2226) decorated with epigraphy very similar to that of the CAM bowl (Watson 2020, 60–61).

67 Hillenbrand 1994.

68 Where this technique is described in Abu'l-Qasem's 1301 treatise on ceramic production, he refers to it as *haft-rang* ("seven colors") while also noting that it was a lost technique by his own time. Matin 2020, 469. A type of ceramic called mina'i was made in Iran in the mid nineteenth century (de Rochechouart 1867, 285), but this seems to be quite a different technique from the medieval enameling practices.

69 Koss et al. 2009, 33–47.

70 See also Simpson 2015, 223–226.

71 Watson 1985, 43; Watson 2004, 519. Recent technical analysis has shown very extensive reconstruction

on the famous mina'i "Muharram bowl" in the British Museum (1945,1017.261), including fragments from at least three different objects as well as new-made glazed and fired replacement sherds (see near-infrared and UV photography and conservation notes at https://www.britishmuseum.org/collection/object/W_1945-1017-261).

72 CAM 1948.109, bought from Kelekian in 1948. I thank Kelly Rectenwald for sharing the results of her conservation work on this piece, conducted after we examined the piece together in 2020.

73 Published preconservation in Riefstahl 1922, 101 and fig. 36, no. 15.

74 Vignier 1928, 84.

75 Simpson 2015, 223–226.

76 Notes from accession card for I.14/64, Museum für Islamische Kunst, Berlin.

77 McCarthy and Holod n.d., and Holod 2012; compare with Pope and Ackerman 1981, vol. 9, plates 674–675, and Lane 1947, plate 70C.

78 This episode also appears on the famous and much-reproduced "Freer Beaker" in the National Museum of Asian Art in Washington, DC (acquired in 1928 from Parish-Watson), first identified as telling the story of Bizhan and Manizeh in D'yakonov 1939. Images of the beaker showing the scene in question—which does not include the fire—were published in black and white in American Art Galleries 1911, no. 327, and Martin 1912, vol. 1, 5, fig. 3; and in color in Rivière and Migeon 1913, vol. 1, plate 45.

79 For example, Brend 2010, 86–87.

80 The palette and the scale and execution of the figures are similar to those on a bottle in the Walters Art Gallery, no. 48.1260, acquired by Henry Walters from Dikran Kelekian in 1922.

81 Likely original sections of the exterior of the Freer "siege plate" are identified in McCarthy and Holod n.d., fig. 13.

82 Mason et al. 2001, 201–207; Koss et al. 2009.

83 Notes from accession card for I.14/64, Museum für Islamische Kunst, Berlin.

84 Hillenbrand 1994; Simpson 1985.

85 McCarthy and Holod n.d. note the same phenomenon of missing bowstrings, indicating that the black overdrawing was not completed when the piece was made.

86 Conservation report dated 31 January 1989, 1952.256, Islamic Near East Object Files, CAM. The report does not make clear which parts of the black retouching were removed.

87 Loan approval form dated 16 July 1912, Nominal File: Kelekian, Dikran, 1892–1912, V&A.

88 Analysis consistently shows that both the underglaze and overglaze blacks of mina'i samples are made with chromium oxide, the latter sometimes including cobalt as well. Koss et al. 2009, 39–40; McCarthy and Holod n.d.

89 Gadoin 2022, 78–95.

90 See the mina'i sherds Godman gave to the British Museum in 1891, which he had bought as part of the Richard collection in 1880: Watson 1999, 426–427.

91 Watson 1999, 427.

92 McClary 2016, 2, n. 10, repeats Watson's assessment. In a subsequent publication he suggests that Calouste Gulbenkian acquired three mina'i sherds and two reconstructed mina'i bowls from Hagop Kevorkian in 1896–98, although the evidence is not conclusive. McClary 2020, 326–328.

93 Reported on doctored ceramics from Attic vases to seventeenth-century German tin-glazed wares. Anonymous 1914; Hüseler 1929. Sometimes the whole surface of a vessel was sanded down and covered with plaster, then painted with an entirely new design and covered with clear varnish or lacquer: **R. S.** 1913. Black varnishes were used to mimic the famous shiny slip of Attic vases and had a greasy or sticky texture that could be pierced with the tip of a needle and removed with alcohol: Zahn 1911; Anonymous 1914; Walters 1905, 39–41; Bulle 1921, 1.

94 Lamboursain 1897, 59–60.

95 Lamboursain 1897, 62; Fearon 2017. A 1901 sale catalogue published by Soehnée Frères exhaustively lists the uses of its varnishes on glass, paintings, and photographs, as well as pills, umbrellas, and bicycles, but makes no mention of ceramics restoration. Soehnée Frères 1901.

96 Examined under handheld UVA light with Kelly Rectenwald, 20 October 2020.

97 Koss et al. 2009.

98 Conservation report from Daedalus Inc., dated March 1992, Toledo Museum of Art curatorial file for 1941.15. A similar handled pitcher is in the NMAA, no. F29.10; like the Toledo example, it was bought from Parish-Watson. Atıl 1973, no. 47.

99 A practice seen on earlier material excavated at Samarra in Iraq, Susa and Nishapur in Iran, and Golden Horde sites, but fairly rare on surviving twelfth- to thirteenth-century Iranian vessels. Sarre 1925, 29–31 and plates 7 and 8; Koechlin 1928, 54–57 and plate X; Mouliérac 1999, 52; Rante and Collinet 2013, 195; Kramarovsky et al. 2005, 145, cat. no. 161; Elnikov and Tihimolova 2017. A piece in the MMA (30.112.51, former Everit Macy collection), attributed to the thirteenth century and reportedly found at Rayy, shows a similar technique with a repeating design in cobalt: Dimand 1931, 8 (not illustrated).

100 Royal Academy 1931, 89, no. 133F (not illustrated); Riefstahl 1922, 183, fig. 60; Pope and Ackerman 1981, vol. 9, plate 685; Ackerman 1940, 218, no. 13D (not illustrated); Anonymous 1941.

101 Other examples cited in Canby et al. 2016, cat. no. 54, n. 4.

102 Komaroff 2012.

103 Examples listed in Watson 2020, 254, n. 149, and further examples in CAM, 1952.257 (former V&A Dikran Kelekian collection, no. 131); Yale University Art Gallery, no. 1953.24.5; Khalili Collection, London, POT 505 (Grube 1994, 219); Keir Collection at Dallas Museum of Art, K.1.2014.319. Spouted and/or handled cups with same: Montreal Museum of Fine Arts, 1939.Dp.12; Gemeentemuseum, h.14.2 (Gemeentemuseum 1956, no. 15); Islamic Art Circle 1969, no. 138; Minneapolis Institute of Arts (Ackerman 1940, 217–218, Case 13, F); Musée des Beaux-Arts de Lyon, no. E 582 (Hellal, Aube, and Brack de la Perrière 2023, 176); and a handled ewer in the Nelson-Atkins Museum of Art, 35-31/5.

104 Loan document dated 16 July 1912, Nominal File: Kelekian, Dikran, 1892–1912, V&A. Now in the CAM (1952.257). Lane 1947, 71C.

105 The same strange bumpy neck is seen on a similar bottle in Tehran: Iran Bastan Museum, Tehran, no. 4753, Koyama and Pope 1978, no. 75.

106 A handled jar with perforated bosses of this type, now in the Brundage Collection of the Asian Art Museum in San Francisco (no. B60P1877), is a pastiche of unrelated fragments. Froom 2008, 8.

107 Martin and Sarre 1912, vol. 2, plate 98, no. 1163; former Parish-Watson collection, Riefstahl 1922, 179, no. 35; online entry for Museum für Islamische Kunst no. I.6210.

108 Herat Museum, no. 01.35.86c, illustrated before and after removal of cosmetic dirt in conservation treatment: Franke and Muller-Weiner 2016, 642.

109 Dumbarton Oaks Collection, object file for Ex. Coll. HC.C.1932.07.(TC). It may have been returned to Kelekian on the advice of Richard Ettinghausen, who prepared a report for the Blisses on their Islamic ceramics collection in 1937 but notably excluded this piece. Ettinghausen 1937, n.p.

110 TL testing performed by Daybreak Nuclear and Medical Systems, Inc., sample taken 18 June 1985, 1948.98, Islamic Near East Object Files, CAM.

111 Watson 2004, 334–336; Aarab et al. 2025.

112 A similar bowl in the V&A has a solid-void tessellation of ogee forms, no. C.61-1953 (former Ernest Debenham collection, Lane 1947, 45–46, plate 90B). Much smaller, sketchier versions of the star-and-cross design can be seen in luster on a sherd acquired by Friedrich Sarre at Rayy in Iran in 1899 and another acquired by the British Museum from Frederick DuCane Godman in 1891 (no. 1891,1020.20): Wallner 2022, 103; Wallis 1891, plate xxviii, no. 2. The star-and-cross design is also seen on some heavily restored mina'i bowls and sherds (McClary 2016), a bowl decorated in overglaze luster in the Bumiller collection (Simeon 2020, plate 88, no. BC 143), and a restored sherd in the Jambyl Region History Museum in Kazakhstan (Duturaeva 2022, 70).

113 Ackerman 1940, 222, shows a similar reserve drawing of a rider mounted on a cow or bull. That bowl is credited to the Lewisohn Collection and I have been unable to find out where it is now.

114 Jones 1990, 28, 34–35.

115 Hannover 1925, 166.

116 Lapatin 2002, 120–139; Gere 2009, 105–139; Beard 2009.

117 Langin-Hooper et al. 2013.

118 EMA 73.46.6. The piece from Rayy is Penn Museum no. 37-11-11, Canby et al. 2016, 245. See also a lobed dish of very similar form in the Ashmolean Museum (EA1978.2315), former Gerald Reitlinger Collection, bought from "Moussa and Meskine, 1939." An undated image of the piece mid-conservation shows that it is very fragmentary, with several areas of significant loss made up in modern times. I thank Francesca Leoni for providing a scan of the accession card and discussing this object with me.

119 The profile of the harpy and some of the painting is reminiscent of that seen on an Iranian bowl decorated with a sphinx in luster in the Munich Völkerkunde Museum (Frembgen 2003, 118).

120 Graves et al. 2023, 2–4, 17, 26–28. The forensic possibilities of artisan's fingerprints are just starting to be explored: Fowler et al. 2020; Sero et al. 2021; Muller 2023.

121 NMAA F1925.6. Watson 2004, 524 and nn. 32 and 33.

122 Toledo Museum of Art 1941.23. Anonymous 1941; Bacigalupi 2009, 99; Anonymous 1941a.

123 American Art Association 1936, n.p., lot 145 (illustrated). The Parish-Watson Company represented Tabbagh's estate in the preparation of the sale and its catalogue; other well-known Islamic ceramics from the 1936 Tabbagh sale passed through Parish-Watson's hands before arriving at their current homes, including the famous "Muharram bowls" now in the Metropolitan Museum, nos. 64.178.1 and 64.178.2.

124 Wrightson 2021, 100–128. For a similar cobalt inscription on white, NMAA S1997.108, Cort, Farhad, and Gunter 2000, 56.

125 For example, Iraqi luster bowl excavated at Nishapur, MMA 40.170.27.

126 Compare with the exteriors of fragments in the Benaki Museum, Philon 1980, 143–162. The facial features of the figures on the Toledo bowl are strikingly similar to those seen on two more bowls of this type. One traded by Parish-Watson is now in the Museum of Islamic Art in Doha, no. PO.428.2006 (Pope 1930a, fig. 28). That piece was sold at auction in 2006 (Christie's 2006, lot 50), at which point the Christie's catalogue entry approvingly noted its similarity to the piece in the NMAA (F1925.6) now reclassified by the museum as a modern forgery on the basis of Watson's research. The other is (or was) in the collection of Kazuo Kurimoto (Mikami 1964, no. 132). From photographs, a further bowl in the Louvre (OA 7807, bought from Charles Vignier in 1924) might also belong to this group (Butler 1926, plate XLIII).

127 Alternatively, there is also the possibility that the piece was refired at a low temperature after the luster-approximating brown substance was painted on. Oliver Watson suggested the latter technique might have been used when I showed him the piece in a photograph, but having examined it in person I think it more likely the technique is overpaint under a lacquer or varnish finish.

128 There is at least one apparently original tenth-century Iraqi figural bowl that combines a cobalt inscription with luster overglaze, V&A C.350-1930, acquired from R. Hormozdiar, Paris, https://collections.vam.ac.uk/item/O7360/bowl-unknown/, accessed 22 March 2025.

129 Thiaucourt 1865, 30–31.

130 Thermoluminescence analysis performed by Oxford Authentication Ltd., using sample taken on 27 May 2016 by Helen Mason.

131 A luster-decorated handled jug excavated at Qal'at Ja'bar in northern Syria might provide some cognates for the design on this piece, but the published image does not show all of the design: Tonghini 1998, plate 37. The Qal'at Ja'bar jar is Tonghini's "fritware 1" (the material of the so-called Tell Minis wares), a fine and white stonepaste body with clear leaded glaze, while the Eskenazi jar corresponds to Tonghini's "fritware 2" (the material of the so-called Raqqa wares), a coarser, grayer stonepaste with clear, leadless alkaline glaze. Tonghini 1998, 38–51.

132 Portable X-ray fluorescence (pXRF) measurements of two areas of luster on the object—one point on the rim and one on the belly inscription—show the significant presence of copper (as would be expected) along with iron (probably coming from the glaze itself, which takes a light green color from ferrous iron). The luster and glaze showed no signs of lead or tin, which accords with excavated fragments of "Raqqa" ware from Syria, notable for leadless, alkaline glazes. Analysis conducted November 2020 by Julie Ribits, Eskenazi Museum of Art. For scanning electron microscopy (SEM) analysis of archaeological sherds, Franchi et al. 1995. See also Pradell et al. 2013 and Pradell et al. 2016, although note that the "Raqqa ware" samples used were not secure archaeological fragments but museum pieces without excavation records.

133 Golombek et al. 2014, 112–117.

134 Carey 2017, 159–167.
135 Smith persuaded Ali Muhammad to share recipes for the *haft-rang* (seven color) ceramic technique in a pamphlet published in English in 1888, and to send samples of raw materials, including pigments, to the Edinburgh museum: Isfahani 1888; Scarce 1976; Matin, Gholamnejad, and Abkenar 2021.
136 Melikian-Chirvani 1966; Ettinghausen 1973, 165. The current location of this piece is not known to me: Melikian-Chirvani stated in 1966 that it was then in a private collection in France, which he believed had entered in the early 1880s (based on the appearance of the wooden frame). For other luster tiles attributed to ʿAli Muhammad Isfahani, Watson 1985a, 169–175; Watson 1975, 77–79.
137 "3937, Lüsterfliese," Museum für Islamische Kunst Inventory Book, *Inventar I.3401—I.4900, Nachweiszeitraum der Zugange 1921–1927 (Inventar I.3401—I.4901)*; Ghouchani 1992, 2. A few pieces of modern Persian lusterware entered the V&A at the beginning of the twentieth century, also bought as exemplars of modern revival techniques. Charles Marling gave the V&A a modern lusterware (797–1909) in 1909 to provide an example of the modern practice: Watson 1985, fig. 6; Watson 2004, fig. 8. Another V&A example (no. 1331–1904) is illustrated in Watson 1985a, plate 145. See also a luster tile in the British Museum, no. G.484, and a bowl in the Khalili Collection, no. POT1535 (Vernoit 1997a, 245).
138 Watson 1985a, plate 37; Pancaroğlu 2007, no. 89.
139 For an example of the former, Woolley and Wallis, *Furniture, Works of Art and Clocks*, 17–18 January 2024, lots 792 and 793, https://www.the-saleroom.com/en-gb/auction-catalogues/woolley-and-wallis/catalogue-id-srwo10378/lot-5056635b-84e3-43cc-bf36-b0d700abb27b, accessed 22 March 2025.
140 Sarre 1907.
141 Falke 1902, 3. Neither of these potters appear in the list of Qajar tilemakers whose names are known from their signed work, compiled in Riazi and Kabiri 2016, 306–324.
142 Brinckmann and Read 1901; Watson 1985, 42.
143 Scanlon 1971, 230 and plate 5; McPhillips 2008, 123; Redlak 2018, 74–76; for pieces excavated in Syria see Bloch, Daiber, and Knötzle 2006, plate 17.
144 Gyllensvärd 1975, 114–115; Krahl and Erbehar 1986, 247–255, nos. 30–57. Redlak (2018, 75–76) states that the hole in the base of the Chinese originals is the result of being built up around a rod on the potter's wheel; Watson (2004, 417) says it was an aid in drying and firing such large bowls.
145 Redlak 2018, 75–76.
146 Watson 2004, 416–418.
147 Thermoluminescence analysis performed by Oxford Authentication Ltd., using sample taken on 27 May 2016 by Helen Mason.
148 Mack 2002, 95–111.
149 Watson 1985; Watson 2004; Watson 1981. See also the detailed instructions on reproducing all kinds of historic wares, including many from the medieval Islamic tradition, in hobbyist manuals: Weiss 1979, 128–163.
150 Pottier 1906; [Brinckmann] 1907; R. S. 1912.
151 Gluck and Gluck 1977, 50, 52.
152 Watson 1985, 43, 46; Watson 2004, 526 and fig. 17; and vase tentatively attributed to a potter called Shah Reza, Gluck and Gluck 1977, 91.
153 McWilliams 2013, 204. McWilliams notes that all of the designs on a modern jar in the Harvard collections (2002.50.66) could have been derived from a single publication, Bahrami 1949.
154 Slitine 1998; Watson 1985, 41; Tornier 2019; St. Laurent 1986; Gerelyes and Kovács 1999.
155 [Brinckmann] 1899; [Brinckmann] 1908; Angst 1900, 4–5.
156 Slitine 2002, 16–17, 76–77; Watson 1985, 41. V&A C.54-2015 is an earthenware bottle with a pseudo-Persian design in black against a turquoise ground, bearing Samson et Cie's pseudo-Arabic mark.
157 Slitine 2002, 12.
158 Benjamin 1887, 299.
159 Olmer 1908, 59.
160 Floor 2009a, 65; Floor 2003, 48; Mahdavi 1999, 88; 199; Mahdavi 2011, 387. Floor 2009 (14) cites two "porcelain factories" in Iran built in the 1880s, one established by Amin al-Zarb at Tehran, and another established by Hajji ʿAbbas ʿAli and Hajji Reza at Tabriz.
161 Floor 2009, 17–18.
162 Zahn 1912, 5–6. See also the incredible process involving sugar, liquid iron, hydrochloric acid, and obsidian that was used in the 1980s to shape Cycladic figurines from marble and provide them with a surface patina, pitting, and discoloration: Tsirogiannis, Gill, and Chippindale 2022.
163 [Brinckmann] 1907a, 4; Hobson 1929; Craddock 1992, 67–68.
164 [Purgold] 1899; Bulle 1921, 3; Gallois 1938.
165 [Brinckmann] 1909; Schmidt 1929; Wakeling 1912, 83, 100. See also the techniques reported in Kelker and Bruhns 2010, 21, and Tremain 2019.
166 A byproduct of silver cupellation: Klesner et al. 2021.
167 Olmer 1908, 60–61.
168 Fry and Vignier 1914, n. 3.
169 CAM 1952.263, Kelekian 1910, no. 70; Lane 1947, plate 93.
170 A jug with this design was sold to Charles Lang Freer by Kelekian in 1908, NMAA F1908.31; other examples are V&A 41–1908 (bowl); Hetjens Museum 1942–26 (bowl); CAM 1952.262 (jar, Kelekian 1910, no. 34); MMA 68.215.11 (gifted 1968); MMA 10.43 (acquired 1910 from Kevark Aharonian); Yale University Art Gallery 1930.472 (bowl) and 1930.482 (jar), both gifted in 1930 and attributed to Raqqa; Ashmolean Museum EA1978.1645 (dish) and EA1978.1587 (bowl), both former Reitlinger Collection; Museum für Kunsthandwerk, Frankfurt, 15307 (dish) (Müller-Wiener 1996, 78); and pieces (formerly) in the possession of Mr. Shinsui Ito, Tokyo (Mikami 1964, no. 177), and Oskar Skaller (Kühnel 1927, plate 19, no. 122). Three more appear in the undated glass negatives from Anton Sevruguin held in the Smithsonian collections: FSA A.4 2.12.GN.11.07; FSA A.4 2.12.GN.59.02; and FSA A.4 2.12.GN.08.04.
171 V&A 619:54–1878; Danti 2004, color plate E; Koval' 2010, plate 32 no. 6, and plate 13 no. 2.
172 McPhillips 2012, fig. 5.2.
173 Attempting to locate the voices of laborers in historical archives is notoriously difficult: Çelik 2016, 135–173; Bohrer 2018, 139–142.
174 Respini and Raad 2015, 148–159.

Chapter 4. The New Babylon: Dealing in an American Century

1 Sarre 1923a, 35; Volait 2021.
2 Sarre 1923, 80.
3 Vignier 1928, 83, n. 1.
4 Stephen Vernoit notes that "for some categories of items, pre-First World War prices were not reached

again until the 1960s": Vernoit 2000, 32. On the constrictions on German museum budgets, especially after WWII, Erduman-Çalış 2020, 12–13.

5 Erduman-Çalış 2020, 12–13.

6 Simpson 2000; Jenkins-Madina 2000; Hallett and Chavak 2019.

7 Arthur Upham Pope to Philip Adams, 12 November 1954, Calligraphic plate 1958.86, Islamic Near East Object Files, CAM.

8 For example, with an invitation to dinner at "a fine new Russian restaurant that will delight your palate": Arthur Upham Pope to Clyde Burroughs, 12 March 1922, Box BUR 22: Administrative Archives 1908–1946, Folder 23, P. Clyde H. Burroughs Records, DIA.

9 For example, Pope and Kevorkian briefed against each other over the so-called Alp Arslan silver salver (Museum of Fine Arts, Boston, 34.68). Correspondence between Ayoub Rabenou and Arthur Upham Pope, 25 December 1933 to 15 February 1934 and 19 June 1934, Box 2: General Correspondence 1930–34, Folder: Personal Corres. 1934 Rabenou, Pope Papers, NYPL.

10 Marchand 1994; Elsner 2002; Grigor 2007.

11 Olin 1996.

12 Josef Strzygowski to Adèle Weibel, 10 August 1923, Box TEX 40, Folder: Weibel Correspondence, Josef Strzygowski 1923 and 1935, DIA. This contradicts the view of Ernst Gombrich that "he [Strzygowski] was not an anti-Semite or anything" (Woodfield 2017, 2, 3). I did not see anything in the Weibel archives to indicate that Weibel shared Strzygowski's anti-Semitism.

13 Mahdavi 1976–77, 201–202, 218.

14 Reilly 1992, 1.

15 Reilly 2001, 84–85.

16 Tahvildar, *Joghrafiya-ye Esfahan* (completed 1891), translated in Floor 2009a, 163; Gatt 1885, 69–73.

17 Floor 2009, 5; Graves 2022.

18 Floor 2009, 6–10.

19 This text has been mined for information by several scholars of art history, most recently and thoroughly Marcus Milwright: Milwright 2008; 2011; 2012; 2012a; 2014; 2022.

20 On Jamal al-Din al-Qasimi, see El Shamsy 2020, 177–181.

21 Al-Qasimi, al-Qasimi, and al-ʿAzm 1960, vol. 1, 40–41, my translation from the Arabic. Alternative translations are given in Issawi 1988, 388, and Milwright 2011, 11.

22 On the shifting valence, circulation, and historicist uses of the term *athar* in late nineteenth-century Islamic literary contexts, Lee 2025.

23 Al-Qasimi, al-Qasimi, and al-ʿAzm 1960, vol. 1, 40.

24 Al-Qasimi, al-Qasimi, and al-ʿAzm 1960, vol. 1, 41; Reilly 1992, 22–23.

25 S.G.W. Benjamin, "Present Conditions of the Turquoise Mines and Pearl Fisheries of Persia, with Remarks About the Manufacture of Spurious Antiques at Isfahan and Hamadan etc.," 16 January 1884, Consul General Dispatch, U.S. Dept. of State. I thank Roxanne Goldberg for sharing this document with me.

26 Volait 2021, 54.

27 For example, Zainab Bahrani has discussed the persistent erasure of Hormuzd Rassam (1826–1910) from the record of Mesopotamian archaeology (Bahrani 2011, 135–138).

28 Veselovsky 1886.

29 Sims-Williams 2000, 116, quoting Hoernle writing in 1899.

30 Vernoit 2000, 6–7; Necipoğlu 2012, 57–60; Goldberg 2025.

31 Graves 2018a.

32 This seems to be reported speech of a presentation by Ernst Kühnel at the 1960 Congress: memo from Peter Pollack to Philip Adams, "The Meeting on the Andarz Name Session Wednesday, April 27, 1960, 10.15 am," Folder Andarz Nama: Gettens Report, Registrar Archives, CAM.

33 Wills 1891, 201.

34 Vignier 1928.

35 Bloom 1975, part 2, vol. 2, 517 (folder sheet for 1910.34); Sarre 1909.

36 Hannover 1925, 64–65.

37 Sigel and McWilliams 2013, 37.

38 Watson 2004, 523, n. 25. Teresa Fitzherbert also recalls "a great deal of patching up of pots being done" while she was researching in Iran between 1968 and 1971 (personal correspondence with the author, 4 April 2014).

39 Lapatin (2002, 170–172) cites early twentieth-century reports of a forgery "factory" near Candia (now Heraklion) to conclude that the workshop for Minoan forgeries was very close to the Minoan sites.

40 Sigel and McWilliams 2013, 49 n. 2.

41 Méchin 1867, 6–8; Foltz 2011, 74–75.

42 Katz 2016, 85; on the formation of a post-French-monopoly antiquities law, and the involvement of minister for culture and purported Hamadan landowner Yahya Qaraqozlu in an earlier version of it, see Mousavi 2005, 461–462; Majd 2003, 55–88.

43 Katz 2016, 85–86.

44 Sigel and McWilliams 2013, 37.

45 Schmidt 1936, 79–80.

46 Mickel 2021.

47 "As you know all Persian faience is very much broken. Paris is the one place where it can be properly repaired. I have there a man who is the more skilful and at the same time the cheapest working anywhere." Arthur Upham Pope to William R. Valentiner, 10 February 1932, Folder: Pope, Arthur Upham, Dealer/Donor Files, DIA Registration Dept.

48 Arthur Upham Pope to Ralph Booth, 4 June 1929, and Arthur Upham Pope to Burrows, 21 July 1931, Folder: Pope, Arthur Upham, Dealer/Donor Files, DIA Registration Dept.

49 Arthur Upham Pope to Ayoub Rabenou, 26 June 1934, Box 2: General Correspondence 1930–34, Folder: Personal Corres. 1934 Rabenou, Pope Papers, NYPL. From Pope's description, it must be Pope and Ackerman 1981, vol. 9, 574 fig. D.

50 Ayoub ran the business primarily from Paris with occasional trips to Tehran, while Khalil seems to have been based initially in Iran, before eventually establishing himself in New York. Khalil was described as a "renowned New York dealer" in the promotional material for the Christie's sale of his daughter's estate: Christie's 2021.

51 George Eumorfopoulos to Arthur Upham Pope, 18 October 1925, Box 1: General Correspondence 1926–29, Folder: Pers. Corres. 1926–7 E, Pope Papers, NYPL.

52 "Mrs Khalil Rabenou," "Louise Rabenou," and "Mrs Yris Rabenou" all have biographical entries on the British Museum collection database. The Rabenou family also gifted a tile panel from an Isfahan synagogue to the Bezalel Museum in Jerusalem in the 1950s: Katz 2016, 165.

53 Gallois 1938.

54 Hoare 2024, 69–70.

55 No. 141 of the Kelekian loan. V&A loan agreement dated 24 March 1922, Nominal File: Kelekian, Dikran, 1912–1954, V&A.

56 Ayoub Rabenou to Arthur Upham Pope, 13 September 1934, Box 2: General Correspondence 1930–34, Folder: Personal Corres. 1934 Rabenou, Pope Papers, NYPL.

57 Pope 1931, captioned "By Courtesy of Oscar Raphael, Esq."

58 Benjamin Mahboubian's sons Mehdi and Houshang Mahboubian were also Persian art dealers. On Houshang Mahboubian's conviction for attempted theft of his own antiquities and allegations of forgeries, Trillin 1987. Some of the Mahboubian family collection is now in the Reza Abbasi Museum in Tehran.

59 McWilliams 2013, 265.

60 Džaparidze 1956, plates xxxix–xlvii; Watson 2004a, 265; Wordsworth 2023. For pieces excavated at Dvin and Ani, Babajanyan 2017, 272; Lessen 1959, 254–270.

61 Arthur Upham Pope to Miss Bryant, Parish-Watson firm, 6 October 1927, Box 1a, Folder: **A. U.** Pope Dealer Corresp. N-O, Pope Papers, NYPL.

62 Arthur Upham Pope to Milson Foss Jr, 25 October 1927, Box 1a, Folder: **A. U.** Pope Dealer Corresp. N-O, Pope Papers, NYPL. See in same folder Milson Foss Jr. to Arthur Upham Pope, 21 October 1927.

63 "Audit of Account of Arthur Upham Pope," 1 March 1932, Folder: Pope, Arthur Upham, Dealer/Donor Files, DIA Registration Dept.

64 Charles Lang Freer to Charles Hecker, 17 June 1908, Folder: Charles Lang Freer Letters to Frank Hecker during foreign travels, 1904–1908, Freer Papers, NMAA.

65 Charles Lang Freer to Vincenzo Marcopoli, 8 May 1911, Box 118, Folder: Vouchers, June–July 1911, Freer Papers, NMAA; Arthur Upham Pope to Ayoub Rabenou, 31 March 1934, Box 2: General Correspondence 1930–34, Folder: Personal Corres. 1934 Rabenou, Pope Papers, NYPL.

66 "[A]ll Rhages pieces have been broken, as you know, and they generally come apart only in the old breaks": M. Parish-Watson to J. Arthur MacLean, 2 January 1935, Curatorial Files: 1935 Persian exhibition, Toledo Museum of Art. See also Hagop Kevorkian to J. Arthur MacLean, 26 December 1934, Curatorial Files: 1935 Persian exhibition, Toledo Museum of Art.

67 Arthur Upham Pope to Ralph Booth, 4 June 1929, Folder: Pope, Arthur Upham, Dealer/Donor Files, DIA Registration Dept.

68 Rudolf M. Reifstahl to William Valentiner, 12 October 1928, Box VAL 11, Folder 8, William R. Valentiner Records, DIA.

69 William Valentiner to Phyllis Ackerman, 21 October 1930, Box VAL 21, Folder 8, William R. Valentiner Records, DIA.

70 Hollis and Milleken 1944, 3.

71 The curator of Oriental art, J. Arthur MacLean, contacted Mehmet Ağa-Oğlu at the DIA for advice about putting together an exhibition on the subject, asking him whom to contact for additional loans. J. Arthur MacLean to Mehmet Ağa-Oğlu, 8 October 1934, Toledo Museum of Art Curatorial Records.

72 Arthur Upham Pope to Dikran Kelekian, 30 November 1926, Box 1a, Folder: **A. U.** Pope Dealer Corresp. K, Pope Papers, NYPL. On Pope's design for the pavilion, Wood 2000, 119–120; Lerner 2016, 173–176.

73 Arthur Upham Pope to Dikran Kelekian, 18 November 1927, Box 1a, Folder: **A. U.** Pope Dealer Corresp. K, Pope Papers, NYPL.

74 Lerner 2016, 173–174.

75 Entries for 1963, 1964, 1970, 1971 in Minassian account book: Sales 1951–1979, Box 14, A98-3, Minassian Archives, Brown University.

76 Quoted in Vernoit 2000, 11–12.

77 When M. Rabenou was mentioned in the *Mitteilungen* in 1938 in association with fake Iranian tiles on the art market in The Hague, he was pitching them as stolen from a remote mosque and wanted by the Iranian authorities. Gallois 1938.

78 Dikran Kelekian to William Valentiner, 7 March 1925, Folder: Kelekian, Dikran G, Dealer/Donor Files, DIA Registration Dept., relating to DIA nos. 25.93.A-C.

79 Kirkor Minassian to William Valentiner, 30 March 1925, Folder: Minassian, K, Dealer/Donor Files, DIA Registration Dept.

80 Hagop Kevorkian to William Valentiner, 9 April 1925, Folder: Kevorkian, H., Dealer/Donor Files, DIA Registration Dept.

81 Arthur Upham Pope to Dr. Valentiner, 9 March 1932, Folder: Pope, Arthur Upham, Dealer/Donor Files, DIA Registration Dept.

82 Arthur Upham Pope to Philip Adams, 12 November 1954, acc. no. 1958.86, Islamic Near East Object Files, CAM.

83 Hassan Khan Monif to Arthur Upham Pope, 20 August 1927, Box 1a, Folder: **A. U.** Pope Dealer Corresp. M, Pope Papers, NYPL.

84 Dikran Kelekian to J. Arthur MacLean, 12 December 1934, Curatorial Files: 1935 Persian exhibition, Toledo Museum of Art.

85 Hagop Kevorkian to J. Arthur MacLean, 26 December 1934, Curatorial Files: 1935 Persian exhibition, Toledo Museum of Art.

86 Hassan Khan Monif to Arthur Upham Pope, 20 August 1927, Box 1a, Folder: **A. U.** Pope Dealer Corresp. M, Pope Papers, NYPL.

87 Arthur Upham Pope to Clyde Burroughs, 1 March 1932, Folder: Pope, Arthur Upham, Dealer/Donor Files, DIA Registration Dept.; see also Wharton-Durgaryon 2020.

88 United States Court of Appeals, *Chester D. Tripp, Chester D. Tripp, Surviving Spouse Etc. v. Commission of Internal Revenue, 337 F.2d 432 (7th Cir. 1964)*, petition no. 14560, Petitioner's appendix, 121–122.

89 "No dealer in the world could supply the things which I got the Institute, at even twice the price." Arthur Upham Pope to Clyde Burroughs, 1 March 1932, Folder: Pope, Arthur Upham, Dealer/Donor Files, DIA Registration Dept.

90 Other dealers sometimes acted as brokers too, and there could be multiple agents involved in a sale. Throughout the 1950s–1970s, Adrienne Minassian recorded multiple transactions where she either paid commission to a broker or acted as a broker herself between one owner and the next. Sometimes the buyer was another dealer, like Fahim Kouchakji, Charles Kelekian, or Nasli Heermaneck, sometimes a final-end private collector like Sadruddin Aga Khan or Edwin Binney, and sometimes an institution. Minassian account book: Sales 1951–1979, Box 14, A98-3, Minassian Archives, Brown University.

91 Dunn-Vaturi and Rugiadi 2023, 432–433.

92 Arthur Upham Pope to Khalil Rabenou, 22 October 1934, Box 2: General Correspondence 1930–34, Folder: Personal Corres. 1934 Rabenou, Pope Papers, NYPL.

93 On the *Andarznama*, Pope 1971; Bloom 2004; Watson 2013; Graves 2018a. On the "Buyid" silks, Blair, Bloom, and Wardwell 1992; Moini and Rollman 2017. Elizabeth Ettinghausen (2005, 595–596) reports from correspondence between Richard Ettinghausen and Ernst Herzfeld in the 1940s that the Paris dealer Indjoudjian was involved in manufacturing "old" Iranian silk textiles through a factory in Lyon, and that this was corroborated by the dealer Joseph Brummer.
94 Lerner 2016, 169.
95 Arthur Upham Pope to Ayoub Rabenou, 19 June 1934, Box 2: General Correspondence 1930–34, Folder: Personal Corres. 1934 Rabenou, Pope Papers, NYPL.
96 See, for example, Force, Biro, and Brennan 2023, 1–2, on Joseph Brummer (1883–1947).
97 Hôtel Drouot 1927.
98 Brocklebank 1931, 220.
99 Mehmet Ağa-Oğlu to Paul Byk, 10 May 1930, Box *ISL 2: Curatorial Correspondence, Folder 14, Islamic/Near Eastern Records, DIA. What might well be the same doors appear in an exchange between Vignier and Arthur Upham Pope in 1927, with mention of Brummer: Arthur Upham Pope to Charles Vignier, 11 August 1927, Box 1: General Correspondence 1926–29, Pope Papers, NYPL.
100 United States Court of Appeals, *Chester D. Tripp, Chester D. Tripp, Surviving Spouse Etc. v. Commission of Internal Revenue, 337 F.2d 432 (7th Cir. 1964)*, petition no. 14560, Petitioner's appendix, 121–122; Bloom 1975, part 2 (catalogue), vol. 1, 366; Jenkins-Madina 2006, 27, n. 41.
101 Riefstahl, shortly after his arrival in the United States from Germany, offered objects for sale to the Detroit Institute of Arts: R. Meyer-Riefstahl to W. P. Stevens, 17 May 1917, Box BUR 7: Administrative Files 1908–1946, Folder BUR 7/9, Clyde H. Burroughs Records, DIA.
102 Laurvik et al. 1917.
103 R.V.D. Magoffin to William R. Valentiner, 16 June 1927, and R.V.D. Magoffin to Mrs Julius Haas, 26 April 1927, Box VAL 9, Folder 7, William R. Valentiner Records, DIA.
104 Attachment to R.V.D. Magoffin to Mrs Julius Haas, 26 April 1927, Box VAL 9, Folder 7, William R. Valentiner Records, DIA.
105 Royall Tyler to Mildred Barnes Bliss, 7 March 1931, Dumbarton Oaks archive online, https://www.doaks.org/resources/bliss-tyler-correspondence/letters/07mar1931-1, accessed 2 April 2023.
106 Undated letter from Phyllis Ackerman to William R. Valentiner, Box VAL 17, Folder 3, William R. Valentiner Records, DIA.
107 Compare for example the pieces in Kelekian 1910 with the very extensively reconstructed and overpainted pieces in Riefstahl 1922.
108 Kelekian 1910.
109 Minute sheet signed C. H. Wylde, 17 November 1909, Nominal File: Kelekian, Dikran, 1892–1912, V&A.
110 Dikran Kelekian to the Director of the V&A, 30 August 1909, Nominal File: Kelekian, Dikran, 1892–1912, V&A.
111 Minute sheet dated 18 September 1909, Nominal File: Kelekian, Dikran, 1892–1912, V&A.
112 Gennari-Santori 2015, 404.
113 Minute sheets signed B. Rackham, 21 September 1909, Nominal File: Kelekian, Dikran, 1892–1912, V&A.
114 Minute sheets signed C. H. Wylde, 27 June 1910, Nominal File: Kelekian, Dikran, 1892–1912, V&A.
115 Dikran Kelekian to Cecil Smith, 23 October 1919, Nominal File: Kelekian, Dikran, 1912–1954, V&A.
116 The last additions to the Kelekian group included ten pieces that had been recently published in Pézard 1920, and a further batch of mostly Egyptian wares bought at the Fouquet sale in Cairo in 1922.
117 Loan agreements dated 24 March 1922, 10 July 1922, 12 October 1922, and March 1926, Nominal File: Kelekian, Dikran, 1912–1954, V&A.
118 Philip Adams to Dikran Kelekian, 24 May 1948, and Philip Adams to Dikran Kelekian, 11 June 1948, Folder: Kelekian, Charles D. and Dikran G, Dealer/Donor Files, CAM.
119 Berger 1951.
120 Telegram from Dikran Kelekian to Philip Adams, 19 January 1951, letters from Dikran Kelekian to Philip Adams, 14, 22, 26, and 29 January 1951, Folder: Kelekian, Charles D. and Dikran G, Dealer/Donor Files, CAM.
121 Philip Adams to Charles Kelekian, 29 March 1951, Folder: Kelekian, Charles D. and Dikran G, Dealer/Donor Files, CAM.
122 Anonymous 1951.
123 Anonymous 1951; Coudert Brothers to Leyt Ashton, 1 March 1951, and memo from Arthur Lane, 22 March 1952, both Nominal File: Kelekian, Dikran, 1912–1954, V&A.
124 Goldberg 2025, 211–212; Wharton-Durgaryan 2020.
125 Minute sheet dated 7 November 1951; Beatrice Kelekian to Leigh Ashton, 2 October 1951; minute sheets dated 8 and 22 October 1951; memo from Arthur Lane, 22 March 1952, all Nominal File: Kelekian, Dikran, 1912–1954, V&A.
126 Extract from codicil dated 14 December 1950, Nominal File: Kelekian, Dikran, 1912–1954, V&A; *In re the Estate of Kelekian, 1 Misc. 2d 886 (1952)*, 17 June 1952, New York Surrogate's Court, 1 Misc. 2d 886.
127 *In re the Estate of Kelekian, 1 Misc. 2d 886 (1952)*, 17 June 1952, New York Surrogate's Court, 1 Misc. 2d 886; *In re the Estate of Kelekian, 281 A.D. 877 (1953)*, 24 March 1953, New York Supreme Court, Appellate Division, 877–878.
128 Beatrice Kelekian to Leigh Ashton, 15 September 1951; Beatrice Kelekian to Leigh Ashton, 2 October 1951, Nominal File: Kelekian, Dikran, 1912–1954, V&A.
129 Beatrice Kelekian to Leigh Ashton, 15 September 1951, Nominal File: Kelekian, Dikran, 1912–1954, V&A.
130 Denton, Hall, and Burgin to the Director of the V&A, 7 April 1952, Nominal File: Kelekian, Dikran, 1912–1954, V&A.
131 The subject of UK death duties was raised explicitly by Charles Kelekian, when he was not yet working with the executors, in a meeting with Leigh Ashton. Memo, 24 August 1951, Nominal File: Kelekian, Dikran, 1912–1954, V&A.
132 Denton, Hall, and Burgin to the Director of the V&A, 7 April 1952, Nominal File: Kelekian, Dikran, 1912–1954, V&A.
133 Leigh Ashton to Denton, Hall, and Burgin, 23 January 1952; Denton, Hall, and Burgin to Leigh Ashton, 25 January 1952, Nominal File: Kelekian, Dikran, 1912–1954, V&A.
134 Memo by Arthur Lane, 8 May 1952, and letter from Leigh Ashton to Denton, Hall, and Burgin, 9 May 1952, Nominal File: Kelekian, Dikran, 1912–1954, V&A.
135 Two pages of untitled and undated notes (May 1952) in Philip Adams's handwriting, Folder: Kelekian, Charles D. and Dikran G, Dealer/Donor Files, CAM.
136 Charles Kelekian to Philip Adams, 22 May 1952,

referring to a formal offer letter sent by Adams to Charles Kelekian on 19 May, Folder: Kelekian, Charles D. and Dikran G, Dealer/Donor Files, CAM.

137 Adding in the Cincinnati side of the story nuances some aspects of the affair as presented in Wharton-Durgaryon 2020, 270.

138 On this piece and related "lajvardina ware" and "Sultanabad ware," Graves 2023.

Chapter 5. The Riddle of Raqqa

1 Jenkins-Madina 2006, 17–18.

2 Theodore Bowie to Ernst Grube, 15 March 1969, "Islamic Art Across the World" Folder 6, Exhibition Records, EMA.

3 Theodore Bowie to Henry Hope, 6 March 1958, Box C349, Folder: Museum Correspondence 1958–68, Henry Hope Papers, IU Archives.

4 He did, however, make a nineteen-minute film of the story of Bahram Gur, using footage of Persianate manuscript paintings in the Metropolitan Museum and New York Public Library: Bowie 1961.

5 Photocopy of unsigned and undated published article, "Islamic Art Across the World" Folder 3, Exhibition Records, EMA; Troelenberg 2012.

6 [Ernst Grube], typewritten manuscript, 22 pp., "Islamic Art Across the World" Folder 8, Exhibition Records, EMA.

7 Grube 1970.

8 Theodore Bowie, typewritten manuscript (history of Bowie's exhibitions), Theodore Bowie Papers, Collection C697, IU Archives.

9 Mango 1986, 23, 28–29. Mango lists Fahim as Habib's son, following de Jerphanion 1926, 18. However, genealogy and family history sites have him as the eldest son of Georges: "Mesjida Kouchakji," *Geneanet.org*, https://gw.geneanet.org, accessed 13 October 2020; http://kouchakji.blogspot.com, accessed 13 October 2020.

10 Anonymous 1908.

11 Anonymous 1910a.

12 MMA 48.113.16, former Havemeyer collection; see Jenkins-Madina 2006, 136.

13 Anonymous 1914a.

14 Anderson Galleries 1927; American Art Association 1928; Frick Collection n.d.

15 Passenger List, United States Lines, SS *Leviathan*, from Southampton and Cherbourg to New York, Tuesday, 1 November 1927. In Kouchakji's 1964 appearance as a court witness in a tax case relating to the valuation of antiquities, he claimed the deceased Kelekian as "a very dear friend of mine" who had at one time bought an intaglio stone from an antique ring from Kouchakji's father. United States Court of Appeals, *Chester D. Tripp, Chester D. Tripp, Surviving Spouse Etc. v. Commission of Internal Revenue, 337 F.2d 432 (7th Cir. 1964)*, petition no. 14560, Petitioner's appendix, pp. 132–133.

16 Anonymous [Ernst Grube] typewritten manuscript, 22 pp., at 10, "Islamic Art Across the World" Folder 8, Exhibition Records, EMA.

17 Fahim Kouchakji to Theodore Bowie, "Islamic Art Across the World" Folder 3, Exhibition Records, EMA. José Pijoán (1881–1963) was a Catalan art historian. Pijoán 1946, vol. 6, 413–419.

18 Bowie 1970a. Several items in Bowie's papers, including a typewritten annotated list of US collectors of erotic art and potential funders for the Kinsey Institute, attest to his interest in this area. Most remarkable is a proposal for publication of a book of updated Bible stories with nude and pornographic images. I thank Elizabeth Tuggle for bringing this last item to my attention. Theodore Bowie Papers, Collection C697, IU Archives.

19 EMA 72.6.16 and 72.6.17. For the examples collected by Freer, NMAA F1911.612; F.1911.613, F1911.614. Grube 1966, figs. 24a and 24b.

20 Theodore Bowie to Fahim Kouchakji, 27 February 1970, "Islamic Art Across the World" Folder 3, Exhibition Records, EMA.

21 The vessels are now EMA 72.6.5; 72.6.6; 72.6.7; 72.6.13.

22 MMA 1956.185.15, Havemeyer bequest; Bowie 1970, cat. no. 162, listed as "Ernst J. Grube Collection." This must be identical with "1 Rhages 13th C. horse and rider pottery," sold to Ernst Grube by Adrienne Minassian on 25 June 1964. Box 14, A98-3, Minassian account book: Sales 1951–1979, Minassian Archives, Brown University.

23 Signed shipping receipts dated 12 November 1970, "Islamic Art Across the World" Folder 4, Exhibition Records, EMA.

24 Theodore Bowie to Fahim Kouchakji, 3 March 1970, Dealer/Donor File for Fahim Kouchakji, EMA.

25 The "Parthian" vase is EMA 71.102. It has a notable publication history under the auspices of Pope and Ackerman: Pope and Ackerman 1981, vol. 4, plate 182 B; Ackerman 1940, 354–355, no. 57C; Pope 1945, 54, plate 34. In all three it is captioned as property of Fahim Kouchakji. In Lane 1947, plate 1, it is labeled "Owner unknown." After it was purchased by Indiana University in 1971, it was published in Indiana University Art Museum 1980, 70. A very similar vase was offered for sale by Kouchakji Frères in 1918: American Art Galleries 1918a, lot no. 315, "The Eros Vase."

26 EMA 72.6.1.

27 Memo from Thomas T. Solley to Herman B. Wells, 15 February 1972, Dealer/Donor File for Fahim Kouchakji, EMA.

28 Moore and Wohl, Attorneys, to Tom Solley, 10 September 1976, Dealer/Donor File for Fahim Kouchakji, EMA.

29 Solley seems to have been quite rigorous about such matters: Tom Solley to Peter Marks, 21 August 1972, Dealer/Donor file for Peter Marks, EMA.

30 Fahim Kouchakji to Tom Solley, 9 May 1975, Dealer/Donor File for Fahim Kouchakji, EMA.

31 Peggy Kouchakji to Tom Solley, 10 December 1975, Dealer/Donor File for Fahim Kouchakji, EMA.

32 Tom Solley to Allen Toby, 12 May 1976, Dealer/Donor File for Fahim Kouchakji, EMA.

33 Moore and Wohl, Attorneys, to Tom Solley, 10 September 1976, Dealer/Donor File for Fahim Kouchakji, EMA.

34 Tom Solley to Peggy Kouchakji, 9 December 1977, with handwritten note "Letter went without my making a xerox, so here is rough draft for file. CC," Dealer/Donor File for Fahim Kouchakji, EMA.

35 Gangoly 1925, 80.

36 Tonghini and Henderson 1998; Henderson 1999; Henderson et al. 2005; Milwright 2005; Heidemann 2006; François and Shaddoud 2013. A waster fragment of black-under-turquoise ware was excavated at Balis in 2002, indicating production there of at least one type of ceramic conventionally attributed to Raqqa (unpublished record from the Princeton excavations, personal communication, Stephennie Mulder). On this last type, category 46 in Rousset 1996.

37 Tonghini 1994, 255 and n. 42; Tonghini 1997; Tonghini 1998, 50; Redford and Blackman 1997; Mason 1997,

169–200; Daiber 2006, 120; McPhillips 2001–2; McPhillips 2012.

38 Sauvaget 1948, 42; Porter 1981, 10, 37–38; Daiber 2006; Jenkins-Madina 2006, 179–187, although see also Milwright 2006.

39 Thiriot and Bernus-Taylor forthcoming; Mulder forthcoming.

40 Migeon 1901, 196–197.

41 Invoice dated 16 August 1902, Vouchers: Art, November 1903, Freer Papers, NMAA.

42 Jenkins-Madina 2006; Yoltar-Yıldırım 2013; Tütüncü Çağlar 2017.

43 Daiber 2006, 119. Alkaline glazes often degrade more during burial than lead glazes, based on comparisons of sherds from the same era excavated at the same site: Molera et al. 2020.

44 Vouchers: Art purchases made during foreign travels, summer 1908, Freer Papers, NMAA.

45 Charles Lang Freer to Stephen J. Warring, 24 April 1908, Correspondence: Warring, Joseph Stephens, 1902–1919, Freer Papers, NMAA.

46 I thank Malcolm Mobutu Smith for his insights on the EMA Raqqa wares when we examined them together, and for explaining to me the likely method of making for this piece.

47 Smith 2006. Note that this study mixes together a small number of archaeologically recovered objects with a much larger number of pieces that surfaced through the antiquities market without provenience information; its conclusions, especially regarding site groupings, must be treated with caution.

48 Pradell et al. 2013, 110. The pieces in this study all surfaced through the antiquities market without provenience information.

49 Maurice Dimand noted the same phenomenon on so-called Rusapha ware bowls from Syria (for example, MMA 41.165.2): Dimand 1931a, no. 172; see also American Art Association 1938, 128, no. 492.

50 Acquired by the Hetjens Museum, Düsseldorf, from private ownership in the 1950s (information supplied by Janine Ruffing, November 2024). See also Sauvaget 1948, 41–42; Jenkins-Madina 2006, 45.

51 Pradell et al. 2016. This study does not state the provenience or provenance of the fragment it analyzes.

52 Fusaro and Allegranzi 2023.

53 Email correspondence from Tim Kirk, 17 December 2014; communication in person with Annick des Roches, 23 March 2016.

54 Kelekian 1910, nos. 21 and 36.

55 I thank Marilyn Jenkins-Madina, who was the first to publish this image, for identifying the EMA jar within it when I contacted her about the spurious Met "accession number" on its foot. Personal correspondence, April 2014. The photograph is held in the Gertrude Bell Archive of Newcastle University and Jenkins-Madina has shown that it, along with a group of other photographs showing Syrian ceramics, must have been given to Bell in Aleppo in 1909; prints of some of the same photographs were sent by Marcopoli to Freer in 1909–11. Jenkins-Madina 2006, 32.

56 This last bit of dealer lore is made stranger by the fact that the two vessels with the supposed Havemeyer pedigree have what appear to be spurious MMA accession numbers on their feet.

57 Jenkins-Madina 2006, 15–16.

58 Prior to TL testing, the collection was surveyed by objects conservator Jennifer Dennis, LLC, who prepared condition reports for each piece. For TL testing, sampling was done in Bloomington by Helen Mason of Oxford Authentication on 27 May 2016. The analysis was performed by Oxford Authentication at their laboratory in the UK; certified results of the analysis for all samples were formally delivered to the EMA in late 2016.

59 One piece in the EMA collection (60.51), a stonepaste multinozzle vase attributed to medieval Iran, could not be dated through TL analysis. The likely cause given by Oxford Authentication was that the relevant minerals were in too low a concentration in the paste, which could lead to random signals unrelated to age or accumulated radiation because of decomposition in the sample. Email correspondence with Doreen Stoneham and Helen Mason, 16 November 2016.

60 Stoneham and Stoneham 2010; Aitken 1991.

61 A Raqqa ware dish in the Koninklijke Musea voor Kunst en Geschiedenis in Brussels returned a date of last firing of 1136 CE plus or minus 124 years: Raemdonck 1999.

62 Inconclusive examples of suggested inconsistencies in TL testing are given in Watson 2004a, 330, and Aidona et al. 2016. Rehydroxylation (RHX) may offer new possibilities for ceramics dating in the future: Galli, Sibilia, and Martini 2020, 2.

63 CT scanning of the EMA wares was performed by IU Health technicians in the radiology department of Bloomington Hospital on 5 and 12 August 2016. The X-rays used in CT scanning add to the radiation dose of the ceramic body and might affect subsequent TL testing, so CT scanning was scheduled only after we had decided that we were not going to attempt a second round of TL testing. Cf. Rasmussen 2008, 21.

64 Analysis was undertaken using portable X-ray florescence (pXRF); inductively coupled plasma mass spectrometry (ICP-MS); molybdenum blue photometry; and atomic absorption spectrometry. Graves et al. forthcoming.

65 Daiber 2006, 119; Franchi et al. 1995; Pradell et al. 2013, 111.

66 The exception is Franchi et al. 1995, drawn entirely from sherds securely excavated at Qal'at Ja'bar. For other studies, see Mason 1997; Mason 2004, 91–121; Smith 2006; Pradell et al. 2008a (two sherds, one of which is from a group reportedly from Ma'arat al-Nu'man, although in chapter 2 see the discussion of this site as a point of entry to the antiquities market; the other is reported to be from Abu Sudairah, i.e., the ancient site of Kish, in Iraq, but the authors do not state the source of this information); Tite, Wolf, and Mason 2011 (one sample from a "Tell Minis" ware, but it is not clear if this piece has a secure provenience or was acquired commercially); Pradell et al. 2013 (three samples of "Tell Minis" ware, three samples of "Raqqa" ware, and two of "Damascus" ware, all from sherds in the Ashmolean Museum that appear to have been acquired commercially by twentieth-century collectors).

67 Personal communication, Abbas Akbari, 3 June 2024; Roberts, Uren, and Murray 1993, 1.

68 al-Qasimi, al-Qasimi, and al-'Azm 1960, vol. 1, 40; Milwright 2011; Milwright 2012a, 18.

69 This is the case for a number of extant wares associated with Raqqa: Jenkins-Madina 2006, 3–5.

70 Riefstahl [1926], no. 3. See also the texts for nos. 1, 2, and 4 in the same publication, and Riefstahl 1922, 83, no. 7 (now Yale University Art Gallery 1958.63.5).

71 Tonghini 1998, 46. Nothing of the kind is visible or mentioned in Grabar et al. 1978, vol. 1, 116–117.

72 Tütüncü Çağlar 2017, 239–240, cobalt-and-luster bowl sent to Istanbul from Raqqa in March 1906. Tütüncü Çağlar says of this piece that the "base has been lightly glazed with a glaze type that has higher content of lead as it is much thinner." It is possible that the "double glazing" is also present on a black-under-turquoise jar of Raqqa-type fabric excavated at Baalbek, but it is hard to tell from the published image (Daiber 2006, plate 15 fig. c.).

73 CAM 1948.118 and 1948.121 (both acquired Kelekian; former is no. 2 in Riefstahl [1926]; Yale University Art Gallery 1958.63.11 (former Parish-Watson); NMAA F1942.5 (acquired 1942, no provenance in online database but is no. 3 in Riefstahl [1926]); Walters Art Museum 48.1044 (acquired 1931, source unknown).

74 NMAA F1908.146; F1908.149.

75 This might also be true of a piece formerly in the Maan Madina collection, now in the Los Angeles County Museum of Art, no. M.2002.1.196. It appears from the online database photo to have a similarly taut design executed entirely in outlining, with cursive inscriptions inside reserve bubbles. This type of inscription appears more often on the pristine and intact Raqqa vessels than it does on fragmentary wares or sherds—although it does occasionally appear on the latter. For a very fragmentary museum object where this type of cursive script in reserve bubbles appears, NMAA F1910.28a-b. For archaeological sherds of this type, Riis and Poulsen 1957, 183, no. 596 (Poulsen's "faïence dite Raqqa," i.e., Tonghini's "fritware 2"), and 201, no. 676 (inscription more neatly written than on any of the museum objects I have seen; paste is Poulsen's "faïence syrienne"); Daiber 2006, plate 13 fig. e. No sherds with this type of inscription are illustrated or discussed in Grabar et al. 1978, vol. 2, 186–195, or Tonghini 1998. It is not seen on any of the pieces recovered in the Ottoman excavations at Raqqa: Tütüncü Çağlar 2017.

76 Mota 1988, 66.

77 Sarre 1909: "Intact vessels are extremely rare; the fragments and the spoilt vessels from the potteries are often most skillfully completed in Aleppo, whence they reach the European and American art markets."

78 Vignier 1928, 84–85; Koob 1998, 53.

79 American Art Galleries 1918a, no. 314. The doctoring in this image rather clumsily tries to eliminate light reflections on the jar: compare Anderson Galleries 1927, no. 293.

80 Riis and Poulsen 1957, 153, no. 479 (Poulsen classed the bowl's paste as "faïence syrienne ancienne," i.e., Tonghini's "fritware 1," sometimes identified with Tell Minis ware).

81 American Art Galleries 1911, no. 148. See also Kelekian 1910, p. 1 of preface; Kouchakji 1923, 515.

82 Jenkins-Madina 2006, 11–12; Hôtel Drouot 1888, lot 55; Roxburgh 2000, 12–14; Labrusse 2011, 139–150.

83 Jenkins-Madina 2006, 11–12 and 116. The bequest from Moore also included two heavily iridized turquoise jars that are now classed as Raqqa-type wares, 91.1.133 and 91.1.132.

84 British Museum G.268.

85 For example, copy of portfolio received from Fahim Kouchakji in 1970 with photographs and typewritten descriptions of objects, Dealer/Donor File for Fahim Kouchakji, EMA.

86 Wallis 1891, plate XXIII and 30.

87 Wallis 1891, 30.

88 Johnston 1999, 144. See the first records in the V&A nominal file Kelekian, Dikran, 1892–1912.

89 Princeton University Art Museum y141, gift of Mary Hollister Prime and William Cowper Prime.

90 Yoltar-Yıldırım 2013, 76; Yoltar-Yıldırım 2006, 195.

91 Yoltar-Yıldırım 2013, 76.

92 Tütüncü Çağlar 2017.

93 Yoltar-Yıldırım 2013; Tütüncü Çağlar 2017, 106–133.

94 Jenkins-Madina 2006, 27.

95 Jenkins-Madina (2006, 22) has already noted that in 1902 the British Museum acquired nine pieces of medieval glazed ceramic, some of them kiln wasters and one of them of "incomplete Raqqa cobalt-and-luster" type, from the London dealer J. J. Naaman. These were said to have come from a factory in Aleppo. Not all of these appear to be wasters, however: for example, 1902,0519.6. See Milwright 2006.

96 Invoices dated 19 November 1902 (Kelekian), and onward, Vouchers: Art, November 1903; Art, June 1904–December 1905, Freer Papers, NMAA.

97 13 September 1904: "Rakka or Persian pieces are getting very scarce. I have bought or received few pieces which I shipped to New York also my brother who made a trip in the interior sent a shipment." 17 February 1905: "These pieces are getting very rare and I not know [*sic*] what shall we do, as there are few pieces in the hand of this Syrians [*sic*] and they want ridiculous prices. We have to make arrangement with M. Bing to get them." Both Dikran Kelekian to Charles Lang Freer. Vouchers: Art, September 1904, and Correspondence: Kelekian, Dikran G., 31 January 1903–7 January 1910, Freer Papers, NMAA.

98 Yoltar-Yıldırım 2013, 76.

99 Yoltar-Yıldırım 2013, 75–76, 82–86; Hamed-Troyansky 2024, 122, notes that the Raqqa refugees were a mix of Circassian, Chechen, and Ossetian families.

100 Vouchers: Art purchases made during foreign travels, summer 1908, Freer Papers, NMAA. The piece bought from Hatoun was never accessioned into Freer's collection, after a disagreement about who was to pay the duty charged for it at New York.

101 Vouchers: Art, September–October 1908; December 1908; List w description of purchases, 1908, Freer Papers, NMAA.

102 Charles Lang Freer to Mr Kennedy, 19 June 1908, Letters to Frank Hecker during foreign travels, 1904–1908, Freer Papers, NMAA.

103 Vouchers: Art purchases made during foreign travels, summer 1908, Freer Papers, NMAA. In a letter to Hecker, Freer speaks freely of antique sculptures he tried to smuggle out of the country that were seized by the authorities at Haifa, including some that he suspected to be forgeries. Charles Lang Freer to Frank Hecker, 27 June 1908, Letters to Frank Hecker during foreign travels, 1904–1908, Freer Papers, NMAA.

104 Vouchers: Art, December 1908—June–July 1911, Freer Papers, NMAA. Jenkins-Madina 2006, 26–28. In a letter to Freer dated 23 September 1910, Marcopoli mentions that he has recently sold three pieces of Raqqa ware to Kouchakji Frères (Vouchers: Art, June–July 1911, Freer Papers, NMAA).

105 Syria diary 1908, transcribed by David Hogge, Freer Papers, NMAA.

106 Mango 1986, 33–34.

107 Mota 1988, 64–67; Hallett 2019, 77–78 and 134–135.

108 Of the pieces Freer bought from Marcopoli, only the

following could make a claim to the kind of condition that came to be attributed to the Great Find: 1908.136 (black-under-turquoise jar); 1908.137 (epigraphic jar); 1908.138 (globular bowl); 1908.140 (handled pitcher); 1908.148 (basin). Of these, three are in exceptional condition (1908.136, 1908.140, and 1908.148) and were all attributed to the "Great Find" by Fahim Kouchakji at a much later date (Bloom 1975, part 2, vol. 1, 366).

109 Martin and Sarre 1912, vol. 2, Tafel 94, Kat nr. 1084 (now MMA 48.113.5); Rivière and Migeon 1913, vol. 1, plates 11 and 12 (now MMA 56.185.6) and fig. 3 (the Raqqa cobalt-and-luster basin they sold to Gulbenkian in 1908); Nöldeke-Hannover 1910–11, plate 10 no. 10.

110 In addition to accepting a shipment of Raqqa ware from Marcopoli in Aleppo, he also bought one piece from the Kouchakji Frères in New York in March 1909; two from the Bauer-Folsom Company, New York; four from N. Ohan, Jerusalem; one from Dikran Kelekian in Paris; and so forth. Vouchers: Art, 1909, Freer Papers, NMAA.

111 Wilpert 2021.

112 Royall Tyler (1910, 640), for instance, wrote in 1910 that "Nothing of importance has been found at Rakka for several years."

113 Anonymous 1908a, 209; Anonymous 1910b; Pier 1908, pl. 1; Barber 1909, 14; Anonymous 1909, 73, referring to two pieces bought using the Otis Norcross fund: 09.1 and 09.2.

114 Jenkins-Madina 2006, 17–19. See also French national museums acquisitions from dealer name "Kouchakji," 31 December 1911 to 22 March 1913, held in the Archives nationales: https://www.siv.archives-nationales.culture.gouv.fr/siv/rechercheconsultation/consultation/ir/consultationIR.action?irId=FRAN_IR_000242&udId=d_11&details=true&gotoArchivesNums=false&auSeinIR=true, accessed 9 June 2024.

115 Kouchakji Frères 1916; American Art Galleries 1918a; American Art Galleries 1917.

116 Powell 1917, 205–206.

117 Gust 2014, 332–337, 424, 509. Deir ez-Zor was the supposed site of origin of some Syrian ceramics purchased by Freer in 1908. Correspondence: Khayat, Azeez, 10 December 1908, Freer Papers, NMAA.

118 Gust 2014, 606.

119 Jenkins-Madina 2006, 27.

120 Yoltar-Yıldırım 2006; Yoltar-Yıldırım 2013.

121 Bell 1911, 59–60.

122 Gertrude Bell, diary entry dated 28 February 1909, Gertrude Bell Archive, Newcastle University, http://gertrudebell.ncl.ac.uk/diary_details.php?diary_id=690, accessed 8 October 2020; Gertrude Bell to her stepmother, 27 February 1909, Gertrude Bell Archive, Newcastle University, http://gertrudebell.ncl.ac.uk/letter_details.php?letter_id=1661, accessed 8 October 2020. See also Burgoyne 1958, 267.

123 Vouchers: Art, June–July 1911, Freer Papers, NMAA.

124 Sarre and Herzfeld 1920, 21. Jenkins-Madina states that this passage appeared in volume 3 of *Archäologische Reise*, which was published in 1911, but it is in fact in volume 4, published in 1920.

125 Weinberg 1976.

126 Carroll 1917.

127 Kouchakji 1923, 515 and 524.

128 Kouchakji 1923, 522.

129 Carroll 1925.

130 Riefstahl [1926]. The publication date can be worked out from circumstantial evidence: Sarre 1925 is described in the text as "just now published," and Garner's cut-and-paste piece came out in 1927, so Riefstahl's book must have been produced ca. 1926.

131 Ağa-Oğlu 1930, nos. 73–77. All seven pieces in the Riefstahl publication were loaned by Jackson Higgs to the 1937 exhibition of Islamic art at the De Young Memorial Museum in San Francisco, also organized by Ağa-Oğlu: Ağa-Oğlu 1937, nos. 104–110.

132 Garner 1927. Garner wrote across a range of topics for the magazine in the 1920s, suggesting he was a staff writer rather than a specialist scholar.

133 P. Jackson Higgs to Mehmet Ağa-Oğlu, 5 November 1930, Box *ISL 1: Curatorial Correspondence, Folder 30: Higgs, J. 1929–1933, Islamic/Near Eastern Records, DIA.

134 For the Doucet collection, he was presumably referring to the dish illustrated in Doucet 1930, plate 27.

135 Vignier 1928, 82, n.

136 The note states that these pieces "owe their good condition to the fact that they were packed inside a large jar at Raqqa, and were brought from there to the Aleppo market." These included three of the five intact pieces acquired from Marcopoli in 1908: 08.136 (turquoise jar), 08.140 (pitcher), and 08.148 (basin). Bloom 1975, part 2, vol. 1, 366, citing "folder sheet."

137 These seem to be copies of Kouchakji's notes sent with the photographs to the museum in 1970. Fahim Kouchakji to Ted Bowie, 28 January 1970, "Islamic Art Across the World" Folder 3, Exhibition Records, EMA.

138 Undated notes in Dealer/Donor File for Fahim Kouchakji, EMA.

139 The pieces originally attributed in this document to the find are the other loaned Raqqa wares—the albarello (Kouchakji's no. 10, EMA 72.6.5), the jar (Kouchakji's no. 11, EMA 72.6.6), the bowl (Kouchakji's no. 12, EMA 72.6.13)—as well as an unidentified pitcher with no image (Kouchakji's no. 13A), and further pieces mentioned for which the EMA collection did not copy the records. Kouchakji's typewritten portfolio notes also report that the "find" included other pieces in the Kouchakji Raqqa ceramics collection sent to Ted Bowie, including at least three pieces now in the EMA, although this information has also been scored out with pen in every instance but one.

140 Undated notes in object file for EMA 72.6.5.

141 Milwright 2008; Milwright 2009.

142 Anderson Galleries 1927, n.p.

Epilogue. Fragile Things

1 Hicks 2020, 1–17; see also Lundén 2024.

2 Masters 2010, 293; Marteau and Vever 1913, 5–6.

3 Macfie 2003; Smith 1761; Graeber 2014, 44.

Bibliography

Aarab, Ali, Ali Shojaee-Esfahani, Siwen Xu, and Yimin Yang. 2025. "Characterizing the Earliest Black and Turquoise Wares in 12th Century Persia." *Journal of Archaeological Science: Reports* 61, 11 pp.

Abdou, Nagib. 1910. *Dr Abdou's Travels in America and Abdou's International Commercial Directory, Especially of the Arabic Speaking People of the World.* Washington, DC., n.p.

Abdulfattah, Iman R. 2020. "A Forgotten Man: Maurice Nahman, an Antiquarian-Tastemaker." In Janice Kamrin et al., eds., *Guardian of Ancient Egypt: Studies in Honor of Zahi Hawass,* vol. 1, 105–123. Prague: Charles University.

Abercromby, John. 1889. *A Trip Through the Eastern Caucasus.* London: Edward Stanford.

Achim, Miruna, and Bertina Olmeda Vera. 2021. "Forgery and the Science of the 'Authentic.'" In Miruna Achim, Susan Deans-Smith, and Sandra Rozental, eds., *Museum Matters: Making and Unmaking Mexico's National Collections,* 55–80. Tucson: University of Arizona Press.

Ackerman, Phyllis. 1940. *Guide to the Exhibition of Persian Art.* New York: Iranian Institute.

Adamova, Adel, et al. 2007. *Persia: Thirty Centuries of Art and Culture.* Aldershot: Lund Humphries.

Adjemian, Boris, and Mikaël Nichanian, eds. 2018. *The Massacres of the Hamidian Period (I): Global Narratives and Local Approaches,* special issue of *Études arméniennes contemporaines* 10.

Ağa-Oğlu, Mehmet, ed. 1930. *Catalogue of a Loan Exhibition of Mohammedan Decorative Arts.* Detroit: Detroit Institute of Arts.

Ağa-Oğlu, Mehmet, ed. 1937. *Exhibition of Islamic Art.* San Francisco: M. H. De Young Memorial Museum.

Aghaie, Ali, et al. 2023. "Radiocarbon Dating of Manuscripts Kept in the Central Library of the University of Tehran." *Radiocarbon,* 1–15.

Aidona, Elina, et al. 2016. "Testing Archaeometric and Thermoluminescence Methods in Archaeologically Dated Structures: The Study of an Early Byzantine Ceramic Workshop in Thessaloniki, Greece." In *41st International Symposium on Archaeometry—ISA2016, Kalamata,* 115–116. Athens: Hellenic Ministry of Culture and Sport.

Aitken, M. J. 1991. "Thermoluminescence Dating." In H. Y. Göksu, M. Oberhofer, and D. Regulla, eds., *Scientific Dating Methods,* 121–140. Dordrecht/Boston/London: Kluwer.

Akbari, Abbas. n.d. *Shakooreh: The Discovery and Restoration of a Kiln in Kashan* (in Persian). Kashan: Ceramic House Institute.

Akbarnia, Ladan, et al. 2018. *The Islamic World: A History in Objects.* London: Thames and Hudson/British Museum.

Alboyajian, Arshag. 1937. *Patmutyun hay Kesario* [History of Armenian Kayseri]. 2 vols. Cairo: Kesario ev Shrjakayits Hayrenaktsakan Miutiun.

Alikhanov, R., and A. A. Ivanov. 1976. *Iskusstvo Kubači/The Art of Kubachi.* Leningrad: Khudozhnik RSFSR Publishing House.

Allan, James W. 1971. *Medieval Middle Eastern Pottery.* Oxford: Ashmolean Museum.

Allan, James W. 1973. "Abu'l-Qasim's Treatise on Ceramics." *Iran* 11, 111–120.

Allan, James [W.]. 1976/77. "Silver: The Key to Bronze in Early Islamic Iran." *Kunst des Orients* 11:1/2, 5–21.

Allen, Lindsay, and Moya Carey. 2021. "*Éminences grises*: Emergent Antiquities in Seventeenth-Century Iran." In Jonathan Ben-Dov and Felipe Rojas, *Afterlives of Ancient Rock-Cut Monuments in the Near East: Carvings In and Out of Time,* 272–344. Leiden: Brill.

Amelia, Pidia, Ichwan Azhari, and Ika Purnamasari. 2023. "Artefacts Evidence of the Entry of Islam in the First History Century (7th A.D.) at the Bongal Site, Badiri District, Central Tapanuli District." In *Proceedings of the 5th International Conference on Innovation in Education, Science, and Culture.* ICIESC. 9 pp.

American Art Association. 1928. *Important Assemblage of Near Eastern and Allied Objects of Art: Egyptian Glass, Roman Sculptures, Antique Jewelry, Persian Miniature Paintings, Rhages, Rakka and Other Potteries, Sold by Order of Kouchakji Freres, Inc.* New York.

American Art Association. 1936. *The Emile Tabbagh Collection: Early Mediterranean and Near Eastern Art.* New York.

American Art Association. 1938. *The V. Everit Macy Collection: Including Rare and Important Persian and Mesopotamian Pottery, Persian and Indian Miniatures, Persian Brocades and Velvet Carpets.* New York.

American Art Galleries. 1911. *An Illustrated Catalogue of the Rare and Beautiful Ancient Faïences, Glass and Other Objects Belonging to Messieurs Tabbagh Frères of Paris and New York.* New York.

American Art Galleries. 1917. *Mr. Thomas B. Clarke's Collection: Beautiful Ancient Pottery Vases of Eastern Origin.* New York, 3–6 January 1917.

American Art Galleries. 1918. *The Important Collection of Persian Musulman Art Formed by the Connoisseur M. C. Filippo of Italy*. New York, 3–6 December 1918.

American Art Galleries. 1918a. *The Kouchakji Frères Collection of Graeco-Roman, Rakka, Persian, Hispano-Moresque Faiences, Italian Majolicas, Persian and Indian Miniatures and Rugs, Egyptian, Ptolemaic, Sidonian, Roman and Arabic Glass, Greek and Roman Bronzes.* New York, March 1918.

Amirhajloo, Saeed, Davoud Agha-Aligol, and Mohammadamin Emami. 2020. "Introducing, Classifying, and Compositional Study of the Luster Tiles from Kerman" (in Persian). *Journal of Research on Archaeometry* 6:2, 1–23.

Amirhajloo, Saeed, Mohammadamin Emami, Davoud Agha-Aligol, and Reza Riahiyan Gohorti. 2020. "Preliminary Studies on Polychrome Lustre Tiles from Qal'eh Dokhtar in Kerman by X-Ray, SEM-EDX and Micro-PIXE Spectroscopy; Insight into a New Production Centre of Lusterware in Southeast of Iran." *Journal of Archaeological Science: Reports* 33, 1–14.

Anderson, Benedict. 2015. "'An Alternative Discourse': Local Interpreters of Antiquities in the Ottoman Empire." *Journal of Field Archaeology* 40:4, 450–460.

Anderson Galleries. 1927. *Liquidation Sale: Rakka, Persian, Rhodian, Damascus, Hispano-Moresque, Faiences; Egyptian, Ptolemaic, Alexandrian, Roman, Arabic, and Syrian Glass; Persian and Indian Miniatures and Manuscripts, Greek and Roman Statuary, Gold and Silver Objects, Persian Rugs and Other Objects of Rarity, The Collection of Kouchakji Freres, Paris & New York.* New York: Anderson Galleries.

Angas, L.L.B. 1937. *Slump Ahead in Bonds: Outlook for Bonds [and Stocks] under Managed Money.* New York: Somerset Publishing.

Angelicoussis, Elizabeth. 2004. "The Collection of Classical Sculptures of the Earl of Arundel, 'Father of Vertu in England.'" *Journal of the History of Collections* 16:2, 143–159.

Angst, [Heinrich von]. 1900. "26. Ueber Fälschungen schweizerischer Alterthümer." *Mittheilungen des Museen-Verbandes als Manuskript für die Mitglieder* (January), 1–13.

Anonymous. 1844. "The Pencil of Nature." *The Spectator* 17:838 (20 July 1844), 685.

Anonymous. 1844a. "The Pencil of Nature." *The Art-Union* 69 (August 1844), 222.

Anonymous. 1845. "The Pencil of Nature, by Henry Fox Talbot, F.R.S., Parts I & II." *The Athenaeum*, 22 February 1845, 202–203.

Anonymous. 1873. "Notes on the Drawings and Copies of Inscriptions from the 'Shapira Collection' Sent Home by Lieut. Conder and Mr. Drake." *Palestine Exploration Fund Quarterly Statement* 5:2, 79–80.

Anonymous. 1874. "The Shapira Collection." *Palestine Exploration Quarterly* 6:2, 114–124.

Anonymous. 1878. "The Moabite Pottery." *Palestine Exploration Quarterly* 10:1, 41–45, and 10:2, 88–102.

Anonymous. 1889. "Persian Tiles." *The Decorator and Furnisher* 15:3, 71–72.

Anonymous. 1900. "33. Ueber Fälschungen von Majoliken" *Mittheilungen des Museen-Verbandes als Manuskript für die Mitglieder* (August), 1–4.

Anonymous. 1906. "M. Minassian, antiquaire, a de belle faïences: Il fut le Premier à les Chercher dans Leurs Pays d'Origine." *New York Herald, Paris*, 31 March 1906, 5.

Anonymous. 1908. "Exhibitions." *American Art News* 6:23, 1.

Anonymous. 1908a. "Principal Accessions." *Metropolitan Museum of Art Bulletin* 3:11, 209–211.

Anonymous. 1909. "Purchases in 1909." *Annual Report for the Year (Museum of Fine Arts, Boston)* 34, 1–115.

Anonymous. 1910. *Austellungen München 1910: Amtlicher Katalog.* Munich: Rudolf Mosse.

Anonymous. 1910a. "Exhibitions." *American Art News* 8:25, 1.

Anonymous. 1910b. "List of Loans." *Metropolitan Museum of Art Bulletin* 5:12, 294–295.

Anonymous. 1914. "417. Über Fälschungen und Verfälschungen von antiken Vasen und Terrakotten." *Mitteilungen des Museen-Verbandes als Manuskript für die Mitglieder* (July 1914), 9–11.

Anonymous. 1914a. "Among the Dealers." *American Art News* 12:32, 6.

Anonymous. 1924. "Proceedings of the Society for the Promotion of Roman Studies, Open General Meetings at Burlington House, 1924–5." *Journal of Roman Studies* 14, 281–287.

Anonymous. 1931. "The Holy Grail." *Syrian World* 5:7, 37–40.

Anonymous. 1941. "Iranian Pottery." *Museum News: The Toledo Museum of Art* 96 (December 1941), n.p.

Anonymous. 1941a. "M. Parish-Watson, Art Dealer Here." *New York Times*, 22 February 1941, 15.

Anonymous. 1951. "Bank to Administer Art Expert's Estate." *New York Times*, 3 February 1951.

Anonymous. 1976. "F. J. Kouchakji, Rare Art Dealer." *New York Times*, 21 August 1976, 24.

Anonymous. 2021. "Stolen İznik Tiles of Mosque Found in Netherlands." *Hürriyet Daily News*, 12 June 2021, https://www.hurriyetdailynews.com/stolen-iznik-tiles-of-mosque-found-in-netherlands-165457, accessed 23 March 2024.

Anonymous. n.d. "Jacques Mosseri Genizah Collection." *Cambridge University Library* [online], accessed 6 January 2023.

Anonymous. n.d.-a. "Persia (1889–1912): The Collections." https://archeologie.culture.gouv.fr/jacques-morgan/en/collections, accessed 12 April 2024.

Anonymous. n.d.-b. "The Story Behind the Sarikhani Collection." https://www.artfund.org, accessed 9 May 2023.

Arnason, H. Harvard. 1941/1942. "The History of the Chalice of Antioch." *The Biblical Archaeologist* 4:4, 49–64, and 5:1, 10–16.

Aslanian, Sebouh David. 2011. *From the Indian Ocean to the Mediterranean: The Global Trade Networks of Armenian Merchants from New Julfa.* Berkeley: University of California Press.

Astvatsaturian, E. G. 1979. "Daghestani Masters of Silversmithing and Armoring in the Cities of the Northern Caucasus and Transcaucasia in the Late Nineteenth and Early Twentieth Centuries." *Soviet Anthropology and Archaeology* 18:2, 84–104.

Atasoy, Nurhan. 1989. "The Survival of Iznik Pottery in Turkey." In Nurhan Atasoy and Julian Raby, *Iznik: The Pottery of Ottoman Turkey*, 14–18. London: Thames and Hudson.

Atasoy, Nurhan, and Julian Raby. 1989. *Iznik: The Pottery of Ottoman Turkey.* London: Thames and Hudson.

Atıl, Esin. 1973. *Ceramics from the World of Islam.* Washington, DC: Smithsonian Institution.

Babajanyan, Astghik. 2017. "The Glazed Pottery of Armenia in the XII–XIV Centuries in the Cultural Context of East and West." In Defne Karakaya and Timothy Glenn Little, eds., *XIth Congress AIECM3 on Medieval and Modern Period Mediterranean Ceramics Proceedings*, 271–287. Ankara: Koç University VEKAM.

Bacigalupi, Don, ed. 2009. *Toledo Museum of Art: Masterworks.* Toledo, OH: Toledo Museum of Art.

Bahrami, Abdallah. 2013. "The Story of the Theft of the Manuscript Books of the Golestan Palace Library, Based on the Memoirs of Abdallāh Bahrāmi, a Deputy of the Nazmiya at the time" (in Persian). *Baharestan* 9–10, 287–306.

Bahrami, Mehdi. 1949. *Gurgan Faiences.* Cairo: Le scribe egyptien.

Bahrani, Zainab. 2011. "Untold Tales of Mesopotamian Discovery." In Zainab Bahrani, Zeynep Çelik, and Edhem Eldem, eds., *Scramble for the Past: A Story of Archaeology in the Ottoman Empire, 1753–1914*, 125–155. Istanbul: SALT.

Bahrani, Zainab, Zeynep Çelik, and Edhem Eldem, eds. 2011. *Scramble for the Past: A Story of Archaeology in the Ottoman Empire, 1753–1914.* Istanbul: SALT.

Bahrani, Zainab, Zeynep Çelik, and Edhem Eldem. 2011a. "Introduction: Archaeology and Empire." In Zainab Bahrani, Zeynep Çelik, and Edhem Eldem, eds., *Scramble for the Past: A Story of Archaeology in the Ottoman Empire, 1753–1914*, 13–43. Istanbul: SALT.

Barakat, Heba, and Zahra Khademi. 2019. *Qajar Ceramics: Bridging Tradition and Modernity.* Kuala Lumpur: Islamic Arts Museum Malaysia.

Barber, Edwin A. 1909. "Notable Examples of Pottery Recently Acquired." *Bulletin of the Pennsylvania Museum* 7:25, 12–15.

Bartol'd, V. V. 1966. "K voprosu ob arkheologicheskikh nakhodkah [On the Question of Archaeological Finds]." In V. V. Bartol'd, *Sochineniia*, vol. 4, *Raboty po arkheologii, numizmatike, ėpigrafike i ėtnografii*, 126–129. Moscow: Nauka.

Baseman, Andrew. n.d. "Scottish China-Mender, c. 1918." *Past Imperfect: The Art of Inventive Repair*, http://blog.andrewbaseman.com/?p=1661, posted 3 June 2010.

Batchen, Geoffrey. 2002. "A Philosophical Window." *History of Photography* 26:2, 100–112.

Batres, Leopoldo. 1910. *Antigüedades mejicanas falsificadas: Falsificación y falsificadores.* Mexico City: Fidencio S. Soria.

Bayard, Émile. 1914. *L'art de reconnaître les fraudes: Peinture, sculpture, gravure, meubles, dentelles, céramique, etc.* Paris: Roger et Chernovitz.

Beard, Mary. 2009. "Knossos: Fakes, Facts, and Mystery." *New York Review of Books*, 13 August 2009.

Beauvais, Guillaume. 1741. *A Dissertation on the Manner of Distinguishing Antique Medals from Counterfeit Ones.* Trans. from French. Knapton.

Be'er, Haim. 2000. "Reflections on the Elusive Charm of the Shapira Affair." In Irit Salmon, ed., *Truly Fake: Moses Wilhelm Shapira, Master Forger*, 11–13. Jerusalem: The Israel Museum.

Bell, Gertrude. 1911. *Amurath to Amurath.* London: W. Heinemann.

Belozerskaya, Marina. 2012. *Medusa's Gaze: The Extraordinary Journey of the Tazza Farnese.* New York: Oxford University Press.

Benjamin, Samuel Greene Wheeler. 1887. *Persia and the Persians.* London: John Murray.

Berger, Meyer. 1951. "Kelekian Plunges 21 Floors to Death." *New York Times*, 31 January 1951, 23.

Bergman, Sidney M. 1974. "Azeez Khayat (1875–1943)—A Noted Collector of Ancient Glass." *Carnegie Magazine* 48:10, 238–244.

Beringer, Johan Bartholomäus Adam. 1726. *Lithographiae Wirceburgensis, Ducentis Lapidum Figuratorum.* Würzburg: Mark Anton Engmann for Philipp Wilhelm Fuggart.

Berlo, Janet Catherine. 2023. *Not Native American Art: Fakes, Replicas, and Invented Traditions.* Seattle: University of Washington Press.

Bevilacqua, Alexander. 2018. *The Republic of Arabic Letters: Islam and the European Enlightenment.* Cambridge, MA: Harvard University Press.

Blair, Sheila S. 1986. *The Ilkhanid Shrine Complex at Natanz, Iran.* Cambridge, MA: Harvard Middle East Papers.

Blair, Sheila [S.]. 2014. "Art as Text: The Luster Mihrab in the Doris Duke Foundation for Islamic Art." In Alireza Korangy and Daniel J. Sheffield, eds., *No Tapping Around Philology: A Festschrift in Honor of Wheeler McIntosh Thackston Jr.'s 70th Birthday*, 407–436. Wiesbaden: Harrassowitz Verlag.

Blair, Sheila S. 2014a. *Text and Image in Medieval Persian Art.* Edinburgh: Edinburgh University Press.

Blair, Sheila S., Jonathan M. Bloom, and Anne E. Wardwell. 1992. "Reevaluating the Date of the 'Buyid' Silks by Epigraphic and Radiocarbon Analysis." *Ars Orientalis* 22, 1–41.

Blake-Coleman, Barrie Charles. 1981. "The Rise of Copper Wire, Its Manufacture and Use to 1900: A Case of Industrial Circumspection." Unpublished MPhil thesis, Open University.

Blakesley, Charlotte. 2016. "Courtroom Pragmatics: Analysis of Questions and Answers in the Tomb Robbery Papyri." Unpublished PhD dissertation, University of Liverpool.

Bloch, Franziska, Verena Daiber, and Peter Knötzle. 2006. *Orient-Archäologie Band 18: Studien zu spätantiken und islamischen Keramik: Ḫirbat al-Minya—Baalbek—Resafa.* Rahden: Marie Leidorf.

Bloom, Jonathan M. 1975. "'Raqqa' Ceramics in the Freer Gallery of Art, Washington D.C." 3 vols. Unpublished master's thesis, University of Michigan.

Bloom, Jonathan M. 2004. "Fact and Fantasy in Buyid Art." *Oriente Moderno*, n.s., 23:84, no. 2, 387–400.

Bobin, O., M. Schvoerer, and C. Ney. 2003. "Where Did the Lustre Tiles of the Sidi Oqba Mosque (AD 836–63) in Kairouan Come From?" *Archaeometry* 45:4, 569–577.

Bohrer, Frederick N. 2018. "Review of Zeynep Çelik, *About Antiquities: Politics of Archaeology in the Ottoman Empire (2016).*" *The Art Bulletin* 100:3, 139–142.

Boldyreva, E. M. 2014. "Keramika s rospis'yu lyustrom na Samosdel'kom Gorodishche [Ceramics with Lustre Decoration at Samosdelka Settlement]." *Bulletin of Moscow University*, series 8, *History* 6, 82–91.

Boucharlat, Rémy. 2005. "Ernst Herzfeld and French Approaches to Iranian Archaeology." In Anne C. Gunter and Stefan R. Hauser, eds., *Ernst Herzfeld and the Development of Near Eastern Studies, 1900–1950*, 429–444. Leiden: Brill.

Bowie, Theodore. 1961. *Seven Wives of Bahram Gur.* Film reel, 16 mm, Indiana University Audio-Visual Center, https://media.dlib.indiana.edu/media_objects/8049g5193, accessed 25 April 2019.

Bowie, Theodore, ed. 1970. *Islamic Art Across the World.* Bloomington: Indiana University Art Museum.

Bowie, Theodore, ed. 1970a. *Studies in Erotic Art (Studies in Sex and Society).* New York: Basic Books.

Braudeau, Michel. 2006. *Faussaires éminents.* Paris: Gallimard.

Brend, Barbara. 2010. *Muhammad Juki's Shahnama of Firdausi.* London: Royal Asiatic Society.

Briefel, Aviva. 2006. *The Deceivers: Art Forgery and Identity in the Nineteenth Century.* Ithaca, NY: Cornell University Press.

[Brinckmann, Justus] J. B. 1899. "23. Die sog. >Indischen Porzellane<." *Mittheilungen des Museen-Verbandes als Manuskript für die Mitglieder* (August), 7.

[Brinckmann, Justus] J. B. 1902. "71. Ueberdecorirtes [*sic*]

Böttger-Steinzeug." *Mittheilungen des Museen-Verbandes als Manuskript für die Mitglieder* (August), 2.

[Brinckmann, Justus] J. B. 1903. "89. Überdekoriertes Böttger-Steinzeug." *Mitteilungen des Museen-Verbandes als Manuskript für die Mitglieder* (July), 12.

[Brinckmann, Justus] J. B. 1907. "192. Über neue Majolikafälschungen." *Mitteilungen des Museen-Verbandes als Manuskript für die Mitglieder* (March), 10–11.

[Brinckmann, Justus] J. B. 1907a. "186. Falschunger prähistorischer Bronzen." *Mitteilungen des Museen-Verbandes als Manuskript für die Mitglieder* (March).

[Brinckmann, Justus] J. B. 1908. "215. Ceramic Forgeries." *Mitteilungen des Museen-Verbandes als Manuskript für die Mitglieder* (May), 3–4.

[Brinckmann, Justus] J. B. 1909. "248. Verschrammung neuer Fayencen zum Zweck der Täuschung." *Mitteilungen des Museen-Verbandes als Manuskript für die Mitglieder* (August), 13–15.

[Brinckmann, Justus] J. B., and C. H. Read. 1901. "56. Fälschung persischer Lüster-Fayencen." *Mittheilungen des Museen-Verbandes als Manuskript für die Mitglieder* (August), 10.

Brocklebank, R.H.R. 1931. "Kubatcha Faience."*Burlington Magazine for Connoisseurs* 59:344, 218–221.

Brodie, Neil. 2011. "The Market in Iraqi Antiquities 1980–2009 and Academic Involvement in the Marketing Process." In Stefano Manacorda and Duncan Chappell, eds., *Crime in the Art and Antiquities World: Illegal Trafficking in Cultural Property*, 117–133. New York: Springer.

Bukina, Anastasia, Anna Petrakova, and Catherine Phillips, eds. 2013. *Greek Vases in the Imperial Hermitage Museum: The History of the Collection, 1816–69*. Oxford: Beazley Archive and Archaeopress.

Bulle, R. [Heinrich?]. 1921. "469. Übersicht über Fortschritte in der Antiken-fälschung." *Mitteilungen des Museen-Verbandes als Manuskript für die Mitglieder* (September), 1–5.

Bulliet, Richard. 1992. "Pottery Styles and Social Status in Medieval Khurasan." In Bernard Knapp, ed., *Archaeology, Annales and Ethnohistory*, 75–82. Cambridge: Cambridge University Press.

Burgoyne, Elizabeth. 1958. *Gertrude Bell, from Her Personal Papers*. Vol. 1. London: E. Benn.

Burnett, Andrew. 1992. "Coin Faking in the Renaissance." In Mark Jones, ed., *Why Fakes Matter: Essays on Problems of Authenticity*, 15–22. London: British Museum Press.

Butler, A. J. 1926. *Islamic Pottery, a Study Mainly Historical*. London: E. Benn.

Canby, Sheila. 2000. "Islamic Archaeology: By Accident or Design?" In Stephen Vernoit, ed., *Discovering Islamic Art: Scholars, Collectors and Collections, 1850–1950*, 128–137. London: I. B. Tauris.

Canby, Sheila, Deniz Beyazit, Martina Rugiadi, and A.C.S. Peacock, eds. 2016. *Court and Cosmos: The Great Age of the Seljuqs*. New York: Metropolitan Museum of Art.

Cannon, Byron D. 2001. "Mortgage Banking Strategies in Egypt, 1880–1914: Crédit Foncier Egyptien [*sic*] Investment and Local Borrowing." *Business History* 43:3, 29–47.

Capezzone, Leonardo. 2020. Introduction to Leonardo Capezzone, ed., *Before Archaeology: The Meaning of the Past in the Islamic Pre-Modern Thought (and After)*, 7–19. Rome: Artemide.

Carboni, Stefano, and Tomoko Masuya. 1993. *Persian Tiles*. New York: Metropolitan Museum of Art.

Carey, Moya. 2017. *Persian Art: Collecting the Arts of Iran for the V&A*. London: Victoria & Albert Museum.

Carney, Mark. 2023. Interviewed on *The Rest Is Politics: Leading*, 5 November 2023, https://www.youtube.com/watch?v=X1E4f9hYFlA, accessed 19 March 2024.

Carroll, Dana H. 1917. "A Foreword, Partly Personal." In American Art Galleries, *Thomas B. Clarke's Collection*, n.p.

Carroll, Dana H. 1925. "A Most Unusual Offering." In *The Private Collection of Mr Thomas B. Clarke, from His Own Residence on Murray Hill*, n.p. New York: American Art Association.

Carswell, John. 2000. "The Greeks in the East: Alexandria and Islam." In Stephen Vernoit, ed., *Discovering Islamic Art: Scholars, Collectors and Collections, 1850–1950*, 138–146. London: I. B. Tauris.

Carswell, John. 2006. *Iznik Pottery*. London: British Museum.

Carswell, John. 2011. "The Bequest of a Gentleman: Magdalen College's Collection of Kütahya Ceramics." *Cornucopia* 46.

Carswell, John, Mina Moraitou, and Melanie Gibson. 2023. *Iznik Ceramics at the Benaki Museum*. London: Gingko.

Casson, Stanley. 1937. "The Great Chalice of Antioch." Review in *Antiquity*, 124–125.

Catterson, Lynn. 2014. *Finding, Fixing, Faking, Making: Supplying Sculpture in '400 Florence*. Todi: Ediart.

Çelik, Zeynep. 1992. *Displaying the Orient: Architecture of Islam at Nineteenth-Century World's Fairs*. Berkeley: University of California Press.

Çelik, Zeynep. 2011. "Defining Empire's Patrimony: Late Ottoman Perceptions of Antiquities." In Zainab Bahrani, Zeynep Çelik, and Edhem Eldem, eds., *Scramble for the Past: A Story of Archaeology in the Ottoman Empire, 1753–1914*, 443–477. Istanbul: SALT.

Çelik, Zeynep. 2016. *About Antiquities: Politics of Archaeology in the Ottoman Empire*. Austin: University of Texas Press.

Çelik, Zeynep, and Leila Kinney. 1990. "Ethnography and Exhibitionism at the Expositions Universelles." *Assemblage* 13, 34–59.

Chaney, Edward. 1993. "Review of *The Late King's Goods: Collections, Possessions and Patronage of Charles I in the Light of the Commonwealth Sale Inventories*, ed. Arthur MacGregor." *English Historical Review* 108:428, 719–721.

Chenciner, Robert, Gabib Ismailov, and Magomedkhan Magomedkhanov. 2006. *Tattooed Mountain Women and Spoon Boxes of Daghestan*. London: Bennet and Bloom.

Chippindale, Christopher, and David W. J. Gill. 2000. "Material Consequences of Contemporary Classical Collecting." *American Journal of Archaeology* 104:3, 463–511.

Choubak, H. 2012. "Islamic Pottery of the Ancient City of Jiroft" (in Persian). *Journal of Archaeological Studies* 4:1, 83–112.

Christian, Kathleen Wren. 2010. *Empire Without End: Antiquities Collections in Renaissance Rome, c. 1350–1527*. New Haven and London: Yale University Press.

Christie's. 2006. *Art of the Islamic and Indian Worlds*. London, 10 October 2006.

Christie's. 2021. *Antiquities*. New York, 12 October 2021.

Clay, Christopher. 1994. "The Origins of Modern Banking in the Levant: The Branch Network of the Imperial Ottoman Bank, 1890–1914." *International Journal of Middle East Studies* 26:4, 589–614.

Clermont-Ganneau, Charles-Simon. 1885. *Les fraudes archéologiques en Palestine*. Paris: Ernest Leroux.

Clermont-Ganneau, Charles-Simon. 1896. "Lychnaria a inscriptions arabes." *Recueil d'archéologie orientale* 2, 19–21.

Clermont-Ganneau, Charles-Simon. 1896a. "Le lychnarion arabe de Djerach." *Recueil d'archéologie orientale* 2, 47–51.

Clermont-Ganneau, Charles-Simon. 1896b. *Archaeological Researches in Palestine During the Years 1873–1874*. Trans. from French by John Macfarlane. London: Palestine Exploration Fund.

Clermont-Ganneau, Charles-Simon. 1899. "Deux nouveaux lychnaria grec et arabe." *Recueil d'archéologie orientale* 3, 41–47.

Cohen, Julia Phillips. 2014. *Becoming Ottomans: Sephardi Jews and Imperial Citizenship in the Modern Era.* Oxford: Oxford University Press.

Colini, Claudia. 2020. "*La invención del Sacromonte*: How and Why Scholars Debated about the Lead Books of Granada for Two Hundred Years." In Cécile Michel and Michael Friedrich, eds., *Fakes and Forgeries of Written Artefacts from Ancient Mesopotamia to Modern China*, 209–262. Berlin: De Gruyter.

Collinet, Annabelle. 2022. "Une nouvelle culture materielle." In Rocco Rante and Yannick Lintz, eds., *Splendeurs des oasis d'Ouzbékistan: Sur les routes caravanières d'Asie centrale*, 189–193. Paris: Musée du Louvre.

Conway, Martin. 1924. "The Antioch Chalice." *Burlington Magazine for Connoisseurs* 45:258, 106–111.

Cooper, Lisa. 2013. "Archaeology and Acrimony: Gertrude Bell, Ernst Herzfeld and the Study of Pre-Modern Mesopotamia." *Iraq* 75, 143–169.

Cooperson, Michael. 2010. "Al-Maʾmun, the Pyramids, and the Hieroglyphs." In John Nawas ed., *ʿAbbasid Studies II: Occasional Papers of the School of ʿAbbasid Studies, Leuven, 28 June—1 July 2004*, 165–190. Leuven/Paris/Walpole, MA: Peeters.

Cooperson, Michael. 2014. "Early ʿAbbasid Antiquarianism: al-Maʾmūn and the Pyramid of Cheops." In Alain Schnapp, ed., *World Antiquarianism: Comparative Perspectives*, 201–211. Los Angeles: Getty Research Institute.

Cormack, Robin, and Maria Vassilaki, eds. 2008. *Byzantium 330–1453.* London: Royal Academy of Arts.

Cort, Louise, Massumeh Farhad, and Ann Gunter. 2000. *Asian Traditions in Clay: The Hauge Gifts.* Washington, DC: Smithsonian Institution.

Craddock, P. T. 1992. "A Short History of the Patination of Bronze." In Mark Jones, ed., *Why Fakes Matter: Essays on Problems of Authenticity*, 63–70. London: British Museum Press.

Crowe, Yolande. 2002. *Persia and China: Safavid Blue and White Ceramics in the Victoria and Albert Museum, 1501–1738.* London: Thames and Hudson.

Dági, Marianna. 2003. "'Tinkers' and 'Patchers': Some Notes on the Ancient Repairs of Greek Vases." *Bulletin du Musée Hongrois des Beaux-Arts/a Szépművészeti Múzeum Közleményei* 99, 31–66.

Daiber, Verena. 2006. "Baalbek: Die mittelalterlichen Feinwaren." In *Orient-Archäologie, Band 18: Studien zur spätantiken und islamischen Keramik, Ḫirbat al-Minya—Baalbek—Resafa*, 111–166. Rahden: Verlag Marie Leidorf.

Daily Sabah. 2019. "Medieval, Seljuk-era Ceramics Unearthed in Ancient Ghost City of Ani on Turkish-Armenian Border." *Daily Sabah*, 7 October 2019, https://www.dailysabah.com/history/2019/10/07/medieval-seljuk-era-ceramics-unearthed-in-ancient-ghost-city-of-ani-on-turkish-armenian-border, accessed 24 April 2024.

Damen, Giada. 2012. "The Trade in Antiquities Between Italy and the Eastern Mediterranean (ca. 1400–1600)." Unpublished PhD dissertation, Princeton University.

Danti, Michael D. 2004. *The Ilkhanid Heartland: Hasanlu Tepe (Iran) Period 1.* Philadelphia: University of Pennsylvania Museum of Archaeology and Anthropology.

David, Jean-Claude, and Thierry Grandin. 1994. "L'habitat permanent des grands commerçants dans les khans d'Alep à l'époque ottomane." In Daniel Panzac, ed., *Les villes dans l'empire ottoman: Activités et sociétés*, vol. 2, 85–124. Paris: CNRS.

de Batz, Georges, and Arthur Upham Pope. 1940. *Persian Art Through Four Millenia; A Check List of Objects Exhibited from January 12, 1940, to February 10, 1940.* Baltimore: Johns Hopkins University.

de Jerphanion, Guillaume. 1926. *Le calice d'Antioche: Les théories du Dr Eisen et la date probable du calice. Orientalia Christiana* 7:27.

DeLanda, Manuel. 2016. *Assemblage Theory.* Edinburgh: Edinburgh University Press.

de Lapérouse, Jean-François. n.d. "Examination and Conservation of Mina'i Ceramics." *Making the Invisible Visible: Conservation and Islamic Art*, http://www.metmuseum.org/exhibitions/listings/2013/invisible-visible, accessed 9 March 2023.

de Lapérouse, Jean-François, Karen Stamm, and Vicki Parry. 2007. "Re-examination and Treatment of Mina'i Ceramics at the Metropolitan Museum of Art." In Lisa Pilosi, ed., *Glass and Ceramics Conservation 2007: Preprints of the Interim Meeting of the ICOM-CC Working Group*, 112–119. Nova Gorica: Goriski Muzej Kromberk.

Deleuze, Gilles, and Félix Guattari. 2006. *A Thousand Plateaus: Capitalism and Schizophrenia.* Trans. Brian Massumi. London: Continuum.

Denny, Walter B. 2004. "Dispersed Ottoman Unified-Field Tile Panels." *Mouseio Benaki* 4, 149–157.

Denny, Walter B. 2006. "Dispersed Ottoman Repeating-Pattern Iznik Tiles, Part 1." In Anna Parzymies, ed., *Studies in Oriental Art and Culture in Honour of Professor Tadeusz Majda*, 165–187. Warsaw: Dialog.

Der Matossian, Bedross. 2013. "Ottoman Armenian Kesaria/Kayseri in the Nineteenth Century." In Richard G. Hovannisian, ed., *Armenian Kesaria/Kayseri and Cappodocia*, 187–230. Costa Mesa, CA: Mazda.

de Rochechouart, Julien. 1867. *Souvenirs d'un voyage en Perse.* Paris: Challamel ainé.

de Voogt, Alex, and Vincent Francigny. 2012. "Opening a Grave in Antiquity—Formation and Interpretation in the Kingdom of Meroe." *Journal of African Archaeology* 10:1, 59–70.

Diehl, Charles. 1926. "Un nouveau trésor d'argenterie syrienne." *Syria* 7, 105–122.

Dieulafoy, Jane. 1887. *La Perse, la Chaldée et la Susiane: Relation de voyage.* Paris: Hachette.

Dimand, Maurice. 1931. "A Recent Gift of Near Eastern Art." *Metropolitan Museum of Art Bulletin* 26:1, 6–12.

Dimand, Maurice. 1931a. *Loan Exhibition of Ceramic Art of the Near East.* New York: Metropolitan Museum of Art.

Directorate General of Antiquities. 1940. *Excavations at Samarra 1936–1939.* 2 vols. Baghdad: Government Press.

Diyab, Hanna. 2022. *The Book of Travels.* Trans. Elias Muhanna. New York: Library of Arabic Literature.

Dolezalek, Isabelle et al., eds. 2022. *Islamische Kunst in Museum für Kunst und Gewerbe Hamburg (1873–1915).* Heidelberg: Universität Heidelberg/arthistoricum.net.

Donabédian, Patrick, and Yves Porter. 2017. "Éghvard (Arménie, début du XIVe siècle): La chapelle de l'alliance." *Hortus Artium Mediavalium* 23:2, 837–855.

Doucet, Jacques. 1930. *Collection Jacques Doucet.* Paris: Galerie Georges Petit.

Dudley, Dennine Lynette. 2004. "Henrietta Louise Jeffreys, Oxford University and the Pomfret Benefaction of 1755: *Vertu* Made Visible." Unpublished PhD thesis, University of Victoria.

Dunn-Vaturi, Anne, and Martina Rugiadi. 2023. "The Brummer Gallery and the Making of Iranian and Islamic Arts." In Yaëlle Biro, Christine Brennan, and Christel H. Force, eds., *The Brummer Galleries, Paris and New York: Defining Taste from Antiquities to the Avant-Garde*, 411–462. Leiden: Brill.

Duturaeva, Dilnoza. 2022. *Qarakhanid Roads to China: A History of Sino-Turkic Relations*. Leiden: Brill.

D'yakonov, M. M. 1939. "Fayansovyĭ sosud s illyustratsiyami k Shakh-name/Un vase en faïence avec des illustrations de Shah-Namé." *Gosudarstvennyĭ Ermitazh Trudy Otdela Vostoka* 1, 317–326.

Džaparidze, Vachtang Varlamovič. 1956. *Keramičeskaja Promyšlennost' Gruzii XI-XIII vekov* [Ceramics Production in Georgia from the 11th–13th Centuries] (in Georgian and Russian). Tblisi: Academy of Sciences of the USSR Georgia.

Edmonds, J. M., and H. P. Powell. 1974. "Beringer 'Lügensteine' at Oxford." *Proceedings of the Geologists' Association* 85:4, 549–554.

Eisen, Gustavus A. 1916. "Introduction to a History of Antique Glass." In *Interesting Examples of Ancient Glass, Including Masterpieces of Glassmakers' Art from All the Representative Periods*. New York: Kouchakji Frères, sale dates 17 November to 23 December 1916.

Eisen, Gustavus A. 1916a. "Preliminary Report on the Great Chalice of Antioch Containing the Earliest Portraits of Christ and the Apostles." *American Journal of Archaeology* 20:4, 426–437.

Eisen, Gustavus A. 1917. "The plate with Seven Loaves and Two Fishes on the Great Chalice of Antioch." *American Journal of Archaeology* 21:1, 77–79.

Eisen, Gustavus A. 1917a. "The Date of the Great Chalice of Antioch." *American Journal of Archaeology* 21:2, 169–186.

Eisen, Gustavus A. 1918. Introduction to *The Kouchakji Frères Collection: Rare Ancient Faiences and Antique Glass and Bronzes, Beautiful Persian Miniatures and Rugs, at the American Art Galleries*. New York: American Art Galleries, sale dates 8 and 9 March 1918.

Eisen, Gustavus A. 1923. *The Great Chalice of Antioch, on Which Are Depicted in Sculpture the Earliest Known Portraits of Christ, Apostles, and Evangelists*. 2 vols. New York: Kouchakji Frères.

Eisen, Gustavus A. 1926. "The Great Chalice of Antioch." *Biblical Review* 11, 40–75.

Eisen, Gustavus A. 1932. *Portraits of George Washington*. 3 vols. New York: Hamilton and Associates.

Eisen, Gustavus A. 1933. *The Great Chalice of Antioch*. New York: Fahim Kouchakji.

Eisen, Gustavus A., and Fahim Kouchakji. 1927. *Glass: Its Origin, History, Chronology, Technic and Classification to the Sixteenth Century*. 2 vols. New York: William Edwin Drudge.

Eldem, Edhem. 1998. *A 135-Year-Old Treasure: Glimpses from the Past in the Ottoman Bank Archives*. Istanbul: Ottoman Bank.

Eldem, Edhem. 1999. *A History of the Ottoman Bank*. Istanbul: Ottoman Bank Historical Research Center.

Eldem, Edhem. 2011. "From Blissful Indifference to Anguished Concern: Ottoman Perceptions of Antiquities, 1799–1869." In Zainab Bahrani, Zeynep Çelik, and Edhem Eldem, eds., *Scramble for the Past: A Story of Archaeology in the Ottoman Empire, 1753–1914*, 281–329. Istanbul: SALT.

Eldem, Edhem. 2016. "The Genesis of the Museum of Turkish and Islamic Arts." In Simon Rettig and Massumeh Farhad, eds., *The Art of the Qur'an: Treasures from the Museum of Turkish and Islamic Arts*, 119–139. Washington, DC: Smithsonian.

Elikhina, Yulia, Pavel Lurje, and Sergey Khavrin. 2021. "Figura 'Zahhaka' i nekotorye drugie poddelki konca XIX v. v Hotanskoj kollekcii gosudarstvennogo Ermitazha" [The Figurine of Zahhak and Some Other Late 19th Century Forgeries in the Khotan Collection of the State Hermitage]. In *Transactions of the State Hermitage Museum 2013–2017*, 375–386. St. Petersburg: State Hermitage Museum.

Elnikov, M. V., and I. R. Tihimolova. 2017. "Relief Decoration Ceramics from the Bolshie Kuchugury Hillfort." In Sergei Bocharov, Véronique François, and Ayrat Sitdikov, eds., *Glazed Pottery of the Mediterranean and the Black Sea Region, 10th–18th Centuries*, vol. 2, 353–362. Kazan: Stratum.

El Shamsy, Ahmed. 2020. *Rediscovering the Islamic Classics: How Editors and Print Culture Transformed an Intellectual Tradition*. Princeton: Princeton University Press.

El Shamsy, Ahmed. 2021. "The Hoax in the ISIS Flag." *New Lines Magazine*, 28 October 2021, https://newlinesmag.com/essays/the-hoax-in-the-isis-flag/.

Elsner, Jaś. 2002. "The Birth of Late Antiquity: Riegl and Strzygowski in 1901." *Art History* 25:3, 358–379.

Emami, Farshid. 2016. "Coffee Houses, Urban Spaces, and the Formation of a Public Sphere in Safavid Isfahan." *Muqarnas* 33, 177–220.

Emami, Farshid. 2019. "All the City's Courtesans: A Now-Lost Safavid Pavilion and Its Figural Tile Panels." *Metropolitan Museum Journal* 54, 62–86.

Enayat, A. n.d. "Amīn-al-Żarb, Ḥājj Moḥammad-Ḥasan." *Encylopaedia Iranica*, http://www.iranicaonline.org/articles/amin-e-dar-al-zarb-hajj-mohammad-hasan, accessed 22 March 2025.

Erdmann, Kurt. 1942. "Die Keramik von Afrasiab." *Berliner Museen* 63:2/4, 18–28.

Erdmann, Kurt. 1946. "Afrasiab Ceramic Wares." Trans. Phyllis Ackerman. *Bulletin of the Iranian Institute* 6/7:6, 102–110.

Erduman-Çalış, Deniz. 2020. *Faszination Lüsterglanz und Kobaltblau: Die Geschichte Islamischer Keramik in Museen Deutschlands*. Munich: Readbox unipress.

Ettinghausen, Elizabeth. 2005. "Ernst Herzfeld: Reminiscences and Revelations." In Anne C. Gunter and Stefan R. Hauser, eds., *Ernst Herzfeld and the Development of Near Eastern Studies, 1900–1950*, 583–615. Leiden: Brill.

Ettinghausen, Richard. 1936. "New Affiliations for a Classical Persian Pottery Type." *Parnassus* 8:3, 10–21.

Ettinghausen, Richard. 1937. "Near Eastern Pottery of the Muslim Period in the Dumbarton Oaks Collection." Unpublished manuscript report, prepared Princeton, NJ.

Ettinghausen, Richard. 1955. "The 'Mesopotamian' Style in Luster Painting." *Artibus Asiae* 18:3/4, 294–306.

Ettinghausen, Richard. 1960. *Medieval Near Eastern Ceramics*. Washington, DC: Smithsonian Institution.

Ettinghausen, Richard. 1973. "Comments on Later Iranian Ceramics: A Review Article." *Artibus Asiae* 35:1/2, 165–169.

Ettinghausen, Richard. 1981. "Dated Faience." In Arthur Upham Pope and Phyllis Ackerman, eds., *A Survey of Persian Art*, vol. 4, 1667–1696. Ashiya: SOPA; reprint.

Eudel, Paul. 1907. *Trucs et truqueurs: Altérations, fraudes et contrefaçons dévoilées*. Paris: Libraire Molière.

Falke, [Otto von]. 1902. "59. Bericht über keramische Fälschungen etc." *Mittheilungen des Museen-Verbandes als Manuskript für die Mitglieder* (June), 1–3.

Fazeli, H., R.A.E. Coningham, and C. M. Blatt. 2004. "Cheshmeh-Ali Revisited: Towards an Absolute Dating of the Late Neolithic and Chalcolithic of Iran's Tehran Plain." *Iran* 42, 13–23.

Fearon, Andrew. 2017. "Copal Resin and the Practice of Oil Varnishing in the Second Half of 19th-Century America." In Mary A. Jablonski and Catherine R. Matsen, eds., *Architectural Finishes in the Built Environment*, 105–112. London: Archetype.

Felch, Jason. 2012. "Robert Hecht Jr. Dies at 92; Controversial Dealer in Classical Antiquities." *Los Angeles Times*, 9 February 2012, https://www.latimes.com/local

/obituaries/la-xpm-2012-feb-09-la-me-robert-hecht -20120209-story.html, accessed 1 May 2024.

Ferrier, Robert W. 1970. "Charles I and the Antiquities of Persia: The Mission of Nicholas Wilford." *Iran* 8, 51–56.

Fiedley, Durr. 1915. "Near Eastern Ceramics." *Metropolitan Museum of Art Bulletin* 10:10, 216–218.

Field, Henry. 1939. "Contributions to the Anthropology of Iran." *Publications of the Field Museum of Natural History: Anthropological Series* 29:1, 1–507.

Fields, John A., and Kenneth R. Seddon. 2002. "Scientific Detection of Fakes and Forgeries?" In Susan Whitfield, ed., *Dunhuang Manuscript Forgeries*, 33–40. London: British Library.

Fischer, Stephanie. 2022. "Der Rekonstruktion der Rekonstruktion/The Reconstruction of the Reconstruction." In Miriam Kühn and Martina Müller-Weiner, eds., *Lüsterkeramik: Schillerndes Geheimnis/Luster Ceramics: Shimmering Secret*, 37–49. Petersburg: Michael Imhof.

Flood, Finbarr Barry. 2006. "Image Against Nature: Spolia as Apotropaia in Byzantium and the dār al-Islām." *Medieval History Journal* 9:1, 143–166.

Flood, Finbarr Barry, and Beate Fricke. 2024. *Tales Things Tell: Material Histories of Early Globalisms*. Princeton: Princeton University Press.

Floor, Willem. 2003. *Traditional Crafts in Qajar Iran (1800–1925)*. Costa Mesa, CA: Mazda.

Floor, Willem. 2009. *Labor and Industry in Iran, 1850–1941*. Washington, DC: Mage.

Floor, Willem. 2009a. *Guilds, Merchants, and Ulama in Nineteenth-Century Iran*. Washington, DC: Mage.

Foltz, Richard. 2011. "Zoroastrians in Iran: What Future in the Homeland?" *Middle East Journal* 65:1, 73–84.

Force, Christel H., Yaëlle Biro, and Christine Brennan. 2023. Introduction to Yaëlle Biro, Christine Brennan, and Christel H. Force, eds., *The Brummer Galleries, Paris and New York: Defining Taste from Antiquities to the Avant-Garde*), 1–30. Leiden: Brill.

Fowler, Kent D., et al. 2020. "Fingerprint Evidence for the Division of Labour and Learning Pottery-Making at Early Bronze Age Tell eṣ-Ṣafi/Gath, Israel." *PLOS* One, https://doi.org/10.1371/journal.pone.0231046.

Franchi, R., Cristina Tonghini, F. Paloschi, and M. Soldi. 1995. "Mediaeval Syrian Fritware: Materials and Manufacturing Technique." In P. Vincenzini, ed., *The Ceramics Cultural Heritage*, 197–205. Faenza: Techna Srl.

François, Véronique, and Ibrahim Shaddoud. 2013. "Nouvel atelier de potier d'époque Abbasside au sud de Tell Abou Ali à Raqqa." *Al-Rāfidān* 34, 21–81.

Franke, Ute, and Martina Muller-Weiner, eds. 2016. *Herat Through Time: The Collections of the Herat Museum and Archive, Ancient Herat*. Vol. 3. Berlin: Staatliche Museen zu Berlin—Preußischer Kulturbesitz.

Frelinghuysen, Alice Cooney, et al., eds. 1993. *Splendid Legacy: The Havemeyer Collection*. New York: Metropolitan Museum of Art.

Frembgen, Jürgen Wasim. 2003. *Nahrung für die Seele: Welten des Islam*. Munich: Staatliches Museum für Völkerkunde München.

Frick Collection. n.d. "Kouchakji Frères." *The Frick Collection: Archives Directory for the History of Collecting in America*, https://research.frick.org/directory/detail/5151 /1, accessed 13 October 2020.

Froom, Aimée. 2008. *Persian Ceramics from the Collections of the Asian Art Museum*. San Francisco: Asian Art Museum.

Fry, Roger, and Charles Vignier. 1914. "The New Excavations at Rhages." *Burlington Magazine for Connoisseurs* 25, 211–218.

Fuchsgraber, Lukas. 2020. "From Auction Catalogue to Museum Archive: The Role of Photographs in the Fight against Forgeries in the Early Twentieth Century." *Mitteilungen des Kunsthistorischen Institutes in Florenz* 62:1, 109–23.

Furlotti, Barbara. 2010. "Connecting People, Connecting Places: Antiquarians as Mediators in Sixteenth-Century Rome." *Urban History* 37:3, 386–398.

Furlotti, Barbara. 2017. "Between Collection and Stock: The Ambiguous Role of Merchants and Artisans in the Sixteenth-Century Roman Antiquities Market." In Christina Anderson, ed., *Early Modern Merchants as Collectors*, 143–155. London: Routledge.

Furlotti, Barbara. 2019. *Antiquities in Motion: From Excavation Sites to Renaissance Collections*. Los Angeles: Getty Research Institute.

Fusaro, Agnese, and Viola Allegranzi. 2023. "A Treasure of Lustrewares from Ghazni (Afghanistan, Mid-12th–Early 13th Century)." *Annali, Sezione Orientale* 83, 61–98.

Gadoin, Isabelle. 2022. *Private Collectors of Islamic Art in Late Nineteenth-Century London: The Persian Ideal*. New York: Routledge.

Galli, Anna, Emanuela Sibilia, and Marco Martini. 2020. "Ceramic Chronology by Luminescence Dating: How and When It Is Possible to Date Ceramic Artefacts." *Archaeological and Anthropological Sciences* 12:190, 15 pp.

Gallois. 1938. "770. Zwei falsche persische Fliesen." *Mitteilungen des Museen-Verbandes als Manuskript für die Mitglieder* (July), 30–32.

Gangoly, Ordhendra Coomar. 1925. "On Some Rakka and Rhages Potteries." *Rupam* 24, 80–86.

Garachon, Isabelle. 2010. "Old Repairs of China and Glass." *Rijksmuseum Bulletin* 58:1, 34–55.

Garachon, Isabelle. 2017. "Fired Infills and Replacement Parts to Ceramics in the Rijksmuseum." *Rijksmuseum Bulletin* (December 2017), 372–385.

García-Arenal, Mercedes. 2009. "The Religious Identity of the Arabic Language and the Affair of the Lead Books of the Sacromonte of Granada." *Arabica* 56, 495–528.

Garner, Julian. 1927. "Ancient Potteries from the Site of Rakka." *International Studio* 87, 52–59.

Gasche, Hermann. n.d. "Susa i. Excavations." *Encyclopaedia Iranica*, https://www.iranicaonline.org/articles/susa-i -excavations, accessed 12 April 2024.

Gascoigne, Alison L., and Rebecca Bridgman. 2010. "Pottery from Jām: A Mediaeval Ceramic Corpus from Afghanistan." *Iran* 48, 107–151.

Gatt, G. 1885. "Industrielles aus Gaza." *Zeitschrift des Deutschen Palastina-Vereins (1878–1945)* 8, 69–79.

Gemeentemuseum. 1956. *Ceramiek uit de landen van de Islam*. The Hague: Gemeentemuseum.

Gennari-Santori, Flaminia. 2015. "An Art Collector and His Friends: John Pierpont Morgan and the Globalization of Medieval Art." *Journal of the History of Collections* 27:3, 401–411.

Gere, Cathy. 2009. *Knossos and the Prophets of Modernism*. Chicago/London: University of Chicago Press.

Gerelyes, Ibolya, and Orsolya Kovács. 1999. *An Unknown Orientalist: The Eastern Ceramics Collection of Miklós Zsolnay*. Budapest: Ministry of National Cultural Heritage.

Ghiasian, Mohammad Reza. 2015. "The 'Historical Style' of Painting for Shahrukh and Its Revival in the Dispersed Manuscript of Majmaʿ al-Tawarikh." *Iranian Studies* 48:6, 871–903.

Ghouchani, Abdullah. 1986. *Inscriptions on Nishabur Pottery/Katibaha-yi sufal-i Nishabur*. Tehran: Reza Abbasi Museum.

Ghouchani, Abdullah. 1371/1992. *Ashʿari-yi farsi-yi kashiha-yi Takht-i Sulayman* [Persian Poetry on the Tiles of Takht-i Sulayman]. Tehran: Iran University Press.

Gibson, Melanie. 2008–9. "The Enigmatic Figure: Ceramic Sculpture from Iran and Syria c. 1150–1250." *Transactions of the Oriental Ceramics Society* 73, 39–50.

Gibson, Melanie. 2010. "Takūk and Timthāl: A Study of Glazed Ceramic Sculpture from Iran and Syria circa 1150–1250." Unpublished PhD thesis, School of Oriental and African Studies, University of London.

Gigante, Federica. 2020. "Medici Patronage and Exotic Collectibles in the Seventeenth Century: The Cospi Collection." In Francesco Freddolini and Marco Musillo, eds., *Art, Mobility, and Exchange in Early Modern Tuscany and Eurasia*, 48–66. New York: Routledge.

Gilman, Ernest B. 2002. *Recollecting the Arundel Circle: Discovering the Past, Recovering the Future.* New York: Peter Lang.

Ginzburg, Carlo. 1979. "Clues: Roots of a Scientific Paradigm." *Theory and Society* 7, 273–88.

Ginzburg, Carlo, and Anna Davin. 1980. "Morelli, Freud, and Sherlock Holmes: Clues and Scientific Method." *History Workshop* 9, 5–36.

Giuzal'ian, L. T. 1960. "Tri iranskich srednevekovych glinianych stolinka [Three Iranian Medieval Ceramic Tables]." *Issledovaniya po istorii kul'tury naradov vostoka: Sbornik v vest' akademika I.A. Orbeli*, 313–319.

Gluck, Jay, and Sumi Gluck. 1977. *A Survey of Persian Handicraft: A Pictorial Introduction to the Contemporary Folk Arts and Art Crafts of Modern Iran.* Tehran: Melli Bank.

Goedicke, Christian. 1994. "Echtheitsprüfung an Tanagrafiguren nach der Thermolumineszenzmethode." In Irmgard Kriseleit and Gerhard Zimmer, eds., *Bürgerwelten: Hellenistische Tonfiguren und Nachschöpfungen im 19. Jh.*, 77–81. Berlin: Staatliche Museen zu Berlin.

Goldberg, Roxanne B. 2025. "Persian Lessons: Islamic Art in America, ca. 1876–1925." Unpublished PhD dissertation, MIT.

Golombek, Lisa. 1999. "The Mystery of Kubachi Wares." In Charles Melville, ed., *Proceedings of the Third European Conference of Iranian Studies, Cambridge (11–15 September, 1995), Part II: Medieval and Persian Studies*, 407–417. Wiesbaden: Reichert.

Golombek, Lisa, et al. 2014. *Persian Pottery in the First Global Age: The Sixteenth and Seventeenth Centuries.* Leiden: Brill.

Gorshenina, Svetlana. 1999. "Premiers pas des archéologues russes et français dans le Turkestan russe (1870–1890): Méthodes de recherche et destin des collections." Trans. Yvette Lambert. *Cahiers du monde russe* 40:3, 365–384.

Gorshenina, Svetlana. 2004. *The Private Collections of Russian Turkestan in the Second Half of the 19th and Early 20th Century.* Berlin: Klaus Schwarz Verlag.

Grabar, Oleg, et al. 1978. *City in the Desert: Qasr al-Hayr East.* 2 vols. Cambridge, MA: Center for Middle Eastern Studies, Harvard University.

Graeber, David. 2014. *Debt: The First 5,000 Years.* London: Melville House.

Graves, Margaret S. 2011. "Arched Surround for a Fireplace." In Margaret S. Graves and Benoît Junod, eds., *Treasures of the Aga Khan Museum: Architecture in Islamic Arts*, 154–155. Geneva: Aga Khan Trust for Culture.

Graves, Margaret S. 2014. "Kashan vii. Kashan Ware." *Encyclopaedia Iranica*, https://www.iranicaonline.org/articles/kashan-vii-kashan-ware, accessed 22 March 2025.

Graves, Margaret S. 2018. *Arts of Allusion: Object, Ornament, and Architecture in Medieval Islam.* New York: Oxford University Press.

Graves, Margaret S. 2018a. "Fracture, Facture, and the Collecting of Islamic Art." In Daniel Becker, Annalisa Fischer, and Yola Schmitz, eds., *Faking, Forging, Counterfeiting: Discredited Practices at the Margins of Mimesis*, 91–109. Bielefeld: transcript.

Graves, Margaret S. 2022. "The Double Bind of Craft Fidelity: Moroccan Ceramics on the Eve of the French Protectorate." In Margaret S. Graves and Alex Dika Seggerman, eds., *Making Modernity in the Islamic Mediterranean*, 117–138. Bloomington: Indiana University Press.

Graves, Margaret S. 2023. "The Evidence of the Earth: Fine Ceramics in the Western Khanates." Paper presented at The Golden Horde: Art, Material Culture, and Architecture conference, Max-Planck-Institut für Wissenschaftsgeschichte, Berlin, 7–8 December 2023.

Graves, Margaret S., Sequoia Miller, Magdalene Odundo, and Vicki Parry. 2023. *Ceramic Art.* Princeton: Princeton University Press.

Graves, Margaret S., Julie Ribits, Erika Elswick, and Shelby Rader. Forthcoming. "Technical Analysis of 'Raqqa Ware' Ceramics in the Eskenazi Museum of Art."

Grbanovic, Ana Marija. 2023. "Lost and Found: The Ilkhanid Tiles of the Pir-i Bakran Mausoleum (Linjan, Isfahan)." *Iran: Journal of the British Institute of Persian Studies* 61:2, 235–254.

Gregory, Sharon, and Sally Anne Hickson, eds. 2012. *Inganno—The Art of Deception: Imitation, Reception, and Deceit in Early Modern Art.* Farnham: Ashgate.

Grigor, Talinn. 2007. "Orient oder Rom? Qajar 'Aryan' Architecture and Strzygowski's Art History." *The Art Bulletin* 89:3, 562–590.

Grigor, Talinn. 2018. "'They Have Not Changed in 2,500 Years': Art, Archaeology, and Modernity in Iran." In Bonnie Effros and Guolong Lai, eds., *Unmasking Ideology: The Vocabulary, Symbols, and Legacy of Imperial and Colonial Archaeology*, 121–146. Los Angeles: Cotsen Institute of Archaeology Press.

Grigoriadis, Ioannis N. 2023. "Develop Archaeology and Museology in the Ottoman Empire, Turkey, and Greece: Théodore Macridy, an Ottoman Greek 'Liminal Scientist.'" *European Journal of Archaeology* 26:2, 209–225.

Grube, Ernst. 1966. "Islamic Sculpture: Ceramic Figurines." *Oriental Art* 12, 165–175.

Grube, Ernst. 1970. "Islamic Art—A Proposed New Classification." In Theodore Bowie, ed., *Islamic Art Across the World*, 7–16. Bloomington: Indiana University Art Museum.

Grube, Ernst. 1994. *Cobalt and Lustre: The First Centuries of Islamic Pottery.* London: Nour Foundation.

Grunwald, Kurt. 1972. "On Cairo's Lombard Street." *Tradition: Zeitschrift für Firmengeschichte und Unternehmerbiographie* 17:1, 8–22.

Guerin, Adam. 1995. "Mosseri Family." In Normal Stillman, ed., *Encyclopedia of Jews in the Islamic World.* Berkeley: University of California Press; published online by Brill.

Guilding, Ruth. 2014. *Owning the Past: Why the English Collected Antique Sculpture, 1640–1840.* New Haven: Yale University Press.

Gust, Wolfgang, ed. 2014. *The Armenian Genocide: Evidence from the German Foreign Office Archives, 1915–1916.* Oxford/New York: Berghahn Books.

Gyllensvärd, Bo. 1975. "Recent Finds of Chinese Ceramics at Fustat. II." *Bulletin of the Museum of Far Eastern Antiquities* 47, 93–117.

Haddon, Rosalind Wade. 2012. "The Middle Islamic Finewares from the Syrian-German Excavations on the Aleppo Citadel." In Roger Matthews and John Curtis, eds., *Proceedings of the 7th International Congress of the Archaeology of the Ancient Near East, Part 2*, 675–690. Wiesbaden: Harrassowitz Verlag.

Hallett, Jessica. 2012. "Pearl Cups Like the Moon: The

Abbasid Reception of Chinese Ceramics and the Belitung Shipwreck." In Venetia Porter and Mariam Rosser-Owen, eds., *Metalwork and Material Culture in the Islamic World: Art, Craft, and Text*, 349–361. London: I. B. Tauris.

Hallett, Jessica, ed. 2019. *The Rise of Islamic Art, 1869–1939*. Lisbon: Calouste Gulbenkian Museum.

Hallett, Jessica. 2021. "A Port of the Sea, Emporium of the Land, and Place of Manufacture: Basra as a Centre of Mobility and Innovation in Ceramics in the Abbasid Period." In Radha Dala, Sean Roberts, and Jochen Sokoly, eds., *The Seas and the Mobility of Islamic Art*, 122–141. London/New Haven: Yale University Press.

Hallett, Jessica, and Maïda Chavak. 2019. "The Gift of Ubiquity: Armenian Art Dealers and Their Networks." In Jessica Hallett, ed., *The Rise of Islamic Art, 1869–1939*, 55–66. Lisbon: Calouste Gulbenkian Museum.

Hamed-Troyansky, Vladimir. 2024. *Empire of Refugees: North Caucasian Muslims and the Late Ottoman State*. Stanford: Stanford University Press.

Hamilakis, Yannis. 2011. "Indigenous Archaeologies in Ottoman Greece." In Zainab Bahrani, Zeynep Çelik, and Edhem Eldem, eds., *Scramble for the Past: A Story of Archaeology in the Ottoman Empire, 1753–1914*, 49–69. Istanbul: SALT.

Hannover, Emil. 1925. *Pottery and Porcelain: A Handbook for Collectors*. Vol. 1, *Europe and the Near East*. Trans. and ed. Arthur Rackham. London: Ernest Benn.

Harari, Ralph. 1939. "Metalwork after the Early Islamic Period." In Arthur Upham Pope and Phyllis Ackerman, eds., *A Survey of Persian Art*, vol. 3, 2466–2529. London/New York: Oxford University Press.

Hay, Jonathan. 2008. "The Value of Forgery." *RES* 53/54, 5–19.

Heidemann, Stefan. 2005. "Die Entwicklung der Methoden in der Islamischen Numismatik im 18. Jahrhundert—War Johann Jacob Reiske ihr Begründer?" In Hans-Georg Ebert and Thoralf Hanstein, eds., *Johann Jacob Reiske—Leben un Wirkung*, 147–202. Leipzig: Evangelische Verlagsanstalt.

Heidemann, Stefan. 2006. "The History of the Industrial and Commercial Area of ʿAbbasid al-Raqqa, Called al-Raqqa al-Muḥtariqa." *Bulletin of the School of Oriental and African Studies* 69:1, 33–52.

Heidemann, Stefan, Jean-Francois de Lapérouse, and Vicki Parry. 2014. "The Large Audience: Life-Sized Stucco Figures of Royal Princes from the Seljuq Period." *Muqarnas* 31, 35–71.

Hellal, Salima, Sandra Aube, and Éloïse Brack de la Perrière. 2023. *Les arts de l'Islam au musée des Beaux-Arts de Lyon*. Gand: Snoeck.

Henderson, Julian. 1999. "Archaeological Investigations of an Islamic Industrial Complex at Raqqa, Syria." *Damaszener Mitteilungen* 11, 243–265.

Henderson, Julian, et al. 2005. "Experiment and Innovation: Early Islamic Industry at al-Raqqa, Syria." *Antiquity* 79:303, 130–145.

Henshaw, Christina M. 2020. "Early Islamic Ceramics and Glazes of Akhsiket, Uzbekistan." Unpublished PhD thesis, University College London.

Hervey, Mary F. S. 1969. *The Life, Correspondence and Collections of Thomas Howard, Earl of Arundel*. Cambridge: Cambridge University Press, 1921; reprinted New York: Kraus.

Hess, Jacob. 1950. "Lord Arundel in Rom und sein Auftrag an den Bildhauer Egidio Moretti." *English Miscellany* 1, 197–219.

Hicks, Dan. 2020. *The Brutish Museums: The Benin Bronzes, Colonial Violence, and Cultural Restitution*. London: Pluto Press.

Hilel, Maayan. 2021. "Cultural Diplomacy in Mandatory Haifa: The Role of Christian Communities in the Cultural Transformation of the City." In Karène Sanchez Summerer and Sary Zananiri, eds., *European Cultural Diplomacy and Arab Christians in Palestine, 1918–1948: Between Contention and Connection*, 127–150. London: Palgrave Macmillan.

Hillenbrand, Robert. 1994. "The Relationship Between Book Painting and Luxury Ceramics in 13th-Century Iran." In Robert Hillenbrand, ed., *The Art of the Saljuqs in Iran and Anatolia: Proceedings of a Symposium Held in Edinburgh in 1982*, 134–145. Costa Mesa, CA: Mazda.

Hillenbrand, Robert. 1999. *Islamic Art and Architecture*. London: Thames and Hudson.

Hillenbrand, Robert. 2010. "Western Scholarship on Persian Painting Before 1914: Collectors, Exhibitions and Franco-German Rivalry." In Andrea Lerner and Avinoam Shalem, eds., *After One Hundred Years: The 1910 Exhibition 'Meisterwerke muhammedanischer Kunst' Reconsidered*, 201–229. Leiden: Brill.

Hoare, Oliver. 2024. *The Exchange: Shahnameh/de Kooning*. London: Looking Glass Press.

Hobson, R. L. 1929. "607. Forgery of a Chinese Metal Figure." *Mitteilungen des Museen-Verbandes als Manuskript für die Mitglieder* (May), 8–9.

Hobson, R. L. 1932. *A Guide to the Islamic Pottery of the Near East*. London: British Museum.

Hoernle, A. F. Rudolf. 1901. "A Report on the British Collection of Antiquities from Central Asia, Part II." *Journal of the Asiatic Society of Bengal* 70, extra no. 1, 1–5.

Hoffman, Eva. 2008. "Between East and West: The Wall Paintings of Samarra and the Construction of Abbasid Princely Culture." *Muqarnas* 25, 107–132.

Hogan, Loretta, et al. 1996. "Reconstructing Major Missing Areas of Ceramics Vessels Using Clay." In Janet Bridgeland, ed., *ICOM Committee for Conservation 11th Triennial Meeting, Edinburgh 1–6 September 1996*, 833–838. London: James and James.

Holcomb, Melanie. 2008. "'Ugly but . . . Important': The Albanian Hoard and the Making of the Archaeological Treasure in the Early Twentieth Century." *Early Medieval Europe* 16:1, 3–22.

Hollis, Howard, and William M. Milleken. 1944. *Islamic Art: Selected Examples from the Loan Exhibition of Islamic Art at the Cleveland Museum of Art*. Cleveland, OH: Cleveland Museum of Art.

Holod, Renata. 2012. "Event and Memory: The Freer Gallery's Siege Scene Plate." *Ars Orientalis* 42, 194–219.

Holt, Frank L. 2021. *When Money Talks: A History of Coins and Numismatics*. New York: Oxford University Press.

Hopkirk, Peter. 2006. *Foreign Devils on the Silk Road: The Long Search for Lost Cities and Treasures of Chinese Central Asia*. Amherst: University of Massachusetts Press.

Hôtel Drouot. 1888. *Catalogue des objets d'art de l'orient et de l'occident tableaux dessins composant la Collection de feu M. Albert Goupil*. Paris: Hôtel Drouot.

Hôtel Drouot. 1927. *Dessins, aquarelles, pastels, tableaux modernes . . . antiquités . . . faïences orientales . . . composant la collection de M. S. Sevadjian, Hôtel Drouot, 1–3 June 1927*.

Howarth, David. 1985. *Lord Arundel and His Circle*. New Haven/London: Yale University Press.

Hsieh, Julia. 2016. "The Practice of Repairing Vessels in Ancient Egypt: Methods of Repair and Anthropological Implications." *Near Eastern Archaeology* 79:4, 280–283.

Hüseler, K. 1929. "606. Eine falsche Hamburger Fayence-Vase." *Mitteilungen des Museen-Verbandes als Manuskript für die Mitglieder* (May), 6–7.

Hylkema, Jacqueline. 2019. "The Rhetoric of Illusion:

Persuasion and Response in Forgery, the Arts and Other Deceptions." Unpublished PhD thesis, Leiden University.

Ibn Khaldun. 1969. *The Muqadimmah: An Introduction to History.* 3 vols. Trans. Franz Rosenthal, ed. N. J. Dawood. Princeton: Princeton University Press.

Ilisch, Lutz. 2015. "The Leipzig Numismatic Contest of 1752—An Incentive from the Imperial Coin Collection to Reestablish the Ability to Attribute Arabic Coins." In Bruno Callagher and Arianna D'Ottone Rambach, eds., *4th Simone Assemani Symposium*, series *Polymnia: Numismatica antica e medievale, studi* 9, 105–129.

Ilyasov, Jangar. 2014. "Exotic Images: On a New Group of Glazed Pottery of the 10th and 11th Century." *Journal of the David Collection* 4, 50–87.

Ilyasov, Jangar. 2016. "'A Celebrated Bowl in the Freer Gallery': Nishapur, Samarqand or Tashkent?" *Tribus: Jahrbuch des Linden-Museums* 65, 157–177.

Ilyasova, Saida R., Jangar Ya. Ilyasov, Ravshan A. Imamberdiev, and E. A. Ishakova. 2016. *Net blaga v bogatstve: Glazurovannaya keramika Tashkentskogo oazisa IX-XII vekov /There Is No Blessing in Wealth: Glazed Ceramics of the Tashkent Oasis in the 9th–12th Centuries.* Moscow: Mardjani Foundation.

Indiana University Art Museum. 1980. *Guide to the Collections: Highlights from the Indiana University Art Museum.* Bloomington: Indiana University Art Museum.

Isfahani, Ali Mohamed. 1888. *On the Manufacture of Modern Kashi Earthenware Tiles and Vases.* Trans. John Fargues. Edinburgh: Museum of Science and Art.

Islamic Art Circle. 1969. *Islamic Pottery 800–1400 AD.* London: Islamic Art Circle/Victoria & Albert Museum.

Issawi, Charles. 1988. *The Fertile Crescent, 1800–1914: A Documentary Economic History.* New York: Oxford University Press.

Jahn, Melvin E. 1963. "Dr. Beringer and the Würzburg 'Lügensteine.'" *Journal of the Society for the Bibliography of Natural History* 4:2, 138–146.

James, Henry. 1907. *The American Scene.* London: Chapman and Hall.

Jefferson, Rebecca. 2022. *The Cairo Genizah and the Age of Discovery in Egypt: The History and Provenance of a Jewish Archive.* London: I. B. Tauris.

Jenkins-Madina, Marilyn. 2000. "Collecting the 'Orient' at the Met: Early Tastemakers in America." *Ars Orientalis* 30, 69–89.

Jenkins-Madina, Marilyn. 2006. *Raqqa Revisited: Ceramics of Ayyubid Syria.* New York: Metropolitan Museum of Art.

Jennings, Justin, April Hawkins, Adam Sellen, and Giles Spence Morrow. 2022. "Fakers and Mold-Makers: The Use of Structured Light Scanning to Detect Forgeries of Pre-Islamic Effigies from Oaxaca." *Journal of Conservation and Museum Studies* 20, 11 pp.

Johnston, William R. 1999. *William and Henry Walters, the Reticent Collectors.* Baltimore: Walters Art Gallery.

Jones, Geoffrey. 1986. *Banking and Empire in Iran.* Vol. 1, *The History of the British Bank of the Middle East.* Cambridge: Cambridge University Press.

Jones, Geoffrey. 1987. "The Imperial Bank of Iran and Iranian Economic Development, 1890–1952." *Business and Economic History* 16, 69–80.

Jones, Mark, ed. 1990. *Fake? The Art of Deception.* London: British Museum.

Jones, Mark, et al. 2003. *Souvenir from Canton: Chinese Export Paintings from the Victoria and Albert Museum.* Shanghai: Shanghai Publishing House.

Juvin, Carine. 2012. "Plat à inscription monumentale." In Sophie Makariou, ed., *Les arts de l'Islam au Musée du Louvre*, 108–110. Paris: Hazan.

Kákosy, László. 1989. "The Plundering of the Pyramid of Cheops." *Studien zur Altägyptischen Kultur* 16, 145–169.

Kalantaryan, A., et al. 2009. *Armenia in the Cultural Context and East and West: Ceramics and Glass (4th–14th Centuries).* Yerevan: Nas Ra "Gitutyun" Publishing.

Kanda, Yui. 2017. "Kashan Revisited: A Luster-Painted Ceramic Tombstone Inscribed with a Chronogram Poem by Muhtasham Kashani." *Muqarnas* 34, 273–286.

Karabacek, Joseph. 1884. "Zur muslimischen Keramik." *Osterreichischen Monatsschrift für den Orient* 10, 281–292.

Karl, Barbara. 2011. *Treasury—Kunstkammer—Museum: Objects from the Islamic World in the Museum Collections of Vienna.* Vienna: Austrian Academy of Sciences Press.

Katz, Brigit. 2020. "All of the Museum of the Bible's Dead Sea Scrolls Are Fake, Report Finds." *Smithsonian Magazine Smart News*, 16 March 2020, https://www.smithsonianmag.com/smart-news/all-museum-bibles-dead-sea-scrolls-are-fake-report-finds-180974425/, accessed 22 March 2025.

Katz, Karl. 2016. *The Exhibitionist: Living Museums, Loving Museums.* New York: Overlook.

Kawami, Trudy S. 1992. *Ancient Iranian Ceramics from the Arthur M. Sackler Collections.* New York: Arthur M. Sackler Foundation.

Kazempour, Mehdi. 2023. "Aghkand and Garrus Ware from Recent Excavations and Surveys in Northwestern Iran." Paper presented at Sgraffito and Champlevé in Islamic Lands (9th–14th Century): Iran, Caucasus and Beyond workshop, Maison de l'Orient et de la Mediterranée, Lyon, 11 May 2023.

Keazor, Henry, and Tina Öcal. 2014. *Der Fall Beltracchi und die Folgen: Interdisziplinäre Fälschungsforschung heute.* Berlin: De Gruyter.

Kelekian, Dikran. 1909. *The Potteries of Persia.* Paris: Dikran Kelekian.

Kelekian, Dikran. 1910. *The Kelekian Collection of Persian and Analogous Potteries, 1885–1910.* Paris: Herbert Clarke.

Kelker, Nancy L., and Karen O. Bruhns. 2010. *Faking Ancient Mesoamerica.* Walnut Creek, CA: Left Coast Press.

Kévonian, Kéram. 1975. "Marchands arméniens au XVII siècle: À propos d'un livre arménien publiée à Amsterdam en 1699." *Cahiers du monde russe et soviétique* 16:2, 199–244.

Kirsch, Otakar. 2015. "Association of Museum Workers in Defence Against Counterfeiting and Unfair Trade Practices: Comments on the Origins of Organised Meetings of Museum Workers on an International Basis." *Museologica Brunensia* 4:2, 48–55.

Kiyani, Muhammad Yusuf. 1973. "Recent Excavations in Jurjan: A Summary." In William Watson, ed., *The Art of Iran and Anatolia from the 11th to the 13th Century A.D.: A Colloquy Held 25–28 June 1973*, Colloquies on Art & Archaeology in Asia 4, 126–133. London: University of London, School of Oriental and African Studies.

Kiyani, Muhammad Yusuf. 1984. *The Islamic City of Gurgan.* Berlin: D. Reimer.

Klein, Rüdiger. 1999. "Aleppiner Handelshäuser zwischen Basar und Börse: Informationssuche und -verarbeitung im Zeichen der Inkorporation (ca. 1780–1920)." In Dietmar Rothermund, ed., *Aneignung un Selbstbehauptung: Antworten auf die europäische Expansion*, 345–372. Munich: R. Oldenbourg.

Klesner, Catherine, et al. 2021. "Investigation of Provenances of Early Islamic Lead Glazes from Northern Central Asia Using Elemental and Lead Isotope Analyses." *Archaeological and Anthropological Sciences* 13:203, 36 pp.

Koechlin, Raymond. 1928. *Les céramiques musulumanes de Suse au Musée du Louvre.* Paris: Ernest Leroux.

Komaroff, Linda. 2012. "369. Basin with Handles." In Wolframm Koeppe et al., eds., *Decorative Arts in the Robert Lehman Collection*, 361. New York: Metropolitan Museum of Art.

Koob, Stephen P. 1998. "Obsolete Fill Materials Found on Ceramics." *Journal of the American Institute for Conservation* 37:1, 49–67.

Koob, Stephen P. 1999. "Restoration Skill or Deceit: Manufactured Replacement Fragments on a Seljuk Lustre-Glazed Ewer." In Norman H. Tennent, ed., *The Conservation of Glass and Ceramics; Research, Practice and Training*, 156–166. London: James and James.

Kopytoff, Igor. 1986. "The Cultural Biography of Things: Commoditization as Process." In Arjun Appadurai, ed., *The Social Life of Things: Commodities in Cultural Perspective*, 64–91. Cambridge: Cambridge University Press.

Koss, Kerith, et al. 2009. "Analysis of Persian Painted *Minai* Ware." In Blythe McCarthy et al., eds., *Scientific Research on Historic Asian Ceramics*, 33–47. London: Archetype.

[Kouchakji, Fahim]. n.d. *Excerpts from Publicly Expressed Opinions on the Great Chalice of Antioch in Two Volumes by Dr. Gustavus A. Eisen*. New York: Kouchakji Frères.

Kouchakji, Fahim. 1923. "Glories of Er-Rakka Pottery." *International Studio* (March 1923), 515–524.

Kouchakji Frères. 1916. *Interesting Examples of Saracenic Art, Chiefly Consisting of Rakka, Syro-Egyptian, Rey or Rhages, Sultanabad, Rhodian, Hispano-Mauresque, Koubatcha Faïences and Arabic Enamelled Glasses*. New York, 28 January–19 February 1916.

Koval', V. Yu. 2010. *Keramika Vostok na Rusi IX-XII veka = Oriental Ceramics in Rus, 9th–17th Centuries*. Moscow: Nauka.

Koyama, Fujio, and John A. Pope, eds. 1978. *Oriental Ceramics: The World's Great Collections*. Vol. 4, *Iran Bastan Museum*. Tokyo: Kodanshah.

Krahl, Regina, and Nurdan Erbehar. 1986. *Chinese Ceramics in the Topkapi Saray Museum, Istanbul: A Complete Catalogue*. Vol. 1. London: Sotheby's/Philip Wilson.

Kramarovsky, M. G., et al. 2005. *Zolotaia Orda: istoriia i kultura = Altyn urda: tarikhy ham madaniiate = The Golden Horde: History and Culture*. St. Petersburg: Slaviia.

Kravchenko, S. A. 2017. "Paradnaya keramika iz raskopok Azaka [Ceremonial Ceramics from the Digs in Azak]." In Sergei Bocharov, Véronique François, and Ayrat Sitdikov, eds., *Glazed Pottery of the Mediterranean and the Black Sea Region, 10th–18th Centuries*, vol. 2, 539–559. Kazan: Stratum.

Kriseleit, Irmgard. 1994. "Fälschungen in der Berliner Sammlung." In Irmgard Kriseleit and Gerhard Zimmer, eds., *Bürgerwelten: Hellenistische Tonfiguren und Nachschöpfungen im 19. Jh.*, 59–69. Berlin: Staatliche Museen zu Berlin.

Kröger, Jens. 2005. "Ernst Herzfeld and Friedrich Sarre." In Anne C. Gunter and Stefan R. Hauser, eds., *Ernst Herzfeld and the Development of Near Eastern Studies, 1900–1950*, 45–99. Leiden: Brill.

Krzhizhanovsky, Sigizmund. 2013 [1927]. "In the Pupil." In *Autobiography of a Corpse*, trans. Joanna Turnbull, 31–60. New York: New York Review of Books.

Kühnel, Ernst. 1927. *Sammlung Oskar Skaller, Berlin: Persische Keramik vornehmlich XIII.–XIV. Jahrhundert*. Berlin: Cassirer.

Kühnel, Ernst. 1931. "Dated Persian Lustred Pottery." *Eastern Art* 3, 220–236.

Kühnel, Ernst. 1934. "Die Abbasidischen Lusterfayencen." *Ars Islamica* 1, 149–159.

Kupferschmidt, Uri M. 1995. "Harari, Sir Victor Pasha and Ralph." In Normal Stillman, ed., *Encyclopedia of Jews in the Islamic World*. Berkeley: University of California Press; published online by Brill.

Kverfel'dt, Ernest Konradovich. 1947. *Keramika Blizhnego Vostoka: Rukovodstvo k raspoznaniiu i opredeleniiu keramicheskikh izdelii* [Middle Eastern Pottery: A Guide to Recognition and Identification of Ceramics]. Leningrad: State Hermitage Museum.

Labrusse, Rémi. 2011. *Islamophilies: L'Europe modern et les arts de l'Islam*. Paris/Lyon: Somogy/Musée des Beaux-Arts de Lyon.

Labrusse, Rémi. 2018. "Modernité byzantine: L'Exposition international d'art byzantine de 1931 à Paris." In Lucile Arnoux-Farnoux and Polina Kosmadaki, eds., *Le double voyage: Paris-Athènes (1919–1939)*, 221–242. Athens: École française d'Athènes.

Lamboursain, Jean. 1897. *Traité de la fabrication et de la réparation des faïences et objets d'art*. Paris: Bornemann.

Lamprakos, Michele. 2017. "Life in the Khans." *Muqarnas* 34, 125–155.

Lamprey, B. L. 1890. "Persian Tiles." *The Decorator and Furnisher* 15:4, 127–128.

Lane, Arthur. 1937–38. "The Early Sgraffito Ware of the Near East." *Transactions of the Oriental Ceramic Society 1937–38*, 33–54.

Lane, Arthur. 1939. "The So-called 'Kubachi' Wares of Persia." *Burlington Magazine for Connoisseurs* 75:439, 156–157, 160–163.

Lane, Arthur. 1947. *Early Islamic Pottery: Mesopotamia, Egypt, and Persia*. London: Faber and Faber.

Langer, Axel. 2020. "Safavid Revival in Persian Miniature Painting: Renewal, Imitation and Sources of Inspiration." In Francine Giese, Mercedes Volait, and Ariane Varela Braga, eds., *À l'orientale: Collecting, Displaying, and Appropriating Islamic Art and Architecture in the 19th and Early 20th Centuries*, 15–27. Leiden: Brill.

Langin-Hooper, Stephanie, S. Rebecca Martin, Mehmet Önal, and Rebecca Molholt, 2013. "Zeugma as the Provenance of 12 Mosaic Fragments at Bowling Green State University." *Journal of Roman Archaeology* 26, 439–455.

Lapatin, Kenneth. 2002. *Mysteries of the Snake Goddess: Art, Desire, and the Forging of History*. Boston/New York: Houghton Mifflin.

Laurvik, J. Nilsen, Arthur Upham Pope, R. Meyer-Riefstahl, and Phyllis Ackerman. 1917. *Catalogue: Mrs Phoebe A. Hearst Loan Collection*. San Francisco: Palace of Fine Arts/San Francisco Art Association.

Lee, Chaeri. 2025. "*Athār*: Visualizing Vestiges of Time in Late Nineteenth-Century Iran." Unpublished PhD dissertation, Indiana University.

Leone, Anaïs. 2021. "New Data on the Luster Tiles of 'Abd al-Samad's Shrine in Natanz, Iran." *Muqarnas* 38, 331–356.

Leoni, Francesca, Dana Norris, Kelly Domoney, Moujan Matin, and Andrew Shortland. 2019. "'The Illusion of an Authentic Experience': A Luster Bowl in the Ashmolean Museum." *Muqarnas* 36, 229–249.

Lepper, Bradley T., and Jeff Gill. 2000. "The Newark Holy Stones." *Timeline* 17:3, 16–25.

Lerner, Judith. 2016. "Arthur Upham Pope and the Sasanians." In Yuka Kadoi, ed., *Arthur Upham Pope and a New Survey of Persian Art*, 169–232. Leiden: Brill.

Lessen, A. A. 1959. *Trudy Azerbaĭdzhanskoĭ (Oren-Kalinskoĭ) ekspeditsii* [Proceedings of the Azerbaijanian (Oren-Kala) Expedition]. Vol. 1. Moscow: Izdatel'stvo Akademii nauk SSSR.

Levenson, Rosemary, and Elizabeth Huff. 1977. *Elizabeth Huff, Teacher and Founding Curator of the East Asiatic Library from Urbana to Berkeley by Way of Peking: An Interview Conducted by Rosemary Levenson*. Berkeley: Regents of the University of California.

Lévi-Strauss, Claude. 1966. *The Savage Mind (La pensée*

sauvage). Unattributed translation [Sybil Wolfram and Ernest Gellner] from the French. London: Weidenfeld and Nicolson.

Losensky, Paul. 2023. "Parts and Wholes, Beyts and Ghazals: Assemblage Theory and the Poetry of Sā'eb Tabrizi." First Frank Lewis Memorial Lecture, University of Chicago, 16 February 2023.

Lovino, Francesco. 2020. "Byzantium on Display: Scholars, Collectors and Dealers at the Exposition Internationale d'Art Byzantin." *Journal of the History of Collections* 32:3, 509–521.

Lundén, Staffan. 2024. "Distorting History in the Restitution Debate: Dan Hicks's *The Brutish Museums* and Fact and Fiction in Benin Historiography." *International Journal of Cultural Property, First View*, 24 pp.

Macfie, A. L. 2003. "The Invisible Hand in the 'Theory of Moral Sentiments.'" In *The Individual in Society: Papers on Adam Smith*, 101–125. London: Routledge.

Mack, Rosamond E. 2002. *Bazaar to Piazza: Islamic Trade and Italian Art, 1300–1600*. Berkeley: University of California Press.

Magomedov, A. D. 2016. "Pervyye fotografii s. Kubachi [The First Photos of the Village Kubachi]." *History, Archaeology and Anthropology of the Caucasus* 12:3, 140–145.

Mahdavi, Ashgar. 1976–77. "Les archives Aminozzarb: Source pour l'histoire économique et sociale de l'Iran (fin du XIXe—début du XXe siècle)." *Le monde iranien et l'islam* 4, 195–222.

Mahdavi, Shireen. 1999. *For God, Mammon, and Country: A Nineteenth-Century Persian Merchant, Haj Muhammad Hassan Amin al-Zarb, 1834–1898*. Boulder, CO: Westview Press.

Mahdavi, Shireen. 2011. "Haj Muhammad Hassan Amin al-Zarb: His World and His Philosophy of Life." *Middle Eastern Studies* 47:2, 379–393.

Mahoney, Daniel. 2019. "Medieval Reports of the Preservation and Looting of Pre-Islamic Burials in South Arabia." *International Journal of Islamic Architecture* 8:1, 71–87.

Maimon, Vered. 2008. "Displaced 'Origins': William Henry Fox Talbot's *The Pencil of Nature*." *History of Photography* 32:4, 314–325.

Mairs, Rachel, and Maya Muratov. 2015. *Archaeologists, Tourists, Interpreters: Exploring Egypt and the Near East in the Late 19th–Early 20th Centuries*. London: Bloomsbury.

Majd, Mohammad Gholi. 2003. *The Great American Plunder of Persia's Antiquities, 1925–1941*. Lanham: University Press of America.

Malley, Shawn. 2011. "The Layard Enterprise: Victorian Archaeology and Informal Imperialism in Mesopotamia." In Zainab Bahrani, Zeynep Çelik, and Edhem Eldem, eds., *Scramble for the Past: A Story of Archaeology in the Ottoman Empire, 1753–1914*, 99–123. Istanbul: SALT.

Mammaev, Mishrikhan M. 2021. "Novyye kamennyye rel'yefy—arkhitekturnyye detali XIV–XVIII vv. Iz Kubachi s ornamentom i arabskimi nadpisyami [New Stone Reliefs—Architectural Details of the 14th–18th Centuries from Kubachi with Ornament and Arabic Inscriptions]." *History, Archaeology and Ethnography of the Caucasus* 17:2, 304–329.

Mango, Marlia M. 1986. *Silver from Early Byzantium: The Kaper Koraon and Related Treasures*. Baltimore: Walters Art Gallery.

Mango, Marlia Mundell. 1992. Introduction to Susan A. Boyd and Marlia Mundell Mango, eds., *Ecclesiastical Silver plate in Sixth-Century Byzantium*, xxi–xxxii. Washington, DC: Dumbarton Oaks.

Maqrizi. 1387 [1967]. *Shudhur al-'uqud fi dhikr al-nuqud* [Pearls of the Divine Ordinances Concerning Money]. Najaf: Al-maktaba al-Haydariya.

Marchand, Suzanne. 1994. "The Rhetoric of Artefacts and the Decline of Classical Humanism: The Case of Josef Strzygowski." *History and Theory* 33:4, 106–130.

Marchand, Suzanne. 2017. "Winckelmann and the Roman Art Market." *International Review of Eighteenth-Century Studies* 3, 55–73.

Margoliouth, David Samuel. 1905. *Mohammed and the Rise of Islam*. New York/London: Putnam/Knickerbocker Press.

Marteau, Georges, and Henri Vever. 1913. *Miniatures persanes, exposées au Musée des arts décoratifs, Juin–Octobre 1912*. Paris: Bibliothèque d'art et d'archéologie.

Martin, Fredrik R. 1899. *The Persian Lustre Vase in the Imperial Hermitage Museum at St. Petersburg and Some Fragments of Lustre Found Near Cairo at Fostât*. Stockholm: Palmquists Aktiebolag.

Martin, Fredrik R. 1912. *The Miniature Painting and Painters of Persia, India and Turkey, from the 8th to the 18th Century*. 2 vols. London: Bernard Quaritch.

Martin, Fredrik R., and Friedrich Sarre. 1912. *Die Austellung von Meisterwerken muhammedanischer Kunst in Munchen 1910*. 3 vols. Munich: F. Bruckmann.

Martin, Meredith. 2020. "Swiss Porcelain and Slavery in the Global Eighteenth Century." In Noemie Etienne et al., eds., *Exotic Switzerland? Looking Outward in the Age of Enlightenment/Une Suisse exotique? Regarder l'ailleurs en Suisse au siècle des Lumières*, 47–62. Zurich: Diaphenes.

Mason, Robert B. J. 1997. "Medieval Syrian Lustre-Painted and Associated Wares: Typology in a Multidisciplinary Study." *Levant*, 29, 169–200.

Mason, Robert B. J. 2004. *Shine Like the Sun: Luster-Painted and Associated Pottery from the Medieval Middle East*. Costa Mesa, CA: Mazda.

Mason, Robert B. J., et al. 2001. "Advances in Polychrome Ceramics in the Islamic World of the 12th Century AD." *Archaeometry* 43:2, 191–209.

Masteller, Kimberley. 2016. "Arthur Upham Pope and Collecting Persian Art for Kansas City." In Yuka Kadoi, ed., *Arthur Upham Pope and a New Survey of Persian Art*, 266–289. Leiden: Brill.

Masters, Bruce. 2010. "The Political Economy of Aleppo in an Age of Ottoman Reform." *Journal of the Economic and Social History of the Orient* 53:1/2, 290–316.

Masuya, Tomoko. 2000. "Persian Tiles on European Walls: Collecting Ilkhanid Tiles in Nineteenth-Century Europe." *Ars Orientalis* 30, 39–54.

Matin, Moujan. 2020. "Appendix: The Technology of Medieval Islamic Ceramics: A Study of Two Persian Manuscripts." In Oliver Watson, *Ceramics of Iran: Islamic Pottery from the Sarikhani Collection*, 459–487. New Haven: Yale University Press.

Matin, Moujan, Mohammad Gholamnejad, and Ali Nemati Abkenar. 2021. "'We Must Send You a Sample'—A Persian European Dialogue: Insights into Late Nineteenth-Century Ceramic Technology Based on Chemical Analysis of Tiles from the Ettehadieh House Complex, Tehran, Iran." *Notes and Records: The Royal Society Journal of the History of Science* 75:1, 5–37.

Matin, Moujan, and Mary Ownby. 2023. "Early Stonepaste Ceramic Technology in Fustat, Egypt." *Journal of Archaeological Science: Reports* 50, 9 pp.

Matthee, Rudolph P. 2013. "Iran's Relationships with Europe in the Safavid Period: Diplomats, Missionaries, Merchants, and Travel." In Axel Langer, ed., *The Fascination of Persia: The Persian-European Dialogue in Seventeenth-Century Art & Contemporary Art from Tehran*, 6–25. Zurich: Museum Rietberg.

Maury, Charlotte. 2012. "Tympans de la mosque de Piyale

Pasha à Istanbul." In Sophie Makariou, ed., *Les arts de l'Islam au Musée du Louvre*, 347–349. Paris: Hazan.

McCarthy, Blythe, and Renata Holod. n.d. "Under a Microscope: The Examination of a Siege Scene Plate." *National Museum of Asian Art*, https://asia.si.edu/essays/under-a-microscope/, accessed 22 March 2025.

McClary, Richard. 2016. "A New Approach to *Mīnā'ī* Wares: Chronology and Decoration." *Persica* 25, 1–20.

McClary, Richard. 2018. "Recontextualizing the Object: Using New Technologies to Reconstruct Lost Interiors of Medieval Islamic Buildings." *International Journal of Islamic Architecture*, 7:2, 263–283.

McClary, Richard. 2020. "Calouste Gulbenkian, His *Mīnā'ī* Ware, and the Changing Islamic Art Market in the Early Twentieth Century." *Muqarnas* 37, 325–343.

McClary, Richard. 2024. *Mina'i Ware: A Reassessment and Comprehensive Study of Iranian Polychrome Overglaze Wares Through Sherds.* Edinburgh: Edinburgh University Press.

McDaniel, Walton Brooks. 1925. "The Great Chalice of Antioch." Review in *Classical Weekly* 18:16, 123–127.

McPhillips, Stephen. 2001–2. "Twelfth Century Pottery from the Citadel of Damascus." *Bulletin d'études orientales* 53/54, 139–155.

McPhillips, Stephen. 2008. "Medelhavsmuseets Samling av Fustat-Skärvor." In *Blåvitt/Blue and White/Mavi Beyaz: Porcelain from the Topkapı Museum and the Museum of Turkish and Islamic Art, Istanbul*, 107–125. Stockholm: Medelhavsmuseet.

McPhillips, Stephen. 2012. "Continuity and Innovation in Syrian Artisanal Traditions of the 9th to 13th Centuries: Ceramic Evidence from the Syrian-French Citadel of Damascus Excavations." *Bulletin d'études orientales* 61, 447–473.

McWilliams, Mary. 2012. "Subthemes and Overpaint: Exhibiting Islamic Art in American Museums." In Benoît Junod et al., eds., *Islamic Art and the Museum: Approaches to Art and Archaeology of the Muslim World in the Twenty-First Century*, 152–172. London: Saqi.

McWilliams, Mary, ed. 2013. *In Harmony: The Norma Jean Calderwood Collection of Islamic Art.* Cambridge MA: Harvard Art Museums.

Measday, Danielle, Charlotte Walker, and Briony Pemberton. 2017. "A Summary of Ultra-Violet Fluorescent Materials Relevant to Conservation." *AICCM Newsletter* 137 (March 2017), https://aiccm.org.au/network-news/summary-ultra-violet-fluorescent-materials-relevant-conservation/, accessed 22 March 2025.

Méchin, Ferdinand. 1867. *Lettres d'un voyageur en Perse: Djoulfa, Yesd, les guèbres.* Bourges: Jollet.

Melikian-Chirvani, Assadullah Souren. 1966. "The Sufi Strain in the Art of Kashan." *Oriental Art* 12:4, 251–258.

Melikian-Chirvani, Asadullah Souren. 1967. "Trois manuscrits de l'Iran Seldjoukide." *Arts asiatiques* 16, 3–51.

Melikian-Chirvani, Assadullah Souren. 1982. "Le rhyton selon les sources Persanes." *Studia Iranica* 2, 263–292.

Melikian-Chirvani, Assadullah Souren. 1985. "The Aesthetics of Islam." In Toby Falk, ed., *Treasures of Islam*, 20–24. Geneva: Musée d'art et d'histoire.

Melikian-Chirvani, Assadullah Souren. 1991. "Les taureaux à vin et les cornes à boire de l'Iran islamique." In Paul Bernard and Frantz Grenet, eds., *Histoire et cultes de l'Asie central préislamique*, 102–125. Paris: Éditions du centre nationale de la recherche scientifique.

Meloy, John L. 2003. "The Merits of Economy: Re-Reading al-Maqrizi's Ighathah and Shudhur." *Mamluk Studies Review* 7:2, 183–203.

Melville, Firuza. 2018. "Zahhak from Cambridge and Bahram Gur from Geneva: Two Unpublished Lustre Tiles with *Shahnama* Verses." In Gabrielle van den Berg and Charles Melville, eds., *Shahnama Studies III: The Reception of the Shahnama*, 319–346. Leiden: Brill.

Ménant, J. 1887. "Forgeries of Babylonian and Assyrian Antiquities." *American Journal of Archaeology and of the History of the Fine Arts* 3:1/2, 14–31.

Merrillees, Robert S. 2017. "Cypriote Antiquities in Late Ottoman Istanbul and Smyrna—I: Luigi Palma di Cesnola, Cyprus and the Ottoman Connection." *Cahiers du Centre d'Études Chypriotes* 47, 43–120.

Michelsen, Leslee Katrina, and Johanna Olafsdotter. 2014. "Telling Tales: Investigating a *Mīnā'ī* Bowl." In David J. Roxburgh, ed., *Envisioning Islamic Art and Architecture: Essays in Honor of Renata Holod*, 66–87. Leiden: Brill.

Mickel, Allison. 2021. *Why Those Who Shovel Are Silent: A History of Local Archaeological Knowledge and Labor.* Louisville: University Press of Colorado.

Migeon, Gaston. 1901. "Céramique orientale a reflets métalliques." *Gazette des Beaux-Arts*, 192–208.

Mikami, Tsugio. 1964. *Islamic Pottery, Mainly from Japanese Collections.* Vol. 2. Tokyo: Chuo-Koron Bijutsu Shuppan.

Milanese, Andrea. 2007. "Pour ne pas choquer l'œil. Raffaele Gargiulo e il restauro di vasi antichi nel Real Museo de Napoli: Opzioni di metodo e oscillazioni di gusto tra 1810 e 1840." In Paula D'Alconzo, ed., *Gli uomini e le cose: Figure di restauratori e casi di restauro in Italia tra XVIII e XX secolo*, Atti del Convegno Nazionale di Studi, 81–101. Naples: Clio Press.

Milanese, Andrea. 2010. "De la 'perfection dangereuse' et plus encore: La restauration des vases grecs à Naples au début du XIXe siècle, entre histoire du goût et marché de l'art." *Techne* 32, 19–30.

Miller, Peter N. 2008. "Peiresc and the Study of Islamic Coins in the Early Seventeenth Century." *Princeton University Library Chronicle* 69:2, 315–369.

Milwright, Marcus. 2001. "Prologues and Epilogues in Islamic Ceramics: Clays, Repairs, and Secondary Use." *Medieval Ceramics* 25, 72–81.

Milwright, Marcus. 2005. "Ceramics from the Recent Excavations near the Eastern Wall of Rafiqa (Raqqa), Syria." *Levant* 37, 197–219.

Milwright, Marcus. 2006. "Review of Marie [*sic*] Jenkins-Madina, *Raqqa Revisited: Ceramics of Ayyubid Syria*." *CAA Reviews*, 16 October 2006.

Milwright, Marcus. 2008. "Imported Pottery in Ottoman Bilad al-Sham." *Turcica* 40, 121–152.

Milwright, Marcus. 2009. "Written Sources and the Study of Pottery in Ottoman Bilad al-Sham." *al-Rafidan* 30, 37–52.

Milwright, Marcus. 2011. "An Arabic Description of the Activities of Antique Dealers in Late Ottoman Damascus." *Palestine Exploration Quarterly* 143:1, 8–18.

Milwright, Marcus. 2012. "Wood and Woodworking in Late Ottoman Damascus: An Analysis of the Qāmūs al-ṣināʿāt al-Šāmiyya." *Bulletin d'études orientales* 61, 545–566.

Milwright, Marcus. 2012a. "Doris Duke and the Crafts of Islamic Syria." *Shangri La Working Papers in Islamic Art* 2, 22 pp.

Milwright, Marcus. 2014. "Glass and Glassworking in Damascus During the Late 19th and Early 20th Centuries." *Journal of Glass Studies* 56, 201–217.

Milwright, Marcus. 2021. "Rubbish, Recycling and Repair: Perspectives on the Portable Arts of the Islamic Middle East." In Robert Hillenbrand, ed., *The Making of Islamic Art: Studies in Honour of Sheila Blair and Jonathan Bloom*, 138–155. Edinburgh: Edinburgh University Press.

Milwright, Marcus. 2022. "The Manual Crafts and the Challenge of Modernity in Late Nineteenth-Century

Damascus." In Margaret S. Graves and Alex Dika Seggerman, eds., *Making Modernity in the Islamic Mediterranean*, 139–154. Bloomington: Indiana University Press.

Mitchell, Timothy. 1991. *Colonizing Egypt*. Berkeley: University of California Press.

Mitchell, Timothy. 1992. "Orientalism and the Exhibitionary Order." In Nicholas B. Dirks, ed., *Colonialism and Culture*, 289–317. Ann Arbor: University of Michigan Press.

Moaveni, Azadeh. 2023. "The Ostrich Defence." *London Review of Books*, 5 October 2023, https://www.lrb.co.uk/the-paper/v45/n19/azadeh-moaveni/the-ostrich-defence, accessed 23 May 2024.

Moini, Mehdi, and Christopher M. Rollman. 2017. "Buyid Silk and the Tale of Bibi Shahrbanu: Identification of Biomarkers of Artificial Aging (Forgery) of Silk." *Analytical Chemistry* 89, 10158–10161.

Molera, Judit, et al. 2020. "Islamic Glazed Wares from Ancient Termez (Southern Uzbekistan): Raw Materials and Techniques." *Journal of Archaeological Science: Reports* 29, 11 pp.

Molina, Gloria, et al. 2014. "Technology of Production of Polychrome Lustre." *Journal of the European Ceramic Society* 34, 2563–2574.

Momdjian, Maran. 2017. "The Levantine Merchant Consuls of Aleppo: The Commercial Elites, 1750–1850." Unpublished PhD dissertation, UCLA.

Momdjian, Mary [Maran]. 2020. "Halabis and Foreigners in Aleppo's Mediterranean Trade: The Role of Levantine Merchants in Eighteenth-Century Commercial Networks." In Stefan Winter and Mafalda Ade, eds., *Aleppo and Its Hinterland in the Ottoman Period/Alep et sa province à l'époque ottoman*, 109–129. Leiden: Brill.

Mota, Maris Manuela. 1988. *Louças seljúcidas, catálogo das louças islâmicas*. Vol. 1. Lisbon: Museu Calouste Gulbenkian.

Motz, Timothy A. 2024. "The Second Life of the Barberini Togatus in Baroque Rome." *Kunstgeschichte* (February), 22 pp.

Mouliérac, Jeanne. 1999. *Céramiques du monde musulman*. Paris: Institut du monde arabe.

Mousavi, Ali. 2005. "Herzfeld, Politics, and Antiquities Legislation in Iran." In Anne C. Gunter and Stefan R. Hauser, eds., *Ernst Herzfeld and the Development of Near Eastern Studies, 1900–1950*, 445–475. Leiden: Brill.

Mouterde, René. 1926. "Review: G. de Jerphanion, 'Le calice d'Antioch: Les théories du Dr. Eisen et la date probable du calice' et Ch. Diehl, 'Un nouveau trésor d'argenterie syrienne.'" *Mélanges de l'Université Saint-Joseph, Beyrouth* 11, 361–367.

Mulder, Stephennie, ed. 2022. *Imagining Antiquity in Islamic Societies*, Bristol: Intellect.

Mulder, Stephennie. Forthcoming. *The Ceramics of Balis*.

Muller, Arthur. 2023. "Les doigts dans le terre. L'exploitation des dactylotypes de coroplathes: Questions, exemples, et perspectives." *Pallas* 121, 23–41.

Müller-Wiener, Martina. 1996. *Islamische Keramik*. Frankfurt: Museum für Kunsthandwerk.

Murphy, Miriam T. 1925. "The Great Chalice of Antioch on Which Are Depicted in Sculpture the Earliest Known Portraits of Christ, Apostles and Evangelists." Review in *Catholic History Review*, 137–138.

Muscarella, Oscar White. 2008. "The Veracity of 'Scientific' Testing by Conservators." In Ernst Pernicka, ed., *Original—Copy—Fake? Examining the Authenticity of Ancient Works of Art—Focusing on African and Asian Bronzes and Terracottas*, 9–18. Mainz: Philipp von Zabern.

Muscarella, Oscar White. n.d. "Bronzes of Luristan." *Encyclopaedia Iranica*, https://www.iranicaonline.org/articles/bronzes-of-luristan, accessed 18 April 2024.

Nasir-i Khusraw. 2001. *Nasir-i Khusraw's Book of Travels (Safarnama): A Parallel Persian-English Text*. Trans. and ed. Wheeler M. Thackston Jr. Costa Mesa, CA: Mazda.

Nasiri-Moghaddam, Nader. 2003. "L'affaire du vol de la Bibliothèque royale du Palais du Golestan à Téhéran, ca. 1907." *Studia Iranica* 32:1, 137–147.

Nasiri-Moghaddam, Nader. 2004. *L'archéologie française en Perse et les antiquités nationales (1884–1914)*. Paris: Connaissances et Savoirs.

Nasiri-Moghaddam, Nader. n.d. "Lesān-al-Dawla." *Encyclopaedia Iranica*, https://www.iranicaonline.org/articles/lesan-al-dawla-mirza-ali-khn, accessed 24 December 2023.

Naumann, Rudolf. 1961. "Die Ausgrabungen am Feuertempel." In Hans Henning von der Osten and Rudolf Naumann, eds., *Takht-i-Suleiman: Vorläufiger Bericht über die Ausgrabungen 1959*, 54–65. Berlin: Gebr. Mann.

Necipoğlu, Gülru. 2012. "The Concept of Islamic Art: Inherited Discourses and New Approaches." In Benoît Junod, Georges Khalil, Stefan Weber, and Gerhard Wolf, eds., *Islamic Art and the Museum*, 57–75. London: Saqi.

Nedashkovsky, Leonard F. 2012. "Golden Horde Antiquities: The Development of Research Ideas." *Acta Archaeologica* 83, 225–255.

Nelson, George. 2024. "Disputed Malevich Painting Tied to Disgraced Dealer Itzhak Zarug Presented as Genuine in Private 'Exhibition' at Centre Pompidou." *ARTnews*, 6 June 2024 , https://www.artnews.com/art-news/news/kasimir-malevich-painting-dispute-co2bit-centre-pompidou-1234708956/, accessed 4 January 2025.

Neuwirth, Angelika. 2022. *The Qur'an: Text and Commentary*. Vol. 1, *Early Meccan Suras: Poetic Prophecy*. Trans. Samuel Wilder. New Haven: Yale University Press.

Nir, Sarah Mislin, Patricia Cohen, and William K. Rashbaum. 2013. "Struggling Immigrant Artist Tied to $80 Million New York Fraud." *New York Times*, 16 August 2013.

Niyazioğlu, Aslı. 2022. "Into the Deep Past of the Ottoman Istanbul: The Bronze Horseman of Constantine in Sixteenth-Century *'Acā'ibs*." *Aca'ib: Occasional Papers on the Ottoman Perceptions of the Supernatural* 3, 13–34.

Nöldeke-Hannover, A. 1910–11. "Zur Kenntnis der Keramik von Raqqa, Rhages, und Sultanabad." *Orientalisches Archiv* 1, 16–17.

Norman, Kirsty. 2004. "Restoration and Faking of Islamic Ceramics: Case Histories." In Oliver Watson, *Ceramics from Islamic Lands*, 69–89. London: Thames and Hudson.

Norris, Dana, and Oliver Watson. 2021. "Illuminating the Imperceptible: Researching Mina'i Ceramics with Digital Imaging Techniques." *Journal of Imaging* 7:233, 11 pp.

Northedge, Alastair, and Derek Kennet. 1994. "The Samarra Horizon." In Ernst Grube, *Cobalt and Lustre: The First Centuries of Islamic Pottery*, 21–35. London: Nour Foundation.

Oddy, Andrew. 1992. Introduction to Andrew Oddy, ed., *The Art of the Conservator*, 7–27. Washington, DC: Smithsonian Institute.

Olin, Margaret. 1996. "Nationalism, the Jews, and Art History." *Judaism* 45:4, 461–482.

Olmer, Louis-Joseph. 1908. "L'industrie persane, rapport sur une mission scientifique." *Nouvelles archives des missions scientifiques et littéraires* 16 (Paris: Ernest Leroux), 1–110.

Osipian, Alexandr. 2022. "Ottoman and Persian Luxury Between Fashion and Politics: The Armenian Merchant Network and the Making of Sarmatian Culture in Early Modern Poland-Lithuania." In Alina Payne, ed., *The Land Between Two Seas: Art on the Move in the Mediterranean and the Black Sea 1300–1700*, 311–333. Leiden: Brill.

Ostapkowicz, Joanna, and Jonathan A. Hanna, eds. 2021. *Real, Recent, or Replica: Precolumbian Caribbean Heritage as Art, Commodity, and Inspiration*. Tuscaloosa: University of Alabama Press.

Overton, Keelan. 2022. "Framing, Performing, Forgetting: The Emamzadeh Yahya at Varamin." *Platform*, 19 September 2022, https://www.platformspace.net/home/framing-performing-forgetting-the-emamzadeh-yahya-at-varamin, accessed 17 March 2024.

Overton, Keelan. 2024. "Jane Dieulafoy in Varamin: The Emamzadeh Yahya Through a Nineteenth-Century Lens." *Getty Research Journal* 19, 57–91.

Overton, Keelan, and Kimia Maleki. 2021. "The Emamzadeh Yahya at Varamin: A Present History of a Living Shrine, 2018–20." *Journal of Material Cultures in the Muslim World* 1:1–2, 120–149.

Pancaroğlu, Oya. 2007. *Perpetual Glory: Medieval Islamic Ceramics from the Harvey B. Plotnick Collection*. Chicago: Art Institute of Chicago.

Pancaroğlu, Oya. 2013. "Feasts of Nishapur: Cultural Resonances of Tenth-Century Ceramic Production in Khurasan." In Mary McWilliams, ed., *In Harmony: The Norma Jean Calderwood Collection of Islamic Art*, 3–13. Cambridge, MA: Harvard Art Museums.

Panzac, Daniel. 1992. "International and Domestic Maritime Trade in the Ottoman Empire During the 18th Century." *International Journal of Middle East Studies* 24:2, 189–206.

Parke-Bernet. 1953. *The Dikran Kelekian Collection, Part 1: Near Eastern Art . . . Public Auction Sale by Order of the Executors of the Estate and the Directors of Dikran G. Kelekian, Inc.* Parke-Bernet Galleries, 21–22 and 23 October 1953.

Parry, Vicki. 2023. "Crazing, Shivering, Golden Cracks and Rivets: Preserving the Value of Flaws." In Margaret S. Graves, Sequoia Miller, Magdalene Odundo, and Vicki Parry, *Ceramic Art*, 47–68. Princeton: Princeton University Press.

Patterson, Orlando. 1982. *Slavery and Social Death: A Comparative Study*. Cambridge, MA: Harvard University Press.

Payaslian, Simon. 2013. "The Fateful Years: Kesaria During the Genocide." In Richard G. Hovannisian, ed., *Armenian Kesaria/Kayseri and Cappadocia*, 281–312. Costa Mesa, CA: Mazda.

Pazaurek, [Gustav E.]. 1929. "603. Fälschungen von Fayence-Signaturen." *Mitteilungen des Museen-Verbandes als Manuskript für die Mitglieder* (May), 4–5.

Pease, Murray. 1958. "Two Bowls in One." *Metropolitan Museum of Art Bulletin* 16:8, 236–240.

Peck, Elsie Holmes. 1997. "Like the Light of the Sun: Islamic Luster-Painted Ceramics." *Bulletin of the Detroit Institute of Arts* 71:1/2, 16–35.

[Petty, William]. 1938. "Of Statues and Antiquities." In *The Works of John Milton*, vol. 18, 258–261. New York: Columbia University Press.

Pézard, Maurice. 1920. *Le céramique archaïque de l'islam et ses origines*. 2 vols. Paris: Ernest Leroux.

Phillip, Filiz Çakir. 2011. "Ernst Herzfeld and the Excavations at Samarra." In Zainab Bahrani, Zeynep Çelik, and Edhem Eldem, eds., *Scramble for the Past: A Story of Archaeology in the Ottoman Empire, 1753–1914*, 383–397. Istanbul: SALT.

Philon, Helen. 1980. *Early Islamic Ceramics: Ninth to Late Twelfth Centuries*. London: Sotheby Parke Bernet.

Pier, Garrett Chatfield. 1908. "Pottery of the Hither Orient in the Metropolitan Museum of Art—I." *Burlington Magazine for Connoisseurs* 14, 120–121, 125.

Pijoán, José. 1946. *Summa Artis: Historia general del arte*. 2nd ed. 18 vols. Madrid: Espasa Calpe.

Pillinger, Renate. 1984. *Studien zu Römischen Zwischengoldgläsern*. Vol. 1, *Geschichte der Technik und Das Problem der Authentizität*. Vienna: Verlag des Österreichischen Akademie der Wissenschaften.

Pope, Arthur Upham. 1930. "Treasures Found in an Earthenware Jar: Fine Seljuk Silver." *Illustrated London News*, 20 September 1930, 480–482.

Pope, Arthur Upham. 1930a. *An Introduction to Persian Art Since the Seventh Century A.D.* London: Peter Davies.

Pope, Arthur Upham. 1931. "Persian Faience of Early Islamic Times." *Illustrated London News*, 10 January 1931, 62.

Pope, Arthur Upham. 1932. Review of R. L. Hobson, *A Guide to the Islamic Pottery of the Near East*. *The Art Bulletin* 14:4, 374–379.

Pope, Arthur Upham. 1940. "Introduction: The Character of Persian Art." In Georges de Batz and Arthur Upham Pope, *Persian Art Through Four Millenia; A Check List of Objects Exhibited from January 12, 1940, to February 10, 1940*, 7–10. Baltimore: Johns Hopkins University.

Pope, Arthur Upham. 1942. "The *Survey of Persian Art* and Its Critics." *Ars Islamica* 9, 169–208.

Pope, Arthur Upham. 1945. *Masterpieces of Persian Art*. New York: Dryden Press.

Pope, Arthur Upham, ed. 1971. *Survey of Persian Art*. Vol. 13, *Fascicle, Addendum A—The Andarz Nama: Proceedings, the IVth International Congress of Iranian Art and Archaeology, April 24–May 3, 1960*. London: Oxford University Press.

Pope, Arthur Upham, and Phyllis Ackerman, eds. 1981. *A Survey of Persian Art*. 16 vols. Ashiya: SOPA; reprint.

Portell, Jean D. 2003. "Prior Repairs: When Should They Be Preserved?" *Journal of the American Institute for Conservation* 42:2, 363–380.

Porter, Robert Ker. 1821. *Travels in Georgia, Persia, Armenia, Ancient Babylonia, &c. &c. During the Years 1817, 1818, 1819, and 1820*. 2 vols. London: Longman, Hurst, Rees, Orme, and Brown.

Porter, Venetia. 1981. *Medieval Syrian Pottery*. Oxford: Ashmolean Museum.

Porter, Venetia. 1996. *Islamic Tiles*. London: British Museum.

Porter, Venetia, and Oliver Watson. 1987. "'Tell Minis' Wares." In James Allan and Caroline Roberts, eds., *Syria and Iran: Three Studies in Medieval Ceramics*, 175–220. Oxford: Oxford University Press.

Porter, Yves. 2011. *Le prince, l'artiste et l'alchimiste: La céramique dans le monde iranien, Xe-XVIIe siècle*. Paris: Hermann.

Porter, Yves. 2021. "'Talking' Tiles from Vanished Ilkhanid Palaces." *Journal of Material Cultures of the Muslim World* 2, 97–149.

Porter, Yves. 2023. *Under the Adorned Dome: Four Essays on the Arts of Iran and India*. Leiden: Brill.

Pottier, E. 1906. "177. Die Fälschung der Schale von Corneto." *Mitteilungen des Museen-Verbandes als Manuskript für die Mitglieder* (September), 12–13.

Potts, D. T. 2020. "'Un coup terrible de la fortune': A. Clement and the Qurna Disaster of 1855." In Irving L. Finkel and St. John Simpson, eds., *In Context: The Reade Festschrift*, 235–244. Oxford: Archaeopress.

Potts, D. T. 2023. *Albert Houtum Schindler: A Remarkable Polymath in Late-Qajar Iran*. Washington, DC: Mage.

Potts, Daniel Thomas, and Gian Pietro Basello. 2022. "The 'Black Stone of Susa:' A Lost *Kudurru*, an Unpublished Drawing and a Line of Middle Elamite Copied in the 1820s." *East and West*, n.s., 3:62, 97–116.

Powell, Edith M. 1917. "Your Home and Its Decoration." *Arts & Decoration* 7:4, 205–206, 208, 210.

Pradell, Trinitat, et al. 2008. "The Invention of Lustre: Iraq

9th and 10th Centuries AD." *Journal of Archaeological Science* 35, 1201–1215.

Pradell, Trinitat, et al. 2008a. "Early Islamic Lustre Wares from Egypt, Syria, and Iran (10th to 13th Century AD)." *Journal of Archaeological Science* 35, 2649–2662.

Pradell, Trinitat, et al. 2013. "Analysis of Syrian Lustre Pottery (12th–14th Centuries AD)." *Applied Clay Science* 82, 106–112.

Pradell, Trinitat, et al. 2016. "Composition of the Lustre Pigment Used in the Production of 13th Century AD Raqqa Lustreware from Syria." *Archaeometry* 58:6, 979–986.

Press, Michael. 2021. "The Myth of Moses Shapira." *Ancient Jew Review*, 1 September 2021, https://www.ancientjewreview.com/read/2021/8/31/the-myth-of-moses-shapira#_edn17, accessed 20 March 2024.

Press, Michael. 2023. "The Career of Moses Shapira, Bookseller and Antiquarian." *Palestine Exploration Quarterly* 155:3, 230–253.

Priestman, Seth M. N. 2011. "Opaque Glazed Wares: The Definition, Dating and Distribution of a Key Iraqi Export in the Abbasid Period." *Iran* 49, 89–113.

Prisco, Gabriella. 2019. "Two Exhibitions and the Project of a Museum Dedicated to Forgery: A History between France and Italy (1930–1955)." In Monica Baggio et al., eds., *Anthropology of Forgery: A Multidisciplinary Approach to the Study of Archaeological Fakes*, 269–285. Padua: Padova University Press.

[Purgold, K.] K. P. 1899. "3. Palissy-Schüssel." *Mittheilungen des Museen-Verbandes als Manuskript für die Mitglieder* (August), 2–3.

al-Qasimi, Muhammad Saʿid, Jamal al-Din al-Qasimi, and Khalil al-ʿAzm. 1960. *Dictionnaire des métiers damascains*. 2 vols. Paris and Le Haye: Mouton.

al-Qazwini, Zakariya ibn Muhammad ibn Mahmud. n.d. *The Wonders of Creation and Marvels of Existence by Zakariya ibn Muhammad ibn Mahmud al-Qazwini*. Trans. Wheeler M. Thackston. Unpublished manuscript of English translation of al-Qazwini, *ʿAjaʾib al-makhluqat wa gharʾib al-mawjudat*.

R. S. 1912. "365. Fayenceschüssel von Schauffele in Schw. Hall." *Mittheilungen des Museen-Verbandes als Manuskript für die Mitglieder* (August), 6–7.

R. S. 1913. "404. Fälschungs-Restaurationen antiker Vasen." *Mitteilungen des Museen-Verbandes als Manuskript für die Mitglieder* (June), 11–12.

Raby, Julian. 1989. "Anno 1582: 'In Nicaea I Was Wrought.'" In Nurhan Atasoy and Julian Raby, *Iznik: The Pottery of Ottoman Turkey*, 269–272. London: Thames and Hudson.

Rackham, [Bernard]. 1931. "656. Fälschungen italienischer Majoliken." *Mitteilungen des Museen-Verbandes als Manuskript für die Mitglieder* (May), 15–23.

Radcliffe, Jane. n.d. "Gustavus Augustus (Gustav) Eisen (1847–1940)." *Illinois Natural History Survey*, https://wwv.inhs.illinois.edu/files/5013/8921/2402/Gustav_Eisen_biov4.pdf, accessed 30 August 2019.

Radnóti, Sándor. 1999. *The Fake: Forgery and Its Place in Art.* Lanham: Rowman and Littlefield.

Raemdonck, Mieke van. 1999. "A Raqqa Lustre Dish Examined." *Bulletin van de Koninklijke Musea voor Kunst en Geschiedenis, Brussel/Bulletin des Musées royaux d'Art et d'Histoire, Bruxelles* 70:142, 135–148.

Rante, Rocco. 2015. *Rayy: From Its Origins to the Mongol Invasion*. Leiden: Brill.

Rante, Rocco. n.d. "Ray 1. Archaeology." *Encyclopaedia Iranica*, https://www.iranicaonline.org/articles/ray-i-archeo, accessed 12 April 2024.

Rante, Rocco, and Annabel Collinet. 2013. *Nishapur Revisited: Stratigraphy and Ceramics of the Qohandez*. Oxford: Oxbow

Rasmussen, Mark. 2008. "Setting the Standard for Due Diligence: Scientific Techniques in the Authentication Process." In Ernst Pernicka, ed., *Original—Copy—Fake? Examining the Authenticity of Ancient Works of Art—Focusing on African and Asian Bronzes and Terracottas*, 19–32. Mainz: Philipp von Zabern.

Ray, Simon. 2000. *Spanish Pottery 1248–1898*. London: Victoria & Albert Museum.

Read, Charles Hercules. 1907. Introduction to *Burlington Fine Arts Club Exhibition of the Faience of Persia and the Nearer East*, ix–xx. London: Burlington Fine Arts Club.

Redford, Scott, and M. James Blackman. 1997. "Luster and Fritware Production and Distribution in Medieval Syria." *Journal of Field Archaeology* 24:2, 233–247.

Redlak, Malgorzata. 2018. "Egyptian Imitations of Chinese Celadon from the 14th–15th Centuries Found at Kom el-Dikka in Alexandria." *Polish Archaeology in the Mediterranean* 26:1, 59–84.

Reilly, James. 1987. "Sharīʿa Court Registers and Land Tenure around Nineteenth-Century Damascus." *Middle East Studies Association Bulletin* 21:2, 155–169.

Reilly, James. 1992. "Damascus Merchants and Trade in the Transition to Capitalism." *Canadian Journal of History* 27, 1–27.

Reilly, James. 2001. "Local and Regional Economies of Ottoman Syria During the Eighteenth and Nineteenth Centuries." In Miura Toru, ed., *Ownership, Contracts and Markets in China, Southeast Asia and the Middle East: The Potentials of Comparative Study*, 61–99. Tokyo: Islamic Area Studies Project.

Reilly, James. 2002. *A Small Town in Syria: Ottoman Hama in the Eighteenth and Nineteenth Centuries*. Berlin: Peter Lang.

Reinach, Salomon. 1882. *Catalogue du Musée Imperial d'Antiquités*. Constantinople: Direction du Musée.

Reinach, Salomon. 1883. "Le vandalisme moderne en Orient." *Revue des deux mondes* 156/239, 132–166.

Reinach, Salomon. 1888. "The So-Called Asiatic Terra-Cotta Groups." *Classical Review* 2:4, 119–123.

Reinach, Salomon. 1888a. "The So-Called Asiatic Terra-Cotta Groups (Continued)." *Classical Review* 2:5, 153–155.

Reinach, Salomon. 1891. *Chroniques d'Orient: Documents sur les fouilles et découvertes dans l'Orient hellénique de 1883 à 1890*. Paris: Firmin Didot.

Respini, Eva, and Walid Raad. 2015. *Walid Raad*. New York: MOMA.

Riazi, Mohammad Reza, and Akram Kabiri. 2016. *Kashi'kari-i Qajari* [Qajar Tiles]. Tehran: Yasaavoli.

Riefstahl, Rudolf Meyer. 1922. *The Parish-Watson Collection of Mohammadan Potteries*. New York: E. Weyhe.

Riefstahl, Rudolf M[eyer]. 1923. "Reiza Khan Monif." In *The Collection of the Late Reiza Khan Monif of Paris and New York*. Anderson Galleries, sale no. 1778.

Riefstahl, Rudolf Meyer. [1926]. *A Collection of Ancient Raqqa Pottery*. n.p.

Riis, P. J., and Vagn Poulsen. 1957. *Hama: Fouille et recherches 1931–1938*. Vol. IV2, *Les verreries et poteries médiévales*. Copenhagen: Nationalmuseet.

Ris-Paquot, Oscar Edmond. 1872. *Manière de restaurer soi-même les faïences, porcelaines, cristaux, marbres, terres cuites, grès, biscuits, émaux, etc.* Paris: Librairie Eugène Delaroque.

Rivière, Henri, and Gaston Migeon. 1913. *La céramique dans l'art musulman*. 2 vols. Paris: Librarie centrale des beaux-arts.

Roberts, Richard G., Christopher J. Uren, and Andrew S. Murray. 1993. *Thermoluminescence Dating Techniques at the Alligator Rivers Region Research Institute.* Canberra: Australian Government Publishing Service.

Rogan, Eugene. 2024. *The Damascus Events: The 1860 Massacre and the Destruction of the Old Ottoman World.* London: Allen Lane.

Rogers, J. Michael. 1974. *From Antiquarianism to Islamic Archaeology.* Cairo: Quaderni dell' Istituto Italiano di Cultura per la R.A.E.

Rogers, J. Michael. 1973/74. "*Art islamique dans les collections privées libanaises,* Musée Sursock, Beirut, May 31st–July 17th, 1974." *Kunst des Orients* 9:1/2, 169–175.

Rogers, J. Michael. 2000. "The Collecting of Islamic Art in Nineteenth-Century Russia." In Stephen Vernoit, ed., *Discovering Islamic Art: Scholars, Collectors and Collections, 1850–1950,* 62–70. London: I. B. Tauris.

Rorimer, James J. 1954. "The Authenticity of the Chalice of Antioch." In Dorothy Miner, ed., *Studies in Art and Literature for Belle da Costa Greene,* 161–168. Princeton: Princeton University Press.

Rose, Vanessa. 2017. "Les fouilles d'Henry Viollet à Samarra." *Annales islamologiques* 51, 167–190.

Rougelle, Axelle. 2023. *Qalhat, a Medieval Port City of Oman: From a Field of Ruins to UNESCO.* Oxford: Archaeopress.

Rousset, Marie-Odile. 1996. "Contribution à l'étude de la céramique islamique: Analyse du matériel archéologique de Rahba-Mayadin (Syrie, vallée de l'Euphrat)." 2 vols. Unpublished PhD thesis, Université Lumière Lyon 2.

Roxburgh, David J. 1998. "Disorderly Conduct? F. R. Martin and the Bahram Mirza Album." *Muqarnas* 15, 32–57.

Roxburgh, David J. 2000. "Au Bonheur des Amateurs: Collecting and Exhibiting Islamic Art, ca. 1880–1910." *Ars Orientalis* 30, 9–38.

Roxburgh, David J. 2001. "The Aesthetics of Aggregation: Persian Anthologies of the Fifteenth Century." In Oleg Grabar and Cynthia Robinson, eds., *Islamic Art and Literature,* 119–142. Princeton: Markus Wiener.

Roxburgh, David J. 2003. "On the Tradition and Reconstruction of Arabic Calligraphy: Ibn al-Bawwab and History." *Studia Islamica* 96, 39–53.

Roxburgh, David J. 2005. *The Persian Album, 1400–1600: From Dispersal to Collection.* New Haven: Yale University Press.

Royal Academy. 1931. *Catalogue of the International Exhibition of Persian Art.* London: Royal Academy of Arts.

Rozantal, A. 1948. *Arts antiques de l'asie occidentale, a partir du IVe millénaire avant J.C., et les origines des motifs de la céramique islamique archaïque.* Nice: G. Mathieu.

Rugiadi, Martina. 2011. "The Emergence of Siliceous-Paste in Iran in the Last Quarter of the 11th Century and Related Issues: The Dated Assemblage from the Southern Domed Hall of the Great Mosque of Isfahan." *Vicino & Medio Oriente* 15, 233–258.

Rugiadi, Martina. 2016. "Nine Stucco Figures and One Fragment from Iran." In Sheila Canby, Deniz Beyazit, and Martina Rugiadi, eds., *Court and Cosmos: The Great Age of the Seljuqs,* 40–47. New York: Metropolitan Museum of Art.

Rugiadi, Martina. 2016a. "Stonepaste Technology in Syria and Iran." In Sheila Canby, Deniz Beyazit, and Martina Rugiadi, eds., *Court and Cosmos: The Great Age of the Seljuqs,* 179–187. New York: Metropolitan Museum of Art.

Rustow, Marina. 2020. *The Lost Archive: Traces of a Caliphate in a Cairo Synagogue.* Princeton: Princeton University Press.

Saba, Matthew. 2012. "Abbasid Lustreware and the Aesthetics of ʿAjab." *Muqarnas* 29, 187–212.

Sabry, Randa. 2018. "Le témoignage d'Amīn Fikrī sur l'Exposition universelle de 1889 et la rue du Caire: Petite polémique avec Timothy Mitchell." *Arabica* 65, 368–391.

Saccocci, Andrea. 2019. "Coin Counterfeiting in Medieval Italy: The Archaeological Evidence (12th–13th Centuries)." In Monica Baggio et al., eds., *Anthropology of Forgery: A Multidisciplinary Approach to the Study of Archaeological Fakes,* 225–234. Padua: Padova University Press.

Sahim, Haideh. 2005. "Jews of Iran in the Qajar Period: Persecution and Persistence." In Robert Gleave, ed., *Religion and Society in Qajar Iran,* 293–310. London: Routledge.

Salmon, Irit, ed. 2000. *Truly Fake: Moses Wilhelm Shapira, Master Forger.* Jerusalem: Israel Museum.

Samavaki, Sheila. 2021. *Les céramiques buff de Nishapur: L'étude iconographique des céramiques polychromes à décor figuratif, IXe–Xe siècles.* N.p.: Editions KPD.

Sambon, Arthur. 1925. "Les faïences ivoirines de Sendjan de la dynastie Bouïde." *Le musée* (December), 113–122.

Sambon, Arthur. 1928. *Images populaires de l'Avesta en Perse, aux XIIe et XIIIe siècles: Description d'une collection de faiences persanes à sujets nationalistes et d'une servie orvietane de style sassanide.* Paris: Bibliothèque du Musée.

Sanderson, David. 2020. "Fakers Make a Right Mesopotamia!" *The Times,* 5 May 2020, 3.

Sarre, Friedrich. 1907. "183. Über Fälschungen persischer Lüster-Fayencegefäße." *Mitteilungen des Museen-Verbandes als Manuskript für die Mitglieder* (March), 2–3.

Sarre, Friedrich. 1909. "Rakka Ware." *Burlington Magazine for Connoisseurs* 14:72, 388.

Sarre, Friedrich. 1922. *Die Kunst des alten Persien.* Berlin: Bruno Cassirer Verlag.

Sarre, Friedrich. 1923. "Die mittelalterliche persische Keramik und die Sammlung Dr Draeger." *Kunst und Künstler* 21, 78–83.

Sarre, Friedrich. 1923a. "Zuwachs der Islamischer Abteilung." *Berliner Museen* 44:5/6, 35–43.

Sarre, Friedrich. 1925. *Forschungen zur Islamischen Kunst. Die Ausgrabungen von Samarra, II: Die Keramik von Samarra.* Berlin: Dietrich Reimer.

Sarre, Friedrich. 1929. "609. Persian Style Forged Precious Metal Work." *Mitteilungen des Museen-Verbandes als Manuskript für die Mitglieder* (May), 10–16.

Sarre, Friedrich. 1939. "Die Fayencen von Nicaea und ihr Export nach dem Abenland." *Pantheon* 24, 341–354.

Sarre, Friedrich, and Ernst Herzfeld. 1920. *Archäologische Reise im Euphrat- und Tigris-Gebiet.* Vol. 4. Berlin: Dietrich Reimer.

Saul, Samir. 2003. "Les agencies du Crédit lyonnais en Egypte: L'insertion d'une banque de dépôts dans une économie d'Outre-Mer (1875–1956)." In Bernard Desjardins et al., *Le Crédit lyonnais (1836–1986): Études historiques,* 521–548. Geneva: Droz.

Saul, Samir. 2013. *La France et l'Égypte de 1882 à 1914: Intérêts économiques et implications politiques,* 295–373. Paris: Comité pour l'histoire économique et financière de la France.

Sauvaget, Jean. 1948. "Tessons de Rakka." *Ars Islamica* 13, 31–45.

Scanlon, George T. 1971. "The Fustat Mounds: A Shard Count, 1968." *Archaeology* 24:3, 220–233.

Scarce, Jennifer M. 1976. "Ali Mohammad Isfahani, Tilemaker of Tehran." *Oriental Art* 22:3, 278–288.

Scerrato, Umberto. 1959. "Summary Report on the Italian Archaeological Mission in Afghanistan: The First Two Excavation Campaigns at Ghazni, 1957–1958." *East and West* 10:1/2, 23–55.

Schevill, Margot Blum. 1993. *Maya Textiles of Guatemala: The Gustavus A. Eisen Collection, 1902.* Austin: University of Texas Press.

Schmidt, Erich F. 1935. "The Persian Expedition." *Bulletin of the Museum of Fine Arts* 5:5, 41–49.

Schmidt, Erich F. 1936. "Rayy Research 1935 ... Part I." *University Museum Bulletin* 6:3, 79–87.

Schmidt, Erich F. 1940. *Flights over Ancient Cities of Iran.* Chicago: University of Chicago Press.

Schmidt, Robert. 1929. "Fayence-Fälschungen." *Mitteilungen des Museen-Verbandes als Manuskript für die Mitglieder* (May), 1–2.

Schnyder, Rudolf. 1972. "Saljuq Pottery in Iran." In *5th International Congress of Iranian Art and Archaeology*, vol. 2, 189–197. Tehran: Ministry of Culture and Art.

Schnyder, Rudolf. 1974. "Medieval Incised and Carved Wares from North West Iran." In William Watson, ed., *The Art of Iran and Anatolia from the 11th to the 13th Century*, Colloquies on Art and Archaeology in Asia 4, 85–95. London: SOAS.

Schwerda, Mira Xenia. 2017. "Iranian Photography: From the Court, to the Studio, to the Street." In David Roxburgh and Mary McWilliams, eds., *Technologies of the Image: Art in 19th-Century Iran*, 81–105. Cambridge, MA: Harvard Art Museums.

Selden, John. 1628. *Marmora Arundelliana.* London: Stanesbeius.

Seraphin Abdullah, R. P., and Frédéric Macler. 1909. *Études dur la miniature arménienne.* Paris: n.p.

Sero, Dzemilo, et al. 2021. "The Study of Three-Dimensional Fingerprint Recognition in Cultural Heritage: Trends and Challenges." *ACM Journal on Computing and Cultural Heritage* 14:4, article 51, 20 pp.

Shaer, Matthew. 2019. "The Invention of the 'Salvator Mundi' Or, How to Turn a $1,000 Art-Auction Pickup into a $450 Million Masterpiece." *Vulture*, 14 April 2019, https://www.vulture.com/2019/04/salvator-mundi-leonardo-da-vinci.html, accessed 25 November 2023.

Shafir, Nir. 2021. "Phanariot Tongues: The Mavrocordatos Family and the Power of the Turkish Language in the Eighteenth-Century Ottoman Empire." *Oriente Moderno* 101, 181–220.

Shafir, Nir. 2022. "Nābulusī Explores the Ruins of Baalbek: Antiquarianism in the Ottoman Empire During the Seventeenth Century." *Renaissance Quarterly* 75, 136–184.

Shanks, Hershel. 2002. "Fakes! How Moses Shapira Forged an Entire Civilization." *Archaeological Odyssey* 5:5, Biblical Archaeology Society Online Archive, https://www.baslibrary.org/archaeology-odyssey/5/5/9, accessed 22 March 2025..

Shaw, Wendy. 2003. *Possessors and Possessed: Museums, Archaeology, and the Visualization of History in the Late Ottoman Empire.* Berkeley: University of California Press.

Shchukin, Pyotr Ivanovich. 1907. *Persidskiye veshchi Shchukinskogo sobraniya* [Persian Goods: Shchukin Collection]. Moscow: A. I. Mamontova.

Sheehi, Stephen. 2016. *The Arab Imago: A Social History of Portrait Photography, 1860–1910.* Princeton: Princeton University Press.

Shishkin, V. A. 1969. "On the History of the Archaeological Study of Samarkand and Its Environs." In *Afrasiabskaia kompleksnaia arkheologicheskaia ekspeditsiia: Afrasiab*, 3–121. Tashkent: "Fan" USSR.

Sigel, Anthony B., and Mary McWilliams. 2013. "History in Pieces: Conservation Issues in Islamic Ceramics." In Mary McWilliams, ed., *In Harmony: The Norma Jean Calderwood Collection of Islamic Art*, 37–49. Cambridge, MA: Harvard Art Museums.

Simeon, Pierre. 2020. *From Ordinary to Luxury: Islamic Ceramics from Iran, Central Asia and Afghanistan.* Wiesbaden: Reichert.

Simpson, Marianna Shreve. 1985. "Narrative Allusion and Metaphor in the Decoration of Medieval Islamic Objects." *Studies in the History of Art* 16, 131–149.

Simpson, Marianna Shreve. 2000. "'A Gallant Era': Henry Walters, Islamic Art, and the Kelekian Connection." *Ars Orientalis* 30, 91–112.

Simpson, Marianna Shreve. 2008. "Mostly Modern Miniatures: Classical Persian Painting in the Early Twentieth Century." *Muqarnas* 25, 359–395.

Simpson, Marianna Shreve. 2015. "Medieval Islamic Ceramics in the Real Academia de Bellas Artes de San Fernando/Cerámica islámica medieval en la Real Academia de Bellas Artes de San Fernando." *Academia: Boletín de la Real Academia de Bellas Artes de San Fernando* 117, 205–237.

Sims-Williams, Ursula. 2000. "Forgeries from Chinese Turkestan in the British Library's Hoernle and Stein Collections." *Bulletin of the Asia Institute* 14, 111–129.

Sjöberg, Fredrik. 2016. *The Art of Flight.* New York: Penguin Random House.

Slitine, Florence. 1998. "C'est un vrai Samson!" *Sèvres: Revue de la Société des amis du musée national de céramique* 7, 66–80.

Slitine, Florence. 2002. *Samson: Génie de l'imitation.* Paris: Massin.

Sluglett, Peter. 2002. "Aspects of Economy and Society in the Syrian Provinces: Aleppo in Transition, 1880–1925." In Laila Fawaz and C. A. Bayly, eds., *Modernity and Culture: From the Mediterranean to the Indian Ocean*, 144–157. New York: Columbia University Press.

Sluglett, Peter. 2002a. "Will the Real Nationalists Please Stand Up? The Political Activities of the Notables of Aleppo, 1918–1946." In Nadine Méouchy, ed., *France, Syrie et Liban 1918–1946: Les ambiguïtés et les dynamiques de la relation mandataire*, 273–290. Damascus: Institut français d'études arabes de Damas.

Smirnov, A. 2013. "The Impact of State Power on Archaeological Science in the Russian Empire." *Complutum* 24:2, 121–130.

Smith, Adam. 1761. *The Theory of Moral Sentiments.* 2nd ed. London and Edinburgh: A. Millar and J. Bell.

Smith, Dylan T. 2006. "Appendix 2: Compositional Analysis of Early Thirteenth-Century Ceramics from Raqqa and Related Sites." In Marilyn Jenkins-Madina, *Raqqa Revisited: Ceramics of Ayyubid Syria*, 221–235. New York: Metropolitan Museum of Art.

Smith, Edmond J. 2015. "'Canaanising Madagascar': Africa in English Imperial Imagination, 1635–1650." *Itinerario* 39:2, 277–298.

Snow, Carol E. 1986. "The Affecter Amphora: A Case Study in the History of Greek Vase Restoration." *Journal of the Walters Art Gallery* 44, 2–7.

Soehnée Frères. 1901. *Notice sur le vernis Soehnée Frères.* Paris: Soehnée Frères.

Sokolovskaia, Ludmila, and Axelle Rougeulle. 1992. "Stratified Finds of Chinese Porcelains." *Bulletin of the Asia Institute*, n.s., 6, 87–98.

Soudavar, Abolala. 2008. "*Le chant du monde*: A Disenchanting Echo of Safavid Art History." *IRAN: Journal of the British Institute of Persian Studies* 46, 253–276.

St. Laurent, Beatrice. 1986. "Léon Parvillée: His Role as a Restorer of Bursa's Monuments and His Contribution to the Exposition Universelle of 1867." In Hâmit Batu and Jean-Louis Bacqué-Grammont, eds., *L'Empire ottomane, la République de Turquie, et la France*, 247–282. Istanbul: Éditions Isis.

Stafford, Barbara Maria. 1984. "Characters in Stones, Marks on Paper: Enlightenment Discourse on Natural and Artificial Taches." *Art Journal* 44:3, 233–240.

Stark, Sören. 2023. "Excavations in the Bukhara Oasis: New Archaeological Data from Bukhara During the Samanid and Qarakhanid Periods." The Hadasseh and Daniel Khalili Memorial Lecture in Islamic Art and Culture, School of Oriental and African Studies, 10 May 2023.
Stedelijk Museum. 1952. *Vals of Echt?* Amsterdam: Stedelijk Museum.
Stedelijk Museum and Corning Museum of Glass. 1953. *True or False: A Special Exhibition, 1953–1954 Season.* Corning, NY: Corning Museum of Glass.
Stein, Aurel. 1903. *Sand-Buried Ruins of Khotan.* London: T. Fisher.
Stoneham, Doreen, and Marshall Stoneham. 2010. "Beating the Forger: Authenticating Ceramic Antiquities." *Contemporary Physics* 51:5, 397–411.
Strohschnieder, Marika. 2021. "A Riveting Past." *National Gallery of Victoria*, 6 October 2021, https://www.ngv.vic.gov.au/essay/a-riveting-past/, accessed 10 March 2023.
Strzygowski, Josef. 1924. "Der Silberkelch von Antiochia, römischer und vorderasiatischer Zeitansatz alchristlicher Denkmäler." *Jahrbuch der asiatischen Kunst*, 157–181.
Suleman, Fahmida. 2003. "The Lion, the Hare and Lustre Ware: Studies in the Iconography of Lustre Ceramics from Fāṭimid Egypt (969–1171 CE)." 2 vols. Unpublished PhD thesis, Oxford University.
Svobodo, Marie. 2013. "Precision and Mastery: Identifying the Work of Raffaele Gargiulo on Four Apulian Vases." In Isabelle Brajer, ed., *Conservation in the Nineteenth Century*, 205–218. London: Archetype.
Sykes, Percy. 1902. *Ten Thousand Miles in Persia or Eight Years in Iran.* London: John Murray.
Talalay, Lauren E., and Margaret Cool Root. 2015. *Passionate Curiosities: Tales of Collectors and Collections from the Kelsey Museum.* Ann Arbor: Kelsey Museum of Archaeology.
Talbot, William Henry Fox. 1844. *The Pencil of Nature.* Fascicle 1. London: Longman, Brown, Green and Longmans.
Tashkhodzhaev, Sh. S. 1967. *Khudozhestvennaia polivnaia keramika Samarkanda IX-nachala XIIIv* [Artistic Glazed Ceramics of Samarkand, 9th—Early 13th Centuries]. Tashkent: "Fan" Uzbek SSR.
Thiaucourt, Prosper. 1865. *Essai sur l'art de restaurer les faïences, porcelaines, terres-cuites, biscuits, grès, verreries, émaux, laques, marbres, albatres, platres, etc.* Paris: August Aubry.
Thiriot, Jacques, and Marthe Bernus-Taylor. Forthcoming. *Les ateliers de potiers de Balis-Meskéné.*
Thomasson, Fredrik. 2010. "Justifying and Criticizing the Removal of Antiquities in Ottoman Lands: Tracking the Sigeion Inscription." *International Journal of Cultural Property* 17:3, 493–517.
Thompson, Erin L. 2021. "That Robby Hobby." *SLATE*, 4 October 2021, https://slate.com/news-and-politics/2021/10/museum-of-the-bible-looted-art-track-record.html, accessed 22 March 2025.
Thurber, James. 1936. "The Talk of the Town: The Great Chalice." *New Yorker*, 4 January 1936, 10.
Ting, Carmen, Martina Rugiadi, and Paul Wordsworth. 2023. "Towards an Integrated Approach to Studying the Stratified Ceramics from the Dandanakan/Daş Rabat, Turkmenistan (9th–12th Centuries a.d.)." *Journal of Field Archaeology* 48:7, 502–517.
Tite, Michael S., S. Wolf, and Robert B. Mason. 2011. "The Technological Development of Stonepaste Ceramics from the Islamic Middle East." *Journal of Archaeological Science* 38, 570–580.
Toll, Christopher. 1970/71. "Minting Technique According to Arabic Literary Sources." *Orientalia Suecana* 19/20, 125–139.
Tonghini, Cristina. 1994. "The Fine Wares of Ayyubid Syria." In Ernst J. Grube, *Cobalt and Lustre: The First Centuries of Islamic Pottery*, 249–257. London: Nour Foundation.
Tonghini, Cristina. 1997. "Ceramica 'Selgiuchide' e ceramica 'di Raqqa': Considerazioni sui criteri di classificazione alla luce di recenti indagini." In Suaro Gelichi, ed., *I congresso nazionale di archeologia medievale*, 428–433. Pisa: Edizioni all'Insegna del Giglio).
Tonghini, Cristina. 1998. *Qal'at Ja'bar Pottery: A Study of a Syrian Fortified Site in the Late 11th–14th Centuries.* London: Council for British Research in the Levant.
Tonghini, Cristina, and Julian Henderson. 1998. "An Eleventh-Century Pottery Production Workshop at al-Raqqa: Preliminary Report." *Levant* 30, 113–127.
Tornier, Étienne. 2019. *Théodore Deck: The Peter Marino Collection.* London: Phaidon Press.
Tracy, James. 2009. "Syria's Arab Traders as Seen by Andrea Berengo, 1555–1556." *Oriens* 37, 163–176.
Tremain, Cara Grace. 2019. "Non-Invasive Techniques to Authenticate the Painted Surfaces of Ancient American Maya Ceramics." In Monica Baggio et al., eds., *Anthropology of Forgery: A Multidisciplinary Approach to the Study of Archaeological Fakes*, 173–180. Padua: Padova University Press.
Treptow, Tanya. 2007. *Daily Life Ornamented: The Medieval Persian City of Rayy.* Chicago: Oriental Institute, University of Chicago.
Trillin, Calvin. 1987. "American Chronicles: Frenchy and the Persians." *New Yorker*, 21 June 1987, 44–67.
Troelenberg, Eva-Maria. 2012. "Regarding the Exhibition: The Munich Exhibition *Masterpieces of Muhammadan Art* (1910) and Its Scholarly Position." *Journal of Art Historiography* 6, 35 pp.
Troelenberg, Eva-Maria. 2014. "On a Pedestal? On the Problem of the Sculptural as a Category of Perception for Islamic Objects." In Gabriele Genge and Angela Stercken, eds., *Art History and Fetishism Abroad: Global Shiftings in Media and Methods*, 159–174. Bielefeld: transcript.
Tsirogiannis, Christos, David W. J. Gill, and Christopher Chippindale. 2022. "The Forger's Tale: An Insider's Account of Corrupting the Corpus of Cycladic Figures." *International Journal of Cultural Property* 29:3, 369–385.
Türker, Deniz. 2014. "Hakky Bey and His Journal *Le miroir de l'art musulman*, or, *Mir'āt-ı ṣanāyi'-i islāmiye* (1898)." *Muqarnas* 31, 277–306.
Türker, Deniz. 2022. "'Angels of the Angels': Abdüllatif Subhi Paşa's Coins, Egypt, and History." *Muqarnas* 39, 193–225.
Turner, Andrew D., and Megan E. O'Neil, eds. 2024. *Collecting Mesoamerican Art Before 1940: A New World of Latin American Antiquities.* Los Angeles: Getty Research Institute.
Tütüncü Çağlar, Filiz. 2017. "From Raqqa with Love: The Raqqa Excavations by the Ottoman Imperial Museum (1905–6 and 1908)." Unpublished PhD dissertation, University of Victoria.
Tyler, Royall. 1910. "Primitive Persian Art." *Saturday Review*, 19 November 1910, 640–641.
Um, Nancy. Forthcoming. "Overland and Underwater: Porcelain Coffee Cups as Cargo in the Red Sea and the Gulf." In Eric Tagliacozzo, ed., *The Twin Seas.*
Uslu, Günay. 2017. *Homer, Troy, and the Turks.* Amsterdam: Amsterdam University Press.
Valiulina, Svetlana. 2021. "Iranian Glazed Ceramics of the 12th–Beginning of the 13th Centuries in the Volga Bulgaria." *Heritage* 4:4, 3712–3730.
van den Bent, Josephine. 2016. "'None of the Kings on Earth Is Their Equal in *'aṣabiyya'*: The Mongols in Ibn Khaldūn's

Works." *Al-Masāq: Journal of the Medieval Mediterranean* 28:2, 171–186.

Vanke, Francesca. 1999. "The Contribution of C.D.E. Fortnum to the Historiography and Collecting of Islamic Ceramics." *Journal of the History of Collections* 11:2, 219–231.

van Koningsveld, Pieter Sjoerd, and Gerard Albert Wiegers. 2023. *The Lead Books of Sacramonte and the Parchment of the Torre Turpiana: Granada, 1588–1606*. Leiden: Brill.

Venice Charter. 1964. https://www.icomos.org/en/participer/179-articles-en-francais/ressources/charters-and-standards/157-thevenice-charter, accessed 23 March 2023.

Vernoit, Stephen. 1997. "The Rise of Islamic Archaeology." *Muqarnas* 14, 1–10.

Vernoit, Stephen. 1997a. *Occidentalism: Islamic Art in the 19th Century*. London: Nour Foundation.

Vernoit, Stephen. 2000. "Islamic Art and Architecture: An Overview of Scholarship and Collecting, c. 1850–c. 1950." In Stephen Vernoit, ed., *Discovering Islamic Art: Scholars, Collectors and Collections, 1850–1950*, 1–61. London: I. B. Tauris.

Vernus, Pascal. 2003. *Affairs and Scandals in Ancient Egypt*. Trans. David Lorton. Ithaca, NY: Cornell University Press.

Veselovsky, Nikolai Ivanovich. 1886. "Sushchestvujut li v srednej azii poddelki drevnostej? [Are There Fake Antiquities in Central Asia?]." *Zapiski Vostochnago otdi͡elenii͡a Imperatorskago russkago arkheologicheskago obshchestva*, 1:2, 110–114.

Vickers, Michael. 1991. "The Views of Persepolis by William Marshall and Wenceslaus Hollar in Sir Thomas Herbert's Travels." In Heleen Sanci-Weerdenburg and Jan Willem Drijvers, eds., *Achaemenid History VII: Through Traveller's Eyes*, 59–69. Leiden: Nederlands Instituut voor het Nabije Oosten.

Vickers, Michael. 2006. *The Arundel and Pomfret Marbles*. Oxford: Ashmolean Museum.

Vignier, Charles. 1925. "L'exposition d'art oriental: Notes sur la céramique persane." *Revue des arts asiatiques* 2:3, 41–48.

Vignier, Charles. 1928. "Sur les truquages des faiences persanes." *Revue des arts asiatiques* 5:2, 82–90.

Vincent Robinson Galleries. 1913. *Exhibition of Persian Art & Curios, the Collection Formed by J.R. Preece Esq. C.M.G.* London: Vincent Robinson Galleries.

Volait, Mercedes. 2021. *Antique Dealing and Creative Reuse in Cairo and Damascus 1850–1890: Intercultural Engagements with Architecture and Craft in the Age of Travel and Reform*. Leiden: Brill.

Volait, Mercedes. n.d. "The rue du Caire at the Exposition universelle in Paris (1889)." *BnF Bibliothèques d'Orient*, https://heritage.bnf.fr/bibliothequesorient/en/street-of-cairo-art, accessed 3 January 2023.

Volmert, Miriam. 2017. "'Framing and Fashioning of Images': The Pictorial Invention of the Art Lover in Daniel Myten's Portrait of Thomas Howard, Earl of Arundel (ca 1618)." *Zeitschrift für Kunstgeschichte* 80:1, 83–107.

von Bothmer, Dietrich. 1998. "Forgeries of Greek Vases." *Minerva* 9:2, 8–17.

Waagé, Frederick O., ed. 1948. *Antioch on-the-Orontes, IV: Part One, Ceramics and Islamic Coins*. Princeton: Princeton University Press.

Wadsworth Athenaeum. 1925. *Loan Exhibition of Near Eastern Art*. Hartford, CT: Morgan Memorial.

Wagner, Esther-Miriam, and Bettina Beinhoff. 2017. "Introduction. Merchants of Innovation: The Languages of Traders." In Esther-Miriam Wagner, Bettina Beinhoff, and Ben Outhwaite, eds., *Merchants of Innovation: The Language of Traders*, 3–18. Berlin: De Gruyter.

Wakeling, T. G. 1912. *Forged Egyptian Antiquities*. London: Adam and Charles Black.

Waksman, Yona. 2023. "Investigations of Sgraffito and Champlevé in Lyon Laboratory." Paper presented at Sgraffito and Champlevé in Islamic Lands (9th–14th Century): Iran, Caucasus and Beyond workshop, Maison de l'Orient et de la Mediterranée, Lyon, 11 May 2023.

Wallerstein, Immanuel. 1979. "Ottoman Empire and the Capitalism World-Economy: Some Questions for Research." *Review (Fernand Braudel Center)* 2:3, 389–398.

Wallis, Henry. 1891. *The Godman Collection: Persian Ceramic Art in the Collection of Mr F. DuCane Godman, F.R.S., The Thirteenth Century Lustred Vases*. London: privately printed.

Wallner, Miriam. 2022. "Friedrich Sarres Geschenk an München: Ein Lüsterkeramikkonvolut aus Rey/Friedrich Sarre's Gift to Munich: A Collection of Lusterware from Rayy." In Miriam Kühn and Martina Müller-Weiner, eds., *Lüsterkeramik: Schillerndes Geheimnis/Luster Ceramics: Shimmering Secret*, 100–109. Petersburg: Michael Imhof.

Walters, H. B. 1905. *History of Ancient Pottery, Greek, Etruscan, and Roman*. New York: Charles Scribner's Sons.

Watenpaugh, Heghnar Zeitlian. 2019. *The Missing Pages: From Genocide to Justice*. Palo Alto: Stanford University Press.

Watson, George Christopher. 2020. "Calouste Gulbenkian and His Coin-Collecting Network." *Journal of the History of Collections* 32:3, 559–571.

Watson, Oliver. 1975. "Persian Lustre Ware, from the 14th to the 19th Centuries." *Le monde iranien et l'Islam: Sociétés et cultures* 3, 63–80.

Watson, Oliver. 1981. "Iznik from Isfahan." *Apollo* 114:235, 176–179.

Watson, Oliver. 1985. "Fakes and Forgeries of Islamic Pottery." *V&A Album* 4, 38–46.

Watson, Oliver. 1985a. *Persian Lustre Ware*. London: Faber and Faber.

Watson, Oliver. 1999. "Museums, Collecting, Art-History, and Archaeology." *Damaszener Mitteilungen* 11, 421–432, plates 54–56.

Watson, Oliver. 2004. "Fakes and Forgeries in Islamic Pottery." *Oriente Moderno*, n.s., 23:84, no. 2, 517–539.

Watson, Oliver. 2004a. *Ceramics from Islamic Lands*. London: Thames and Hudson.

Watson, Oliver. 2006. "Almost Hilariously Bad: Iranian Pottery in the Nineteenth Century." In Doris Abouseif and Stephen Vernoit, eds., *Islamic Art in the 19th Century: Tradition, Innovation, Eclecticism*, 333–362. Leiden: Brill.

Watson, Oliver. 2006a. "Lustre Wasters: Attribution, Provenance, and Art-Historical Politics." In Patricia Baker and Barbara Brend, eds., *Sifting Sands, Reading Signs: Studies in Honour of Professor Géza Féhérvari*, 231–249. London: Furnace.

Watson, Oliver. 2013. "Authentic Forgeries?" In Alexander Geurds and Laura Van Broekhoven, eds., *Creating Authenticity: Authentication Processes in Ethnographic Museums*, 59–71. Leiden: Sidestone Press.

Watson, Oliver. 2014. "Revisiting Samarra: The Rise of Islamic Glazed Pottery." *Beiträge zur Islamischen Kunst und Archäologie* 4, 123–142.

Watson, Oliver. 2020. *Ceramics of Iran: Islamic Pottery from the Sarikhani Collection*. New Haven: Yale University Press.

Weinberg, H. Barbara. 1976. "Thomas B. Clarke: Foremost Patron of American Art from 1872 to 1899." *American Art Journal* 8:1, 52–83.

Weis, Friederike. 2016. "A Persianate Drawing of the Tazza Farnese: A Work by Muhammad Khayyam?" In Julia Gonnella, Friederike Weis, and Christoph Rauch, *The Diez Albums: Contexts and Contents*, 380–426. Leiden: Brill.

Weiss, Gustav. 1979. *Alte Keramik neu entdeckt*. Berlin: Ullstein.

Wen, Wen. 2021. "Preconceptions of the Samarra Horizon, Green Splashed Ware and Blue Painted Ware Revisited Through Chinese Ceramic Imports (Eighth to Tenth Centuries)." *Journal of Material Cultures in the Muslim World* 2, 150–183.

Westgarth, Mark. 2020. *The Emergence of the Antique and Curiosity Dealer in Britain, 1815–1850: The Commodification of Historical Objects*. Abingdon /New York: Routledge.

Wharton-Durgaryon, Alyson. 2020. "'I Have the Honour to Inform You That I Have Just Arrived from Constantinople': Migration, Identity, and Commodity Disavowal in the Formation of the Islamic Art Collection at the V&A." *Museum & Society* 18:2, 258–279.

Whitcomb, Donald. 2012. "Lusterware Jug from Rayy, Iran." In Jack Green, Emily Teeter, and John A. Larson, eds., *Picturing the Past: Imaging and Imagining the Ancient Near East*, 143–144. Chicago: Oriental Institute.

Whitcomb, Donald. 2016. "Archaeology in Iran and the Experience of Arthur Upham Pope." In Yuka Kadoi, ed., *Arthur Upham Pope and a New Survey of Persian Art*, 97–109. Leiden: Brill.

Whitehouse, David. 1994. "Two 19th-Century Forgeries of Gold Glasses in the Corning Museum of Glass." *Journal of Glass Studies* 36, 133–135.

Whitfield, Susan. 2002. "Introduction." In Susan Whitfield, ed., *Dunhuang Manuscript Forgeries*, 1–21. London: British Library.

Whitney, T. B. 1910. *Catalogue des anciennes faïences persanes, Damas, Rhodes et Koubatcha, composant la collection T. B. Whitney*. Paris: Georges Petit.

Whittlesey, Charles. 1872. "Archaeological Frauds: Inscriptions Attributed to the Mound Builders, Three Remarkable Forgeries." *Western Reserve Historical Society Historical and Archaeological Tracts* 9 (February), 1–4.

Whittlesey, Charles. 1881. "Inscribed Stones, Licking County, Ohio." *Western Reserve and Northern Ohio Historical Society* 53 (March), 129–133.

Wilkinson, Charles K. 1973. *Nishapur: Pottery of the Early Islamic Period*. New York: Metropolitan Museum of Art.

Williams, Daniela. 2018. "Osman Bey of Constantinople: A Late 18th-Century Forger of Ancient Coins." *Revue numismatique* 176, 361–383.

Willis, Michael D. 1987. "Tiles from the Mosque of Rüstem Paşa in İstanbul." *Artibus Asiae* 48:3/4, 278–284.

Wills, Charles James. 1891. *In the Land of the Lion and the Sun, or, Modern Persia, Being Experiences of Life in Persia from 1866–1881*, new. ed. London: Ward, Lock, and Co.

Wilpert, Joseph. 1926. "Early Christian Sculpture; Its Restoration and Modern Manufacture." *The Art Bulletin* 9:2, 89–141.

Wilpert, Sebastian. 2021. "A German-Ottoman Scramble for Objects in ar-Raqqa: Antiquities, Trade, Archaeological Looting and Museum Rivalry in the Late Ottoman Empire." *Orient-Institut Istanbul Blog*, 23 April 2021, https://www.oiist.org/a-german-ottoman/, accessed 9 June 2024.

Wilson, Timothy. 2009/2010. "La contraffazione delle maioliche all'inizio del Novecento: La testimonianza del Museen-Verband." In Lucio Riccetti, ed., *1909 tra collezionismo e tutela* (Perugia), 267–280, also published in an undated English translation on the author's website, "Faking Maiolica in the Early Twentieth Century: The Evidence of the Museen-Verband," https://timothywilsoncouk.files.wordpress.com/2020/03/imbertandfakingmaiolica.pdf.

Wood, Barry. 2000. "'A Great Symphony of Pure Form': The 1931 International Exhibition of Persian Art and Its Influence." *Ars Orientalis* 30, 113–130.

Woodfield, Richard. 2017. "Gombrich on Strzygowski." *Journal of Art Historiography* 17, 7pp.

Woolley, Leonard. 1924. Letter to the *Times Literary Supplement*, 10 July 1924, 431.

Wordsworth, Paul. 2023. "Archaeological Approaches to Art Historical Problems: Rethinking the Date and Production of So-called 'Aghkand' and Associated Wares." Paper presented at Sgraffito and Champlevé in Islamic Lands (9th–14th Century): Iran, Caucasus and Beyond workshop , Maison de l'Orient et de la Mediteranée, Lyon, 11 May 2023.

Wrightson, Rebecca. 2021. "Legibility, Visual Ambiguity, and the Patterning of Arabic Script: Epigraphic Ceramics of the Early Islamic World." Unpublished PhD thesis, Oxford University.

Wulff, Hans E. 1966. *The Traditional Crafts of Persia*. Cambridge, MA: MIT Press.

Yenişehirlioğlu, Filiz. 2004. "Ottoman Ceramics in European Contexts." *Muqarnas* 21, 373–382.

Yenişehirlioğlu, Filiz. 2013. "A Digital Database for Tiles at the Topkapı Palace Museum Storage Rooms." In Frédéric Hitzel, ed., *14th International Congress of Turkish Art: Proceedings*, 13–23. Paris: Collège de France.

Yildirim, Sefa, and Fatih Öztep. 2019. "The Protection of Historical Artifacts in Ottoman Empire: The Permanent Council for the Protection of Ancient Artifacts." *Universal Journal of Educational Research* 7:2, 600–608.

Yoltar-Yıldırım, Ayşin. 2006. "Appendix 1: The Ottoman Response to Illicit Digging in Raqqa." In Marilyn Jenkins-Madina, *Raqqa Revisited: Ceramics of Ayyubid Syria*, 191–220. New York: Metropolitan Museum of Art.

Yoltar-Yıldırım, Ayşin. 2013. "Raqqa: The Forgotten Excavation of an Islamic Site in Syria by the Ottoman Imperial Museum in the Early Twentieth Century." *Muqarnas* 30, 73–93.

You, Yao-Fen. 2016. *Coffee, Tea, and Chocolate: Consuming the World*. Detroit: Detroit Institute of Arts.

Zahn, Robert. 1911. "306. Gefälschte griechische Vasen." *Mitteilungen des Museen-Verbandes als Manuskript für die Mitglieder* (June), 14–15.

Zahn, Robert. 1912. "349. Silberner Widder." *Mitteilungen des Museen-Verbandes als Manuskript für die Mitglieder* (March), 5–6.

Ziaii-Bigdeli, Layah. 2017. "Nīshāpūr Figural Buffware Pottery: Facing Unprovenanced Objects." Unpublished MA thesis, Rutgers University.

Index

Page numbers in *italics* refer to illustrations.

Photo Credits

After Atıl 1973, cat. 32: Fig. 3.14
After Koob 1999, p. 160: Fig 3.15
After Melikian-Chirvani 1966: Fig. 3.50
Archives of American Art, Smithsonian Institution: Fig. 4.2
© Les Arts Décoratifs: Fig. 1.12
Photo courtesy of the author: Fig. 3.7, Fig. 3.20, Fig. 5.33
Photo: Author, by permission of the Detroit Institute of Arts: Fig. 5.20, Fig. 5.21
Photo: Author, by permission of the Hetjens Museum: Fig 2.14, Fig. 5.25
Photo: Author, by permission of the Museum für Islamische Kunst: Fig. 3.43
Photo: Author, by permission of the Toledo Museum of Art: Fig. 2.47, Fig. 3.11, Fig. 3.12
Photo: BnF: Fig 1.10
Brooklyn Museum/Harry Debauche: Fig. 3.17, Fig. 3.18
Photo: Courtesy Cincinnati Art Museum, photography by Rob Deslongchamps: Fig 2.5, Fig. 2.24, Fig. 2.25, Fig 2.26, Fig 2.28, Fig. 2.42, Fig. 2.46, Fig. 2.53, Fig. 2.54, Fig. 3.9, Fig. 3.23, Fig. 3.24, Fig. 3.26, Fig. 3.27, Fig. 3.31, Fig. 3.33, Fig. 3.34, Fig. 3.35, Fig. 3.39, Fig. 3.41, Fig. 3.42, Fig. 3.55, Fig. 4.4, Fig. 4.7, Fig. 4.16, Fig. 5.24, Fig. 5.29
Photo: Cincinnati Art Museum/Daderot/Wikipedia: Fig. 4.6
Photo: Courtesy Cincinnati Art Museum/Kelly Rectenwald: Fig. 3.25
Cleveland Museum of Art Archives: Fig. 4.9
Photo © The Courtauld/Bridgeman Images: Fig. 3.44
Photo: Detroit Institute of Arts: Figs. 1.6a-g, Fig. 2.45, Fig. 2.51
Photo: Detroit Institute of Arts/Christina Bisulca: Fig. 2.52
Courtesy of the Doris Duke Foundation for Islamic Art, Honolulu, Hawai'i; Photograph: David Franzen, 2012: Fig 2.17
Photo: Hughes Dubois: Fig 2.38
Photo: Eskenazi Museum of Art: Fig 2.19
Photo: Eskenazi Museum of Art Archives: Fig. 5.1, Fig. 5.2, Fig. 5.10, Fig. 5.11
Photo: Eskenazi Museum of Art/Kevin Montague: Fig. 1.1, Fig 2.20, Fig. 2.35, Fig. 2.37, Fig 2.39, Fig. 2.41, Fig.3.1, Fig. 3.3, Fig. 3.4, Fig. 3.5, Fig. 3.6, Fig. 3.19, Fig. 3.21, Fig 3.22, Fig. 3.45, Fig. 3.46, Fig. 3.47, Fig. 3.49, Fig. 3.52, Fig. 3.53, Fig. 5.4, Fig. 5.5, Fig. 5.6, Fig. 5.7, Fig. 5.8, Fig. 5.9, Fig. 5.12, Fig. 5.13, Fig. 5.14, Fig. 5.15, Fig. 5.16, Fig. 5.17, Fig. 5.18, Fig. 5.19, Fig. 5.22, Fig. 5.23, Fig. 5.27, Fig. 5.34, Fig. 5.35, Fig. 5.36, Table 1 (all photos)
Photo: Fitzwilliam Museum: Fig. 3.13, Fig. 4.8
Geneanet/lucevemimi: Fig 1.9
Photo: Melanie Gibson: Fig. 2.7
Photo: Peppe Guida/Wikipedia: Fig. 1.1
Harvard Art Museums/Arthur M. Sackler Museum, Photo: © President and Fellows of Harvard College: Fig. 1.6
Harvard Art Museums Archives: Fig. 4.5
Historic Images/Alamy Stock Photo: Fig. 2.6
Courtesy of the Institute for the Study of Ancient Cultures, University of Chicago: Fig 2.32
©IsIAO archives Ghazni/Tapa Sardar Project 2014, by permission: Fig 2.23
Photo: International Dunhuang Project/Wikipedia: Fig. 1.9
Photo: Johnson-Humrickhouse Museum, Coshocton, Ohio/ Ben Croghan: Fig. 1.5
Photo: courtesy of the Joukowsky Institute for Archaeology and the Ancient World, Brown University: Fig 2.8
© The Metropolitan Museum of Art. Image source: Art Resource, NY: Fig. 3.38
Minassian Collection, John Hay Library, Brown University: Fig. 2.10, Fig. 2.11, Fig. 2.12
Mitteilungen des Museen-Verbandes als Manuskript für die Mitglieder: Fig. 1.15
Photograph © 2026 Museum of Fine Arts, Boston: Fig. 2.31, Fig. 4.12
Photo: Museum of Mediterranean and Near Eastern Antiquities: Fig. 2.44, Fig. 3.54
National Museum of Asian Art, Smithsonian Institution, Freer Collection, Purchase—Charles Lang Freer Endowment, F1957.24: Fig 2.36
National Museum of Asian Art, Smithsonian Institution, Freer Collection, Gift of Charles Lang Freer, F1908.145: Fig. 5.31
Ernst Herzfeld / National Museum of Asian Art Archives, Smithsonian Institution, Ernst Herzfeld Papers, FSA A.06 04.PF.20.077: Fig. 2.40
Antoin Sevruguin / National Museum of Asian Art

Archives, Smithsonian Institution, Myron Bement Smith Collection, FSA_A.4 2.12.GN.26.05: Fig. 1.11
Antoin Sevruguin / National Museum of Asian Art Archives, Smithsonian Institution, Myron Bement Smith Collection, FSA_A.4 2.12.GN.10.08: Fig 2.27
Antoin Sevruguin / National Museum of Asian Art Archives, Smithsonian Institution, Myron Bement Smith Collection, FSA A.4 2.12.GN.30.09: Fig. 1.8
Antoin Sevruguin / National Museum of Asian Art Archives, Smithsonian Institution, Myron Bement Smith Collection, FSA_A.4 2.12.GN.05.05: Fig. 3.8
Image © National Museums Scotland: Fig. 2.21
© National Portrait Gallery, London: Fig. 1.3
© Natural History Museum, London, 2014–2015, photographed by kind permission of the trustees of the Natural History Museum, London: Fig. 6.1
Bell (Gertrude) archive, Newcastle University Library: Fig. 5.28
Niedersächsische Staats- und Universitätsbibliothek Göttingen/Public domain: Fig. 1.4
Photo: Keelan Overton: Fig 2.15
Palestine Exploration Fund, London: Fig 1.7, Fig. 1.8
© Walid Raad, by permission of the artist: Fig. 6.3
Photo: Julie Ribits: Fig. 6.4
© Agop Kaledjian, Courtesy Sfeir-Semler Gallery (Beirut / Hamburg) and permission of Walid Raad: Fig. 3.57
Courtesy of the Artist and Sfeir-Semler Gallery Beirut / Hamburg: Fig. 6.2
Staatliche Museen zu Berlin, Museum für Islamische Kunst / Nico Becker: Fig. 2.49, Fig 2.50
Staatliche Museen zu Berlin, Museum für Islamische Kunst / Johannes Kramer: Fig. 3.29, Fig. 3.30, Fig. 3.51
Photo: Toledo Museum of Art: Fig 3.28, Fig. 3.37, Fig 3.48, Fig. 4.10
Toledo Museum of Art, curatorial archives: Fig. 3.10
© The Trustees of the British Museum: Fig. 2.1, Fig 2.3, Fig. 5.38
© Victoria and Albert Museum, London: Fig 2.2, Fig 2.4, Fig 2.9, Fig 2.29, Fig 2.34, Fig. 3.2, Fig. 3.32, Fig. 3.56, Fig. 4.1, Fig. 4.15
The Walters Art Museum, Baltimore: Fig. 2.22
Photo: wikipedia/Beneathtimp: Fig. 4.11
Photo: Yale University Art Gallery: Fig. 3.40, Fig. 5.26